JAROSLAV PÁNEK, OLDŘICH TŮMA ET ALII
A HISTORY OF THE CZECH LANDS

Fig. on page 5: *Bohemiae Rosa*. A Baroque map of the Bohemian Kingdom stylized as a rose. It symbolized the expected flourishing of the country after the mid-17th century. The rose is seen sprouting from Austria, with Vienna under its stem. The leaves on the right symbolize Moravia, the left ones part of Austria. Prague is in the centre of the flower. Above the rose, near the royal crown and sceptre, there is Emperor and King Ferdinand III's motto "Iustitia et pietate" (With Justice and Piety), on the right is the emblem of the Bohemian Kingdom – two-tailed lion. At the bottom of the picture is a numbered list of regions and Latin texts reminding of the previous wars that swept through the Bohemian Kingdom. Texts also express hope in the peaceful future of the country. Engraving by Christian Vetter from 1668 was used in Bohuslav Balbín's *Epitome historica rerum Bohemicarum* (1677).

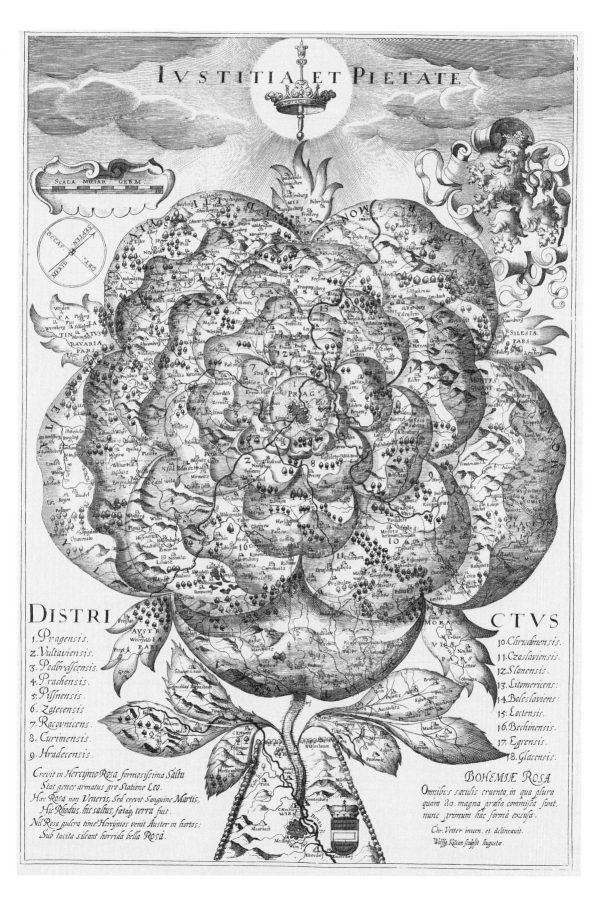

IVSTITIA ET PIETATE

SCALA MILIAR. GERM.

Chr. Vetter inven. et delineauit.

Wolffg. Kilian sculpsit Augustæ.

DISTRI CTVS

1. Pragensis.
2. Vultaviensis.
3. Podbrdscensis.
4. Prachensis.
5. Pilsnensis.
6. Zatecensis.
7. Racovnicensis.
8. Curimensis.
9. Hradecensis.

10. Chrudinensis.
11. Czaslaviensis.
12. Slanensis.
13. Litomericens.
14. Boleslaviens.
15. Loctensis.
16. Bechinensis.
17. Egrensis.
18. Glacensis.

Crevit in Hercinio Rosa formosissima Saltu
Stat penes armatus pro Statione Leo.

Hæc Rosa non Veneris, Sed crevit Sanguine Martis,
Hic Rhodus, hic saltus, fataq; terra fuit.

Nil Rosa pulcra time! Hercinnes venit Auster in hortos;
Sub tacita sileant horrida bella Rosâ.

BOHEMIÆ ROSA

Omnibus sæculis cruenta, in qua plura
quam 80. magna prælia commissa sunt,
nunc primum hac formâ excusâ.

JAROSLAV PÁNEK
OLDŘICH TŮMA
ET ALII

A HISTORY OF THE CZECH LANDS

Charles University in Prague
Karolinum Press 2011

Main authors and editors: Prof. PhDr. Jaroslav Pánek, DrSc.
PhDr. Oldřich Tůma, Ph.D.

Authors: PhDr. Jaroslav Boubín, CSc. PhDr. Pavel Cibulka, CSc.
                      PhDr. Jan Gebhart, CSc. PhDr. Martina Ondo Grečenková
                      PhDr. Jan Hájek, CSc. Doc. PhDr. Josef Harna, CSc.
                      Prof. PhDr. Milan Hlavačka, CSc. Doc. PhDr. Jiří Kocian, CSc.
                      Doc. PhDr. Martin Kučera, CSc. Doc. PhDr. Jiří Mikulec, CSc.
                      PhDr. Jiří Pernes, Ph.D. PhDr. Miloslav Polívka, CSc.
                      Prof. PhDr. Eva Semotanová, DrSc. PhDr. Jiří Suk, Ph.D.
                      Prof. PhDr. František Šmahel, DrSc. † PhDr. Dušan Třeštík, CSc.
                      Prof. PhDr. Josef Žemlička, DrSc.

Reviewed by: Prof. PhDr. Zdeněk Jirásek, CSc.
                      Prof. PhDr. Josef Petráň, CSc.
                      Prof. PhDr. Josef Válka, CSc.

ISBN 978-80-246-1645-2

Historical emblem of the Bohemian Kingdom. A two-tailed jumping lion was an emblem of the Bohemian Kingdom from the 13th century. It has been used till today as part of the state emblem of the Czech Republic. Engraving from a new edition of the Renewed Land Ordinance for the Bohemian Kingdom from the 18th century. *Verneuerte Landes-Ordnung deroselben Erb-Königreich Böheim*, Prague 1753.

Contents

Introduction

At the beginning of May 2004, the Czech Republic joined the European Union. The histories of the individual states in this community are both perceived and known to varying degrees. When the European past is narrated, a small number of states dominate, either because of the extraordinary culture they produced or the power that they wielded; while the others are either occasionally remarked upon or completely overlooked. Nearly every child in primary school knows at least something about the former, while the latter remain vague or utterly unknown even to most educated people. The former are usually and automatically perceived as the axes of any framework of a common European history, while generally speaking even renowned experts have little to say about the latter. To this group belong mainly those states that seem at first glance "young", including the new members of the European Union. Little is known of them, and thus these countries have no choice but to strive to show that they too have indisputably belonged to Europe for a very long time. Some of these countries at least have the advantage of a name that has not changed for centuries: Poland and Malta, to give two instances, have held the same appellation for over a thousand years and thus they are generally identifiable.

Czechia (*Česko*) however does not have that advantage. Although the historical lands which constitute it – that is, Bohemia (*Čechy*), Moravia (*Morava*) and the southern part of Silesia (*Slezsko*) – have belonged together for many centuries now, the framework of their state has changed many times in that period. Sometimes the change was profound, on other occasions it was only formal; but each change destabilized these countries in the eyes of Europe. After Great Moravia (*Velká Morava*; 9th century) there came the Bohemian Principality (*České knížectví*) whose ruler occasionally donned a royal crown (9th to 12th centuries); and the Bohemian Kingdom (*České království*; from the end of the 12th century), which in the 14th century spread its territory to the north and took the title of the Crown of the Bohemian Kingdom (*Koruna Království českého*) or the Bohemian Crown (*Česká koruna*). In 1526 this state, made up of five crown lands, entered a confederation with the lands of Austria and Hungary, becoming one of the three main parts of the Habsburg Monarchy. After an unsuccessful attempt to re-arrange Europe on the basis of the Estates (which was meant to be founded on the Bohemian Confederation; 1619–1620), the Habsburg conception of Central Europe was established. The Czech state was ever more firmly bound to the Viennese governing centre, until the year 1804 when it almost dissolved into the Austrian Empire in the long process of centralization. After the dualistic transformation of the Habsburg monarchy into Austro-Hungary in 1867, Bohemia, Moravia and Czech (at that time Austrian) Silesia became part of the western half of the monarchy, named Cisleithania (*Předlitavsko*).

Austro-Hungary was defeated in World War I, with Czechoslovaks participating politically and militarily in anti-Habsburg resistance. This enabled the establishment of the independent Czechoslovak Republic (*Republika československá*), which in the years 1918–1938 became an active element in the system of European states. The Munich Agreement of 29 September 1938 limited this independent state to the reduced Czecho-Slovakia (*Česko-Slovensko*), which under the pressure of Nazi Germany collapsed with the creation of the Slovak Republic (14 March 1939). The remainder of Bohemian and Moravian territory was occupied by the German army on 15 March 1939, and the following day the Protectorate of Bohemia and Moravia (*Protektorát Čechy a Morava*; in German, *Protekorat Böhmen und Mähren*) was established. After liberation by the Soviet and American armies at the beginning of May 1945, the restored Czechoslovak Republic (*Československá republika*) emerged. As a consequence of a Communist putsch in February 1948, it became one of the satellites of the Soviet Union and in 1960 changed its name to the Czechoslovak Socialist Republic (*Československá socialistická republika*). The federalization of this state led at the beginning of 1969 to the administrative unification of the Czech Lands under the name the Czech Socialist Republic (*Česká socialistická republika*). The fall of the Communist regime in November 1989 brought several smaller changes to the country's name: it was now the Czech and Slovak Federal Republic (*Česká a Slovenská Federativní Republika*), which at the close of 1992 was divided into two independent states through agreement between Czech and Slovak political representatives. On 1 January 1993, our overview of Czech history ends with the birth of the independent Czech Republic (*Česká republika*).

These regular transformations of the state's framework paradoxically had little impact on historical Czech territory. The Czech Republic occupies more or less the same tract of land as the territory ruled by the Bohemian princes roughly one thousand years before. It was then, as it is today, inhabited by Slavs who from ancient times took the common appellation of Czechs (*Češi*) and who – in view of the traditions of the historical lands – sometimes refer to themselves as Czechs, Moravians (*Moravané*) and Silesians (*Slezané*). However, important national minorities also lived on this territory, helping to create the history of this space – mainly Germans, Poles and Jews, and in the modern era Romanies and Slovaks. National minorities represent fully fledged subjects of the history of this space, just as all the inhabitants of all the historical lands (including those who for longer periods in the past belonged to the territorially expanded Czech state). This given state of affairs, like the integral connection of Czech history with that of Europe, was crucial to the preparation of this book.

Those who initiated and organized the work, like the authors of individual chapters, are members of two institutes of the Academy of Sciences of the Czech Republic – the Institute of History, which is concerned with the period from the beginning of the Middle Ages to

World War II, and the Institute of Contemporary History, which concentrates on research from the 1940s to the contemporary period. The authors are for the most part also lecturers at Charles University in Prague, and in some cases at Masaryk University in Brno. Thanks to this, they were able to exploit their pedagogical experience with university students in drawing up the individual chapters, and so present a text which would have been impossible without the close co-operation of the institutes of the Academy with the foremost Czech universities. The aim of such a large collective of authors was not to continue long-standing, endless debates about the sense, interpretation and periodization of the events of this country's past, but to present a domestic readership, as well as readerships in several foreign languages, with an overview of Czech history that was as factually accurate and as cogent as possible. They concentrated on the development of the state and the inhabitants with special emphasis on social, cultural and political metamorphoses, as well as religious and national aspects.

For some time now there has been no capacious single-volume overview of Czech history in its entirety for a domestic readership. More serious however is the absence of such a work for foreign readers. While all our neighbours have already published such works in the main languages, Czech historical writing has lagged behind. It was this gap that motivated our work and in this volume we thus attempted to summarize and present the fruits of recent research on Czech history for a wider public.

Since a publication of this kind cannot present all the information that might be expected, we placed especial emphasis on the bibliographies, both to this introduction and the individual chapters. These are not merely lists of all the important works, but a selection of mainly book-length publications that offer syntheses and other approaches, and we combined works that are now classics of the genre as well as more recent research. Apart from major monographs and studies, we also draw attention to books that, while maintaining a reliable standard of expertise, are also accessible to a wider readership thanks to the style in which they were written. Readers, encouraged to study Czech history more deeply as a result of our overview, should find sufficient sources in these bibliographies for their further explorations.

Jaroslav Pánek – Oldřich Tůma

Bibliography

AGNEW, Hugh LeCaine: *The Czechs and the Lands of the Bohemian Crown*, Stanford, California 2004.
Atlas československých dějin, Jaroslav Purš (ed.), Praha 1965.
BAHLCKE, Joachim: *Schlesien und die Schlesier*, 2nd edition, München 2000.
BAHLCKE, Joachim (ed.): *Geschichte der Oberlausitz. Herrschaft, Gesellschaft und Kultur vom Mittelalter bis zum Ende des 20. Jahrhunderts*, Leipzig 2001.
BĚLINA, Pavel – ČORNEJ, Petr et al.: *Dějiny zemí Koruny české*, I–II, Praha 1992.
BERÉNGER, Jean: *Histoire de l'empire des Habsbourg 1273–1918*, Paris 1990.
Biografický slovník českých zemí, I–II (A–Č), Praha 2004–2008.
BOHATCOVÁ, Mirjam et al.: *Česká kniha v proměnách staletí*, Praha 1990.
Die böhmischen Länder zwischen Ost und West, München 1983.
BRÁZDIL, Rudolf – KOTYZA, Oldřich et al.: *History of Weather and Climate in the Czech Lands*, I–V, Zürich 1995 (I); Brno 1996–2002 (II–V).
BRUCKMÜLLER, Ernst: *Sozialgeschichte Österreichs*, 2nd edition, Wien–München 2001.
BŘEŇOVÁ, Věra – ROHLÍKOVÁ, Slavěna: *Czech and Czechoslovak History, 1918–1999: A Bibliography of Select Monographs, Volumes of Essays, and Articles Published from 1990 to 1999*, Prague 2000.
Co daly naše země Evropě a lidstvu, I–II, Vilém Mathesus (ed.), Praha 1939, 1940; III, Ivan Havel – Dušan Třeštík (eds.), Praha 2000.
CZAPLIŃSKI, Marek – KASZUBA, Elżbieta – WĄS, Gabriela – ŻERELIK, Rościsław: *Historia Śląska*, Wrocław 2002.
ČECHURA, Jaroslav – MIKULEC, Jiří – STELLNER, František: *Lexikon českých panovnických dynastií*, Praha 1996.
České korunovační klenoty, Praha 1993.
Československá vlastivěda, IV, *Dějiny*, Praha 1932–1933.
Československá vlastivěda, II/1–2, *Dějiny*, Praha 1962–1969.
Československé dějiny v datech, Praha 1986.
Češi a Jihoslované v minulosti. Od nejstarších dob do roku 1918, Václav Žáček (ed.), Praha 1975.
Češi a Poláci v minulosti, I–II, Josef Macůrek – Václav Žáček (eds.), Praha 1964–1967.
Česká literatura od počátků k dnešku, Jan Lehár – Alexandr Stich – Jaroslava Janáčková – Jiří Holý, Praha 1998.
Český ekumenismus. Theologické kořeny a současná tvář církví, Praha 1976.
ČORNEJOVÁ, Ivana – RAK, Jiří – VLNAS, Vít: *Ve stínu tvých křídel... Habsburkové v českých dějinách*, Praha 1995.
DANIEL, Bartoloměj: *Dějiny Romů. Vybrané kapitoly z dějin Romů v západní Evropě, v Českých zemích a na Slovensku*, Olomouc 1994.
Dějiny bankovnictví v českých zemích, Praha 1999.
Dějiny české literatury, I–IV, Praha 1959–1995.
Dějiny českého divadla, I–IV, Praha 1968–1983.
Dějiny českého výtvarného umění, I–VI, Praha 1984–2007.
Dějiny exaktních věd v českých zemích do konce 19. století, Praha 1961.
Dějiny Prahy, I–II, Praha–Litomyšl 1997–1998.
Dějiny Rakouska, Václav Veber – Milan Hlavačka – Petr Vorel – Miloslav Polívka – Martin Wihoda – Zdeněk Měřínský, Praha 2002.
Dějiny techniky v Československu do konce 18. století, Praha 1974.
DENIS, Ernest: *La Bohême après Montagne-Blanche*, Paris 1901.
DENIS, Ernest: *Fin de l'indépendence bohême*, Paris 1890.
Deutsche Geschichte im Osten Europas. Böhmen und Mähren, Friedrich Prinz (ed.), Berlin 1993.
Frankreich und die böhmischen Länder im 19. und 20. Jahrhundert. Beiträge zum französischen Einfluss in Ostmitteleuropa, Ferdinand Seibt, Michael Neumüller (eds.), München 1990.
GAWRECKI, Dan et al.: *Dějiny Českého Slezska 1740–2000*, I–II, Opava 2003.
GOOD, David G.: *The Economic Rise of the Habsburg Empire 1750–1914*, Berkeley 1984.
Grossbritanien, die USA und die böhmischen Länder 1848–1938. Eva Schmidt-Hartmann, Stanley B. Winters (eds.), München 1991.

HAMANNOVÁ, Brigitte: *Die Habsburger. Ein biographisches Lexikon*, München 1988.

Handbuch der Geschichte der böhmischen Länder, I–IV, Stuttgart 1967–1974.

Handbuch der historischen Stätten – Böhmen und Mähren, Joachim Bahlcke, Winfried Eberhard, Miloslav Polívka (eds.), Stuttgart 1998.

Handbuch der historischen Stätten – Schlesien, Hugo Weczerka (ed.), Stuttgart 1977.

HOENSCH, Jörg K.: *Geschichte Böhmens. Von der slavischen Landnahme bis ins 20. Jahrhundert*, München 1987.

HOENSCH, Jörg: *Geschichte der Tschechoslowakei*, 3rd edition, Stuttgart–Berlin–Köln 1992.

HORČÁKOVÁ, Václava – REXOVÁ, Kristina – POLANSKÝ, Luboš: *Select Bibliography on Czech History. Books and Articles 1990–1999*, Jaroslav Pánek (ed.), Prague 2000.

HORČÁKOVÁ, Václava – REXOVÁ, Kristina: *Select Bibliography on Czech History. Books and Articles 2000–2004*, Jaroslav Pánek (ed.), Prague 2005.

HORSKÁ, Pavla – MAUR, Eduard – MUSIL, Jiří: *Zrod velkoměsta. Urbanizace českých zemí a Evropa*, Praha–Litomyšl 2002.

HREJSA, Ferdinand: *Dějiny křesťanství v Československu*, I–VI, Praha 1947–1950.

HUSA, Václav – PETRÁŇ, Josef – ŠUBRTOVÁ, Alena: *Homo faber. Pracovní motivy ve starých vyobrazeních*, Praha 1967.

JANÁK, Jan: *Dějiny Moravy*, III/1: *Hospodářský rozmach Moravy 1740–1918*, Brno 1999.

JANÁK, Jan – HLEDÍKOVÁ, Zdeňka: *Dějiny správy v českých zemích do roku 1945*, Praha 1989.

Die Juden in den böhmischen Ländern, Ferdinand Seibt (ed.), München 1983.

KADLEC, Jaroslav: *Přehled českých církevních dějin*, I–II, 2nd edition, Praha 1991.

KADLEC, Karel: *Přehled ústavních dějin Moravy*, Praha 1926.

KALOUSEK, Josef: *České státní právo*, 2nd edition, Praha 1892.

KANN, Robert A.: *A History of the Habsburg Empire 1526–1918*, Berkeley 1974.

KAPRAS, Jan: *Právní dějiny zemí Koruny české*, I–II, Praha 1913–1920.

KAVKA, František – PETRÁŇ, Josef (eds.): *A History of Charles University*, I–II, Prague 2001.

KNOBLOCH, Erhard J.: *Deutsche Literatur in Böhmen, Mähren, Schlesien von den Anfängen bis heute. Kleines Handlexikon*, 2nd edition, München 1976.

Kontakte und Konflikte. Böhmen, Mähren und Österreich: Aspekte eines Jahrtausends gemeinsamer Geschichte, Thomas Winkelbauer (ed.), Horn–Waidhofen an der Thaya 1993.

KŘEN, Jan: *Konfliktgemeinschaft. Tschechen und Deutsche 1780–1918*, München 1996.

KUBÍČEK, Tomáš et al.: *Literární Morava*, Brno 2002.

KUČA, Karel: *Města a městečka v Čechách, na Moravě a ve Slezsku*, I–VI (A–S), Praha 1996–2004.

KUTNAR, František – MAREK, Jaroslav: *Přehledné dějiny českého a slovenského dějepisectví. Od počátků národní kultury až do sklonku třicátých let 20. století*, Praha 1997.

KVAČEK, Robert et al.: *Dějiny Československa II. 1648–1918*, Praha 1990.

LEDVINKA, Václav – PEŠEK, Jiří: *Prague*, Praha 2001.

MALÝ, Karel – SIVÁK, Florian: *Dějiny státu a práva v Československu*, I (do roku 1918), Praha 1988.

MALÝ, Karel et al.: *Dějiny českého a československého práva do roku 1945*, 2nd edition, Praha 1999.

MAUR, Eduard et al.: *Dějiny obyvatelstva českých zemí*, 2nd edition, Praha 1996, 1998.

MĚŠŤAN, Antonín: *Geschichte der tschechischen Literatur im 19. und 20. Jahrhundert*, Köln–Wien 1984.

MÍKA, Alois: *Československé dějiny v obrazech*, Praha 1971.

NOVÁK, Arne: *Přehledné dějiny literatury české*, Olomouc 1936–1939; 2nd edition: Brno 1995.

OKEY, Robin: *The Habsburg Monarchy c. 1765–1918. From Enlightenment to Eclipse*, London 2001.

PALACKÝ, František: *Dějiny národu českého v Čechách a v Moravě*, I–V, Praha 1848–1876, 3rd edition, 1876–1878.

PÁNEK, Jaroslav (ed.): *Czech Historiography in the 1990s*, Prague 2001 (In: Historica. Historical Sciences in the Czech Republic, Series Nova 7–8, 2000–2001).

PÁNEK, Jaroslav – Vorel, Petr (eds.): *Lexikon současných českých historiků*, Praha 1999.

PÁNEK, Jaroslav et al.: *Idea českého státu v proměnách staletí*, Praha 2008.

PÁNEK, Jaroslav – RAKOVÁ, Svatava – HORČÁKOVÁ, Václava: *Scholars of Bohemian, Czech and Czechoslovak History Studies*, I–III, Prague 2005.

PĚKNÝ, Tomáš: *Historie Židů v Čechách a na Moravě*, 2nd edition, Praha 2001.

PETRÁŇ, Josef: *Český znak. Stručný nástin jeho vzniku a historického vývoje*, Praha 1970.

PETRÁŇ, Josef et al.: *Dějiny Československa I. Do roku 1648*, Praha 1990.

PETRÁŇ, Josef et al.: *Dějiny hmotné kultury*, I/1–2, II/1–2, Praha 1985–1997.

PODIVEN (Pithart, Petr – Příhoda, Petr – Otáhal, Milan): *Češi v dějinách nové doby (1848–1939)*, 2nd edition, Praha 2003.

POHL, Walter – VOCELKA, Karl: *Die Habsburger. Eine europäische Familiengeschichte*, Graz–Wien–Köln 1992.

POLIŠENSKÝ, Josef: *History of Czechoslovakia in Outline*, Praha 1991.

PRINZ, Friedrich: *Geschichte Böhmens 1848–1948*, Frankfurt am Main–Berlin 1991.

Přehled československých dějin, I–III Praha 1958–1960.

Přehled dějin Československa, I/1–2, Praha 1980–1982.

RENNER, Hans – SAMSON, Ivo: *A History of Czechoslovakia since 1945*, London–New York 1993.

ŘÍČAN, Rudolf: *Dějiny Jednoty bratrské*, Praha 1957.

RYANTOVÁ, Marie – VOREL, Petr (eds.), *Čeští králové*, Praha–Litomyšl 2008.

SCHENK, Hans: *Die Böhmischen Länder. Ihre Geschichte, Kultur und Wirtschaft*, Bielefeld 1993.

SEDLÁČEK, August: *Hrady, zámky a tvrze království Českého*, I–XV, Praha 1882–1927; 3rd edition, 1993–1998.

SEIBT, Ferdinand: *Deutschland und die Tschechen. Geschichte einer Nachbarschaft in der Mitte Europas*, München 1974.

Sejm czeski od czasów najdawniejszych do 1913 roku, Marian J. Ptak (ed.), Opole 2000.

SERKE, Jürgen: *Böhmische Dörfer*, Praha 2001.

SKÝBOVÁ, Anna: *České královské korunovační klenoty*, Praha 1982.

SPUNAR, Pavel: *Kultura českého středověku*, Praha 1985.

TAPIÉ, Victor-Lucien: *The Rise and Fall of Habsburg Monarchy*, London 1971.

TEICH, Mikuláš (ed.): *Bohemia in History*, Cambridge 1998.

TOMEK, Wácslaw Wladiwoj: *Dějepis města Prahy*, I–XII, Praha 1871–1901, 2nd edition: 1882–1906.

URBAN, Otto: *České a československé dějiny do roku 1918*, Praha 1991.

VÁLKA, Josef: *Česká společnost v 15.–18. století*, I–II, Praha 1972–1983.

VÁLKA, Josef: *Dějiny Moravy*, I–II, Brno 1996.

VOCELKA, Karl – Heller, Lynne: *Die Lebenswelt der Habsburger. Kultur- und Mentalitätsgeschichte einer Familie*, Graz–Wien–Köln 1997.

VOCELKA, Karl – Heller, Lynne: *Die private Welt der Habsburger. Leben und Alltag einer Familie*, Graz–Wien–Köln 1998.

VOREL, Petr: *Od pražského groše ke koruně české. Průvodce dějinami peněz v českých zemích*, Praha 2000, 2nd edition, 2004.

VOREL, Petr: *Od českého tolaru ke světovému dolaru. Zrození tolaru a jeho cesta v evropském a světovém peněžním oběhu 16.–20. století*, Praha 2003.

WANDYCZ, Piotr S.: *The Price of Freedom. A History of East Central Europe from the Middle Ages to the Present*, London–New York 1992.

WINTER, Eduard: *Tausend Jahre Geisteskampf im Sudetenraum*, Salzburg–Leipzig 1938.

WOLKAN, Rudolf: *Geschichte der deutschen Literatur in Böhmen und in den Sudetenländern*, Augsburg 1925.

I. Territorial Development
and the Transformation of Landscape

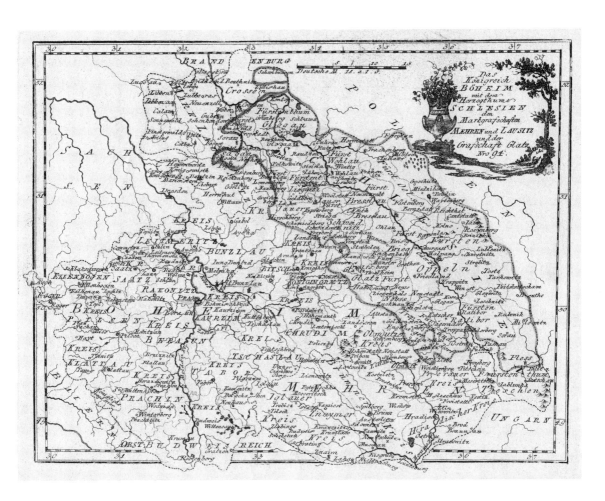

Czech crown lands on the map by Franz Johann Joseph von Reilly from the year 1791. Viennese cartographer F. J. J. Reilly produced the 1:2000000 scale map of the Czech crown lands for the atlas *Schauplatz der fünf Theile der Welt*. The map shows not only Bohemia, Moravia, but also the whole of Silesia, whose major part belonged to Prussia from 1742, and Upper and Lower Lusatia, ceded to Saxony in 1635. The title of the map is adorned with a Rococo cartouche, copperplate.

1 The Formation of the Geographical Core of the Czech State

A range of lands or regions – in various modes of dependence, both closer and looser or in the form of personal union – have been connected with the geographic core of the Czech state in the course of the preceding centuries. However, during the thousand years of its history, not only did the boundaries of the state, lands, regions, local and other forms of administration change, but so too did the terms and names which expressed Czech statehood. The original political designation of individual state entities are recorded in maps and written sources – above all in Czech, Latin and German. Deeds and bills from the Middle Ages, and documents from the Modern Era capture the transformations and variations of the political and geographical nomenclature.

The geo-political and military-strategic significance of Bohemia, Moravia and Silesia has always been influenced by its "classic position in the heart of Europe". From prehistoric times, the Czech Lands have been distant from the economic, cultural and, later, political centres, even though an important trade route crossed the territory of today's Moravia and Slovakia (the Amber Road which joined the Mediterranean region with the Baltic coast). Protected by mountains at its border, in the notional centre of the continent, with no marine harbours and without access to the large waterways (excepting the Elbe which rises here and the Danube nearby), without extensive fertile lowlands, the Czech Lands remained for centuries rather at the margins of the great political, economic and social processes of Europe. For the most part these were manifest in the Czech Lands after something of a delay and often less intensely.

František Palacký, the most important Czech historian of the 19th century, in the introduction to *The History of the Czech Nation in Bohemia and Moravia*, cogently expressed the mutual bonds of natural conditions and developmental opportunities of both the society and, to an extent, the geo-political standing of the Czech Lands, mostly Bohemia, within the European framework: "Nature itself, having completed and formed Bohemia as a particular unit, thus predetermined the main character of Czech history… Distance from the sea, lack of great navigable lakes and rivers in the land, and that very wreath of border mountains which obstructs commerce and connection with the rest of Europe: these factors isolated

Bohemia, and this lack of natural routes into the country was only compensated when artificial ones were carved out later."

The Czech state, its core and borders, were formed from the beginning of the 10th to the beginning of the 11th centuries. However, before this, there were two attempts to constitute a state in the Czech basin and the Moravian valleys: Samo's realm and Mojmír's Great Moravian Empire. The Frankish merchant Samo, leader of the rebellious Slavs against the Avars in the first half of the 7th century, created a strong tribal union of Slavs after a series of victories over the Avars in Central Europe around the year 623 or 624. It is not possible to determine the exact territorial extent of the union, named Samo's Realm (*Sámova říše*), due to the lack of written information and archaeological sources. As the experts differ, we can only demarcate Samo's tribal union vaguely. Its centre was most likely located in Moravia. Members of the union included Slavic tribes in Bohemia, Serbs of Prince Dervan, along the Elbe (Polabian) and the Saale rivers, northwest of Bohemia, and perhaps even part of Carinthia, also inhabited by Slavs. The borders of the tribal union were not stable, but changed in response to the political situation of the moment in Central Europe. Samo's realm joined in common battle against the Avars and later against the Frankish king Dagobert I. After Samo's death around 658 the historical sources are silent on the subject of the continuity or dissolution of the realm, and we can neither assert nor rule out the possibility of further political events in the former centre of Samo's realm during the 8th century.

In the first half of the 9th century, we know of another power centre that began to form on our territory in southern Moravia around Valy near Mikulčice and Staré Město near Uherské Hradiště, and in Slovakia in the environs of Nitra. With the connection of the two regions by Mojmír I after Pribina was run out of the Nitra region around 833–836, the core of what would become Great Moravia (*Velká Morava*) was formed, including the settled territory of the Moravian valleys and the Nitra region. Its southern border reached into today's Austria in the area to the south-west of the confluence of the rivers Morava and Dyje (Thaya).

The Great Moravian Empire reached its utmost territorial and political extent in the era of Prince Svatopluk. Most probably after 883, Svatopluk expanded his influence to Bohemia, as well as to the Serbian tribes settled along the river Saale and apparently in the years 874–880 encroached upon the region of the Silesian tribes around the upper Oder and Vistula. In the years 883–884 Svatopluk took control of Pannonia; in the east his power probably reached as far as the upper Tisza after fighting in the years 880–882. Although the Great Moravian Empire was more powerful and its political system firmer than Samo's tribal union, the demarcation of Great Moravia's border remains a theoretical construct, founded as in the case of Samo's empire, upon available archaeological and written sources. It is not possible to draw on a map with any degree of exactitude those regions which are presumed to have formed part of the empire.

By the beginning of the 10th century after the fall of the Great Moravian Empire, the centre of political life shifted to Bohemia, where the Czech state (*Český stát*) began to form through the expansion of the Central Bohemian Přemyslid domain. Boleslav I began the unification process after 935 and to the end of the 10th century the Přemyslids controlled the entire territory of Bohemia including the eastern Bohemian domain of the Slavníkovecs. Under Boleslav's governance there were also territorial conquests among his princes: in northern Moravia, to the Váh region, Silesia, Lesser Poland (the Cracow region), Sandomierz and further east to Červonograd. It seems that the Piasts pushed the Přemyslids back to Bohemia by the end of the 980s, and in the years 1003–1004, the Polish prince Bolesław the Brave controlled Bohemia. Only in 1019 did the Přemyslid Oldřich win Moravia back (that is, mostly the northern part of the country), joining it to the Bohemian principality and entrusting its administration to his son Břetislav. The territorial core of the Czech state, which was strongly influenced by natural conditions, had been formed for the centuries ahead.

The natural barrier, protecting the inhabitants of the Czech Lands and its seats, was created by a mountain zone covered by impassable woods, and with a notional border running through its middle. In the territories unprotected by mountains with dense forests, a natural border was lacking and it was mainly the south-eastern border of Bohemia and the southern border of Moravia that changed most often, and differ most from the present state.

In the time of Břetislav's reign in the years 1035–1055, Kłodzko (presumably from the 10th century), the regions of Zittau, Weitra and Zagost were part of Bohemia; however the regions of Cheb, Aš, Nová Bystřice and Landštejn did not belong to it. In southern Moravia the border with Austria was further south, and only about half-way through the 11th century did it settle on the river Dyje. In north Moravia, Břetislav conquered the territory around Hradec nad Moravicí and thus laid the foundations of the future region of Opava. Beyond the Moravian Pass, he penetrated to the rivers Ostravice and Pszczyna. For a short period after his invasion of Poland in 1039 he controlled Silesia, the Cracow region and part of Greater Poland, including Gniezno and Poznań; but he had to give up this conquered territory over time. The Přemyslid princes gained several further lands during the 11th and 12th centuries for a transition period: in the years 1075–1076, the Dohna region; in the years 1076, 1085 and 1158 (to 1256) the Bautzen region; and from Hungary in 12th century on the right bank of the Olšava and Morava south of Uherský Brod in the direction of Hodonín. They forfeited the Sušice region (1124–1265) and part of the Weitra region (1179 saw the loss of territory in the regions of Vitoraz-Weitra; in 1186 the region to the west of Weitra was made over in fief to the line of Kuenrings).

By the end of the 12th century, the integrity of the Czech state was profoundly disturbed by the dissensions of the Přemyslids. Emperor Frederick I Barbarossa made over Moravia to Conrad Otto in 1182 as an imperial appanage and declared it a free margraviate independent of Bohemia. In 1187 Barbarossa also raised the Prague bishopric to the level of imperial principality. However after the death of the Bohemian prince Frederick (*Bedřich*) in 1189, when the Moravian Margrave, Conrad Otto ascended to the prince's throne in Prague, the Czech Lands were again unified. The independence of the Prague bishopric came to an end in 1193, since at that time Bishop Jindřich Břetislav from the Přemyslid line became Bohemian prince.

The territory of the Czech state was further enlarged in the second half of the 13th century and the beginning of the 14th during the reigns of Přemysl Otakar II, Wenceslas II (*Václav*) and Wenceslas III. The expansionist policies of Přemysl Otakar II, motivated by the desire to strengthen his family and the ruler's power, turned to the south. In 1251, Přemysl Otakar II took Upper and Lower Austria, Styria (to 1254, and again to 1260), in 1253 Pitten and 1269 Carinthia, Carniola and most of Friuli (1270). To the west of Bohemia he gained the Cheb region for ten years (1266–1276). However he had to give up all these territories to Rudolf I of Habsburg in 1276. In 1256 the Bautzen region was yielded to Brandenburg; in contrast however the Sušice region was returned to Bohemia in 1265. Kłodzko briefly became part of the Piast region of Wrocław in 1278.

Wenceslas II, with his desire for greater power, turned his interests to the north-east and south-east. In 1290 he regained Kłodzko and in the years 1289–1292, gradually, the regions of Bytom, Opole, Těšín and Cracow; in 1291 also the western part of Cheb. In 1296 however he definitively lost the remainder of the Weitra region, over which Rudolf I of Habsburg gained control. As Polish king Wenceslas II extended his lands to Greater Poland (1300–1306), for his son, later Wenceslas III, he accepted the Hungarian crown in 1301. The emergent Přemyslid confederation which, in 1305 at the beginning of Wenceslas III's reign, was still made up of the Czech Lands, Poland and part of Hungary, collapsed with the death of the last Přemyslid in 1306.

In the 10th century the establishment of secular power together with the guarantee of the material and social standing of the ruler and his retinue led to the division of the country into two smaller appanages (úděl; in Latin documents "pars"), administrated by members of the ruler's line. These were not administratively independent territories, and in Bohemia, unlike Moravia, their sizes were not fixed and they were not heritable. For instance from the 10th century and the beginning of the 11th, we know of the appanage belonging to Wenceslas's brother, Boleslav, in Stará Boleslav; also to Boleslav III in Žatec or to Jaromír and Oldřich in the Kouřim region. In the 1030s, Jaromír had land in the Plzeň region, and in the beginning of the 13th century also in the regions of Chrudim and Čáslav. Hradec Králové and Kłodzko are also mentioned.

After Prince Oldřich took control of Moravia, the first appanage was established; during the reign of Vratislav II two (of Olomouc and Brno); and by the end of the 11th century, three appanages (of Olomouc, Brno and Znojmo). The Moravian appanages were politically and territorially more stable than those of Bohemia. The Olomouc appanage possessed the castle network of Olomouc, Přerov, Spytihněv, Břeclav and Hradec nad Moravicí; the Brno appanage only the castle network of Brno; the Znojmo appanage of Znojmo and Bítov. The appanages ceased to administrate the regions half-way through the 12th century. In Moravia, they came to an end in 1197; in Bohemia only at the beginning of the 13th century. One of the reasons for the disappearance of these appanages was the extinction of the Děpoltic line, the last auxiliary branch of the Přemyslids, in 1223, and the coronation of Wenceslas I as the younger king in 1228.

Along with the appanages, there was also a castle administration in Bohemia and Moravia, or, in other words, a castle system. In the Bohemian crown lands of the early Middle Ages, the castle system formed the foundation of state power and administration. Executive functions and, gradually, those connected with tax were taken over by castles; presumably by the end of the 10th century, by the year 993, there is proof of the existence of castle provinces belonging to some of the new Přemyslid castles, for instance in the regions of Bílina, Děčín and Litoměřice. At the close of the 10th century among the administrative castles were Mělník, Kouřim, Čáslav, Mladá Boleslav, Žatec, Litoměřice, Bílina and Děčín; by the end of the 11th century also Chrudim and Hradec (Králové). Gradually castles that had been established earlier but in more remote places were joined with the administrative castles which were located in old settled territory, the fertile lowlands. Among the former there was above all Plzeň (Stará Plzeň or Starý Plzenec), and by the end of the 11th century and the beginning of the 12th, Sedlec, Prácheň, Netolice, Doudleby, Chýnov and perhaps Bechyně. About mid-way through the 12th century the castle of Vraclav near Vysoké Mýto, founded by Břetislav I, became the centre of the castle province; in Moravia the castles of Olomouc, Přerov, Brno, Spytihněv, Břeclav, Bítov, Hradec nad Moravicí and Znojmo were of administrative level. The castle system, which created the basis of the state administration in Bohemia and Moravia from mid-way through the 11th century, began to fall apart in the second half of the 13th century during the rule of Přemysl Otakar II. Only at the end of the 14th century and the beginning of the 15th was the function of the castle network taken over by the regions (*kraj*). What were originally tax regions gradually turned into multifunctional administrative units.

2 The Bohemian Crown Lands

The next significant territorial transformations of the Czech state are connected with Luxemburg dynasty on the Bohemian throne, and mainly the dynastic policies of Charles IV. John of Luxemburg regained the Bautzen region in 1319; for helping the Roman King Ludwig of Bavaria the Cheb region also in 1322; and the purchase of the Görlitz region in 1329 (all of upper Lusatia – this name began to be used for the Bautzen and Görlitz regions from the 15th century – was added in 1363). The regions of Aš and Selb were integrated into the Cheb region in 1331. Among John of Luxemburg's significant successes in the area of foreign military activities was the addition of Upper and part of Lower Silesia in the years 1327–1335. The jural relationship of the Silesian principalities and Moravian enclaves in Silesia to the Bohemian crown lands developed and metamorphosed in the following centuries. The Czech state inherited Luxemburg itself through the father of John of Luxemburg, Henry VII.

During the rule of Charles IV, and then continuously from the 15th century, the terms Bohemian crown lands (*země Koruny české*), the Crown of the Bohemian Kingdom (*Koruna českého království*), *Corona regni Bohemiae*, or in short, the Bohemian Crown (*Koruna česká*) began to be used. Already on May 19, 1329, John of Luxemburg employed this general designation of the state for the group of lands under his rule. From 1348 Charles IV used this designation for both the original territory of the Czech Lands as well the added lands and foreign fiefs. The crown of St Wenceslas became the symbol for all the territories which made up the Czech state under one ruler. The basis of this territorial complex was the Bohemian kingdom; other territorial units began to be commonly referred to as auxiliary or incorporated lands. Charles IV, whose territorial gains were facilitated above all by his marriage policy, joined two further Silesian principalities to the Czech state, Świdnica (1353, through marriage; 1368 through inheritance) and Jawor (1368), Lower Lusatia (1368), and Brandenburg, which he purchased in 1373. In 1353 he gained the greater part of the Upper Palatinate, and two years later he definitively added it to the Czech state. At the same time through purchases and liens of castle, domains and towns in Vogtland, Meissen, Thuringia, Mecklenburg and Upper Palatinate, he created a dense network of foreign fiefs (in Latin called *feuda extra curtem*). He built a systematic zone of fiefs in Bavaria which linked to fiefs in the Upper Palatinate. In the 18th century, František Martin Pelc, historian and representative of the Enlightenment and national awakening, designated the Czech territory of the Upper Palatinate in the time of Charles as New Bohemia (*Nové Čechy*).

Near the end of his life, Charles IV in 1377 arranged the administration of territories of the Bohemian crown lands in such a way that the unity of the Crown would be maintained after his death. Wenceslas IV however was unable to hold together the crown lands he inherited from his father. In 1401 he lost the Upper Palatinate. In 1402 the Margrave of Meissen gained Dohna as fief. The same year Sigismund ceded the territory of Neumark to the Teutonic Knights, and part of Brandenburg from the 1140s; in 1415 he gave Brandenburg in lien to the Hohenzollerns and in 1423 Moravia also in lien to his son-in-law Albrecht of Austria (to 1437). The territory of Cheb was gradually reduced, almost to its present extent. During the Hussite wars the following areas were given in lien to the Meissen margraves: around Most (1423–1456), Duchcov (1423–1450) and Osek (1423–1450). In the 1420s the border between Bohemia and Zittau assumed its final form, the latter definitively merging with Upper Lusatia.

From the beginning of the 14th century, regions gradually emerged in the Bohemian crown lands which were autonomous in their administration and economy. By the beginning of the 15th century, Bohemia was divided into twelve regions: of Bechyně, Boleslav, Čáslav, Hradec, Chrudim, Kouřim (Prague), Litoměřice, Plzeň, Prácheň, Rakovník, Slaný and Žatec. However, because of the frequent transformations of the territorial extent of the peripheral domains, their borders were not fixed. No natural formation of regions took place in Moravia during the Middle Ages.

Neither the emergence of important Central European units of power – Great Moravia in the 9th century, and the Czech state in the 10th century – nor the numbering of the Bohemian crown lands with the great powers of Europe in the time of Přemysl Otakar II, and more significantly in the time of Charles IV in the 14th century, promoted Central Europe to the level of geo-political centre of the continent. Nevertheless, the Czech state was always an important crossroads of cultural currents, political interests and conflicts.

From the end of the 15th century and in the course of the 16th, the uneven development of European economics affected the Bohemian crown lands. The great geographical discoveries brought with them, among other things, the shift of commercial centres from southern Europe to its western coast. New trade routes crossed the world, the influx of American silver and a range of other political and economic aspects together with the continental position of the Bohemian crown lands unfavourably influenced relations with the more advanced European states.

In the 15th century, the territorial extent of the Czech state partially changed, mainly due to the personal unions. Under Sigismund (*Zikmund*) of Luxemburg, a personal union was established between the Bohemian crown and Hungary (1436–1437); under Albrecht of Habsburg (of Austria, r. 1437–1439) and Ladislav Posthumous (r. 1453–1457) between Hungary and the Austrian lands; under the Jagiellons Vladislav II and Louis (*Ludvík*) again with Hungary (1490–1526). George of Poděbrady (*Jiří z Poděbrad*) regained some foreign fiefs, and also in 1462 Lower Lusatia, which had been given in lien in 1445 to the margraves of Brandenburg, although with the territory around Cottbus and Picń. The territories of the regions of Opava and Krnov were gradually disengaged from Moravia, drawing closer to the Silesian principalities. In 1468, George was forced to transfer the rule of Moravia, both Lusatias and Silesia to Mátyás Corvinus, just as Vladislav of Jagiellon had to during the years 1471–1490 (according to the Olomouc agreement for the years 1478–1490). Only after Mátyás's death were the Bohemian crown lands integrated within the framework of the personal union of the Jagiellons (1490–1526).

The number of regions was increased to fourteen after the Hussite wars under the rule of George of Poděbrady (Podbrdy broke away from the Rakovník region; the Vltava region from that of Bechyně), and it remained thus to the beginning of the 18th century. From the outset, the towns of Prague formed a special administrative unit outside the framework of the regions. The regions which were referred to as outer – Cheb, Kłodzko, Loket and Trutnov – established according to fief law, had at the same time exceptional jural standing. The Trutnov region was administratively joined to that of Hradec mid-way through the 16th century. Under the Turkish threat in the 16th century, four regions – Brno, Hradiště, Nový Jičín and Olomouc – were established as defensive units in Moravia in 1529. In 1569 their number was fixed at five – Brno, Hradiště, Jihlava, Olomouc and Znojmo. The largest, the Olomouc region, was divided in 1735 into the Kolštejn-Třebová and Přerov-Bruntál districts.

The emergence of the Czech-Austrian-Hungarian confederation under the Habsburgs in 1526 entailed the integration of the Bohemian crown lands into the multinational Habsburg monarchy for a period of four centuries. In the time of the early Modern Era – the 16th–18th centuries – the tempo of economic growth in various parts of Europe diverged further. A network of commerce and transportation, enabling dynamic economic relations between the Mediterranean, Western Europe and the Baltic, as well as other continents, created the great harbours, river transport and a relatively dense network of overland routes. The location of the Bohemian crown lands in the continental interior again enabled connection with the economic activities of the Low Lands, England, France and, in Germany, above all the lower Rhineland. The Bohemian crown lands were reliant on commercial dry-land conveyance or on the waterways of the Elbe or Danube. Despite the considerable efforts of the Austrian state to implement mercantile ideas, principles and reforms to cathect the economy of the monarchy, the Bohemian crown lands, dependent for the most part on domestic circumstances, lagged behind the countries of Western Europe as these latter developed quickly.

There were significant territorial losses in 1635 when both Upper and Lower Lusatia were lost to Saxony (given in lien before that in 1623). Further changes to the territorial extent of the Czech state date from 1742: after defeat in the Silesian wars, Maria Theresia gave Prussia Kłodzko in its entirety (measuring about 1635 km^2), Lower Silesia and part of Upper Silesia, Opole, Racibórz with Bytom, Pszczyna and, from Bohumín, territory on the right bank of the Olše river (Olza in Polish) measuring roughly 35,000 km^2. The remaining part of Silesia, Těšín, part of the regions of Opava, Krnov, Nisa, began to be designated as Czech (or Austrian) Silesia. To 1815, all foreign fiefs were gradually lost (the last in 1815: Marktredwitz [Ředvicko] to Bavaria).

Administrative reforms of 1714 reduced the regions in Bohemia to twelve. The regions of Vltava and Podbrdy were merged with that of Beroun; Slaný was joined to that of Rakovník. The Cheb region merged with Žatec and Loket, whose privileged standing was gradually pared back after the Thirty Years' War. Bohemia was divided into the regions of Bechyně, Beroun, Boleslav, Čáslav, Hradec, Chrudim, Kouřim, Litoměřice, Plzeň, Prácheň, Rakovník and Žatec, from 1714.

There was a further change in 1751 when the four largest regions were divided (Žatec into that of Žatec and Loket, Plzeň into Plzeň and Klatovy, Bechyně into Tábor and Budějovice, and Hradec into Hradec and Bydžov) to ensure that all regions were of the same size. New regions from the outset were designated as sections (podíl), but in the same year they then became regions. The sixteen Bohemian regions lasted for an entire century. In Moravia a sixth Moravian region was established from the Přerov-Bruntál district of the Olomouc region – that of Přerov. The independent territorial-administrative development of Silesia, mainly along the Moravian border, ended in 1742 when only part of Silesia, referred to as Czech (or Austrian) Silesia, remained within the Habsburg monarchy. It was divided into the principalities of Krnov, Nisa, Opava and Těšín. Regions were created in Silesia only in 1783 when the regions of Opava and Těšín were established.

In the 19th century, the entire economic life of Europe, as well as many countries beyond, was influenced by the Industrial Revolution. It came in phases from England through France and the western part of Germany to Central and Eastern Europe, and this meant that the Bohemian crown lands, because of their geographical position, felt its effects only after the more advanced European states. Begun in England at the close of the 18th century, the process of urbanization, linked with the quick growth of the towns, with the development of the industrial agglomerations and growing sections (podíl) of the population in towns, affected the Bohemian crown lands more markedly only a century later – in the last decades of the 19th century and the beginning of the 20th. Inside the Habsburg monarchy however, the territorially stable Bohemian crown lands held an important position in relation to the greater part of the lands in the confederation as an industrially developed region. There were no further large territorial changes to the Czech state until the emergence of Czechoslovakia in 1918. The collapse of Austro-Hungary marked the end of the jural existence of the macro-region of the Bohemian crown lands.

After the abolishment of serfdom in 1848, along with the patrimonial offices, the territorial division of the Czech Lands changed once again. With effect from 1850, seven regions were established in Bohemia: of Budějovice, Česká Lípa, Cheb, Jičín, Pardubice, Plzeň and Prague. The regions were further divided into political districts (*okres*). The new reform of 1855, divided Bohemia into thirteen smaller regions: of Boleslav, Budějovice, Čáslav, Hradec, Cheb, Chrudim, Jičín, Litoměřice, Písek, Plzeň, Prague, Tábor and Žatec. The capital city of Prague retained its administrative independence.

After administrative reform, Moravia was divided into two regions with effect from 1850 (of Brno and Olomouc, and political districts); from 1855 to 1868 into six regions (of Brno, Znojmo, Jihlava, Olomouc, Uherské Hradiště, and Nový Jičín). Silesia was to be one region with political districts from 1850; it was briefly joined with Moravia in the years 1860–1861.

1862 witnessed the abolishment of the regional executives in Bohemia, and for Moravia and Silesia in 1860, but they retained some of their powers to 1868. In the further administrative reforms of 1868, the regions were not restored, and the regional executives were abolished; after almost five centuries, the regional system ceased to exist. Political districts remained, although their number changed.

3 Czechoslovakia in Central Europe

The establishment of Czechoslovakia in 1918 fulfilled Czechs' and Slovaks' aim of independence. The post-war arrangement of Europe however held many risks, which climaxed in a further military conflict, and, after 1945, in the division of the European continent into new spheres of political interest.

During World War I, the Czech resistance both at home and abroad anticipated the creation of the Czechoslovak state. Ideas concerning the territorial extent of the future state were first expressed by Tomáš Garrigue Masaryk in London in 1916, and he sent his outline on the map of Europe for further negotiation to the United States of America. He integrated Bohemia, Moravia and Czech Silesia with their borders of that time, along with Slovakia as the northern area of Hungary, settled for the most part by Slovak nationals; also Vitoraz, Valtice and the southern part of Kłodzko, part of Lusatia, inhabited by the Lusatian Serbs (approximately according the Sorbian-speaking borders from the end of the 19ᵗʰ century) and Racibórz. At the same time he proposed the creation of a corridor in today's Burgenland between the Czechoslovak state and the southern Slav territories. At the margin of the map Masaryk noted: "Corridor connecting Bohemia with Serbo-Croatia. Established by numerous Croatian colonies, in the south Slovenes. It would either belong in its entirety to Serbia, or in part to Hungary, in part to Serbia." Even before the establishment of Czechoslovakia, the Commission of Czechoslovakian Affairs in Paris prepared further variants of the territorial extent of the future republic. Some of these included the possibilities of connecting

Kłodzko, Racibórz and the region of Lusatian Serbia, as well as the course of the border between Hungary and Slovakia.

After World War I, the legal form of the new state, the Republic of Czechoslovakia (*Republika československá*), was fixed in the series of agreements called the Paris Peace Conference. There were peace agreements with Germany made on June 28, 1919 in Versailles, with Austria in Saint-Germain on September 10, 1919 and with Hungary in Trianon on June 4, 1920. The settlement of the Czechoslovak state borders however took until 1924. The demands of Czechoslovakia with respect to the recognition of its state borders proposed during the war, were presented by Edvard Beneš to the session of the peace conference on February 6, 1919. A conclusive resolution was approved by the Council on April 4, 1919, and it integrated them into the three treaties of the Paris Peace Conference. The basis of the republic became the historical territory of the Czech Lands, and, with smaller changes, the old land borders of Bohemia, Moravia and Czech Silesia, and furthermore the territories of the former Upper Hungary (*Horní Uhry*). With no reservations, the regions of Hlučín, Valtice (known as the Moravian-Dyje triangle) and part of Vitoraz (the upper reaches of the Lužnice river). The region of Těšín and, in Slovakia, the northern border with Poland in the areas of the Spiš and Orava was the subject of further negotiation. Czechoslovakia disputed the Těšín region with Poland, and this was concluded through arbitrage of the involved powers in Spa on June 10, 1920. According to this, the state border led along the river Olše, so the eastern part of the Těšín region, including most of the town of Těšín, fell to Poland, while the western part of what was once the Těšín principality, with the smaller part of the town (now Český Těšín), became part of Czechoslovakia.

The northern border of Slovakia (*Slovensko*) was essentially the northern border of the former Hungary, that is, Transleithania; border arrangements above all concerned the ceding of part of the territory of Poland in the regions of Spiš and Orava and went on till 1924. The southern, Slovak-Hungarian border had to be jurally determined by the Treaty of Trianon of June 4, 1920 because of the absence of a historical border. In the framework of the peace negotiations, Czechoslovakia gained the disputed territory of the Veľký Žitný island and smaller territory near Bratislava on the right bank of the Danube, named Petržalka. In the years 1922 and 1924, it ceded the territory around Suny, Somoskö and Somosköújfalu. This left a population of almost half a million ethnic Hungarians in Slovakia, mainly in the south.

Through the Treaty of Saint-Germain in 1919, Subcarpathian Ruthenia (*Podkarpatská Rus*), for centuries part of Hungary, became part of the Czechoslovak Republic. This union was preceded by the negotiation of several groups of the political representatives of the Ruthenian population in the USA and Subcarpathian Ruthenia, who in May 1919 definitively expressed their agreement to joining Czechoslovakia.

The founding of Czechoslovakia on October 28, 1918 considerably aggravated the Sudeten Germans living mainly in the border areas of the new state. A group of German deputies from the Czech Lands requested the establishment of an autonomous province, Deutschböhmen, within the framework of the Habsburg monarchy. (They made this request in connection with the negotiation of the Czech declaration (*Tříkrálová deklarace*) in the Imperial Council of January 1918.) On October 29, 1918 the province of Deutschböhmen was declared a part of the new Austrian state, Deutsch Österreich (German Austria), which included territory from Aš and Cheb through the regions of Most and Liberec to the Orlice Mountains, with its administrative centre in Liberec. Immediately after this on October 30, 1918, the province of Sudetenland was established on the territory of northern Moravia and Czech Silesia, with its centre in Opava. Finally on November 3, 1918 two further provinces were established, Böhmerwaldgau in the area of Český Les and the Bohemian Forest (*Šumava*), with its centres in Vimperk and Český Krumlov, and Deutschsüdmähren in southern Moravia with its centre in Znojmo. Apart from the four provinces, the towns of Brno, Olomouc and Jihlava (all with a strong German minority) were meant to be attached to Austria. However the attempt to strip away these provinces, created approximately in the space of the territories that would be occupied after the Munich agreement in 1938, was unsuccessful. After the failure of negotiations between the Czechoslovak government and representatives of the provinces, the territory of the provinces was occupied by Czechoslovak military units. In 1919 the Treaty of Saint-Germain brought to a close the attempts of the Sudeten Germans to break away.

In the years 1920–1928, the new state was divided into five administrative entities, called lands (*země*): Bohemia, Moravia, Silesia, Slovakia and Subcarpathian Ruthenia. The individual lands were made up of political districts (in Bohemia, Moravia and Silesia) and in Slovakia and Subcarpathian Ruthenia into districts called *župas*. Although the Župa Act of February 29, 1920 (in force from January 1, 1923) introduced *župa* system on the entire territory of Czechoslovakia, it was only brought into effect in Slovakia, where six new *župas* were established, two towns with controlled municipal councils and districts. In the Czech Lands, the original pre-war division of political districts remained in force; in Subcarpathian Ruthenia the old Hungarian *župa* system. According to the Political Administration Act of 1927, the new territorial division came into force on December 1, 1928, and this determined the Czech Land (*Země Česká*), by the joining of Moravia and Silesia into the Moravian-Silesian Land (*Země Moravskoslezská*), the Slovak Land (*Země Slovenská*; in Slovak, *Krajina Slovenská, Slovenská krajina*), and Subcarpathian Ruthenian Land (*Země Podkarpatoruská*). The *župa* system was abolished and replaced by political districts throughout Czechoslovakia.

The end of the twenty-year existence of the Czechoslovak Republic began with the Munich Agreement of September 29, and its acceptance on September 30, 1938. Czechoslovakia was forced to cede the border territories, what were referred to as Sudeten areas, about 28,000 km² in extent, in the days October 1–10, 1938. It also ceded about two-thirds of the Těšín region, and smaller territories in Slovakia to Poland in the period November 2–30, 1938; furthermore, and in accordance to Viennese arbitrage of November 2 it was to cede border territories of southern Slovakia and part of Subcarpathian Ruthenia to Hungary in the period November 5–10, 1939. The extent of the ceded territories in the space of the Czech Lands almost equalled the extent of the provinces of Deutschböhmen, Sudetenland,

Böhmerwaldgau and Deutschsüdmähren, as they were declared after the establishment of Czechoslovakia in autumn 1918 when those areas attempted to join Austria.

Most of the occupied territory of the Czech Lands became a special *župa*, Sudetenland, with its centre in Liberec. The southern areas of Bohemia, Moravia and in Slovakia in the area of Petržalka and Devín belonged the imperial *župas* Oberdonau and Niederdonau. The ceded territories made up about 29% of the original extent of the Czechoslovak state – of nearly 141,000 km^2 there remained only about 99,000 km^2. On October 6, 1938, Slovakia gained full autonomy with its own government; and on October 11, 1938 Subcarpathian Ruthenia likewise. The autonomy of the two lands was approved by the House of Deputies on November 19, 1938, and they also changed the official title of the state, the so-called second republic, to Czecho-Slovakia (*Česko-Slovensko*).

With the establishment of the Protectorate of Bohemia and Moravia *(Protektorát Čechy a Morava)* on March 16, 1939 after the German occupation of the Second Republic on March 15, 1939, Czechoslovakia was definitively abolished. The German occupation was preceded by the break away of Slovakia and the establishment of the Slovak State (*Slovenský štát*) on March 14, 1939; Subcarpathian Ruthenia was occupied by Hungary by March 18, 1939.

The Munich Agreement and the occupation of Czechoslovakia by Nazi Germany on March 15, 1939 also brought a fundamental change to the territorial division of the state. The ceded territories were gradually subordinated to the German imperial administration. The border areas of southern Bohemia, southern Moravia and Hlučín were joined to the existent administrative units in neighbouring land, to *župas* (Oberdonau, Niederdonau and Oberschlesien). From the rest of the ceded territories the so-called Reichsgau Sudetenland was created (Imperial Sudetenland *župa*), which was divided into fifty-three rural districts (*Landkreise*) and five town districts. The town districts (*Stadtkreise*) were Liberec, Ústí nad Labem, Cheb, Karlovy Vary and Opava.

On the territory of the Protectorate the original political districts remained, designated as "autonomous", and newly established *oberlandräte*. Established in the course of the first year of the occupation's administration, the *oberlandräte* were directly subordinate to the Reichsprotektor. Their number changed during World War II; after the administrative reform of Reinhard Heydrich there were seven *oberlandräte*, and after September 1, 1944, there were six.

Even during World War II, the Czechoslovak President-in-Exile Edvard Beneš considered several variants of the future borders of post-war Czechoslovakia. His ideas evidently originated in the period before the Munich Agreement, and then during the existence of the Second Republic. The extant sketch of the Czech Lands by Jaroslav Drábek from January 1939 contains three areas in western and northern Bohemia, and in Silesia with about 900,000 inhabitants of German nationality, which Beneš was thinking of ceding to Germany, along with three small territories in southern Bohemia and southern Moravia. The new map of May 1941 moreover captures the areas of southern Slovakia – these were meant to be ceded to Hungary. The territory meant to be ceded in southern Bohemia and southern

Moravia was, *pace* Drábek's sketch, greatly expanded. As compensation, Beneš demanded part of Kłodzko along its historical south-western borders.

So, as the political and military situation in Europe changed, so too did Beneš's decisions concerning the presumed Czechoslovak territories. In February 1945, the new proposal of border arrangements almost corresponded with pre-Munich borders, but without the regions of Aš, and without the Šluknov and Frýdlant Hook, and with a demand for part of the territory of Kłodzko. Diplomatic negotiations in the years 1945–1946 demanding the joining of Kłodzko in its entirety to Czechoslovakia, as in the peace conference of 1919, met with failure because of Czechoslovak-Polish relations of the time.

After World War II, Czechoslovakia was restored to its pre-Munich borders, without Subcarpathian Ruthenia, which, in accordance with agreements between the Czechoslovak Republic and the USSR, became part of the Soviet Union – the Ukrainian Soviet Socialist Republic. The state borders between Czechoslovakia the Soviet Union led along the former land border of Slovakia and Subcarpathian Ruthenia with smaller changes in the area of Čop. Czechoslovakia ceded the iron centre of Čop to the Soviet Union, thirteen municipalities to the north and in 1946 regained the cadastral territory of Lekárt (from 1948 Lekárovce). In 1947, Czechoslovakia received three municipalities from Hungary on the right bank of the Danube – Jarovce, Rusovce, Čunovo and part of the municipality of Rajka, which are today part of Bratislava. In 1959, small adjustments were made to the border with Poland to the benefit of both states. The new name of the republic from 1960, Czecho-Slovak Socialist Republic (*Česko-slovenská socialistická republika*), brought no change to the territorial extent of the state, and neither did the establishment of the Czechoslovak Republic (*Československá republika*) by constitutional law on March 6, 1990 nor the Czechoslovak Federal Republic (*Československá federativní republika*) on March 29, 1990 nor the Czech and Slovak Federal Republic (*Česká a Slovenská Federativní Republika*) on April 20, 1990.

The territorial division of the restored Czechoslovakia was based on the state of affairs up to September 29, 1939, without Subcarpathian Ruthenia. Three Lands (*Země*) – Bohemia, Moravia-Silesia and Slovakia – were divided into districts according to the Decree of the President of the Republic on October 27, 1945. From January 1, 1949, when the Regions Act came into effect, nineteen regions were established, divided into districts (of Prague, Ústí nad Labem, Karlovy Vary, Plzeň, České Budějovice, Jihlava, Pardubice, Hradec Králové, Liberec, Brno, Gottwaldov, Ostrava, Olomouc, Bratislava, Nitra, Žilina, Banská Bystrica, Košice and Prešov). In 1960 new territorial divisions were created with ten regions: Central Bohemia, Eastern Bohemia, Northern Bohemia, Western Bohemia, Southern Bohemia, Northern Moravia, Southern Moravia, Western Slovakia, Central Slovakia and Eastern Slovakia. The capital city of Prague gained the status of region. The Federalization of the Republic Act of October 27, 1968 (which came into effect on January 1, 1969) did not change the number of regions. In 1990, the national regional councils were abolished.

4 The Czech Republic in the Heart of Europe

With the division of the Czechoslovak state on January 1, 1993 into two independent states – the Czech Republic and Slovak Republic – the Czech Republic's extent returned to that of Břetislav's medieval principality. After many transformations, the Czech Republic (*Česká republika*), in its position and the demarcation of its borders, reminds us of the Czech Lands in the time of Břetislav's rule after 1035, when the first political crisis of the Přemyslid principality of that time ended, and its territory stabilized. The agreement about the demarcation of the borders between the Czech Republic and the Slovak Republic was signed on January 4, 1996.

The new Czech Republic was divided into seventy-five districts (*okres*) in the years 1993–1995; from January 1, 1996, this number rose to seventy-six. On January 1, 2000 constitutional law concerning the establishment of higher territorial autonomous entities came into effect, and this restored the regional system, and demarcating the extent of the fourteen new regions (*kraj*): of Prague, Central Bohemia, Liberec, Ústí, Karlovy Vary, Plzeň, Southern Bohemia, Pardubice, Hradec Králové, Moravia-Silesia, Vysočina, Southern Moravia, Olomouc and Zlín (this nomenclature valid from 2001). By January 1, 2003 the district offices were abolished and in their place commissioned municipalities were established.

The geographical position of the Czech Republic has not changed. In contemporary advanced society, the significance of the position of the Czech Lands is apparently smaller than in the past; nevertheless even after important changes during the 1980s and '90s, Central Europe remains a sensitive gold-leaf indicator of European stability, and the geopolitical aspect continues to shape the relations between European states and lands.

5 Metamorphoses of the Landscape

By the term "landscape" we understand a naturally or artificially defined part of the earth's surface whose elements are pedogenic rocks, land, skies, water, flora, fauna and mankind. Landscape, mainly the cultural landscape, in which to a considerable degree the activities of human society have participated, has changed dramatically in the Czech Lands in the course of the centuries, influenced by both natural conditions and mankind. The Czech landscape has its own dynamic. Over decades and centuries there have been changes caused by natural processes and human activity in the landscape; it also has its own ecological stability. In Central Europe the ecological stability of the landscape is defined by a relatively dense amount of forests, meadows, pasturage, tillage and built-up areas.

The historical landscape, or landscape as memory, is often talked of in connection with historical development. The historical landscape is every landscape of the past, but at the same time, in the sense of landscape as memory, the exceptional parts of past landscapes, where the preserved signs of human activity are singular and unique. The attribute "historical" is thus given by the object of study, i.e., landscape existing in the past (as opposed to the contemporary cultural landscape), preserved traces – remnants of landscape elements –

which helped create this landscape (and today document it), and historical information concerning the landscape. The significance of the phrase "landscape as memory" expresses a group of specific, identifiable relicts of the historical landscape, significant because they preserve the cultural heritage of the country. Here we always mean the cultural landscape, which is what mankind has helped create. Historical approaches discern in the landscape more a space for the realization of life and ideas of society, and the projection of the values of human civilizations.

The form of the historical landscape from various periods, in the contemporary cultural landscape, is preserved to a certain degree in both larger and smaller traces, some of which are hidden while others are easily apparent. Traces of the historical landscape (as distinct from natural influences) capture many political, economic, social and cultural events. The greater the distance in the past, the fewer the traces. In some cases, mainly when the landscape has been greatly damaged, the traces of human activity of even recent decades disappear.

6 Landscape of the Czech Lands in the Neolithic Age and Early Medieval Colonization

To the end of the Mesolithic Age, people hardly affected nature at all; they were an integral part of it. In the Neolithic Age however, the warm, moist Atlantic climate contributed to the creation of favourable conditions for the emergence of agriculture and permanent human settlements. In the Neolithic period, about 5000 BCE, the cultural landscape began to form on the territory of the Czech Republic in the space of today's central and north-western Bohemia, and south-western Moravia with permanent settlement and cultivated chernozem land to a height of 300 m above sea-level. Neolithic man cultivated land was not forested, and at the same time gradually transformed forest into agricultural land. The process of the separation of man from nature had begun, along with his active participation in the transformations of landscape.

At the beginning of the millennium, the climate was exceptionally favourable, warmer and humid, and this peaked in the 13th century and the first half of the 14th. Up to the 12th century, the Czech Lands were almost completely covered by predominantly broadleaf forests, surrounding small tracts of initially sparsely populated unforested lowlands. Mountains with primeval forests made a natural border of the Czech state, apart from the border regions of southern Moravia, the division between forest and the cultivated landscape was less obvious than it is today.

From the 11th century and especially from the second half of the 12th, with the growth of settlement caused by the internal and later external colonization, people penetrated to the higher, forested areas, and the unforested tracts gradually began to expand. Settlement gradually moved from the lowlands in the catchment area of the central and lower Elbe, the lower Ohře and lower Vltava, from the valleys of the rivers Morava, Svitava, Svratka and Dyje to the higher, more remote areas. The colonization movement was directed towards the forested areas, first to a height of 300 m above sea-level and later 500 m. New colonies with enclosed structures in fields, interrupted by smaller broadleaf forests, imprinted a new character on the landscape. From the first half of the 13th century, towns were founded in the Czech Lands, climaxing in the second half of the 13th century. The number of inhabitants rose, agriculture and crafts advanced, and the German settlers brought new legal norms to the land. By the close of the 14th century, settlement was almost complete, with the exception of those areas that were difficult to access. The process of gradual deforestation of the landscape was mitigated by the dilapidation and extinction of some settlements as a consequence of war, famine and plague, as well as natural disasters.

Waterways in the lowlands of the Elbe, the lower Vltava and Ohře, and the Moravian valleys constantly changed their beds and meandered. Influenced by erosion, spring floods and severe summer rains, these rivers formed numerous distributaries, pools and wetlands. Sluiced farmlands, timber and, in the summer, cereals and hay were swept along the original bed and the strong current created a new one. With the development of medieval river navigation and timber rafting, mainly on the Vltava and Elbe, fairly intense water-engineering activity began in the Czech Lands (weirs were built, river-beds were adjusted). The first artificial reservoirs – ponds – were established by the damming of streams and smaller rivers, probably from as early as the 13th century. The demand for fish grew (this was due among other factors to their higher consumption in times of fast). For instance the monastery in Louka near Znojmo obtained a decree permitting it to build ponds from as early as 1227, and there is mention of ponds in the founding document of the monastery of Zlatá Koruna in 1263.

By the passes (through border forests) important strategic and commercial land routes entered Bohemia and Moravia. They aimed above all for Prague, Brno and Olomouc and connected the Czech Lands with Europe. The network of land routes gradually branched out, becoming denser, and some changed according to the accessibility of the terrain as well as with the establishment of new economic and commercial centres. Land routes homed in on Prague from all sides. From the north, there were roads from Zittau, Chlumec (Serbian) and Most; from the west the Via Magna and from Domažlice. From the south-west, there was the well-known Gold Road, also named the Via Aurea, from Austria the Austrian road. From Prague to the east, there were the main routes to Poland (the Kłodzko road, or Silesian, the Polish or the Náchod road); to the south-east to Brno, named the Trstená road; and through Jihlava, the Habry road. From Moravia, there were further land routes to Vienna, Hungary and Poland.

In some areas the earth's surface was affected by the mining of minerals – before the first half of the 13th century, prosperous silver mines were opened near Jihlava and Německý (now Havlíčkův) Brod; in the last decade of the 13th century, rich silver lodes were discovered at the newly founded Kutná Hora. The Czech-Moravian highlands became the main production area of silver, even though silver mines were to be found also at Stříbro, Příbram and in Moravia at Jeseníky. Apart from silver, gold, copper and pewter was also mined.

In the Bohemian crown lands, the cultural landscape took on a new appearance towards the end of the 13th century. This was due to three basic types of settlement: villages, towns and aristocratic seats (castles, forts and monasteries), as well as a fairly stabilized communication network. Generally speaking, this state of affairs persisted to the Modern Era.

7 The Great Transformations of the Landscape in the Early Modern Era

In the course of the 16th century, in many places the landscape of the Bohemian crown lands took on a new character. Large systems of ponds were established; mining of high-grade ores penetrated the mountain regions; rich broadleaf forests in some areas thinned out or vanished completely. As soon as some of the terrible consequences of the Thirty Years' War were removed in the second half of the 17th century, the process of transforming the landscape continued. To a certain degree this was affected by political and economic changes, new intellectual currents (for instance mercantilism, and the advancement of science and technology). In the 18th century, these changes affected most the economic state of forestry and waterways, along with agricultural production; a century later they also impacted on the mining of minerals and the construction of new transport routes.

One of the prospering branches of the economy became fisheries on large aristocratic farmsteads towards the end of the 15th century and into the 16th. The greatest and most important pond basins in the Bohemian crown lands were established in the areas of Pardubice, Poděbrady and Třeboň. In Pardubice, the level territory of the Pernštejn domain, kept extremely wet by the meandering Elbe, had good conditions for the construction of a pond system. The ponds were linked by two long artificial canals – the Opatovice canal, built from the end of the 15th century to 1513, and Počaply canal of the same period. Together with the Golden Canal and New River in Třeboň, and the Sány Canal and the New Canal in Poděbrady, these artificial canals were an index of how advanced water construction was. The important Czech pisciculturist and knight, Kunát of Dobřenice, worked in the service of the Pernštejns, and Štěpánek Netolický was one of his students. The Pardubice pond system was completed half way through the 15th century. Now there was hardly any further space to be found in the landscape for new water reservoirs. In the environs of Pardubice and the Mount Kunětice, there were about 230, of which the largest was some hundred hectares (the largest pond in Pardubice, Čeperka, measured about 1,000 hectares, constructed in 1491–1496, submerged several villages).

The Poděbrady region, much flooded and soaked by the waters of the Elbe, the Cidlina and the Mrlina, was originally one of the less fertile, marshy areas. At the turn of the 15th and 16th centuries, a system of ponds was established here, and this was connected to the rivers Cidlina, Mrlina and the canals of Sány and the New Canal. The Sány canal channelled water to the pond of Blato near the village of Pátek, which was about 990 hectares in size. (This pond no longer exists.)

In Třeboň, the Lužnice river brought a large amount of surface water which was used to construct a further water system in Bohemia. In the 16th century a grand plan for a giant pond system was put into effect by Štěpánek Netolický, who was active in southern

Bohemia in the first third of the 16th century. Jakub Krčín of Jelčany and Sedlčany, continued Netolický's work in the period 1560–1580. The Golden Canal, over 45 km in length, constituted the axis of the pond system. In the second half of the 16th century, Jakub Krčín established the monumental ponds of Rožmberk measuring about 1,060 hectares: Svět (earlier named Nevděk), and an artificial canal New River (*Nová Řeka*), connecting Nežárka river with the Lužnice. While Netolický's ponds were for the most part small and shallow, though excellent for fish-farming, Krčín built deeper water reservoirs over larger areas, and with lower yields.

During the 16th century, ponds were established even in less advantageous areas. The territory of south-western, southern and south-eastern Bohemia was interlaced with water systems, which began in the regions of Blato, Lnáře and Rožmitál, and continued across the areas of Písek, Vodňany, Strakonice and Netolice, Budějovice, Nový Hrad, Třeboň, Soběslav and Nová Bystřice to that of Jindřichův Hradec. Other smaller areas with ponds were to be found in western Bohemia in the areas of Klatovy and Rokycany, near Bor at Tachov, near Nýřany, Jesenice, Planá and Teplá. In northern Bohemia, pond management was successful in the region of Most and around Doksy in central Bohemia at Žebrák, Mýto, Konopiště, Neveklov, Sedlčany and in the Kouřim region. In eastern Bohemia the pond area began in the regions of Mladá Boleslav and Jičín, continuing across the regions of Městec Králové, Poděbrady, Pardubice to Hradec Králové. The total number of ponds in Bohemia in the 16th century is estimated at 78,000 with an area of about 120,000 hectares, i.e., probably two thirds more than at present.

In northern and central Moravia large systems were established in the Šumperk region, around Uničov, Tovačov and Kroměříž. Further ponds were established in southern Moravia in the region of Mikulov and Hodonín – Kobylí, Čejč pond, Nesyt, and in the region of Znojmo on the river Jevišovka. On the Czech-Moravian highlands Velké Dářko was built, and a number of smaller pond areas existed near Hlinsko, Polná, north-west of Jihlava and between Humpolec and Lipnice.

Despite the decline of pond-building, caused by the fall in prices of fish and the gradual transformation of husbandry, the pond system persisted into the second half of the 18th century almost unchanged (the Josephine Land Register states that around 1788 there were in total 76,815 hectares of ponds in Bohemia). From the end of the 18th century, the number of ponds began to fall. The growing need for agricultural land contributed to their elimination, the intensification of cereal-farming and pasturage, and later, mainly around Pardubice and Poděbrady, the cultivation of new crops – sugar beet. Arable land on the tracts of former large ponds of Blato and Čeperka (of Poděbrady and Pardubice) are crossed today by reclamation canals; in many places in this area new water reservoirs were established – flooded mine shafts of sand quarries. The least affected in this respect were the southern Bohemian ponds: the lower quality of the agricultural land there saved them from widespread eradication.

The 16th century is connected in the Bohemian crown lands also with the development of mining, above all after the discovery of silver lodes in Jáchymov. In the region of the

EVA SEMOTANOVÁ

Ore Mountains (*Krušné Hory*), apart from silver, high-grade ores such as copper, led, iron, pewter, tungsten and molybdenum were mined, as in the regions of the Giant Mountains (*Krkonoše*) and Jeseníky. In the Bohemian Forest (*Šumava*) region, from the 16th century iron ore was extracted until it was exhausted in the second half of the 17th century. The development of this mining of minerals and the smelting associated with it was a great strain on forest management. To a considerable degree, forests in central Bohemia near the regions of Slaný, Kladno and Sázava, as well as in the regions of the Elbe in Chlumec, in southern Bohemia in the region of Český Krumlov and Netolice. Also the woods near the border, the Bohemian Forest, the Ore Mountains the Giant Mountains and the Orlice Mountains met the same fate. Groups of forests with their own forestry management were set up to service the high consumption of wood fuel and charcoal in mining and smelting. For instance, wood was freighted from Přísečnice to the mines at Jáchymov; to Kutná Hora from Trutnov and Rychnov; to Rudolfov from Hluboká.

By the end of the 17th century and in the first half of the 18th century, mining was revived, and glassmaking and ironworks began to enjoy a boom. This branch of the economy required even greater amounts of wood for its operation, whether timber or charcoal. There was intensive felling of forest growth, many forests thinned out, many clearings spread and the production of timber fell. Oaks and firs vanished from the forests; hornbeams, aspens, birch and pine began to dominate. Because of the lack of usable timber it was necessary to plant trees that grew quickly – above all pine, spruce, larch, poplar, maple and ash. In many places, a conifer monoculture replaced the broadleaf forests (the former were mainly of spruce and pine as they were more resistant to forest pests). In reserves or mountain forests the first forestry plans appeared which fixed the provisions and permissible annual lumber quotas. Pasture, burgeoning above all in the mountain regions, contributed to the gradual devastation of the forests.

In the 17th century, rivers were increasingly made navigable. Water was for man from the beginning of his existence a source of livelihood. It brought comestibles; a sufficiency of water meant a good crop, while drought meant poverty and famine. The great waterways were transport arteries to remote lands; they created borders between territorial units; and in times of danger they were natural obstacles in the way of the enemy. The chroniclers wrote of the most important Bohemian and Moravian rivers; the oldest official sources and local histories mention them; land surveyors and cartographers drew their courses. In the first half of the 17th century, the Abbot of Strahov, Kryšpín Fuk, personally oversaw the work on the Vltava to make it navigable in the Svatojánské currents, and made a number of detailed manuscript maps of the Vltava. At the turn of the 17th and 18th centuries, Lothar Vogemonte undertook a systematic investigation of the network of watercourses, especially of the Vltava, the Morava and the Oder. He was the author of proposals to make further rivers navigable and the construction of canals as one way to encourage the economy of the Habsburg monarchy.

Water management continued mainly with the work of making the Vltava navigable. The implementation of scientific ideas in water engineering was promoted by for instance

Jan Ferdinand Schor, who in 1726–1729 constructed engineering works which were unique for their time, i.e., the boat storage ponds on the Vltava at Županovice and at Modřany. In the second half of the 18th century because of the construction of the military fortresses in Hradec Králové and Terezín, technically difficult adjustments were carried out on the Ohře, Elbe and Orlice, shifting their courses. The construction of a fortress at Hradec Králové began in 1766. It required extensive regulation of the Elbe and Orlice, the straightening of their courses, the filling in of their distributaries and the building of systems of sluice-gates to allow the level of both rivers to rise and flood the fields in front of the fortress. The fortress of Terezín, founded in 1780 to support the defensive capabilities of military transfers across the Lužice Mountains, and the protection of the Elbe waterway, was founded on the left bank of the Ohře in the place of the villages of Německé Kopisty and Travčice. The Ohře river, about 4 km distant from its debouchure in the Elbe, was divided into two channels, of which the western, so-called the New Ohře (*Nová Ohře*) became the main riverbed, and the original, Old Ohře (*Stará Ohře*), the side channel. Water management work, changing the appearance and direction of waterways of the Bohemian crown lands, continued through the 19th century.

The structure of the main dry-land routes did not change considerably up to the first half of the 18th century, and basically followed the directions of the old land routes. With the increased importance of a high-quality communication network for the economy, transport and posts, as well as for strategic purposes, it became clear that communications would have to be re-constructed, and this was done first with the six main land roads – to Linz, Zittau, Vienna, Nuremberg, Leipzig and Silesia. Building adjustments also affected the Gold Road. However, the Silesian wars and the Seven Years' War considerably exhausted the Habsburg finances, and it was not until the end of the 18th century was there interest again in improving the state of land communication.

After the second half of the 18th century, the number of inhabitants of the Bohemian crown lands rose. In order to secure them sustenance it was necessary to increase agricultural productivity, and one way was to extend the arable lands. The transformation of woodland into tillage continued, necessitating the removal of common pasturage, the elimination of vineyards and even the drainage and elimination of ponds to the mid-19th century (though some of these were restored later in the 19th century). To the end of the 18th century the three-field fallowing method of crop rotation with cereals dominated. Only with the gradual changeover to the alternating method, the introduction of new crops (mainly clover, lucerne, potatoes, turnip, later sugar beet) and more plentiful manuring by natural and artificial fertilizers led to the improvement of yields in the course of the 19th century. It also resulted in a change in rotational patterns and the extent and structure of the available tilth.

One specific manifestation of the creation of cultural landscape in the Bohemian crown lands in the 18th century was what is referred to as "Czech Baroque Landscape" – an organized landscape, economically purposeful and also aesthetic, expressing the harmonic connection of man and nature. The Baroque landscape was employed economically – new crops were introduced, ponds were drained in order to gain new arable land, or deforestation took place to service glassworks, smelting and mining enterprises. Nevertheless the Baroque landscape was extremely aesthetic, and filled with the harmonic relations and ideas of Baroque man. Its traces are preserved in the Bohemian landscape to this day and offer the opportunity of an intense encounter with the spirit and heritage of the Baroque landscape.

The Baroque landscape is characterized by undulant terrain with a mosaic of smaller fields, a dense network of roads and paths, alleys lined by trees, sacral village architecture dominated by Baroque churches, smaller architecture in the open landscape (wayside shrines, crosses, chapels) and aesthetic re-arrangements of the landscape – Baroque gardens and the landscape parks of castle buildings. Three of the most important examples of landscaping are, first, the castle and baths at Kuks between Dvůr Králové and Jaroměř from the end of the 17th century and beginning of the 18th, built in the eastern Bohemian domain of Count František Antonín Špork; second, Wallenstein's early Baroque demesne; and third, the Schlick Baroque demesne in the Jičín region. However these Baroque landscaped gardens have not been preserved in their entirety.

8 Landscape in the Time of Industrialization, Urbanization and the Rise of Transport

In the 19th century the landscape changed at an even faster rate. The managed renewal of forestry continued apace, mitigating to a greater degree the long-term affects of the lumber industry. The systematic afforestation of clearings and the more frequent use of coal instead of charcoal, especially in connection with the introduction of steam engine in production and transport: these two factors contributed to the partial improvement of the critical state of the forests. In the lower regions, oak, hornbeam, birch, alders and aspens predominated, but continuous broadleaf growths disappeared. They were replaced by conifers, mostly pine, spruce and larch, for instance in the areas of Zbraslav, Mladá Boleslav and Litomyšl. Floodplain forests in the catchment areas of the Morava, Dyje, Elbe and lower Ohře retained their specific composition. In the submontane and montane areas, with less lumber activity, the original woods grew, untouched by spruce monocultures, apart from spruce firs, beech, maple, ash, pine, and in the Jeseníky region larch also.

The Forestry Act of 1852 introduced state supervision of forest management and forbade the reduction of forest lands. Together with the support of cultural organizations (for instance the Bohemian Forestry Units or the Moravian Forestry Society), new progressive silvicultural technologies were gradually implemented. There was extensive education on the subject and the next generation of experts was trained. Apart from the economic importance of forestry, its functions both as a crucial element of the landscape and for recreation were also recognized.

With the gradual shift from the fallowing system to that of alternation of agricultural management, and the domestication of new agricultural crops, areas of specific agricultural production began to be established in Bohemian crown lands. Up to the mid-19th century, cereal production was one of these (the Elbe region, the lower Ohře, the Lower Moravian valley, as well as that of the Dyje and Svratka), hops another (the regions of Žatec, Rakovník and Louny) and viticulture (south Moravia, around Prague and Mělník). Towards the close of the century, beet production was added to these (in the regions of Hradec Králové, Pardubice, Kolín, Prague, Mělník and Litoměřice), cereal and potato production (above all the Bohemian-Moravian highlands) and fodder crops (the submontane area of the border mountain zones). The Všetaty, Brno and Znojmo regions and the area around Prague were designated for the cultivation of vegetables. The use of the available land and its structure changed – during the first half of the 19th century, the extent of agricultural land was still expanding by about 10%. In the second half of the 19th century, the tracts of agricultural land remained almost unchanged; however the acreage of arable land, garden, orchards and vineyards expanded at the expense of pasturage and meadows.

In order to improve the state of forestry and agriculture, much land reclamation took place in the Bohemian crown lands from the mid-19th century (and mainly towards its close). This activity contributed to the more intensive use and cultivation of plots and affected the value of the soil. The work was connected with the adjustment of waterways and served as protection against the effects of natural disasters – strong gales, torrents and floods. Land reclamation also changed the extensive drainage and irrigation of the subterranean water.

The Lanna firm above all devoted itself to systematic water management, even through-out the 19th century, in connection with the development of timber rafting. Up to the mid-19th century, it carried out important adjustments to the upper flows of the Lužnice, Nežárka, Blanice, Malše and Otava. There was also work on the Vltava and Elbe, with exten-sive regulation of its bed from 1819. The bed of the river between Kolín and Poděbrady was adjusted, beyond Nymburk, between Brandýs nad Labem and Kostelec nad Labem, and at the confluence of the Elbe and Vltava, where the main and auxiliary channels of both rivers were intertwined in a complex way before they were regularized. From the 1880s, Lanna made the Vltava in Prague navigable. It reconstructed the solid weirs, and built moving weirs beneath Prague, which were meant to facilitate the passage of timber along the bed. They built wharfs in Holešovice and in Smíchov; the wharf at Karlín was restored. The river was embanked by the first quay. In Bohemia and Moravia many projects to connect river flows were revived – for instance, the Danube-Oder canal, the Danube-Vltava canal, the connec-tion of the Danube-Oder canal with the river Vistula and the canal from Přerov to Pardubice, to join the Danube-Oder canal with the Elbe. However these were never realized. The idea of the Vltava-Danube canal was definitively shelved with the construction of horse-drawn rail from České Budějovice to Linz in the years 1825–1832.

From 1896, the Board for the Canalization of the Elbe and Vltava planned and orga-nized canal construction in the Bohemian crown lands. The first large-scale construction program of waterways, mainly of the Elbe, Vltava and Oder, was enabled by the Waterways Act of 1901; in 1903 the Land Regulation Board was set up. Regulatory interventions also meant the partial restriction of destructive floods which repeatedly filled the flood-plains

EVA SEMOTANOVÁ

of streams and rivers, changing their banks and their currents, and swept away islands or created new ones.

At the beginning of the 20th century, locks were built at Klecany, Libčice, Troja, Mirovice and Vraňany nad Vltavou with a canal to the sluice gate in Hořín near Mělník. On the Elbe locks were built at Dolní Beřkovice, at Roudnice, Litoměřice and Lovosice before World War I; the first dams were built on the Chrudimka near Hamry and on the Doubravka near Pařížov. In Moravia, the Land Board looked after the adjustment of rivers, and oversaw the regulation of the Morava, Bečva and Ostravice rivers and the planning of dam-systems.

Nevertheless, most of the rivers in the Bohemian crown lands were still not navigable at the beginning of the 20th century. Steam-boats were in operation only on the Vltava and the Elbe from Štěchovice through Prague and Mělník to Děčín, and then along the Elbe. Boats without steam could pass on the Vltava from České Budějovice to Mělník; on the Elbe along the current of the river from Obříství. The Vltava above České Budějovice through Prague to Mělník was made navigable for regular timber rafting, and from there on along the Elbe to the border of the country, as well as the larger tributaries of the Vltava, i.e., the central and lower Otava, Nežárka, Lužnice, Sázava and the lower flow of the Stropnice. The Elbe from Hradec Králové to Mělník, and the central and lower flows of the Morava and Bečva, were navigable for timber only in some seasons when the water level was high enough.

In the 19th century, the face of the landscape was marked by the mining of minerals and its expansion was accompanied by the advancement of mine surveying and cartography. The areas of the Berounka river, especially in the regions of Beroun and Rokycany, were among the most important for the mining of iron ore in the Czech interior; from the 1840s the Nučice region and, in the Bohemian-Moravian highlands, the region of Žďár. With the progress of industry, other minerals were increasingly used. Graphite was mined in southern Bohemia; bismuth, nickel, cobalt, arsenic and lead mainly in the Ore Mountains. Coal mines were opened mainly in the region of Ostrava, Kladno and near Nýřany. In the second half of the 19th century, brown coal began to be mined in below the Ore Mountains (in the regions of Most, Chomutov and Teplice); while uranium was extracted at Jáchymov. The long-term boom of coal mining soon caused the devastation of the landscape in the immediate proximity of the coal mining district. Nevertheless at the turn of the 19th and 20th centuries, interest increased in the re-cultivation of the undermined territories (the brown-coal mines especially negatively marked the character of the landscape below the Ore Mountains at that time).

The fundamental transformations of the transport network in the Bohemian crown lands were connected with the economic development of society, with the process of the Industrial Revolution and with general technological progress. After 1804 road engineering saw the introduction of a new system of "voluntary competition", which divided authorities and subjects into domains. The authority paid the expense for walled road construction – for instance, ditches, bridges and protective walls, and subjects within a radius of two miles of these shared in the construction through road subject labour (transport of materials and work). The more expensive projects were paid by the state from the transport fund and the Road Directorate oversaw the construction work. Up to the 1840s, the construction of a network of main imperial roads was completed, and the quality and density of regional communications improved. In Moravia and Silesia, however, voluntary competition did not work out: to the mid-19th century the road network advanced slowly. From the mid 1860s, the network of state roads was made even denser by district and municipal roads. They linked the regions with the railways – the main transport arteries of the country.

Rail, the new transport phenomenon, imprinted itself upon the landscape in the second half of the 19th century (the foundations of the rail network were laid in the period 1850–1880). It enabled more people to be transported faster over greater distances, not to mention materials and industrial products, thus connecting Czech commerce with foreign markets, influencing the quick growth of towns, and affecting the geographic locations of economic activities and accessed less developed regions. Among the oldest lines were the Northern Line of Emperor Ferdinand from Vienna to Břeclav and Brno from 1839 (continuing to Přerov, Olomouc, 1841 and Opava, 1855), and from Olomouc to Prague (1845), from Brno to Česká Třebová (1849), from Prague to Ústí nad Labem (1850) and from Ústí nad Labem to Dresden (1851). By the mid-1870s, the construction of the main lines was completed. Railways did not cover the Bohemian crown lands evenly: the lines were concentrated in northern, north-western and eastern Bohemia and northern Moravia in that time. This corresponded to the location of important economic regions, predominantly the coal, engineering, textile and sugar-refining industries. The least dense rail network was to be found in southern and south-eastern Bohemia and southern Moravia, i.e., agricultural areas for the most part. However, new routes, serving rail, water and road transport, took into consideration natural conditions in each region.

Up to the mid-19th century, mankind co-operated with nature to a certain degree, as yet unable to damage it significantly through its activities. Only with the onslaught of the Industrial Revolution, accompanied by large-scale encroachments on the landscape, did a new phase of its development begin after many centuries. The construction of railways, progressive mining of minerals (mainly black and brown coal), and the process of urbanization, left patent and permanent traces of human activity on the landscape. In north-western and northern Bohemia and in northern Moravia, industrial, urbanized areas sprang up connected with a new type of agriculture in the countryside, which lasted up to the mid-20th century.

9 The Landscape in Conflict with Modern Society

In the 20th century the development of the Czech landscape was linked more closely than in previous periods with political events, technological progress and the newest methods of management. Society tried to shape the modern geographic environment according to its ideas and requirements.

After 1918, the participation of man in the shaping of the landscape grew, both in positive and negative respects. The systematic electrification of rural areas began in Czechoslovakia,

EVA SEMOTANOVÁ

and this was dependent on the construction of power stations and pylons. Intense reclamation work – drainage of marshes and the cultivation of infertile and devastated lands – improved almost a quarter of a million hectares in the Czech Lands alone. The regulation of waterways continued. Among the most important areas of agricultural production was beet-farming on the Bohemian stretch of the Elbe, and in Moravia in the regions of Prostějov, Kroměříž and Kojetín; cereals (as much as 60% of arable land here was sown with cereals), and cereal and potato farming, mainly in the Bohemian-Moravian highlands. Hops, fruit, vegetables, flowers and medicinal herbs, and vines to a lesser degree, were cultivated. In the mountain regions where fodder was produced, sheep-dairy farming as a form of Alpine management. The Forestry Protection Act of 1918 helped improve the state of the forests (in the Czech Lands conifers predominated). The reconstruction of the transport system focussed on the support of routes to sea ports and on securing the transport connections of Slovakia and Subcarpathian Ruthenia with other parts of the Republic. In both countries the forest areas were also made accessible by the construction of forest routes.

During World War II, the domestic population was evacuated in many places in the Czech Lands. The space that was freed up in the areas of Sedlčany, Benešov, Neveklov, Milovice, Vyškov, the Drahany highlands, Jihlava and Brdy to the extent of about half a million hectares served to establish military training camps or the settlement of German immigrants. Military operations and air bombardment of military factories at the end of World War II led to the devastation of the landscape, not to mention loss of life and property. For instance, industries in Prague, Plzeň, Záluží near Most, in Moravia the engineering centre in Brno and nearby manufacturing in Zlín and the Ostrava area were all hit.

Agricultural collectivization after 1949 strongly affected the landscape of post-war Czechoslovakia. With the ploughing away of the balks, the elimination of many tracks and the integration of fields and meadows, more extensive plots were established. The structure of settlement changed. A considerable number of people moved to the towns and smaller towns. Extensive urbanized territories around the large industrial centres sprang up: Prague and its environs, north-western Bohemia, the regions of Plzeň, Liberec, Hradec Králové and Pardubice; in Moravia the regions of Brno, Olomouc and Ostrava; in Slovakia the regions of Bratislava, Trnava, Nitra, Košice and Prešov. In the rural municipalities the share of non-agricultural land grew. The construction of new high-ways, dam reservoirs and entire water-management systems left their mark upon the landscape. But it was mainly the reconstruction of Czechoslovak industry (with the economic orientation on mining and smelting, engineering and extensive agriculture with high energy consumption and the use of poor quality raw materials) which posed the greatest threat to the landscape, disrupting its balance and ability to regulate itself. Urbanization, industrialization and the building of communications together with farmers' improper methods of working the land led to the uninterrupted reduction of available land. Surface mining of brown coal in northern Bohemia, where whole mountain-tops and hillsides were mined away, the flooding of abandoned mines and the elimination of residences, transformed part of the landscape into a wasteland which can be re-cultivated only with great difficulty. The higher production of sulphuric acid due to the burning of brown coal and other emissions contributed to the pollution of the air, water and land, and the damage to forestry. The landscape was also destroyed in those places where the Soviet army resided in 1968–1991.

In the last decade of the 20th century and the beginning of the 21st it is already possible to see many beneficial activities of society in the landscape. Extensive re-cultivation of regions and micro regions is taking place where the mining of some minerals has ended. All eyes are on the protection and creation of the landscape, sustainable development of the landscape, landscape-planning and the creation of urbanized spaces in the landscape. Landscape, the form of which man's activities have helped create in the Czech Lands from the Neolithic Age for seven millennia, is an integral part of the life and development of society. The transformations of the landscape are, to a greater or lesser degree, preserved in its present appearance, that is assuming that the ecological stability was not markedly disturbed or if the identity of the landscape was not lost. Those elements of the landscape that have been preserved, or the remnants of human activity, create the memory of the landscape, reminding us of society's roots in nature and express the mutual relationship of both the phenomena which make history.

Bibliography

BOGUSZAK, František – Císař, Josef: *Mapování a měření českých zemí od poloviny 18. století do počátku 20. století, Vývoj mapového zobrazení Československé socialistické republiky*, III, Praha 1961.

BOHÁČ, Zdeněk: *Atlas církevních dějin českých zemí, 1918–1999*, Kostelní Vydří 1999.

BRAZDIL, Rudolf – KOTYZA, Oldřich: *History of Weather and Climate in the Czech Lands*, I, Period 1000–1500, Zürich 1995.

GOJDA, Martin: *Archeologie krajiny*, Praha 2000.

Historická geografie, pp. 1–34, Praha 1968–2007.

HLAVAČKA, Milan: *Dějiny dopravy v českých zemích v období průmyslové revoluce*, Praha 1990.

HORSKÁ, Pavla – MAUR, Eduard – MUSIL, Jiří: *Zrod velkoměsta. Urbanizace českých zemí a Evropa*, Praha–Litomyšl 2002.

HOSÁK, Ladislav et al.: *Historický místopis Moravy a Slezska v letech 1848–1960*, I–XV, Ostrava 1966–2008.

HOSÁK, Ladislav: *Historický místopis země Moravskoslezské*, Olomouc 1932–1938 (2nd edition, Praha 2004).

HOSÁK, Ladislav: *Přehled historického místopisu Moravy a Slezska v období feudalismu do roku 1848*, Ostrava 1967.

HOSÁK, Ladislav – Šrámek, Rudolf: *Místní jména na Moravě a ve Slezsku*, I–II, Praha 1970–1980.

JAKUBEC, Ivan: *Železnice a Labská plavba ve střední Evropě 1918–1938*, Praha 1997.

JANÁK, Jan – HLEDÍKOVÁ, Zdeňka – DOBEŠ, Jan: *Dějiny správy v českých zemích od počátků státu po současnost*, Praha 2007.

KAŠPAR, Jaroslav: *Vybrané kapitoly z historické geografie českých zemí a z nauky o mapách*, Praha 1990.

KLÁPŠTĚ, Jan: *Paměť krajiny středověkého Mostecka*, Most 1994.

KLÁPŠTĚ, Jan: *Proměna českých zemí ve středověku*, Praha 2005.

KREJČÍ, Oskar: *Geopolitika středoevropského prostoru*, Praha 2000.

KUBŮ, František – ZAVŘEL, Petr: *Der goldene Steig*, Passau 2001.

KUČA, Karel: *Města a městečka v Čechách, na Moravě a ve Slezsku*, I–VII, Praha 1996–2008.

KUCHAŘ, Karel: *Mapy českých zemí do poloviny 18. století, Vývoj mapového zobrazení Československé republiky*, I, Praha 1959.

KVĚT, Radan: *Duše krajiny. Staré stezky v proměnách věků*, Praha 2003.

LIPSKÝ, Zdeněk: *Sledování změn v kulturní krajině*, Kostelec nad Černými lesy 2000.

LÖW, Jiří – MÍCHAL, Igor: *Krajinný ráz*, Kostelec nad Černými lesy 2003.

LUTTERER, Ivan – ŠRÁMEK, Rudolf: *Zeměpisná jména v Čechách, na Moravě a ve Slezsku*, Havlíčkův Brod 1997.

NEKUDA, Vladimír: *Zaniklé osady na Moravě v období feudalismu*, Brno 1961.

OLIVOVÁ-NEZBEDOVÁ, Libuše – KNAPPOVÁ, Miloslava – MALENÍNSKÁ, Jitka – MATÚŠOVÁ, Jana: *Pomístní jména v Čechách. O čem vypovídají jména polí, luk, lesů, hor, vod a cest*, Praha 1995.

PANTOFLÍČEK, Jaroslav (ed.): *Atlas Republiky československé*, Praha 1935.

PROFOUS, Antonín: *Místní jména v Čechách, jejich vznik, původní význam a změny*, I–IV, Praha 1954–1957; V. SVOBODA, Jan – ŠMILAUER, Vladimír, Praha 1960.

PURŠ, Jaroslav (ed.): *Atlas československých dějin*, Praha 1965.

Retrospektivní lexikon obcí Československé socialistické republiky 1850–1970, I/1–1, II/1–2, Praha 1978.

ROUBÍK, František: *Přehled vývoje vlastivědného popisu Čech*, Praha 1940.

ROUBÍK, František: *Příručka vlastivědné práce*, Praha 1941–1947.

ROUBÍK, František: *Silnice v Čechách a jejich vývoj*, Praha 1938.

ROUBÍK, František: *Soupis a mapa zaniklých osad v Čechách*, Praha 1959.

ROUBÍK, František: *Soupis map českých zemí*, I–II, Praha 1951–1955.

SÁDLO, Jiří – POKORNÝ, Petr – HÁJEK, Pavel – DRESLEROVÁ, Dagmar – CÍLEK, Václav: *Krajina a revoluce. Významné přelomy ve vývoji kulturní krajiny českých zemí*, Praha 2005.

SCHALLER, Jaroslav: *Topographie des Königreiches Böhmen*, I–XVI, Prag 1785–1790.

SEDLÁČEK, August: *Místopisný slovník historický Království českého*, Praha 1909.

SEDLÁČEK, August: *O starém rozdělení Čech na kraje*, Praha 1921.

SEMOTANOVÁ, Eva: *Atlas českých dějin*, 1–2, Praha 1998–2002.

SEMOTANOVÁ, Eva: *Atlas zemí Koruny české*, Praha 2001.

SEMOTANOVÁ, Eva: *Historická geografie českých zemí*, Praha 1998 (2nd, updated edition 2002, 2006).

SEMOTANOVÁ, Eva: *Kartografie v historické práci*, Praha 1994.

SEMOTANOVÁ, Eva: *Kartografie v hospodářském vývoji českých zemí v 19. a na počátku 20. století*, Praha 1993.

SEMOTANOVÁ, Eva: *Mapy Čech, Moravy a Slezska v zrcadle staletí*, Praha 2001.

SEMOTANOVÁ, Eva et al., *Česko. Ottův historický atlas*, Praha 2007.

SEMOTANOVÁ, Eva – FELCMAN, Ondřej: *Kladsko. Proměny středoevropského regionu. Historický atlas*, Hradec Králové–Praha 2005.

SEMOTANOVÁ, Eva – CHODĚJOVSKÁ, Eva – ŠIMŮNEK, Robert – ŽEMLIČKA, Josef (eds.): *Historický atlas měst České republiky 1–18*, Praha 1995–2008.

SEMOTANOVÁ, Eva – ŠIMŮNEK, Robert: *Lexikon mapových archivů a sbírek České republiky*, Praha 2000.

SOMMER, Johann Gottfried: *Das Königreich Böhmen, statistisch-topographisch dargestellt*, I–XVI, Prag 1834–1849.

SVOBODA, Jiří – VAŠKŮ, Zdeněk – CÍLEK, Václav: *Velká kniha o klimatu zemí Koruny české*, Praha 2003.

ŠIMŮNEK, Robert (ed.): *Historická krajina a mapové bohatství Česka. Prameny, evidence, zpřístupňování, využívání*, Praha 2006.

ŠIMŮNEK, Robert (ed.): *Regiony – časoprostorové průsečíky*, Praha 2008.

ŠMILAUER, Vladimír: *Atlas místních jmen v Čechách*, Praha 1969.

ŠMILAUER, Vladimír: *Osídlení Čech ve světle místních jmen*, Praha 1960.

ŠMILAUER, Vladimír: *Úvod do toponomastiky*, Praha 1963.

VALENA, Tomáš: *Město a topografie*, Praha 1991.

VELÍMSKÝ, Tomáš: *Trans montes ad fontes! K roli újezdů při středověké kolonizaci středních a vyšších poloh na území severozápadních Čech*, Most 1998.

Výběrová bibliografie historické geografie Čech za léta 1961–1970, Historická geografie 7, Praha 1971.

WANNER, Michal – HORA, Josef: *Soupisy vedut vzniklých do roku 1850*, II/1–2, *Státní oblastní archivy*, Praha 1999–2001.

WANNER, Michal – HORA, Josef: *Soupisy vedut vzniklých do roku 1850*, II/3, *Státní okresní archivy*, Praha 2003.

WOLNY, Gregor: *Die Markgrafschaft Mähren topographisch, statistisch und historisch geschildert*, I–VI, Brünn 1835–1842.

II. Prehistory and Beginnings
of Slavic Settlement (to the 8th Century)

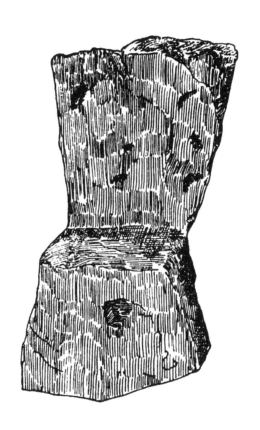

Picture of a stone throne as general documentation of the Indo-European ritual of enthroning of the ruler. Pictured here a medieval throne belonging to the O'Neills of Clannaboy in Ireland. The original is deposited in the Belfast Museum.

1 The Significance of the Neolithic Revolution

If history is that part of the past that has some significant relationship to the present, then for the Czech Lands this surely begins in the period that archaeologists refer to as Neolithic. It is the time of the first farmers, men who were no longer only parasites on nature and the environment in general, but actively created it. Their work was the cultural landscape which in its fundamental outlines remains with us to this day. Their work was also foundational because despite the many transformations – of the economy, of settlement, of ethnicity – there is an indisputable continuity to be found in the prehistoric period of the Czech Lands to the Neolithic Age (of course not an ethnic continuity, but a continuity in patterns of settlement, and to a degree the economy also).

The Czech Neolithic Age is dated, according to the most recent findings, in the period between 6000–5500 to 4000 BCE. The first farmers came from the "fertile crescent" in the Near East. However they penetrated to our territory in a kind of intermediary phase in their movement, created by the Balkan-Ukrainian Neolithic circle. From there they spread mainly along the enormous flow of the Danube as far as eastern France, but also to the north, up to the Baltic. Their culture (characterized by what is called Linear Pottery) then developed a range of local variations. The finest of these was the culture of what is called Moravian Painted Pottery (4700–3700 BCE), which emerged from north-western Hungary. Its main features were superbly painted pottery, exuberant statuettes of female deities typical of the matrilineal cults of ancient farmers, as well as numerous annular cult objects.

At the turn of the 4th and 3rd millennia, a fundamental transformation took place mainly due to the appearance of metal-processing (copper was first) and also to agriculture, which was improved immeasurably by the implementation of tillage. At the same time, fundamental ethnic changes took place. Although in these troubled times the old ethnic group of the first farmers still survived, a new people emerged from very distant regions. The most significant of these was a mounted people with battle axes and cups decorated with the print of a comb, or cord. In the Czech Lands this culture is called the culture of Comb Ceramics, 2900–2800–2600 BCE, elsewhere it is referred to as Battle Axe culture. These warriors occupied the vast territory between the Volga and the Rhine. There is little doubt that, ethnically, they were Indo-Europeans. But at the same time, a pedestrian archer people with marvellously decorated bell-like cups (2700–2400 BCE) spread from somewhere on the Pyrenean peninsula to the Carpathian basin; these were definitely not Indo-European.

The cultural synthesis of these two currents most likely took place on Czech territory, and from this emerged the distinctive Únětice culture (2400–1550 BCE), which occupied Central Europe in its entirety – Germany, Poland, Austria and Slovakia. There is no doubt that the Indo-Europeans were the bearers of this, with their typical social organization of the "triple people" – kings, warriors and priests – even though in Únětice culture itself we see only a distinctive class of chieftains – "king-rexes" (the Indo-European word for "king" was *reg*).

Únětice culture (named after Únětice near Prague) was the first culture of the Bronze Age, a culture of farmers and metallurgists. It gained knowledge of bronze processing from the Near East and the eastern Mediterranean. In the civilizational context, it was a kind of distant northern outpost of advanced Aegean civilization. Some time in the period 1550–1200 BCE, the centre of gravity moved to Moravia, where the central Danubian Barrow culture emerged (it was named after its burial-mounds), and from where it consequently spread. Another barrow culture appeared in south-western Bohemia and in Bavaria. In the course of the Bronze Age, two areas of culture become apparent: the culture of the western barrow culture and that of eastern "Lusatia". It seems that this division was the basis of the ethnogenesis of various groups of Indo-Europeans; to the east, of Veneti, an extinct people about whom little is known, and to the west, in the territory from the Rhineland to western Bohemia, originally Italics and Celts. After the exit of Italics to Italy, the Celtic ethnogenesis took place in the area where the barrow culture had been.

2 Celts in the Czech Lands

Nothing fundamental changed even with the onset of the Iron Age (what is referred to as Hallstatt Civilization; 750–400/300 BCE). The processing of iron spread and the cultural influence of the Mediterranean grew significantly, from which standpoint Central Europe was still a little known barbaric region. In society, mounted warriors evidently rose beside chieftain-kings, whose characteristic feature was the carriages. A stunning site of findings from that time (*c.* 500 BCE), the cave of Býčí Skála in Moravský kras (not far from Brno), has still to be decoded. Here under a layer of boulders and gravel, forty skeletons were discovered, mainly of young girls, who had neither been sacrificed nor died violent deaths. The discovery of the objects was extremely valuable: not for any treasure found, but because of the metal workshop and provisions that were present. It could not have been a residence because the cave was almost inaccessible. The mystery of the site remains unresolved. The place belonged to the "Veneti". A similarly important "Celtic" locality was Závist near Prague from the second half of the 5th century. Here an extensive holy place was established on a large artificial plateau ("nemeton") – evidently along Mediterranean, Etruscan or Greek lines.

The huge Celtic expansion to Italy and across the Carpathian basin in the Balkans in the 4th century BCE brought with it the thorough-going Celticization of the Czech Lands. An advance culture developed, characteristic of which was the "town" *oppidum* and unfortified commercial emporia, as well specialized "industrial zones", bartering and coin-minting. After a certain time, the tribe of Boii (whose name – *Boiohaemum* – has stuck to this day) took control of Bohemia, while the tribe of the Volcae-Tectosages resided in Moravia. The population of the Celts in the area was constantly augmented with the arrival of Celtic groups from the west, mainly from France and Switzerland. (This was why the conquest of Gaul by Caesar in 58–51 BCE, interrupting contacts with the west, initiated the decline of the Bohemian and Moravian Celts.) Towards the end of what is called La Tène period (500–0 BCE), the civilization of *oppida* died out and Bohemian and Moravian Celts disappeared. They neither left the country nor were they expulsed or subjugated by the newly arrived Germans: they evidently died out as an ethnicity together with their political organization and culture.

However the tradition of Celtic La Tène civilization continued. Not in its "high" expressions but rather in simple everyday manifestations, and all the more markedly for that. Although the *oppida* (the best known are Hradiště above Závist near Prague and Stradonice near Beroun) died out, the tradition of settlement, and perhaps even production and commerce with the emporia and "industrial" zones (mainly iron) survived the political and economic transformation of the following centuries. La Tène was a civilization based on iron in the fullest sense of the word. Iron instruments produced in large quantities, with the most recent technology, were "standardized" and optimized; in many cases the standard of design that was reached then has not been outstripped.

At the beginning of the Common Era, the border of the Roman Empire moved as far as the Danube and came closer to the northern Barbarians. After the following centuries, to the fall of the Empire, the life of the Barbarian societies to the north of the border was defined by multifaceted relations to the Roman Empire. The Celts were replaced in Bohemia and Moravia by the much more primitive Germans. The Marcomanni occupied Bohemia, led by King Marobudus, while Moravia, along with part of Slovakia, was held by the Quadi under King Tudrus. Marobudus soon subjugated the Quadi and began to build his great realm, which provoked the justified fears of the Romans. However he was deposed in the year 19 by the magnate Catualda, who soon after met the same fate in 21. The Romans transferred Marobud's and Catualda's armies to the dependent Quadi kingdom of Vannia, with which they maintained amicable relations at the time. Only in the years 166–180 did the great Marcomanni wars take place, which peaked with the expeditions to the north from the border to the Barbarian territory and in connection with this to the establishment of foot-holds on German territory. Several Roman infantry camps and permanent garrisons were discovered in south Moravia, the most noteworthy of which was Mušov, where the X. legion from Vindobona (Vienna) was located, with a number of first-class Roman findings. Not far from there the richly equipped grave of a German king was recently found – this dated from the time of the Marcomanni wars and evidently he was in some way dependent on the Romans.

3 The Transmigration of Nations

At the beginning of the first millennium, the centre of culture and power in our part of the world was the still wealthy and, in relative terms, peaceful Roman Empire, arranged around the Mediterranean. Beyond its borders, in Europe beyond the Rhine and Danube, poor tribes of Barbarians lived, attempting to plunder the Romans' wealth. From the 3rd century, it was ever more expensive to defend against these, and developing towns were impoverished under the pressure of taxes; markets went into decline and rural areas became self-sufficient. The urban civilization of antiquity, founded on market economics, was coming to an end and changing into a civilization of farmers. The self-possession and confidence of citizens, the belief in reason and in the municipality was transformed into uncertainty and restlessness; people no longer depended on philosophy but searched for consolation in various eastern religions which promised redemption or salvation. Among these, the teachings of the small Jewish sect of Jesus of Nazareth, who was meant to become the Saviour of his faithful, eventually came out on top. Christianity spread quickly among the urban population. It was organized and formed its church. Eventually Constantine the Great (r. 306–337 CE) transformed it from a persecuted anti-state religion to the *de facto* established Church.

It was intended to consolidate the Empire, but it was too late for that. The Barbarian masses beyond the Danube and Rhine were on the move after 375, pushed from the east by the itinerant Huns, and fell upon the Empire, not it would seem in order to destroy it but rather to settle there as "allies" (*federati*). The western part of the Empire with its centre in Rome could not withstand this pressure and collapsed into a number of smaller states founded on its territory by German marauders. Only the eastern part, with its centre in Constantinople (Byzantium) remained. Far beyond these German tribes, somewhere in the expansive regions of the central Dnieper, a new Slavic-speaking people emerged at some stage during the 2nd to 4th centuries. The Romans knew nothing of them and neither does modern research have any clear ideas about their origins. All that can be said is that archaeologists are researching the existence of the oldest Slavic settlements from the end of the 5th century in the Ukraine and confirm that about the year 530 masses of Slavic marauders appeared at the border of Byzantium on the Lower Danube. The Slavic transmigration had begun, and in a relatively short period (from the 6th to 7th centuries) it poured into the greater part of Central and Eastern Europe and the entire Balkans.

The population reserves of the German transmigration were at that time exhausted and the area between the Rhine and Volga was an uninhabited waste land. Similarly, on the territory of what would become the Czech Lands there remained only a scattering of Germans. Most of them probably left Bohemia around the year 530, and some would have participated in the origin of the tribe of Bavarians, giving them their name (*Baiuwarii* – "men from the land of Baia-Boiohama"), and in western Moravia some of the Lombards settled, who at that time owned Lower Austria and western Hungary. When a strong current of settlers came from the Ukraine making across the Cracow region and the Moravian Pass to the rich south some time soon after 530, they found free territory only in that stretch of land beside the mountains, from the Carpathians to the Sudets, the Giant Mountains (*Krkonoše*) and the Ore Mountains (*Krušné Hory*). The Carpathian basin was occupied in the east by the German Gepids and in the west the Lombards. It was impossible to penetrate to the wealth of Italy and the Balkans. The Slavs had already come up against the Lombards in Italy, and some of them thus made for Bohemia, and from there along the Elbe to the later Serb territory between the Saale and Elbe. In 547 all these new settlers presumably received a pledge from the Gepids of safe passage across their territory, and for several years they mercilessly looted the Byzantine territory in the western Balkans. The Gepids however joined in war with the Lombards and the passage to the Balkans was closed to these Slavs. The last expedition took place in 551.

The Lombards eventually called upon the itinerant Avars, recently arrived from Central Asia, for assistance against the Gepids in 567. Although they defeated the Gepids with their help, they themselves preferred to leave for Italy, leaving the Carpathian basin to the Avars. However together with the Avars, further Slavs came from the east and these were the military allies of the Avars. They were also farmers, and because they were subjects of the Avars, they were responsible for provisioning them. At the turn of the 6th and 7th centuries there were so many of them in the Carpathian basin that they had to migrate from there. In only a few years the military groups of settlers occupied Carinthia, Croatia, southern Serbia, Moravia and western Slovakia, Bohemia, and from there Serbia between the Saale and Elbe. They mixed with the older Slavic population here, and perhaps with the remnants of the Germans, arranging their internal relations so that they joined with the large tribes. In Bohemia the tribe of Czechs emerged, and in Moravia the Moravians.

From the start the Avars supported the conquests of their Slavs, but would not tolerate their independence. When the Avars suffered a heavy defeat in 626 in their campaign against Constantinople, the Slavs, who had just organized themselves in new tribes in the occupied territories, rose up against them. The nucleus of the rising was made up of Moravians, who were joined by the Czechs and probably the Carinthians. Later the Serbs from between the Saale and Elbe joined the confederation. The leaders of the tribes elected a foreigner as leader, the Frankish merchant Samo, evidently to ensure that no one tribe dominated in the confederation. The weakened Avars were unable to suppress Samo's rebellion, and when the Merovingian king Dagobert I made his claims on Samo's territory, the latter was also able to resist successfully. In 631, in a battle lasting three days beneath the castle at Wogastisburg (perhaps somewhere in north-western Bohemian, in recent times thought to be at the summit of Rubín near Podbořany), he repulsed the attack of the main body of Dagobert's army, which was making across Bohemia for southern Moravia, where Samo's domain was most likely located. After Samo's death (658/659) the confederation fell apart and the tribes became independent.

In continental trans-Alpine Europe from about the Bronze Age, a particular type of agriculture was established which ensured the survival of people despite the fluctuations of nature. Farmers tilled land in plots almost the size of small gardens, which provided them with relatively large returns of valuable foodstuffs (for instance pulses); they also collected forest fruits and hunted. When there were fewer people, they could plough the fields lying fallow and sow grain on them. Work productivity was of course low: peasants had to do much work to gain a small amount of provisions. Economic growth was slow, and so people embarked on uncertain migrations in pursuit of better livelihoods. After this transmigration of nations there remained overgrown islands of original agricultural land in a sea of forests covering Central Europe.

The Slavs settled there. They were few and territory was plenteous. They could thus plough tracts of fertile fallow lands and sow wheat and rye on them, neither of which had to be laboriously weeded and tended. They killed off most of the cattle which they brought from the old country and began to breed pigs which grazed in the oak forests untended and did not require much work. Of course the yields were small: 2–4 grains from each planted, but they did not have to work so much on the fields, thus productivity rose markedly. Although they production techniques were primitive, it was easy work carried out on large tracts, so that soon they had at least twice what they had before, and it is not to be wondered that they quickly began to multiply.

They lived scattered in small settlements of about 7–10 square half-buried sod cabins with an oven in the corner. They kept cereals and other items in holes in the ground. There were no other structures in the village. (The present type of village emerged only during the transformations of the 13th century.) For many years now the lands of the colonies had not been been commonage: individual families (not lines) owned them freely and privately. This ownership and freedom was protected by the tribe which had been established not through some organic growth, but through the "political" decision of all free men, owners of the village (*dědina*). This was because a miscellaneous group made up of remnants of the old tribes (in Bohemia for instance the Czechs, Doudlebs and probably Croatians) had come to the new settlements, and they were joined by the older settlers and perhaps also some Germans. It was necessary to unify all these and create a community which, first, would empower judicial assemblies; second, organize defence (mainly against the Avars) and conquest; third, arrange publicly beneficial works such as the establishment of roads and bridges; fourth, construct and man the border regions; and, fifth, perhaps as early as this time, but certainly from the 8th century, build typical Slavic castles of wood and earth. The assembly of all free men, the diet of the tribe, decided these issues.

The diets met at regular intervals dictated by the phases of the moon. At first one diet was enough for the tribe, but later when the tribe grew and occupied an extensive territory, diets were established for individual territories. Common matters were decided by the central diet. The diet normally elected a prince from the better and highborn families; he was above all a military commander and presumably also had responsibility for the victims sacrificed to the gods who guaranteed pieces and good crops. The main god was the pan-Slavic Perun ("Parom" is to this day a curse in Slovakia), the ruler of thunder, who resided in the heavens. His opposite, hiding beneath the ground and in the waters, was Veles; the female deity was Mokoš. The tribe was the frame for the lives of all its people, their home and "nation", guarantor of their ownership and freedom.

Bibliography

Archeologie pravěkých Čech, I–VIII, Praha 2007–2008.

BUCHVALDEK, Miroslav: *Kultura se šňůrovou keramikou ve střední Evropě*, Praha 1986.

DOBIÁŠ, Josef: *Dějiny československého území před vystoupením Slovanů*, Praha 1964.

DRDA, Petr – RYBOVÁ, Alena: *Keltové a Čechy*, Praha 1998.

DROBERJAR, Eduard: *Věk barbarů*, Praha – Litomyšl 2004.

FILIP, Jan: *Keltská civilizace a její dědictví*, Praha 1963.

LABUDA, Gerard: *Pierwsze państwo słowiańskie. Państwo Samona*, Poznań 1949.

POHL, Walter: *Die Awaren. Ein Steppenvolk in Mitteleuropa 567–822 n. Chr*, München 1988.

Pravěké dějiny Čech, R. Pleiner, A. Rybová (eds.), Praha 1978.

Pravěké dějiny Moravy, ed. V. Podborský et al., Brno 1993.

RULF, Jan: *Neolitic agriculture of central Europe – review of the problems*, Památky archeologické 82, 1991, pp. 376–384.

TEJRAL, Jaroslav – BOUZEK, Jan – Musil, Josef: *The fortification of the Roman military station at Mušov near Mikulov*, Archeologia 45, 1994, pp. 57–68.

TEJRAL, Jaroslav: *Morava na sklonku antiky*. Praha 1982.

III. Great Moravia and the Beginnings of the State (9ᵗʰ and 10ᵗʰ Centuries)

Picture of an Avar warrior with a captive, beat into a golden jug no. 2 from the treasure found in Nagyszentmiklós. The original is deposited in the Kunsthistorisches Museum, Antikensammlung, Vienna

1 Beginnings of Great Moravia

After the death of Samo, the important events of the Czech Lands are veiled in darkness. But Europe at this time was undergoing fundamental transformations. Thus at the turn of the 8th and 9th centuries Moravian and Bohemian Slavs found themselves in a completely different situation. Their relative prosperity led to a marked growth in their numbers and to the widespread planting of new farm lands; they grew in both economic and military terms. Throughout the Central Danube basin during the 8th century many princes emerged, settling with their followers in newly built castles. In each tribe there was a whole range of princely families which both intermarried and married far beyond the tribe. However they did not rule over clearly demarcated territories, rather they formed part of a tribe. The power of the Slav princes also grew because the heretofore strong Avar rule was weakened by internal differences. However a new potent neighbour emerged in the Empire of Charlemagne.

In the second half of the 8th century the Empire of the Franks, ruled now by the Carolingians, became the most powerful empire in Europe. Even the popes resident in Rome sought its protection, which in 800 CE resulted in the coronation by the Pope of the Frankish king, Charlemagne, as Emperor of the western part of the Roman Empire. Thus began the co-operation and competition of the two supranational powers and authorities of Western Christianity, which lasted throughout the Middle Ages. Charlemagne's empire, after its division in 843, laid the foundations for the arrangement of nations and states in Europe which has persisted to this day. To the east, on the Elbe, the Saale, the Bohemian Forest (or Šumava) and on the plains of Central Danube basin, in the Eastern Alps to the Adriatic, Charlemagne's empire clashed with the Slavic tribes. From this encounter, Central Europe emerged as an area defined by its position between western and eastern Europe.

Charlemagne, in protracted and repeated battles, subjugated Saxony, annexed Bavaria and clashed with the Avars. In order to secure the new border from the Baltic to the Adriatic, he created a chain of dependent Slavic tribes. In 805 it was the turn of the Czechs. Charlemagne's troops invaded the "Czech plain" in the Ohře (*Eger*) region, and laid unsuccessful siege to Canburg Castle. Although Lech, an important Czech leader, fell in battle, the Franks were not victorious. Their campaign had to be repeated the following year and the Czechs, having suffered the repeated devastation of their lands, submitted and swore to pay tributes to the Empire. The Moravians in similar fashion recognized Frankish formal sovereignty some time in this period.

In the years 791–805 Charlemagne was able to destroy the Avars with surprising ease. However it was not Charlemagne who reaped the fruits of this victory, but the Slavic princes in that area, who invaded the Avars and collected much booty in the form of people, livestock and valuables. The Moravian princes who resided in castles on the Morava river, and in Mikulčice, Uherské Hradiště and Olomouc mainly gained the most. It strengthened their standing to such an extent that they were able to attempt to take power in the tribe and establish a state of the kind they had seen in the Frankish Empire. The princes began to build stone churches and to establish priests there from Bavaria, Northern Italy and from Byzantine Dalmatia. At their head stood Mojmír I (r. c. 830–846), who not only succeeded in breaking the power of tribal institutions, but also in pushing through the "official" baptism "of all Moravians", which was carried out by the Bishop of Passau in Bavaria (831).

Under the leadership of Mojmír, the Moravians expanded into the Avar territory of south-west Slovakia and also into the region of Slavic Nitra north of there. Pribina, probably a Moravian, became prince in Nitra, and he had promised to embrace Christianity and also build his church, but he came into conflict with Mojmír and was expelled from the land some time in the years 833–836. After many adventures and wanderings, he eventually wound up as a Frankish vassal at Balaton, where he built up his own principality about his new castle Blatnohrad-Mosaburg.

The Empire of the Franks was at this time even further weakened by internal disputes, and thus it lost control of the Bohemians and seemingly also of the Moravians. However when these struggles ended with the division of the Empire in the Treaty of Verdun in 843, the energetic Louis the German received the newly emerged eastern Germanic sector. He immediately proceeded to renew the authority of the Empire among the tribes on the eastern border. As early as 844 he prepared an offensive against the Polabian Slavs and there was little doubt that the Bohemians would be next. Surmising that Christianity might provide them with defence, as it had the Moravians, in 845 they sent fourteen of their princes to Louis the Great in Regensburg to be christened. Louis, surprised by this, agreed. However the Bohemians were bitterly disappointed the next year. Louis attacked Moravia in 846, regardless of the fact that they were Christians, and deposed Mojmír I, who was replaced by his nephew Rostislav (r. 846–869). The disappointed and insulted Bohemians rejected Christianity, which had proved to be no protection, and fell upon Louis's troops returning from Moravia. From that time they continued to revolt against the Empire and also remained allies with the Moravians.

Rostislav used his good relationship with Louis the German to consolidate his rule and mainly to build up the structures of the state. We know little of this, except that he understood the importance to the state of an independent ecclesiastical institution. The Pope was required to establish this and it was subordinate to him alone; bishoprics were subordinate to an archbishop in the Empire. But this was a long way off. First it was necessary to unify and arrange ecclesiastical instruction and practice in the land and above all acquire a sufficient number of educated priests. Thus Rostislav turned to the Pope in 861 with a request for a teacher to whom these very tasks could be entrusted. Receiving no answer, he then requested a teacher from Byzantine.

Emperor Michael III and Patriarch Photios chose two brothers for this task – Constantine and Methodius. Although Greeks, they were from Salonica where Slavic was in everyday use, so they knew this language well. Constantine carried out the task conscientiously and during his time with Methodius in Moravia in the years 863–867 he trained a large number of priests. Their education was facilitated by the use of their native tongue. There was nothing particularly unusual about this – similar attempts to raise the status of vernacular tongues were under way in the same period in the Empire of Louis the German. Constantine however created a special alphabet to accommodate the speech sounds of the Slavic language, i.e., Glagolitic. Most importantly, the brothers began to use Slavic in the liturgy, that is, during the celebration of mass, in a period when only Latin or Greek was permitted. This led to differences with native clerics who were subordinate to the Bishop of Passau.

The disputes ended when Constantine and Methodius declared their task complete in 867 and set out for Constantinople. With them they brought their disciples who they wished to have ordained. On their way they stopped at Pribina's principality, which at that time was governed by his son Kocel, and there they won his admiration and friendship. While waiting in Venice for the ship that would take them to Constantinople, they heard that Emperor Michael III had been murdered and Patriarch Photios removed, and so in fact they had no-one to return to. This is why they gratefully accepted an invitation to Rome from Pope Nicholas I. Before they reached the city, Nicholas died; however his successor Hadrian II received them with the same favour. Constantine secured the ordination of his students as well as the acceptance of his methods of instruction, i.e., above all his alphabet, if not the liturgy in the Slavic language. Constantine, now ailing, and having fulfilled his task, entered a Greek monastery in Rome, dying on February 14, 869. The brothers' mission was to end there and Methodius awaited the fate of an emigrant.

We are unsure why, but in the spring of 869 Methodius became a key player in the political machinations which the Papacy was engaged in with the Patriarchate in Constantinople concerning claims to the northern Balkans (old Roman Illyria) and in which the Bulgar khan Boris was involved (he was at that time in the process of being received into Christianity and was balancing between Rome and Constantinople). Whether it originated with the Pope, or with Methodius himself (though it was unlikely to have been Kocel, and certainly not Rostislav, who knew nothing of these matters), the idea emerged to renew the old Roman archbishopric in Sirmium (Sremska Mitrovica near Belgrade). However, at this time, it was held by the Bulgars who had not yet decided for ecclesiastical obedience to Rome. The true seat was then to have become Blatnohrad, which however was not located in Illyria, but in Old Pannonia. Methodius thus became Archbishop of Sirmium with its seat in Pannonia.

He truly did wish to settle in Blatnohrad, but this meant that he would encroach upon the rights of the Frankish church in Pannonia, which had gained the territory with the agreement of the Pope after the defeat of the Avars. This did not seemingly refer to Moravia, which in any case had other worries.

The dispute between Rostislav and Louis the Great came to a point in 864, when Louis besieged Rostislav in Děvín (near Bratislava) and forced him into subjection. But he refused to give in, allying himself with neighbouring tribes, above all the Bohemians and Serbs, who together successfully resisted the Empire. However, they weakened from within. From at least the year 867, Rostislav's nephew Svatopluk became the governor of one administrative territory of the Great Moravian state, and he soon tried to instigate his own policies there. We are not sure where Svatopluk's territory exactly lay, but it was probably in Nitra. In 869, Louis the German, with a combined attack on Serbia, the Bohemia, Moravia and Svatopluk's territory, attempted to defeat Rostislav. In military terms it was, in the end, something of a fiasco, but the Bohemians and Svatopluk above all brokered a separate armistice. With Svatopluk's independent activity, Great Moravia thus fell apart. Although Rostislav attempted to deceive and murder Svatopluk, he himself fell into a trap, and Svatopluk handed him over to the Empire. Louis the German had him tried, blinded and imprisoned in a monastery, where Rostislav most likely died soon after. Svatopluk however did not succeed him as governor, because Louis's son Carloman attacked Moravia and occupied it, encountering no resistance. He had Svatopluk imprisoned in 870 and the Moravians, who supposed that he had died, rose up and proved their allegiance to Mojmír's line by electing as their prince Slavomír, Rostislav's relation (regardless of the fact that he was an ordained priest). It seemed to Carloman that the situation would calm down if he placed Svatopluk at the head of the army which was to pacify Moravia. However when the troops besieged "Rostislav's old town", the castle of Valy at Mikulčice, Svatopluk crossed over to the side of the besieged and together they beat back the Frankish troops.

In the following two years, together with the Czechs and Serbs, Svatopluk resisted all the Empire's attempts at subjugation. However, he did not try to exploit his victory and wisely made peace with Louis the German in Forchheim in 874. He swore allegiance to him and an annual payment in exchange for Louis leaving him freedom in his dealings.

2 Great Moravia between Byzantium and the Empire of the Franks

Relations with the Empire settled down after the peace made at Forchheim in 874, and Svatopluk systematically took advantage of this situation to make widespread military expeditions. At some stage in the period 874–880 he attacked the Vistulans in southern Poland (in the greater Cracow area), capturing the local prince and sending him to be christened in Moravia. It was merely one of the wars with "pagans" which he was engaged upon at that time. The hardest was clearly the struggle for eastern Slovakia and the watershed of the upper Tisza around the year 880. Svatopluk forced the local tribe, or tribes, to accept Christianity. An extremely large struggle took place in the years 882 and 883 for Frankish Pannonia; however we do not know if he annexed it to his territory. He exploited the emergent enmity for the Empire in order to occupy Bohemia, which the Empire considered its subject land. Again, he used the policy of Christianization; in 883 he had one of the Bohemian princes, Přemysl Bořivoj, christened, and he placed him at the head of the other Bohemian princes as his second-in-command.

Together with the Bohemians he most likely took control of Serbia. Whether and how he took power in Silesia and in Lusatia we do not know. Nevertheless by the year 880, a great empire had emerged, far surpassing the territory of Moravia. A significant role was played by the Christianizing of the subjugated tribes. At first there were difficulties with this policy. In 871 he expelled the Bavarian priests from the land and the Moravian church once again suffered from a lack of priests. He thus turned, like Rostislav before him, to Rome. Here John VIII drew attention to the fact that somewhere in Swabia an archbishop who had once sojourned in Moravia was imprisoned. It was Methodius, who had been captured by the Franks in Blatnohrad (Moosburg, today Zalavár) and sentenced by the Bavarian bishops for illegally seizing their territory in Pannonia. He had vainly attempted to defend himself by claiming he had been entrusted with the task by the Pope; the bishops were able to present evidence that the Pope had endorsed their possession of Pannonia much earlier. He ended up imprisoned in a monastery in Swabia (most likely Ellwangen) and tried without success to send secret messengers with complaints to Rome, where the plan to establish the Pannonian-Sirmian archbishopric had already been abandoned.

Only in 872 when Svatopluk asked John VIII to resolve ecclesiastical relations in Moravia, did the Pope take up the cause of Methodius and work for his release. Some time in the year 873 Methodius was in Moravia, not however as the Archbishop of Moravia, but of Sirmium, which he had never seen, and Pannonia, which he was not permitted to enter, even though he tried to function as Bishop of Pannonia from Moravia. In Moravia Svatopluk made priests and churches subordinate to him "on all castles", that is, the entire Moravian church. This, however, did not mean the whole people, many of whom were to a degree still pagan, not only in outlying rural areas, but also in part in the castle centres. In Mikulčice, only 500 m from the main basilica, there stood a pagan sacrificial site that was in constant use throughout the whole time that Methodius was there. We do not know if the state was forced to make some kind of compromise and if the church went along with this.

Methodius did not fight the pagans, or at least not to the best of our knowledge. However he was engaged in constant conflicts with local priests and did not get on well with the ruler. The cause of this was, once again, the Slavonic liturgy. Although Methodius, when released, had promised the Pope that he would relinquish it, he did not keep this promise and thus gave his opponents an opportunity to accuse him of breaking with orthodoxy. At the heart of these conflicts was Methodius's claim on Pannonia which he had not given up, and which was repellent to the Bavarian clergy, and the claim of the Bishop of Passau on Moravia. The deepest cause however was the profound differences between – in Methodius's view the primitive, though, in Central European terms, more germane – practice of Western Christianity, and the resilient Byzantine orthodoxy, which he would not and could not adjust to suit the barbarians.

When Christianity became the established religion in the Roman Empire in the fourth century, court theologians justified the Emperor's rule of the Church by saying that he had personal responsibility for the salvation of his subjects, and that thus his measures were not merely administrative and political actions, but directly served God's plan. Also following from this was the idea that only those loyal to the Emperor could be saved. This however turned out to be an illusion in the Western Empire: the Empire fell apart and demonstrated that it was not a decisive agent in God's plan for the salvation of humanity. Western theologians, above all St Augustine, thus proclaimed that the state and earthly powers are of no significance in God's plan, designating responsibility for salvation to each human individual with free will. Later this emphasis on free individuals became the basis of western Christianity, including its political culture. Even when the Church co-operated with the state, it maintained its distance from the latter. In the eastern part of the Empire, in Byzantium, things did not move in this direction: the older view of the role of the Emperor and the state was strengthened. Thus Byzantium did not even attempt to send a mission to the barbarians. After all, only those who were loyal to Caesar and also sufficiently cultured (i.e., shared the Hellenic culture of the Empire) could be saved.

Of course, Constantine and Methodius, the educated sons of a lower imperial clerk, shared these opinions. However, when Methodius was confronted with the task of professionally preparing priests to serve a state of unknown Slavic barbarians, he was able to rise above usual prejudices to such an extent when he justified his attempt with the profoundly humanistic idea of the equality of all nations before God (even those of the barbarians), an idea which had its roots in early Christianity. In his view, this could be achieved by means of the transmission of Christian education in their own language. The spreading of Christianity thus would also be the spreading of education. This was an exceptional approach in Byzantium, where no-one bothered about the barbarians, as well as in the west where Christianization was for the most part a practical business of introducing "Christian morality". Constantine held a deep conviction that the Word stored in books could elevate people and should be made available to all, and this is a timeless and universal message, valid even now.

On the other hand, Constantine and Methodius's values were typical of Byzantine education insofar as they understood their idea as orthodoxy and as they declared their opponents heretics for holding to the widespread teaching that mass could be served only in the three holy tongues – Hebrew, Greek and Latin. They conducted a bitter struggle about the serving of mass in the Slavic tongue, which of course complicated their mission greatly. There were no objections to orthography in vernaculars – the Church of the Eastern Franks had already made such an attempt.

These arguments were not of much importance to Svatopluk, and in fact along with his princes he favoured the Latin mass. He required Methodius above all so that he could implement Rostislav's old plan of establishing an independent archbishopric in Moravia.

Thus Methodius, as already noted, was not the Archbishop of Moravia: his archdiocese was in Pannonia. Svatopluk achieved this in 880 with a deft diplomatic manoeuvre, as he handed over his lands to St Peter, the patron saint of the Papacy, extricating himself thus from the bonds upon earthly rulers, freeing himself above all from the Empire. Great Moravia thus became a full and equal member of the family of European Christian states. To consolidate this position for the future, it had its own archbishopric, answerable only to the Pope. Methodius became the Archbishop of Moravia and received a subordinate bishop with a seat in Nitra. The Pope's permission to use the Slavonic liturgy in addition to the Latin was also a personal victory for Methodius.

At the same time, this was the beginning of Methodius's defeat. Latin priests in Nitra, with Bishop Wiching at their head, were not to be reconciled with this new state of affairs and brought the conflict before the Pope. In 884 this dispute with Wiching went so far that Methodius excommunicated him. Stephen V, who Svatopluk designated as judge in the matter, decided in the end against Methodius and the Slavonic liturgy. While acknowledging the usefulness of Slavonic orthography, he forbade its use in the liturgy. Methodius was unable to appeal the decision as he died on 6 April 885. Svatopluk, tired of the arguments of his priest, which brought only difficulties, resolved the matter by releasing all priests in his empire who kept the Slavonic liturgy. Most of them made their way to Bulgaria, where the Old Slavonic orthography was preserved and by that means transmitted from there to Russia. Croatia became the second centre of Church Slavonic.

The political power of the Papacy in this time weakened and Svatopluk thus gradually returned to the old policy of settlement with Kingdom of the Eastern Franks. In 890, he agreed with King Arnulf that the latter would acknowledge Svatopluk's conquest (mainly his occupation of Bohemia), and that Svatopluk would remain loyal to him. But Arnulf did not intend to hold to this and he attempted (in the years 892 and 893) to establish military domination. Although Svatopluk was able to withstand this easily, he died in 894 and this event was a greater threat to his realm than foreign armies.

It turned out that the state had been held together more by Svatopluk's strong personality that any functioning institutions. Mojmír II (r. 894–906), on his accession to his father's throne, met with great difficulties. There was strong opposition in support of his younger brother; dependent tribes also tried to break away; and of course the threat of the Eastern Franks. Although Mojmír was unable to prevent the breakaway of the Czechs (895) and the Serbs (897), he launched a promising campaign to regain them. The Magyar army, which appeared in 896 in the Carpathian basin, driven from its settlements on the steppe of southern Russia by the Pechenegs, became his allies and assigned him to camps near the Tisza. He eventually succeeded in implementing Rostislav's and Svatopluk's old plan, when Pope John IX in 898 named a new archbishop and ordained four further bishops. Their names are not known to us and we do not know where they resided; we only know that they were Latin bishops.

All seemed to be going well. Mojmír was able to rid himself of the troublesome Magyars who, bribed by Arnulf with large sums in 898, left for Italy to fight against his opponent

Berengar. But then Arnulf suddenly died in the year 899 and the Magyars returned and occupied Pannonia in 900. It was clear that they were dangerous. For this reason Mojmír agreed in 901 with the Bavarians on a joint effort against the Magyars, who in the mean time had brought their people into the country (up to this they had remained beyond the Carpathians) and began taking control. In the year 906, they struck against Moravia and most likely in a single great battle (perhaps somewhere in the area of the Slovak stretch of the Danube) they broke Mojmír's army and slaughtered many of his magnates. Perhaps it was here also that Mojmír himself fell. The Bavarians recovered only in the following year; their great campaign was however defeated utterly on 4 August 907 near Bratislava. The fall of Great Moravia was thus confirmed. Everything went, all that had made it a state: ruler, princes and magnates, many of whom fled to neighbouring countries. Of the entire Moravian territory, the Magyars occupied only the southern parts of Slovakia; normal life continued in Moravia despite the frequent ravages and regardless of the Magyars. The state structures however were completely destroyed, presumably because the disintegration of the state was accelerated by the pagan uprising. Along with the Moravians' state, the Moravians themselves as an ethnicity died out. Today's ethnic group, Moravian and also Slovak, emerged much later with no direct connection with these old Moravians.

* * *

The rise and fall of the Moravian state, with its population growth and relative agricultural prosperity, enabled the maintenance of a substantial fighting force, magnates and other inhabitants of castle towns. The axis of the settlement were the valleys with great rivers and the most fertile lands (which were, however, difficult to plough). Lands with softer soil were in short supply, which necessitated more intense tillage with better implements. For this reason the iron plough prevailed and iron instruments also. The production of iron significantly rose. Iron, in the form of axe-shaped talents, also became a substitute form of specie, alongside fine woven linen scarves (the Czech word to pay, *platit*, thus comes from the word for linen, *plátno*). A brisk business was done in the markets, and the most important market went on for three days, and took place monthly in Svatopluk's seat (evidently in Mikulčice). This contributed also to the development of crafts for the market and also for princes and magnates.

At first glance, the emergence of the state did not have a profound effect on Moravian tribal society, but it did change its foundations. Outside this society, there were only slaves and chattels: the personal freedom of the Moravians remained intact. On the one hand each prince merely levied taxes and duties, and on the other relieved them of part of their executive power over shared concerns. However, given that the ruler took part of his usufruct from their villages and that he forced them to this, it meant that he infringed some of their proprietorial rights and restricted their freedoms. Because the princes stripped the tribal diet of its powers, ordinary Moravians could not defend themselves against these restrictions or decide otherwise about them. The extent of Moravia was thus ensured by this involuntary loss of freedom and restriction of Moravians' property rights.

DUŠAN TŘEŠTÍK

The emergence of the state also impacted upon its organization. Those princes who joined together to rule the tribe ruled the state. Together with the ruler, they decided on all matters of state and they also had the main share in its administration. Apart from the princes, there was a class of rich magnates, resident not only in castle towns, where we find their courts and churches, but also in the countryside. However they did not have any large farmsteads on which to base their power: rather they lived on state pensions. The core of the state was formed by a group of castle towns in southern Moravia, Nitra being the important centre of these connected territories. Smaller marginal territorial units were connected to this core, administered by the magistrates of the ruler, and called by the title of *župa*, originally an Avar word. The ruler's representative was one of these magistrates, most likely called a duke. The main task of the territorial administration was the collection of taxes. The castles were also the centres of ecclesiastical administration. During the rules of Mojmír and Rostislav this administration was answerable to the Bishop of Passau, who established in Moravia his archipresbytery (office of the bishop's representative). During Svatopluk's rule, ecclesiastical administration was transferred to Methodius.

State finances served above all to build up a large state retinue, a well armed and well trained professional army, which was fed, armed and maintained by the ruler. This was made up of the armoured equestrian core of the army, supplemented by infantry regiments of normal Moravians. The castle towns served most of the needs of the army (one specialized base of the standing army was Pohansko Castle near Břeclav). It is however possible that Svatopluk already had begun to assign individual settlements the responsibilities attendant on the army's needs, establishing what could be called a service organization, which became known later in the Přemyslid state.

3 Political Unification of the Czech Lands

The collapse of Great Moravia after 906 was only one part of the general collapse of Charlemagne's organization of Europe. The constant forays of Magyars and Normans from Scandinavia were only an external cause. The method of government itself had caved in, which had been inherited from the Late Roman Empire and which granted the state, with the Emperor at its head, the right to rule the lives of all his subjects. Among those were the members of an emergent aristocracy. They were state magistrates and lived above all from their share of the finances collected by the state. In the west, in France, the collapse of the state led to almost complete lawlessness, from which the rule of former magistrates, who "privatized" what remained of the state, slowly emerged. Later in Germany, power was concentrated around the duchies which had come from the tribes of Bavaria, Saxony, Swabia and the Franks. These joined in a loose arrangement with a king at its head, from which emerged the empire of the Ottonian dynasty.

Bohemia entered this crucial time as a tribe, but soon there were relatively strong princedoms within it. While the rich and powerful Moravian princes joined together and created a state as early as the beginning of the 9th century, in Bohemia they were as yet too weak.

They closed themselves off with their retinues in the new castles and gradually built up their position in the surrounding territories. Within the tribe princedoms thus emerged, but these princes were not untrammelled governors since the people still had some measure of democratic, tribal freedom. Thus no principality could prevail over another: the princes always negotiated in matters of Bohemian interest as one, and also collectively commanded the Bohemian army.

The Bohemians supported Great Moravia in their fight with the Kingdom of the Eastern Franks. However during the rule of Svatopluk this alliance segued into dependence, which was sealed by the Moravian ruler in about 883 with the violent annexation of Bohemia. He was unable to rule them directly as he did not have sufficient warriors, so he chose Bořivoj I, of the Přemyslids, as ruler of the Central Bohemian principality (from 872–889). He had him christened probably by 883 by Methodius and made him his deputy in Bohemia, with the other princes subordinate to him. Bořivoj resided in Levý Hradec, where he also had the first church built in Bohemia. The diet of princes however did not approve of its superior's daring manoeuvre and removed him from his position. Bořivoj had to flee to Moravia, returning the following year with Svatopluk's army. In order to confirm his victory over his people's paganism and the tribal structures, he first constructed the Church of the Virgin Mary on the site which was both the old sacrificial field and the site of the princes' diet. Some time later in this place his son Spytihněv had a new castle built – Prague. None of this would have been possible without the example and support of Great Moravia. The emergent Czech state, in the newly founded Prague, was linked directly to the statehood of Great Moravia.

In 895, the Bohemians threw off the rule of Great Moravia and joined with the Kingdom of the Eastern Franks. The Přemyslids however maintained their position among the Bohemian princes (in the words of the Frankish annals, *duces Boemanorum*). Bořivoj's son, Spytihněv I (894–915) consolidated his inherited statelet by building a chain of castles, centres of "state" and ecclesiastical administration on the pattern of Great Moravia. He subordinated his principality to the Bavarian bishopric in Regensburg, which then set up its archipresbytery. The other Bohemian princes evidently formally recognized his government, while maintaining their own independence. During the rule of Vratislav I (r. 915–921) and Wenceslas (*Václav*; r. 921–935), the grandson of Bořivoj, Bohemia was constituted of state-organized Central Bohemia and loosely dependent principalities, living in tribal conditions and paganism. The Přemyslids depended upon Bavaria, the core of the decaying Kingdom of the Eastern Franks, competing under the governance of Duke Arnulf with Saxony, whose duke, Henry I (r. 919–936), became king in 919. Fearing Saxony, the Bohemians fully supported Arnulf. However, in 921, he unexpectedly closed an agreement with Henry I, and recognized his sovereignty.

Vratislav had just died in Prague and since Wenceslas had not yet come of age his mother Drahomíra ruled in his name. She refused Arnulf's decision to recognize the sovereignty of Henry I, but Ludmila, Bořivoj's widow, opposed her; Ludmila was supported in this by Bavarian princes active in Prague. The dispute came to a head in 921 when Drahomíra had Ludmila murdered and expelled the Bavarian princes from the country. However, the following year Arnulf, with military aid, forced her to recognize his alliance with Henry I and receive the expelled princes once again. Among those very princes Ludmila gained the reputation of saint. Wenceslas, although he fully supported co-operation with Western Christendom, also hesitated in a similar fashion, and was cautious in his relations with aggressive Saxony. Although in 929 he was forced by the combined armies of Henry and Arnulf to give his allegiance to Henry's kingdom and pay a tribute as a mark of this, they granted him a standing similar to that of the other dukes of Henry's kingdom.

It was thus necessary to decide whether, with Bavaria, to join in the emergent supernational empire (the German nation did not yet exist) or to go the way of full or limited independence. The disparate, half statist, half Christian gathering of principalities which made up Bohemia at that time could not assert itself. In any case it was necessary to remove the other non-Přemyslid principalities by force, build a unified state administration and gain the means to create an army capable of resisting the powerful neighbour. Wenceslas was against such a risky undertaking, proposed by his brother Boleslav. The disputes ended on September 28, 935 with Boleslav's murder of his brother in the castle of Stará Boleslav.

The tragedy of Stará Boleslav meant the end of the process of the emergence of the Czech state, begun by Bořivoj I. Boleslav I (r. 935–972) more than succeeded in building a unified state. Although some Bohemian princes looked to Henry's successor Otto I for support, he was able to destroy all the principalities. He build new castles all over Bohemia in which his magistrates resided and where there were also churches. A large unified state administration thus emerged and concomitantly the whole country, if only in formal terms, was finally baptized. Boleslav made all freemen liable to a tax called the peace tax, i.e., a payment for the prince's protection and more generally for his administration of public matters. It was paid in part in silver coins (denars brought by merchants), in part in the local substitute specie, fine-woven scarves, which were ten to a denar. Soon after, before 965, Boleslav then began to mint his own denar coins, after the Bavarian fashion.

From the taxes and contributions of the people collected in the castle, Boleslav now had the means to build a large retinue. He succeeded in gathering several thousand excellently armed and trained warriors, a number that was prodigious for that time. There was further revenue especially from considerable international trade. It was at this time, in the second decade of the 10th century, that the large trade road moved from the Danube to Prague. This led from the Cordovan caliphate in what is today Spain, through France, Mainz and Regensburg to Prague, and from there through Silesia, then Moravia to Cracow and from there on to Kiev to the market of the Khazars on the lower Volga, which was in turn connected to the Middle East and China. Merchants paid ten percent of the value of their goods for protection, and so Boleslav attempted to gain control over as much of the road as he could.

All this, however, was not sufficient for the upkeep of the army and retinue; booty and tributes from subjugated lands were necessary, and to a degree the army had to maintain itself. Conquests were thus of crucial importance to Boleslav's state. His army conquered

Silesia, the northern part of Moravia along with regions of the Slovak Váh river and Cracow, to the Bug and Styr rivers, where the borders of the Czech state met with Kievan Russia. Thus there emerged a kingdom reminiscent of Svatopluk's with its centre in Bohemia and with subordinate territories governed evidently by garrisons in the main castles, such as Wrocław, Olomouc and Cracow.

Up to the mid-10th century, this formation was not threatened from without. The entire territory between the Elbe and the Bug was settled by tribes that were weaker; although the Magyars undertook raids throughout Europe, they did not thus fundamentally threaten the unity and stability of the states there. The single serious force was the emergent kingdom of Otto I, whose enmity Boleslav had incurred from the first moments of his rule. For fourteen years he fought with Otto I and only in 950 did he subjugate himself to him, recognizing Otto's sovereignty, and like Wenceslas agreeing to pay him tribute. In fact he favoured the policy for which he killed his brother. He acknowledged that the new Czech state could not exist beside a powerful neighbour, even after regularizing relations with it. The fundamental difference was however that Bohemia in those fourteen years became a strong state, in no danger of disappearing into the other kingdom.

The situation became complicated very soon. Otto I, with Boleslav's assistance, defeated the Magyars in a battle on the Lech river near Augsburg and definitively brought an end to their incursions. The Magyars were forced to begin to build their own state. At the same time, in the region of Poznań and Gniezno in Greater Poland, another state began to form under the Piast dynasty. A serious competitor for the Czech state and kingdom thus emerged. In 963 Mieszko I clashed with the margraves of Otto I on the Oder, who governed the subjugated territories of the Polabian Slavs, and joined in alliance with Otto. He also joined in alliance with Bohemia, and sealed this in 965 through marriage with Doubrava, the sister of Boleslav I. Thus the division of spheres of influence was established, albeit at the expense of the Polabian Slavs.

Part of the agreement was that Mieszko would be baptized. This was done with the participation of the Bohemian church and in 968 the first bishop was appointed to his land. Mieszko thus all at once gained more than Boleslav, whose territory was still subject to the bishopric in Regensburg. Thus, through his sister Mlada in Rome and in person with Otto, who in the meantime had become Emperor (962), he negotiated bishoprics for Prague and Moravia. He evidently justified his request with reference to the fact that the Moravian bishopric (and archbishopric) already existed and need only be renewed. However he did not live to see the results, dying in 972. Agreement between the Pope and the Emperor on the Prague and Moravian bishoprics (with its seat in Olomouc) was reached in 973 by his son Boleslav II (r. 972–999). In 976 the first Prague bishop, Thietmar of Saxony (*Dětmar*), was ordained, in addition to an unknown Moravian bishop.

After Thietmar's death in 982 Vojtěch (later known as St Adalbert), the son of Prince Slavník, was elected Bishop of Prague. Since Slavník was allied with the Přemyslids, Boleslav I entrusted him with the administration of Libice, and thus also Boleslav II gave priority to a native son over foreigners when filling the post of bishop. The new bishop felt

DUŠAN TŘEŠTÍK

himself to be a prince in the same way that bishops in Otto's kingdom were, and attempted to enjoy the same rights. He minted his own specie according to their example and attempted above all to reform long-standing, lax ecclesiastical practices (which had originated to an extent in Great Moravia) along the lines of reforming demands made at that time in the Empire. He suppressed the sale of Christian prisoners to pagans, as well as to Jewish and Arab merchants; he opposed polygamy, the marriage of priests and the unconscientious establishment of feast days. However he met resistance, mainly from the magnates, who had enriched themselves by trading in slaves, and alienated the princes and their ruler himself. The disputes went so far that Vojtěch eventually had to resign his office and in 988 left for Rome, where he entered a monastery.

4 The Crisis of 1000 and Its Resolution

Some time before the year 990, Mieszko I suddenly attacked and conquered Silesia and Cracow; Boleslav II never succeeded in winning back these territories. To consolidate the victory, Mieszko I dedicated his lands to St Peter in 990, and thus positioned them directly under the protection of the Papacy. This however involved Vojtěch in complex issues, as Silesia and greater Cracow were in part his diocese, and he had to canonically agree to any changes. The Pope evidently applied pressure and Vojtěch eventually agreed. From the Bohemian point of view he thus became a traitor. Boleslav II however despite this recalled Vojtěch, conceded to his demands and set up the first Benedictine monastery in Bohemia in 993 in Břevnov near Prague.

The cessation of conquests and losses of rich territories provoked alarm among the magnates, and tension rose in the country; this was accompanied by disputes with the bishop and his brother, Soběslav, in Libice. In 994 Vojtěch once again left the land for his monastery in Rome. Immediately after this in 995, Boleslav's regiments attacked Libice and murdered Vojtěch's brothers resident there at the time. In Rome Vojtěch met with the young Otto III (r. 983–1002) on the occasion of the Emperor's coronation. He talked long with the Emperor of plans for the renewal of the Western Empire in close political and ideological co-operation with the Papacy. The Empire had already been reinstated by Otto I in 962, but in practical terms it meant only the "German" empire. Otto III was thinking about an empire that was in fact Roman, and recognized throughout the West. Vojtěch proposed that the Emperor would look for recognition among the rulers of the new Christian states in Central Europe, Bohemia, Poland and Hungary.

Because the Emperor had to rule over kings, these rulers had to be crowned. They had to be directly subject to the Pope through the establishment of archbishoprics in their countries, and these archbishoprics, unlike bishoprics, would be directly answerable to the Pope. Vojtěch was clearly thinking of his diocese and of the Bohemian ruler, of a kingdom and archbishopric for Bohemia, but not only of these things. He knew that the new arrangements would be complex throughout the entire space of Central Europe, which was now joining Europe proper. Vojtěch's plan recognized the sovereignty and the peculiar nature of the new states, while at the same time creating for them a supra-national framework of co-operation under the authority of the Emperor and the Pope.

In Bohemia however at this time there was no place for Vojtěch. He thus went to Bolesław the Brave, the successor of Mieszko I, to whom his brother Soběslav had also fled. In 997 Vojtěch died on a mission to Prussia. Otto III had him canonized in 999, and began to carry out his earlier intention. In 1000, on a pilgrimage to Vojtěch's grave in Gniezno in Poland, he honoured Bolesław the Brave by placing on his head his imperial diadem and established an archbishopric in Poland, naming Vojtěch's brother Radim-Gaudentius as its head. At the same time he ensured the coronation of Stephen I of Hungary and the establishment of an archbishopric for Hungary; Vojtěch's assistant, the abbot of Břevnov Astrik-Anastasius, became archbishop there. Bohemia received nothing, and in the following centuries the country would campaign for an archbishopric and the status of kingdom.

The country's lead was thus frittered away. After Silesia, Greater Cracow was lost. The expansion that had been achieved collapsed, fiduciary sources and tributes dried up, there was no means to maintain a large retinue, and dissatisfaction spread. When Boleslav II died in 999, the state went into a deep crisis. The sons of Boleslav II, Boleslav III (r. 999–1003), Jaromír (r. 1004–1011) and Oldřich (r. 1012–1034) competed for governance, and were deposed and expelled by Bohemian magnates and Henry II or Bolesław the Brave. Bolesław the Brave placed Vladivoj (r. 1002–1003) on the Bohemian throne, and in the years 1003–1004 he ruled himself in Bohemian crown lands. A consolidation of sorts was reached during the rule of Oldřich, who succeeded in winning back Moravia from Bolesław the Brave. He entrusted its administration to his son and successor Břetislav I (r. 1035–1055).

Bibliography

BENDA, Kliment: *Mittelalterlicher Schmuck. Slawische Funde aus tschechoslowakischen Sammlungen und der Leningrader Ermitage*, Praha 1966.

Boleslav II. Der tschechische Staat um das Jahr 1000. P. Sommer (ed.) (Colloquia mediaevalia Pragensia 2), Praha 2001.

CHARVÁT, Petr: *Zrod českého státu 568–1055*, Praha 2007.

CIBULKA, Josef: *Velkomoravský kostel v Modré u Velehradu a začátky křesťanství na Moravě* (Monumenta Archaeologica 7), Praha 1958.

Das Grossmährische Reich, F. Graus, J. Filip (eds.), Praha 1966.

DEKAN, Ján: *Velká Morava. Doba a umění*, Praha 1976.

DITTRICH, Zdeněk R.: *Christianity in Great Moravia*, Groningen 1962.

DOSTÁL, Bořivoj: *Břeclav – Pohansko. IV. Velkomoravský velmožský dvorec*, Brno 1975.

DVORNÍK, Francis: *Byzantské misie u Slovanů*, Praha 1970.

DVORNIK, Francis: *The Making of Central and Eastern Europe*, London 1949.

Europas Mitte um 1000. Beiträge zur Geschichte, Kunst und Archäologie, II, A. Wieczorek, H.-M. Hinz (eds.), Stuttgart 2000.

FRIED, Johannes: *Otto III. und Boleslaw Chrobry. Das Widmungsbild des Aachener Evangeliars, der "Akt von Gnesen" und das frühe polnische und ungarische Königtum* (Frankfurter Historische Abhandlungen, Bd. 30), Stuttgart 1989.

GALUŠKA, Luděk: *Uherské Hradiště – Sady. Křesťanské centrum říše velkomoravské*, Brno 1996.

GRAUS, František: *L'Empire de Grande-Moravie, sa situation dans l'Europe de l'époque et sa structure intérieure*, in: Das Grossmährische Reich, Praha 1966, pp. 133–226.

DUŠAN TŘEŠTÍK

Grossmähren – Slawenreich zwischen Byzantium und Franken (Ausstellungskatalog 1. des Römisch-Germanischen Zentralmuseums), Mainz–Bonn 1966.

HAVLÍK, Lubomír E.: *Der päpstliche Schutz und die slawischen Völker. Zur Problematik der den Herrschern in den Ländern Südost- und Osteuropa gewährten päpstlichen patronatus-protectio*, Annales Instituti Slavici II/1, 1969, pp. 10–32.

HAVLÍK, Lubomír E.: *Constantine and Methodius in Moravia*, in: Sborník prací filosofické fakulty brněnské university C 11, 1964, pp. 27–50.

HAVLÍK, Lubomír E.: *The Relationship between the Great Moravian Empire and the Papal Court in the Years 880–885 A. D.*, Byzantinoslavica 26, 1965, pp. 100–152.

HRUBÝ, Vilém: *Staré Město. Velkomoravské pohřebiště Na valách*, Praha 1955.

JAN, Libor: *Václav II. a struktury panovnické moci*, Brno 2006 (= Knižnice Matice moravské, 18).

LABUDA, Gerard: *Pierwsze państwo słowiańskie. Państwo Samona*, Poznań 1949.

LABUDA, Gerard: *Święty Wojciech. Biskup – męczennik, patron Polski, Czech i Węgier*, Wrocław 2000.

LUTOVSKÝ, Michal: *Bratrovrah a tvůrce státu. Život a doba knížete Boleslava I.*, Praha 1998.

LUTOVSKÝ, Michal – Petráň, Zdeněk: *Slavníkovci, mýtus českého dějepisectví*, Praha 2004.

Magna Moravia (Spisy University J. E. Purkyně v Brně, Filosofická fakulta 102), Praha 1965.

MARÁZ, Karel: *Václav III. (1289–1306). Poslední Přemyslovec na českém trůně*, České Budějovice 2007.

MATLA-KOZŁOWSKA, Marzena: *Pierwsi Przemyślidzi i ich państwo (od X do połowy XI wieku)*, Poznań 2008.

MĚŘÍNSKÝ, Zdeněk: *České země od příchodu Slovanů po Velkou Moravu*, I–II, Praha 2002–2006.

NOVOTNÝ, Václav: *České dějiny*, I/1, Praha 1912.

NOVÝ, Rostislav: *Die Anfänge des böhmischen Staates*, I (Acta Universitatis Carolinae, Philosophica et Historica, Monographia XXVI), Praha 1968.

NOVÝ, Rostislav: *Ilustrované české dějiny/Illustrated Czech History, 2. The State of Bohemia in the 10th–12th Centures*, Praha–Bělehrad 1996.

Origins of Central Europe, P. Urbańczyk (ed.), Warszawa 1997.

PETRÁŇ, Zdeněk: *První české mince*, Praha 1998.

Přemyslovci. Budování českého státu, P. Sommer, D. Třeštík, J. Žemlička (eds.), Praha 2009.

POHL, Walter: *Die Awaren. Ein Steppenvolk in Mitteleuropa 567–822 n. Chr.*, München 1988.

Siedlung und Verfassung Böhmens in der Frühzeit, F. Graus, H. Ludat (eds.), Wiesbaden 1967.

SLÁMA, Jiří: *Střední Čechy v raném středověku III: Archeologie o počátcích přemyslovského státu*, Prag 1988.

SLÁMA, Jiří – VAVŘÍNEK, Vladimír: *Ilustrované české dějiny/Illustrated Czech History, 1. Slavic Settlement in the Czech Lands and Great Moravia*, Praha–Bělehrad 1996.

SOMMER, Petr: *Začátky křesťanství v Čechách. Kapitoly z dějin raně středověké duchovní kultury*, Praha 2001.

Svatý Vojtěch, Čechové a Evropa, D. Třeštík – J. Žemlička (eds.), Praha 1998.

TŘEŠTÍK, Dušan – KRZEMIEŃSKA, Barbara: *Wirtschaftiche Grundlagen des frühmittelalterlichen Staates in Mitteleuropa (Böhmen, Polen, Ungarn im 10.–11. Jahrhundert)*, Acta Poloniae Historica 40, 1979, pp. 5–31.

TŘEŠTÍK, Dušan: *Počátky Přemyslovců. Vstup Čechů do dějin (530–935)*, Praha 1997.

TŘEŠTÍK, Dušan: *"Eine große Stadt der Slawen namens Prag". Staaten und Sklaven in Mitteleuropa im 10. Jahrhundert*, in: Boleslav II. Der tschechische Staat um das Jahr 1000, ed. P. Sommer (Colloquia medievalia Pragensia 2), Praha 2001, pp. 93–138.

TŘEŠTÍK, Dušan: *Die Gründung Prags*, in: Burg–Burgstadt–Stadt. Zur Genese mittelalterlicher nichtagrarischer Zentren in Ostmitteleuropa, H. Brachmann (ed.), Berlin 1995, pp. 228–240.

TŘEŠTÍK, Dušan: *The Baptism of the Czech Princes in 845 and the Christianization of the Slavs*, Historica 2, Nova series, 1995, pp. 7–59.

TŘEŠTÍK, Dušan: *Von Svatopluk zu Bolesław Chrobry. Die Entstehung Mitteleuropas aus der Kraft des Tasächlichen und aus einer Idee*, in: The Neighbours of Poland in the 10th Century, ed. P. Urbańzyk, Warszawa 2000, pp. 111–145.

TŘEŠTÍK, Dušan: *Vznik Velké Moravy. Moravané, Čechové a střední Evropa v letech 781–871*, Praha 2001.

TUREK, Rudolf: *Čechy v raném středověku*, Praha 1982.

Velká Morava a počátky československé státnosti, ed. J. Poulík, B. Chropovský et al., Praha 1985.

ŽEMLIČKA, Josef: *Das "Reich" der böhmischen Boleslaws und die Krise an der Jahrtausendwende*, Archeologické rozhledy 47, 1995, pp. 267–278.

ŽEMLIČKA, Josef: *Ilustrované české dějiny/Illustrated Czech History, 3. The Rise of Bohemia among European Powers (1173–1253), 4. The Czech Lands during the Reign of the Last Premyslids (1253–1310)*, Praha–Bělehrad 1996.

IV. The Czech State in the Era of Přemyslid Princes and Kings (from the Beginning of the 11th Century to 1306)

A drawing of a seal of Vítek III of Prčice, the founder of one of the most important Czech noble families – Víteks and Rožmberks. The seal is affixed to a document from 1220; the drawing is from August Sedláček's estate deposited in the Institute of History of the ASCR, v.v.i., Prague

1 Consolidation of the Czech State
in the Era of the Princes

The crisis had been resolved. However it was necessary to make the transition from plunder-ing to farming, and also to restore the shaken international standing of the Czech state. The situation changed after the death of Bolesław the Brave and the Hungarian king, Stephen, when Poland and Hungary found themselves in difficulties similar to Bohemia. A pagan uprising broke out in Poland, which allowed Břetislav to occupy Silesia and to take posses-sion of the remains of St Vojtěch (Adalbert) in Gniezno in the year 1039. He wished to set to rights two of the heaviest losses suffered by Bohemia – Silesia and the archbishopric (the latter had in fact been the archbishopric of St Vojtěch, designated originally for Bohemia). At the same time, in Rome he also attempted to gain the Pope's consent to this arrangement of affairs. However he met with resistance from King Henry III, who considered the growth in Bohemia's power at the expense of Poland undesirable.

The conflict with the King turned into war. In 1040, Břetislav put up a successful de-fence in a battle at Brůdek at the Domažlice Pass; however the next year he was defeated and forced to accept Bohemia as a fief from the King. He then supported Henry in his fight with Hungary, attempting to use the opportunity to win back the Slovak part of old Moravia (the Váh region and probably greater Nitra) which Stephen I had taken, but he was unsuccessful. He was unable even to retain Silesia, which he ceded to Poland in 1054 for payment. Nevertheless he consolidated the Czech state very effectively within its borders, and these latter would change only to a small extent in the following centuries. His main work was the economic and administrative consolidation of Moravia as a special region of the Czech state. He had five sons and, aware that this could cause serious conflicts for the throne after his death, he divided the governance of Moravia among his young sons in such a way that Vratislav received the Olomouc half, and the Conrad and Ota the other Brno half. The middle son Jaromír was to become a bishop. All were to be subordinate to the eldest, Spytihněv II (r. 1055–1061), who would govern the whole state from Prague. Furthermore, the chief prince of Bohemia and Moravia would always be the eldest of the Přemyslid family. Although this law of primogeniture was later broken, its validity was generally acknowledged and it allowed the ambitious development of Břetislav's policy of consolidation of the Czech state.

Although Spytihněv attempted to overturn his father's decision and strip his brothers of their appanages, his successor Vratislav II (r. 1061–1092), set up appanaged principalities again in Moravia, and Jaromír was forced to accept ordination. His supreme authority over Moravia was secured with the renewal in Olomouc of the special Moravian bishopric in the year 1063. He attempted to block the election of Jaromír as bishop in Prague, but he had to give in to the pressure of the magnates in 1068. It was only then that a Přemyslid ascended to the see who understood his bishopric as his brothers understood their appanages in Moravia; he thus wished to prevent the restriction of his finances through the renewal of the Moravian bishopric. The protracted conflict with Vratislav was resolved by the Pope in 1075 when he decided in favour of the Olomouc bishopric. Pope Gregory VII thus tried to win Vratislav II to his side in the conflict with Henry IV in the matter of what was called the investiture; the conflict about the confirmation of ecclesiastical dignitaries by the Emperor was in fact a fight for the liberation of the church from the bondage of the state. Vratislav however decided in favour of Henry IV and assisted him in suppressing the rebellion in Saxony and also on his Italian campaign.

He was rewarded for this in 1085 with a royal crown. But this was only for himself and not his successor. In addition to the Bohemian royal title, he also held the Polish title, most likely in order to emphasize Czech claims on Silesia. However, he had to concede to Jaromír once again by joining the bishoprics of Prague and Moravia. When Jaromír died in 1090, Vratislav renewed the Olomouc bishopric.

One of the main and enduring results of Břetislav's efforts was the organization of the Bohemia and Moravia in a common state. This jural entity was *de facto* made up of two parts, his own Bohemia and Moravia as a kind of independent, internally unified annex. In 1055 Břetislav I determined that the eldest living Přemyslid should rule both parts of the Czech state in such a way that Moravia was to be governed by several princes who were the issue of his younger sons. From the year 1061, this was the family of Ota I of Olomouc and Conrad I of Brno. In 1092, Conrad's heirs split their appanage in such a way that in addition to the appanage of Brno, there was also one of Znojmo. None of these princes however was ever given the title of Olomouc, Brno or Znojmo, but always that of Prince of Moravia.

Moravia was a unified land, governed in common by several princes who divided its regions in such a way that the Olomouc prince held two and the Brno and Znojmo princes one each. Any of the Moravian princes had the right to the Bohemian throne if he was the eldest of the Přemyslids. The opposite was not the case: the family of Vratislav II's successors did not have any claim on the government of Moravia, because that was hereditary and exclusive to the families of the heirs of the younger sons of Břetislav I. If one of these died without adult heirs, his domain could be ceded by the chief prince in Prague for governance to one of the other Přemyslids, but only until the rightful heir came of age. These rules were abused, but this did not change the jural situation. The Moravian Přemyslids could always rely on the prospect of the Bohemian throne, and thus they never attempted to break away, even though they understandably defended their rights. Thus the integrity of the state was guaranteed.

From the outset, the emergent Czech state recognized its subordination to "German" rulers, expressed in the form of tribute, evidently harking back to the original tribute paid to the Frankish Empire from the year 806. In 1002 Prince Vladivoj was enfeoffed with Bohemia by Henry II and gradually this state of affairs was established as the relationship between the German ruler and Bohemia. It behooved the Bohemian prince to provide "advice and assistance" to his liege lord; fulfilment of this role depended of course on the given set of circumstances. It decidedly was not a responsibility that was enforceable. The German king or emperor had the right to confirm the formal enfeoffment of the prince, elected in Bohemia. Otherwise, he did not involve himself in Bohemian affairs. He also had the right to confirm the investiture of the election of the Bishops of Prague and Olomouc, because both bishoprics were subordinate to the imperial archbishopric in Mainz.

When the Ottonian kingdom became the Roman Empire in 962, drawing upon the inheritance of the Western Roman Empire of antiquity, the Czech state was integrated into its grouping, exceeding the actual dominions of the German king. The territories of today's Germany, Holland, Belgium, Switzerland, Austria, Eastern France and Northern and Central Italy belonged to this. The Emperor never directly ruled Bohemia and Moravia; and he did not have his farmlands or administrators there. He was only recognized as the supreme earthly authority. The Empire was more an ideological grouping which expressed the unity of Western Christendom, even though its authority was not recognized everywhere; the situation did not change even when its ideology became an instrument of aggressive Hohenstaufen policy in the 12th century.

The internal structures of the three Central European states which had emerged in the 10th century – Bohemia, Poland and Hungary – were so similar that they indubitably were run on a pattern common to all. This was a type of state administration with its origin in antiquity which had however guttered at the end of the 9th century along with the Carolingian Empire, and so the Bohemian Přemyslids, the Polish Piasts and the Hungarian Árpáds could not have been familiar with it and could not have organized themselves according to its example. Neither did the Ottonian Empire of their own time provide an example. The state which mediated this example of Charlemagne from the 9th century for the new states of the 10th century was evidently that of Great Moravia. Bohemia drew upon its tradition as early as the rule of Bořivoj I and his sons; the Hungarian state probably became acquainted with remnants of the Great Moravian state organization in Slovakia; and Poland ran itself from the second half of the 10th century along Bohemian lines. The emergent statehood of the Central European states thus drew upon the Great Moravian inheritance.

All of these states were established in a similar fashion: the ruler removed the old tribal institutions, levying taxes, contributions and duties on freemen. Their personal freedom and proprietorial rights remained safe and furthermore they were all equal – if only in theory. By taking part of the yield of their farmlands, the ruler in practice became co-owner, a kind of supreme owner of all the land in the country. He had a free hand only in that land that was unsettled. His subjects had to be forced into this arrangement which effectively limited their freedoms, directly or indirectly. The instrument of state administration was a relatively extensive state apparatus. Although its officers did not have any hereditary privileges, and thus were not an aristocracy, they nevertheless made up a kind of aristocratic retinue governing the people. The existence of the state was a necessity accepted and recognized by relatively large parts of society, above all because the state was able to assert and defend common interests more effectively than the old tribal structures. František Palacký compared this with the case of the Polabian Slavs who clung to the tribal system, and thus perished.

Above all the existence of the state understandably raised the economic question. Even though the agriculture of that time was relatively inefficient, it nevertheless produced some surplus, while the farmers generally kept only what they needed to support their families. From these small amounts exacted in taxes, contributions and work duties, it was necessary to support warriors and administrators who did not plough and did not sow. In Charlemagne's Empire this situation was resolved by the ruler's lending of land in fief to his vassals along with the people who worked that land in exchange for military and other services. In Central Europe the ruler could not treat his freemen in such a fashion. All that was collected was thus gathered in administrative castles to maintain the state apparatus. The amounts were however limited, and thus it was necessary to inventory carefully all these sources (in Hungary this was done in writing) and use them systematically.

As in tribal times, society was divided principally in two groups – freemen and slaves. A brisk trade was done in the latter, and they served as domestic menials in the courts of rich magnates; some of them received land from their masters so that they could support themselves. They had no rights, and they were subject exclusively to their masters. Freemen were the only *sui juris* members of society, but there were significant differences in wealth and standing between them. The class of high-born magnates was not restricted in any way: it had no hereditary privileges and was not thus an aristocracy, even though in terms of wealth and prestige the difference between magnate and farmer was great. Although magnates had more landed property and serfs than ordinary people, they had in fact no large farmlands. The source of their standing and power was above all their service to the ruler and their share of the state revenues arising from it.

The largest section of the population was made up of farmer-heirs, who resided in their villages (*dědina* in Czech, cognate with the verb *dědit se*, inherit) and paid state taxes; first and foremost there was the peace tax, which was an important symbol of their social standing. That a man was free was evident from the fact that he paid this tax. Those who did not own their land rented it from other owners as "guests" of a kind. These too were freemen, and thus paid the peace tax, which in the 12th century was probably 60 denars per annum. A special group of freemen was formed by the warriors of the "second class", who although involved in agriculture, served in the army in times of need, either as infantry-men ("shield-bearers") or equestrian warriors. All freemen were otherwise subject to military obligations. These made up the main body of the army; the prince's own warriors were however his retinue – armoured, well trained warriors, some of them magnates, who were maintained by the prince. These were considered warriors of the "first class". Beyond this social order were foreigners, above all merchants who enjoyed the special protection of the ruler as his "guests", who were subject to their own law. This held also for Jews, who began to settle in Prague as early as the 10th century.

The internal organization of all Central European states depended upon castles, and for that reason it is referred to as the castle system. Castles built from wood and clay were more or less equally spread throughout the land, inhabited by garrisons and administrators. At their head stood the castle administrator, appointed by the ruler regularly for short periods (this was intended to prevent their gaining great influence over the region). All free inhabitants of the region were attached to the castle, and they went to war in that grouping, as well as to its market regularly each week (originally on Sundays) and its court of law. Public works also took place there (referred to as serjeanty), such as the construction and repair of castles, their guard, the construction of roads and bridges, border posts (at the passes). The oldest churches also stood within the castle precincts and the castle catchment area was the original greater parish. These churches were staffed for the most part by priests with an archipresbyter. The princes' farmsteads were administrated from the castles and pertinent courts, and tilled by serfs. Taxes or payments in kind collected from the castle's population were also gathered here. They paid for the upkeep of administrators and retinue. However the greater part was stored in granaries and cellars for the ruler and the members of his court who constantly travelled from castle to castle.

The paladin was the foremost figure in the prince's court to the 11th century. He was the prince's deputy in all matters, especially those concerning the military. Other administrators from the first had to look after the economic and organizational logistics of the travelling court. Beverages were looked after by the Cup-Bearer, food by the Butler, horses and more generally travel logistics by the Marshall. The numerous hunters were looked after by the Master of the Hounds. In the 12th century, the court modernized itself, and the office of chancellor was created, who was usually the Provost of the Vyšehrad chapter; revenue was looked after by the Vice-Chamberlain, while the Chamberlain had responsibility for the courts of law. The title used to refer to all these administrators, of both castle and court, was *župa*, a title used earlier in Great Moravia and which occurred also in Hungary (*ispán*).

It was necessary to ensure a range of craft products and services for this apparatus. A concentration of artisans and servants in the castles would have increased consumption and upkeep expenses. If the prince had gathered the required number of artisans and servants in the castles, he would have had to maintain them and they would have consumed the greater part of provisions in the castle granaries and beer cellars. Thus he did this only rarely, for instance in the case of textile workshops (gyneceum), made up of female serfs who wove materials for the needs of the castle and who were supervised by the castle's matron (*bába*). He solved the problem with a measure that was as simple as it was effective: he settled specialist artisans on lands adjacent to the castles so that they could maintain themselves. He collected some of their products or demanded work from them. In the case of simpler services, he exempted some villages of his "heirs" from tax, requiring from them special services in perpetuity. Thus specialized villages arose which provided one particular service, and some of these villages have retained those reputations to the present day. All villages with the name of Ovčáry (*ovce*, sheep), Vinaře (*víno*, wine), Psáry (*pes*, dog – as these villages fed the prince's dogs), Práče (*prádlo*, washing – they washed the castle's clothes), Kobylníky (*kobyla*, mare – they tended the prince's thoroughbreds), Dehtáře (*dehet*, pitch), Sokolníky (*sokol*, falcon – they trained the prince's falcons), Struhaře (*strouhat*, to scrape – they were the lathe-hands who produced for the most part wooden bowls), Šřítary (*štít*, shield – they produced shields for the army from wood and leather) and many other similar activities from the period of 10th–12th centuries; these are the remnants of what was referred to as the service organization. From the economic point of view, this arrangement was not particularly efficient as it employed only a tiny part of the work force, but it was the only one possible.

The prince was the sole governor. Not only was he the head of the state but the state itself. All the inhabitants of the land from the first magnate to the last farmer were his subjects. The prince was the one "lord" (*pán*) in the land who was addressed thus. It might then seem that his rule was untrammelled, almost like that of a tyrant. In practice however he had to take into account his loyal subjects and all Bohemia, i.e., at least the politically active parts of society, i.e., those magnates who were his administrators and shareholders in the state; in exceptional situations, the people themselves. This was especially apparent in the matter of his election. The prince was chosen only from the line of Přemyslids, and according to the directive of Břetislav I of 1055 he had to be the eldest of the family; ultimately however, the crucial factor was the support that individual candidates received from the magnates. Princes did not reign long (on average, 12 years), and all long-term directives had to be endorsed by the magnates, often under oath. This formally took place at so-called *colloquia*, advisory assemblies that would gather regularly on the Feast of St Vitus (June 15) and St Wenceslas (*Václav*; September 28).

The prince counted priests among his executive officers. They helped him in the administration of the state, and above all they oversaw the observances of the dictates and prohibitions of the new Christian morality. Christianity, which the priests introduced to the people, was significantly different from the Christianity of theologians. It was a collection of dictates and prohibitions covering all areas of life, from food to sexual behaviour. Christening introduced one to the "Christian way of life", not to faith in our understanding of it. The most important figure was not God, but the powerful king Christ, beneath whose leadership Christians fought the devil; and above all they ensured that on certain days fasting took place, that every seventh day was a day of rest, and that women were chosen according to the rules laid down by priests. The actual "Christian army" were the monks, whose main job was to fight with prayer against the diabolic powers. The saints were Christ's disciples and mediators between him and the people. At christening, people accepted the "yoke of servitude" and pledged that they would remain true to Christ by strictly observing the dictates of Christian morality, even when they found those dictates to be incomprehensible (for instance, when their interests were harmed by not ploughing on Sundays). The Christian mode of life was diametrically different from the old tribal morality and tradition.

Upholding it thus meant that the old world of freedom and equality was dead, just as the old gods were dead; it convinced the people that Christ now ruled in heaven, just as the prince ruled on earth.

Neither the prince nor his people had much interest in the spiritual basis of Christianity, and Vojtěch came to grief when he attempted to assert it. Through the early Middle Ages the written culture of the Church existed beside the oral culture of the illiterate lay population, and there was little mutual interaction. The main centre of this high ecclesiastical culture in Bohemia became the Prague bishopric, where an outstanding school was founded. Of the monasteries, Sázava was the finest. It was founded about 1032 by Prokop, who came from an indigenous noble line, and who received a Slavonic education abroad. His monastery was in close contact with Kievan Russia mainly, which preserved a large range of Old Slavonic writings which had originated or been translated in Sázava. In 1054 when the Western and Eastern churches split, the Slavic monks from Sázava were expelled (1055). Vratislav II recalled them later, and although in 1080 he tried to gain recognition of the Slavonic liturgy from the Pope, he was unsuccessful. In 1096 the Slavic monks of Sázava were definitively expelled. Slavic literature had a longer tradition in Bohemia, because many Slavic priests found their way there after the fall of Great Moravia, and the legacy of their learning persisted to the end of the 10th century. At the very least, one legend of St Wenceslas (the first Old Slavic legend about him) originated from these originally Moravian priests. Latin literature also for the most part concentrated on legends of Ss Wenceslas and Ludmila, who had played an important role in the justification of the Prague bishopric, pointing out the maturity of Czech Christianity by reference to its martyrs. The most significant of these was the collection of legends written in 992–994 by a monk in the St Emmeram monastery in Regensberg and also the son of Boleslav I, Kristián.

The marked proliferation of the Přemyslids – the heirs of the four sons of Břetislav I – necessarily led to disputes about the throne. This resulted in the increased power of the magnates, on whom the individual candidates were dependent, providing neighbouring rulers with opportunities to attack. A crisis in the dynasty came to pass, significantly weakening the state. This began as early as the rule of Břetislav II (r. 1092–1100), when he attempted to bypass both the law of primogeniture and the electoral rights of the magnates. In the first years of the 12th century, against a background of constant in-fighting for the Bohemian throne, Bořivoj II, Svatopluk (of the Olomouc Přemyslids) and Vladislav I ruled in quick succession.

The internal situation stabilized only with the rule of Soběslav I (r. 1125–1140), even though he had no right to the throne. King Lothar tried to establish the rightful heir, Ota II of Olomouc; however his military campaign was defeated in 1126 by Soběslav in the Battle of Chlumec, near Chabařovice. He did not prosecute the conflict to the bitter end and was enfeoffed with Bohemia by Lothar in order to insure himself against imperial attacks as well as to allow him to attempt to curb the powers of the magnates.

In 1140, the emergent aristocracy itself elected Vladislav II (r. 1140–1172) as their prince; he was intended as the instrument of the nobles. Konrád (Conrad) II of Znojmo had a greater claim to the throne at that time, and he tried to make good this claim with the support of all Moravia and part of Bohemia. Vladislav was defeated by the Moravians in the Battle of Vysoká (near Čáslav) and then besieged in Prague. The Bishop of Olomouc, Jindřich Zdík, mediated the help of King Conrad III and Vladislav prevailed. At the instigation of Zdík, Vladislav founded a number of monasteries (mainly Augustinian and Norbertine). In 1146 Vladislav II rewarded him by removing the farmlands of the Olomouc bishopric from the authority of the Moravian princes and freeing them from tax and serjeanty. Thus began the long road of the Czech church to free itself from secular power.

Vladislav II allowed himself to be drawn into the adventurous policies of Emperor Frederick I Barbarossa, who was trying to assert imperial governance in Northern Italy. Diplomatic negotiations were led by an outstanding politician, Daniel, Bishop of Prague. He reached an agreement whereby Vladislav's participation in the Italian campaign would be rewarded by the royal crown. The Bohemians excelled in the campaign (above all in 1158 in the siege of Milan), and Frederick crowned Vladislav before the siege was even over. This time the title was hereditary. Moreover, Frederick again recognized the Bohemian claim on Silesia and confirmed Vladislav's possession of the Bautzen region. Vladislav was at the height of his power. In 1172 he voluntarily gave up his rule and set his son Frederick (*Bedřich*; r. 1172–1173, 1178–1189) on the throne, once again bypassing electoral rights of the magnates. They rose up, surprisingly receiving support from Frederick, who claimed that the enthronement of Czech Frederick was invalid, as he had not been elected. In 1173 Frederick of Bohemia was deposed, and Oldřich, the son of Soběslav I, was enfeoffed with Bohemia. Thus for the first time the Bohemian throne was occupied by a ruler installed by the power of the Emperor.

Although Oldřich immediately renounced the office in favour of his brother Soběslav II (r. 1173–1178), who was also crowned without an election. He thus looked for support from the warriors of the lower orders. For this reason it was said of him that he was more a prince of farmers than of *župas*. Barbarossa once again supported Frederick, whom he had previously removed from the throne. Although Soběslav defeated him in a battle near Loděnice in 1179, he himself was defeated immediately after in a battle outside Prague.

Frederick was soon deposed. Barbarossa again intervened and compelled the Bohemian representatives to accept Frederick, leaving Moravia, however, to Conrad Otto. At that time he ruled all the appanaged principalities and began to call himself the Margrave of Moravia. After heavy fighting, agreement was finally reached in negotiations at Knín in 1186 that Conrad Otto would recognize Frederick's supreme rule and he in turn would guarantee Conrad's succession to the throne. Frederick's cousin, Jindřich Břetislav whom Frederick had made Bishop of Prague, immediately rose against him, and succeeded insofar as Barbarossa recognized the Prague bishopric as an imperial principality in 1187. Even though this did not change much in practice, the integrity of the state was threatened. The situation was resolved by the death of Frederick, who was then succeeded by the duly elected Conrad Otto (r. 1189–1191). Immediately after his accession to the throne, he issued what is known as the Statute of Conrad, which favoured the emergent aristocracy, guaranteeing the peaceful possession of its farmlands, and establishing a judiciary. After his death, dynastic conflicts were renewed with the attempt of Přemysl Otakar to take over the governance in 1192. After Jindřich's brief rule (r. 1193–1197), Přemysl Otakar I definitively gained power, and this initiated a new epoch in the history of the medieval Czech state.

The constant in-fighting among the Přemyslids for the throne in the 12th century consisted of contests of the magnates for greater shares of state revenue and remunerative office. This weakened the state, and peace was disturbed in the country. However Bohemian and Moravian society survived these upheavals since the state was no longer necessary for its maintenance and development. It was gradually moving towards a looser dependency on the ruler.

The number of inhabitants grew constantly and the acquisition of new tillage by forced clearance was increasingly difficult. The so-called internal colonization (in distinction to the *Ostsiedlung*, colonization by external settlers called in from abroad, which was typical of the 13th century) speeded up significantly. During the 12th century extensive tracts of forest bordering on territory that had been inhabited from earliest times were tilled. These efforts were successful, and there was once again sufficient agricultural produce. This is witnessed by the extraordinary growth of markets, and the growth of the role of money and commerce. Because country people made purchases at markets, we must assume that they had goods to sell there, and therefore that they had surpluses.

Czech coin, which in the 10th and 11th centuries was used mainly for commerce with distant countries, became territorialized from the time of Vratislav II, and circulated only within the Czech state. In Moravia, mainly in the south, Hungarian denars were used as well as the coinage of the Moravian princes. The number of coins in circulation rose dramatically. It is estimated that at the beginning of the 12th century there were probably one million denars in circulation at any one time. The prince's coiners travelled to all the markets several times a year, enforcing the exchange of old denars for newly minted ones (although these were of lower quality, with a smaller silver content). Contemporaries complained about this "shaving"; however this renewal of coinage was an important source of revenue for the state. The frequent exchange of coinage entailed the frequent change of images on the coins, the creation of which was entrusted to outstanding artists in the 12th century. Thus it was that the exploitative practices of the ruler have left us in coinage miniature art works of the highest level. In their time, these denars were specie in markets in all castles of the principalities, but even beyond them, at fords, bridges and important roads. Markets took always place at least once a week, most frequently on Fridays, but on other days also, with the exception of Saturday and Sunday. Today's names of settlements like Pátek (Friday), Úterý (Tuesday) and Středa (Wednesday) are the remnants of these very markets.

The main goods at market were not luxury items such as slaves, expensive textiles and hides, but everyday craft goods, which were purchased for the most part by normal farmers. Great treasures of coin were to be found also in country cottages as money was common in the countryside. Artisans concentrated mainly in the environs of the large castles. Although they were mostly the servants of the prince, they only worked for him part of the time; this left them enough time to work for the market. Around the mid-12th century, the castle environs of Prague, Žatec, Litoměřice, Brno, Olomouc and Znojmo and other castles were lively market centres with many goods produced there. Merchants from German and Romance countries or Hungary, as well as Jews, settled in these places in specialized autonomous communities.

Prague was the exception to all this. A large number of aristocratic and ecclesiastical dignitaries who wished to be close to the ruler were concentrated in the city, and they built their courts there to provide for their accommodation. Also, a church was usually to be found nearby. In the 12th century Prague, with its two chapters (in Prague Castle and Vyšehrad), thus became the place where a large number of educated priests was concentrated. All this created a market for merchants dealing in imported goods, as well as for local artisans and farmers who supplied Prague with provisions. From the 11th century, an extensive constellation of settlements of merchants, artisans, fishermen and farmers, as well as courts of the magnates and ecclesiastical dignitaries spread out between the two castles of Prague, Vyšehrad and Prague Castle. The main market also moved here, established on the Lesser Town (*Malá Strana*) in the 10th century. In today's Týn a merchant's court was established in the 12th century, which served both as a place where the merchants could congregate and also be subject to inspection. A permanent settlement of German merchants existed from as early as the 11th century near the ford of Maniny at St Peter's at Poříčí; the Jewish settlement was "between Prague and Vyšehrad"; there is also evidence of a settlement of Romani. All these settlements fell under the special protection of the ruler, and written privileges were provided for the Germans by Vratislav II. At the end of the 12th century many stone houses were built in the vicinity of the market in the Old Town (*Staré Město*), and by 1172, through the offices of Judith, Vladislav II's wife, a stone bridge was built, the second oldest in Europe.

This economic growth created a new situation in society, above all in the aristocratic retinue, that is, the Bohemian and Moravian magnates. In order to support the people who did not work directly in the fields, taxes and contributions from many farmers were no longer necessary: the lord could be supported at a fitting level by only a smaller farmstead. There was not enough land. Many people had to support themselves by working on other people's land; however for the most part they tried to obtain land by clearing forests. In this way the richest magnates who already had courts with relatively large economic turnovers and who above all controlled the property of the lord through their administrative positions, obtained forest lands that had not yet been tilled. Former warriors began to manage their interests (made up of their booty gained in war and revenue from the offices entrusted to them). Up to this, they did not permanently reside in their country courts and were always on the move with the ruler. However, in the last quarter of the 12th century these people came to be identified with their country seats. From the second half of the century, widespread construction of expensive stone churches near their courts began. Before this, from the 1130s, many monasteries had been founded, and not by the ruler as before, but by rich magnates. The Bohemian and Moravian magnates already had in their possession a

DUŠAN TŘEŠTÍK

substantial amount of land and people, however the greater part was not their property. It all still belonged to the "state", that is, the prince.

Probably from the time of Vladislav II, an exclusive group of magnate families formed in order to execute all castle and courtly offices. From this arose the great aristocratic lines of the pre-Hussite period. We know them as the Vítkoveces, Hrabišices, Markvartices, Ronoveces, and so on. The first known ancestors of these lines lived in the second half of the 12th century and for the most part came into the possession of the primary family property in those places where they held the castles of the principality. Their farmsteads evidently made up the original appurtenances of the castle; they were the property of the prince and castle administrators or court officers took over their ownership simply by dealing with them as their own. At the same time they colonized the forests of the principalities and treated the land gained as their own. Although they frequently requested some of these farmsteads from the ruler as reward for services rendered, the ruler did not give out these gifts with full transfer of property rights: he could always request them back.

These gifts were not the main source of property for the emergent aristocracy: this came from administrative positions. In the 10th and 11th centuries, all the retinue and administrators lived from the castle, where they got their bread and meat, as it were. In the 12th century however there was not enough bread and meat to go around. For this reason they vied furiously for offices by offering their services to those Přemyslids who were fighting for the throne, and quite often they themselves provoked these struggles. At that time, the contents of the principality's chambers, granaries and cellars at the castle were no longer divided, rather the sources of the revenue themselves were. The retinue received its income from the castle environs, from several villages, in part from the peace tax levied on a demarcated territory, from certain duties, income from ferries on rivers; but mainly the salaries which were fixed for particular offices. All these were called the benefices (*beneficium*) or *župa*, which was the salary of the *župa* or administrator. Originally the ruler provided the benefices only for a fixed period; by the end of the 12th century however these offices were hereditary for certain families. Rulers were replaced, each dependent on the magnates, and they lost control over the *župas*, which became the property of the administrators. However they did not own them outright, and they constantly faced the threat that the next, and perhaps stronger, ruler, would take them away. This was the reason that they exploited their resources in the worst possible manner. They abused their judicial powers in order to maximize their court fines; taxes were extorted not collected. The arrival of the bailiffs of the castle administrators in a village was not dissimilar to that of a marauding army. Free farmers, "heirs" and guests thus preferred to seek protection from various lords and gave up their freedoms (which were of little advantage to them in any case as they only exposed them to the despotism of the *župas*). Uncertainty resulted from this. The aristocracy was not yet an aristocracy. It held farmlands which it did not own. Freemen paid dearly for their freedom, and the number of free farmers decreased. Although the ruler governed, he had ever fewer resources for this, because the administrators took control of them. Nevertheless society improved, and was ever more autonomous and less dependent on the state.

The church now came to play an increasingly important role. Not only did the number of priests and ecclesiastical institutions rise, but their significance did also. Up to 1100, only seven monasteries were founded in Bohemia and Moravia, and these through the offices of the ruler. However between the years 1100–1205, twenty-seven rich monasteries funded by the magnates were established. Above all a large number of churches sprang up in the countryside distant from the castles. There were many more priests and monks, all of whom however were dependent on the founders of their churches. The latter considered the churches and monasteries as their property and made claims on their revenues, most importantly on the tithes. The bishops of Prague and Olomouc had the right to educate and ordain priests, as well as consecrate churches, but they had no influence over the appointment of priests to churches or even over the tithes arising from them. Even the churches with castle parishes were dependent rather on the prince and his administrators rather than on the bishop.

An independent organization subordinate to no external power was built up by the Bishop of Olomouc, Jindřich Zdík (in office, 1126–1150), one of the most important personalities of Czech history in the 12th century; the Bishop of Prague joined him in his efforts in the sixth decade of the century. The bishop selected his special administrators and archdeacons from the chapters, and assigned regions to them for the oversight of the lower clergy. They resided for the most part in the bishops' courts and received their salaries from the same. The old, large castle parishes went into decline and from some colleges of priests there emerged rural chapters.

Increasing numbers of priests were required – both spiritual pastors for the ordinary rural churches and educated priests capable of occupying important positions at the court of the bishop or the ruler. The education of simple priests was not that sophisticated: they could read and write, and they had basic knowledge of Latin and the practical liturgy. Frequently they came from the lower levels of society, in some cases from the ranks of the serfs, and thus they were all the more connected with the life of the people. In earlier times, the higher offices were occupied mainly by foreigners, above all from the German lands, and indigenous priests were in the minority. From the second half of the 11th century however, in ever greater numbers the capitularies of the Bohemian and Moravian chapters began to send their sons to study at famous schools in French and German territory (celibacy had not yet been established and lay priests were married). These people then occupied the key positions in the ecclesiastical administration and in the service of the ruler. They formed a fraternity joined by bonds of blood and friendship, a community of educated people, a professional intelligentsia. They felt themselves to be Czech, not least because foreigners competed with them in their homeland by taking many important and lucrative positions. However, many became chancellors of the ruler, diplomats in his service and some even reached the level of bishop, as for instance Daniel in Prague and Jindřich Zdík in Olomouc.

This intelligentsia's opinions on the situation in Bohemia and Moravia and the measures required to right them was expressed best in his Latin Chronicle of the Bohemians by the dean of the Prague chapter, Kosmas (c. 1045–1125). He surmised that the holder of sovereignty was the land of the Bohemians, which was not however only a territory, but the politically active group of all Bohemians – a political nation, in fact. This sovereignty had been transferred at some stage by the Bohemians to the first prince, Přemysl, with whom they had agreed that they would voluntarily subordinate themselves to him with all their property and freedom. From the end of the 11th century, Kosmas's followers promulgated the idea that Bohemia was not subject to the temporal governing prince, but the eternal prince, who would never die – St Wenceslas. On the seals of Vladislav II and his heirs there appeared the inscription "The Peace of St Wenceslas in the Hands of the Prince". This meant that St Wenceslas was the holder of the government, order and laws; and he merely gave those attributes of power to the prince in trust. Such ideas dominated Bohemian art and spiritual life in the 12th century and hammered home for Bohemians that they were a political nation concentrated about the eternal prince. It was an expression of the confidence of society, of the "Bohemia" or "tribe of St Wenceslas", as this grouping was also referred to. This society became the sovereign holder of the state.

The worlds of the church and of the warriors began to mutually influence and interpenetrate one another. The emergent aristocracy built churches on their farmlands, looking after their artwork and statuary; aristocrats undertook pilgrimages and participated in crusades. They imitated the style of life abroad, looking mainly to French and German models.

This was expressed most remarkably in building works. New Romanesque basilicas were constructed above all by monasteries (in Tismice, Doksany, Louka, Třebíč, etc.); the aristocracy built simpler churches, frequently decorated in a rich fashion. The tendency was towards a raised tribune for the aristocrat and his family, while the people remained in the nave (St Jakub's in Kutná Hora, the church in Červená Řečice, in Záboří nad Labem and many others). On the whole, Czech architecture in the Romanesque style manifested a respectable level in the Central European context; its uniqueness however resided in its expression of the contemporary ideology of the state and the Czech land.

2 Royal Titles and Their Historical Significance

There was a turn in affairs during the rule of Přemysl Otakar I (r. 1197–1230). From the beginning Přemysl energetically joined in the struggle for the Empire which broke out immediately after the death of Henry VI in September 1197. While the camp of the House of Hohenstaufen elected Philip of Swabia, brother of the deceased Emperor, as the Roman king, the opposition favoured young Otto IV of Brunswick, the son of Henry the Lion from the line of Guelphs and a close relation of the English kings. The alternating support of the imperial line of Hohenstaufen along with the enemy Guelphs enabled Přemysl to gain the hereditary royal title in 1198, recognized gradually by all the competing parties including the Pope. At that time the Empire was not able to keep up the pressure on its eastern neighbours. On the contrary Přemysl with his warriors was a welcome ally and a feared opponent of all contenders for the Roman throne. His assistance was appreciated most of all by the Hohenstaufen Frederick II, the Warlike (r. 1211–1250) of Sicily, who was just ascending to the throne of Roman king, and who awarded Přemysl what was called the Golden Bull of Sicily.

This extraordinary charter, issued on 26 September 1212 in Basel and endorsed by Frederick II with his royal Sicilian seal, is one of the founding documents of Czech statehood. Before this, Philip of Swabia (in 1198) and Otto IV of Brunswick (1203) issued binding *privilegia* for Přemysl and "his" kingdom; these however have not survived and to a great extent are incorporated into the Golden Bull of Sicily. In it Frederick confirmed the royal title of Czech rulers, allowing Přemysl and his heirs to use it hereditarily and without any tribute to the Empire. Furthermore he recognized the right of Bohemian kings to approve native bishops. To these articles, most likely contained in the earlier *privilegia* of his forebears, Frederick evidently added new freedoms. Neither the Bohemian king nor his successors were enjoined to attend the Imperial Diets other than in Bamberg, Nuremberg and, under certain conditions, in Merseburg. For imperial coronal journeys to Rome they had to send either 300 armoured soldiers or pay 300 silver talents.

With the Golden Bull of Sicily Přemysl achieved his main political goals. The Empire formally recognized that the election of the Czech ruler was an internal matter, and that therefore all previous interventions (mainly in the years 1172–1197) were of an invasive nature. The Bohemian kingdom, without seceding from the Empire, remained in practical terms an independent formation. Since the Bohemian king was at the same time one of the foremost imperial princes, in the future he could influence his western neighbours more assertively than the Emperor could the Bohemian crown lands. The issue of the Golden Bull of Sicily was a step of fundamental constitutional significance; but the circumstances surrounding the granting of the hereditary kingdom had even wider ramifications. The royal title was at this time generally seen as a feature of independence and sovereignty. In the tradition of Czech foreign policy it had even deeper roots.

As early as 1000, Central Europe witnessed the first wave of granting of royal titles, which affected Hungary and partly Poland. The emergence of a kingdom at the turn of the millennium connected with universal pan-Christian ideology of Emperor Otto III. Bohemia, convulsed by dynastic conflicts and a general crisis, was unsuccessful. The next wave was triggered by the struggle of the Empire and the Papacy in the second half of the 11th century. Spytihněv II (r. 1055–1061) was only partially successful in gaining the right to wear a mitre. That honour, which was evidently connected with Rome's attempt to gain greater influence in Europe, was granted by the Pope. It was not until Vratislav II received the crown from the hands of Emperor Henry IV, did a Czech become king. This happened in the coronations in Mainz in 1085 and thereafter on June 15 in Prague, most likely in 1085. The royal Estate of Vratislav II was not however hereditary, so his successors ruled again as princes. Not even the title of Vladislav II, granted by Emperor Frederick I Barbarossa in 1158 in Regensburg, was generally recognized and enduring. In the fighting after 1172, hopes of maintaining it quickly disappeared, and so Přemysl's success in 1198 was quite surprising.

Royal coronations introduced a new quality not only in terms of conspicuous prestige, but also from the viewpoint of constitutional symbolism. The royal Estate of the Přemyslids

JOSEF ŽEMLIČKA

meant a break in the traditional ideology of principalities; previously the ruler was merely the physical representative of the true ruler of the country – the eternal and immortal prince St Wenceslas, who was lord of the dynasty and the state. With his election and coronation on the old stone throne which stood at the centre of Prague Castle, the prince was bound to "all Bohemians", that is, all the more to the early medieval aristocracy, which had begun to make the saint's cult their own. With the elevation to royal Estate, Přemyslid rulers rid themselves of the burden of the past, free now of the tight framework of being "merely" deputies of the distinguished saint, who then gradually became the symbolic property of the aristocracy. They began to build his charisma on another ideology. From the former prince, whose dark "pagan" roots were obscured by the ideology of St Wenceslas, there sprung a king who ruled at the mercy of God. He was no longer a representative of the holy prince, but Christ and God themselves. Here is yet another of the differences between the era of princes and that of kings.

It was only a question of time before the Přemyslids became aware of the double dimension of the royal Estate. The title and coronation had for them from the first a greater value than anointment. Even the fact that the first coronation took place outside Prague bears witness to the international political prestige over domestic relations. The first royal coronation in the new style took place on 6 February 1228 in St Vitus Cathedral in Prague. King Přemysl saw his son crowned on that occasion, who soon after became an independent ruler, Wenceslas I (r. 1230–1253). The ceremony was carried out by the Archbishop of Mainz, who was the metropolitan of the dioceses of both Prague and Olomouc until 1344. In 1228 he thus initiated the continuous series of royal Bohemian coronations according to the ecclesiastical liturgical model. Ecclesiastical anointment and coronation made of the ruler the lord designated by God's will and emphasised the sacred aspect of his person. The ruler thus became independent of his magnates and chiefs. The old Bohemian electoral diet came to an end, and the stone throne of Prague Castle was forgotten so quickly that not a trace was left. The continuity of the extraordinary place remained: the celebration was merely moved to Prague Cathedral.

Among the lordly features of Bohemian princes was the throne; further symbols were the sceptre and above all the staff with pennant, which was transformed in the 12th century into the staff of St Wenceslas. The most outstanding insignia was however the head gear. The princes originally wore a hood from the hide of a beast of prey on celebrations and sometimes a kind of feathered diadem. There are several visual representations of the crown of Vratislav II. From its band there rose four crosses. Vratislav's successors wore a simple prince's hat with narrow veil at the back, until Vladislav II introduced the crown again. We can get an idea of the crown of Přemysl Otakar I from his gold seal dating from 1224. Here we see the enthroned king with his sceptre and an apple. He wears a perfectly shaped crown, formed from a band of lilies. It is not unlike the crowns of the last of the Přemyslids, which were modelled according to the French style.

The achievement of hereditary royal Estate was not just a formal affair. The ruler with royal Estate brought together the "land" (*terra*) and the "kingdom" (*regnum*) in a truly institutional kingdom. Closely connected with him was also the symbolism of the saintly and immortal Prince Wenceslas. The terms land and kingdom took on political content, beyond the direct influence of the ruler, and an aristocracy arose from its holders. The Přemyslid lands (i.e., Bohemia and Moravia) were constituted as a jural corporation, in which the aristocracy played the decisive role – Bohemian in Bohemia, and Moravian in Moravia. In the course of the 13th century, this was apparent in the titles of the supreme administrators. Previous "private" commissars of the prince and king became dignitaries of the "land" and "kingdom". The term "Bohemian Kingdom" (*regnum Bohemiae*) began to express the supra-territorial union of the Přemyslid lands. This developed directly into the "Crown of the Bohemian Kingdom" of the Luxemburgs (*Corona regni Bohemiae*), or the Bohemian crown lands.

3 The Czech Lands in the Time of the Great Colonization

In the course of the 13th century what was once the princely House of Přemyslid became a power in the centre of Europe. Without colonization, without the mass emergence of towns, without widespread mining and internal consolidation of royal power, the role of the last Přemyslids in foreign affairs would have been much weaker. In a relatively brief period, Bohemia and Moravia underwent dynamic development which brought them closer to the more advanced areas of Western Europe. The more developed areas of France, the German Rhineland and the Danube Basin, Southern and Central England and most of all Northern and Central Italy had a not inconsiderable head start on Central and Eastern Europe. From the second half of the 11th century, brisk economic and social change spread through the area, connected with urbanization, with the metamorphoses of settlement and the consistent rise of market-finance exchange. Things began to look up for regions which produced specialized goods and were able to export them. Textiles from Florence, Flanders and Brabant; silks from Lucca in Italy; wines from France – all these became renowned. The markets in the town of Champagne in France became an important crossroads of international trade. Merchants settled their debts there and closed new agreements. Roads from Italy to the Netherlands, and onwards to the Baltic, became important trade routes; the Rhine also became a significant route. Even though the Crusades did not renew direct connections between Europe and the Far East, contacts with the Near East were at least strengthened. War with the Arabs as well as the growing requirements of sea trade necessitated the mass construction of ships. At the forefront of these ever demanding financial operations stood Italian bankers. An integral part of this great change, which did not proceed equally everywhere and was retarded in some places till the late Middle Ages, was the reform of monetary systems, climaxing in Bohemia with the minting of the Prague *groschen* in 1300.

A key role in these systemic metamorphoses was played by the towns. The Romans had founded their municipalities in Gaul, Germany and other provinces. The early Middle Ages also had their mercantile centres; but only in the 11th century did the first free and autonomous town centres of a new type begin to emerge. The highest echelon of urban society, made up mainly of merchants and rich artisans, gradually began to demand economic as well as political privileges. This took place in various ways, from co-operation with territorial powers with municipalities to confrontations between bishops and urban communes. The greatest degree of freedom was gained by the large cities in Northern Italy – Milan, Florence, Venice, Pisa and others.

While the more advanced parts of Europe developed quickly, in the East the changes were less intense. This marginal zone, along with Central and Eastern Europe in its entirety, belonged to the monarchy of the Czech Přemyslids. Their territory could not draw upon the traditions of late antiquity. Nevertheless, profound changes took place there from as early as the end of the 12th century. The gradual inhabitation of the Bohemian and Moravian interior disturbed the natural self-sufficiency of medieval economics, in which agricultural production prevailed. Large populations settled in the administrative castles of princes and on the crossroads of important routes, and these concentrated crafts, trade and local markets. The further development of Bohemia and Moravia was profoundly influenced by the way that settlement progressed. The interior uplands were inhabited and in some places the population reached to the foothills of mountainous borders. From the Bohemian and Moravian side, the forests of the previously inaccessible highlands were encroached upon. This colonizing progress was accompanied by significant metamorphoses in socio-legal areas. The settlers in these expansive forest tracts, building their new estates, received various types of relief and freedom from their lords. These provided important stimuli which helped old Czech society to transform itself and begin to catch up with the more advanced regions of Europe.

In tandem with this transformation of Czech society, all of Central and Eastern European society encountered the phenomenon of *Ostsiedlung*, or German eastward expansion. This too was part of much wider processes in which man from early times expanded the reach of culture and society. From the 11th century however the movement of settlers accelerated in unwonted fashion. Enormous unbroken tracts of forest disappeared; settlers drained swamps and marshes in order to build towns and villages. The higher table lands and littorals of France, Flanders and Friesland and even German territory were occupied. Colonization transformed the aspect of rural Italy, the Pyrenees and England. The interest of rulers joined with that of the colonizers. New managers were given various personal advantages and were often freed for a time from payment of tax and interest.

Colonizing activities provoked ethnic removals also. Friesians and Dutch from the 11th and 12th centuries were active in the cultivation of land in the Northwestern coasts of Europe, and beyond the Pyrenees French farmers searched out new homes. Flemings and the Dutch, prompted by bishops and margraves, settled in the newly established German principalities on the right shore of the Elbe. The most noteworthy element of the multifaceted phenomenon was however the movement from the German lands to the east and southeast. The political and ethnic pressure in this direction had older roots, since as early as the beginning of the 9th century the Franks and later the medieval Roman Empire attempted to expand its influence over the western Slavs. A new phase began at the turn of the 13th century. Extremely dense settlements and difficult living conditions forced farmers, townspeople and miners from Saxony, Francia, Bavaria, Rhineland and Swabia towards Silesia, Poland, Bohemia and Moravia, central Hungary, Transylvania and the Baltics. They still had dependent status in these places, since they had settled on the lands of their new lords, but they received advantages which raised them above the indigenous population. They found support from the princes and kings of the regions, as these latter wished to encourage economic growth, and the settlers allowed them both to improve their finances and also more generally consolidate their positions.

Priests and monks from Bavaria or Saxony were active in the Přemyslid lands from as early as the 10th century. Part of the prince's retinue was often made up of foreigners with German names and settlements of German merchants brought variety to Romanesque Prague, Litoměřice, Brno, Olomouc and Znojmo. But only at the beginning of the 13th century did Bohemia and Moravia open up to the tide of German colonists. This was not a mass tendency up to the accession of Přemysl Otakar II (r. 1253–1278) to the throne. For a longer period German settlements had dissolved into the larger internal colonizations, which had encroached upon remote and less fertile highlands from the end of the era of princes. The significance of *Ostsiedlung* however lay in another aspect: through its mediation our country became acquainted with advanced forms of legal systems and institutions.

In rural areas, the so-called German code of law (*ius teutonicum*), known gradually also as the inheritance law, commercial law, *purkrecht* or Law of Emphyteusis. As a collection of customs and legal regulations, employed by the German, Flemish and even Dutch colonists during their progress eastwards, it reached its definitive form at the beginning of the 13th century in the Meissen region and Silesia. The first mentions of German law began to appear in Moravia and a little later in Bohemia. In return for regular payment of his fixed tax and contributions, the holder of these rights enjoyed the use of his farmlands heritably; he also enjoyed a greater measure of personal freedom and autonomy. A prominent feature of German law was the pressure of market production and exchange, realized in specie. The advantages of German law both for the emergent rulers and their subjects were that the older, indigenous forms of staggered duties and taxes (what was referred to as *lhotní právo*) lost their significance. German law, granted first of all in likelihood to German settlers, became in time the means for dealing with the indigenous Czech peasantry. It spread particularly in the environs of the emergent towns, where a subject could exchange his produce more easily at market.

The spread of German law, the Law of Emphyteusis, was a long-term process climaxing at the end of the 13th century and in the course of the 14th. In this period the two sources of colonizing populations more or less reached parity. Settlements of German farmers in many places spread out into larger surrounding tracts (the areas around Broumov, Trutnov, beneath Ještěd, near Loket, Svitavy, in some parts of the Bohemian-Moravian highlands and south Moravia), and accepted Emphyteusis in large numbers; for them it was the ideal arrangement of villages and their farmlands. The wave of indigenous colonization on the contrary continued rather in the old manner. Its villages were not as extensive and there was a looser arrangement of farmsteads and fields; Emphyteusis often bypassed these areas

JOSEF ŽEMLIČKA

completely. Generally speaking however, in the territory of the Přemyslid state, colonization went forward with a mixture of nations, occupying not only bordering mountains in the mid-14th century, but filling up the empty areas in the vicinity of Prague.

Since the population was continually growing and larger towns in particular were demanding in consumer terms, attention turned once again to the old, fertile settled territory. From the previous scattering of smaller settlements and isolated farms there emerged in the environs of some large towns a network of populous villages with regularly shaped tillage, which offered better usage of three-field crop rotation. These changes spread in northwestern Bohemia (near the towns of Litoměřice and Most) before the mid-13th century (the three-field crop system was best mainly for grain production). Of grains, rye was cultivated the most, and after that barley and oats, while wheat fell behind. Organizational changes in agricultural production were assisted by the modification of the shape of fields into long belts in which it was easier to employ a heavy plough. Further technical improvements followed, not only in the work on the land, but also in the harnessing of animals. All this was reflected in the general growth of farm and livestock production.

The conquest of new land for cultivation, the construction of dwellings and all types of agricultural work were facilitated by the enormous expansion of high-quality and affordable iron instruments. These were supplied to rural areas from the workshops of urban artisans. Thus it was that the town became an integral part of all these changes during the era of the last Přemyslids.

The expanding settlements, concentrated about the large castle of princes, were well known in Bohemia and Moravia before the 13th century. These centres, made up of a wreath of settlements in the enceinte, courts of the magnates with chapels and markets, might at first glance have seemed like medieval towns in some respects, but in fact they were different. They lacked two key features: the subordination of all inhabitants of the town to a special municipal law and the existence of a free municipal artisans, who supplied products to the market. From the 13th century however, the future belonged to the municipalities, whose institutions had come into existence in Western Europe and reached the Přemyslid lands in the course of the *Ostsiedlung*. Chartered towns were also to be found in Bohemia, as in Poland and Hungary, constituted by *locatio*. Tasks of a technical nature relating to the settlement such as demarcating the market place, streets or planning the boundaries of the town involved the jural relations to the lord of the town, to municipal law and even to the individual rights and duties of the population. Unlike the rural colonization, the German settlers played a stronger role in the organization and founding of the towns from the beginning. Not only did they have the necessary experience in the organization of such ventures, but they also possessed the financial means to realize them.

The urbanization of Bohemia took place mostly in the 13th century. The towns spread first from Silesia to north Moravia. It was perhaps in the year 1213 that Bruntál was cleared, and, shortly after this, Uničov. Opava was constituted as a municipality by 1224, and in 1226, in the outlying fields of the important principality's castle, Znojmo was established. At the same time, the first town *locatio* began in the Czech territory (Hradec Králové, Litoměřice,

Kladruby). Know-how concerning town organization travelled from Silesia across Kłodzko to the Polabian region, as well as from Saxony, the Cheb region and the Bavarian Upper Palatinate. Hodonín in southeastern Moravia underwent *locatio* according to the Hungarian model. In the third decade of the 13th century the Old Town of Prague (*Staré Město*) was incorporated, and Brno and Olomouc followed soon after. Only in the era of Přemysl Otakar II and Wenceslas II however did a number of Bohemian and Moravian towns expand and improve. One significant enterprise in the mid-13th century was the founding of Jihlava, which became the centre of a dynamically developing mining district; in Bohemia to the south the grand *locatio* of České Budějovice in 1265 was also of note. In economic terms the most influential towns created an infrastructure of village settlements about themselves, and so in some areas it is possible to refer to real municipal regions as early as the 13th century. In the time of the first Luxemburgs, significant municipalities were founded only on rare occasions, the most important of which was that of the New Town (*Nové Město*) in Prague in 1348.

Favourable starting positions were to be found especially where the future towns could draw upon older settlements near beneath the prince's administrative castle (Hradec Králové, Litoměřice, Žatec, Brno, Olomouc, Znojmo, etc.). A new municipality could maintain the high degree of services to be found in the older castle centre; it could exploit and, according to its needs, re-mold the older structure of the settlement in its area. At other times, the lord had founded his town on "greenfield land". Such town estates usually had a regular ground plan (České Budějovice, Litovel, Uherské Hradiště, etc.); but it required more work to establish it economically. The dominating feature of most towns was the parish church. In larger towns Dominican and Conventual Franciscan monasteries were established and these were usually part of the town's fortifications. From the outset town construction was straightforward, for the most part using wood and mud, and it was only much later that the great Gothic stone buildings were erected.

The ruler equipped the towns with various privileges so that they could prosper economically and vie with the always tough competition from the aristocracy. The right to a market, whether weekly or, later, annually, was one of the basic privileges, and its granting was an index of prestigious status. By concentrating market turnover from all surrounding areas in the town marketplace and by dictating prices, the towns began to abuse their dominant position over the villages. A further measure intended to strengthen various town monopolies was the mile-right (German, *Meilenrecht*), which forbade trades and inns within a mile of the town. Among common freedoms was also the right to build battlements or turnpikes (merchants had to go through the town and offer their goods at the local market). If the town was affected by war or natural catastrophe (fire was particularly common among the wooden buildings), the lord released his town and its citizens from the multifarious payments and duties. Each town had to establish its rights and privileges individually, and assert them independently of others. Royal towns, frequently established upon the older castle centres, usually asserted themselves as the real economic centres of the outlying regions. In contrast, the greater number of aristocratic or monastic towns remained limited in their development, never surpassing their narrowly local framework. By the end of the 13th century, the next phase began with the emergence of conflicts between independent towns, provoked by competitive economic factors. These concerned the restriction of market catchment areas, trade profits or dates of annual or weekly markets.

Towns differed from rural areas above all in their internal organization. The shared life of a relatively large number of people in an enclosed urban space placed high demands on legal authority, for instance, on the execution of heritable and proprietorial matters, the defence of citizens' freedoms, the trial and punishment of torts and criminal offences. Unlike the rest of the country, the towns were governed by municipal law. This code of law was not unified, but varied according to different models. Most towns in the northern half of Bohemia and also in northern Moravia employed the code of law from Magdeburg, whose indigenous authority was Litoměřice in Bohemia. Prague's Old Town took its code of law from the south German model, and Brno from the Vienna and the Austrian towns. In the Přemyslid part of Silesia and in northern Moravia the code of law from Hlubčice (now Głubczyce in Poland) prevailed. For mining towns the extent of law of the town of Jihlava was important.

From the outset, it was the royal towns which had the most influence and prestige. At their head was the magistrate (*rychtář, richter*), the king's officer. Not only did he run the town administration, but also chaired the town court. Apart from the magistrate, the town council soon became a grouping of influential citizens, which the ruler regularly appointed in the royal towns. It was from these councils, run by the mercantile and financial patricians, that pressure came to expand the autonomy of towns. The balance of power between magistrate and council turned in favour of the latter only at the beginning of the 14th century.

The richest group in the large towns was the patrician class who were involved in international trade or financial and mining ventures. Because of its economic position, this class could influence the running of the town and municipal affairs, which brought it into conflict with the artisans, who made up the base of municipal society. Since these patricians were German in character for a long time, and the artisans for the most part spoke Czech, the tensions were not merely social, but took on a national aspect also. The character of urban production and its protectionist measures gradually forced the craftsmen into various associations. First, there emerged religious brotherhoods, and then from the end of the 13th century and throughout the 14th the guilds made up of masters of the same or related crafts. Through these associations, artisans increasingly affected the life of their towns. On the lowest rung of this layered urban society stood hired labourers, servants, grooms and maids. Since the elderly and infirm remained at a low social level throughout the Middle Ages and there were few hospitals, they usually wound up among the beggars and cripples.

For a long period, the means of exchange could not not keep up with this dynamic economic development. The frequent withdrawal of denars from circulation and their exchange for "new" money, often of lower quality, weakened confidence in minted coins. Contemporary accounts draw attention to this. The state of affairs did not change even with the mass minting of bracteate in the 13th century. Thus most normal payments still were made with unminted pieces of silver, measured in talents. The necessary conditions for improvement began to emerge after the discovery of silver in the environs of Jihlava. However it was only with the substantial silver lodes discovered during the reign of Wenceslas II near the Cistercian monastery in Sedlec that Czech mining and minting embarked on a new phase. A populous town sprang up almost overnight directly above the mining galleries – Kutná Hora. Very soon, miners from all over Central Europe made their way there. Entitlement to the organization of mining work caused the need to introduce a unified legal code relating to this activity. At the request of Wenceslas II, a mining code of law was drawn up (*Ius regale montanorum*). Its creator, the Italian lawyer Gozzius of Orvieto, was able to draw upon his earlier experience with Jihlava law. In 1300 Wenceslas II undertook radical minting reforms. The minting of new and now more permanent coins was concentrated in the main royal mint in Kutná Hora. The silver from this town was issued only in the form of the Prague (Czech) *groschen*, and this was divided into twelve smaller coins. It became the basis of the new exchange system in the Czech Lands for the next few centuries.

Within a relatively short period many changes took place that would otherwise have taken much longer. Society underwent transformations which were still to be felt during the time of the first Luxemburgs. The tripartite world of warriors, princes and peasants no longer obtained. The confident citizen stepped onto the historical scene. Success began to be measured not only by birth, as it had been heretofore, but also through wealth and profit. One can see new ideas also in the aristocracy. The retinue and magnates of the "princely era", who lived on pensions from the prince or "state", became regular landed authorities. Though the highest placed of the "new" landed aristocracy claimed continuity with the circle of former court and castle ranks, they held and owned their farmsteads heritably. This was another of the fundamental results of the 13th century.

Those magnates' families who earlier enjoyed the favour of their prince now had the best prospects of gaining large amounts of land. Their representatives were the former holders of castellar ranks and other high benefices, and so when the time was right they could use their administrative standing for private appropriation. In the course of the 13th century they became an influential ruling group. In Bohemia, the southern Bohemian family of Vítkovec were among the foremost originary lines, soon splitting into the lords of Rožmberk, Hradec (Jindřichův), Landštejn and Ústí. In north-eastern Bohemia from the Hrabišic line came the Rýzmburks, and further, there were the originary lines of Markvartic (of Vartenberk, Valdštejn, et al.), Ronovec (of Lichtenburk, Lipá, Dubá, et al.), Buzic (of Valdek, Házmburk, et al.), Bavor of Strakonice, Švamberk and many others. In Moravia, the foremost positions were taken up by lords from Pernštejn, Boskovice, Kunštát, Cimburk, Žerotín and others, but also families with wider Bohemian-Moravian reach (of whom the most famous were the Šternberks). By means of their political influence and extensive property these families pushed the mass of lower aristocracy into the background, leaving them later to be called squires, yeomen or knights.

Such "privatizing" pressures quickly brought an end to the old castle administration. The landed wealth of Bohemia and Moravia scattered into farmsteads belonging to the aristocracy, the Church and the ruler; their boundaries were unclear and they often changed owners. More continuous tracts of property emerged only in some places, for instance in southern Bohemia with the strong position of the lords from Rožmberk. The king could no longer interfere at will in proprietorial relations; neither could he any longer alienate aristocratic or ecclesiastical goods. His direct influence remained limited to royal castles, towns and other properties. Another part of the royal revenue was the income from tariffs, the exclusive right to mint specie as well as mining (the claim on precious metals located in the ground).

The changes directly affected laws. The old Slavonic laws which had never been firmly codified, but which had emerged from a collection of continuously updated customs, began to be arranged according to the kind of people using them. Members of the aristocratic class claimed that the Land Law applied to them (placing themselves thus under the jurisdiction of the Land High Court). The sessions of this representative body were run by the supreme Land regents – the Supreme Chamberlain, Land Judges and the Land Clerk; and in the 14th century, the Supreme Burgrave held the most privileged position. Property transfers of free farmsteads and the criminal matters of the aristocracy were recorded in the Land Rolls. Clerics fell under canon law, which was based on old Roman law and was unified for all Latin Europe. Life in the towns, where a relatively large amount of people were concentrated in small spaces, also began to organize itself. Municipal law was valid there, and was most advantageous for the inhabitants of royal towns. Subjects of the king, aristocrats and the Church were subject to land authorities, which usually transferred part of their powers to the village magistrates. These last were equipped with lower court powers. On the larger Estates burgraves oversaw the individual areas.

New forms of business activity were introduced into Bohemia and Moravia by voracious individuals who had both experience and ambition. The first generation usually came from neighbouring German lands, and only later did native businessmen join them. These people were active as *locatores* in the founding of villages and towns. They negotiated with the future authority about the conditions of the settlement, they brought the settlers, vouched for the success of the project, measured out the extent of the future estates. For their services they received profitable magistrate offices in the towns and in the villages also. Soon they were active in mining, minting and finance. They gained the favour of the king because they were able to provide his eternally needy court with large loans. They belonged above all to the patrician class of the big royal towns (Prague, Brno, Jihlava and, from the end of the 13th century, Kutná Hora), and they wished to vie with the aristocracy in their style of living. Not only did they adopt court fashions and indulge in conspicuous consumption, but the most prominent built their own castles.

This economic and social boom in Bohemia however had firmly defined limits. One basic disadvantage was the lands' position in the interior, with access neither to the sea nor any of the large European rivers (the Rhine and Danube). Bohemia moreover was distant from the main overland routes. No specialized centres of production were established. Only in a small number of large towns (Prague, Brno, Olomouc, Jihlava) did merchants engage in international trade. While most of the imports were luxury goods (cloths and textiles) and some types of comestibles (salt, good wine, sea fish), the meagre export trade for the most part consisted of agricultural surplus or some uncomplicated animal or natural products (hides, honey, wax, resin, etc.). Economic changes, moreover, spread unevenly, for the most part concentrated in the fertile hinterlands of the larger towns or in the newly colonized regions. The peripheral regions were neglected for many years. Nevertheless, in the 13th century a decisive step was made and Bohemia and Moravia broke many of the barriers which had separated them from the more advanced parts of Europe.

4 The Realm of Přemysl Otakar II and Wenceslas II

After his accession to the throne in December 1197, Přemysl Otakar I primarily faced the distrust and resistance of the magnates who over generations had grown used to controling the choice of king. He managed to pacify Moravia, where only recently a group opposed to the power centre of Prague had come together. The administration of Moravia, with the rank of margrave, was assumed by Přemysl's younger brother Vladislav Jindřich, even though he most likely took control over the extensive region of Olomouc only later. Until his death in 1222, this margrave was one of Přemysl's most reliable adherents, always acknowledging the supreme authority of royal power over the rank of margrave.

The magnates, dissatisfied with Přemysl's autocratic interpretation of governance, now gathered around the Děpoltic clan, one of the auxiliary lines of the Přemyslids. They later exploited the problems in the Přemyslid family. The competition between the two Roman kings, Philip of Swabia and Otto IV of Brunswick, for the governance of the Empire provided them with a good opportunity for this activity. In 1212 the situation became critical when Emperor Otto IV, at the diet of princes in Nuremberg, declared Přemysl dethroned. At the same time Vratislav, the son of King Přemysl and his first wife Adléta, was enfeoffed with Bohemia. Only Otto's swift defeat and the victory of Frederick II of Hohenstaufen (at the Battle of Bouvines in 1214) prevented deeper upheavals.

One result of the king prevailing was the election of Přemysl's son Wenceslas in 1216 in Prague. Only one branch of the dynasty remained on the political scene; moreover this was narrowed down to Přemysl's issue with his second wife Konstancia of Hungary. The rebellious Děpoltics were exiled. After their expulsion from Bohemia they drifted to the court of the relations of the Piasts in Wrocław, and died out before the end of the 13th century. In 1216, the Prague bishop Ondřej accused Přemysl and the Bohemian magnates of breaking ecclesiastical regulations and, in agreement with the Pope, demanded the end of the continuous interference of the laity in ecclesiastical matters. In a long dispute, Ondřej failed to win even the support of the domestic clergy, since his reforming demands tended towards the observance of celibacy, moral probity and other restrictions. The dispute ended in 1222 with the issue of Přemysl's *privilegia* for the Czech church. Bishop Ondřej formally pushed through his demands, however Přemysl deftly ensured that the landed possessions of the chapters, cloisters and other institutions fell under the rule of the king and the emergent

106

offices in Prague. Thus centralizing power in the Bohemian kingdom managed to maintain the unity of the monarchy and also consolidated its positions inside the state. It was able to unmoor itself just in time from unilateral dependence on the crumbling castle system and the still quite numerous castle beneficiaries who still lived on designated "state" pensions and privileges.

Wenceslas I (r. 1230–1253) took over direct governance of Bohemia, while the administration of Moravia was entrusted for two years to his younger brother, the Margrave Přemysl. The complex relationship between the siblings provoked conflicts, during which the margrave would occasionally appeal to Austria for support. But relations with Austria drew the attention of Czech politicians for other reasons. Since Duke Frederick II, who ruled in Austria and Styria, was the last living Babenberg, this line was threatened with extinction. The interest of neighbouring countries in the future of the two duchies increased. Its importance resided in the strategic position on the Alpine routes between the German part of the Empire and Italy. Wenceslas I assiduously tried to gain the western part of the Austrian Danube basin and forge a family connection with the Babenbergs. He frequently clashed with Frederick II, which brought suffering to the broad borderlands about the Dyje (Thaya) river, which were subject to the raids of the Bohemians and Moravians on Austrian territory, and likewise of the Austrians in southern Moravia. In the dispute between the Hohenstaufen Emperors and the Roman papacy, Wenceslas manoeuvred deftly, but refrained from clearly aligning himself with either side. He ignored the elections of the anti-kings, of the Landgrave of Thuringia Henry Raspe (r. 1246–1247) and after his early death William II of Holland (r. 1247–1256).

The prestige of the Bohemian king rose significantly during the Mongol invasion of 1241. Wenceslas was the only one of all the princes and kings of Central Europe to realize the extent of the Mongol threat, and he undertook vigorous preparations to repulse it. The Mongols were victorious in Lesser Poland and in Silesia and their second force destroyed the Hungarian army. Bohemia however was spared the invasion and only Moravia suffered from the quick movement of the Mongols from Silesia to the Hungarian lowlands. From there they drew back to the east early in 1242.

Halfway through the fourth decade Frederick permitted the marriage of his niece Gertrude with the Moravian margrave Vladislav, the eldest son of Wenceslas I. Frederick fell soon after in a battle with the Hungarians (1246). The way was open for the Přemyslids to the duchies of Austria and Styria, but the early death of young Vladislav and internal warring in Bohemia foiled these prospects.

In 1248 a group of rebellious representatives of King Přemysl elected the son of Wenceslas I. This second son was about fifteen at the time and he accepted the title of Moravian Margrave after the death of his brother. While the "younger" King Přemysl, whom the real leaders of the rising used as a foil, was supported mainly by the beneficiaries of lower and middle ranks, the "older" king was backed by the prominent families of the landed aristocracy. After the initial surprise and concessions in Přemysl's favour, King Wenceslas, who also received important support from abroad, finally gained the upper hand. After several turnabouts, Wenceslas was victorious and the alleged leaders of the rising, who were said to have deceived Přemysl, were executed. The consequences were clear. The property and power of the ruling families was consolidated, and from this moment the mass construction of their stone castles of the new western type began. The aristocracy started to function as an independent political force.

The consolidated self-confidence of the aristocracy was reflected also in the external expressions of their style of life. The royal court of Prague began to be numbered among the important centres of knightly culture, which had come from southern France, through German territory to the lands of Central Europe. There were famed poets and singers in Prague, as well as minnesingers, who praised love and bravery and extolled their generous patrons. Knights' tournaments were another part of the court revels. A typical manifestation of knightly fashion was the fondness for splendour – beautiful weapons and symbolic rituals (dubbing of knights, etc.). A natural-born knight had to live according to certain principles, which distinguished him from the rest of the population. The wave of refined court culture spread from the Prague court through the newly emergent aristocratic castles. They were marked by German titles and soon the aristocratic families became to take their names from their places of residence (e.g., Lichtenburk, Rýzmburk, Rožmberk, Pernštejn, etc.). The Romanesque and Late Romanesque style was gradually replaced by Gothic, whose fundamental features were crystallized in northern France and spread to the east through German territory. The new artistic style first appeared in Prague buildings (St Agnes of Bohemia cloister, the Old-New Synagogue), and penetrated to places further afield more slowly, where thus the Romanesque style still survived for some time longer. The beginnings of Gothic architecture also marked the boom in sculpture (the portal of the cloister in Tišnov), but the Romanesque artistic tradition persisted in book-making and murals.

Only after domestic relations had settled down could Wenceslas and Přemysl begin again to enter the field for the Babenberg inheritance. They had to come to terms with the claims of the Hungarian Árpáds and the Bavarian Wittelsbachs. In the end, however, the Austrian aristocracy leaned in favour of the Přemyslids. At the end of 1251, an offer came from Austria to Wenceslas, who sent the Margrave Přemysl to that land. With some hesitation, the Styrian aristocracy recognized him as their king. To strengthen his claim, Přemysl joined in marriage with the much older Margaret, the sister of the deceased Duke Frederick.

The Hungarian king, Béla IV, was unhappy with these disturbances of the balance of power in Central Europe. War came, which brought great losses to Moravia and Austria above all. The Přemyslids, in order to fend off further political pressures, had to swear allegiance to the Church and Pope. The war with Béla ended in 1254 with a temporary armistice. Přemysl was to keep Austria while the Hungarian king would receive Styria. As Wenceslas I died suddenly in 1253, Přemysl made these agreements already as Bohemian king.

The protracted fracas for the Babenberg inheritance demonstrated the extent to which relations in Central Europe had moved beyond of the control of the Empire. The intensifying struggle with the Pope, with the towns of Lombardy, with the anti-kings and also with the attempt of the princes to gain more independence, greatly undermined the position of Emperor Frederick II (r. 1211–1250). His power, in comparison with the 11th and 12th centuries, had significantly declined. Princes, bishops, margraves, landgraves and counts in the German regions of the Empire claimed for themselves unlimited powers of governance and became almost untrammelled lords in their territories. In the long struggle for primacy in Western Christendom the Papacy had seemingly emerged victorious over the Hohenstaufen emperors, however it could not act in accordance with its wishes. New contenders challenged it. Sicily and the Province of Naples were taken by the French Angevines and the Spanish Aragons. The society of northern and central Italy, politically frustrated, would not relinquish the idea of renewing imperial power. Neither did the rich Italian towns intend to give up any of their rights. In all this fragmentation of contending power interests, France began to surpass all the other forces in Europe. Its kings from the Capetian line, step by step, took the lead in attempts to liberate the Holy Land again. In tandem with the disintegration of centralized power in the Empire, the power of the Bohemian king increased. While the Empire crumbled into a chaotic tangle of secular and ecclesiastical properties, the Přemyslids proved capable of maintaining the territorial integrity of the Bohemian kingdom, integral to which was the Moravian margraviate. Even though Moravia had created its own domestic institutions and had developed along its own path to a degree, the Přemyslid state remained the most extensive and integrated formation in Central Europe. Though it was loosely a part of the Empire, the influence of the latter's rulers was manifest only in the formal enfeoffment of the Bohemian kings. The office of the imperial Cup-Bearer, documented first in the relations to the Přemyslids in 1114, enabled the Bohemian kings to join the circle of exclusive electors of the Roman king that was forming in the course of the 13th century. Among these imperial dignitaries were also the Count Palatine of the Rhine, the Duke of Saxony, the Margrave of Brandenburg; of the spiritual electors the Archbishops of Mainz, Cologne and Trier. In the election of 1257, two Roman kings emerged – Richard of Cornwall, brother of the English king, and the Castilian king, Alfonso X. Neither of these however gained the respect required and thus the Empire remained ungoverned.

Přemysl Otakar II (r. 1253–1278) maintained good relations with both Roman kings and broke through to the Alpine region with their tacit agreement. After some time, even the Roman Curia was favourable to Přemysl. Neither the weakened imperial position nor the Papacy offered any resistance to the Czech pressure, while the Hungarian kings and Bavarian dukes were extremely dissatisfied with this. In 1260, war was joined with Hungary, and it ended with Přemysl's victory in Kressenbrunn (Groissenbrunn near Marchegg in Lower Austria). Béla IV, defeated, had to accept terms, agreeing to give up Styria. In order to assuage the enmity of the Hungarians, Přemysl divorced the ageing Margaret of Babenberg and joined in marriage with Kunigunda, grand-daughter of King Béla. In Austrian and Alpine politics, Přemysl depended on the support of the Bavarian episcopate. The archbishopric of Salzburg was especially strong in its backing of the Czechs. When Přemysl was named by King Richard "defender of the property of the Crown to the right of the Rhine", he took control of the imperial town of Cheb and its surrounding region in 1266. At the same time, his prospects opened towards Carinthia, Carniola and the Windic March. He made good use of the fact that he was closely related to the Carinthian Sponheims. When Duke Ulric of Carinthia died in 1269, Přemysl occupied his land. The influence of the Bohemian king now reached to the shores of the Adriatic sea.

Přemysl's power interests were directed also towards the north-east. With the promise of military assistance from a range of German knights, the Bohemian king wished to break through to the Baltic, especially to Lithuania. The bishopric which was to be established there was meant to be subject to the Olomouc bishopric, which would consequently be raised to the status of archbishopric. However, since the Papacy did not favour these aims, Přemysl drew back from them. In contrast, political and cultural ties of the Prague court to the Polish and above all Silesian princes continued. The result of this was the penetration of Czech influence in Silesia, which took the form of political protection which the young Henryk IV, prince in Wrocław, requested of the Bohemian king.

However the extensive federation of states, created by Přemysl Otakar II, remained only a loose collection of independent countries, each of which continued to function according to its customs. They were joined only by the person of the Bohemian king, who in Austria, Styria, Carinthia and elsewhere ruled as the Duke of Austria, Styria, Carinthia, etc. He had to take into account the historical traditions of each country, its legal code and the status of the indigenous aristocracy. He frequently appointed trusted people from Bohemia and Moravia as governors. This approach provoked disagreement and resistance beyond the Czech borders. More serious however was renewal of war with Hungary after the death of Béla IV in 1270, and the forces engaged for the most part in what is now Slovakia. The counts of Gorizia-Tyrol, along with other smaller rulers in the area, began to fear Přemysl's presence in the Alpine area. The Archbishop of Salzburg, who wished to release his new metropolis from the influence of Přemysl, stood to the fore of these dissatisfied groupings.

The new Roman king, Rudolf I of Habsburg, succeeded in exploiting these circumstances to his advantage. As early as his election in 1273, he came into serious conflict with Přemysl, resulting in the questioning of the Bohemian elector's vote. Rudolf, previously a count from Swabia, could not compete with Přemysl in terms of property. He thus all the more intensively searched for a territory which could become the power base of his line. Referring to the fact that Přemysl took control of properties beyond the Czech borders at the expense of the Empire and without its confirmation, he uncompromisingly demanded that Přemysl give them up. When the Bohemian king refused, he placed Přemysl under the ban of the Empire. The Roman Curia turned its back on Přemysl, preferring the generous promises of the new Roman king. Within a short period a coalition formed against the Czechs, made up of King Rudolf, the imperial princes, the dissatisfied Alpine aristocracy and Hungary. All of its members were joined in their fear of the growing power of King Přemysl.

In the Alpine countries the aristocracy, perceiving itself to be too closely bound to the strong rule of Přemysl, rose up in 1276. King Rudolf was able to exploit this development. With the imperial army, he marched on Vienna, which had remained loyal to Přemysl. Battle was not joined however, as Přemysl was forced to capitulate by nobility's rebellion in the Czech rearguard. In peace negotiations outside Vienna, the Bohemian king was forced to

JOSEF ŽEMLIČKA

acknowledge Habsburg as Roman king and renege his claim to all properties beyond Bohemia. Only after this did Rudolf rescind the ban of Empire, enfeoffing him with Bohemia and Moravia.

Relations between the king and the noble families had been disintegrating for a long period, especially in Bohemia. With the consolidation of the proprietorial ownership of the aristocracy, royal power also began to defend consistently its remaining proprietorial positions. New royal castles sprang up, royal towns and the domain of the crown became ever more firm. Since many of the once landed castles of the nobles had been silently transferred to the hands of the aristocracy, Přemysl did not hesitate to take them. At the same time he built new centralized institutions which limited the influence of the aristocracy in the regions. Although influential noble families were offered administrative careers in the Alpine countries, the king retarded their further progress. He ruled, rather, with a circle of selected confidantes. The powerful Vítkovec family line were especially displeased by this, as Přemysl deliberately broke up their integrated properties in southern Bohemia with the establishment of the royal towns of České Budějovice and the cloister at Zlatá Koruna.

Not even after the peace of 1276 did relations between Přemysl Otakar II and Rudolf I improve. On the contrary, both kings readied themselves for battle again. Přemysl searched for allies, but his increased diplomatic efforts came to nothing. Although he acted forcefully against the rebellious nobles, Rudolf left him with no time to gather his forces. In the end, Přemysl had to depend on his royal regiments, troops of the unreliable aristocracy and foreign mercenaries. The decisive battle came in 26 August 1278 at Marchfeld in Lower Austria. The smaller Czech army was defeated by Rudolf's superior numbers, reinforced with extra regiments from Hungary. Přemysl himself died in the battle after putting up a brave fight.

The consequences were catastrophic. The nobility, exploiting the king's death, began to appropriate crown properties. The administration of the Bohemian kingdom along with the guardianship of Přemysl's son, Wenceslas who was not yet of age, was given to the Margrave of Brandenburg along with Wenceslas's cousin Otto V of Brandenburg. Rudolf of Habsburg was to retain power over Moravia for the same period. Otto's "Brandenburg" government struggled with anarchy in its lands as teams of mercenaries attempted to seize what wealth they could. The internal integrity of the state declined. Only when a group of patriotic and constitutional-minded aristocrats gathered about Tobiáš of Bechyně, the Bishop of Prague, and Purkart of Janovice, did the prospect of a remedy to these difficulties arise. Negotiations with Margrave Otto resulted in an agreement that Wenceslas, held in Brandenburg, would be brought back to Bohemia. However, the margrave did not fulfil his side of the bargain for a long time, and general upheaval and economic decline intensified when Bohemia and Moravia were hit by a wave of famine and epidemics. Only in 1283 when Otto released Wenceslas, having exacted extensive concessions from him, did matters take a turn for the better.

Two enemy camps in the nobility soon began to compete for high functions and influence over the king. The southern Bohemian family of Vítkovec stood against the followers of Bishop Tobiáš. Their leader, the capable Záviš of Falkenštejn, managed to gain the sympathy of the widowed Queen Kunigunda and his knightly bearing drew the sympathy of young Wenceslas also. Within Bohemia war raged again, and the Vítkovec group gained the upper hand. Marriage with Kunigunda (who died in 1285) and then with Elisabeth, sister of the Hungarian king, merely intimated Záviš's high ambitions. He even began to be considered the uncrowned king of Bohemia. This was a disturbing development for the Habsburgs, since Záviš's predatory politics could threaten their governance of Austria. In these circumstances young Wenceslas finally inclined to the opposition and in 1289 had Falkenštejn arrested. He suppressed the resulting rebellion of the shocked Vítkoveces and in 1290, Záviš was beheaded before the besieged castle of Hluboká.

Only then could Wenceslas II (r. 1283–1305) begin to rule independently. He maintained tactical good relations with the Habsburgs, who in the mean time consolidated their power in Austria and Styria. In 1290 Rudolf I of Habsburg confirmed the electoral vote of the Bohemian king (which had earlier been called into doubt) and the office of imperial Cup-Bearer. Despite these concessions, Duke Albrecht of Austria, Rudolf's son, was to be disappointed. When Rudolf of Habsburg died, Wenceslas II supported his adversary, Adolf, the Count of Nassau, in the election of 1292. The candidacy challenging the Habsburgs was successful and Albrecht had to withdraw from political life.

The circumstances surrounding the imperial election indicated that Wenceslas II wished to restore the Bohemian kingdom to its previous powerful position. His attention turned to the north, as the south was blocked by the Habsburgs. As early as 1138 the Piast monarchy in Poland had disintegrated into a range of mutually competing principalities. Close cultural and blood ties, which had traditionally developed between Prague and Silesia, especially with the princes of Wrocław, significantly eased the entrance of Wenceslas II onto the political scene there. In 1289, several Piasts in Upper Silesia recognized the Bohemian king as their liege lord, and after this Wenceslas subjugated the Cracow and Sandomierz regions. After the violent death of the Polish king, Przemysł II of Greater Poland (1296), the Přemysl candidacy gained support from the Polish aristocracy. Shortly after his marriage with Richenza (in Bohemia referred to as Rejčka), daughter of the murdered king Przemysł, Wenceslas II gained the Polish crown in Gniezno (1300).

In the meanwhile Wenceslas II greatly contributed to changes in the governance of the Empire. Since Adolf of Nassau (r. 1292–1298) did not hand over Meissen to the rule of the Bohemian king, as he had earlier promised, Wenceslas again became closer to the Habsburgs. The voracious territorial policies of King Adolf provoked resistance from other imperial princes. So in 1298 he was deposed, and in a battle with the newly elected Roman king, Albrecht of Habsburg (r. 1298–1308), he died.

In 1301, Andrew III, the last legitimate heir of the Árpáds, died. Some of the Hungarian magnates wished to give the empty throne to the Přemyslids. Wenceslas II accepted the offer for his son of the same name, later Wenceslas III, who after his coronation in Székesfehérvár at the end of August 1301 governed as Hungarian king under the name of Ladislaus V. This move was freighted with risk. The Prague court had to overcome many difficulties already in Poland, and in volatile Hungary there was the prospect of even greater problems. Claims to the Hungarian throne were made also by Charles Robert from the line of the Neapolitan Angevines.

Czech policies could count on the well established respect for the royal line of Přemyslids and the economic strength of their hereditary lands. Bohemia and Moravia had quickly recovered from the catastrophic consequences of the bad years and renewed royal power was able actively to capitalize on this economic improvement. The discovery of rich silver lodes near Kutná Hora contributed to this, and raised the international prestige of Wenceslas II in no small way. In the eyes of contemporaries, he was a ruler whose resources seemed unlimited and inexhaustible. Stories went about that thousands and thousands of miners brought up silver ore to the earth's surface for the Bohemian king. With opulent gifts and promises, the Bohemian king influenced the decisions of the Polish and Hungarian magnates. The political interests of the Prague court were looked after by a group of experienced diplomats who Wenceslas II had brought in from abroad. Among others, Peter of Aspelt, both Bishop of Basel and later Archbishop of Mainz.

In his dealings with the aristocracy, Wenceslas II avoided the errors of his father. He did not reappropriate alienated farmsteads and offered attractive offices in Poland and Hungary to the prominent families of the nobility. He respected the rising significance of the Land Diets, which had evolved from the *colloquia* of the early Middle Ages, now became a political platform of the emergent aristocratic constituency.

The luxuries and refined tastes of the Prague court found expression in the pageantry of royal majesty. Splendour bordering on profligacy was perhaps most apparent at the coronation of Wenceslas II in 1297. Prague welcomed thousands of honoured guests, and instead of water wine flowed from the municipal fountains. The celebrations went on for several days and drew heavily on the royal coffers. Minnesingers were treated especially well and brought into the royal presence; it is said that Wenceslas himself composed love poems. The wave of knightly fashion burgeoned also. Although the nobility had taken German names and re-named their castles in a similar fashion, they viewed with distaste the entrepreneurship and financial prowess of the German patricians in the big towns, mainly Prague, Brno, Jihlava and soon Kutná Hora. The aristocracy began to emphasize its prerogative rights in the land. Latin writing and German courtly poetry was now accompanied by the Czech language. The Church was mainly to thank for its more notable literary works ("Island Song" [*Ostrovská píseň*], "Kunigunda's Prayer" [*Kunhutina modlitba*]). The Gothic style was now employed in the construction of monumental castles (Zvíkov, Bezděz, Brno – Špilberk Castle), cathedrals (Kolín, Vyšší Brod) and also in the towns. It quickly spread to outlying areas also. In painting and sculpture the style was less apparent.

At the beginning of the 14th century, the Přemyslids gained the three crowns of the Central European monarchies. To hold them, and above all to hold on to them, was however a more difficult task. In Hungary and Poland, centrifugal forces prevailed and the aristocracy was all too easily won over to the enemy camp. Huge outlays were necessary for the administration of Poland and Hungary, for gifts to be given to the dissatisfied aristocracy, and the maintenance of armies. Only the German patrician class of the large towns (Cracow, Buda) enjoyed a degree of protection in the extensive federation of the Přemyslids, and they were loyal to the latter to the end. The Habsburgs were anxious about the disturbance of the balance of Central European power, and neither did the Papal Curia favour the Czech Wenceslas, openly supporting the Angevines in Hungary.

In 1303 the Roman King Albrecht of Habsburg called on the Přemyslids to give up Hungary. At the same time, they denied them all rights to Poland, and forced them to retreat from the regions of Cheb and Meissen. They went so far as to demand revenue from the silver mines of Kutná Hora. Charles Robert gained control over Hungary in the mean time. In order to strengthen the chances of his son, Wenceslas marched on Hungary in 1304. Although he gained nothing by this (since the Czech government in Hungary was falling apart), he at least brought his only son and heir back to safety. In August, Albrecht of Habsburg attacked Bohemia. Together with the Hungarians, his armies reached as far as Kutná Hora, which Albrecht wanted to control for its silver. On this occasion however the Bohemian aristocracy were loyal to their king and Albrecht had to retreat, suffering heavy losses.

After Albrecht's failure, many erstwhile enemies sought to establish good relations with Prague. However, these good prospects of dignified peace foundered when Wenceslas II fell seriously ill. In order to facilitate his son's entrance on the stage of governance, he was prepared to make large compromises. However in 1305, aged only 34, Wenceslas II died. His successor, the young Wenceslas III (r. 1305–1306) had garnered experience in Hungary, but he lacked his father's confidence and tenacity. He gave up his rights to the Hungarian crown, presuming that he would at least keep Poland. But there too the situation had deteriorated to such an extent that military action was required. In the campaign against Władysław I Łokietek, who was energetically vied for the Polish throne, he was treacherously stabbed to death in Olomouc August 1306. To this day it is not clear who was responsible for his death.

The murder of Wenceslas III brought an end to the old dynasty of princes and kings which was closely connected with the beginnings and rise of Czech statehood. It was a huge blow to the whole kingdom, and it would take many years to recover from the event. While resistance occasionally gathered against the rulers from the line of the mythical Přemysl Oráč (the Ploughman), and many were indeed deposed, neither the line's right of succession, the realm nor the indigenous aristocracy was ever called into doubt. Now however the situation was changed utterly. The Bohemian throne was empty and it was not clear who would ascend to it.

Bibliography

APPELT, Heinrich: *Böhmische Königswürde und staufisches Kaisertum*, in: Aus Reichsgeschichte und Nordischer Geschichte. K. Jordan zum 65. Geburtstag. H. Fuhrmann, H. E. Mayer, K. Wriedt (eds.), Stuttgart 1972 (Kieler Historische Studien, 16), pp. 161–181.
BLÁHOVÁ, Marie: *Die Beziehung Böhmens zum Reich in der Zeit der Salier und Frühen Staufer im Spiegel der zeitgenössischen böhmichen Geschichtsschreibung*, Archiv für Kulturgeschichte 74, 1992, pp. 23–48.

BLÁHOVÁ, Marie: *Staročeská kronika tak řečeného Dalimila (3) v kontextu středověké historiografie latinského kulturního okruhu a její pramenná hodnota. Historický komentář. Rejstřík*, Praha 1995 (Texty a studie k dějinám českého jazyka a literatury, 6).

BLÁHOVÁ, Marie – FROLÍK, Jan – PROFANTOVÁ, Naďa: *Velké dějiny zemí Koruny české*, I. Do roku 1197, Praha–Litomyšl 1999.

CHARVÁTOVÁ, Kateřina: *Václav II. Král český a polský*, Praha 2007.

DRAGOUN, Zdeněk – ŠKABRADA, Jiří – TRYML, Michal: *Románské domy v Praze*, Praha 2002.

Dvory a rezidence ve středověku, II. Skladba a kultura dvorské společnosti, Dana Dvořáčková-Malá – Jan Zelenka (eds.), Praha 2008 (= Mediaevalia Historica Bohemica, Supplementum 2).

DURDÍK, Tomáš: *Ilustrovaná encyklopedie českých hradů*, Praha 2000.

FIALA, Zdeněk: *Přemyslovské Čechy. Český stát a společnost v letech 995–1310*, 2nd edition, Praha 1975.

HILSCH, Peter: *Die Bischöfe von Prag in der frühen Stauferzeit. Ihre Stellung zwischen Reichs- und Landesgewalt von Daniel I. (1148–1167) bis Heinrich (1182–1197)*, München 1969 (Veröffentlichungen des Collegium Carolinum, 22).

HLAVÁČEK, Ivan: *Die Formung der westslawischen Schrift-, Buch- und Bibliothekskultur unter dem Einfluss der lateinischen Kirche*, in: Settimane di studio del Centro italiano di studi sull'alto medioevo 30, 1983, pp. 701–743.

HLAVÁČEK, Ivan: *Die böhmische Kurwürde in der Přemyslidenzeit*, in: Königliche Tochterstämme, Königswähler und Kurfürsten. A. Wolf (ed.), Frankfurt am Main 2002, pp. 79–106.

HOFFMANN, František: *České město ve středověku*, Praha 1992.

HOFFMANN, Hartmut: *Böhmen und das deutsche Reich im hohen Mittelalter*, Jahrbuch für die Geschichte Mittel- und Ostdeutschlands 18, 1969, 1–62.

HOENSCH, Jörg K.: *Přemysl Otakar II. von Böhmen. Der goldene König*, Graz–Wien–Köln 1989.

KEJŘ, Jiří: *Zwei Studien über die Anfänge der Städteverfassung in den böhmischen Ländern*, Historica 16, 1969, pp. 81–142.

KEJŘ, Jiří: *Böhmen und das Reich unter Friedrich I.*, in: Friedrich Barbarossa. Handlungsspielräume und Wirkungsweisen des staufischen Kaisers. A. Haverkamp (ed.), Sigmaringen 1992 (Vorträge und Forschungen, 40), pp. 241–289.

KEJŘ, Jiří: *Vznik městského zřízení v českých zemích*, Praha 1998.

KLÁPŠTĚ, Jan: *Proměna českých zemí ve středověku*, Praha 2005.

KOPIČKOVÁ, Božena: *Eliška Přemyslovna. Královna česká*, Praha 2003.

KOUŘIL, Pavel – PRIX, Dalibor – WIHODA, Martin: *Hrady českého Slezska*, Brno–Opava 2000.

KRZEMIEŃSKA, Barbara: *Wann erfolgte der Anschluß Mährens an den böhmischen Staat?*, Historica 19, 1980, pp. 195–243.

KRZEMIEŃSKA, Barbara: *Břetislav I. Čechy a střední Evropa v prvé polovině XI. století*, 2nd edition, Praha 1999.

KRZEMIEŃSKA, Barbara – MERHAUTOVÁ, Anežka – Třeštík, Dušan: *Moravští Přemyslovci ve znojemské rotundě*, Praha 1996.

KRZENCK, Thomas: *Die politischen Beziehungen Böhmens zum Reich in der Stauferzeit (1158–1253)*, Jahrbuch für Geschichte des Feudalismus 14, 1990, pp. 159–179.

KUTHAN, Jiří: *Česká architektura doby posledních Přemyslovců. Města, hrady, kláštery, kostely*, Vimperk 1994.

KUTHAN, Jiří: *Gloria Sacri Ordinis cisterciensis*, Praha 2005.

KUTHAN, Jiří: *Přemysl Otakar II. Král železný a zlatý. Král zakladatel a mecenáš*, Vimperk 1993.

MARÁZ, Karel: *Václav III. (1289–1306). Poslední Přemyslovec na českém trůně*, České Budějovice 2007.

MERHAUTOVÁ, Anežka – SPUNAR, Pavel: *Kodex vyšehradský. Korunovační evangelistář prvního českého krále*, Praha 2006.

MERHAUTOVÁ, Anežka – TŘEŠTÍK, Dušan: *Románské umění v Čechách a na Moravě*, Praha 1983.

NOVOTNÝ, Václav: *České dějiny*, I/2, I/3, I/4, Praha 1913–1937.

NOVÝ, Rostislav: *Přemyslovský stát 11. a 12. století*, Praha 1972 (AUC, Philosophica et Historica, Monographia, 43/1972).

Ottokar-Forschungen. Jahrbuch für Landeskunde von Niederösterreich, Neue Folge 44/45, 1978/1979, Max Weltin – Andreas Kusternig (eds.), Wien 1979.

PLAČEK, Miroslav: *Ilustrovaná encyklopedie moravských hradů, hrádků a tvrzí*, Praha 2001.

PRINZ, Friedrich: *Böhmen im mittelalterlichen Europa. Frühzeit, Hochmittelalter, Kolonisationsepoche*, München 1984.

Přemyslovci. Budování českého státu, P. Sommer, D. Třeštík, J. Žemlička (eds.), Praha 2009.

RICHTER, Miroslav – VELÍMSKÝ, Tomáš: *Die archäologische Erforschung von Stadtwüstungen des 13. Jahrhunderts in Böhmen*, Siedlungsforschung. Archäologie – Geschichte – Geographie 11, 1993, pp. 83–110.

SMETÁNKA, Zdeněk: *Legenda o Ostojovi. Archeologie obyčejného života v raně středověkých Čechách*, 2nd edition, Praha 2004.

SOMMER, Petr: *Svatý Prokop. Z počátků českého státu a církve*, Praha 2007.

SOMMER, Petr: *Sázava und böhmische Klöster des 11. Jahrhunderts*, in: Der heilige Prokop, Böhmen und Mitteleuropa, Petr Sommer (ed.), Praha 2005 (= Colloquia mediaevalia Pragensia, 4), pp. 157–171.

SOUKUPOVÁ, Helena: *Anežský klášter v Praze*, Praha 1989.

ŠUSTA, Josef: *Poslední Přemyslovci a jejich dědictví. 1300–1308*. Praha 1917 (Dvě knihy českých dějin, 1).

ŠUSTA, Josef: *České dějiny*, II/1, Praha 1935.

TŘEŠTÍK, Dušan: *Kosmova kronika. Studie k počátkům českého dějepisectví a politického myšlení*, Praha 1968.

TŘEŠTÍK, Dušan: *Slavische Liturgie und Schrifttum in Böhmen im 10. Jahrhunderts. Vorstellungen und Wirklichkeit*, in: Der heilige Prokop, Böhmen und Mitteleuropa, Petr Sommer (ed.), Praha 2005 (= Colloquia mediaevalia Pragensia, 4), pp. 205–236.

TŘEŠTÍK, Dušan – KRZEMIEŃSKA, Barbara: *Zur Problematik der Dienstleute im frühmittelalterlichen Böhmen*, in: Siedlung und Verfassung Böhmens in der Frühzeit. F. Graus, H. Ludat (eds.), Wiesbaden 1967, pp. 70–98.

TŘEŠTÍK, Dušan – KRZEMIEŃSKA, Barbara: *Wirtschaftliche Grundlagen des frühmittelalterlichen Staates in Mitteleuropa (Böhmen, Polen, Ungarn im 10. und 11. Jahrhundert)*, Acta Poloniae Historica 40, 1979, pp. 5–31.

Umění doby posledních Přemyslovců, Jiří Kuthan (ed.), Praha 1982.

URBAN, Jan: *Lichtenburkové. Vzestupy a pády jednoho panského rodu*, Praha 2003.

VANÍČEK, Vratislav: *Vratislav II. (I.), první český král*, Praha 2004.

VANÍČEK, Vratislav: *Velké dějiny zemí Koruny české*, II–III. 1197–1250, 1250–1310, Praha–Litomyšl 2000–2002.

VELÍMSKÝ, Tomáš: *Hrabišici, páni z Rýzmburka*, Praha 2002.

Wegener, Wilhelm: *Böhmen/Mähren und das Reich im Hochmittelalter. Untersuchungen zur staatsrechtlichen Stellung Böhmens und Mährens im deutschen Reich des Mittelalters*, Köln–Graz 1959 (Ostmitteleuropa in Vergangenheit und Gegenwart, 5).

WIHODA, Martin: *Zlatá bula sicilská. Podivuhodný příběh ve vrstvách paměti*, Praha 2005.

WOLVERTON, Lisa: *Hastening Toward Prague. Power and Society in the Medieval Czech Lands*, Philadelphia 2001.

ŽEMLIČKA, Josef: *Origins of Noble Landed Property in Přemyslide Bohemia*, in: Nobilities in Central and Eastern Europe: Kinship, Property and Privilege. J. M. Bak (ed.), History and Society in Central Europe 2, Budapest–Krems 1994, pp. 7–24.

ŽEMLIČKA, Josef: *Čechy v době knížecí (1034–1198)*, Praha 1997 (Česká historie, 2).

ŽEMLIČKA, Josef: *Století posledních Přemyslovců*, 2nd edition, Praha 1998 (Historia Bohemica).

ŽEMLIČKA, Josef: *Böhmen – von den slawischen Burgzentren zum spätmittelalterlichen Städtenetz*, in: *Städtelandschaft – Städtenetz – zentralörtliches Gefüge. Ansätze und Befunde zur Geschichte der Städte im hohen und späten Mittelalter*. M. Escher, A. Haverkamp, F. G. Hirschmann (eds.), Mainz 2000 (Trierer Historische Forschungen, 43), pp. 233–253.

ŽEMLIČKA, Josef: *Počátky Čech královských 1198–1253. Proměna státu a společnosti*, Praha 2002 (Česká historie, 10).

JOSEF ŽEMLIČKA

V. The Expansion of the Czech State during the Era of the Luxemburgs (1306–1419)

The oldest seal of the Charles University represents the symbolic acceptance of the founding charter of the university. Bohemian King Charles IV is kneeling in front of the most important Bohemian saint and land patron saint (W – Wenceslas). The two-tailed lion symbolizes Bohemia, the eagle stands for Moravia. Mid-14th century.

1 The European Dimension of Czech Politics

After the ascension of Wenceslas II (*Václav*) to the throne (r. 1283–1305) it seemed as though the Bohemian kingdom would soon regain its economic strength and, if handled skilfully, enjoy once more the same international prestige that it had before the final defeat of Přemysl Otakar II. However, the turn of the 13th and 14th centuries witnessed a range of power upheavals in Central Europe linked to dynastic and geopolitical changes. The aim of the interconnected contracts of inheritance of the Central European ruling families – the Árpáds in Hungary, the Habsburgs in the Austrian principalities, the Polish Piasts and Czech Přemyslids – was to protect the interests of the dynasties in each country, and, at the same time, ensure a degree of stability in the region. In addition to the centuries-long experience of dynasties and their competition for thrones, it was now necessary to prevent the expansive policies of the Holy Roman Empire and the interests of the Papal Curia.

The first decade of the 14th century tested these agreements, some of which were fully discharged, others of which changed with the new circumstances and yet others were abandoned completely. With his marriage to Eliška Rejčka (1300) of the scion-less line of the Polish Piasts, Wenceslas II gained the Polish crown. In order to smooth matters over with the Habsburgs, he assisted them in deposing Albrecht of Nassau from the Roman throne (1298) and the crowning of Albrecht I of Habsburg (r. 1298–1308). In 1301 the last of the Árpád line, Andrew III, died unexpectedly and the Hungarian magnates arranged the coronation of the youthful heir to the Bohemian crown, Wenceslas III, who took the name Ladislaus V. They wished not only to thwart the Habsburgs' ambitions for the Hungarian throne, but also those of the Neapolitan candidate Charles Robert of Anjou who was backed by the Pope. The Přemyslids now had the opportunity to govern the whole region of Central Europe. However, the fact that they gained the support of many Czech and foreign magnates began to aggravate their opponents. The Curia along with the court of the King of the Romans had other ideas about the division of this part of the continent. It was therefore not difficult to find allies in aristocratic and ecclesiastical circles in Poland, Hungary and in the Bohemian crown lands themselves who were willing to stand against the Přemyslids, either openly or in secret, and, together with the Curia and the King of the Romans, set in motion a plot to halt the rise of the Přemyslid dynasty in Central Europe. This led to the murder of Wenceslas III in Olomouc in 1306, the circumstances of which remain vague to this day, and which opened the Bohemian throne to the competing adjacent dynasties.

The importance of the Bohemian throne to neighbouring rulers became apparent very soon. Before his Polish campaign and sudden death, the seventeen year-old Wenceslas III entrusted his brother-in-law Henry of Carinthia with the office of Supreme Governor of the Bohemian crown lands. Immediately after Wenceslas's death, Henry put himself forward for the Bohemian throne, and thus did not hesitate to recognize the freedom of the Bohemian nobility and its right to elect the ruler, as was affirmed in the Gold Bull of Sicily from 1212. Henry had just been elected in September 1306, when King Albrecht I of Habsburg expressed his dissatisfaction with this outcome. In October 1306, he brought his army to Prague and expelled Henry from the Bohemian crown lands, to the latter's surprise. In order to place his son Rudolf on the Bohemian throne, he too recognized the ancient rights of the Bohemian nobility, including that of election of the ruler. He also had to promise Bohemian nobles that he would marry Eliška Rejčka, Wenceslas II's widow, so that the Bohemian kingdom could keep its claim to the Polish crown through her. Nothing then stood in Rudolf's path to become Bohemian king on October 16, 1306.

Dramatic developments, which for years had disturbed the lives of the inhabitants of the Bohemian crown lands and provoked conflicts in its ruling classes, were nowhere near at an end. King Rudolf of Habsburg became a victim of these, when he fell in battle with the opposition elements in the Czech aristocracy only a year after his election. Some weeks later Henry of Carinthia once again became the head of the country. His further political concessions indicated that as ruler, mishandling his powers and unable to orient himself in events, he would not be able to manage the country for long. A pro-Habsburg group among the Bohemian and Moravian aristocracy again fuelled the interest of Albrecht I in expanding into the Czech region. However his military campaign was interrupted by his sudden violent death. Albrecht was murdered in May 1308 and his less-than-surefooted son Frederick gave up the claims on the Bohemian throne. Henry of Carinthia retained the Bohemian crown for the time being, but the incompetence that he displayed in dealing with his subjects was also manifest in his international policies in the period when a contest, conducted through diplomatic channels, arose concerning the election of the head of the Roman Empire. When Henry VII was elected Roman King at the end of 1308, a man stood at the head of the Empire who knew the German situation intimately and enjoyed close and friendly relations with the French court. The compromise reached in the Empire raised the hope of eliminating the Habsburgs from the power struggles and the pacification of affairs in Central Europe.

Skirmishes between individual groupings of the aristocracy and towns continued in the mean time in the Bohemian crown lands (with Henry of Carinthia helplessly looking on). He did not attend to the administration of royal finances, and neither taxes nor profits from mining (mainly from the silver mines of Kutná Hora) were properly collected. The political upheavals brought economic stagnation and international merchants were even more reluctant to transport their goods over uncertain roads. Transit commerce dropped, and with it, the incomes of towns and authorities from tariffs and tolls. The aristocracy began to appropriate the landed property of the royal chamber, as well as that of ecclesiastical institutions (mostly monasteries) and the towns. Military campaigns, violence and robbery were a part of everyday life in Bohemia and Moravia. Administrative structures disintegrated and the law was no longer enforced. The lower levels of society, unable to protect themselves from the consequences of the upheavals, suffered a radical drop in their standard of living.

The situation of the time was documented by two chronicles of outstanding literary quality which were written in the Czech Lands at the beginning of the 14th century. The author of the first of these was referred to as Dalimil, who wrote in verse using Old Czech (*Dalimil Chronicle*). The anonymous poet, drawing on his personal experience and also his knowledge of Czech history, was anti-German and against the towns also, even while he accused the representatives of neighbouring states of causing much of the difficulties of his own land. The second document, *The Zbraslav Chronicle*, written in Latin by Ota and Petr Žitavský (of Zittau), educated abbots of the Cistercian monastery in Zbraslav near Prague, takes a more sober approach and characterizes the events of this dramatic period with a firm knowledge of international contexts.

It was Konrád, an abbot in Zbraslav, who belonged to the group of spiritual leaders who joined with representatives of the aristocracy and towns who wished to stabilize the situation in the Czech state. The frequent negotiations of the Cistercian abbots in the Empire and in France acted as a conduit for important knowledge to the Bohemian crown lands about events in Europe. The contact between the heads of the order and the circles of court and Curia enabled them to influence political developments directly. The group about Abbot Konrád was able to exploit these opportunities to negotiate with the court of the Roman ruler and the electors, the most important imperial princes, both secular and spiritual, in the matter of the election of the new Bohemian king. Talks climaxed at the Imperial Diet in Frankfurt am Main in July 1310. The Czech mission led by Konrád of Zbraslav and the magnate Jan of Vartemberk, along with representatives of several towns, received permission from Henry VII to crown his son John (*Jan*). The dynastic connection of the two lines was to be secured by the marriage of the fourteen year-old John with the eighteen year-old Eliška Přemyslovna, daughter of Wenceslas II.

The entry of the Luxemburg dynasty to Czech affairs quickened the pace of events. As early as September 1310, the wedding took place in Speyer, after which the newly weds made their way to Prague accompanied by a group led by the experienced diplomat and expert on Czech issues, Peter of Aspelt, Archbishop of Mainz. Henry of Luxemburg ensured that imperial regiments accompanied and protected the couple on their journey from Nuremberg to Prague, and these finally helped Czech forces to gain control of Prague and expel Henry of Carinthia on December 3, 1310.

Prague Castle was uninhabitable so John took up residence in one of the houses on the Old Town Square and with the help of his advisors and supporters began to stabilize affairs in the Czech state. One of his first steps was to attempt to re-establish royal authority and secure peace in the country, where various aristocratic groupings still contended with one another. In 1311 he reached agreement with the Bohemian and Moravian aristocracy in the matter of mutual relations and codified this in what are referred to as "inaugural diplomas", in which he restricted the relations of the ruler and aristocracy, including the confirmation of their ancient privileges. The aristocracy would retain the right to elect the king and decide in the matter of extraordinary taxation, as well as the heritable right to their property and the right to choose freely whether to offer military support to the king in foreign wars. On the other hand the aristocracy was obliged to raise an army when peace in the land was threatened. Royal powers were also to be restricted insofar as the king could no longer appoint foreigners to high office. The resulting agreement with the Czech aristocracy seemed to John to provide a sound basis for the consolidation of the ruler's power in the Bohemian kingdom.

Issues were complicated, however, when the ruler attempted to regain the royal properties which had been appropriated by the Czech aristocracy in the midst of all the chaos at the beginning of the 14th century. An insufficiency of funds forced the king to apply fiscal principles consistently in the matter of tax collection as well as in the assertion of the royal patents on mining and its profits (mainly those from silver). The constant need of finance for the administration of the Bohemian crown lands and for the realization of Czech interests abroad led John of Luxemburg to support the towns. The royal coffers filled with a large amount of funds that resulted from the administrative and commercial privileges he granted to the towns. He negotiated in a similar fashion with some towns beyond the Czech borders (e.g., Regensburg, Bautzen and Görlitz). One of the most extensive and profitable privileges was granted to the imperial town of Nuremberg in 1326 when its merchants were allowed to trade freely in the Bohemian crown lands. The main transit routes across Bohemia and Moravia were renewed after many years and the profits from this flowed not only to the royal chamber, but also to the coffers of the towns and aristocracy. John's steps also contributed to the rise of the Czech economy and provided the opportunity to renew the network of international trade in Central Europe.

From the outset, King John played a role in international politics. With the help of Henry of Luxemburg he succeeded in pressuring the Habsburgs to reach an agreement over Moravia, and also in pressuring the House of Wettin, princes of Saxony, in the matter of the territory lying to the northern border of the Czech state. He also launched upon the job of calming relations with the Silesian principalities, which had become closer, both economically and politically, to Bohemia and Moravia. It was foreign, rather than Czech, politics that attracted John of Luxemburg, and he was unusually gifted in this field. His activities in the international arena also were helped by the fact that his father named him General Vicar, his deputy for the governance of the Empire. John was to contribute to the preparations of his trip to Rome for the imperial coronation, and also help with the conclusion of the wars in the Italian territory. This promising co-operation between father and son was however brought to an end when Henry died suddenly in 1313 on his way to coronation in Rome.

John was suddenly among the candidates for the imperial crown along with Frederick of Habsburg and finally Ludwig of the Bavarian ducal line of Wittelsbach, who was chosen by the electors. John of Luxemburg himself voted for Ludwig at the diet of electors as he was aware of the resistance of the Roman Curia and some electors to the alliance of Luxemburgs with France; but at the same time he did not wish to support Frederick of Habsburg, who embodied the Habsburg ambition to rule again over Central Europe. For helping Ludwig of Bavaria, John received a promise from the new Roman king of support in the territorial claims of the Czech state in Silesia and Meissen, but also in the region of Cheb and the Upper Palatinate.

These aims could not be carried out immediately however. John of Luxemburg was bound not only by relations with the Empire, but he also had to take into account the troubled state of the Bohemian crown lands. His agreements with the leaders of the Bohemian and Moravian aristocracy had not been as successful as both sides had hoped. The King continued to employ the services of foreign advisors and bureaucrats, as it was difficult for him to adapt to the Czech situation, the language and culture of which was quite alien to him, more accustomed as he was to life in France and the Rhineland. The Czech aristocracy equally did not intend to surrender its properties and the influence it had gained after the death of Wenceslas II. The domestic politics of the Bohemian crown lands presented great difficulties to John, and not even his closest advisors were able to orient him in the struggles of various interest groups among the aristocracy and towns.

The difficulties were increased by John's frequent absences from the country and inadequate communication with the Bohemian and Moravian lords, which adversely affected the relationship of the royal couple. The competition between the two strongest parties of the Czech aristocracy climaxed when the representative of one camp, Jindřich of Lipá, gained the trust of the King, while Jindřich's opposite number, Vilém Zajíc of Valdek, convinced the Queen that it was the wish of the Lord of Lipá to ruthlessly overthrow the King. John had Jindřich imprisoned in 1315, but while the former was engaged in activities abroad, his wife attempted to influence developments in the country independently of him. John joined in battle with the representatives of the nobility, which concluded in 1318 with reconciliation in Domažlice. There the King acknowledged the rights of the aristocracy and also took a further step on the long road to the establishment of the dualism of the Estates, to the division of government between the ruler and the aristocracy in the country.

The royal couple broke up soon after this when John sent his wife Eliška with her children to the castle of Mělník. He later sent his son Wenceslas, the future King Charles IV, to be raised at the French royal court in Paris. The decision was influenced not only by his fear that the Czech aristocracy would use his heir as a political hostage, but also certainly by John's high ambitions for his successor. When Charles returned from France at the beginning of the 1330s, John transferred ever more powers to him. Finally a kind of double government evolved in which the heir played an increasingly important role.

After 1318, when his standing in the Bohemian crown lands was weakened, John of Luxemburg was still concentrating on foreign politics. He was involved in the cause of the Roman King and later Emperor Ludwig of Bavaria, both in the Empire itself and Italy, and spent a long period outside the country. With Ludwig's support, he gained the Cheb region as imperial encumbrance (1314–1322), and after the Brandenburg House of Ascania died out, he gained control once again of the one-time Czech fief of the Bautzen region (1319) and the Görlitz region (1329), i.e., Upper Lusatia. In 1327, John undertook a military campaign to Upper Silesia and with the support of a range of German knights succeeded within two years in subduing the principalities of the region, which heretofore had belonged to the confederacy of the Polish Kingdom. The greater part of the Silesian Piast princes (of Těšín, Racibórz, Opole and Oświęcim-Zátor). He later gained control over the regions of Głogów and Wrocław. During the integration of Görlitz into the Bohemian kingdom, the phrase "Crown of the Bohemian Kingdom" (*Corona Regni Bohemie*) was first used in 1329, which in the subsequent period became the official title of the Czech state. However, individual crownlands, with their own issues and customs, continued independently. The ruler was now joined with the centre of the state along with the governor (*hejtman, fojt*), for whom the king was liege lord.

John of Luxemburg also inherited the Polish crown from his predecessors, however he could not enforce his claim in practice. The Bohemian, Polish and Hungarian kings met in Trenčín and later in Visegrád because of the need to consolidate contractually the possession of Silesia and to stabilize relations between the Hungarian Kingdom and thus ensure peace throughout Central Europe. John of Luxemburg, Kazimierz the Great and Charles Robert signed there a three-page peace agreement in 1335 which ensured the status quo by recognizing John's accession of Silesia, and at the same time his renunciation of all claims to the Polish throne.

Like the Přemyslids before him, John was thinking of expansion to the south, particularly to the Tyrol, Carinthia and Northern Italy. He counted on the assistance of Emperor Ludwig, who he himself tried to support in the struggle between competing groups of Guelphs and Ghibellines in Italy. He bore in mind his own interests and tried to strengthen his position even in those areas where Ludwig was unwelcome. In the northern parts of Italy – in Lombardy, Emilia and Tuscany – John gained the favour of several towns and city-states (mainly Bergamo, Pavia, Mantua and Papal Bologna), which formed the pro-Luxemburg signoria. However, this turned out to be illusory. The diplomats of the Italian towns wished above all to protect their own independence from Italian contenders, and they were merely exploiting the unreal ambitions of the Bohemian king for their own ends when they allowed his highly paid troops to battle with their local enemies. The distance of the Bohemian crown lands, the logistical barrier of the Alps, the unwillingness of the Czech aristocracy to support John's ambitions far from the borders of the kingdom and the high costs of war, led to the failure of Luxemburg's efforts. John involved his son Charles in the Italian battles, and while this provided the young man with an opportunity to see the beauty and richness of this part of the Apennine peninsula, he nevertheless also witnessed the suffering of war. In his autobiography *Vita Caroli*, he recorded how difficult it was for him to reconcile himself with this and the lesson he learned from the whole pointless exercise. The Italian experience seems to have led him always to give priority to diplomacy over war in his future life as a ruler. John failed to gain control even over the Tyrol and Carinthia for more than a short period, nevertheless he married his second-born son, Jan Jindřich with Duchess Margaret of Carinthia, who had the soubriquet "blubber-lip", and who because of her ugliness became a legendary figure.

King John remained the loyal ally of the French rulers for his whole life. From his birthplace of Luxemburg, to which he travelled occasionally, he visited Paris, where he lived in a house of some splendour that had been given him by the French king, Charles IV, in gratitude for his diplomatic and military help. He gave his sister Marie in marriage to the future French King Charles IV and entrusted his eldest son – originally named Wenceslas – to be brought up by the French court. The heir to the Bohemian throne on his confirmation took the name of his royal godfather, Charles, which he would use from that point on. John's second wife, Beatrix of Bourbon, also came from the circle of the French court, and John's daughter Jitka-Bonne became the wife of King John II and mother of the next French king, Charles V. These links brought the two countries closer, and Charles IV would continue this, and thus balanced his policies with respect to both the Papal Curia and the German lands. John of Luxemburg supported the French ruler, Philip VI, in his fight with England, and eventually was killed in his service in one of the most important clashes of the Hundred Years' War, in the Battle of Crécy in 1346.

The life and heroic death of the Bohemian king, who was at that time ill and blind, along with most of his retinue became for contemporary chroniclers, especially Jean Froissart, a shining symbol of medieval knighthood. Some later historians designated John of Luxemburg as "foreigner king", reproaching him for his minimal attention to the domestic issues of the Bohemian kingdom. By nature an adventurous man, it was in truth difficult for him to accommodate himself to circumstances other than those he grew up in; he was dismayed by his ignorance of the language of the country he ruled, as well as by the behaviour of the aristocratic constituency and the disintegration of his family. However, his attempts to consolidate the state in the international context and to expand its borders demonstrated his desire to connect his line with that of the Bohemian kingdom. It was this same aim that motivated him when he handed over governance in the lands of the Bohemian Crown to his son Charles, whose way was subsequently opened to the supreme earthly rank of Christendom at that time, the title of Roman King and Emperor.

It was a daring idea, since the preceding history of struggles for the Roman crown showed the unreliability of the election results. However, Charles IV, born in 1316, from a young age had gained great experience and perhaps because of this would, in propitious circumstances, experience on three occasions the exaltation of the ritual of coronation. Charles most likely had no fond memories of his childhood in the Bohemian crown lands, since at the age of three he was taken with his mother and siblings to a castle at Mělník, where they remained in isolation from the royal court. At the age of seven, his father took him to Paris to be brought up at perhaps the greatest centre of courtly culture of the time. Although he almost lost all knowledge of Czech there, he learned French, Latin, Italian and also German. His father and French tutors took special care that the Czech prince fitted into his French surroundings. One of the clearest indices of this was the fact that on his confirmation in

1323 he took the name Charles, after his godfather Charles IV of France, abandoning the name Wenceslas, which was connected with the Přemyslid line. Shortly after this the seven year-old prince was married to Blanche of Valois, who was the same age. The diplomatic reasoning behind this was that it would be wise to join both kingdoms dynastically. However, many years passed before the union of the two children was happily consummated, during which their lives were separate and Charles continued his education.

At the beginning of the 1330s, the Bohemian king John involved his son in politics. First he brought him to the Luxemburg duchy where Charles was acquainted with imperial affairs by his grand-uncle Balduin, Archbishop of Trier nearby and a prominent European politician. Immediately after, in 1331, John called his son to Italy, where Charles was to help him in the administration and defence of the towns and territories that John had governed earlier. Apart from the fact that the heir to the throne had to use his knowledge of the arts of war, theories of which he had learned at the French court, he also became acquainted with a range of personalities who would later support him in his imperial policies, when they themselves occupied important offices in Italy and the Empire (Louis of Savoy, Orlando Rossi and others). This left John free to participate in important negotiations with the Papal Curia and the Emperor, Ludwig the Bavarian. His relations with the Emperor however deteriorated when Ludwig wished to gain control over the Tyrol and Carinthia, thus crossing John's plans in that matter.

Charles was burdened greatly with the administration of the Northern Italian provinces, where the city-states, with short-term memories, were no longer grateful for John's support when they were threatened some years before. Despite this, Charles remained there to the end of 1333. At that time, he had his own chancellery in which, along with Italian, French and German clerks, Czechs were employed. Moreover, at its head was Chancellor Mikuláš of Brno, who informed Charles about political developments in the Czech state, supplementing the information Charles received from his father. It seems that Mikuláš mediated the negotiations of the deputies of the Bohemian and Moravian aristocracy with Charles in Merano (1333), in which an urgent demand was made of Charles that as heir to the throne he should return to the Bohemian kingdom and assist with its internal consolidation, which had for many years now been neglected by his father.

Military victories and defeats, endless diplomatic negotiations and the back-room intrigues of Italy had exhausted the young Charles to such an extent that they haunted him in dreams, as he would later write in his autobiography. A further reason for his decision to leave for the Bohemian kingdom was perhaps his feeling that it was futile to attempt to realize his father's ideas about the control of part of Northern Italy. A desire to return to the land where he was born, which he would rule in the near future and which according to the account of the Czech mission was in a deplorable state, also played a role. Apart from the curiosity of a seventeen year-old youth there was indubitably a sense of responsibility for his own country. John of Luxemburg, preoccupied with imperial politics, did not prevent his son in this, and so Charles entered Prague in autumn of 1333, after an absence of fourteen years. And now the situation that his father before him experienced repeated itself.

Prague Castle was uninhabitable and Charles had no relations who would provide him with familial hospitality.

In order to secure formally his son's standing in the Bohemian crown lands and ensure necessary fiscal resources, John named Charles Margrave of Moravia at the beginning of 1334. This title did not however limit his heir's powers to Moravia, but during the long periods of John's absence, Charles governed the kingdom in its entirety, as well as neighbouring countries which were subject to him. In the subsequent period, the margrave carried out a range of changes in the Land and court offices, to which he named outstanding figures drawn from the Czech aristocracy, who had surrounded him from the time of the negotiations in Merano, offering support in his efforts to renew the country. Thus for instance Petr of Rožmberk became Supreme Chamberlain, and Vilém of Landštejn Vice-Chamberlain. Unlike his father, Charles forged close links with the ecclesiastical hierarchy, mostly with the Bishop of Prague, Jan IV of Dražice, who had recently returned from Avignon and certainly enjoyed the favour of the margrave for his attempt to stabilize the organization and work of the Church, but also for the fact that he brought knowledge of architecture and art from France, which was far in advance of the Bohemian crown lands in these matters. In Moravia, he could depend on the newly named Bishop of Olomouc Jan Volek, who also held important offices in the Bohemian crown lands. Several foreign adherents provided Charles with substantial support, mainly the Archbishop of Trier, Balduin, and his former teacher, bishop, member of the royal council, Pierre de Rosière, the future Pope Clement VI. And last but not least, his wife Blanche played a significant role in encouraging Charles's efforts; she came to Prague in 1334 to set up house for him. This was a further reason for Charles to renovate Prague Castle quickly: he wished to offer his spouse a seat of fitting dignity and splendour.

Although the start of his governance was not without difficulty, the young margrave very soon displayed his ability to comprehend his new circumstances and find allies, and with unusual energy initiate the renewal of the country. His policies required both finances and a power-base in the kingdom. The source of Charles's money is not apparent. There was some profit from the silver mines, especially in Kutná Hora, but these were divided between himself and his father. Whether he received loans or gifts is not known to us, but he seems to have used the occasion of his accession to the throne and arrival of his wife in order to levy an extraordinary tax. A significant sum must have resulted from the confirmation of the ancient privileges of both the aristocracy and above all the towns, not only in Bohemia and Moravia, but also in the neighbouring countries, which his father had gained. The towns were certainly willing to buy the good-will of the future king in order to develop their commercial ties and in order for their merchants to exploit the transit routes criss-crossing the Bohemian crown lands.

Charles IV managed to regain the encumbered royal properties, which included a large number of towns and castles, relatively quickly. Among the most important in Bohemia were Křivoklát, Hradec Králové, Písek, Tachov and Trutnov; in Moravia, Telč, Veveří and the castles of the prominent royal towns. The systematic construction of a whole collection of farmsteads, towns and castles, over which the margrave managed to re-assert his proprietorial rights, demonstrated that at the very beginning of his governance he wished to establish control evenly over the whole land as well as assert the ruler's power. A range of selected localities lay near the land borders and thus served for their protection; other fortified places were concentrated on the defence of Prague; in the Moravian margraviate, Charles gained control over the main centres of Brno and Olomouc, and also Znojmo, strategically positioned near the border with Habsburg power in Austria.

John of Luxemburg also involved his son in the negotiations concerning the countries adjacent to the Bohemian kingdom and the treaties with the neighbouring rulers. This was why Charles participated in the negotiations in Trenčín and Visegrád in 1335, and also in the mid-1330s in the recuperation of the Wrocław region, in the military expeditions of his father on the Moravian-Austrian border, as well as in John's break with Ludwig the Bavarian over Carinthia. In these uncertain situations, the margrave took ever greater care to emphasize the integrity of the kingdom and inalienable nature of the lands incorporated into it through frequent use of the unifying concept of the Bohemian crown lands or the Crown of the Bohemian kingdom. Those terms known already from the era of John now were employed consistently.

In 1339, John, at this stage already blind, under pressure from Ludwig the Bavarian and his allies, decided to write his political will and divide his inheritance. Charles was to receive Bohemia, the Bautzen and Görlitz regions, Silesia, while his younger brother Jan Jindřich would receive Moravia, and the youngest, Wenceslas, the Duchy of Luxemburg. Two years later John named Charles as his successor, thus providing a clear jural framework for the double governance of the Bohemian kingdom, which in practice had obtained from the first years after the return of the eldest to the country.

At the end of John's life the Luxemburgs found themselves in a serious conflict with Ludwig the Bavarian over properties in southern Germany. The clash threatened to become militarized, but new changes in the European arena prevented them. Of first importance was the accession of Charles's former teacher in France, Rosière, to the Papal See as Clement VI in 1342. The Pope emphatically supported the Luxemburgs against Ludwig the Bavarian, who was in conflict with the Curia over his refusal to subordinate earthly authority to that of the Church, and violently effected the imperial coronation. The position of the new Pope brought substantial support to his former student both in the Czech context and international politics. Clement VI fulfilled Charles's request that the Prague bishopric be raised to an archbishopric, which came about in the spring of 1344. Arnošt of Pardubice, a confidante, advisor and supporter of Charles, occupied the office. Ecclesiastical structures in the Czech state were overhauled, adding the newly established bishopric of Litomyšl. The establishment of the Prague archbishopric itself was the decisive factor in the Bohemian crown lands unhitching themselves from ecclesiastical subordination to the archbishops of Mainz and further loosened their relation to the Roman Empire.

Charles's political rise continued. Through the deft policies of his father and the Papal Curia, he became a candidate for the imperial throne, and was successful in the election

MILOSLAV POLÍVKA

which took place in Königstuhl Castle in Rhineland in 1346. Afterwards he joined John and the French forces participating in the unfortunate Battle of Crécy, in which his father fell. On the journey home, he became aware that a significant section of the imperial aristocracy would adhere to Ludwig and refuse to recognize his election as Roman King, as they placed many obstacles in the way of himself and his company. Some German chroniclers state that the elected Roman King wandered in disguise and hid in monasteries. Charles prepared with unusual care for the subsequent Czech coronation in September 1347. He had a new Bohemian crown made, and prepared the Coronal Procedure of Bohemian Kings and the Blessing of Queens including the ceremony which connected the Luxemburg dynasty with the old Přemyslid customs, among which was the journey on foot from Prague Castle to Vyšehrad, the change of the ancient chorale "Lord, Have Mercy on Us" (*Hospodine, pomiluj ny*) and other rituals.

Ludwig of Bavaria died soon after this and the attempts of enemies to run other candidates had little chance of success against Charles IV, who had in the mean time been crowned in Bonn as King of the Romans. Furthermore, two coronations in a short period had certainly raised Charles's confidence and the Bohemian and Roman King unfolded his plans in all directions. One of these was the fulfilment of the supreme grade of his career, through imperial coronation, which did not come about until 1355. Immediately after his coronation Charles IV issued privileges which gained him supporters and delimited the position of the Bohemian kingdom within the framework of the Roman Empire, thus paving the way for the issue of the Golden Bull (of Charles). Its proclamation in Nuremberg in 1356 rendered in law the concept and internal structure of the Empire as well as its superiority over all countries which it included; at the same time, however, he delimited the privileges which in the imperial framework had given the Bohemian kingdom its status as an independent and self-governing state. He confirmed the pre-eminent standing of the Bohemian king among the electors and enjoined them to learn the Czech language. In negotiations with the Polish and Hungarian kings, as well as with the Habsburgs, he tried to secure the borders of his countries, which for him were the firm dynastic base of the Luxemburgs. Charles's marital policies contributed greatly to the expansion of his international influence and the territorial extent of his properties. After the death of his first wife Blanche (1348), he would marry three times, and with each marriage he expanded the territory of the Czech state.

His marriage with Anna of the Palatinate cleared Charles's way to the west and facilitated his attempt to gain control over towns and castles between Tachov and Nuremberg, where a new group of fiefs were established, creating what was referred to as New Bohemia (*Nové Čechy*) from 1356. At Lauf Castle nearby, where Charles liked to stay, he had a unique gallery of 114 shields of the crownlands, aristocratic lines and towns painted. The imperial town of Nuremberg was to become its centre, which Charles connected with all the parts of the Empire, and thus enjoyed his extraordinary favour. He began to summon the Imperial Diets there, and gave the townspeople generous commercial privileges, allowing them to conduct business in the mining of precious metals – silver, copper, pewter and lead. The citizens of Nuremberg built an astronomical clock in his honour, and to this day one can see the electors circle the Emperor seated on his throne every twelve hours. From here, over other fiefs, the King's policies aimed towards the Rhine and, further, to Luxemburg and France. But also in the regions of Thuringia and Mecklenburg and elsewhere he acquired other foreign fiefs (*feuda extra curtem*) and finally gained Lower Lusatia. His third wife, Anna of Świdnica, brought with her the Świdnica-Jávor principality in Silesia, and his fourth, Alžběta of Pomerania, supported Charles's interest in the northern regions of Europe, which he achieved with the purchase of Brandenburg in 1373.

The Emperor had seven children and his decisions about their marriages served the aims of his dynastic policies and the security and expansion of the Czech state. Markéta married Louis of Hungary, Kateřina Rudolf IV of Habsburg and later Otto of Brandenburg, Eliška Albrecht III of Habsburg, Václav Johanna and then Sophia of Bavaria, Anna the English king Richard II, Sigismund (*Zikmund*) Maria of Hungary, Jan of Görlitz Richardis of Sweden, and Markéta Johann of Hohenzollern. These dynastic alliances bear witness to Charles's political grasp and perspicuity. In France he had his closest supporters, from Italy he gained invaluable experience and the knowledge that it was impossible to control it militarily and unify it; in the Austrian lands he succeeded in pacifying the influential Habsburgs with whom he reached agreement in 1364 about mutual succession if either of the lines died out. The western connection was important for the Emperor as it allowed him access to the political, economic and cultural hub of Europe, that is, the Rhine from which it was possible to reach his family home of Luxemburg and his beloved France. He also maintained good relations with the Curia, but disputes within the Catholic Church itself prevented him from becoming more fully engaged, though the Papacy helped him to the title of King of the Romans and over the years provided him with diplomatic support at home and, most importantly, in the international arena.

Around his sixtieth year, the successful ruler was, however, tired and ill, and judged that he had only a few years of life left to him. If he looked back over the work of two generations of Luxemburgs, he would have been satisfied. The Bohemian crown lands, which at the beginning of the 14th century were fighting for their survival, and, after the extinction of the Přemyslids, had lost the greater part of their international prestige, had now become the centre of the Roman Empire. Charles was the first Bohemian king to gain the Roman and Imperial Crown and be numbered among those who influenced European politics over several decades. Both Luxemburgs worked to transform the Bohemian kingdom into the line's permanent feudal home. Unlike his father, Charles was more at home in the new country and he was also more successful in his dynastic activities. By pacifying the disputes with the domestic opposition, he was able to engage upon an agile foreign policy, but also to establish order in his country and nurture its expansion.

Although Charles IV was not always in agreement with the foremost members of the Czech nobility, thanks to the international recognition which the ruler enjoyed, the aristocracy were willing to respect him both as their representative abroad and in domestic administration, even though they did not wish to give up their ancient rights. Charles IV however came into open conflict with some members of the Czech nobility, for instance in 1352 when he clashed with the Rožmberks, who sought support for their political plans in the Empire. The balance of power between the ruler and the nobility was manifest when Charles wished to bring into force the first written code of law in the Bohemian kingdom, referred to as *Maiestas Carolina*, in 1355. In accepting it the nobility would no longer have been able to "find the rights" of each individual case according to ancient custom, and would thus have had to subordinate themselves to the legal regulations as defined by centralized power. As soon as Charles saw that his proposal would not fly, he withdrew it making the excuse that the written version had been lost by mischance in a fire.

The recognized seat of the Bohemian kingdom was always Prague, but in taking the title of ruler of the Roman Empire, the city was stabilized for a long period as imperial residence for the first time in its history and its foreign policies shone forth on a grand level. Charles devoted unusual attention to the construction of Prague. As early as the establishment of the Prague archbishopric, he laid the foundation stone of St Vitus Cathedral in 1344, in which the bodies of the royal dynasts were to be interred. Situated within Prague Castle, the cathedral symbolized the conjunction of royal and spiritual power, and at the same time provided safe housing for the coronal insignias. The Bohemian crown jewels are there behind the walls of the Chapel of St Wenceslas to this day.

The Old Town (*Staré Město*) in Prague was the economic and commercial centre of the area and together with the Lesser Town (*Malá Strana*) and the Castle area (*Hradčany*) and it benefited hugely from the fact that visitors came to the imperial seat and court from all corners of Europe. Moreover, Bohemian and Moravian nobles built their palaces there in order to be near their ruler's court. Room for the metropolis's further expansion was provided by Charles in 1347 when he founded the Emmaus monastery (*Na Slovanech*) on the open space between the Old Town and Vyšehrad, the second royal fortress, on the right bank of the Vltava facing south. This was to be where the Slavonic liturgy would be fostered as contribution to the reconciliation of the conflict between the Western Church, the focal point of which was the Papal seat in Avignon in the south of France for most of the 14th century, and the Eastern Church, with its centre in Constantinople. With the foundation of Emmaus, the ruler emphasized the degree to which he valued Czech cultural and religious traditions, which formed a part of his aim to anchor the Luxemburg dynasty in the Bohemian kingdom. In the southeast of Prague, which was gradually fortified with thorough-going ramparts to defend the newly planned agglomeration of the New Town (*Nové Město*), he proposed a further endowment of the church of Karlov. The cathedral was built according to the example of the ancient German cathedral in Aachen, in which a great number of German kings had been crowned. By means of this symbol, Charles clearly emphasized the continuity between Charlemagne and Prague as the imperial seat of Roman tradition.

In this matter, Charles IV entrusted the French builder Matthias of Arras with the construction of the castle at Karlštejn. A fortress of great splendour amidst the forest, completed after nine years in 1357, it was only a half-day's ride from Prague. It was intended to provide the ruler on the one hand with a sumptuous privacy for meditation and prayer, and on the other, as a retreat for discreet diplomatic negotiations with domestic councillors, imperial advisors and diplomats from all of Europe. The main aim was however to house securely the imperial and Bohemian jewels in the tower of Karlštejn in its symbolically decorated Chapel of the Holy Cross. This chapel was illuminated on days of celebration by candlelight which reflected off hundreds of precious and semi-precious stones, lighting up the paintings of Master Theodoricus, and it symbolized the heavenly firmament and the host of saints. The remains of saints were also laid to rest there, as Charles was famed throughout Europe for his passion collecting of reliquaries. Whoever wished to gain his favour contributed gifts to his rich collection. This tradition, which was more current in the Empire than in the Bohemian crown lands, was introduced by the Emperor in Nuremberg midway through the 1350s. The Nurembergers drew up a list of jewels and reliquaries which were to be housed in Karlštejn, and described the marches and processions which took place in connection with their presentation. From 1382, these treasures were exhibited on Corpus Christi in the eponymous chapel in the New Town in Prague. The Brotherhood of Corpus Christi, to which the centrally positioned sanctuary belonged, connected the court, the Empire and Prague town. The tradition of exhibition of reliquaries and insignias was interrupted by the disturbances before 1419, and the ensuing removal of the valuables and jewels across Hungary to Nuremberg and later to Vienna.

To consolidate his power in the land and to protect it, Charles IV had a number of further fortresses built, and some took his name. To the north there was, for instance, Karlsfried in the region of Zittau, but the king also took an interest especially in ensuring the defences and vulnerability of the border with southern German along with New Bohemia. From Karlík, Karlštejn and Točník it was easy to reach Karlskrone (Radyně near Plzeň), and from there to Přimda or further south to Karlsberg (Kašperk). The castle system was also based upon castles of older origins, for instance the town castles of Tachov and Domažlice, as well as the large castle at the land border (Leuchtenberg), thus speeding up travel, improving security and the transfer of information both by means of messengers or smoke signals. Such paths were well appointed with fortresses which provided greater security, above all to merchants' caravans which were often the target of attacks by bandits on both sides of the border in the difficult mountain regions.

In 1348, Charles founded the New Town in Prague, endowing it with many privileges and thus enabling the influx of artisans and merchants, while also connecting the town with European markets all the more closely. He thus reduced the influence of the patriciate of the Old Town in Prague, which up to this time held the monopoly on the commercial centre of the Bohemian crown lands with foreign trade. The European significance of Prague grew after 1348, when, with the help of the Pope, Charles IV was able to realize his old dream of establishing a university, which today carries his name. In founding this, he took into account the experience and organizational structure of the most renowned European universities – Bologne in northern Italy and the Sorbonne in Paris. Its importance grew with the appointment of the Prague archbishop as its chancellor, and of outstanding foreign scholars as professors. The Charles University thus became the first centre of advanced learning north of the Alps and east of the Rhine, where students from all over Central Europe, as well as from the north and east, would seek education for centuries to come.

From the accession of Charles IV, the ruler's court drew the political and intellectual elite, numbering several hundred people who were at the disposition of the ruler as councillors, diplomats, property administrators and servants of higher or lower standing. The court was run by the Master of the Court, documentation was looked after by the Chancellor along with a team of clerks, who kept records of the documents issued and managed incoming correspondence; fiscal matters were dealt with by the Supreme Chamberlain; the king and his family were cared for by the Master of the Kitchen; physicians, pharmacists and others were available to offer professional services. Some of the courtiers travelled about the kingdom and beyond with the ruler to ensure the continued functioning of the royal office. The queens had their own, though far smaller, court, accommodating their needs, as did the archbishops, bishops and affluent representatives of the nobility. For many young aristocrats, a sojourn at court when they were old enough to serve as a page, was an education in life as well as a platform for a career in various offices.

Although the hub of progress in the Holy Roman Empire still remained in the Rhineland, the transfer of central imperial power to the Bohemian crown lands, and above all to Prague, in the middle of the 14th century marked an important change in the decades ahead. It led to the ever more intense connection of the eastern parts of the Empire with those in the west, which was apparent economically and culturally. A further profound shift in these affairs occurred with the Hussite revolution.

2 Society and Culture in the Era of the Luxemburgs

An index of the successful governance of the two first Luxemburgs on the Bohemian throne was the significant territorial gains which influenced the development of the Czech state and its society. Bohemia itself had an area of approximately 55,000 km², Moravia about 27,000 km² and the Bohemian crown lands all together (omitting Brandenburg and Luxemburg) 125,000 km². All adjacent lands thus made up 43,000 km². Information about the population numbers of these extensive territories can only be estimated; for the Bohemian kingdom the figure is about two and half to three million people.

In the years 1348–1350 Bohemia and Moravia were struck by plague, which was referred to as the Black Death. While in Italy and other southern countries in Europe, where it entered from Asia Minor, it became a pandemic that decimated the populations of large towns and whole territories; in the Bohemian crown lands it was not as intense. To the end of the 14th century, the fall in population numbers evened out and since the Bohemian crown lands had not been afflicted by any wars, a certain increase in population occurred.

The national division of the Czech population can only be guessed. While the central Bohemian and Moravian territory was settled mainly with people of Czech ethnicity, nearer the borders and in adjacent lands, the German population had risen; in northern regions there were also Lusatian Serbs and Poles. Rough estimates are based on the fact that over

60% of the inhabitants of the Bohemian crown lands were Czechs, almost 25% Germans and the rest made up of Lusatian Serbs, Poles and members of other minorities, among which the Jews had special standing.

Jews worked for the most part in commerce and finance, and, as in Europe in general, they met with significant problems in the Czech state. On the one hand they were welcomed for usury and pawn-broking (i.e., activities that were forbidden to Christians), but at the same time they were hated for their wealth and different faith, which was apparent in their features, clothing and religious rituals. Jews of course paid large amounts to the royal coffers, which helped run the royal court and its investments, but they also contributed to the towns. Their wealth and religious difference often became the stimulus for expression of rancour against the Jewish communities. Alleged arson or ritual murders, or the suspected responsibility of the Jews for the spread of the plague (1348–1350) served as to ignite anti-Semitic pogroms, for instance in the nearby German towns of Augsburg and Nuremberg, in Silesian Wrocław and in Cheb at the western Czech border; but in Bohemia and Moravia themselves, such activities from the outset were not as intense.

The pograms had an economic backdrop as they provided an opportunity to destroy notes of credit and encumberment on nobles and burghers. Taking this into consideration, Charles IV allowed the Jewish town in Prague to be ransacked, to appease the Bohemian nobles who were unhappy about the proposal of the law of *Maiestas Carolina*. Midway through the 1380s, his son Wenceslas IV froze Jewish property and walled off the houses of the Jews; nevertheless this did not prevent a large pogrom against them in 1389, which spread from Prague to further towns including Bautzen and Görlitz. To prevent further expressions of hatred, the Bohemian king gave the Jewish population the privilege of allowing them to protect themselves against attacks, but at the same time allowed the royal chamber to draw upon the funds of Jewish merchants.

The spectrum of nationalities in Prague and other Bohemian and Moravian towns was widened by the arrival of businessmen from Germany, Austria, Italy, Poland, Hungary and other countries. Bohemian and Moravian society, up to this time somewhat closed to foreigners, now saw the advantages of opening up to the European world. While at the beginning of the 14th century, merchants from Regensburg did the most business with the Bohemian crown lands, from the mid-century they were replaced by merchants from Nuremberg, who settled in Cheb and Plzeň, dominating commerce with the eastern parts of the Empire. The burghers of Nuremberg and Saxony, as well as the miners of Kutná Hora and Jihlava played a special role, the latter also becoming important vendors of silver and other ores in Central Europe up to the outbreak of the Hussite revolution in 1419. Cheb was a German-speaking town, like many of the towns and villages in the border areas (Tachov, Trutnov, Znojmo, etc.); moreover, the German burgher class was extremely important in Prague and Brno.

Along with the ruler, the most influential group in the Czech state were a number of families of the Bohemian and Moravian high nobility. Rožmberks, Házmburks, Lichtenburks, Cimburks, Šternberks and further members of the higher aristocracy built secure, and splendidly appointed castles as their family seats, done in the Gothic style common in

Western Europe. The nobility co-existed with their client towns and supported their construction in the vicinity of their castles. For instance Český Krumlov, which belonged to the Rožmberks, developed into the economic and cultural centre of an expansive aristocratic dominion, and took on significance beyond its own region on the Bohemian-Austrian border. We learn much about the care that the nobility devoted to its farmsteads in the period immediately before and during that of the Hussites, mostly from the correspondence of the magnates of south Bohemia – the lords of Rožmberk.

The high nobility of the 14th century wished to consolidate its influence over the administration of the land and reduce its dependence on rulers. In accordance with the agreement with the constituency of Czech nobles from 1310, King John named his most important Land officials – i.e., the Supreme Burgrave, Supreme Chamberlains and the Land Judges – from the ranks of the noble lines. The first of these took executive power as the ruler's deputy; the others looked after finances of the country and ran the Land court, generally considered the foundation of legal order in the country. The nobility could be arraigned only before a Land court of the larger kind; due to the growing number of disputes, a new smaller Land court was established alongside these in 1383 which dealt with less serious cases, and for the most part became the forum for the legal problems of the lower nobility. The courts kept systematic records of their sessions (Land rolls); these however were destroyed in the fire of 1541 in Prague. The development of the executive and system of justice in Moravia was in part different from that of Bohemia. If the office of margrave was not filled, the governor (*hejtman*) looked after the running of the country (a similar office was established also in the newly gained neighbouring territories, for instance, the governor in both Lusatian margraviates); the Moravian judicial system was divided into the areas of Brno and Olomouc. Land Diets did not meet regularly in the Bohemian crownlands, rather only on the occasions for the approval of extraordinary taxes. For the maintenance of law and order there were special agreements between the ruler and the members of the Estates – "territorial peace" (*landfrýd*); in 1388 the first of these became valid for the whole land.

In the course of the 14th century distinctions within the nobility in the Bohemia crownlands developed. The circle of high aristocracy narrowed to about twenty or thirty families who were able to prove a genealogy reaching back to the distant past, in addition to possessing substantial wealth, of varying sizes. These noble lines occupied the supreme offices of the provinces and court (in some cases heritably). Beyond these, the remaining free-born men (*zeměnínové*) made up the lower aristocracy in Bohemia and Moravia. Members of this class did not have the financial means to participate in protracted diets, legal and diplomatic negotiations connected with the administration of the country, and also of the Land offices, which remained the concern of the nobility (they could only reach the office of Supreme Clerk). The family seats of the lower nobility were unimpressive (small castles and forts), and for the greater part their standing – apart from the freehold farmstead – was not very different from that of the richer farmers. While lords had more opportunities to employ the profits of their farmsteads in commercial, religious and official activities, the lower nobility often became vassals of the king and of the higher ecclesiastical dignitaries or lords. The most significant of the vassal circles was that of royal Vyšehrad, and vassalage was also in place in Karlštejn and other royal castles. Vassal systems with tens and even hundreds of clients were set up around the Margrave of Moravia, the Archbishop of Prague, the Bishop of Olomouc, as well as the most powerful noble families. Clients served in the protection of castles and in the military; they sat in the royal courts of their liege lords and held offices in the administration of their farmsteads, which improved their own economic standing as well as their social prestige.

An important phenomenon in Czech society in the late Middle Ages were the towns which were now centres of production and commerce. They were divided according to laws and freedoms into royal towns (of which there were 56 at the beginning of the 14th century in the Bohemian crown lands and Silesia), subject towns (60) and smaller towns again (136). Although at the beginning of the 15th century the number of royal towns hardly changed (in Moravia it even decreased), the numbers in the other categories almost doubled. At the turn of the 14th and 15th centuries, Bohemia, Moravia and Silesia had in total 556 town centres, which made for a relatively dense urban network.

The towns had held on to their rights and administrative principles, as well as their judicial code, from the 13th century, but where possible they tried to gain further economic and political privileges. They especially canvassed for the strengthening of autonomous town councils at the expense of the authority's representative, the magistrate (*rychtář*). As a result of this pressure, the right to establish a town hall as the centre of autonomous administration was given first to the Old Town in Prague (1338), and inside ten years, to the Moravian towns of Brno and Olomouc; of the Bohemian towns, Slaný, Žatec, Most and others. As for population, that of Prague most likely rose to 35,000 by 1400, and thus joined the largest imperial towns such as Nuremberg, Frankfurt am Main and Cologne. Other Czech royal towns had between one and four thousand inhabitants, with the exceptions of Cheb and Kutná Hora, which were larger. Responsibility for the royal towns was the Vice-Chamberlain's, who had to levy taxes for the royal chamber. Subject towns for the greater part had less than a thousand inhabitants and were subordinate to an aristocratic or religious authority.

The number and structure of towns in Bohemia and Moravia answered to their economic strength. Urban production and commerce was however concentrated for the most part on local or regional demand. Only rich merchants looked to markets through which ran the transit routes to neighbouring countries and to towns with the right of compulsory storage. In the bigger towns, there were clashes of interest between the patriciate and artisans (or the guilds representing the latter); but John of Luxemburg as well as Charles IV and his son Wenceslas IV, by intervening personally or via their magistrates, were able to resolve these problems. In Prague, the threat of conflict was greatest, where during the 14th century the newly rich patriciate in part blended with the lower aristocracy, when its members bought freehold farmsteads, or succeeded in the new class of artisans, which had emerged after the founding of the New Town in Prague. While in Prague the large, originally German ethnic patriciate blended with the Czech population, in Moravian towns the Germans remained distinct up to the Hussite period, outnumbering Czechs.

In the towns, those crafts and commerce developed most which were dedicated to meeting local demands (for provisions, clothing and footwear, common metal implements and pottery, and further basic goods). Merchants in the larger towns, who were in contact with foreign businessmen, purchased goods from the countryside (honey, leather, freshwater fish, game) and ordered foreign products, mostly spices, wines (from Italy, Austria, Franconia, the Rhine), salted sea-fish, fabrics and jewels. Cattle and horses came from Hungary and Poland, the smaller part of which remained in the Bohemian crown lands, and the rest was sent on to the West. The Gold Road, along which flowed carriages from salt chambers of Austria loaded with sacks, became an important source of income. Fruit from the south was also available, as well as the paper necessary for the ever-growing work of administration and correspondence (as opposed to pergamon, which was expensive). These types of goods were imported mostly from the Low Lands, Germany and Italy. Prague took on special importance in this area of commerce, as it had the most advantageous storage rights, and also because it drew upon the presence of the royal court and its guests, for whom it provided luxury goods. Markets in the other Bohemian and Moravian residential towns (mostly Brno and Olomouc) responded to higher levels of consumption.

Mining of and trade in precious and other metals played an important role in the economics of the Bohemian crown lands. While gold lodes and alluvial deposits of gold did not return especially large profits, the Bohemian lands became one of the greatest powers in the mining of silver. Kutná Hora took on this leading role from the end of the 13th century, and by the beginning of the next century it was the main mint of the country for the production of Czech *groschen*. Since the profit from the mining of precious metals and minting of coins was one of the ruler's rights, the coffers of the Luxemburgs were enriched, enabling them to finance their policies, both at home and abroad, as well as undertake new construction work and cultural enterprises. Although the value of the Czech *groschen* fell with the lower silver content throughout the 14th century (gradually half of what it originally was), this specie remained in demand in all neighbouring countries as late as the Hussite period. On the reverse of the Czech *groschen* a number of German towns impressed their mark as evidence of its high quality. However, the affluence of the Czech state was increased by the mining of other metals, and pewter, copper and lead – partly the by-products of silver mining – were exported to the German lands.

The prosperity of the towns was reflected in the construction of prestigious buildings, and as a rule about the main square. The Old Town in Prague was outstanding in this respect, and its wealth at that time is instanced by the reconstruction of the House at the Stone Bell. This building, like many others there, underwent reconstruction by the mid-point of the 14th century, and was modelled on the Western European style. Houses around the Old Town Hall, the palace of the lords of Kunštát, parts of the university residences and a number of churches of the time provide indices of an extraordinary amount of construction activity, influenced by western architecture. Gothic cathedrals were built in a number of towns (Brno, Olomouc, Hradec Králové, Plzeň and elsewhere), as well as in the subject towns (foremost of which was Český Krumlov, which belonged to the Rožmberks). In contrast, Cheb, which gravitated to the neighbouring area of the Empire, did not undergo such extensive change and for a long time maintained its older architectural style.

The countryside was structured in a similar way to the towns, where along with the patriciate there were more numerous classes of artisans and poorer commoners. In the villages, alongside the small numbers of rich farmers, owners of iron and saw mills, and above all of flour mills, there was the more numerous class of labourers of small to middling wealth, whose rents ensured the income of their authorities. While urban craft production gradually perfected its techniques (e.g., the production of paper and firearms, or the refinement of iron ore to a high level), such developments came later to the villages. The slow development of agricultural production and the stagnation of social relations in the countryside were connected with the dependence on the quality of the year's harvest, which according to reports in the chronicles was various.

The Church, which enjoyed special social and jural status, was an integral part of medieval society and affected all social classes. In the Bohemian crown lands during the rule of the Luxemburgs, the bond of secular society with ecclesiastical organization was significantly consolidated. Not even John of Luxemburg, whose election was ensured by Cistercian abbots, wished to avoid co-operation with the Church which favoured him to a greater extent than the nobility. Charles IV maintained an even closer alliance with the Church, both within and without the borders of the Czech state. The king supported the expansion of ecclesiastical organization, which he succeeded in establishing as an independent archdiocese in 1344. The Silesian territory however was still subordinate to the Bishop of Wrocław, and thus also to the archbishopric of Gniezno, which in the first decade of the 15th century became, in addition to language differences, the main cause for priests not to be sent to parishes (from the period of their studies in Prague they sympathized with the reform movement). In Lusatia the situation was similar, where the ecclesiastical administration was subordinate to the Bishop of Meissen, while foreign fiefs were divided between the dioceses of Bamberg and Regensburg.

Charles IV, in co-operation with Archbishop Arnošt of Pardubice, devoted no small amounts of time and energy to the expansion of ecclesiastical institutions and provided an example to the nobility and burghers by his generous support of church endowments. New, splendidly constructed, or reconstructed, monasteries and churches sprang up, as well as numerous urban brotherhoods which cared for chapels, which had been built apart from or adjacent to existing churches. Arnošt of Pardubice himself oversaw the fine-tuning of the ecclesiastical executive, which was not completed till the time of the episcopate of Jan of Jenštejn in the 1380s, when the administration (vicariate) and judicial institution (officialate) of Czech religious life were established and functioning.

This ecclesiastical hierarchy was a social pyramid. While its upper echelon was provided for by richly endowed benefices of episcopates, chapters, monasteries, churches and chapels, the lower religious, despite their material security and exceptional social status, did not leave them many resources. Since the ubiquitous Church was more visible to all inhabitants than the burghers and nobility, the members of the other classes took note of the growth of its property and riches, as well as its shortcomings in the fulfilment of its religious duties. This became the object of criticism both from the laity and inside the Church itself in the last decades of the 14th century. The growing tension foreshadowed the conflict over the reformation of the Church and all society, which resulted in a long and ruthless battle at the beginning of the 15th century. This situation was further complicated by the Papal Schism, which came about as a result of the breach among the cardinals and the subsequent election of two heads of the Catholic Church half way through 1378. While one pope continued to govern in Avignon under the protection of the French king, the other returned to the traditional seat of Rome. Ecclesiastical administration and the internal struggle for power which affected secular crown heads influenced affairs throughout Europe and shook moral values not only among simple believers, but throughout the religious community. Emperor Charles, seriously ill, undertook a journey to France to help resolve the situation in the Empire and Paris, but was unsuccessful.

The Church, through its parochial and monastic schools, which were more numerous than urban schools, contributed to the spread of basic education throughout the social classes. From the foundation of the Prague university in 1348, it was closely connected with its administration and pedagogy, since the theological faculty was the supreme faculty, ranked above the faculties of arts (philosophy), law and medicine. Thanks to contacts with top European scholars, Prague gained influential teachers, who brought to the intellectual, cultural and social circles of the city ideas and theories that were current in the west. These would help create the basis for the next attempt to reform the Church and Czech society. This came about not only through professors from abroad but students of Czech origin who had studied in Paris, Montpellier, Avignon, Oxford and the Italian universities of Bologne, Perugia and Padua. When they returned to their homeland, they brought to Prague the ideas of Marsilius of Padua and his contemporaries, who were working on the relations between secular and ecclesiastical power, as well as the ideas of the English theologian John Wycliffe. At the turn of the 14th and 15th centuries it was Wycliffe's teaching above all that most influenced the intellectual development of the Czech reformation, at whose head stood Master Jan Hus (John Huss). Numerous educated men emerged from the university and many of these were concerned with questions about the fair division of society, the mutual relations of social groups and moral standards. Among these was the educated yeoman Tomáš Štítný, who wrote a range of books in Czech on philosophical and religious issues.

The court of the Luxemburgs became a very important focal point of cultural life, mediating influences and experience from Western Europe to further courts, both secular and ecclesiastical, in the Bohemian crown lands. From their journeys in Italy, France, the lands of Austria and Germany, as well as Poland, the ruler along with his courtiers, lords and religious, brought ideas which they wished to put into effect in their seats. This was manifest in the life of the royal court, in the construction of castles and their furnishings, in literature, music and the visual arts. The Luxemburgs, when encountering western courts, understood the significance of prestige and splendour. As they increasingly became a part of the Czech context, they exploited cultural relations with the countries that were close to their own sympathies. Above all they depended on their knowledge of Italy, Rhineland and France, and they decided to use their cultural inheritance to emphasize their dynastic mission as well as for the overall expansion of the Czech state, which was to become the permanent base of their line.

While the university was the educational centre which connected the Bohemian kingdom with all of Europe, the royal and imperial court became a cultural centre in the wider sense of the word. Alongside the educated ruler, there were important Church dignitaries whose horizons extended over the European continent, and consequently had large networks of international contacts. The last Bishop of Prague Jan of Dražice spent most of his life in Avignon; the first archbishop, Arnošt of Pardubice, had studied in Italy; Jan of Středa, from 1353 chancellor of the royal and imperial chancellery and later Bishop of Olomouc, was famed for his contacts with Italian humanists, and under its influence he developed a penchant for illuminated manuscripts. The most outstanding work in his collection was the *Liber viaticus*. The representatives of important monasteries and secular institutions were also to be found at court, and these were able to further their ambitions under the strong foundational activities of Charles IV. Wenceslas IV followed in Charles's footsteps. The former had an unusual interest in the book and created a collection of superlative illuminated manuscripts, of which are preserved only a handful scattered through European libraries and galleries.

Charles IV corresponded with such personages as the Italian humanists Francesco Petrarch and Cola di Rienzo, who visited the king in Prague in 1350 and unsuccessfully tried to win him over for his grand if unrealistic plan to renew the great Empire with its head in Rome. Apart from these pre-eminent men of the age, the spirit of the imperial court was also influenced by Italian masters at the Prague university; these acquainted courtiers with cultivated Latin and humanist ideas. This is why the Prague court during the era of the Luxemburgs is considered the main centre of early humanism beyond the Alps. Whether the Emperor was taken by all these ideas is not certain, but it seems that he gave priority to the late medieval religious world over the emergent idea of "sweet new style" (*dolce stile nuovo*), which placed greater emphasis on opening up to secular life. Nevertheless this influence would be effectively reflected in the upbringing of Charles's sons, Wenceslas and Sigismund.

The elements of humanism which penetrated the Czech context opened up possibilities for the use of national languages, which were already employed at various levels. German was the first to be used in the chancelleries and private correspondence of nobles and burghers, and shortly after that Czech. Gradually however, and mainly during the era of Charles IV, Czech came into use in the ruler's chancellery, even though German was given priority because of the frequent official contact with imperial addressees. In the opinion of some linguists, it was in the context of the royal chancellery in Prague that the first attempts at unification of German (New High German) orthography are to be found, which was important especially for the lands of southern and central Germany. The refined style is to be found in the translation of the Old Testament into German from the time of

Wenceslas IV, and the famed work *Ackermann aus Böhmen*, which reached Czech readers in an adapted translation as the well known work *Tkadleček*.

Czech did not lag behind either, developing dynamically even beyond the court environment. In the second half of the 14th century, the first Czech translation of the Bible was made (entitled the *Leskovec* or *Dresden Bible*; in Moravian it overlaps with the Olomouc version), and so the Czechs were numbered after Italy and France among the first nations to undertake such a task. Bartoloměj of Chlumec, known as Klaret, along with several assistants and most likely supported by the Emperor, concentrated on lexicographical works which throw light on the scientific terminology of the time, which up to this employed mostly Latin. Works which dealt with the Czech language itself increased, peaking at the beginning of the 15th century with the attempt to simplify it by rejecting digraph orthography: this was proposed in the small work *Ortographia Bohemica* from the Emmaus monastery (1412). The overall result of these efforts was that in all areas of cultural life there was now an opportunity to employ the national language, which was marked progress from the time of the writing of *Chronicle of Dalimil* at the beginning of the 14th century. The work of the above-mentioned Tomáš Štítný and later some of Hus's writings mark the rise of the Czech language. Ondřej of Dubá's work, Bohemian Land Rights (*Práva zemská česká*) (1400) successfully used the riches of Czech legal terminology. The court, the Church and the towns ensured a range of translations of well known literary works into Czech; also, university students created nursery rhymes and songs.

It is striking that especially in the areas of religious arts (song and preaching), but also in the translation of Latin liturgical texts, that Czech penetrated not only Silesia after the first half of the 14th century and into the 15th century, but also beyond the borders of the Czech state, mainly into Poland. Along with the entire texts of religious songs, the terminology used in legal documents was also important as it ensured clarity for Slavic inhabitants there. Linguistically, the Czech influence spread also to the south, as far as Croatia, mainly due to the activities of the Emmaus monastery in Prague.

Charles IV himself contributed to literary life with his autobiography *Vita Caroli* and in his proposals relating to the imperial and Czech jural code, as well as further works on religion, where he emphasized the continuity between the Luxemburgs and the Přemyslid dynasty from the time of St Wenceslas, thus stressing the continuity of his line back to ancient Czech history. For him, as for other rulers, history was an instrument for the celebration of his own personage and dynasty. This is why he supported so strongly a range of chronicle works which at that time originated under the auspices of the court and thus propagated these ideas (the works of František of Prague, Přibík Pulkava of Radenín, the Italian Marignolli and others).

Construction activity was more visible, and with the growing prosperity of the Bohemian crown lands and the increase of its European contacts this was evident in the reconstruction of royal castles and palaces, as well as of the seats of the nobility, the houses of burghers, churches and monasteries. Because of the influence of the Bishop of Prague, Jan IV of Dražice, the Bohemian crown lands embraced the new French Gothic style in the first half of the 14th century. Supported by the Augustinians, whose expansion in the Bohemian kingdom was due in large part to him, Bishop Jan IV transformed his seat in Roudnice to the north of Prague into an example of modern architecture, in which airy French influences (large windows, rose windows and light interior supports in towards the roof) prevailed over the heavy elements of old Gothic architecture. Similar approaches were taken by the Cistercians, who maintained contact with the Rhineland and France, in the construction of their monasteries. With the arrival of the architect Matthias of Arras, who oversaw the first phase of the construction of St Vitus's Cathedral and the Emmaus monastery, the French architectural style spread further. His influence was strengthened by the arrival of Peter Parler from Gmünd in Swabia, who had gained much experience abroad and continued in the work of his predecessor. He was responsible for the construction of the choir in St Vitus's Cathedral and the reconstruction of a range of further ecclesiastical buildings. This experience spread through Moravia and Silesia, as well as to Vienna which was another destination for the pupils of Parler's construction school. Gothic architecture in the Bohemian crown lands reached its zenith at the end of the 14th century, and its quality was acknowledged in neighbouring countries by their abundant imitation of it.

Extensive architectural work and above all the construction of new prestigious edifices required the development of arts and crafts for the decoration of the more complex secular buildings as well as those of the Church. Apart from the exquisite work of Master Theodoricus, whose most important contribution was to the decoration of Karlštejn, there were outstanding achievements by artists of icons and church panels from southern Bohemia, the Masters of the altars of Třeboň and Vyšší Brod.

During the 14th century, Czech society underwent fundamental changes. The consolidation of royal power and the international prestige of the ruler's line, as well as the harmony between Charles IV and the Church, eased the conflicts with the nobility. The latter's representatives were temporarily satisfied by appointments to important offices and the easing of the pressure that they experienced under the Přemyslids. This peaceful state of affairs enabled the nobility to improve their position, which relied on the economic prosperity of the Bohemian crown lands and their political and cultural blossoming. The Czech state found itself at its zenith at the end of the 14th century and it was recognized throughout Europe not only as the heart of the Holy Roman Empire but also as one of its engines of political and cultural change.

3 Before the Revolution

Even a ruler as perspicacious as Charles IV made mistakes which had fateful consequences for his life's work. One of the steps which created problems in the domains of the Luxemburgs was the Emperor's will. As was the custom in medieval times, only the birth of a son was a guarantee of dynastic continuity. So Charles – in 1349 still without male issue – gave the Moravian margraviate to his younger brother Jan Jindřich in order to introduce him to the politics of the Bohemian crown lands in the same way that his father John had before him. Jindřich's son Jošt took over the governance of Moravia in 1375. Near the end of his life Jošt was elected King of the Romans for a short time. Afterwards, when Charles's first son was born, symbolically named Wenceslas, the Emperor worked very hard for him to be crowned Bohemian king in 1363 while still only a child of two, and in 1376 as King of the Romans. Charles IV gave his younger sons important parts of the crown territories that had only recently been unified – Sigismund received the region of Brandenburg and Jan the region of Görlitz. He thus provided ambitious members of his family with the opportunity to engage in endless internecine struggles for power and status in the Bohemian crown lands as well as in imperial politics.

After Wenceslas IV was deposed in 1400, the Roman throne was occupied by his cousin Jošt (r. 1410–1411) and then his younger brother Sigismund (r. 1411–1437), who also gained the Hungarian crown in 1387. The skilful Sigismund became the deputy of Wenceslas IV despite his support of the opposition against his brother. In the end Sigismund was twice crowned Bohemian king in the tumultuous Hussite period. After Charles's death in 1378 the principle of unitary dynastic governance in the Empire collapsed, which very much weakened the position of the Luxemburgs and enabled the nobility and clergy to enter politics, and further the interests of their own Estates.

The stability of the kingdom was upset and the young king Wenceslas IV felt even more uncertain because the older generation of his fathers' advisors, who had influence not only in the Bohemian crown lands but also in the Empire, had also departed. The ruler increasingly looked for support to his retinue who for the most part came from the ranks of the lower nobility and who were materially dependent on him. These were the origin of the phrase the "king's darlings". As a consequence of this step, distrust grew between Wenceslas and the heretofore pro-royal elements of the nobility and clergy. In the Bohemian crown lands criminality increased and the aristocracy and religious did not hesitate to take an open stance against the ruler in the 1390s. While the deputies of the aristocratic constituency engaged in massacre because of the excessive growth in the power of some royal courtiers, the exemplary case in the matter of the conflict with the church became the murder of John of Pomuk (in later tradition St John of Nepomuk, or Nepomucene). Wenceslas IV had this General Vicar drowned in the Vltava in 1393 because he prevented him from establishing a new bishopric in western Bohemia, which the king imagined would give him greater influence over the church. The ruler decided to confront the Czech ecclesiastical hierarchy, headed by the internationally renowned Archbishop Jan of Jenštejn. John of Pomuk became the symbol of the struggle of secular and religious powers, and later – mostly after his canonization in the 18th century – honoured in Europe and further afield as a saint in the Baroque period, designated as a martyr for the Seal of the Confessional.

Tension in Czech society was most likely increased by the gradual fall in income, not only of the royal coffers, but also of the purses of entrepreneurial aristocrats and religious. This was perhaps the first cause of the lack of consistency of the pertinent ruler's offices, along with insufficient control over finances and the corruption of the disoriented court of Wenceslas IV. Moreover this is proved by the dramatic increase in the property holdings of Wenceslas's court favourites, for example Zikmund Huler, administrator of the royal finances. Taxes collected in the country and profits from precious metals were mishandled to such a degree that the king had to have Huler condemned and removed. His own removal from the imperial throne in 1400 must have been an even greater blow to Wenceslas's budget, as it meant the loss of extremely large incomes from the imperial finances – taxes, gifts and payments from the people of outlying territories. Financial breakdown did not however occur during Wenceslas's rule, since the court, nobility, burghers and other members of the lower classes had a good lifestyle, at least until revolution erupted. The chiliastic beginnings of Hussite Tábor can be illustrated by one example: the poorer part of the population as well as the lower nobility took to filling tubs with money and valuables from spring 1420.

At the turn of the 14th and 15th centuries, Czech society faced further problems, arising from the fact that over three generations the country had undergone transformations incomparable with those in neighbouring states. The end of the Přemyslid dynasty, a period of decline followed by the unusual rise to the level of European politics and culture, provided it with the determination to attempt to right those affairs which were in conflict with generally accepted principles. Fragmented secular power had to compromise in part with the ideas of the Luxemburg Emperor concerning the arrangement of the Empire and the state. The Church, which wished to maintain its ostensible unity, did not have enough internal strength to manage this task. It entered into a conflict which concerned not only itself but took on European proportions and strongly affected the Bohemian crown lands to the degree that its rulers were drawn into it on the imperial level. When Wenceslas IV returned together with his father from France in 1378, no-one could have anticipated that the rupture in the Church (which they wished to prevent through diplomacy), along with political and intellectual tensions, would gather to breaking point so quickly in the Czech context.

What contributed significantly to this was the fact that after Charles's death, the new advisors of Wenceslas IV were not closely linked with European diplomacy. The growing conflicts in the Bohemian kingdom and the king's lack of information about international developments increased his apathy towards political events in general and led him to avoid the consideration of their possible consequences. Charles IV chose Prague as his residence, diverging thus from the custom of his predecessors to administer the Empire through constant travel. Nevertheless his itinerary shows that his travels were consciously spread through the territories under his power. Moreover he relied on Nuremberg in imperial matters, and for this town he created extraordinarily favourable conditions by granting a range of political and especially economic privileges. The Imperial Diets also met in this town and its burghers provided the Prague court with information about events throughout Europe. Wenceslas IV, on the contrary, buffered himself from imperial and international affairs and restricted himself to a circle which suited only his personal interests. He limited his contacts with the Empire to such a degree that he was stripped of the throne in 1400 because he was designated a ruler of "no use". Wenceslas IV's vacillation when resolving the Papal Schism, the more shadowy aspects of which he became acquainted with on his trip to Paris in 1378 as well as in the consequent negotiations with ambassadors of the Avignon and Roman Popes, prevented him from reaching the rank of Emperor. This failure strengthened the king's distrust towards the Czech ecclesiastical hierarchy.

Though it is true that Wenceslas IV would escape domestic problems by turning to the cultural interests of his court or by trips to his favourite castles of Žebrák, Točník and Křivoklát, which lay deep in the forests to the west of Prague, he did not systematically refuse to resolve them. Together with his circle of favourites he prevented the rise in the nobility's influence, and when in the 1380s he began to support a new understanding of the spiritual life along the lines of *devotio moderna*, he clearly indicated his differences with the official Church. Neither did he distance himself from reform groups in the university, who in the spirit of Wycliffe's ideas gained in popular standing above all through their preaching in the Bethlehem Chapel, founded in 1391. From the beginning of the 15th century, the reform movement intensified and started to divide Czech society. Constant conflicts among the nobility, the religious and the burghers took on a new dimension which obviously suited the ruler since it weakened the threats to his power.

Before the Council of Pisa, convened in 1409 with the aim of ending the double papacy, Wenceslas IV secured the promise of one of the candidates for the Papal See that he would again receive the imperial crown. A new conflict flared up between the Czech clergy and the high nobility. The reform side, with Jan Hus at its head, promised to help Wenceslas by getting the university to favour his papal candidate. As a consequence of this, a dispute over votes broke out in the university in Prague, which was resolved by the king in 1409 in favour of Hus's followers by the Decree of Kutná Hora. He thus weakened the university's followers of the Roman Church (the university "nations" of Bavaria, Saxony and Poland) and strengthened the influence of the Czech university nation. At the same time he intimated that he would stand on the side of the followers of Wycliffe and Hus's ideas about the reform of church and society in their dispute with the Papal Curia. The king's position incensed the anti-ecclesiastical mood to such a degree that the property of Church dignitaries began to be appropriated.

The Council of Pisa did not resolve the question of the schism and Wenceslas IV was left without the support of the Church. When the electors met after the unexpected death of the recognized King of the Romans, Ruprecht of the Palatinate, who had ruled for 10 years, they elected Wenceslas's brother Jošt, who however died unexpectedly immediately afterwards at the beginning of 1411. Wenceslas suffered yet another political defeat soon after when his younger brother Sigismund was crowned Roman King. As a consequence of this Wenceslas resigned virtually all active participation in politics and left the course of events in freefall. The divided inhabitants of the kingdom, competing in faith as well as language, prepared for conflict, and this came about with the sentencing of Jan Hus in Constance in 1415. It was only four years to the outbreak of a war which would take on significance for all of Europe.

Bibliography

BARTOŠ, František Michálek: *Čechy v době Husově*, Praha 1947 (České dějiny II/6).

BAUM, Wilhelm: *Kaiser Sigismund. Konstanz, Hus und Türkenkriege*, Graz–Sien–Köln 1993.

BENEŠOVSKÁ, Klára (ed.): *King John of Luxembourg (1296–1346) and the Art of His Era*, Praha 1998.

BOBKOVÁ, Lenka: *Velké dějiny zemí Koruny české*, IV (1310–1402), Praha–Litomyšl 2003.

ČECHURA, Jaroslav: *Lucemburkové na českém trůně*, I–II, Praha 1999–2000.

ČORNEJ, Petr: *Velké dějiny zemí Koruny české*, V (1402–1437), Praha–Litomyšl 2000.

DRDA, Miloš – HOLEČEK, František Jindřich – VYBÍRAL, Zdeněk (eds.): *Jan Hus na přelomu tisíciletí*, Tábor 2001.

ENGEL, E. (ed.): *Karl IV. Politik und Ideologie im 14. Jahrhundert*, Weimar 1982.

FAJT, Jiří (ed.): *Magister Theodoricus. Dvorní malíř císaře Karla IV.*, Praha 1997.

FREY, Beat: *Pater Bohemiae – Vitricus Imperii. Kaiser Karl in der Geschichtsschreibung*, Bonn 1978.

FUDGE, Thomas: *The First Reformation in Hussite Bohemia*, Aldershot 1998.

HERGEMÖLLER, Bernard-Ulrich: *Maiestas Carolina. Der Kodifikationsentwurf Karls IV. für das Königreich Böhmen von 1355*, München 1995.

HERGEMÖLLER, Bernard-Ulrich: *Der Nürnberger Reichstag von 1355/56 und die „Goldene Bulle" Karls IV.*, Münster 1978.

HLAVÁČEK, Ivan: *Das Urkunden- und Kanzleiwesen des böhmischen und römischen Königs Wenzel (IV.) 1376–1419*, Stuttgart 1970.

HOENSCH, Jörg K.: *Die Luxemburger. Eine spätmittelalterliche Dynastie gesamteuropäischer Bedeutung 1308–1437*, Stuttgart–Berlin–Köln 2000.

JURITSCH, Georg: *Handel und Handelsrecht in Böhmen bis zur hussitischen Revolution*, Leipzig-Wien 1977.

KAVKA, František: *Am Hofe Karls IV.*, Leipzig 1989.

KAVKA, František: *Vláda Karla IV. za jeho císařství (1355–1378)*, I–II, Praha 1993.

KLASSEN, John Martin: *The Nobility and the Marking of the Hussite Revolution*, New York 1978.

KRÁSA, Josef: *Rukopisy Václava IV.*, Praha 1974.

KUBÍNOVÁ, Kateřina: *Imitatio Romae. Karel IV. a Řím*, Praha 2006.

LEGNER, Anton (ed.): *Die Parler und der Schöne Stil 1350-1400*, I–V, Köln 1978.

LIPPERT, Julius: *Sozialgeschichte Böhmens in vorhussitischer Zeit*, I–II, Prag–Wien–Leipzig 1896–1898.

MARQUE, Paul (ed.): *Le rêve italien de la maison de Luxembourg aux XIVe et XVe siècles*, Luxembourg 1997.

MEZNÍK, Jaroslav: *Praha před husitskou revolucí*, Praha 1990.

MEZNÍK, Jaroslav: *Lucemburská Morava 1310–1403*, Praha 1999.

PAULY, Michel (ed.): *Johann der Blinde, Graf von Luxemburg, König von Böhmen 1296–1346*, Luxembourg 1997.

Prague – The Crown of Bohemia 1347–1437, ed. by Barbara Drake Boehm and Jiří Fajt, New York–New Haven–London 2005.

SEIBT, Ferdinand: *Karl IV. Ein Kaiser in Europa 1346–1378*, München 1978.

SEIBT, Ferdinand (ed.): *Kaiser Karl IV. Statsmann und Mäzen*, München 1978.

Sigismund von Luxemburg. Kaiser und König in Mitteleuropa 1387–1437, J. Macek – E . Marosi – F. Seibt (eds.), Warendorf 1994.

STEJSKAL, Karel: *České umění gotické (1350–1420)*, Praha 1970.

STOOB, Heinz: *Kaiser Karl IV. und seine Zeit*, Graz–Wien–Köln 1990.

SWOBODA, Karl M. (ed.): *Gotik in Böhmen*, München 1969.

ŠMAHEL, František: *Die Hussitische Revolution*, I–III, Hannover 2002.

ŠMAHEL, František: *Cesta Karla IV. do Francie 1377–1378*, Praha 2006.

WELTSCH, Ruben Ernst: *Archbishop John of Jenstein (1348–1400). Papalism, Humanism and Reform in Pre-Hussite Prag*, Den Haag 1968.

ZEMAN, Jarold K.: *The Hussite Movement and the Reformation in Bohemia, Moravia and Slovakia (1350–1650)*, Ann Arbor 1977.

146

VI. The Hussite Revolution (1419–1471)

John Huss preaching to the multitudes in the Betlehem Chapel. Woodcut, from *Processus consistorialis et de victoria Christi*, Strasbourg c. 1525, page 4.

1 Beginnings of the Reform Movement

The Bohemian crown lands quickly caught up with other advanced areas of Western and Southern Europe in the course of the 14th century. On more than one occasion, however, this process strained affairs to breaking point, especially when some external factors (foremost among them the Papal Schism) brought further new problems. Several other countries were more advanced in their arrangements of the relations between church and state, and the same is true of relations with their Estates. As a consequence of the revolutionary events which would shake the Czech state in the 15th century, great progress was made in this matter. The co-existence of two ethnic groups, each with its own language – Czech and German – within the same state, had no small impact on the course of events.

The political geography of the next revolutionary phase had already been established in the second half of the rule of Wenceslas IV (*Václav*). The ruler was at once both the head and the single authority of the Bohemian crown state, since the Estates of the individual crown lands had independent political structures, without the unity that general diets would have provided. The volatile nature of the internal bonds became apparent in the critical months after the death of Wenceslas IV. While Bohemia opposed the successor to the throne, Moravia, the Silesian principalities, both parts of Lusatia (Upper and Lower), and the city of Cheb accepted the Roman and Hungarian king Sigismund (*Zikmund*) as the rightful lord of the land. This checked the concerted advancement of Czech nobility, which up to this had given both jural validity and a power base to the reform movement.

By 1419, there were many settlements across the land, with a hundred larger towns and roughly three times more lesser towns; alongside this there was a dense network of 2084 parishes, 122 monasteries and 29 convents. One parish in the Prague archdiocese was about 28 km^2, with one priest for 200 people. From this it is clear that high the number of clergy brought difficulties to the economic potential of the Bohemian crown lands. Although 30% to 40% of all useable land belonged to ecclesiastical institutions, some monasteries and convents, even episcopal farmsteads, were on the edge of economic collapse. The vigorous activities of the Archbishop of Prague, Jan of Jenštejn (d. 1400), to complete the centralization of the administration and create from the Czech Church a state within the state came to grief when it was opposed by Wenceslas IV. In consequence, the power of the clergy was reduced in part. Relations between ecclesiastical and secular powers escalated into violent conflicts in the last decades of the 14th century in Moravia also.

The Czech nobility, clashing with the ruler in an attempt to limit his power, initially saw an ally in the upper echelons of the Church hierarchy, and for the most part remained on the sidelines of the reform movement. The new men who were appointed to Land and court offices shortly before 1410 were more open to compromise and took greater notice of voices demanding rectification of ecclesiastical affairs. The convergence of the standpoints of the king, the court and Land offices helped deflect the first wave of violent attacks against the leaders of the reform movement. In the years 1415–1418, a group of influential representatives of the Bohemian and Moravian nobility suppressed a second, more dangerous onslaught from the Council of Constance and Pope Martin V. In contrast with this, the lower nobility, with the exception of a small group at court, who on some occasions supported the reform movement behind the king's back, played a secondary role in political life up to 1419.

Although signs of crisis continued to threaten the prosperity of the urban economy as well as the standard of living of the middle and lower classes, internal social disputes seldom erupted into open clashes. From the end of the 14th century, the national emancipation of the Czech population became a pressing issue in ethnically mixed towns. This also explains why reform demands found support in just under a third of royal towns with a Czech majority in their population and in their autonomous organs. In the case of the Moravian royal towns, which in their entirety opposed attempts at reform, the conflictual relations with local lords and knights, who sooner or later took the side of the Hussite-Utraquist group, played no small role.

Extensive areas of the countryside in Bohemia and Moravia remained outside the reform movement which would later become a revolution. Throughout the whole governance of Wenceslas IV, feeble expressions of social protest did not escalate into outright resistance. The undercurrent of social unrest in some rural areas (mainly southern Bohemia) was created by the climate of increased uncertainty: neither life nor limb was safe in an environment racked by the consequences of small wars, power struggles and virulent plague epidemics. The ambiguity of social disputes in the Czech state's period of crisis found expression in all classes of society as well as in the anti-ecclesiastical tendency of reform ideology, which became the focus of widely differing interests, ranging from the desire for partial reform to general transformation of a revolutionary character.

Attempts to correct the secularized Church and to foster an internal rebirth of religious life took various forms in the Bohemian crown lands. The "new devotion" (*devotio moderna*), as it was known, was practiced in both the newly founded monastic house of Augustinians in Roudnice and the Cistercian monastery in Zbraslav, where one of the most widely known religious writings originated, the allegorically titled *Malogranatum* (Garnet Apple). Emphasis on the spiritual experience of the individual was complemented by an attempt at a complete translation of the Bible into the national language. In this matter, Bohemia was ahead of most

FRANTIŠEK ŠMAHEL

European countries. Thanks to anonymous translators, in the last quarter of the 14th century a wider circle of educated laity could encounter the Bible's message in Czech and partly in German. Religious non-conformity in the manner of what was called folk heresy in Bohemia found expression at first only among the Waldensian sectarians, who had settled here along with other colonists. However, soon the Inquisition arrived, establishing its permanent seat in Prague. In the years 1335–1355 alone about 4,000 people suspected of heresy were interrogated, of which over 200 were burnt. What was left of the families of the Waldensians of German origin were outlaws until the beginning of the movement in Tábor.

The preaching of the Augustinian Konrad Waldhauser (d. 1369), who had been invited to Prague by Charles IV himself, was noteworthy for its sharp criticism of mendicant orders and ecclesiastical fiscal policies. Under this preacher's influence Milíč of Kroměříž (d. 1374) resigned his office in the royal chancellery; in contrast with his predecessor he gathered about him a retinue of disciples of the indigent Christ. He gave his property to the poor, and devoted all his energy to building an exemplary parish in Prague named Jerusalem. In a chapel with a refuge for aged prostitutes, he founded a school for reform preachers. Milíč died in Avignon, where he defended himself against the accusations of Prague's parish priests before the Papal judicial court. Milíč, with his demand for free preaching of the word of God, adumbrated one of Hussite articles, and his successor Master Matěj of Janov (d. 1394) pioneered the idea of the frequent receipt of holy sacraments. He thought the individual's path to salvation lay in a return to the early Church, which he justified in his Latin tract about the rules of the Old and New Testaments (*Regulae veteris et novi testamenti*).

At the end of the 14th century, the first writings of the Oxford professor John Wycliffe (d. 1384) made their way to Prague, and their philosophical assertiveness captured the imagination of young Czech masters at the Prague university. As soon as Wycliffe's opinions about the Church and the necessity of the corrective intervention of secular power became known, the majority of foreign masters condemned his 45 erroneous theses in 1403. In the ensuing disputes about Wycliffe's teachings the principles of the Hussite reform program gradually matured. A further element of this struggle was the strenuous efforts of the Czech "nation" in the university to gain exceptional prerogatives in domestic scholarship.

Disputes at the university peaked in the years 1408–1409. One of the crucial moments was the refusal to agree on the summons of the ecumenical Council of Pisa. The German masters, gathered in three of the four university "nations", crossed the political plans of King Wenceslas IV in this matter. On January 18, 1409 in Kutná Hora, the angered ruler, prompted by his Czech councillors, assigned three votes to the Czech university nation, against one for the combined remaining nations of foreign professors and students. Through this change in its internal constitution resulting from the Decree of Kutná Hora, the Prague university opened itself fully to the elements canvassing for profound reform of both church and society. On the other hand however, the exodus of seven to eight hundred foreign masters, bachelors and students considerably weakened the international significance of the Prague university. Former Prague professors immediately began sounding the alarm about Czech heresy in neighbouring countries.

The spokesman of the university reformers, generally recognized from the outset, was Jan Hus (John Huss; *c.* 1370–1415) who from 1402 was active as a preacher in Prague's Bethlehem chapel. This spacious chapel, intended exclusively for preaching in the Czech tongue, had been built in the 1390s by a circle of Czech patriots who also supported the association of the domestic nation at the Prague university. Hus's criticism of the Church was a thorn in the side of many parish priests in Prague. Archbishop Zbyněk of Házmburk defended Hus at first from their complaints. However when accusations directed against the Prague defenders of Wycliffe's errors reached the Roman Curia, the archbishop tried to suppress the contagion by forbidding all preaching and folk song in Bethlehem chapel. The burning of Wycliffe's writings in July 1410 provoked especial outrage in the archbishop's court. The king and his wife, along with representatives of the higher nobility and three Prague towns, immediately sent an epistle to the Pope and his cardinals defending Hus and his reform group.

The extensive reform association, with Jan Hus at its head, suffered a profound setback in spring 1412 when King Wenceslas gave his agreement to the sale of fully authorized indulgences in support of Pope John XXIII's military undertakings. Strident expressions of simony provoked a strong wave of protest among the incensed crowds of Hus's followers. Students, under the leadership of Jeroným of Prague organized a masked demonstration to protest the indulgences, and the streets of Prague were for the first time filled with the followers of the Bethlehem preacher from among the commoners. In July 1412, three journeymen who were executed on the king's order as examples, gave the movement its first martyrs. After a brief hesitation Hus decided to defend the principles of the reform program, while several of the former Wycliffites went over to his opponents' side. Just as he had previously opposed the archbishop and Pope, he now stood against the king. The rupture at the university foreshadowed the profound division of the entire national polity in the matter of the true faith. This became the supreme value to which the interests of nation and country were subordinated for a long period. All the competing parties presented themselves as the sole representatives of true Czechness.

Increasingly severe ecclesiastical punishments forced Hus to remove to the countryside, where he wrote among other tracts *De ecclesia* and in Czech Short Treatises on Simony (*Knížky o svatokupectví*). The reforming nobility, who had extended its Estate's responsibility for the "general good" of the land to the area of spiritual freedom, protected him. The reasons that motivated some magnates to the reform movement were various. Some were attracted by the selfish prospects of appropriating Church farmlands; others listened to Wycliffe and Hus's interpretations of God's law because it resonated in their souls. Similar positions were taken up by the lower nobility which later would employ its professional military experience under the Hussite standards. However only a small part of the Bohemian and Moravian nobility aligned itself behind the chalice, which thanks to the radical theologian Jakoubek of Stříbro (Jacobellus de Misa d. 1429) had become the symbol of Hussitism in its entirety. Communion in both kinds (*sub utraque specie*), which was called Utraquism, not only reduced the difference between the laity and clergy, but also expanded the sacred connection with the realm of the divine, as the blood of Christ in the form of wine was previously reserved for the priests alone. Jakoubek here stood side by side with Nicholas of Dresden, one of the foreign reformers dwelling in the Prague university residence of The Black Rose (*U Černé růže*).

The Council of Pisa, which elected a new pope in 1409, did more harm than good since both preceding popes refused to resign. The Church, divided by three heads, once again had to be unified by yet another council, convened at the initiative of the King of the Romans, Sigismund of Luxemburg, in Constance at the end of 1414. Sigismund intended to resolve the question of Czech heresy finally in Constance, and that is why he attached a guarantee of safe conduct to Hus's invitation. Hus accepted the offer, but soon came to understand in jail in Constance that the truths of his faith did not correspond to the ideas of the Council. The promised public hearing became the trial of a heretic who did not hesitate to sacrifice his life for his beliefs. Hus's death at the stake on July 6, 1415 ignited the flame of revolt in Bohemia and Moravia, and this was fuelled further by the burning of Hus's friend Master Jeroným of Prague at the end of May 1416. In the mean time, the Council embarked upon a long struggle with Czech heresy through its ban on the chalice for the laity.

In 1415, the seals of 452 nobles were attached to an epistle protesting Hus's execution, among which were representatives of roughly a third of the 90 aristocratic families. Thanks to the Land governor Lacek of Kravaře a large number of seals from Moravia were there. In addition to the league of Hussite nobles, a league of Catholic lords had been created in 1416, which supported the offensive of the officers of the archbishopric (i.e., the consistory) against the swiftly growing reform movement. The Hussite nobles, with the Supreme Burgrave of Prague Čeněk of Vartenberk at their head, again took the Prague university under its protection, which in March 1417 opposed the authority of the Council of Constance with a decree of the True faith of the chalice. Čeněk of Vartenberk, also guardian to the heir of the enormous landed property of Oldřich of Rožmberk, was able to preserve a considerable number of parish churches for Utraquist priests. Thanks to this, Hussitism in southern Bohemia was radicalized more quickly than in other areas. Fears of the spread of reforming demands consolidated the links between representatives of the Hussite nobility and the university masters gathered about Jakoubek of Stříbro. Both these leading groups began to waver and with the onslaught of radical currents temporarily withdrew from the forefront.

From 1412, the reform movement increasingly asserted itself in royal towns in the countryside. In roughly one third of them, Hus's followers controlled the town halls within just a few years. Beyond the Prague towns, the movement's main bases were Plzeň, Hradec Králové and Žatec. Of the non-royal towns that were influenced by Hus's time in southern Bohemia Sezimovo Ústí was the most prominent, providing shelter for the retinue of radical preachers from Bohemia and Moravia. Symptoms of the long-term political and economic crisis were reflected in feelings of uncertainty and fear of the future, which were further increased by the virulent plague epidemic. Faith in the assistance of a supernatural agent gathered force among the adherents of a thorough purge of the secularized Church.

The obstinacy of both the Council of Constance and the newly elected pope, Martin V – whose accession brought the Church schism to an end – served to unify the competing reform currents into one defensive phalanx. Under pressure from his brother Sigismund (who had already begun to gather his Czech followers) and threatened by the Papal legation of Fernando, King Wenceslas IV returned the churches of Prague and other towns to Roman priests. Though the Prague Hussites soon extracted partial concessions from the ruler, in the countryside the Utraquists lost control of one church after another. This was why they were forced to gather on higher ground for religious services, to which the radical preachers gave biblical names. The most significant of these assembly areas was the hill of Tábor (today, Burkovák) in southern Bohemia between Sezimovo Ústí and Písek. In defiance of prohibitions by Catholic authorities, there was an enormous gathering of Hussite pilgrims from the regions of Bohemia and Moravia on July 22, 1419, at which, in addition to services, secret councils took place on further action.

Several days later, on Sunday July 30, 1419, the radical New Town preacher Jan Želivský called his listeners to accompany him to the Church of St Stephen, from where he had been expelled in January. After violently breaking into the church, the crowd took strength from communion in both kinds and made for the New Town Hall nearby to liberate their brethren imprisoned there. The armed attack on the town hall, during which eleven opponents of the Utraquists, among them several aldermen, were thrown from windows and massacred, was in all likelihood planned in advance with the help of the experienced soldier of fortune and passionate Utraquist Jan Žižka of Trocnov. The hurriedly convened assembly of the New Town elected four governors who were to remain in power until a new council was formed, entrusting these with the seal and all powers. After several days, the deputies of the insurgent faction formally bowed down before the king, who then approved the newly elected New Town council. Such upheavals in Prague and in the countryside disturbed King Wenceslas to such a degree that he died of a violent stroke on August 16, 1419. The unrestrained storm of reaction which broke out in Prague's towns on the news of his death announced the imminent revolution.

2 The Hussite Wars in the Years 1420–1434

The interim government after the death of Wenceslas IV was run by a confederacy of lords at whose head stood the widowed Queen Sophie of Bavaria (d. 1428). Sigismund, heir to the throne, was at that time occupied with the defence of the southern Hungarian border against the Turks. He was in no rush to get back to the insurgent country and left the demands – religious and otherwise – of the Utraquist nobles and of the Prague towns unanswered. The leaders of the Hussite pilgrims who gathered towards the end of September 1419 at Křížky near Ládví (northeast of Prague) thus convened another Land Diet at Prague. Some of the Hussites from rural areas used this opportunity to visit the capital city where their preachers clashed with university professors over the next tasks of the movement. Revolutionary calls for the election of their own bishop and perhaps also of their own ruler affrighted the town aldermen to such a degree that they joined the confederacy of Queen Sophie at the beginning of October. The occupation of Prague Castle and part of the Lesser Town by the queen's mercenaries forced the followers of the preacher Želivský at the end of October to occupy the fortress at Vyšehrad under the leadership of Jan Žižka. Small skirmishes heralded war in rural areas also. German miners from Kutná Hora flung Utraquists they had arrested down a shaft; at Živohošť Hussites from Sezimovo Ústí engaged Catholic knights in violent battle. At the beginning of November, there was fighting again in Prague, which the Catholic nobility and the towns of central Bohemia declaimed as its enemy. In these unfavourable conditions, the representatives of the Prague towns sent the royal regiment to Vyšehrad.

Along with Utraquists from western Bohemia with Václav Koranda (d. after 1452) at their head and the disappointed soldier of fortune Žižka, their brethren from southern Bohemia left Prague, though their return journey was blocked by the royal cavalry. Plzeň became the temporary focal point of the radical Hussite campaign, from which prophetic visions spread in all directions, along with excited calls to flee to the five "chosen" towns. Expectations of the end of the world, the advent of the saviour and his reign of a thousand years (chiliasm) grew out of the depressed, uncertain atmosphere of flights, failures and disappointed hopes, which at the turn of 1419 and 1420 paralyzed the Táborite movement in southern and western Bohemia. Chiliastic propaganda was less apparent in the regions of Žatec and Louny. There was not enough time to get through to the Hussites of eastern Bohemia (called Orebites after their mountain of pilgrimage near Třebechovice). Earlier ideas of spiritual victory over the enemy quickly faded as the Táborites had to protect their lives with weapons in their hands at many junctures. In the area of Plzeň, Jan Žižka resisted the attacks of the regional war faction, and also won the first victory at Sudoměř on March 25, 1420 for "God's warriors" although outnumbered by royal forces. This came about after the forced retreat of the determined Hussites of Plzeň who went over to the enemy and thus formed an important base for the Catholic side. Žižka's warriors turned from Sudoměř to the newly founded revolutionary fortress of Hradiště on the mountain of Tábor.

After the departure of the Hussite groups from Sezimovo Ústí to Prague at the end of October 1419, government over this subject town was grasped by the Catholic authorities. At first the expelled radicals awaited the end of the world, announced for the February 14, 1420. When Christ did not come to their aid, they took their fate into their own hands on 21 February and, led by the preachers Petr Hromádka of Jistebnice and Jan of Bydlín, ran the opponents of Utraquism off the castle's battlements. Since the town was hard to defend, they began to build a fortified estate adjacent to the castle of the lords of Ústí, which was on a headland and at the end of March burnt Sezimovo Ústí to the ground. Reports of the foundation of a community of brethren without lords and subjects, in which "mine is yours and yours is mine", soon brought several thousand farmers and artisans from near and far to Hradiště on the mountain of Tábor. The new settlers gave up their provisions and small valuables to a common fund, which was divided by the preachers overlooked by the four elected captains. Apart from the knight Mikuláš of Hus, Jan Žižka again proved himself in the fighting against the surrounding enemies. Led by both these governors most of the Táborite brothers and sisters set out in May for Prague, threatened by the army of the first crusade.

The Roman and Hungarian king, Sigismund appeared in Brno in 1419, where along with the Czech Catholics, several Hussite magnates and representatives of Prague and other towns, the Moravian lords swore allegiance to him. Since the representatives of the Estates of other lands of the Bohemian crown (i.e., the Silesian principalities, and all of Lusatia) followed suit, Hussite Bohemia found itself totally isolated. Sigismund hurried to the Imperial Diet in Wrocław, during which the Papal legation declared a crusade against the Hussite heretics on March 17, 1420. Two days earlier, Sigismund had the Utraquist Jan Krása of the New Town tortured to death as a warning to others; his death roused the Prague councils to the defence of Utraquism and the metropolis. In mid-April Čeněk of Vartenberk officially handed over the royal Castle to Praguers; on 20 April the leading representatives of the Hussite Estates issued a call to arms against the heirs of the throne, and finally at the beginning of May the Orebites of eastern Bohemia appeared in the city. The hopes of Prague fell again when Čeněk, vacillating, gave Prague Castle over to the royal governors and the city's ambassadors returned from Sigismund with unacceptable conditions half way through May. With a request for assistance addressed to governors and radical brethren in the regions of Louny and Žatec, the representatives of the Prague towns decided definitively for revolutionary struggle. Because of its wide social implications, its territorial extent, its protracted nature, the responses it provoked from abroad and its long-term consequences, the Hussite movement, in the spring of 1420, had become one of the first revolutions on the European continent.

The arrival of over three thousand Táborite brothers and sisters intensified the religious purge of Prague and accelerated its preparations for war. The revolutionary groups, at their common diet of May 27, 1420 appointed new town councils, elected supreme governors and declared their common demands, which became the basis for the pan-Hussite program of the four Articles of Prague. The first of these demanded freedom to preach the word of God; the second ordered communion in both kinds for believers regardless of age or state; the third forbade both a life of luxury and secular power to the religious; and fourth and last, demanded the punishment of mortal sins and other iniquities by appropriate revolutionary bodies. Three of the Prague Articles expressed the fundamental principles of the Czech reform school, while the fourth was added by the Táborites, for whom these four articles remained the essentials of their program for years to come.

The fruitless conquering of Prague Castle burdened the defence of the insurgent metropolis, which at the end of June was besieged by a crusading army of about 30,000 men. After some skirmishing, mounted crusaders broke through the fortifications on Vítkov hill on July 14, 1420. The brave resistance of the Táborite garrison led by Captain Žižka with the help of reinforcements from Prague forced the crusaders into retreat and to an extent thus decided the entire failure of the first crusade. Negotiations of the university masters with the Papal nuncio Fernando behind the backs of the radical allies also ended in failure for Sigismund. To cap all these troubles, a fire in one of the siege camps created a panic among disgruntled crusaders. Sigismund had himself hurriedly crowned Bohemian king in St Vitus's Cathedral and at the end of July 1420 along with his crusading forces abandoned an unbowed Prague.

Hardly had this danger passed when the Utraquists of the Old Town and the university masters attempted to grasp definitive power over the country. Although they gained the agreement of Jan Žižka to offer the empty throne to the Polish king Władysław (*Vladislav*) of Jagiellon, in all other matters they met with the determined resistance of the Táborite leaders and their allies in the New Town. Through their attempts at suppression and new attacks on monasteries, the Táborites forced not only the acceptance of twelve severer demands, but also a change of aldermen in the Old Town hall. The balance of power which favoured the radical Hussite front did not last long. After the departure of the Táborites for the battlegrounds of southern Bohemia, the revolutionary councils in the Prague towns held on for only three further months. Their victory over King Sigismund, which the Praguers had achieved with the help of the eastern Bohemian Orebites on November 1, 1420 at the battle at Vyšehrad, foreshadowed the sharp rise of their power in the next three years.

In the mean time, the levelling principles of the Táborite revolutionary faction quickly faded. The necessity of military organization pushed to the fore leaders from the ranks of the lower nobility. Apart from this, lack of provisions forced the Táborites in autumn 1420 to exact subject tributes from surrounding peasants. Dreams of a fair society were replaced by the day-to-day struggle for survival. A range of Táborite preachers and priests found it difficult to compromise on original chiliastic ideas and, oblivious to prevailing conditions, began to declare the beginning of an age of complete freedom of body and mind. Although the unsystematic teaching of the Táborite sects (referred to as the Picards and Adamites) in some articles explicitly demolished the basis of social relations, their utopian visions weakened the internal cohesion and fighting capability of the Táborite brethren. The situation disintegrated at the turn of 1420–1421 when a group of priests gathered about the Moravian preacher Martin Húska denied the sacrament of communion in both kinds. Now the Hussites, as well as the Catholics, had a heretic within their ranks.

The first violent clash of the Picards and the moderate party, with Jan Žižka at its head and the elected elder Táborite priest Mikuláš of Pelhřimov, followed Húska's imprisonment. A minority of two to four hundred Picards refused to submit and moved to the small town beneath the castle at Příběnice. The onset of resistance within his own army forced Žižka to intervene strogly. In the second half of April 1421, with the help of allies, he attacked the settlement at Příběnice and had about fifty of the former brothers and sisters burned as a warning to others. Fragmented groups of sectarians, who put up a good fight, were defeated by Žižka's army in the autumn months. The violent extermination of freethinking Táborites brought about the first serious shift of forces within the Hussite grouping, on whose radical wing the Táborite brotherhood now found itself together with the Orebites and the Prague followers of Jan Želivský.

After the victory at Vyšehrad, the association of fully fledged citizens (what was referred to as the great assembly) of the Prague towns pushed through a range of revolutionary privileges, which expanded the powers of the elected councils. A considerable part of Church property found its way in this manner into the hands of the burghers of the Old Town and other towns. Extensive confiscations of Church farmsteads took place at this time throughout Bohemia. In Catholic territory they took the form of appropriation of monastic and other properties, which King Sigismund had given to his numerous creditors. The powerful position of burgherly Prague as the "head of the kingdom" was consolidated by a massive spring offensive of Hussite armies. Within a few weeks during April and May 1421, Prague had created around it a league of twenty-one royal and other towns. The political weight of the Prague league was soon apparent at the Land Diet in Čáslav in June 1421, which declared the four Articles constitutional law and stripped Sigismund of Luxemburg of his right to the Bohemian throne. Although the twenty-member land government soon fell apart, its composition indicated just how profound the revolutionary intervention was in the representation of the Estates. The lords had to be satisfied with five members and the remaining places were shared between eight members of the lower nobility and seven burghers.

The rise of the conservative Utraquists in the Old Town, who secured the Lithuanian prince, Sigismund Korybut, as a candidate for the Bohemian throne, was a thorn in the side of the New Town party of Jan Želivský. Dissatisfaction with the division of Church property and other privileges became so extreme that New Town radicals deposed the governing council in the summer 1421, joined both towns and appointed its own representatives to the council. At the beginning of August the Prague army, led by Želivský, suffered a severe defeat at Most. The consequences of this for his power base in Prague did not even serve to reduce some of his outgoings to less well-to-do burghers. Thus Želivský, in a further upheaval, gave full power to his loyal governor Jan Hvězda of Vicemilice on October 19. The dictatorship of both men lasted till the beginning of February 1422, when a conciliatory board made up of the representatives of the Hussite leagues supported the Old Town opposition, headed by the influential Master Jakoubek of Stříbro. A month later Jan Želivský, along with nine of his followers, was beheaded at the Old Town hall. News of his death provoked the people of Prague to a storm of destruction, during which the houses of aldermen were destroyed, as well as the masters' residences and the Jewish ghetto.

In the meantime, Hussite Bohemia had repulsed the second crusade: its crushing onslaught was halted in September 1421 on the battlements of the northern Bohemian town of Žatec. When the imperial princes received no support from King Sigismund after an entire month of siege, they withdrew at the beginning of October. Sigismund's delayed army met with a much worse end in January 1422, when the combined Hussite armies, under the supreme command of Jan Žižka, roundly defeated it in a number of battles from Kutná Hora to Německý Brod (today's Havlíčkův Brod). The recently blinded military leader was able to exploit the bellicose mood of his folk army, to whom he adapted both armaments and tactics of defensive battle with surprising strikes from armoured wagons. Žižka's permanent military retinue foreshadowed later field armies of the radical Hussite leagues, whose manoeuvrability and operational procedures would dominate not only the Bohemian crown lands but also neighbouring regions for long years.

The tempestuous situation in the capital city calmed in May 1422 after the acceptance of Sigismund Korybut as the administrator of Prague and its league. Although Captain Žižka recognized the Lithuanian prince, he eyed with distrust his suspicious links with representatives of the Utraquist nobility. Well before Korybut's recall to Poland at the end of 1423, he recognized the danger which threatened the radical Hussite leagues in the premature peace with King Sigismund, and tried with all his force to prevent it. Since he could not depend on the Táborite league because of its internal fragmentation, Žižka transferred his base to eastern Bohemia in spring 1423. The towns of Domažlice, Klatovy and Sušice, along with several Táborite governors and allies, gradually joined the new brotherhood. After a brief term as governor in Tábor, Jan Hvězda of Vicemilice became the adjutant of the blind military leader, and was responsible for the defeat of the Praguers at Malešov on June 7, 1424. Žižka prepared for an attack on Prague. However half way through September he was persuaded to close an armistice on what is called the Hospital Field (*Špitálské pole*, in today's Karlín, a suburb of Prague), which was followed by the first agreements with the Catholic side in Zdice. Žižka did not wait for their result, but made for Moravia with his army. However he died on October 11, 1424 at Přibyslav.

The expedition to Moravia was intended to strengthen the Utraquist nobility there, which after the transfer of the margraviate to the Habsburg duke, Albrecht, on March 5, 1423, was no longer bound in allegiance to his father-in-law Sigismund of Luxemburg. An attempt of local proportions to establish a Moravian Tábor in Nedakonice at the turn of 1420–1421 soon foundered. However radical Hussitism in some south Moravian areas ardently held out against Sigismund and Albrecht's soldiery until the time of the permanent Táborite garrisons in Ivančice, Třebíč, Moravský Krumlov and Břeclav. These garrisons closely co-operated with the Moravian Hussites, especially the lords of Pernštejn and Lipá. Hussite lords from Tovačov, Boskovice and Kravaře took control over most of central and north-eastern Moravia, where in the second half of the 1420s the Orebites frequently operated (after Žižka's death they were referred to as Orphans).

The new rise to power of Tábor accelerated its transformation into an autonomous municipality in which the governors of the domestic armies had decisive influence. Due to the work of Jan Hvězda of Vicemilice, not only was the Tábor league once again unified after the death of Žižka, but it was also temporarily joined with the Orebite-Orphan brethren. In a large offensive in spring and summer 1425 the army of this radical union occupied a number of towns of the Prague league, at whose head stood Sigismund Korybut. After Hvězda died of his wounds in October 1425, his successor, Bohuslav of Švamberk, one of the two barons among the Táborite captains, died a month later on his raid on Austria. The death of two advocates of unificatory policy foreshadowed a new crisis in the relations between the individual elements of the radical grouping. The Písek region created its own league, and separatist forces strengthened in eastern Bohemia. The supreme commanders of the Orphans came and went in quick succession; of their religious administrators Ambrož of Hradec and Prokůpek (Little Prokop) excelled. The danger of a new invasion of crusaders brought the Hussite party together again. In a victorious battle over the army of Meissen in June 1426 at Ústí nad Labem, the religious administrator of the Táborite field army, Prokop Holý (the Bald, also known as Prokop the Great) proved his leadership abilities.

Mobile troops were detached because of the necessity of military operations over the whole territory of the Bohemian crown lands. While the radical leagues were dependent both economically and militarily on the towns, the field armies provided them with a reaction force that could be employed against domestic and foreign enemies. The standing armies, because of their manoeuvrability and fighting capability, were superior to both the urban home guard and the mercenary corps of the Catholic side. On the other hand, it required a constant supply of provisions and other services. For this reason the field armies, with increasing frequency, undertook raids on adjacent countries from which they almost always returned with much plunder. Temporary or permanent garrisons of field forces in Moravia, Silesia and even Slovakia were at most a day's march from each other, which facilitated surprising military operations of the radical leagues. With the exception of Slovakia, where the Czech reform movement already had some scattered followers, the raids of the Hussite armies – what were referred to as "magnificent rides" – did not encounter favourable responses abroad.

After the crushing onslaught of the radical armies in the second half of the 1420s, Prague, controlled by Korybut, was able to defend only Kolín, Chrudim and Mělník of the towns in its league. The détente of the prince with the Catholic side as well as a sharp attack of the conservative masters on some principles of Hussite teaching, provoked the rising of the two disgruntled Prague towns on April 17, 1427. A number of university masters had to go into exile. Korybut was arrested and imprisoned in the countryside for a long time. He never returned to Prague and temporarily established himself, surprisingly, with the Táborite garrisons in Silesia. Attempts to unify the spiritual and secular administration soon clashed with the conflicting interests (economic and other kinds) of the Prague towns. The New Town enforced its demands with the help of the Orphan league, which it joined in 1429. In contrast, the autonomous administration of the Old Town looked to Prokop's bloc for help, co-operating with it occasionally. The central role of Prague in this period was taken over temporarily by Kutná Hora as the combined seat of the leaders and offices of the field armies.

The dilatory approach of King Sigismund in his battles with the Hussite heretics provoked dissatisfaction both in the Papal See and the Empire. The organization of further military expeditions was thus taken up by several electors at the Imperial Diet of April 1427. They fared no better, however, since their crusading corps, after failing to take the western Bohemian town of Stříbro, fled from Tachov without offering any resistance to the unified Hussite armies. The Hussites crowned their military success by taking Tachov in August 1427. The defeat of the third crusade accelerated the change in military strategy of the field armies, which shifted from defence of their own territory to permanent offensive on the territory of the enemy. Attempts at a peaceful solution of the Czech question met with the stiff resistance of Papal diplomacy, which also froze the negotiations of King Sigismund with a mission from the Hussite leagues in Bratislava in April 1429.

Only with the ensuing great expeditions to all the surrounding countries did the representatives of the Catholic world acknowledge the superiority of Hussite weapons. After raids on Slovakia, Silesia, Upper and Lower Lusatia and Austria, the combined armies of

FRANTIŠEK ŠMAHEL

the Hussite leagues penetrated to Franconia through Meissen in December 1429, from which it returned laden with plunder in February of the following year. Soon further expeditions were made to Slovakia and Silesia. The Catholic world tried once more to stop the Hussite offensive. After declaring the fourth crusade at the Imperial Diet in Nuremberg in March 1431, responsibility for war preparations was taken by the Brandenburg elector Frederick of Hohenzollern. At the end of July, the crusaders from the west marched on Tachov, while the northern corps from Meissen crossed the border with a delay of some days. The Hussite armies set out to engage the enemy on August 12 and after two days of forced march reached Domažlice. The crusaders did not stay to meet them, and fled in chaos on August 14, 1431.

A new ecumenical council, which shortly before had convened in Basel, invited a mission of Czech Hussites in October 1431. In February 1432, a Bohemian diet accepted the invitation and sent its representatives to Cheb for preparatory negotiations with the council's messengers. Here in May of the same year, the Hussites enjoyed their greatest success in their struggle of many years with the representatives of the Roman Church when they established God's law as the deciding authority in the dispute over the four Articles, and the practice of the early Church along with the corresponding teaching of the Church fathers (what was referred to as the Cheb Judgement). The public hearing of the Hussite mission, with Prokop Holý at its head, took place in Basel from the second half of January to the beginning of April 1433. Differences between the defendants and opponents of the Hussite articles were not overcome, and so both sides agreed to further negotiations in Prague.

The restriction of military operations brought about by partial peace agreements raised the question of how the field armies would be further employed. For this reason in summer 1433 the Hussite military leaders besieged Plzeň; by taking the town they wished to force both the members of the council and King Sigismund to greater compliance. The council however did not remain idle and by means of its skilful diplomats set breakdown and betrayal working through Bohemia. With the heavy defeat of a Táborite provisioning expedition to Bavaria old disagreements between the captains resurfaced. The removal of Prokop Holý from his position of supreme commander soon proved to be a gross error, since his successors were not quick enough to spot the crisis signs in the fields of war and politics. This was true even of Captain Jan Čapek of Sány, who together with Orphans' field army reached Plzeň after their return from a great expedition to the Baltic coast at the end of September or beginning of October.

Failure to take Plzeň, increasing problems with provisions, betrayals by bribed captains and disgruntlement across the social spectrum with the rule of the radical brethren all contributed to the unification of the opposition of the Catholic and Utraquist nobility. When the armies of the "noble" units, assisted by allies from the Old Town, took control over Prague's New Town on May 6, 1434, the field armies had to give up any notion of further siege of Plzeň, and secure the urban areas that it depended on to the rear. Not even the return of Prokop Holý to the head of the Táborite bloc could prevent the coming defeat of the field armies. When all attempts at peace collapsed, a decisive battle took place at

Lipany on May 30, 1434, in which, along with many other Táborites and Orphans, Prokop Holý was killed. While the fall of the radical brethren brought to a close the revolutionary chapter of Hussite history, it was by no means the defeat of Hussite Bohemia.

3 The Era of Restoration and Interregnums after Lipany (1434–1452)

The unity of the victors immediately collapsed after the return from the battleground of Lipany. Disputes on religious points and other matters between the temporary allies were so serious that they would be resolved only much later. Leaders of the weakened radical brethren attempted to defend their position at the Land Diet. However they came up against the interests of the Utraquist nobility and the Old Town league. The importance of the Land Diets now grew, since their prime aim was to reach an agreement satisfactory to both sides at the council in Basel and with King Sigismund. While the theologians of the council, with reservation, only accepted communion in both kinds for the laity, the aging Sigismund was better disposed to the demands of the diet, as he wanted the Bohemian throne as soon as possible.

The dramatic decline in the power of the radical leagues after the crushing defeat of their field armies at Lipany caused another profound shift in the make-up of the Hussite fraternity. The moderate ground held by Prague, which attracted many victors from Lipany, now became the central exponent of the Czech reformation in the eyes of the council. Most of the participants in the Land Diets comported themselves consistently and in defending the demands of the Estates they did not forget the religious freedoms of the four Articles. To a degree recognition of communion in both kinds for Bohemia and Moravia included the free profession of God's word in the moderate interpretation of Prague Hussite teaching. The election of Jan Rokycana (d. 1471) as Prague archbishop at the Diet of October 1435 was intended to secure power for the Hussite majority in the Prague diocese before Sigismund was received as king. However for the representatives of the council acknowledging Rokycana was just as unacceptable as agreeing with the appropriation of ecclesiastical property in the spirit of the third Hussite article. Only in the matter of the punishment of mortal sins was there no dispute, since the edge of this Táborite article had already been blunted earlier.

Massive transfer of land holdings was one of the most profound long-term consequences of revolutionary Hussitism. The Catholic Church suffered most in this respect, losing roughly four fifths of its farmsteads in Bohemia. The losses of the Church in Moravia were not so great. Not even those parts of the Catholic nobility which had confiscated monastic and other properties claiming that they wished to protect them had any interest in a return to the *status quo ante*. The royal coffers suffered great losses during the period of war as the king's property, including castles and financial revenues, almost faded away. The Bohemian nobility could not have been happier. As well as a poor Church it had a poor king, bound by conditions regarding succession. The combined interests of the Bohemian nobility had become an obstacle to attempts by the council and King Sigismund of total restoration of the pre-Hussite state of affairs. On the other hand, religious differences arising from the consequences of the recent bloody past, as well as the newly forming power blocs, further divided the nobility and other social classes.

The group of radical preachers and captains about Jan Roháč of Dubá did not intend to put up with the state of affairs after Lipany, and Roháč succeeded in founding a Unity of Táborite and Orphan towns. The interim government, led by the Land administrator Aleš of Vřešťov, took the military initiative away from this war party within several months. While Captain Roháč continued his armed resistance against Sigismund up to his execution in September 1437, the new leader of the remaining Táborite league, Bedřich of Strážnice (d. 1459) gave priority to advantageous treaties with the heir to the throne. In return for a promise of obedience, Tábor gained from Sigismund enlarged privileges of a royal town and lands to the extent of a middling to large domain. With the exception of the Old Town and Louny, the other Hussite towns emerged from the revolution without any large material gains. In contrast, captains and soldiers of fortune from the lower nobility multiplied their properties. These people now wished to insure their rise with increased influence over political life in the country.

Agreements were reached with the Táborites after the ceremonial acceptance of Sigismund of Luxemburg as Bohemian king in the square at Jihlava on August 14, 1436. Although Sigismund confirmed most of the demands of the Czech Estates concerning succession, along with political privileges and religious agreements with the council of Basel (the *Compactata*, or Compacts of Basel), soon after his arrival in Prague he began to rule without regard for his previous promises. Utraquist fears increased with king's negative stance towards Archbishop Rokycana, who decided to flee to the safety of the Hussite fortresses in eastern Bohemia half way through 1437. Added to the complaints of the Utraquist party were the open expressions of disobedience to the ruler from the end of September 1437, whose hurried return from Bohemia to Hungary somewhat resembled flight from a heretical land. Sigismund's death on December 9, 1437 ended the reign of the Luxemburg dynasty in the Bohemian crown lands.

The election of Sigismund's son-in-law, Albrecht II of Habsburg (r. 1437–1439), as Bohemian king was pushed through by the Diet of December 1437 by the Catholic party with the help of the Prague Utraquist group around the Supreme Burgrave Menhart of Hradec. Apart from this duplicitous lord, the Catholic magnate Oldřich of Rožmberk was one of the most important figures in Czech politics. The Utraquist nobility of eastern Bohemia, with Hynek Ptáček of Pirkštejn at its head, rejected the December election and after brief hesitation, together with the Táborite city league, decided to support the succession of Prince Kazimierz, the brother of the Polish king Władysław. The Polish court sent a smaller war party to Bohemia to support Kazimierz's candidacy, but it could not counter Albrecht's more powerful army. The struggle for the throne resulted in war, and this took place in August 1438 near Tábor. The fort held back the huge numbers of the enemy, but the Austrian party succeeded in destroying the Polish candidacy.

The unexpected death of King Albrecht II in October 1439 caught the country at a time when none of the power groupings were able to achieve their goals. A way out of the emergency was found in the Diet of January 1440 in what was referred to as the "Epistle of Peace", by which the nobility and towns of both persuasions enjoined to keep the peace and the present state of affairs in the country until the next ruler was elected. In Moravia, the "territorial peace" (*landfrýd*) played a similar role from 1440. The central government of the land continued to be substituted by the region groupings with elected captains at their heads. Oldřich of Rožmberk remained the head of the Catholic side, and among the Utraquists the governor of four of the eastern Bohemian regions, Ptáček of Pirkštejn, had the deciding word. The remaining towns of the Táborite league, with their bellicose policies, found themselves in total isolation. George of Poděbrady (*Jiří z Poděbrad*), who after the death of Ptáček of Pirkštejn, stood at the head of the eastern Bohemian regions, followed with distrust events in the capital, where the governing group of Menhart of Hradec was easing the way for gradual reconversion. On the night of September 3, 1448, George of Poděbrady attacked Prague and took control there, thus bringing an end to the division of power.

The rise of George of Poděbrady to power on the stage of a Bohemia rent by religious difference marked the entry of a deliberating yet determined statesman of noble origin, who resolutely continued in Ptáček's policies of unifying the Utraquists with Jan Rokycana at their head. The counterweight to the Poděbrady side became in February 1449 what was referred to as the Catholic league of Strakonice, and Oldřich of Rožmberk was able to bring the majority of the nobility from southern and western Bohemia to this side. George of Poděbrady faced them successfully on both the fields of war and politics, and with the assistance of Roman King Frederick III (r. 1440–1493) gained the office of Land Regent for a period of two years at the Bohemian Diet of April 1452. While the lords of Rožmberk vainly searched in Austria for support for the domestic opposition, military corps of the Land Administrator forced the representatives of rebellious Tábor, members of the Strakonice league and even the lords of the *landfrýd* of Plzeň into obedience during September. However with the acceptance of Albrecht's son, Ladislav Posthumous (who was not yet of age), as Bohemian king and his coronation in October 1453, the fourteen-year interregnum was at an end.

4 Kingdom of Two Peoples

The accession of the Catholic ruler promised the consolidation of the loose bonds between the Bohemian kingdom and the other crownlands. The Moravian Utraquists had ensured their religious freedoms earlier in the middle of the 1430s when they accepted Albrecht of Habsburg as their margrave with the condition that the *Compactata* of Basel would remain in force. After Albrecht's death, the Hussite Jan Tovačovský of Cimburk (d. 1464) became Land Governor. The pacification of domestic affairs in Moravia was helped by the good relations of the provinces with the Bishop of Olomouc, as well as regular diets, in which representatives of the royal towns participated from 1440. Such an advanced organization of the Estates was also to be found in both Lusatias, while fully fledged participation at the Silesian central Diet was possible only for princes. After the recognition of Ladislav Posthumous in Lusatia and Silesia, the land administrator appointed members of Czech Catholic noble families as royal officers in the king's name, thus binding them to him in personal obligation.

Within just a few years, the Land Regent, George of Poděbrady, succeeded in revising the extent of appropriations of royal property, ensuring the security of trade routes, easing the tension between religious parties and last but not least strengthening his personal power. This was to his advantage when Ladislav Posthumous died in November 1457 soon after coming of age. Although a range of important rulers vied for the throne which had the first vote in the college of imperial electors, the Bohemian Diet, with the agreement of the prominent Catholic lords, elected George of Poděbrady king on March 2, 1458 (r. 1458–1471). The struggle to acknowledge the royal title in adjacent lands and further abroad at first went well for George. However as soon as it became apparent that he would continue to defend the *Compactata* as the basis of co-existence of "two peoples", the Papal Curia decided to use all means at its disposal against him. The unilateral revocation of the *Compactata* of Basel by Pope Pius II, which took place in March 1462 in the presence of the Czech mission to Rome, flung the country back into religious war and revived the dispute over the spiritual principles of the Czech reformation.

The main conduit between the scholarly reformers and their followers among the people, most of whom had no formal education, were the preachers. Even written propaganda, whether programmatic declarations, manifestoes, verse compositions, collections of sermons (postils), or even satires and polemics – all were now accommodated to the simplicity and comprehensibility of the spoken word. Hymns were made more accessible to commoners, along with marching songs and simple chants which either conveyed religious teaching, braced them for battle with the enemy (i.e., "All Ye Warriors of God", *Ktož jsú boží bojovníci*) or mocked opponents and their weaknesses. The language of scholarly exchange, refutation and manifestoes addressed to foreign audiences remained in Latin, which Vavřinec of Březová favoured for his Hussite chronicle. Apart from this masterwork of contemporary history writing, many valuable records, of various length and written in Czech, concerning events from the beginning of Wenceslas IV's government to the 1520s (entitled Old Czech Annals; *Staré letopisy české*) were preserved. The omnipresent force of intellectual considerations was apparent not only in the refusal of the external forms of religious rituals, but also in the principled opposition to overly ornate cathedrals and devotional icons or statues of saints. The greatest and often irreparable losses resulting from Hussite iconoclasm were suffered by Church architecture. As the vehemence of purging reform gradually fell off, interest in artworks and greater ornamentation of functional objects began to resurface among the Utraquists. Progress in all areas of artistic endeavour had in the mean time come to a standstill, with the exception of book illustration in manuscripts with Biblical texts and topical religious themes (Codex of Jena; *Jenský kodex*).

The original reform demands had lost their appeal during the long years of war, although disputes over them between the Prague masters and their Táborite opponents continued to the 1450s. The desire for deeper religious experience in the era after Lipany brought together small groups of dissatisfied Utraquists from all parts of Bohemia and Moravia. A number of them were the former pupils or followers of the southern Bohemian governor Petr Chelčický (d. by 1460). Petr remained loyal to the principles of spiritual battle from the period of the Hussite pilgrimages to the mountains and, oblivious to the changed circumstances, spoke out sharply against all expressions of violence. Chelčický entered the history of European thought with his refusal of Church scholastic teaching about the triple division of society, i.e., the unchanging hierarchy of rulers, priests and those who provision them. Archbishop Rokycana at first supported the retinue of his followers, led by Brother Řehoř, and he was joined in this by George of Poděbrady, who allowed its members to settle in the village of Kunvald at the edge of the Orlice mountains in 1457. However as soon as the Kunvald brethren and their successors expressed their dissatisfaction with the Utraquist church by calling for an independent religious corps, Rokycana together with King George hunted them down as heretics. Beginning in 1467, the brethren began to ordain their own priests. Their Unity of Brethren, unlike other Hussite groups, completely broke from the Roman Church and became the first independent church of the European reformation.

The Catholic Church was in a state of profound disintegration after the Hussite wars. The higher religious had forfeited their political influence for two centuries, the archbishopric in Prague remained empty to 1561, the bishopric in the eastern Bohemian town of Litomyšl disappeared completely, most of the monasteries were razed or used for secular purposes. The situation could not have been more different in Moravia, where along with the bishopric in Olomouc most of the monasteries and convents survived. Religious dignitaries had nothing to live on when they returned to Prague from their years-long emigration since Church properties had for the most part dwindled away. A lack of priests on both sides resulted in a considerable number of unstaffed rural parishes. One of the consequences of religious division of the country was the development of regional cultural centres. In western Bohemia, Plzeň was one example of this; the town became the seat of Catholic administrative offices (i.e., the consistory) for a period; while in the south České Budějovice and Český Krumlov played a similar role. Similarly in the Moravian Catholic towns, internal relations were almost the same as they were before the Hussite period, and this was why the repair or completion of ecclesiastical buildings began earlier than in Utraquist territory.

After Sigismund's accession to the Bohemian throne, the Prague university was open again to Catholics. The arrival of a considerable number of foreign students in the 1440s improved the level of instruction and facilitated the re-affirmation of university privileges by the Papal See. Although the conquest of Prague by George of Poděbrady in September 1448 prematurely ended the sojourn of foreign students, indigenous Catholics soon returned to the university. Small squabbles between the university Utraquists and the Catholics escalated beyond tolerable proportions when the dissenters among his students sharply opposed Archbishop Rokycana at the end of the 1450s and the beginning of the next decade.

One of these was Hilarius of Litoměřice, author of belligerent polemics and later one of the supreme administrators of the Catholic consistory. The king's intervention in university matters led to the introduction of a mandatory Utraquist oath which closed the university to Catholics. Developments in the university reflected the heightened religious tension in the land, which was threatened with the renewal of Utraquist war after the revocation of the *Compactata*.

The first phase of the clash with the Papacy took place on the stage of foreign policy. In 1462, George succeeded in winning Frederick III over to his side, as well as reaching an agreement of amity with the Polish king, Kazimierz. Pressed on by his foreign advisors, George supported plans to reform the imperial executive and the mustering of expeditions against the Turks; the aim of these efforts was to turn attention away from the question of the Czech heresy to matters of a more serious kind. This intention was pursued also in the founding of an international peace league of European rulers, which through its mission and permanent parliament foreshadowed the United Nations. After preparatory negotiations in the Polish and Hungarian courts, George's mission presented a plan for a Peace Union in summer 1464 to the French king, Louis XI. Papal diplomacy soon stymied this initiative, but the Czech mission did return with an agreement of friendship with France. George would also favour the peaceful settlement of war disputes and other matters later when confronting enemies both at home and abroad. He tried to gain the support of the Moravian Estates in January 1464 by raising Moravia to the same legel status as Bohemia, revoking its previous status as fief, while at the same time asserting the "indivisibility" of both countries.

The repeated summons of King George to the Papal judicial court emboldened the Czech Catholic lords to oppose him openly when they founded an auxiliary league on Zelená Hora in 1465. At the head of the rebels from southern and western Bohemia stood George's former ally Zdeněk of Šternberk, now governor of the Zelená Hora group. The situation escalated at the end of 1466 with the declaration of the interdict upon the Bohemian king and his family. Affirming Zdeněk of Šternberk as governor of the Zelená Hora league, Pope Paul II issued a call to arms against the heretic on the throne in March of the following year. After a vain attempt to broker peace, George declared war on the rebellious lords and within several months had taken control of several of their seats. The League of Zelená Hora in contrast brought to its side the large Moravian towns, Plzeň in western Bohemia and several Catholic courtiers who had heretofore remained loyal to the king. In the adjacent countries George had mixed results; however overall he remained in control of the situation.

George of Poděbrady encountered greater difficulties when the Hungarian king Mátyás Corvinus took command of the anti-Hussite crusade with a declaration of war in March 1468. In the following months, George lost a considerable part of Moravia and several fortresses in adjacent countries. Events turned in his favour only at the beginning of 1469 at Vilémov when Mátyás was able to stave off a crushing defeat only by making peace. George released his opponent on parole and also in return for mediating an agreement with the Papal See promised to support his candidacy for the imperial throne. Mátyás did not keep his promise, and when the Zelená Hora leaders offered him the Bohemian crown, and he was elected

Bohemian ruler in May 1469 in Olomouc. The kingdom of two peoples now had two kings. Renewed fighting brought mixed results and setbacks for both sides until George's death on March 22, 1471.

Czech Hussitism foreshadowed the European Reformation by a century. In attempting to correct both Church and society, the movement remained isolated and, in its defensive activity against all opponents, lost its messianic energy. The changes which the Hussite period brought were of a epochal character. After decades of brutal wars and internal disputes, the Bohemian crown lands became one of the few islands of religious toleration in a continent racked by strife over spiritual and ecclesiastical issues. Living conditions of commoners in the towns and villages were not improved by Hussitism, but neither did they deteriorate. The Prague towns, as well as the Táborites and Orphans of the military republic, proved themselves capable of autonomy, only however within their own leagues. In a number of Hussite towns the Czech nationality had become stronger, while in contrast the Catholic towns of Moravia still had a German majority in their councils and communities.

The impoverishment of the Church enriched the nobles above all. While the nobility alone competed for power with the ruler, the post-Lipany monarchy already had two fully complete Estates of the higher and lower aristocracy, and a third was now preparing to enter the political stage. The combined rise of the nobility after the religious peace of 1485 forced the royal towns of both persuasions, led by Prague, to join in their common defence. It was the next era, rather than Hussitism, that saw the birth of the urban Estate in the full sense of the word. The shift to a monarchy of Estates was accelerated by the death of King Mátyás in 1490 and the election of Vladislav II of Jagiellon to the Hungarian throne.

Bibliography

BAUM, Wilhelm: *Kaiser Sigismund. Hus, Konstanz und Türkenkriege*, Graz–Wien–Köln 1993.

BETTS, Regainald Robert: *Essays in Czech History*, London 1969.

BREDEKAMPF, Horst: *Kunst als Medium sozialer Konflikte. Bilderkämpfe von der Spätantike bis zur Hussitenrevolution*, Frankfurt am Main 1975.

BRETHOLZ, Berthold: *Die Übergabe Mährens an Herzog Albrecht V. von Österreich im Jahre 1423* (Archiv für österreichische Geschichte 80, 2), Wien 1893.

GRAUS, František: *The Crisis of the Middle Ages and the Hussites*, in: S. E. Ozment (ed.), The Reformation in medieval Perspectives, Chicago 1975, pp. 77–103.

GRAUS, František: *Pest – Geißler – Judenmorde. Das 14. Jahrhundert als Krisenzeit*, Göttingen 1987, 2nd edition 1988.

KALIVODA, Robert: *Revolution und Ideologie. Der Hussitismus*, Köln–Wien 1976.

LAMBERT, Malcolm: *Medieval Heresy. Popular Movement from the Gregorian Reform to the Reformation*, Oxford, 3rd edition 2002.

MOLNÁR, Amedeo: *Réformation et Révolution. Le cas du senior taborite Nicolas Biskupec de Pelhřimov*, Communio viatorum 13, 1970, pp. 137–153.

MOLNÁR, Amedeo: *Jean Hus, témoin de la vérité*, Paris 1978.

MOLNÁR, Amedeo: *I Taboriti. Avanguardia della rivoluzione ussita*, Torino 1986.

NECHUTOVÁ, Jana: *Matěj of Janov and his Work Regulae Veteris et Novi Testamenti*, The Bohemian Reformation 2, 1998, pp. 15–24.

PALACKÝ, František: *Geschichte von Böhmen* II/2–IV/2, Prag 1842–1860.

FRANTIŠEK ŠMAHEL

PATSCHOVSKY, Alexander – ŠMAHEL, František (eds.): *Eschatologie und Hussitismus*, Praha 1996.
POLÍVKA, Miroslav: *The Bohemian Lesser Nobility at the Turn of the 14th and 15th Century*, Historica 25, 1985, pp. 121–175.
ŠMAHEL, František: *The Idea of the "Nation" in Hussite Bohemia*, Historica 16, 1969, pp. 143–247; 17, 1969, pp. 97–197.
ŠMAHEL, František (ed.): *Häresie und vorzeitige Reformation im Spätmittelalter* (Schriften des Historischen Kollegs, Kolloquien 39), München 1998.
ŠMAHEL, František: *Die Hussitische Revolution*, I–III (MGH Schriften 43, 1–3), Hannover 2002.
WERNER, Ernst: *Jan Hus. Welt und Umwelt eines Prager Frühreformators* (Forschungen zur mittelalterlichen Geschichte 34), Weimar 1991.
ZEMAN, Jarold K.: *The Hussite Movement and the Reformation in Bohemia, Moravia and Slovakia (1350–1650).* A Bibliographical Study Guide, Ann Arbor 1977.

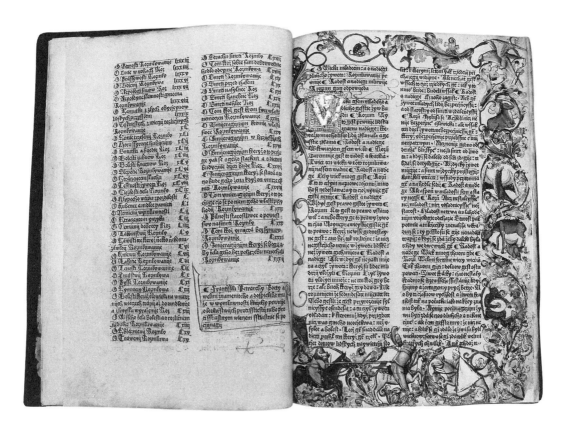

Czech translation of Petrarch's *De remediis utriusque fortunae* (Remedies Against Luck and Bad Luck), one of the oldest translations of works by Italian humanists into Czech. It was translated by Řehoř Hrubý of Jelení, printed in 1501.

1 The Czech-Hungarian Personal Union

The death of George of Poděbrady (*Jiří z Poděbrad*) opened the way for a new dynasty on the Bohemian throne. During the half-century of Jagiellon rule Czech and European society more generally underwent a deep transformation. The Bohemian crown lands once again fully integrated into the community of Western Christianity from which, to a degree, it had been divided by severe religious conflicts. At the same time European civilization was no longer closed within its old borders. Courageous Portuguese voyages around Africa to India and to the countries of the Far East, like the Spanish expeditions to American shores, definitively broke what had heretofore been the isolation of the old continent and led to the confrontation of two completely distinct civilizations. With the regeneration of economically advanced western European countries as colonial powers the old balance of political and economic power in Europe shifted and its hub was transferred from the Mediterranean to the Atlantic shores, as the other states could not keep up.

News of the discoveries that dislodged medieval views of the world were attentively followed in the Bohemian crown lands, but from the Czech viewpoint a different encounter with a closer, non-Christian country was of greater significance. The Ottoman Empire, which took control of Constantinople in 1453, quickly penetrated through the Balkans to the Danube Basin, and this pressure influenced affairs in Central Europe. Awareness of the proximity of the Turkish danger helped ease the disputes between Rome and the Czech Hussites.

Not long after the death of George of Poděbrady the Land Diet assembled in Kutná Hora to elect a new king. In the two foreign candidacies for the Bohemian throne the clashing ambitions of two great Central European rulers were manifest. Although the Hungarian king Mátyás had the support of the aristocracy and already governed a large part of Moravia, Silesia and Lusatia, he was unacceptable to a crucial part of the Bohemian Estates because of his involvement in the fight against Czech Utraquism. Success was vouchsafed in this case to the more tactical strategies of the Polish Jagiellons, who had had their eye on the Bohemian throne for a long time. The Polish king Kazimierz IV exploited the weakened position of George of Poděbrady by persuading the Bohemian king shortly before his death to forego any ambition to found his own dynasty, as well as to agree to the subsequent accession of the Jagiellons to the Bohemian throne. The Bohemian Estates preferred this arrangement and on May 27, 1471 they elected Kazimierz's son Vladislav. Mátyás and his followers refused to recognize the result of the election and the very next day in Jihlava the Papal Nuncio declared Mátyás Bohemian king.

Vladislav, fifteen-years of age on his accession to the throne, accepted the new electoral conditions of the Bohemian Estates and enjoined that he would respect the wide-ranging political freedoms they enjoyed, including the *Compactata*. With his promise not to infringe the rights of either of the two main religious parties in Bohemia, along with his military engagement with Mátyás, he provoked an enraged reaction from the Papal Curia, which declared the young king a heretic.

Although the military conflict of the two quarrelling sides continued, it exhausted both and its initial intensity waned. It was played out for the most part on Bohemian crown lands, especially in Silesia. Not even the military encounters of 1474, in which the Polish army also participated, brought a decisive blow. Vladislav still had the upper hand in his own Bohemia and Mátyás in the other lands. Diplomatic negotiations went on for many years and eventually resulted in a compromise called the Peace of Olomouc in 1478. The two rulers retained the title of Bohemian king. Vladislav became the lord of the Bohemian kingdom while Mátyás gained the neighbouring lands (Moravia, Silesia and both Lusatias). In the case of Mátyás's death, these four Bohemian crown lands could be purchased for the price of 400,000 Hungarian florins and once again be joined with the Bohemian kingdom under a single ruler.

The consequences of the long Czech-Hungarian war were soon manifest on the international scene. The new state of play was exploited by Mátyás above all, whom the Peace of Olomouc allowed to engage in ambitious policies, mainly against the Habsburgs. Vladislav was less successful: it was not until 1487 that the Pope lifted his interdict and recognized him as Bohemian king. Not long after this he was accepted among the imperial electors.

After the unexpected death of Mátyás on April 6, 1490, the Hungarian Estates elected Vladislav as their king. The first job of the new ruler was to wage war with the failed candidates. Although the peace agreements which he reached with his younger brother Jan Albrecht and the King of the Romans Maximilian I of Habsburg, ensured him the Hungarian crown, they also necessitated that he resign any hope of creating a great Polish-Czech-Hungarian confederation under the government of a Jagiellon ruler; moreover the agreements increased the political influence of the Habsburgs in that area of Europe.

The Czech-Hungarian personal union was an extensive state formation which had already appeared on the political stage of the 15th century on several occasions. This time however its creation entailed a significant decline in the international authority of the Czech state. The Hungarian kingdom, greater in extent and population than the Bohemian crown lands, occupied the first position in the entire confederation. The king moved his seat to Buda and spent most of his time in Hungary, where he addressed himself for the most part to Hungarian matters. The Jagiellon rulers seldom visited the Bohemian crown lands.

Vladislav came to Prague on only three occasions after 1490, and his son Louis (*Ludvík*) only once during his decade-long governance. The occasional delegations sent from the Bohemian crown lands along with the presence of some Czech administrators were not sufficient to balance the much greater influence of the Hungarian nobility and prelates on the weak rulers. Hungarian advisors influenced the king's decisions in Czech matters also. Internally fragmented according to their religious and provincial affiliations, the divided Estates of the Bohemian crown lands were not capable of holding their own against the stronger and more concerted Hungarian Estates in the jockeying for influence over the ruler, especially when their position was weakened by the vague constitutional standing of the neighbouring lands.

The disputed standing of Moravia, Silesia and both Lusatias was the consequence of the Czech-Hungarian wars of 1468–1478 and the Peace of Olomouc. From the viewpoint of the Bohemian Estates, these countries were part of the Bohemian crown, while the Hungarian side understood them to be the undischarged lien owing to Hungary. On his accession to the Hungarian throne, Vladislav had to promise the Hungarian Estates that Moravia, Silesia and the Lusatias would remain subject to the Hungarian crown until the agreed sum was paid. Against this the Bohemian Estates claimed, also with reference to the Peace of Olomouc, that this directive did not apply in the case where all the lands of the Bohemian and Hungarian crowns were under a single ruler. In their view, Moravia, Silesia and the Lusatias automatically returned to the lands of the Bohemian crown as soon as Vladislav became Hungarian king. The vacillating standpoints of the two Jagiellon rulers, now agreeing with one side and now the other, did not help resolve the problem.

The Estates were largely successful in winning for themselves a lot of political autonomy and in loosening their bond with the Bohemian kingdom, and this contributed to the ambiguous constitutional standing of the neighbouring countries. In the Jagiellon period, the old system of the Czech state, based on the fief principle, disintegrated even further. From the 15th century a new interpretation was established which understood the Bohemian crown as a set of equal states with a common ruler at their head. Although the Bohemian Estates continued to assert that their position was superior to the Estates of neighbouring countries, they ran up against ever stronger resistance. Weakening of the bonds between the crownlands accelerated the long-term transformation of the Czech state. The drift towards the integration of Bohemia and Moravia on the one hand, and Silesia and both Lusatias on the other, gathered momentum. The national make-up of these lands played no small role in this tendency. At the end of the 15th century, Czech became the first official language in the supreme Estates institutions of Bohemia and Moravia. In Silesia and the Lusatias – in contrast with the expansion of Czech in the period – German became more prevalent.

The strong Estates and their constant jockeying, together with the weakening of the ruler's power – these were the main causes of the inability of the Czech-Hungarian personal union to assert itself more strongly on the international political stage. Czech-Hungarian rulers from the House of Jagiellon, in many of their disputes and aims, remained isolated from the Polish branch of the family, drawn away as they were by Habsburg politics. The Viennese congress of 1515 confirmed the unrelenting ambition of the Habsburg dynasty to anchor itself firmly in both Central European kingdoms, leading to marital alliances between both ruling lines. In 1521, the agreement was fulfilled by the marriages of the Czech and Hungarian king Louis with Maria of Habsburg and the Austrian Archduke Ferdinand with Anna of Jagiellon.

Neither did the international prestige of the Czech-Hungarian confederation increase during the decade-long rule of Vladislav's son and successor Louis (r. 1516–1526). Louis ascended to both royal thrones at the age of ten, and the nobility openly usurped supreme power for itself when he was not yet of age. Although the young ruler tried to consolidate his power half way through the 1520s, he had to come to terms with a highly complex international situation. The Ottoman Empire, under Suleiman I, energetically renewed its expansion across the Balkans to Central Europe. In 1521, Belgrade in Serbia was taken and the way was clear for the Turks to the Hungarian interior. On August 29, 1526, the Hungarian army, with the help of Czech regiments, was defeated by stronger Turkish forces at Mohács. King Louis was also killed while fleeing after the rout. With his death, the Czech-Hungarian personal union collapsed.

2 The Estates and Society in the Jagiellon Period

From the 15th century, Estates monarchies began to be established in Central Europe. Their main characteristic was a power dualism, a system in which the Estates shared supreme power with the ruler. The ratio of forces between the two competing powers was not clearly defined and could, depending on the situation, tend towards one side or the other. The distinctive form of the Bohemian Estates was of course affected by the social and economic consequences of the Hussite revolution.

In Czech history, the period of Jagiellon rule marked the completion of the formation of the Estates monarchy. The structure of the Estates' society was crystallized and in individual lands its grouping was clearly superior to the ruler. Young King Vladislav, on his arrival in Bohemia, did not have enough forces at his disposal to assert himself against the strong Estates. The most influential members of the latter were the relations and close allies of the former king, and Vladislav of Jagiellon was materially dependent on them in the military conflict which was taking place at that time. One index of the Estates' strength is that in the diet at Benešov in 1473, the Bohemian Estates of both sides elected four Land Regents who were to rule the kingdom till peace was brokered between the two kings. A similar solution was accepted also in Moravia, and only in Silesia and the Lusatias did it prove impossible to push through. Both kings, for a specified time, had to be satisfied with only their titles and their royal incomes.

The Jagiellon rulers were unable to face down the power of the Estates even in the peace which followed. As a consequence of the Hussite revolution, royal property was much reduced. Neither did the Jagiellons, in their power struggle with the strong nobility,

176

find support from ecclesiastical institutions or the towns. The standing of the Catholic Church had in large part been eroded by Hussitism, while the relation of the royal towns to the ruler had become looser. Occasional attempts of the Jagiellon kings to strengthen the Catholic Church and enforce greater subordination from the royal towns did not meet with much success. On the contrary, they brought the threat of the ruler's humbling defeat, as witnessed in the Prague uprising of 1483. The long-term absence of the king from the land during the period of the Czech-Hungarian union thus only capped the profound decline of his power.

The Estates' success in gaining the upper hand over the ruler resulted soon in open confrontation. Serious conflict between the royal towns and the nobility was one of the dominating features of the internal political scene during the Jagiellon period. The regrouping of forces and interests within the Estates paved the way for this. The religious peace of Kutná Hora contributed to the pacification of the religious disputes which up to this had divided the Estates. The alliance of both lower Estates, which had for the most part aligned themselves with Utraquism, collapsed, since the lower nobility found in the prevalently Catholic higher nobility a common interest in the fight against the strong royal towns.

The nobility exploited the marked limitation of the ruler's power and attempted to codify the gains which it had accrued over the course of the 15th century. The Vladislav Land Ordinance resulted from this in 1500. This set of privileges, decrees of diets and findings of the Land Court, arranged into a kind of Land Constitution, was intended to confirm finally the hegemonic standing of the Estates, and above all the nobility, in the Bohemian kingdom. The Ordinance, in its directives, ensured the dominance both of the Estates over the ruler, as well as of the nobility over other competitors within the Estates (royal towns and the Church). The royal towns were denied the right of a third vote at the diet and were subordinated to the powers of the nobility's Land Court.

Although the ruler endorsed the Vladislav Land Ordinance, the town Estate refused to respect it and began mobilize; its military force would come to be respected by the nobles. Numerous armed skirmishes, as well as the determination with which the towns began to execute thieving aristocrats and lay waste to their farmlands, forced the nobility to retreat in part. The Estates gradually accepted several compromises, among which St Wenceslas's Treaty of 1517 was of special importance. The towns achieved recognition of their right to vote at diets and defended their partial independence of the Land Court; however they had to submit in economic issues and reconcile themselves with commercial competition from the nobles.

In the neighbouring countries of the Crown, the disputes between the nobility and the Estates were not as dramatic as in Bohemia. Nevertheless, the nobility of the greatly urbanized Upper Lusatia attempted to deny political rights to the towns (mostly the right to vote at the diet), but they met with failure. In contrast, in Moravia, where the nobility had characteristically greater dominance over the royal towns, the development of the relation between the Estates was much calmer, dictated from the end of the 15th century by their compromising agreement of 1486 and the deposition of King Vladislav in 1493.

The consolidation of the power of the Estates in the Bohemian crown lands led to the jural crystallization and demarcation of individual Estates, between which there had been no clear borders before. The hierarchical relations within the landed Estates were also strengthened. Both the higher nobility and the more numerous, if more socially fragmented, lower nobility clearly divided into old and new families. Within the framework of a particular Estate, the older, more noble, families were accorded greater rights than new families. Also, a narrow class of armorial burghers, to whom the ruler had granted noble titles, now disengaged themselves from the rank and file of the urban population. In the Bohemian aristocracy, the leading position was accorded to the Rožmberks, while among the towns the leading position was maintained by the Old Town of Prague.

Representatives of all the Estates sat at the Land Diets, which were the most important organ of Estates' power. Diets took place in each land and their decrees became law. Important political, religious, economic questions were discussed, with special emphasis on the approval of taxes, which were the ruler's most significant source of income. Voting took place in accordance with the Estates curia.

The Bohemian Diet, which in the whole confederation had the greatest political weight (for instance, it played the decisive role in the election of the new ruler), had three curias: in the first, the lords sat; in the second, the lower nobles; and in the third, the representatives of the royal towns. Religious representatives were excluded from their negotiations, which was a unique situation in Europe at that time. Although prelates sat in the Moravian Land Diet, they were assigned to the third curia, together with the burghers. The first two curias of the Moravian Diet were occupied by the members of the higher and lower nobility.

The situation was different in Silesia. That land was broken up into a number of small principalities, some of which belonged directly to the Bohemian king, while others had their own princes of various dynasties, but which were subordinated to the supreme power of the Czech ruler. The complex composition of the Silesian Diet was reflected in the intricate jural and constitutional relations there. Its first curia belonged to the princes and persons of similarly high standing; the second to the nobility of the principality, subordinate directly to the king; and the third to the towns of that principality. Here the prelates had the most prestigious position, since they stood with the nobility. In Upper Lusatia, in which the landed nobility had strong towns, the Diet had only two curias. In the first were the nobility and prelates, while the burghers sat in the second. The Diet of Lower Lusatia had in contrast four curias: one each for the prelates, the higher and lower nobles and the towns. Special standing was reserved for both religious dignitaries of the Bohemian crown lands – the bishops of Olomouc and Wrocław – who had the right to sit in the first curia of the pertinent Land Diets, i.e., those of Moravia and Silesia.

On only two occasions during the rule of the Jagiellon dynasty did general diets take place in which representatives of all the Bohemian crown lands met. However, as a consequence of the loosening of bonds between individual crownlands, the diet was of no great significance.

JAROSLAV BOUBÍN

In addition to the Land Diets there were the so-called dietines, with smaller scope and powers, which met in the individual Silesian principalities and in some of the outlying areas of the Bohemian kingdom. In the individual Czech regions, regional congresses took place, delegating for instance the representatives of the lower nobility to the Land Diet. Representatives of the burghers were in contrast elected at what was referred to as the large assembly of the individual royal towns, which for the most part were made up of a wide spectrum of the artisanal classes.

Apart from attendance at diets, which met from time to time, the Estates continuously participated in the politics of both their region and the state by means of the supreme land officers, who were responsible both to the ruler and the pertinent Estate grouping. At its head in Bohemia was the Supreme Burgrave of Prague (*nejvyšší purkrabí pražský*); in Moravia, the Land Governor (*zemský hejtman*); in Silesia the Supreme Governor (*nejvyšší hejtman*), and in Lusatia the Land Governors (*zemský fojt*).

Supreme judicial power in the country remained almost exclusively in the hands of the nobility. And since the Supreme Land Officers and members of the Land Court in Bohemia made up the royal council, the noble Estates controlled even that important institution.

The privileged Estates made up only a minority of late medieval society. Its most numerous part was that of the clients, which was extremely various. Although the greater part of these lived in rural areas, an ever increasing share was made up of urban settlements. In Bohemia and Moravia alone, in the era of the Jagiellons, there were about 600 client towns. So, by the measure of urbanization, the Bohemian crown lands had the clear lead on nearby Poland and Hungary, and were approaching the state of affairs to be found at the time in a number of German countries.

In contrast with the pre-Hussite period, there were no larger changes in the responsibilities of clients. Although there were still payments in kind and subject labour (*robota*), the monetary form of rents dominated. Both the authorities and clients themselves (especially the wealthier classes) benefited from the long-term prosperity of agriculture and the economic rise of the client towns. Not even the deterioration of the jural standing of the clients, when the authorities tried to gain control over them and restrict their movements, led to the enormous social conflicts that we know of from neighbouring Hungary (1514) and from the German and Austrian lands (1524–1526).

In the Jagiellon period the largest land owner remained the aristocracy. Its land-holdings in Bohemia and Moravia, in contrast with preceding times, had grown, mainly at the expense of the ruler's property and that of the Church. The royal towns also forcefully established themselves as landed authorities. The largest dominions in Bohemia were held by the lords of Pernštejn, Rožmberk, Rožmitál, and the knights Trčka of Lípa – generally speaking, the aristocrats who held the foremost offices in the kingdom. In Moravia, alongside the Pernštejns, the lords of Cimburk, Boskovice, Lomnice, Žerotín, Kunovice and others established themselves

The ever decreasing real income from landed property, which was a consequence of the long-term rent at a fixed nominal level, forced the aristocracy to search for new financial sources. After the aristocratic warlord (who was typical of the period from Hussitism, George of Poděbrady to the beginning of Jagiellon rule), there appears a new sort of aristocrat around the 1480s – the aristocrat as man of business. Lords began vigorously to build up the economic prosperity of their domains. They did so not only with the support of their clients' economic activity, when they helped develop their client towns, but also when they embarked upon business undertakings of their own. Fisheries especially were expanded at the turn of the 15th and 16th centuries. The greater part of Bohemia and Moravia were covered in a dense network of ponds, whose construction was accompanied by striking technical and technological innovations.

The royal towns protested the infringement of their long-standing economic monopolies, but because of St Wenceslas's Treaty of 1517 they had to put up with the rising competition of the large noble farmsteads. Their artisanal production was not supposed to exceed the limits given by the guilds and only rarely were their goods in demand beyond the local and regional markets.

Only at the beginning of the 16th century did Czech foreign commerce begin to develop more distinctly. It had suffered a range of tough restrictions as a consequence of the long wars and continuous Church interdicts. Although the economic embargo against Hussite Bohemia was never consistently enforced, the Pope enabled the expansion of international trade with his revocation of the prohibition of Church trade with Bohemia in 1495. Salt, spices, fruits from the south, iron products, rare textiles and livestock were the main imports to the Bohemian crown lands, while cheap fabrics, glass, grain, rare and precious metals and further products associated with mining (copper, pewter, silver, gold, mercury) made up the main exports. The new growth of mining in Kutná Hora as well as the discovery of rich veins of silver near Jáchymov in the Ore Mountains (*Krušné Hory*) ensured the continuing importance of Bohemia in the production of those metals.

3 On the Eve of the European Reformation

As a consequence of the Hussite revolution, the monopoly of one faith and one – Catholic – church that had existed up to this in Bohemia and Moravia collapsed. The search for new forms of co-existence of mutually competing faiths was an exceptional experience and striking process, foreshadowing by over a hundred years the similar developments which were to take place on a larger stage after the European reformation. The demands of everyday life, the experience of long wars which brought no clear victor, the generally increasing secularization of social life – these were the factors that contributed to the decline in the authority and influence of ecclesiastical institutions and to the abatement of religious disputes.

Although the Czech-Hungarian war of the 1460s and '70s was the last attempt at a military takeover of the Czech Hussites, the religious aspects of the quarrel were nowhere near as prominent as they had been in the conflicts of fifty years before. On the contrary the open entrance of the Jagiellons into the conflict, as well as the changeable position of the Roman Emperor Frederick III of Habsburg, made it ever more clear that this was above all a struggle for hegemony in the eastern part of Central Europe.

The Peace of Olomouc (1478) removed the acute threat of Czech Utraquism from abroad, but complicated its standing within Bohemia itself. The return of the erstwhile followers of King Mátyás to the Land Diet and the Land and court offices significantly strengthened the role of Catholics in the area which was now subordinate to King Vladislav. The Catholic nobility regained the farm-holdings which it had lost during the war, and again took control in the crucial Estate of lords.

King Vladislav, as a Catholic, sympathized with his fellow believers and so gave the go ahead to open attempts at reconversion of the lapsed. After the Peace of Olomouc he no longer had to take the Utraquists into account, who up to this had been his vital political bulwark. On the contrary, he attempted to co-operate as closely as possible with the Catholic Estates, since he could thus legitimize his government as that of a Catholic ruler in the eyes of Europe and the Papal Curia.

Vladislav exploited his powers over the royal towns in the onslaught of the reconversion campaign. He began to strip the Utraquist aldermen of their functions and in their place he appointed determined Catholics. After several warning signals from the Utraquist side, there was an open uprising in Prague in September 1483. The aldermen appointed by the king were murdered or run out and the Utraquists once again took power. Vladislav had no option but to reconcile himself with the situation. He confirmed the victorious rebels in their offices as aldermen and had to abandon his policy of reconversion.

The success of one of the largest Hussite uprisings in Prague tested the viability of Utraquism. It was once again apparent that neither side could hope for outright victory in the religious conflicts of Bohemia. Moreover fears of the political strength of the towns, which had increased during this conflict, forced both the Utraquist and Catholic nobility to come to terms with each other, rather than continue their long-standing rivalry. The Diet which took place in Kutná Hora in March 1485 thus declared religious peace, the basis of which would become the renewed recognition of the *Compactata*. Regardless of the opinion of the Papal Curia the Bohemian Estates arrogated the power of deciding on fundamental religious questions and made relative religious tolerance law on the territory of the Bohemian kingdom. The Utraquists and Catholics were still neither able to accuse each other of heresy nor attack each other on religious grounds. In contrast to the later Peace of Augsburg (1555), clients were not obliged to adopt the faith of their lords. It was the first time in European history that the lowest classes of society were allowed freedom of faith. The Decree of Kutná Hora was at first accepted for a period of 31 years; however in 1512 it was prolonged *in eternitas*. A similar solution to the tensions between Utraquists and Catholics was reached in Moravia.

The circumstances of the enforced principle of mutual toleration was explicitly declared only for Catholics and Utraquists. In Bohemia the Utraquists dominated, especially to the east and in the centre of the land. Among the Estates, the greater part of the lower nobility implemented it and almost all of the royal towns. In Moravia Utraquism was weaker, and was rooted above all in the western areas adjacent to Bohemia, and in the midlands. Even here it found much support amidst the lower nobility, while the royal towns remained firm bastions of Catholicism. Most of the Estate of lords in both countries belonged to the Catholics. Religious affiliation followed national lines also: while the Czech-speaking population was for the most part Utraquist, the Germans were Catholic.

The Catholic Church in Bohemia and, in part, Moravia was still finding it difficult during the Jagiellon period to recover from the trauma of Hussitism. A number of its institutions died out. Of the four episcopal sees which were to be found in the Bohemian crown lands at the beginning of the Hussite revolution, only two were occupied in the second half of the 15th century – those of Olomouc and Wrocław. The Litomyšl bishopric came to an end and the Prague archbishopric went unoccupied for a long period. The upper consistory, as it was called, took over its administration along with its entire apparatus which returned from Catholic Plzeň to Prague after temporary exile during the Czech-Hungarian war. The monastic houses suffered a particularly crushing blow. Many ceased to exist, and some only succeeded in getting by. Nevertheless the monasteries became the fulcrum of the Counter Reformation offensive. The convent of the Dominican order in Olomouc took on especial importance, where the Inquisition established its office for Bohemia and Moravia. New monasteries and convents emerged, mainly Franciscan. Although in Silesia and Lusatia the Catholic Church maintained its old position, the arrival of the Lutheran reformation would radically change this as early as the end of the Jagiellon era.

The Utraquist church was administrated by what was called the lower consistory, made up in part by the clergy and in part by the laity. At its head stood the administrator, who for many years in the Jagiellon period was Václav Koranda the younger, of Plzeň, Rokycana's pupil and successor. The Utraquist church was not confident enough to break all ties to the Catholic Church and violate what was called apostolic succession, according to which a true priest can only one who has been ordained by a bishop, who has in turn been or-dained by the Pope. This was why the Utraquists did not set up their own bishop, and their candidates for the priesthood had go abroad in order to be ordained by benevolent or less curious bishops. The presence of two Italian bishops, both of whom hoped that they would be looked after better in Bohemia than in their poor Italian dioceses, only helped this situation temporarily.

In the arguments about how best to resolve the unfavourable position of the Utraquist Church, Utraquism began to split into two camps. In a series of negotiations with the Ro-man church, the more conservative part tried to reach accords which would not diverge from the *Compactata*; the more radical part however had resigned all hope of agreement with the Catholic Church and looked for other allies. They were particularly sympathetic to the Unity of Brethren (which was now stronger), and, after 1517, to the German reformer Martin Luther.

The church which developed most dynamically in Bohemia and Moravia in the Jagiel-lon period was, in the end, the church which had been excluded from the Decree of Kutná Hora. Although the Unity of Brethren was periodically persecuted (in 1508 the St James

Mandate was issued against it), but general forbearance in religious questions had reached such proportions that a new religious group could grow relatively quickly. It created its own organization, independent of the Utraquists and of the Catholic Church, and had its own bishops and clergy. It was distinctive for its emphasis on strict moral discipline. Intellectually it was anchored in old Táborite pacifism, as expressed in the work of Petr Chelčický. According to the Táborite example, it limited the number of sacraments, it consecrated no religious feasts and refused to honour the saints, it reduced the length of the service, etc. In the 1490s it abandoned its earlier negative attitude to secular power and the requirement of its members to voluntary poverty, and began to welcome affluent burghers and nobles into its ranks. Lukáš Pražský (of Prague), the prominent theologian of the Unity, developed its new theology, which opened up the way for its further growth and dialog with Reformation beyond the borders of Bohemia.

The actions of Martin Luther in 1517 and the beginning of European Reformation provoked profound changes in the arrangement of confessions in the Bohemian crown lands. The new faith caught on not only in Silesia and Lusatia, but also in the Catholic and especially German regions of Bohemia and Moravia. It brought substantial change to both the Utraquists and the Unity of Brethren. Luther publicly declared his allegiance to Hus as his predecessor and established contact with representatives of the Czech Reformation. Czech Hussitism thus definitively broke through its century-long international isolation and entered into dialog with the newly emergent confessions as a recognized equal.

At the same time, the disunion inside the Utraquist church came to a head. While its conservative wing wished to be unified with the Catholic Church, even at the price of significant compromises, its more radical members were closer to Luther in matters of faith. They thus tried to set up their own ecclesiastical order and organization which would have been independent of Rome. The conservative Utraquists and Catholics managed to gain control over Prague temporarily in the 1520s, as well as key positions in the country, and began to persecute all followers of the new religious faiths. However, agreement on the final unification of the Utraquists and Catholics, which was accepted at the Land Diet of 1525 and which was intended to initiate the victorious counter-Reformation in all lands of the Bohemian crown lands, proved impossible to implement because of the resistance of the opposition.

The Jews formed a small religious minority in the Bohemian crown lands. Because they were not persecuted to the same extent as their fellow believers in Western Europe, a greater number resided here. The royal towns especially tried to have them expelled, as they saw in the Jews a dangerous commercial competitor. However the Jagiellon kings appreciated the financial advantages to the royal coffers and tried to protect Jewish residents. Similar motives were to be found amidst the nobility who gave them shelter on their farmsteads.

4 Education and Culture in the Jagiellon Era

The consequences of the Hussite revolution were manifest in the specific characteristics of education and culture in the Bohemian crown lands. In contrast with the pre-Hussite period in Bohemia and Moravia, we encounter a colourful mosaic of variously oriented schools of confession – alongside the Catholic and Jewish schools, there emerged schools of Utraquism and the Unity of Brethren. As a result of the drop in parishes, which came about during the 15th century, mainly in Bohemia, schooling in rural areas went into decline, but developed in the towns. The education of the urban population was thus fundamentally higher than in the countryside, comparable perhaps with that of German towns. Students in the lower schools learned firstly to read, write and count; in the senior schools (referred to as particular schools) they were given a command of more advanced subjects including the basics of Latin. In neighbouring countries and in the Catholic areas of Bohemia, education was accessible both in the monasteries and other ecclesiastical institutions. In contrast with the Utraquist context, the schools in those countries were in the hands of the Church, but the town councils often succeeded in gaining control over them.

In the territory of the Bohemian crown lands there was only one university. Advanced scholarship in Prague was controlled by the Utraquists and remained limited to a faculty of arts. Each of its members was obliged to swear to the *Compactata*, so foreigners steered clear of it and Catholics of the Bohemian crown lands went elsewhere for an advanced education – to Vienna, Leipzig or Cracow. As a consequence of this exclusivity of confession and nation, the level of instruction at the university fell; however it was sufficient for the needs of the Czech towns, for whom it educated bureaucrats and teachers.

Since the Prague university and lower schools (especially those of the Utraquists) remained for the most part closed to the newer trends in European intellectual life, the latter made their way into the Czech context by other routes. On their journeys through Italian and other countries nearby, educated Czech gentlemen and aristocrats met with the phenomenon of humanism. The Buda court from the time of King Mátyás played a special role in its transmission. This current of new ideas and style of living, which spread from Renaissance Italy to the other countries of Europe and whose early forms penetrated to the Czech context as early as the rule of Charles IV, represented a new attempt at the synthesis of antique thought with the Christian view of the world. The morality of the Stoics began to influence norms of behaviour and pushed medieval asceticism into the background. Interest in the natural world and mankind drew the attention of the humanists away from earlier preoccupation with God.

Humanism in the Bohemian crown lands was restricted to small groups of scholars, joined by their passion for antiquity and classical education. Even though humanist authors came to the attention of an international audience through their works in Latin (Bohuslav Hasištejnský of Lobkowicz, Augustin Käsenbrot, et al.), humanism developed also in works written in the national languages. In the 1490s the lawyer Viktorin Kornel of Všehrdy formulated a demand for a Czech humanist vocabulary, emphasizing the need to transmit the

JAROSLAV BOUBÍN

significant works of antiquity and humanist literature into the Czech language. Within a short time a number of noteworthy translations were made, among which was the oldest translation of Erasmus's *In Praise of Folly* into the national language.

A further epochal change was the advent of printing. The discovery of Johann Gutenberg, the German goldsmith, appeared in Bohemia before any other lands of the Bohemian crown lands. A printing-house in Plzeň was already at work in 1476, and very soon there were others, for the most part in Prague. Because small in number, these houses were not able to supply all domestic demand; thus a range of books, targeted to the Czech market, were printed abroad, both in adjacent countries and Italy. While in the neighbouring countries *incunabulae* (i.e., books published before 1500) were mostly in Latin and German, in Bohemia almost all books printed were in Czech.

The long period of peace after the conclusion of the Czech-Hungarian war brought dramatic developments in the fine arts. In the Jagiellon period the late Gothic style in Czech art reached its zenith. While in Bohemia itself artistic development was disrupted as a consequence of the long religious wars of the 15th century, in the neighbouring countries of the Bohemian crown lands it continued unbroken in the pre-Hussite tradition, enjoying the fruit of many foreign contacts. In this the Prague court of King Vladislav provided the main impulse, mainly in the development of large-scale art. Very soon after the conclusion of the Czech-Hungarian war, the ruler embarked upon the renovation of Prague Castle, which had been uninhabited for many decades (the preceding Bohemian kings had moved their seat to Prague's Old Town). In order to implement his plans, he invited a range of artists from abroad, the first of which was Benedikt Ried from the German Danube Basin. After a long period, Prague again became a metropolis where culture prospered, and it remained so even after the removal of King Vladislav to Buda in Hungary.

Ried's supreme works in Prague Castle (Vladislav Hall, Louis's Palace) are a unique example of the combination of late Gothic and Renaissance architectural elements. Ried's services were also employed by the nobility, which entrusted him with the reconstruction of its castles (Švihov, Blatná), as well as the patriciate, for which he built grand cathedral spaces (Louny, Kutná Hora). The Jagiellon period was a time of hectic construction activity of noble seats and town cathedrals, town-halls and private residences. Because of the ornate style of these buildings it has come to be known as Vladislav Gothic.

Developments as intense as those in architecture can be seen in other areas of the visual arts (i.e., murals, panels and book illumination, as well as statuary and other arts and crafts). The work of an anonymous artist known as the Master of the Litoměřice altar reached remarkable levels. Of Czech origin, he displayed his familiarity with the ideas of Renaissance art through a range of panels on the Litoměřice altar, as well as through the decoration of St Wenceslas's Chapel in Prague Castle and the first Renaissance portrait of Czech origin dated 1506.

In the neighbouring countries of the Bohemian crown lands there was continuity in the development of the visual arts and for this reason it has different characteristics. In contrast with the Czech context, the Catholic Church was one of the main sources of the commission of artworks. One important feature was also the permanent close links with the major cultural centres of Central Europe in the Danube Basin, in the Buda court of Mátyás Corvinus and his Jagiellon successors, in the Meissen region and elsewhere. The sculptor and architect, Anton Pilgram, who participated in the construction of the town-hall and St James's Cathedral in Brno was one of the most significant artists working in Moravia. In Silesia the most noteworthy artistic achievement was the reconstruction of the town-hall in Wrocław.

In the course of the Jagiellon period, Czech art succeeded in keeping in step with other parts of Central Europe. Though various social classes were involved in Czech culture of the time, it was the burghers and nobles who were above all responsible. In this respect the development of Czech culture under the Jagiellons was fundamentally different from the grand cultural blossoming of the Bohemian crown lands under the rule of the Luxemburgs in the 14th and the beginning of the 15th centuries.

Bibliography

BACZKOWSKI, Krzysztof: *Walka Jagiellonów z Maciejem Korwinem o koronę czeską w latach 1471–1479*, Kraków 1980.

BACZKOWSKI, Krzysztof: *Zjazd wiedeński 1515 roku*, Warszawa 1975.

BAHLCKE, Joachim – BÖMELBURG, Hans-Jürgen – KERSKEN, Norbert (eds.): *Ständefreiheit und Staatsgestaltung in Ostmitteleuropa. Übernationale Gemeinsamkeiten in der politischen Kultur vom 16.–18. Jahrhundert*, Leipzig 1996.

BAHLCKE, Joachim – STROHMEYER, Arno (eds.): *Konfessionalisierung in Ostmitteleuropa. Wirkungen des religiösen Wandels im 16. und 17. Jahrhundert in Staat, Gesellschaft und Kultur*, Stuttgart 1999.

BROCK, Peter: *The Political and Social Doctrines of the Unity of Czech Brethren in the Fifteenth and Early Sixteenth Centuries*, Gravenhage 1967.

ČORNEJ, Petr: *Království dvojího lidu. České dějiny let 1436–1526 v soudobé korespondenci*, Praha 1989.

ČORNEJ, Petr – BARTLOVÁ, Milena: *Velké dějiny zemí Koruny české*, VI, Praha–Litomyšl 2007.

DENIS, Ernest: *Fin de l'indépendence bohême*, I, Paris 1890.

DMITRIEVA, Marina – LAMBRECHT, Karen (eds.): *Krakau, Prag und Wien. Funktionen von Metropolen im frühmodernen Staat*, Stuttgart 2000.

EBERHARD, Winfried: *Konfessionsbildung und Stände in Böhmen 1478–1530*, München–Wien 1981.

ENGEL, Evamarie – LAMBRECHT, Karen – NOGOSSEK, Hanna (eds.): *Metropolen im Wandel. Zentralität in Ostmitteleuropa an der Wende vom Mittelalter zur Neuzeit*, Berlin 1995.

HARDER, Hans-Bernd – ROTHE, Hans (eds.): *Studien zum Humanismus in den Böhmischen Ländern*, Köln–Wien 1988.

HLAVÁČEK, Petr: *Čeští františkáni na přelomu středověku a novověku*, Praha 2005.

HLOBIL, Ivo – PETRŮ, Eduard: *Humanism and the Early Renaissance in Moravia*, Olomouc 1999.

HOMOLKA, Jaromír – KRÁSA, Josef – MENCL, Václav – PEŠINA, Jaroslav – PETRÁŇ, Josef: *Pozdně gotické umění v Čechách (1471–1526)*, Praha 1978.

HUSA, Václav: *Tomáš Müntzer a Čechy*, Praha 1957.

JANÁČEK, Josef: *Řemeslná výroba v českých městech v 16. století*, Praha 1961.

KREUZ, Petr – MARTINOVSKÝ, Ivan: *Vladislavské zřízení zemské*, Praha 2008.

LANGER, Andrea – MICHELS, Georg (eds.): *Metropolen und Kulturtransfer im 15./16. Jahrhundert.* Prag–Krakau–Danzig–Wien, Stuttgart 2001.

MACEK, Josef: *Jagellonský věk v českých zemích*, I–IV, Praha 1992–1999.

MACEK, Josef: *Tři ženy krále Vladislava*, Praha 1991.

MACEK, Josef: *Víra a zbožnost jagellonského věku*, Praha 2001.

JAROSLAV BOUBÍN

MALÝ, Karel – PÁNEK, Jaroslav (eds.): *Vladislavské zřízení zemské a počátky ústavního zřízení v českých zemích (1500–1619)*, Praha 2001.

MAREK, Jaroslav: *Společenská struktura moravských královských měst v 15. a 16. století*, Praha 1965.

MAŤA, Petr: *Svět české aristokracie (1500–1700)*, Praha 2004.

MÍKA, Alois: *Poddaný lid v Čechách v první polovině 16. století*, Praha 1960.

MILLER, Jaroslav: *Uzavřená společnost a její nepřátelé. Město středovýchodní Evropy (1500–1700)*, Praha 2006.

MITTENZWEI, Ingrid: *Der Joachimsthaler Aufstand 1525, seine Ursachen und Folgen*, Berlin 1968.

MÜLLER, Joseph Th.: *Geschichte der Böhmischen Brüder*, 1–2, Herrnhut 1922–1931.

PESCHKE, Erhard: *Kirche und Welt in der Theologie der Böhmischen Brüder*, Berlin 1981.

PESCHKE, Erhard: *Die Theologie der Böhmischen Brüder in ihrer Frühzeit*, I, Stuttgart 1935.

POŠVÁŘ, Jaroslav: *Politický vývoj ve Slezsku v letech 1471–1526*, Opava 1960.

ŘÍČAN, Rudolf: *The History of the Unity of Brethren. A Protestant Hussite Church in Bohemia and Moravia*, transl. C. Daniel Grews, Bethlehem 1992.

SEIBT, Ferdinand – EBERHARD, Winfried (eds.): *Europa 1500. Integrationsprozesse im Widerstreit: Staaten, Regionen, Personenverbände, Christenheit*, Stuttgart 1987.

ŠMAHEL, František: *Die Hussitische Revolution*, III, transl. Thomas Krzenck, Hannover 2002.

VÁLKA, Josef: *Přehled dějin Moravy II. Stavovská Morava (1440–1620)*, Praha 1987.

VOREL, Petr: *Páni z Pernštejna. Vzestup a pád rodu zubří hlavy v dějinách Čech a Moravy*, Praha 1999.

VYBÍRAL, Zdeněk: *Politická komunikace aristokratické společnosti v českých zemích na počátku novověku*, České Budějovice 2005.

VIII. The Czech Estates
in the Habsburg Monarchy (1526–1620)

Land Court of the Bohemian Kingdom in the mid-16th century. Bohemian King Ferdinand I is sitting in the centre surrounded by leading Estates representatives – the highest Land officials (members of the Land Government) and lay judges of the major land court. Woodcut, from *Zemské zřízení Království českého z roku 1549* [Land political system of the Bohemian Kingdom from 1549] (published in Prague in 1550).

1 Integration of the Czech State into the Central European Monarchy of Habsburgs

The transition from the Middle Ages to the early Modern Era, which in Czech history is symbolically linked to the events of 1526, entailed not only the entrance of the Czech state into the framework of the Central European Habsburg monarchy. It was also a time in which dramatic changes came about in the idea of the world, and the place of Europe in it. The voyages of discovery, engaged upon by the nations of the western European littoral, led to the unprecedented expansion of the great Atlantic powers, to the establishment of commercial links between continents and to the commencement of the colonial system, and with that, the future form of the world's economy. This enormous expansion of Europe's geographical horizons affected the countries of Central Europe also, even though their inhabitants did not directly participate in these expeditions overseas.

Czechs, along with their neighbouring lands, also took good note of the newly forming interrelationships between states and continents. They began to feel the tremors of change in price-levels and in the heretofore settled rhythms of economic life, provoked by the influx of precious metals from America. They came to know the political and financial force of the sea-going nations, whose interests played out in Central Europe more than at any time before this. Aristocrats who were publicly active and the representatives of the more important towns understood the significance of keeping up-to-date and began to read the European gazettes in order to gain regular information about affairs in the distant focal points of European politics and war. Ever more frequently, they themselves made journeys so that they could see European countries and also those overseas. These tours served not only to orient them, but also allowed them to become active participants in events. If the Bohemian crown lands opened up once again to Europe in the preceding Jagiellonian period, a characteristic feature of the 16th century was the inhabitants' desire to establish a wide range of international contacts and participate directly in the development of, at the very least, Central Europe. It was not only a desire to further their own interests, but a pressing material necessity since Central Europe itself in the second quarter of the 16th century was radically transformed before the very eyes of its inhabitants.

To the close of the Middle Ages, the central part of the old continent was still divided into several relatively stable states controlled by their dynasties. Czech, Polish, Austrian and Hungarian rulers had of old competed for dominance, and from mid-way through the 13th century repeatedly attempted to unify this space under one sceptre. However neither the last Přemyslids and Luxemburgs in the 13th and 14th centuries, nor the Polish-Lithuanian Jagiellons nor the Hungarian king Mátyás Corvinus in the 15th century, achieved any lasting success. On two occasions – after the extinction of the Přemyslids (1306) and Luxemburgs (1437) – the Austrian Habsburgs took up this task, but they too came to grief. Affairs took a turn only after the Habsburg dynasty pursued a high-powered marriage policy which expanded its holdings far into the west of Europe and, in the person of Charles V, reached the level of King of Romans and Emperor, along with the Spanish crown (1516), which brought with it extensive territory from Italy to the Low Countries, together with profitable colonies overseas. Only this noble line, with the above advantages and supported by a power base and finance in the western continent, could hope to implement its hegemonic intentions in the heart of Europe.

Ferdinand I, the younger of two brothers who were members of the founding generation of Habsburgs, was able to exploit these unique opportunities to the full. Educated in Spain, and having ruled the Austrian lands as archduke from 1521, the young man, thanks to his exceptional intelligence and organizational gifts, was able to orient himself quickly in Central European politics. He exploited the chaos brought by the defeat at Mohács and the death of the Bohemian and Hungarian king Louis (*Ludvík*) on August 29, 1526, and consistently pursued his main aim of acquiring the Bohemian and Hungarian crowns permanently. Although backed up by the Vienna agreements of 1515 between the Habsburgs and Jagiellons about mutual accession, he did not bring this argument to Bohemia. The confident Bohemian nobility had fought for a free election, in which along with Ferdinand I they entertained candidates from Bavaria, Saxony and Poland (domestic magnates from the ranks of the Bohemian Estates or the lower Silesian princes were also considered). However, the only contenders with a realistic chance against Ferdinand were the dukes Ludwig and Wilhelm from the Bavarian House of Wittelsbach, the single dynasty which had tried to halt the dramatic rise of the Habsburgs in Central Europe with the support of France and the Papal Curia. None the less, Ferdinand I, who had to agree to significant restrictions of his powers of government in his electoral capitulation, was successful in the election of October 23, 1526.

There was one serious drawback to the election in Prague: only representatives of the Bohemian kingdom participated in it. The entire state – the Bohemian Crown – was however made up of five countries. In the symbolism of the time, apart from the "head" (the Bohemian Kingdom), there was also the "principal limb" (the Moravian Margraviate) and three further "limbs", each parts of the one body, that is, the Silesian Duchy, the Upper and Lower Lusatian Margraviates. Czech nobles, in their deliberations over the crown, were guided by the conviction that they alone were the guarantors of state unity, and thus the only entitled electors of the king. Moravians, Silesians and Lusatians in contrast pushed forward the viewpoint of the lands, which was based on the principle that all five lands of the Crown were equal, and they considered the action of the Bohemian electors an expression of inadmissible arrogance. In protest against the infringement of their rights, the Estates diets of the four "adjacent" or "incorporated" lands recognized the hereditary claim of Anna of Jagiellon, wife of Ferdinand I, and in this way accepted his succession to the Bohemian throne. They thus enlarged the new ruler's room for manoeuvre, as the next time he would be able to exploit the disputes between the Bohemian crown lands for his own ends.

Ferdinand I was prepared to go to war over the Bohemian and Hungarian crowns. While he was able to coerce his way to the Bohemian crown, in Hungary he faced a serious candidate, János Szapolya, who was backed by the Ottoman Empire. Even though Habsburg was successful in the end, he initiated a long series of Habsburg-Turkish wars, which drew heavily on the financial and military resources of the Bohemian crown lands and the rest of the monarchy. The Bohemian nobility was well aware of this danger, and thus did not wish to join the Czech and Hungarian lands. It had bad memories of the personal union from the Jagiellonian era, when the ruler resided in Buda, and Hungary took the precedence in the confederation at the expense of Bohemia. In this respect also their suspicions turned out to be justified. The lands of the Crown of St Stephen gained priority in the ruler's titulary of the Habsburgs and the same was true of the Hungarian coat-of-arms, which held the permanent place of honour rather than that of Bohemia. This reflected the long-term decline of the Czech state's international prestige, and the symbolic arrangement was retained even after the greater part of Hungary was occupied by Turks from 1541 and taken away from the Habsburg monarchy for over 150 years.

War and diplomacy established the bases of the Habsburg monarchy, which was an extraordinarily complex confederation made up of three historically independent entities – the Bohemian crown, the Hungarian crown and various sets of heritable Austrian lands. It was a vast territorial entity which took up a considerable part of Central Europe. When the monarchy was established in 1526–1527, the lands of Hungary exceeded all others: it was more extensive and its population larger (about 3.5 million inhabitants, while the Bohemian crown lands and the Austrian lands lagged behind with around 2.7 million and 2.1 million respectively). The situation changed very soon when, as a result of the Turkish conquest, Hungary lost most of its territory and was now limited to Royal Hungary (roughly speaking, today's Slovakia, the western part of Hungary, Burgenland and Croatia), which had about 2 million people. The Austrian state also divided into three parts four decades later after the death of Ferdinand I in 1564 (Ferdinand's sons, and lines rising from them ruled these). While the Inner Austrian lands (Styria, Carinthia, Carniola and Littoral) and Upper Austrian lands (the Tyrol and Vorarlberg) gained administrative, fiscal and military autonomy under the rule of the younger Habsburgs, the common fate of the Bohemian crown lands was still directly linked only to Lower and Upper Austria in the Danube Basin. It was these two countries (with about 800,000 inhabitants) which created with their neighbours in the north (Bohemia and Moravia) the core of the Habsburg monarchy. Its main axis was between Vienna and Prague, the two alternating residences of the Habsburg rulers.

In a situation where most of Hungary remained occupied by Turks till the close of the 17th century, the Inner and Upper Austrian lands were divided for a long period and moreover even the northern territory of the Bohemian Crown was later lost (Upper and Lower Lusatia, in the Peace of Prague in 1635, and Silesia after the defeat of the Austrian-Prussian wars in the middle of the 18th century), the Central European confederation was nowhere near as impressive as it appeared ideally to Ferdinand I. Its absolute centre of gravity remained those four central countries – Bohemia, Moravia, Upper and Lower Lusatia. The Habsburg monarchy would stand or fall by these. In this reduced constellation however the real significance of the two Czech lands rose markedly. Since the Bohemian crown lands made up approximately a third of the population of the new monarchy, in the context of the Czech-Austrian core of Habsburg power, they constituted more than two thirds. Because this was the regular fiscal source of the Habsburg monarchy in the first century of its existence, the Bohemian crown lands took on for the Habsburgs and their confederation crucial importance.

With the acquisition of the Bohemian crown lands, the Habsburgs' standing in Central European was consolidated on all sides. The Czech ruler was a member of the college of electors of the King and Emperor of the Holy Roman Empire, which helped stabilize the standing of the Habsburg dynasty in this large supranational formation. In addition, he remained the one crowned king among the electors, which raised his international political prestige. The Bohemian crown lands were more advantageously positioned in the centre of the Empire than Austria, and this facilitated the Habsburgs' political and military interventions in relation to nearly all the independent heads of the German territorial states and the imperial towns. The relatively dense population of the Bohemian crown lands with their valuable economic potential, especially in silver mining and minting, became one of the pillars of Habsburg power.

At the same time however the Czech state presented a particularly difficult task to a ruler who intended to centralize power. Bonds between the five crownlands were so loose that it was not possible to govern them effectively from one centre of the expansive monarchy. In each country, above all in Bohemia and Moravia, the Estates had their own diet, land government and independent judiciary, and acted with confidence in their powers. In Silesia the interests of the Bohemian king, who was also at the same time supreme Silesian duke, clashed with those of the Silesian princes, who ruled in several smaller principalities, which however belonged to influential Central European dynasties (*inter alia*, the Hohenzollerns of Brandenburg and the Wettins of Saxony) who often had their own foreign policies.

Moreover the greater part of the population of the Bohemian crown lands, whether it belonged to the Czech Utraquists, the Unity of Brethren, the German Lutherans or other more radical currents of the European Reformation, took a fundamentally negative position on Habsburg attempts at reconversion. This was yet another obstacle placed in the way of the Catholic ruler whose aimed to gradually unify all his subjects in the faith, and he repeatedly came into conflict with the nobility and burghers over their stance on the church and religion, which at the beginning of the Modern Era still legitimated political power. During the fighting in Hungary and afterwards during the exhausting wars on the

Habsburg-Ottoman border, military, religious and financial problems, as well as difficulties with the state centralization of the executive, constantly overlapped in the relationship of the Habsburg ruler with the Estates of the Bohemian crown lands. The basic line which the king took was to strengthen central power, making it more efficacious, while the nobility and burghers wished above all to maintain Estates freedoms, as well as other political freedoms, and religion. A ruler such as Ferdinand I, always taking the initiative, had no intention of letting things drift (as his Jagiellon predecessors had done), but rather attempted to construct new bases of central power.

2 Land of the King and the Estates

The government of Ferdinand I (r. 1526–1564) was of epochal significance for the further development of Central Europe. Although for most of his life the Bohemian and Hungarian king remained in the shadow of his older brother, Emperor Charles V on a formal level, and on occasion barely avoided conflicts with him, he conducted himself as an independent statesman of international standing. He understood early on the unrealistic nature of Charles' ideas of the creation of a universal Christian monarchy and instead concentrated on the strengthening of the bonds between the Czech, Austrian and Hungarian lands. Moreover he increased his influence in the Holy Roman Empire, becoming its joint ruler in 1531 and, after Charles's resignation in 1556, emperor. This represented an important victory for the younger Austrian branch of the Habsburg dynasty over the older Spanish line, which gave up hope of retaining the imperial crown. Although Spain, in its efforts to achieve hegemony over western Europe and colonies overseas, remained the more powerful partner, developments in the following centuries showed that the consolidation of power in Central Europe held greater potential for the Habsburg dynasty.

Ferdinand I depended on the international prestige of the Habsburg dynasty and its strong position in the system of European powers, as well as on considerable fiscal sources, including loans, which European banking houses of the first rank furnished him with (e.g., Fugger and Welser in Augsburg). An outstanding organizer and politician, capable of thinking in the long-term, he drew on his western European experience with the modernization of a centralized administration, adapting that knowledge to the situation of Austria and the Bohemian crown lands. Backed by important Austrian nobles who devoted their careers to dutiful service of the Habsburgs (the Hofmanns of Grünbühl, the Roggendorfs, counts of Salm and others), he began to put into effect his idea of firm royal power over allied countries immediately after his accession to the Bohemian throne. For the first time in the history of Central Europe there appeared a centralizing direction of rule which exceeded the borders of the state.

The means to unify gradually the various elements of the confederation became the new system of monarchic administration, which was independent of the will of the Estates and subordinate only to the ruler. This reform was implemented through the issue of the order of the court (*Hofstaatsordnung*) of 1527, which established new institutions beside the existing Estates offices, and thus introduced a two-track state administration. Although on one side the old institutions remained, beside them, and *de facto* above them, now stood new institutions. In the years ahead, the Privy Council, the supreme advisory body of the ruler, and the Court Chamber, the supreme office for the royal fiscal matters, took on especial significance. Along with the Court War Council, established later in 1556, these institutions became the basis of the central administration which in its fundamental outlines remained in place to the mid-19th century.

The ruler alone decided on appointments to the central council, but it was in his own interests to have the nobility of the Bohemian crown lands represented there as much as possible. However its leaders – unlike the more experienced Austrians – from the outset refused membership in the Viennese bodies. It would take over two decades, i.e., an entire generation, before they realized that it was through these institutions they could strengthen their influence. Gradually the Privy Council was staffed by the supreme chancellor of the Bohemian kingdom, Heinrich IV of Plauen, Jáchym of Hradec and Vratislav of Pernštejn, and later further dignitaries from Bohemia and Moravia. Over time these magnates abandoned their prejudices against this organization and came to identify with the idea of centralized bureaucratic rule. Most importantly this entailed, first, running the executive from one power-centre; second, a systematic approach to the relatively complex affairs of chancellery; third, regular administrative tasks carried out punctually; fourth, a clear hierarchy of compe-tence; and, fifth, increased expertise of the executive bureaucracy. On the threshold of the Modern Era, bureaucratization contributed to effectivity in the running of society and the economy, and thus it was implemented not only from above (from the ruler to the Estates), but also from below (from the economic administration of the large farmsteads and towns to the land administration). General bureaucratization, from the mid-16th century, became the main agent which brought more precision to official activities and to dependency on dealing with matters in writing rather than orally, as was previously the custom, but also to the gradual overwhelming of the offices with an excess of written business.

Of great practical impact was the bureaucratization of the state finances by means of a central Court Chamber in Vienna, along with land chambers subordinate to it. On the ter-ritory of the Czech state, the Bohemian chamber was established in Prague and later the Silesian chamber in Wrocław. The chamber administration grew into an instrument to satisfy the growing fiscal needs of the monarchy (military, foreign policy, administrative apparatus and the grandiose ruler's court), which could not be covered from existing sources. More so than their Jagiellon predecessors, the Habsburgs systematically exploited the royal patent rights to mining and minting activities, on tariffs and further perquisites; and Ferdinand I did not hesitate to enter into conflicts with the nobility (mostly with the Schlick counts of western Bohemia), to implement his renewal of royal rights. From the time of Ferdinand's accession, pressure also increased on the regular taxation of the population. Although taxes were approved by privileged Estates at the diets, the burghers and rural clients were taxed most heavily. With the monarchy's higher outgoings, the tax burden on the Bohemian crown lands was greater; in the period of the Hungarian wars and the building of a line of defence along the Habsburg-Ottoman border, fiscal demands rose to levels that were previously unimaginable. Estates politicians were well aware of the dependence of the ruler on tax revenues, and so they jealously guarded their rights to set their extent and tried to keep their collection in the hands of region and land officers. Finance thus became the pivotal subject in diet negotiations, and the main instrument of resistance against the inordinate rise of royal power.

The Estates opposition, even after the accession of Ferdinand I, was able at least to maintain the general outlines of the division of power between the ruler and the Estates. Apart from the new monarchical institutions, the land bodies, which were influenced strongly by the Estates, continued to function. Although the ruler could not dissolve them or staff them with foreigners, in propitious circumstances he was able to appoint his loyal followers from the ranks of the domestic nobility, for instance the lords of Hradec, the Popels of Lobkowicz, the Berkas of Dubá and further lords and knights. These nobles built their political careers in royal service, and although they never left the Estates, as a rule in conflict situations they favoured the interests of the king over the defence of traditions and Estates privileges.

The opinions and behaviour of the aristocracy from the Bohemian crown lands (like that of Hungary) influenced the ruler's court over the long-term. The latter was located predominantly in Vienna during the rule of both Ferdinand I and his son Maximilian II, but occasionally moved to Prague for protracted periods. It was in this socially attractive and politically inspiring court environment that nobles from all lands of the Habsburg monarchy and other parts of Europe met and conversed. Depending on their origins, birth, wealth, personal abilities and social ambitions, they served there as high officers, courtiers or, in the earliest instance, pages gaining their first experience of the court. Longer sojourns at the royal court made them somewhat sympathetic to the integration ambitions of the Habsburg dynasty and offered opportunities to forge contacts with influential personages in the monarchy, dignitaries in the bureaucracy or the ruler himself. This intercourse expanded the horizons of politicians from the nobility beyond the borders of their individual lands, but as yet did not lead them to join heart and soul with the Viennese environment, as would later come about in the 17th century. Personal acquaintances from the ruler's court or direct Habsburg intervention facilitated marriage alliances between prominent nobles of the Czech, Austrian and Hungarian lands, and even – as the examples of the Rožmberks and Pernštejns demonstrate – marriages with imperial princesses or members of the Italian and Spanish aristocratic lines. The power elite of the Bohemian crown lands thus overcame its previous isolation within the framework of its own state, and in harmony with the Habsburg interests – and sometimes even against them – converged with the rest of Europe.

At the very beginning of the Habsburg monarchy the religious orientation of the ruling dynasty and its policies had been decided. Ferdinand I was not a fanatical bigoted Catholic; on the contrary in his youth he was quite close to the moderate interpretation of the Catholic faith in the spirit of Erasmus. At the same time he considered himself the protector of the Catholic Church, and this brought a responsibility for the unification of all subjects in the faith, which he considered was one of the principles of correct government. His policy of reconversion was influenced also by the alliance with Spain and the bond of confession with the Papal Curia. On the other hand he was a pragmatic politician who acknowledged extant jural relations in the Bohemian crown lands; he respected the earlier legalization of Utraquism, even while he tried with its backing to prevent the spread of radical Reformation churches. Ferdinand I's negative position, which hardened with the passage of time, raised the religious question to the status of crucial theme in the development of the Habsburg monarchy and marked the first century of Habsburg rule in the Bohemian crown lands.

The Bohemian Estates made the acceptance of Ferdinand I as king in 1526 conditional on the ruler's acknowledgement of the principle of the elective throne and the inviolable nature of political freedoms and Estates privileges. However the principle of election was damaged immediately after by the independent act of the adjacent lands, which also later complied with the ruler's demands when he wished to dominate the Bohemian Estates. Ferdinand I deftly profited from the disputes between the Bohemian crown lands and their Estates, and despite his difficulties with the Moravians, Silesians and Lusatians, he concentrated above all on Bohemia. He devoted much energy to securing the Bohemian throne for his heirs. He exploited the fire in Prague Castle in 1541 when the Land Rolls and the records of the decrees of the diets and Land courts were destroyed, as well as all Land privileges. In the diet of 1545 which dealt with the new record of the Estates patents, he brought such pressure to bear on the Estates that he succeeded in changing his own coronal undertaking and through skilful legal argumentation coerced them into recognizing the hereditary rights of the Habsburgs to the Bohemian throne.

In his contest with the Estates, Ferdinand I refused to be bound by old regulations. However, he strongly fought the Estates on any attempt to revise the laws in force at the expense of royal power. In the diets, he left them with little space to negotiate political issues and overwhelmed them with applications for arms taxes. By his authoritative negotiating style and references to the necessity of the common struggle against the Turkish threat, he prevented the Estates from resolving the pressing questions of religion and ecclesiastical politics. He unswervingly insisted that the antiquated *Compactata* of 1436 remain unchanged, and apart from Catholicism, he would not recognize any other religion but Utraquism in its old form, which was now distant from the views of most Czech Protestants (in the mean time they had moved towards the more radical currents of the Reformation). First he stymied the attempt to win legal recognition for the Unity of Brethren in 1535, after which he suppressed attempts to organize Czech Utraquism into a Land church of the Lutheran variety (1539–1543).

The lack of a clear and unified program was the most serious weakness of the Estates opposition throughout the 16th century; not until the Bohemian Confederation of 1619 would the Estates of the Bohemian crown lands achieve this. The purposeful ruler thus exploited the internal disputes of the Estates' corporations and persons, and from the beginning of his Czech reign thwarted the partisan interests which stood in the way of the consolidation of royal power. In 1528 he moved against the knights, forbidding them to organize regional conferences without the special permission of the ruler. The Estate of the towns was also weakened by the division of the unified towns of Prague and the prohibition of the so-called great councils of burghers at which up to this all fully fledged inhabitants of royal towns had assembled. He also moved against individuals who deviated from the usual framework of the aristocratic Estate – he took the profitable Jáchymov mines from the counts of Šlik in 1528 and two years later he dismissed Zdeněk Lev of Rožmitál, the most influential noble of the Jagiellon era, from the position of Supreme Burgrave (chair of the Land government). Even though these uncompromising measures did not provoke concerted resistance, tension and mutual suspicion surfaced between the king and a significant part of the Bohemian Estates. This was compounded by the malice of the domestic nobility against outsiders and bureaucrats who had gained material and political advantages in the service of the Habsburgs. However, this negative attitude changed in time as several of the outsiders – such as the long maligned councillor of the Bohemian chamber Florian Griespek, who constructed Renaissance chateaux in Kaceřov and Nelahozeves – invested their wealth in the support of domestic culture and as early as the next generation blended into the Czech environment.

However, the Bohemian Estates' opposition, which was made up of lords and knights, as well as leaders of the royal towns, gradually strengthened. Two extreme poles formed in the opposition – lords who were economically and politically the strongest element of the Estates, and the royal towns who were goaded into fighting by the systematically anti-urban policies of Ferdinand I. Such an incongruous grouping of disgruntled elements did not have great hope of success, even though it attempted to exploit the first serious setback of the Habsburg monarchy, which came when foreign, domestic and financial troubles mounted.

The opposition of the Bohemian Estates tried to halt the long-term growth of royal power during the Schmalkaldic War of 1546–1547. Ferdinand I was at that time engrossed in war on German territory, where the Lutheran princes led by the Saxony elector, John Frederick I, rebelled against his brother Charles V in order to limit imperial power and achieve status for Lutherans equal to that of Catholics. The opposition in Bohemia had similar aims and counted on the support of the imperial princes, but it did not dare engage in war against its own ruler. Most of the lords acted with discretion and waited for an opportunity to extract concessions from the king without great risk. The knights were more radical, but even they did not have a clear-cut program. Only the representatives of the royal towns were convinced that the decline of their significance had become critical, and their fate was now hanging in the scales. Moreover, the rebellious Bohemian towns found sympathizers among some of the burghers of Silesia and Upper Lusatia in this matter. In contrast, only Jihlava in Moravia joined the Bohemian Estates, for fear that it would lose its landed property in Bohemia if the rebellion were successful.

In February 1547 a league of Estates opposition was set up, the leaders of which made emphatic protests at the March diet against the limitation of their rights. However, apart from the royal towns, only a handful of radical nobles were willing to risk confrontation with the king; these wished either to obtain legal recognition for the Unity of Brethren or to regain the privileges which had been lost. This radical core, gathered in the Estates commission, was unable to establish a sufficient counter-weight to the ruler's power. Although it tried to employ the Land army, led by Kašpar Pluh of Rabštejn, to defend itself against their own king, neither its numbers nor determination sufficed for an armed conflict against the Habsburgs. After the defeat of the German Schmalkaldic forces in the battle at Mühlberg on April 24, 1547 it was obvious that the erratic Bohemian rebels would remain isolated. The Estates league collapsed; the nobles left the royal towns to their own fate, seeking to cover their actions in professions of loyalty to Ferdinand I.

This enabled the victorious king to punish the seditious parties severely and to disarm the opposition elements in the Bohemian Estates both politically and economically. Most of the guilty parties were pardoned by Ferdinand I, and in determining punishments he took into account not so much the degree of real guilt as the significance and danger of individuals in the Estates. He instigated political trials only against those nobles whom he considered too radical or whose property he intended to confiscate, as well as against the rebellious royal towns. The execution of two knights and two burghers, carried out with great ceremony on Hradčany Square in Prague on August 22, 1547 on the eve of the Land Diet's session, and the punishments meted out to the fugitives were intended to engender an atmosphere of fear and compliance.

Certain noblemen were punished by home arrest in their chateaux and the confiscation of their farmlands. On the other hand, the king levied heavy fines on towns in Bohemia (and similarly in Upper Lusatia, where the Lusatian League, led by Görlitz and Bautzen, was the greatest opposition force), removing their privileges, weapons, territories and other fiscal sources. He temporarily stripped them of all legal standing, and sank the town councils into permanent debt. Although he later returned some privileges and properties to the towns, he did not relent in his main aim, which was to break the political and economic strength of the royal towns. Ferdinand I shackled the autonomous executives of the towns with the supervision of newly appointed monarchical officers – royal magistrates and, in the Prague towns, governors appointed from the ranks of the nobility. The supreme judiciary of the towns was also limited by the establishment of a court of appeal in Prague Castle, which became the first true professional chair of law in the Bohemian crown lands and contributed to the modernization of judicial practice here.

As a consequence of these repressive measures the towns were transformed into dependencies of the royal property and their erstwhile significance, based on their unrepeatable actions in the Hussite revolution, was irreversibly lost. "The prostration of the Estate of towns", which was described resonantly by the former chancellor of Prague's Old Town, Sixt of Ottersdorf, meant an extensive shift in the Bohemian Estates and in their opposition in which the nobility now clearly dominated. If representatives of the royal towns played a role later on in political affairs, it was of secondary importance. They no longer defended the interests of urban artisans, but only a narrow class of the commercial and official patriciate. The interests of one part of that patriciate were linked with the ruler; the others' interests, as a rule non-Catholic, with the influential nobles of the Estates opposition.

Overshadowed by these severe punishments, the Bartholomew Diet of August 1547 took place. The nobles renounced the right to independent confederation, which would in the future cramp any opposition activity. The Estates also declared their agreement with the coronation of the next ruler during the lifetime of the incumbent. With this they enabled the Habsburg dynasty to fix itself on the Bohemian throne and would no longer be able to exploit short-term interregnums between the death of the incumbent and the accession of the new king in order to freely formulate a political program and vigorously implement their own claims. However the nobility as a whole did not suffer and it was only a question of time before favourable domestic and international circumstances allowed it to regroup.

Of the conflicts that were in the offing, the religious question was ever more important; this would come to a point in the second half of the 16th and beginning of the 17th centuries throughout Europe. The Catholic Church, aware of the necessity of an inner spiritual renewal and of the favourable conditions for the restoration of its previous power, engaged in the struggle to regain lost ground, mainly through the offices of the combative Jesuit order. After the Council of Trent (1545–1563), in which the Church formulated a clear program, it embarked on the reconversion of those areas affected by the Reformation.

At the same time however the bonds of Reformation confessions with many secular rulers and magnates in Central Europe were consolidated: each of these considered himself the head of the pertinent church in his land or as the protector of Protestants in his own domain. Both Catholic and Protestant confessions were now legitimized by governing power, and where appropriate could justify their opposition activities, or even armed resistance against a ruler who violated the principle of religious freedom. This tendency which accompanied the division of Western Christendom along the lines of both politics and the confessions, was obvious to the west of the Bohemian borders. Lutheran princes in the Roman-German Empire won equal status for their religions and the right to implement Lutheranism on their territories as the one recognized faith in the Peace of Augsburg in 1555. However it was not long before princes of a Calvinist bent also began to implement a similar policy, suppressing both Catholicism and Lutheranism in their lands. Although it was not until the decrees of the Peace of Westphalia in 1648 that Calvinists won full legalization, as early as the second half of the 16th century a very ruthless power struggle between states and statelets of all three confessional-political orientations took place in the immediate neighbourhood of the Bohemian crown lands. Non-Catholic Protestantism also spread in Austria and Hungary, as well as further European countries. Radical Calvinism, with which the Unity of Brethren gradually converged, gained its main support in Switzerland, the Low Countries and the Palatinate. These states became hot spots of European politics, from which intellectual stimuli radiated as well as new sources of tension in the Czech environment.

Unlike other states in Central and Western Europe, Bohemia and Moravia had more than a century of experience behind them of armed conflict over the two competing religions. The Hussite revolution and the wars which followed, along with the consequent social upheavals, showed that neither the Hussites nor their Catholic opponents had sufficient strength to establish their religion exclusively. Realizing this, they became relatively accustomed to peaceful co-existence, and with the years, there were attempts to codify that co-existence in law. A noteworthy development in Moravia was the separation of politics from religion over a period of time; religion was to remain protected from external interventions in the area of personal, inner spiritual life. Thanks to the similar outlooks of a number of aristocrats there, Moravia – along with Poland and Transylvania – became one of the oases of religious freedom in the turbulent European theatre in the second half of the 16th century.

However, the peaceful co-existence of a range of confessions went against the Habsburg policy of reconversion. Ferdinand I contributed to the deterioration of relations when he attempted to use his increased authority after 1547 to implement Catholicism in order to cement the position of the monarchy. He moved against the Unity of Brethren most harshly, whom he blamed above all others for the anti-Habsburg rebellion, forcing many of their members into exile. The Brethren left Bohemia for Moravia, as well as for Poland, where they founded a new centre in Leszno. Displaying a similar ruthlessness but with no lasting effect, Ferdinand I tried to run out the Anabaptists who settled in southern Moravia under the protection of the nobility from the 1520s.

As soon as Ferdinand I began to threaten the religious freedom to which the people had become accustomed, he encountered angry resistance. In 1549, Bohemian nobles foiled the king's manoeuvre to integrate the Utraquists into the Catholic Church. Immediately after, in 1550, the Moravian Estates let him know that they had no intention of tolerating the ruler's interventions in the country's religious affairs. He failed also in his crackdown against the Lutherans in other parts of the Bohemian Crown, particularly in north-western Bohemia, which is especially evident from the fact that Luther's followers occupied an unshakeable position in Silesia and both Lusatian margraviates around the middle of the 16th century. Thus from the 1550s Ferdinand I opted for a different tactic. He abandoned one-off administrative interventions against other faiths and began systematically to strengthen the Catholic clergy, in which he saw an important Habsburg ally in the decades ahead. In 1556 he introduced the Jesuits to Bohemia, members of the Society of Jesus, who distinguished themselves through their strict discipline, single-minded orientation on the re-education of young nobles and wealthy burghers, as well as through their excellent results as school-teachers and preachers. The king founded the first college in Prague's Clementinum, the role of which was educate the spiritual and secular exponents of a thorough-going reconversion policy. With the renewal of the Prague archbishopric in 1561, which had guttered during the Hussite revolution, he laid the foundations of the systematic renewal of the Catholic Church's administration. In contrast, the ruler made it impossible for the Protestants to build their necessary ecclesiastical organization and in 1562 stripped the non-Catholic Estates of their right to run the ancient so-called Lower Consistory, the central administration and judicial body of the Utraquist Church.

The non-Catholic Estates understood that a whole set of their privileges were in the balance along with freedom of confession. This realization was reflected in the transformation of the opposition's policy. It was now no longer in conflict with government centralization alone, but also with religious unification, which was pushing to join the whole population in a single permitted faith. While most lords and knights were in agreement on the first issue, on the second the viewpoints of individual nobles varied according to their confession. Members of the old noble lines, who in the third quarter of the 16th century worked in the Land governments, for the most part had not given in to religious zealotry, and occupied mediating positions. Under the leadership of the Supreme Burgrave Vilém of Rožmberk, who was the most influential figure in Czech politics from the 1550s to the beginning of the 1590s, they tried to retard the escalation of religious-political disputes. They used this tactic also during the reign of Ferdinand's son Maximilian II (r. 1564–1576), an educated and tolerant ruler, but unenterprising and capable only of continuing the long-term Habsburg strategy in his government of the country. Since Maximilian became bogged down in massive state debt and misfortunes abroad, the nobility's opposition in the diet grew stronger, and they were partially successful in returning to the *status quo ante* 1547.

Along with the expansion of the widespread Estates opposition, there also emerged a narrower grouping of nobles who did not wish to be demoted in importance, or suffer persecution, purely because they belonged to an unlawful church. These were Neo-Utraquists who had broken away from the Old Utraquists, having abandoned attempts to reach agreement with the Catholic Church, and accepted many of the stimuli of the Lutheran Reformation; also there were orthodox Lutherans, mainly nobles from the border regions with German-speaking populations, and members of the Unity of Brethren. These all made up the majority of the Bohemian Estates, but they were not sufficiently represented in the most influential offices. The Protestant opposition's program became one of absolute equality with Catholics, which they achieved at the Land Diet of 1575. With Bohuslav Felix Hasištejnský of Lobkowicz at their head, they accepted as their intellectual and organizational base the newly formulated common confession – the Bohemian Confession – which aptly joined the Hussite tradition with the newer Lutheran principles of respect for the specificities of the Brethren's faith. At the same time they agreed on an ecclesiastical system whereby a Land Church would be established in Bohemia under the auspices and power of the Protestant Estates. They presented the Bohemian Confession and ecclesiastical system to Maximilian II for approval. The king however did not accept the proposals as the Czech Catholics and Old Utraquists were against them, as were the main Catholic powers – the Papal Curia and Spain. Disciples of the Bohemian Confession did not in the end broker any fundamental resolution with the ruler, receiving only his oral promise that he would continue to preserve religious tolerance.

The main result of the months-long negotiations was the creation of a narrower, Estates opposition of Neo-Utraquists and Brethren, with a clear program for the conflicts ahead concerning the legal standing of non-Catholics. This aim was not achieved by the Protestant Estates until 1609 with the Letter of Majesty on religious freedom. At that point the long stand-off between the ruler and the Estates reached its final stages, and the way to a conclusive solution was open.

3 Society and Culture in the Century Preceding the Thirty Years' War

The Bohemian crown became part of the Habsburg monarchy as a typical composite state of the Modern Era made up of autonomous lands, and which had a population of several nationalities and religions on its territory. Czechs and Germans lived there; in the northern half, Poles and Lusatian Serbs; and in all the lands Jews were settled; as well as other minorities in the larger towns. Although in Bohemia and Moravia – especially in the border regions – there was a considerable German minority, Czechs clearly predominated in all social classes here. It was the Czech-speaking nobles themselves who considered the language crucial to cement the whole state. Thus the lords and knights emphasized the privileged standing of Czech, which was by law the only language of the administration, above all at the Diet and the Land Court – in Moravia from as early as 1480 and from 1495 in Bohemia. In the course of the 16th century the significance of German grew as a generally accepted means of communication in all lands of the Habsburg monarchy, and this language became for Czechs travelling abroad the most frequently used. The German-speaking population of the Czech state of course used its language both in local administration and in contact with the central executive.

The influx of foreigners to the Bohemian crown lands, both in the Habsburgs' service and for economic reasons, seemed to the indigenous population so strong that at the beginning of the 17th century, literary defences of the Czech language appeared, the most famous of which was The Scolding of the Slipshod Czech (*Okřik na nedbalého Čecha*) by Pavel Stránský in 1618. These efforts received institutional support in the Prague diet of 1615, where a law was even passed to protect the Czech language (though this was not very effective). Although language differences provoked occasional tension between members of individual nations, at the same time they created an interesting bedrock for the blending of social and cultural influences. By no means did they become for the Bohemian crown lands a difficulty as serious as the division of the population into the Protestant majority and the privileged Catholic minority. However even these problems of confession were drowned out by the pressing social and economic worries of everyday life.

For most of the population the basic livelihood was agriculture. At the beginning of the Modern Era, there were no great technical changes which would have increased agrarian production. However, the constant growth of population numbers, marked in Central Europe from the middle of the 15th century, increased the demand for agricultural crops, raised their prices and stimulated the expansion of production. The growing towns, the mining regions (mostly the Ore Mountains; *Krušné hory*), military camps and fortresses on the Habsburg-Ottoman border in Hungary, as well as the densely populated areas neighbouring Bohemia to the west and south – all these offered large markets. Favourable conditions for the expansion of grain tillage and regional specialization, mainly fruit and hop farming, and in southern Moravia vineyards.

It was above all mid-level farmers and the richer ones who dedicated themselves to the profitable business of foodstuffs, and their standing generally improved. In contrast, families of peasants and lacklands lived on the poverty line. Many of them made their living as menials on large farmsteads and the land holdings of the nobility, or joined the ranks of the village and town poor without regular shelter. Some entered the military and left the country, mainly for Hungary or the Low Countries, where they were hired in whole regiments of Czech sappers. Others found themselves on the very edge of society, wandering through the country, stealing, or in groups of bandits threatening the life and limb of respectable burghers and villagers on public roads. The unsettled Romany population found themselves in a similarly marginal position, beyond the law, in the 16th century. While to the east (in Poland, Hungary and the Balkans) the settlement of Romanies who earned their living by artisanal or commercial activity was tolerated, in Western Europe these itinerants were cruelly persecuted. The Bohemian crown lands became a transit land for them, mainly when these itinerants were fleeing persecution and murder in the German territorial states. From the 1530s, measures were repeatedly taken by both the ruler and the diets forbidding them residence in Bohemia and Moravia. Although the propaganda of the time occasionally referred to the Romanies as Turkish spies and incendiaries because of their complexion, for the most part the itinerants were not murdered. However in an environment that tended towards the legal restraint of those classes of society without privileges, there was little chance of even beginning the integration of Romanies in the settled population.

In rural areas which were controlled administratively by noble authorities, besides small village producers there was now a new dynamic agent. This was the large farmstead of the nobleman. The owners of these farms were no longer satisfied with the collection of fixed rents and goods from their subject peasants, but wished to establish large-scale production which they ran directly. The most entrepreneurial lines of the lords and knights – the families of Pernštejn, Rožmberk, Trčka of Lípa, Smiřický and others – exploited the large transfers of property during the Hussite period and after, and from lands which had been split up before, gradually created expansive economically cohesive domains. For these authorities the main measure of wealth was no longer the number of castles and forts, or the amount of rent-paying client settlements, but commercial profit in ready money. Rents, moreover, were not sufficient for the growing demands of the nobility, since the real value of currency had fallen and at the same time the requirements for the reconstruction of aristocratic seats for official functions, for travel and for political activities had risen at an unusual rate. Nobles had to search for more substantial sources of profit and found them in production and commercial activities, whether run by themselves or their subject burghers.

Lords and knights supported the brewing of beer in both the large and small towns under their authority, which disturbed the long-standing privilege of the royal towns; but the nobles made a lot of profit from this. They established their own sheep-folds, they built ponds and in areas with large ponds – mainly in southern and eastern Bohemia and southern Moravia – they amply benefited from the sale of fish, in both domestic and foreign markets. After the mid-point of the 16th century, they set up their own breweries, mills, farmsteads, which supplied large amounts of grain, in some places even glassworks, lime-kilns and iron mills. In this fashion the lords' financial income was multiplied in the course of several decades. It paid to export some types of goods on carts or river boats (mainly on the Elbe to Saxony); in general however expensive transport over land made the development of commerce with foreign lands more difficult.

Owners of large demesnes depended upon domestic markets above all. They exploited their lordly powers to set up monopolies in purchasing, production and sale, at the expense of their own subjects, the royal towns and foreign merchants. They systematically overhauled their large farmsteads, transforming them into independent economic units, in which the nobles' businesses were connected with the subjects' settlements and with market centres of the demesne in the vicinity of the towns. The lords also claimed the right to cheap labour. Permanent menials and wage labourers no longer sufficed, and thus they began to exact subject labour (*robota*), the significance of which had fallen greatly in the preceding period of the rent economy (13th–15th centuries). The situation differed from one demesne to another; however taken in the entirety in the course of the 16th century and the beginning of the 17th, there was an unmistakable increase of subject-labour duties.

This effort to exploit the subject work-force effectively on the large farmsteads led to the gradual restriction of villagers' movements and to the general deterioration of their legal standing. However, the long-standing agricultural boom, which from the close of the 15th century to the beginning of the 17th, provided a living to the greater part of the subject peasantry, and maintained the social contract in the Bohemian crown lands. This social balance was disturbed only by the events of the Thirty Years' War (1618–1648), when the consequences of economic decline bore down on the peasantry along with violent reconversion and the ravages of war.

The inhabitants of towns, socially and legally, were fundamentally different from villagers. From as early as the High Middle Ages the Bohemian crown lands were numbered – mainly in comparison with their eastern neighbours – among countries with a fairly dense urban network. Although almost all the important towns had been established before the 14th century, in the following period, especially in the second half of the 15th century and the 16th century, the number of towns markedly grew. Many villages were furnished with market and production privileges; they gained autonomy and became lesser towns. Some thriving lesser towns were raised to the level of towns. Around the year 1600, in the five lands of the Bohemian crown there were about 1,000 towns and lesser towns whose size depended on the location, economic prosperity and the political significance of individual localities.

In the environment of Central Europe more generally, and not just in the Bohemian crown lands, there was no city of truly global importance with over 100,000 inhabitants, like the most important metropolises of western and southern Europe. According to Central European measures, there were two large towns in the Czech state each with over 20,000 inhabitants. Prague held the first place: at the end of the 16th century it had become the largest Central European metropolis with roughly 60,000 inhabitants, and this was mainly due to the imperial residence of Rudolf II, whose presence stoked the big consumption boom and immigration to the group of Prague towns. For a long period the second place in the Czech state had been occupied by Wrocław, the political, ecclesiastical and cultural centre of Silesia, which had about 23,000 inhabitants in the middle of the 16th century. Thanks to the short-lived silver rush in the Ore Mountains, the newly founded town of Jáchymov sprang up and with 18,000 inhabitants became the second largest town in Bohemia. But after the lodes were effectively exhausted – as in Schwaz in the Tyrol, the southern area of the Habsburg monarchy – its significance steeply declined once more. Two Silesian towns (Głogów and Świdnica) hovered around the 10,000 mark, while the other significant localities in the Bohemian crown lands as a rule only came up to the 5,000 mark.

The greater part of municipalities were made up of artisanal and artisanal-agricultural localities specializing in certain foods, clothing and other crafts, which supplied routine needs. A small number of towns diverged from this mean due to their involvement in foreign trade (for instance Wrocław in Silesia, Görlitz in Upper Lusatia, Olomouc in Moravia), or because of their exceptional consumption (Prague) or, on the contrary, their extraordinary production strength. In this group were towns with a developed woolen cloth industry targeted for export (Jihlava, Broumov) as well as mining towns.

Mining and the refinement of ore was one of the most important branches of production. Its development influenced the whole economy of the Bohemian crown lands. The mining towns of Bohemia were famed for their extraordinary production of silver and pewter. From the yield of the mines at Jáchymov, the silver *thaler* was minted from 1519, an important coin of international trade (after which the American dollar was later named, along with the currency of roughly a further thirty states throughout the world). Czech pewter, along with that of England, also occupied a leading position in Europe. However in the course of the 16th century, there wert technical difficulties linked to sub-surface mining. It also suffered from a lack of capital and with competition from American imports of precious metals. These blows affected the Czech state, whose international trade balance was maintained by those very exports of metals and coins. The decline of mining, which came about in the second half of the 16th century, led to the lowering of holdings of silver, and thus the general impoverishment of the Bohemian crown lands.

The development of towns was permanently influenced by the growth in the power of the nobility. From the turn of the 15th and 16th centuries the subject towns, and later also the lords' business enterprises, offered serious competition to the free royal towns. The nobility exploited their political dominance by favouring their own or their subjects' production at the expense of the royal towns. They limited the supply of raw materials to these towns from rural hinterlands and forbade the purchase of their products on their demesnes. The inhabitants of the royal towns were not able to compete, as their products – because of pricing and quality – were never in demand in foreign markets. Thus they were restricted to local and regional markets and could not establish themselves in international commerce.

The entrepreneurism of the burghers was hamstrung by lack of capital, and they preferred to close themselves within guilds for protection and familiar material certainty. Although the class-levelling of the guilds guaranteed a living, it led artisans to complacency, leaving them happy with a humble and undynamic mediocrity. It prevented technical and organizational development like that of the expansion of production in southern and western Europe. In the towns, as a rule only those big merchants who participated in the transit trade and the export of luxury goods became richer. However these patricians invested their money in land holdings rather than business ventures in the towns.

The poor economic development of Czech towns was still furthered by the decline of the export of the products of Czech mercery, which at the close of the 16th century suffered from a serious lack of raw materials. This deepened the economic stagnation of the Bohemian crown lands, which was not reversed by the expansion of the linen industry in the northern border region of Bohemia and Moravia, in Silesia and Lusatia. The general situation was not changed even by indications of more advanced manufacturing in a small number of glassworks, paper mills and iron mills which emerged outside the framework of the towns. The unequivocal dominance of the nobles' large farmsteads in economic life, sealed also by the political defeat of the royal towns in 1547, and the restriction in the guilds of artisanal production became the characteristic features of trade and production in the Bohemian crown lands. Thus the Czech state, even before the Thirty Years' War, was closer to the stagnant areas of Central and Eastern Europe, and its development after 1620 only confirmed this.

* * *

In this social environment, which was economically limited and situated between the more dynamic western Europe and the more conservative eastern continent, the cultural life of the Bohemian crown lands developed in the first century of Habsburg rule. Despite its regional, confessional and national diversity, it generally equalled the cultural standards of Central Europe. The latter absorbed the stimuli of western Europe and literary and artistic production burgeoned. But only seldom did it influence the fundamental directions of spiritual development, as happened in Italy, France, Spain, the Low Countries and England in the Modern Era. The style of the period, defined by the last echoes of late Gothic and later by the unequivocal dominance of the Renaissance, was in the Bohemian crown lands marked by the inertia of the schools' variants of Renaissance humanism, by the dissemination of the German and Swiss Reformation and eventually the Catholic Counter-Reformation offensive. In this atmosphere, there were no epochal political or philosophical ideas, or profound artistic innovation; however, favourable circumstances were created for the reception of tried and tested paradigms.

Omnipresent religious themes took precedence over the solution of secular problems even at a time when didactic and travel writing about Palestine, the Ottoman Empire, Russia and America, introduced new horizons and far-flung vistas from overseas. This tendency was reflected in contemporary cosmographic literature, which through the combination of historical and geographical findings mediated a complex world picture. The largest printed Czech book of the 16th century became the Czech Cosmography (*Kozmografia česká*), the

JAROSLAV PÁNEK

work of the Catholic scholar Zikmund of Puchov, printed in Prague in 1554. This enormous work originated from the recently published Latin text of the Basel polymath Sebastian Münster *Cosmographia Universalis* (1550), but it was no mere translation of a bestseller. On the contrary it attempted to adapt that book to the Czech context and to emphasize the significance of the Bohemian crown lands in the Europe of the time, while also criticizing the loose style of Renaissance life. At the same time it reflected the idea that the role of the combined forces of the Czechs and Poles was to push back the Turkish invasion that was threatening, and protect Central Europe from the onslaught of militant Islam.

The impulse to transmit such a world view came, it seems, from the ruler's court, which through its support of literary and artistic activities usually pursued a politically oriented representation of the Habsburg dynasty. At the same time, however, this court environment in its extent and financial resources created a space for artistic, literary and musical activities and the satisfaction of the highest cultural demands. Whether it resided in Vienna or Prague, the Habsburg court provided extraordinary conditions for relatively unfettered artistic creation, which was sufficiently funded and at the same time free of the guild limitations of burgher life. The court environment was in essence cosmopolitan and facilitated the encounter of artists and scholars from all over Europe. As early as the reign of Ferdinand I, who often resided in Prague with his court, Italian Renaissance architecture was in fashion, best exemplified by the royal summer palace of the Belvedere near Prague Castle. Also a new style of life emerged, fundamentally different from that fostered by the provincial isolation of the last decades of Jagiellon rule. The Renaissance court in the Czech metropolis stabilized in the years 1547–1566 during the vice-regal government of the ruler's second-born son Ferdinand II of Tyrol. Surrounding himself with Czech and European nobles, he enlivened Prague and Plzeň in western Bohemia with court celebrations and tournaments, but also displayed artistic ambitions in the symbolic figuration of the Hvězda summer palace west of the Prague battlements.

The cultural significance of the Prague Habsburg court reached its zenith at the turn of the 16th and 17th centuries during the reign of Rudolf II, when it became one of the centres of European mannerism. The imperial residence then hosted a large amount of diplomats and courtiers, many outstanding scholars and artists, but also adventurers and conmen. True creators shared the Emperor's desire to create a great laboratory and an all-inclusive museum, which was embodied in the vast, systematically supplemented collections of Prague Castle. Among those active in the city were the most important astronomers of the age (Tycho Brahe of Denmark and Johannes Kepler of Germany), the English mathematician John Dee, outstanding musicians, artistic craftsmen and connoisseurs of art, especially painters, engravers and sculptors. Bartolomaeus Spranger, Hans von Aachen and Josef Heinz along with other Dutchmen, Italians and Germans created an original style, which combined Italian and Dutch stimuli. Through an emphasis on the inner world of man and dream representations (including explicit revelation of the erotic) this style – Rudolfine Mannerism – reflected the intellectual uncertainty and imbalance of all values, characteristic of the end of the Renaissance and the gradual transition to the emotionally exalted Baroque period.

Rudolfine mannerist culture drew upon ancient traditions of thought; however its works resulted from the intercourse of the intellectually oriented Emperor with humanist intellectuals of noble and burgherly birth, who created a "republic of letters" (*respublica litteraria*). In this environment, while the ruler was supreme patron (a new Hermes Trismegistos – god of the word, numbers and books), artists and scholars of various dispositions also held privileged positions. Together they sought to understand the world in all its facets, and regardless of religion they wished to find a way to both the primal origin of balance in interpersonal relations and to divine harmonies. They based their explorations on Neo-Platonic philosophy, Hermeticism and the Cabbalistic studies; they experimented in the natural sciences in a way which often pointed to the future, but they also attempted to find answers in the occult and esoteric teachings. They believed that the world was organized hierarchically on the idea of the analogy of every partial microcosm with the universal macrocosm, and that it was thus possible to interpret and rectify it by discerning the basic principles which were expressed in a symbolic language. Supporters of the idea of the similarity of all things based their thought on magic, hoping to find the key to the understanding of the systematic arrangement of the cosmos and afterwards also the mode of harmonious life within it. By gaining this wisdom, not only would they be capable of transforming ordinary metals into gold, discovering the elixir of youth or constructing artificial beings, but it would most importantly allow them to discern the entire magic universe, and express this through scientific or artistic means. It was intended to lead to the general rectification of human affairs, as Jan Amos Komenský (Comenius) would write, in synthesis, several decades later in his pansophical and all-emendating texts. Even though the method of analogical thinking and faith in an all-embracing conception of society was not confirmed by later developments, Rudolfine Mannerism joined the ranks of the great epochs of European cultural history. Its main contributions were to liberate intellectual creators from disadvantaged social and religious backgrounds, and, in a period of dramatic intellectual and political upheavals, to seek a universal world order and a peaceful path to understanding between people.

The presence of the ruler's court markedly raised the allure of Prague, which in the minds of foreigners became one of the undisputed centres of the contemporary world. At the beginning of the 17th century a new map of Europe appeared in the famous Dutch atlases of Johannes Blaeu which represented the standing of Bohemia and its metropolis. A *veduta* of Prague was to be found there among the nine most significant cities of the old continent, alongside Rome, Constantinople, Venice, Paris, London, Amsterdam, Toledo and Lisbon. Also, in the symbolic representation of the inhabitants of the land – Czechs (*Bohemi*) – were ranked among the ten main nations of Europe, alongside the English, French, Dutch, Spanish, Italians (Venetians), Germans, Poles, Hungarians and Greeks.

In the preceding period the Bohemian crown lands, and especially Prague, were accustomed to the influx of numerous foreigners for reasons of trade, short-term work or permanent residence. In the Rudolfine period however their number and significance was multiplied. Foreigners began to create distinctive communities which were in contact with the home countries, while at the same time building institutional structures in Bohemia

JAROSLAV PÁNEK

(mainly their own churches and schools). Above all this was true of the Germans, especially the Lutherans, who were closely connected with Saxony, but at the same time wished to establish German churches in all three important parts of the Prague agglomeration – the Old and New Towns, and the Lesser Town. They acted as the Prague German-speakers (*Germani evangelici Pragae*), but they managed to gain moral and material support not only abroad but also among ethnic Czech fellow-believers.

The Italian minority was of exceptional cultural and economic importance. They created Catholic institutions including hospitals and religious congregations, and gradually concentrated in Prague's Lesser Town in the environs of today's Vlašská (= Italian) Street. One of their leaders – the extraordinarily wealthy merchant of Mantuan origin, Ercole da Nova – through his social contacts, marriages and bequests clearly demonstrated the degree to which the Italian minority had successfully penetrated the Czech environment, while maintaining its cultural independence. More or less peaceful co-existence was facilitated by the fact that Italians brought to their new home knowledge required in the fields of architecture, art, chimney work, in commerce and finance, as well as in services otherwise unavailable, and thus were a welcome addition which in no way competed with the inhabitants. Long before the accession of Rudolf II, their skills opened the way to a number of towns in the Bohemian crown lands, where they became irreplaceable co-creators of the Czech variant of the late Renaissance.

The Dutch community was predominantly Calvinist in orientation. Although not large, it included important painters, goldsmiths and other artists, but also scholars, merchants and bankers. At the close of the 16th century, these belonged to the widespread international sect of Family of Love (*Huis der Liefde, Familia Amoris*) which linked an eschatologically coloured messianism with neo-stoicism; through correspondence its members maintained contact between the Low Countries and the cultural centres of the Habsburg monarchy – Prague, Vienna and Wrocław. After the issue of the Letter of Majesty on religious freedom of 1609, Dutch Protestants grew closer to the followers of the Bohemian Confession and established a small reformed church. This religious and cultural centre, which was joined by French men, Walloons, English men and Scots resident in Prague, created a striking cosmopolitan community which, during the anti-Habsburg uprising, stood unequivocally on the side of the Bohemian Estates.

Social life in Prague, and especially in the royal court, to a certain degree inspired the courtly environment of the prominent magnates – mainly the lords of Rožmberk, Pernštejn, Hradec, Lobkowicz, Liechtenstein, Žerotín and others. The same was true of the courts of the prelates, above all the bishops of Olomouc and Wrocław, who were for the most part men of international horizons, actively connected with Central European diplomacy and possessed of ecclesiastical and cultural contacts with Italy. In their main residences they all built ostentatiously decorated palaces in which they arranged public festivals; some of them employed not only a number of officials, courtiers and servants, but they also had their own musicians, painters and writers. The role of the courtiers was not only to service the opulent life of the magnates, their security and entertainment, but also their ceremonial representation through occasional or more demanding literary and artistic works. The most advanced aristocratic courts started up collections of artistic works and curiosities, extensive libraries and galleries of family portraits. While the Pernštejns, and later the Lobkowiczes, were noteworthy for their passionate interest in contemporary painting (especially from Spain), the Rožmberks created a marvellously organized archive and one of the best stocked libraries in Central Europe (approximately 11,000 volumes), which the Švamberks then took over from them. The last lord of the Rožmberks, Petr Vok, even had his own court historian, Václav Březan, who learned the critical method of Jean Bodin and composed the enormous *Rožmberk History* (*Historia rožmberská*) in five volumes (1610–1615). Among the aristocrats and the prelates, various forms of presentation of the role of particular person and line in history were established. A highly subjective approach was taken by the visionary and well-travelled critic of contemporary mores, Jan Zajíc of Házmburk in his memoirs *Sarmatia* (1553). In contrast, the Polish-Czech writer and genealogist Bartoloměj Paprocký used an objectivized approach to honour his topic, and in that spirit composed extensive works about the Estates of the individual lands of the Bohemian crown (the Moravian *Zrcadlo*, Mirror; 1593; the Bohemian *Diadochos* [1602]; the Silesian *Štambuch*, Album Amicorum, 1609).

The Bohemian, Moravian and Silesian nobility found unique cultural inspiration in the tour of Italy undertaken by fifty lords and knights together in the years 1551–1552. After a number of months spent in Lombardy and Liguria, they saw what life was like in the princely residences of Mantua, Milan and Genoa. Later leading politicians and patrons of the arts, Vilém of Rožmberk, Vratislav of Pernštejn, Zachariáš of Hradec, Burian Trčka and Jaroslav Smiřický together with others, thoroughly examined the supreme creations of Renaissance architecture, sculpture and painting. They came to know Italian music, but also fashionable dress and the gastronomic arts. And because they encountered this splendour at the very beginning of their public careers, their northern Italian experience profoundly and permanently influenced their subsequent attitudes to art and culture. In the second half of the 16th century, Renaissance residences sprang up in their demesnes (chateaux in Český Krumlov, Litomyšl, Opočno, Telč and elsewhere), exquisite summer palaces in the style of the Italian Renaissance villas and palaces in Prague. The decoration and furnishings of these and many other seats, whose owners had been indirectly inspired by Italy, were an index of the imitation of the Italian style of life. The humanist interest in antiquity, which found literary inspiration in ancient and contemporary Italy, contributed to this, just as it prompted readers to undertake study trips abroad.

Less wealthy lords and knights, in their own humbler seats, were only able to attempt a more distant imitation of the magnates' residences, but nevertheless they could actively participate in court life at the side of their powerful patrons. They thus became dependent on the lords, but some, through their expert services, bureaucratic activities or independent entrepreneurism, were able to amass liquid assets which they lent to permanently indebted magnates. In this way a web of interests was established, and this facilitated the wider dissemination of the courtly style of life and the reception of the architectural heritage in simplified form among the other social classes. The members of the lower nobility above all shared Renaissance interests in travel and art. Exceptionally gifted personages at the turn of the 16th and 17th centuries were able to encourage highly cultivated literary and musical creation – e.g., the political leader of the Unity of Brethren and writer of the *Anti-Alkorán* Václav Budovec of Budov or Václav Vratislav of Mitrovice, the author of the Adventures (*Příhody*) about his sojourn in the Ottoman Empire, or the travel writer and musical composer Kryštof Harant of Polžice.

The large towns such as Olomouc, Wrocław, Görlitz, Jáchymov, and especially Prague, provided excellent opportunities for culture. The great advantage of Prague was the existence of two schools of high learning which reflected the religious and political plurality of the Bohemian crown lands. While the older university founded by Charles IV was basically restricted to one faculty (that of Arts, or Philosophy), the newly founded Clementinum (1556) attracted the interest of the foremost personages of the Jesuit order and educated a new Catholic intelligentsia in the spirit of post-Tridentine renewal. The competition between two great educational institutions emphasized the contrast between the links of the Jesuits with the centres of the European Catholicism on the one hand and the impoverished Carolinum (the Prague university, named after Charles IV) as the Protestant-oriented Land university, catering for a relatively dense network of high-level Latin (particular) schools in the Bohemian and Moravian towns. However, there were also solid secondary schools, mainly thanks to the Lutherans (Jihlava and Velké Meziříčí in Moravia; Görlitz in Upper Lusatia or Brzeg and Goldberg (Złotorya) in Silesia) and the Unity of Brethren. Their *gymnasium* (particular school) in Ivančice was internationally renowned because of Esrom Rüdiger, a former professor of the University of Wittenberg, who around 1580 modernized teaching methods. The greatest support of the ruler and Catholic magnates was given of course to the Jesuit colleges with their psychologically and didactically developed system of teaching and upbringing. The colleges of Prague and Olomouc were promoted to the level of university soon after their founding, but Jesuit colleges also spread to further royal and subject towns, creating not only a pedagogical basis for reconversion, but missions also for that purpose.

One of the most important aims of education – apart from the teaching of religion and orientation in basic subjects from writing to mathematics and astronomy – was mastery of three languages: Czech, which had priority not only as the main means of communication, but also in the land institutions of Bohemia and Moravia; German, predominantly in common use in Silesia, Lusatia and the neighbouring territories of Germany and Austria; and Latin, the language of the Catholic Church, the universities and generally of European learned men. Apart from widespread tri-lingualism, Romance languages were also to be found among the most educated of nobles and burghers (mainly Italian and Spanish); some university scholars knew classical Greek and Hebrew. Active Czech-German bilingualism became the priority not only of those nobles and burghers whose first language was Czech, but also some native-German speakers who came to study in Czech schools and who for reasons of diplomacy, administration or trade became involved in relations which surpassed the borders of countries and languages.

The supreme form of education became the grand tour. This was intended to lead to the practical mastery of foreign languages, to education in law, medicine and theology, but also to familiarity with social customs, court etiquette and establishing useful personal acquaintances. Sufficiently endowed young men were sent to famous universities; nobles were also sent to royal courts and those of principalities. They most frequently made for the countries of Central Europe and Italy, less so to Spain, the Low Countries and England; in some cases they went to Palestine and Egypt to see the sights. During the second half of the 16th century the given confession of the traveller began to dictate the destination: while Catholics generally made for Bavaria and Italy, Protestants preferred the northern German and Swiss towns. After returning from the tour, they maintained correspondence with foreign friends, kept up with news in the weekly papers, read topical reports and specialized literature from abroad. In the period of the Renaissance the scope of the culturally and politically ambitious inhabitants of the Bohemian crown lands considerably exceeded the borders of their land, as these people took it for granted that they were participants in the common fate of Europe.

Access to culture for the inhabitants of the towns and lesser towns was much more restricted. For the most part it was possible to receive rudimentary education there, provided by the town or church school of Catholic or Protestant orientation; and the private schools in the rural seats of nobles were open only to a handful of high-born students. Nevertheless in this environment the small class of clergy and wealthier burghers became consumers of affordable literature and visual arts. Renaissance influences were also to be found there, often mediated by Italian builders and artisans; religious and didactic literature also made an impression. Some members of the local ascendancy not only read, but also tried to create works themselves, such as occasional Latin verses, and became part of the literary brotherhood which encouraged church music.

The burgher class was notably conservative and its cultural life was devoted to the maintenance of fixed values, which was in line moreover with the levelling tendency of the guilds in urban society. Whoever diverged too much from convention and did not have a powerful protector, came into conflict with the educated burghers. Such was the case of the extraordinarily talented creator of Latin love poetry and epigrams, Pavel of Jizbice, who turned even the masters of the Prague university against him, before his untimely death in 1607.

The intellectually unenterprising environment of the towns did not stop expressions of the Renaissance from making themselves at home there in the second half of the 16th century. Not only marvellous town-halls (for instance in Plzeň, Olomouc and Wrocław), but also Renaissance agglomerations of towns in Český Krumlov and Nové Město nad Metují in Bohemia, Slavonice and Telč in Moravia, Nysa in Silesia or Görlitz in Upper Lusatia: all these show that the original Gothic urban lay-out of towns was adjusted according to the Renaissance interpretation of beauty and public splendour. The Italian Renaissance was the most important influence in the Bohemian crown lands, but the Northern Renaissance was also of note, and for the most part domestic taste in Bohemia and Moravia adapted to this. So with the co-operation of foreign and domestic builders and artisans, the distinctive

Czech version of the Renaissance emerged and its construction is distinguished by its richly articulated gables and graceful ornamental decoration on facades.

In some cases, cultural interests overcame social differences between the Estates and led the nobility and burghers to joint endeavours. When carrying out especially demanding projects, the best printers – in the second half of the 16th century, outstanding among them were Jiří Melantrich of Aventinoe and his son-in-law Daniel Adam of Veleslavín – turned to the wealthiest aristocrats, receiving support from them for publications of the foremost works of Czech and European humanist learning. Book printing helped the spread of books about astronomy (the works of Tadeáš Hájek of Hájek), botany (the translation of Mattioli's renowned *Botany*), law, politics and other fields. Of the great historical works, Václav Hájek of Libočany's Bohemian Chronicle (*Kronika Česká*) became an especial favourite (1541).

The attempt to promote the faith and propagate particular confessions contributed to the hectic publication of religious texts; sometimes however it stimulated literary works of permanent value. This was especially true in the case of the Unity of Brethren, a minority unrecognized in law until 1609. Its attention to the native tongue reached its peak in the large translation work which surpassed a number of older Biblical texts in Czech. In the years 1579–1594, the Unity published a six-volume translation with commentary in a secret printing shop in Kralice in southern Moravia (The Kralice Bible, *Bible kralická*), which drew upon the Hebrew, Aramaic and Greek originals. The Czech text of the New Testament was prepared by the Brethren's bishop Jan Blahoslav, author of theoretical works on language and music; while a group of theologians and Hebrew scholars, among them converts of Jewish origin worked on the Old Testament in five volumes. These laid the grand foundations for the Czech language, which would support the revival of the Czech tongue at the turn of the 18th and 19th centuries, and at the same time was one of the pillars of Czech culture in the Modern Era.

In Bohemia and Moravia, in addition to the predominant Czech element, a number of German humanists of domestic or foreign origin found a home in the 16th century, working in the border towns or leaving for Prague and other cultural centres. The town doctor of Jáchymov, mineralogist and metallurgist, Georgius Agricola, and the analyst of metallurgic processes Lazar Ercker, were outstanding internationally recognized experts in the area of mining and metallurgy; Agricola's work *De re metallica libri XII* (1556) was ranked among the classic works of that field. Some writers – such as the physician and poet Georg Handsch, close colleague of the patron Jan Hodějovský – wrote in Latin and also knew Czech. Other literary men directly drew on Czech literature in their works, especially when they wrote about the history of Bohemia. Martin Boregk considered his *Behmische Cronica* (1587) the first attempt at a German treatment of Czech history on the basis of the Latin text of Jan Dubravius, and Johann Sandel translated Václav Hájek of Libočany's *Bohemian Chronicle* into German in 1596. Local German historians created chronicles of Cheb, Trutnov and other border towns which were of great documentary value.

Czechs and Germans met in the field of culture and this was manifest on different levels. Under the patronage of the Czech magnate Petr Vok of Rožmberk, the lyrical works of his secretary Theobald Hoeck *Schönes Blumenfeld* (1601) were published, a book which foreshadowed the rise of German Baroque poetry. The texts of several German authors from the Bohemian crown lands gained however a Czech readership through translation. For instance several Czech translations appeared in book form at the turn of the 16th and 17th centuries of the works of the zealous disciple of the Lutheran Reformation and parish priest of Jáchymov, Johannes Mathesius, author of the renowned collection of sermons *Sarepta oder Bergpostill* (1562). Nevertheless, there were also works which displayed the strong tensions between Czechs and Germans. Among these, for its dramatic treatment a special place is reserved for the play The Terrible and Unique Tragedy of Two Czech Lords (*Eine crunser seltzambe Tragoedi von zweyen böhmischen Landtherren*; 1594). This work captured the recent hate-filled collapse of relations between the German burghers of Chomutov, an important centre of Lutheranism from Saxony in Bohemia, and their nobility, the Czech Catholic lord Jiří Popel of Lobkowicz.

Songs, broadsheets and above all distinctive chronicle texts (*Geschichts-Bücher*) of Anabaptists of Hutterite orientation became a truly unique expression of Germanophone culture. These advocates of pacifism and radical ideas about social equality, after earlier persecution in German and Austrian lands, found shelter in tolerant Moravia. From the 1520s, they settled on the demesnes of the southern Moravian nobility and lived there in their distinctive communes to the year 1622 when they were run out as a result of Habsburg reconversion. Anabaptists, whose numbers reached 20,000, were distinguished by their unparalleled mastery of several specialized crafts (mainly, in cutlery and the production of artistically crafted faiences), and agricultural techniques and services. This was why they were welcomed by the new authorities and enjoyed their protection. From the Moravian Estates, they even received a unique privilege: the tax revenue from Anabaptists was not used for military purposes (which would have been in conflict with their Hutterite pacifism), but for the financing of local doctors. Despite the exceptional nature of their opinions and organization, for which they were persecuted and burned in other European countries, the Anabaptists became a part of Moravian society. Although this process was violently interrupted, the north American Anabaptists, descendants of the Moravian Hutterites, consider the 16th and the beginning of the 17th centuries the golden age of their agitated history to this day.

Those crown lands with a German majority in the population stood out for their distinctive cultural life. Silesia and Lusatia were criss-crossed by foreign trade routes which were punctuated by economically important towns which quickly absorbed the stimuli of Lutheran reform. In the turbulent beginnings of the Reformation it was here in Legnica in Silesia (thanks to Prince Frederick II of Legnica) that the first Protestant university in Europe was established. However because of the disputes between theologians there, and also because of a lack of funding, it foundered after three years (1526–1529). Silesian and Lusatian humanists, which were educated in local *gymnasia* and in foreign centres of high learning, worked in their native countries or made for Prague and Vienna, Poland and western Europe. Outstanding among these were the representatives of the early Silesian Reformation, Johannes Hess, author of the lost historical work *Silesia Magna* (before 1547), and Johann Crato of Krafftheim, who in his role of the personal physician to Ferdinand I, Maximilian II and Rudolf II importantly influenced the spiritual life of the Habsburg court in the second half of the 16th century. The self-made religious visionary of Lutheran orientation, Jacob Böhme, originally a Görlitz shoemaker, with his philosophical-mystical system (*inter alia*, the text *Aurora*,1612), made his mark on European thought and influenced not only his contemporaries but later the Pietists and Romantics also. Also in Silesia and Lusatia occasional humanist poetry developed abundantly as an instrument of social communication. From that environment there arose a writer who broke free of Latinate poetic mannerisms and laid the theoretical foundations of German Baroque literature. Martin Opitz, who programmatically stood against those who scorned the use of the vernacular (*Aristarchus*,1617, *Buch von der deutschen Poeterey*,1624), and in his consolatory verse of the years 1620–1621 presented one of the first critical views of the beginnings of the Thirty Years' War.

The Polish population of Silesia was made up for the most part of peasants. There was no nobility and only a small number of them among the burghers. Such a social structure corresponded to the use of Polish mainly in religious texts for rural people. The significance of this literature rose in the 16th century with the use of book-printing in the service of the Reformation and Counter-Reformation, when Polish hymnals, prayer books, catechisms and postils were printed above all in Brzeg and Oleśnica. Polish however was also used in the executive, mainly in the bureaucratic records of smaller towns and villages. The Polish-speaking Silesian intelligentsia were concentrated in nearby Cracow and its university, which further emphasized the fact that Silesia was peripheral in the development of Polish, especially in contrast with the dramatic developments in the neighbouring territory of the Polish-Lithuanian state.

This ethnically diverse picture of the Czech state is rounded out by the Lusatian Serbs in the territory of Upper and Lower Lusatias, from the first half of the 14th century to the year 1635, the two smallest lands of the Bohemian crown. The remnants of a former Slavic settlement in the northern regions of German Elbe and Baltic, they inhabited villages along a wide band of territory between the northern border of Bohemia, Dresden and Berlin (the number of Serbs in both Lusatian margraviates is estimated at 120,000–150,000 midway through the 16th century, of which about 50,000 lived in Upper Lusatia). Subject peasants predominated in the Lusatian-Serbian population, but a considerable number of Serbs lived in towns with mostly ethnic German in the dense urbanization of Upper Lusatia. The social and national make-up of the population of both Lusatias contributed to the establishment of Latin and German as the languages of writing. Nevertheless through study in the *gymnasia* of Bautzen, Görlitz and other towns, and at the Saxon university in Wittenberg, a Sorbian intelligentsia emerged among which theologians played an influential role, and who in their pastoral services employed Sorbian, the Slavic language of the Lusatia. Some of the Lusatian humanists endorsed their native tongue, though they used Latin in their literary works. One example of this was the physician and polymath Caspar Peucer, author of the Upper Lusatian verse chronicle *Idyllium patria seu historia Lusatiae superioris*, published in Bautzen in 1594. The attempt to employ the native tongue to promote the Lutheran

Reformation gradually laid the groundwork for the next stage in the development of the two written languages in the course of the 16th century. In Lower Sorbian there appeared, among others, a translation of the New Testament (manuscript from 1548) and a hymn book as the first proven printed book (1574); in Upper Sorbian a collection of translated spiritual songs appeared at the end of the 16th century. Both contacts with the Czech-language environment and the cultural stimuli of the German Reformation thus contributed to the retardation of long-term Germanization and the constitution of two small but viable Slavic nations in Central Europe.

In all five countries of the Bohemian Crown the distinctive culture of the Jewish diaspora lived and flourished, although its standing was ambivalent. The Habsburg rulers confirmed the privileges of the Jews and in an attempt to maximize income from the profits of their commercial activities they formally protected them. But they could not consistently prevent discrimination against them. For reasons of religion and political opportunism, Ferdinand I expelled the Jews from Bohemia on two occasions (1541, 1557), but he did not stop their gradual return. However many Jews from Prague, which was the largest Hebrew community in the Czech state, left for Moravia: in that freer atmosphere they did not come into commercial conflict with the burghers and won the protection of the noble authorities. The golden age of Czech Judaism was the reign of Rudolf II, who at the close of the 16th century expanded their commercial privileges and strengthened the autonomy of the Jewish Town in Prague, which was becoming one of the most important centres of Ashkenazi Jews.

The economic and social rise of Prague Jews was embodied by their primate and privileged "court Jew" Mordechai Maisl (1528–1601), one of the richest merchants and bankers of Rudolfine Prague. This financier, with a deep sense of civic duty, was responsible for the extraordinary construction and overall urbanistic form of the Jewish Town, and he also supported Jewish science and literature. He became the patron of the renowned Talmudic school led by Judah Löw ben Bezalel (1512–1609), the former Moravian provincial rabbi of Mikulov. Rabbi Löw, whose later legend was linked to the artificial creature, the Golem, was one of the most important thinkers of late Humanism in the Bohemian crown lands, and left after him extensive pedagogical and religious-philosophical works. Among his students, David Gans (1541–1613) was outstanding, who as an astronomer and mathematician forged contacts with Tycho Brahe and Johannes Kepler; but his lasting place in Jewish science is due to *Cemah Dawid* (Bough of David; 1592), which stands at the beginning of Modern Era Jewish historiography. In the environment of Jewish Prague, politically uncertain but culturally fruitful, Hebrew book production from 1512 also developed, reaching exceptional levels, both in terms of typography and content. In addition to religious literature, it was capable of producing beautiful editions of the works of the prominent Jewish scholars, such as Rabbi Löw himself or David Gans, and through this means influenced Jewish communities in other countries of Central Europe.

The society of the Czech state at the beginning of the Modern Era corresponded to the specific standing of Central Europe in the history of the old continent. Although its culture was not – with the exception of Rudolfine Mannerism – influential further afield, it did have

218

fundamental significance for the nations of this territory or those that were newly forming. The Bohemian crown lands learned from the tragic experience of the religious wars of the 15th century and in the following age of the 16th century advanced to a relatively high level of toleration. Moravia above all became a land of unusual religious and intellectual freedom where social, religious and ethnic influences from central, southern and western Europe came together and blended. It was no coincidence that at the beginning of the great European catastrophe of the Thirty Years' War an attempt to establish constitutionally a free confederation of Central European countries emerged from Bohemia and Moravia; or that one of the most significant thinkers of the 17th century Jan Amos Komenský (Comenius) came from there in precisely that period. His thinking attempted the general improvement of things human, and if he was unable to do this for his own generation, then he wished to achieve it at least through education of the next.

4 The Approach of Conflict and the Bohemian Estates Rebellion, 1618–1620

Although the Bohemian kingdom was both one of the pillars of the Central European monarchy and its territory was home to the strongest Estates opposition, this in no way meant that the fuse of the Thirty Years' War would necessarily be lit there. The more important epicentre of potential conflict lay somewhere else entirely. The ruler's residence and the monarchy's administrative centre, in the first five decades of Habsburg reign and again from 1612, was in Vienna in Lower Austria. On the threshold of the Thirty Years' War, this was the effective centre of political power in Central Europe. The largest Central European battle-ground remained Hungary, in which, with short breaks, the ceaseless struggle against Ottoman expansion took place. The focal point of Central European political life was transferred to Bohemia at the beginning of the 1580s when the Holy Roman Emperor and Bohemian King Rudolf II (r. 1576–1611/1612) moved permanently to Prague. In one stroke the largest metropolis in the greater Czech-Austrian-Hungarian confederation became the centre of diplomatic life in Europe, and the Bohemian crown lands were transformed into the place where the confessional politics of Catholics, Lutherans and Calvinists collided. These foreign stimuli blended in many ways with the clashing interests of the domestic aristocracy and patriciate, and cathected the tension in domestic politics with wider European conflicts.

Bohemian nobles wished to transfer the Habsburg residence to Prague as early as the election of Ferdinand I since, after their negative experience with the Jagiellonian kings in Buda, they thought it would be more advantageous to have their king close and, circumstances permitting, control the ruler's court. Rudolf however was the first ruler whom it suited, as he valued the strategic advantage of Prague and the greater safety it provided in contrast with Vienna, which had been repeatedly threatened by Turkish invasions. When Rudolf II came to Prague he was a widely cultured ruler with occasionally peculiar methods of governance, which were influenced on the one hand by his weak health and festering mental illness, and on the other were in line with his intention to continue the Habsburg policy of reconversion.

From the end of the 1570s, and especially after the Emperor's move to Prague in 1583, the advancement of the Bohemian kingdom became the measure of success of the Habsburg dynasty and Catholicism in Central Europe. The key to reconversion was meant to be control over the most important Land offices by radical Catholics of the rising generation, already trained in the uncompromising Jesuit ethos. After previous failures, one turning point came in 1599 when an unusually capable bureaucrat, Zdeněk Vojtěch Popel of Lobkowicz, was appointed head of the Bohemian Court Chancellery, the most important office of the Czech state. After long preparations along the political axis of the Prague court and the Olomouc bishopric in the years 1598–1603, a similar turn of events took place in Moravia. In the two key lands of the Bohemian Crown and of the Habsburg monarchy in its entirety both the offices of the monarch and the Estates were brought into the service of the Counter Reformation. A new wave of persecution of the Unity of Brethren began and trials threatened the leaders of the Protestant opposition.

The further struggles between Catholics and Protestants were marked by the epochal events in Hungary, where the Ottoman attackers, taking the military initiative, provoked the outbreak of what were called the long Turkish wars of the years 1593–1606. In an effort to gain further revenue for the army, Rudolf II raised taxes and in Hungary went as far as to confiscate the demesnes of the Protestant nobility. Dissatisfaction with Habsburg policies and with the violence of the Emperor's forces resulted in rebellion in 1604–1606, at whose head stood the Transylvanian magnate, Stephen Bocskay. Hungarian rebels attempted to gain allies in the Bohemian crown lands, but their destructive raids on Moravia dissuaded Czech fellow believers from direct alliance. Nevertheless, the Hungarian rebellion shook the Habsburg monarchy and roused the Estates opposition in the Bohemian and Austrian lands.

On behalf of the ailing Rudolf II, his younger brother, Archduke Matthias, negotiated with the Hungarian rebels. He exploited every opportunity to weaken the standing of the incumbent ruler in order to get the throne for himself. The question of succession thus grew into a dynastic crisis. The Peace of Vienna, which Matthias negotiated with Bocskay's plenipotentiaries on June 23, 1606, fixed the political and religious freedoms of the Hungarian Estates, which represented a fundamental compromise of the Habsburgs' central idea. For a long time Rudolf II refused to recognize the peace negotiations, and thus provided Matthias with an excuse for open alliance with the Hungarian Estates. For the first time, a member of the ruling line stood at the head of a military rebellion to further his personal ambition at the cost of profound upheaval of dynastic positions. It was the most serious threat to the unity of the Habsburg monarchy up to the outbreak of the Thirty Years' War.

The actions of Archduke Matthias suited the Estates opposition in the lands neighbouring Hungary perfectly. At the end of 1607, he was joined by disgruntled elements in the Austrian lands and in April 1608 also by the Moravian Estates led by Karel the Elder of Žerotín, of the Unity of Brethren, and the Catholic convert Karl of Liechtenstein. Thus the

JAROSLAV PÁNEK

Hungarian-Austrian-Moravian confederation was formed, and its military forces made for Bohemia to force Rudolf II to abdicate. However the Bohemian Estates correctly presumed that the continuation of the dynastic crisis would ensure them greater gains than its abrupt completion in Matthias's favour. Through the compromise of the Peace of Libeň of June 1608, they protected the imperial crown of Rudolf, and the Bohemian crown lands, with the exception of Moravia, which Matthias continued to rule, just as he did Hungary and Lower and Upper Austria. Even though there was still hope of their re-unification after Rudolf's death, the unity of the Czech state was profoundly disrupted.

Estates confederations and leagues were up to this an unusual form of concerted action by the opposition in the Habsburg lands. The opposition now overcame the borders of individual countries and found a shared program and organizational base in the fight against their own ruler. The merging of the Estates multiplied their force and self-confidence, which was necessary for the coming struggle with the Habsburgs. This was why the Moravian and Austrian Estates brokered a secret agreement to co-operate in the struggle against Matthias. In a similar fashion the Bohemian Estates ensured themselves against Rudolf through a confederation with the Silesians. At the beginning of the 17th century, the outlines formed of the possibility of a constitutional connection of Central European lands on the basis of the Estates and not a dynasty.

The division of the Empire between two sovereigns and the weakening of the ruler's authority allowed the Estates to implement their aims even more vigorously. The Czech opposition's attempt to secure religious and Estates freedoms gathered focus. The Letter of Majesty on the non-confiscation of land-holdings (1608) firstly confirmed the inviolability of the nobility's property even when their political guilt was proven. Having gained this advantage, the Czech opposition, led by Václav Budovec of Budov, placed pressure on Rudolf II. Since he refused to codify in law religious freedom for Protestants, the opposition opted for a government of thirty directors, raised an army and negotiated with the Estates of neighbouring countries for assistance. Fears of military conflict, for which the Emperor was not prepared, and the mediation of moderate Catholic nobles, forced Rudolf II to issue the Letter of Majesty on religious freedom. The ruler's official seal attached to the document of July 9, 1609, along with an Agreement on relations between the Protestant Estates and the more conciliatory elements of the Catholic nobility, meant the jural establishment of the Bohemian Confession of 1575 as one of the fully-fledged religious communities in the land. An independent church was created with noble and burgherly protectors (defensors), with a Neo-Utraquist-Brethren consistory as its administrative and judicial centre, and the Prague university as the intellectual hub of Czech non-Catholics. The Letter of Majesty brought legal protection to non-Catholics, which made up 85–90% of the Bohemian population. It was a historic victory for tolerance over bigotry, and even more valuably, it ensured that religious freedom – just as in the Peace of Kutná Hora of 1485 – extended to the subject peasantry.

The unswerving advocates of reconversion, led by Chancellor Zdeněk of Lobkowicz, refused to recognize the Letter, but with the support of the ruler and other Catholics they nevertheless remained in government. A paradoxical situation emerged in which the leading representatives of executive power denied the new constitutional arrangements in the country and tried to overturn them. Not even Rudolf II could reconcile himself with the Letter, which he had been coerced into signing, and its political consequences: at the first opportunity he used violent means to attempt its reversal. With the help of the army of his adventurous cousin, Leopold, Bishop of Passau, he tried to gain control of Bohemia at the beginning of 1611 and humiliate the opposition as well as his hated brother Matthias. However his poorly thought-out plan collapsed against the resistance of the Estates and Rudolf II had to give up the Bohemian throne.

In May 1611, with the coronation of Matthias (r. 1611–1619) as Bohemian king, the Habsburg monarchy was once again unified, but its basic problem remained unresolved. Matthias returned to the centralizing and Counter-Reformation politics of his predecessors, and increasingly clashed with the Estates opposition. Although he moved the ruling seat back to Vienna after Rudolf's death (1612), the epicentre of tension remained the Bohemian kingdom.

On the one hand, an anti-Habsburg coalition of western European states was forming, from which the Protestant Estates in the Habsburg Empire expected assistance, and on the other the Catholic Habsburg camp had consolidated itself. However, on the threshold of the first pan-European conflict, the Thirty Years' War, the ruling circles of the western European powers of the Low Countries, England and France were occupied with their own internal political problems and direct intervention in Bohemia was not on the cards. The burden of the contention fell mainly on the Estates opposition in the Bohemian, Austrian and Hungarian lands, and on the Palatinate Elector's land, whose rulers from the Calvinist line of the House of Wittelsbach were the most consistent opponents of the Habsburgs in the Holy Roman Empire. In contrast, the Habsburg camp was better integrated. Apart from the Austrian and Spanish branches of the Habsburgs, it could count on the Papal Curia and the Catholic League of German princes, led by Duke Maximilian of the Bavarian branch of the Wittelsbach dynasty. Despite financial difficulties and political and military defeats in the preceding period, the Habsburgs remained the chief European dynasty whose ambition was to dominate the entire continent.

The question of whether the Habsburgs would succeed in maintaining the Bohemian throne even after the death of the childless Matthias became crucial. Members of the Spanish line could become candidates for the succession, or the junior Styrian branch of the family; the uncompromising Catholicism of both sides provoked serious fears among the Protestant Estates. Representatives of the dynasty agreed that they would support the candidacy of Ferdinand of Styria with their combined forces, who had much experience with the suppression of the Reformation in the interior lands of Austria. Backed by the Jesuits, the Habsburgs embarked on an intense propaganda campaign part of which was a grand theatrical performance at Prague Castle and the Clementinum, while at the same time single-mindedly terrorizing their opponents. Although Czech opposition leaders were ready to reject the Styrian candidacy, when they clashed with the Habsburgs and Chancellor

Lobkowicz in 1617, they faltered. With the exception of two lords and two burghers, all the intimidated members of the Prague electoral diet voted to accept Ferdinand, thus sealing his legal claim to the Bohemian crown.

This easy victory over the opposition encouraged the advocates of reconversion to ratchet up the suppression by a notch. They violently attacked Protestants and their churches in two border towns in northern Bohemia (Broumov and Hrob), unintentionally provoking the anti-Habsburg opposition into feverish activity. In March 1618, the opposition met at a conference in Prague and complained about the infractions of the Letter of Majesty on religious freedom. Matthias responded with the banning of further conferences, thus denying the non-Catholic Estates the right of lawful self-defence and called into doubt the rickety legal order in the country. The radical Protestant representatives no longer saw any other option than to take government into their own hands and resort to violence in order to resolve the conflict.

In May 1618, the Protestant Estates called another conference and their leaders staged the trial of the hated royal lieutenants Vilém Slavata and Jaroslav Bořita of Martinice, which concluded with their ejection from the window of the Czech Chancellery in Prague Castle. The event of May 23, 1618, which history records as the second defenestration of Prague, was the signal for the anti-Habsburg rising. Government was seized by the thirty-member Directorate with equal representation by lords, knights and towns; but real power was held by a small number of lords. Among them, Václav Vilém of Roupov, chairman of the Directorate, was outstanding for his insight, and Jindřich Matyáš Thurn was able to employ his military experience. They attempted to mobilize their forces, win over the Protestant knights and the patriciate, but prevent the resistance of the population of the towns and villages. In terms of their program the anti-Habsburg conflict of the years 1618–1620 remained a typical Estates rising, the basic aim of which was to re-distribute power in the Czech state in favour of the non-Catholic Estates opposition.

The Protestant Estates of Silesia and Lusatia were positively disposed towards the Bohemian rebels, but the anti-Habsburg nobility in Austria also became sympathetic. In contrast, Moravians remained loyal to the Habsburgs, which was above all due to their intellectually oriented leader Karel the Elder of Žerotín, who on principle refused the violent resolution of religious disputes and at the same time did not hide his lack of confidence in the rebellion's prospects. Only the turnabout of May 1619 in Brno changed the situation: the radical opposition led by Ladislav Velen of Žerotín, supported by Thurn's division, joined Moravia with the rebels.

The unification of the Bohemian crown, as it battled with the Habsburgs, enabled a new arrangement of constitutional relations. At the Prague general diet of July 31, 1619, a new constitution of the Czech state was approved – the Bohemian Confederation (*Česká konfederace*). It modified the relations between the five countries of the Bohemian crown, putting them on an equal footing; it determined common institutions and a chain of command to ensure the unified defence of the state. The guiding idea of the confederation was the dominance of the Estates over the ruler, who was to be freely elected at a general diet by the representatives of all the confederate countries and whose executive power would remain under the control of representative Estates bodies. The constitution also fixed the privileged standing of the Protestant majority over the previously favoured Catholic minority. However this did not entail the dictatorship of Protestants over Catholics or the latter's expulsion from the country, but was only to ensure the loyalty of all the population to a multi-confessional state, in which the Bohemian Confession and the Letter of Majesty on religious freedom became the unquestioned pillars of the jural order. The sophisticated, clearly formulated confederate document, in one hundred articles, its conceptions close to Western European anti-absolutist Monarchomachism, ranks among the most significant creations of Czech legal thinking in the early Modern Era.

The new constitutional set-up of the Czech state was based on experience with the confederate movement from the beginning of the 17th century. This was why it remained open to possibilities of alliance and contact with neighbouring countries and their Estates. The Estates of Upper and Lower Austria really did accede to the expanded interpretation of the confederation, and in its Bratislava diet of January 1620, the Hungarian Estates opposition also joined it; together with Transylvanian duke, Gabriel Bethlen, they governed almost all of the territory of Slovakia. Given these circumstances, the Habsburg monarchy *de facto* ceased to exist and changed into a loose grouping of countries run by Estates governments.

During the war with the Habsburgs, the rebels depended on substantial help from abroad. From spring 1619, they did in fact receive financial and military support from the Low Countries, and Charles Emmanuel, Duke of Savoy, sent a mercenary army to Bohemia. In contrast, France, England and even the league of Protestant princes in the Empire remained neutral. The one ally ready to join its fate with the Czech rebels was the twenty-three year old Calvinist elector, Frederick V of the Palatinate, for whom the royal Bohemian crown was the supreme achievement of the foreign policy of his small imperial principality. After the death of Matthias and the dethronement of Ferdinand II (r. 1619–1637), Frederick was elected Bohemian king on August 26, 1619. In comparison with the Habsburg camp, supported from the north also by Catholic Poland and Lutheran Saxony, the Bohemian-Palatinate personal union was definitely the weaker party.

For over two years, there was fighting on Bohemian and Moravian territories between the armies of the Estates and the Habsburgs. The rebels' two attempts to take Vienna in 1619 failed. The decisive factors were the short-comings of the Estates army and ineffective co-operation with the other anti-Habsburg forces, especially Bethlen's divisions. The imperial army however at the very outset of the rebellion occupied the southern regions of Bohemia, establishing there a base from which to attack Prague. War operations disrupted the economic life of the Bohemian crown lands and brought their inhabitants hardship and unbearable financial burdens.

A handful of nobles displayed unusual generosity by drawing on their own resources to support the military divisions. However the greater part of the lords and knights underestimated the extent of the looming danger and continued to look to their short-term personal gain. Especially harmful was the inability to abandon a limited prejudice against the towns and fairly divide the burden of war, or even completely revoke the burden of serfdom upon farmers who were otherwise willing to support their fellow believers from the nobility. At the beginning of the war, the nobility had to treat the royal towns with favour and acknowledge the return of their jural standing from before 1547. The burghers were represented in the Directorate government. However after the accession of King Frederick, the nobles returned to the traditional division of supreme offices and pushed out the town deputies from the Land and regional executives. Legal discrimination and excessive financial burdens on the towns caused the great majority of burghers in the second half of the rising to lose all interest in providing it with more substantial material support. The war leaders also extracted further finances and military service from the subject peasantry, but offered them in return only hardship from mercenaries on both sides. One expression of the detached position of the rural people from the Estates government was the armed insurgencies in the regions of Žatec and Tábor, which became the spontaneous self-defence of villagers against the violence of the soldiery of both the Empire and Estates.

A narrow social base and insufficient support from abroad – these were the decisive factors in the collapse of the Estates rebellion. In the course of 1620, the Habsburg-Catholic coalition, which was able to mobilize more funds than its opponents, had clearly taken the lead. The imperial and Bavarian forces made their way to the centre of Bohemia from the south; the Saxon army occupied Lusatian territory to the north. Badly paid and often undisciplined Estates regiments had to withdraw to Prague. On Sunday November 8, the armies joined battle at White Mountain, to the west of the metropolis. The Estates had a force of about 20,000–21,000 and their enemies about 23,000–28,000, the greater part of which did not see any fighting. The two-hour battle nevertheless was a catastrophic defeat for the Estates. This military fiasco uncovered the internal breakdown of the rebels' camp and Frederick of the Palatinate's incompetence in governing. The "winter king", thus named because he spent only one winter on the throne, fled from Bohemia, never attempting to retake the country. Immediately after, the neighbouring countries capitulated, and although several garrisons in fortified positions held on for a few more months, the fate of the rebellion was sealed.

The immediate consequences of the defeat were manifest in the pillage of the Bohemian crown lands by the victorious army; great loss of life, property and cultural heritage; the elimination of the representatives of the Estates opposition *en masse*, and further punishments; enormous property transfers in the form of confiscations and expulsions of non-Catholics from the country. The crushing of the Estates resistance also had very serious long-term effects. Bohemia and Moravia, by right of victory, became more dependent than ever on the Habsburg dynasty, which transformed these countries' internal relations: the central government was strengthened, religious freedom was suppressed and the population was subject to violent reconversion. This meant the end of a political culture based on religious plurality and of the active participation of the Estates in the running of the state. The privileged position of the Czech language in public life came to an end, which together with wide-ranging transformations within the Estates of lords and knights led not only to the marked decline of the communicative and cultural significance of Czech, but also to the long-term waning of the cultural development of the Bohemian crown lands in all respects.

All these extensive changes were traditionally associated with White Mountain, which became a landmark in the history of the Czech nation. However the Battle of White Mountain, while it brought a tragic close to the Estates rising, was decidedly not the conflict of Czechs with Germans that it would later be presented as. On both sides, mercenaries, hired from various parts of Europe, were involved in the fighting. On the Catholic side mostly there were commanders and soldiers whose origins were German, Italian, Spanish, Walloon and Polish, as well as others from other European countries. On the Czech-Palatinate side there were Czechs and Germans, from Bohemia, Moravia, Silesia and Lusatia, as well as soldiers from Austria, imperial principalities (above all from the Palatinate and other Protestant states), from Hungary and other distant lands. The Battle of White Mountain, with its variegated representation of nations was a faithful reflection of the Thirty Years' War, which grew into the first great conflict of pan-European proportions.

In the following centuries "White Mountain" became a symbol also because in the wake of the military defeat and the executions of June 21, 1621, the leading representatives of the Czech intelligentsia were brought to the scaffold – the writer Václav Budovec, the composer Kryštof Harant and the natural scientist of Slovak origin Jan Jessenius. For radical Catholics "White Mountain" became a symbol of the deserved humiliation of heretics, under the auspices of the Virgin Mary Victorious, in whose honour many churches in Bohemia and abroad were consecrated. In contrast, for Protestants and Czech nationalists it was a strong reminder of lost freedom, a national disaster and injustice. Out of the clash and development of these conflicting views, the myth of White Mountain grew, which is a part of Czech historical memory to this day.

Bibliography

BAHLCKE, Joachim: *Regionalismus und Staatsintegration im Widerstreit. Die Länder der Böhmischen Krone im ersten Jahrhundert der Habsburgerherrschaft (1526–1619)*, München 1994.

BAHLCKE, Joachim – Bömelburg, Hans-Jürgen – Kersken, Norbert (eds.): *Ständefreiheit und Staatsgestaltung in Ostmitteleuropa. Übernationale Gemeinsamkeiten in der politischen Kultur vom 16.–18. Jahrhundert*, Leipzig 1996.

BAHLCKE, Joachim – DUDECK, Volker (eds.): *Welt – Macht –Geist. Das Haus Habsburg und die Oberlausitz 1526–1635*, Görlitz–Zittau 2002.

BAHLCKE, Joachim – STROHMEYER, Arno (eds.): *Konfessionalisierung in Ostmitteleuropa. Wirkungen des religiösen Wandels im 16. und 17. Jahrhundert in Staat, Gesellschaft und Kultur*, Stuttgart 1999.

BEIN, Werner: *Schlesien in der habsburgischen Politik. Ein Beitrag zur Entstehung des Dualismus im Alten Reich*, Sigmaringen 1994.

BIBL, Viktor: *Maximilian II. Der rätselhafte Kaiser*, Hellerau bei Dresden 1929.

BIDLO, Jaroslav: *Jednota bratrská v prvním vyhnanství*, I–IV, Praha 1900–1932.

BLEKASTAD, Milada: *Comenius. Versuch eines Umrisses von Leben, Werk und Schicksal des Jan Amos Komenský*, Oslo–Praha 1969.

BOBKOVÁ, Lenka (ed.): *Život na šlechtickém sídle v 16.–18. století*, Ústí nad Labem 1992.

BOBKOVÁ, Lenka – NEUDERTOVÁ, Michaela (eds.): *Cesty a cestování v životě společnosti*, Ústí nad Labem 1997.

BŮŽEK, Václav: *Ferdinand von Tirol zwischen Prag und Innsbruck. Der Adel aus den böhmischen Ländern auf dem Weg zu den Höfen der ersten Habsburger*, Wien 2009.

BŮŽEK, Václav: *Rytíři renesančních Čech*, Praha 1995.

BŮŽEK, Václav – HRDLIČKA, Josef et al.: *Dvory velmožů s erbem růže. Všední a sváteční dny posledních Rožmberků a pánů z Hradce*, Praha 1997.

BŮŽEK, Václav – HRDLIČKA, Josef – Král, Pavel – Vybíral, Zdeněk: *Věk urozených. Šlechta v českých zemích na prahu novověku*, Praha–Litomyšl 2002.

BŮŽEK, Václav – Král, Pavel (eds.): *Aristokratické rezidence a dvory v raném novověku*, České Budějovice 1999.

BŮŽEK, Václav – Král, Pavel (eds.): *Slavnosti a zábavy na dvorech a v rezidenčních městech raného novověku*, České Budějovice 2000.

BŮŽEK, Václav – Král, Pavel (eds.): *Šlechta v habsburské monarchii a císařský dvůr (1526–1740)*, České Budějovice 2003.

BŮŽEK, Václav – ŠTEFANOVÁ, Dana (eds.): *Menschen – Handlungen – Strukturen. Historisch-anthropologische Zugangsweisen in den Geschichtswissenschaften*, České Budějovice 2001.

ČECHURA, Jaroslav: *Adelige Grundherren als Unternehmer. Zur Struktur der südböhmischer Dominien vor 1620*, München–Wien 2000.

CHALINE, Olivier: *La bataille de la Montagne Blanche (8 novembre 1620). Un mystique chez les guerriers*, Paris 2002.

CHUDOBA, Bohdan: *Spain and the Empire 1519–1643*, Chicago 1952.

DAVID, Zdeněk V.: *Finding the Middle Way. The Utraquists' Liberal Challenge to Rome and Luther*, Washington–Baltimore–London 2003.

DEVENTER, Jörg: *Gegenreformation in Schlesien. Die habsburgische Rekatholisierungpolitik in Glogau und Schweidnitz 1526–1707*, Köln–Weimar–Wien 2003.

DILLON, Kenneth J.: *King and Estates in the Bohemian Lands (1526–1564)*, Bruxelles 1976.

DMITRIEVA, Marina – LAMBRECHT, Karen: *Krakau, Prag und Wien. Funktionen von Metropolen im frühmodernen Staat*, Stuttgart 2000.

DOEBEL, Günter: *Johannes Kepler*, Graz–Wien–Köln 1983.

DWORZACZKOWA, Jolanta: *Bracia Czescy w Wielkopolsce w XVI i XVII wieku*, Warszawa 1997.

EBERHARD, Winfried: *Konfessionsbildung und Stände in Böhmen 1478–1530*, München–Wien 1981.

EBERHARD, Winfried: *Monarchie und Widerstand. Zur ständischen Oppositionsbildung im Herrschaftssystem Ferdinands I. in Böhmen*, München 1981.

VAN EICKELS, Christiane: *Schlesien im böhmischen Ständestaat. Voraussetzungen und Verlauf der böhmischen Revolution von 1618 in Schlesien*, Köln–Weimar–Wien 1994.

ENGEL, Evamaria – LAMBRECHT, Karen – NOGOSSEK, Hanna (eds.): *Metropolen im Wandel. Zentralität in Ostmitteleuropa an der Wende vom Mittelalter zur Neuzeit*, Berlin 1995.

EVANS, Robert J. W.: *The Making of the Habsburg Monarchy 1550–1700*, Oxford 1984.

EVANS, Robert J. W.: *Rudolf II and his world. A study in intellectual history*, Oxford 1973, 1997.

FELLNER, Thomas – KRETSCHMAYR, Heinrich: *Die österreichische Zentralverwaltung*, I/2, Wien 1907.

FICHTNER, Paula Sutter: *Ferdinand I of Austria. The Politics of Dynasticism in the Age of the Reformation*, New York 1982.

FICHTNER, Paula Sutter: *Emperor Maximilian II.*, New Haven and London 2001.

FORBELSKÝ, Josef: *Španělé, Říše a Čechy v 16. a 17. století. Osudy generála Baltasara Marradase*, Praha 2006.

FRANZL, Johann: *Ferdinand II. Kaiser im Zwiespalt der Zeit*, Graz–Wien–Köln 1978.

FUČÍKOVÁ, Eliška (ed.): *Rudolf II and Prague. The Court and the City*, Prague–London–Milan 1997.

FUČÍKOVÁ, Eliška – BUKOVINSKÁ, Beket – MUCHKA, Ivan: *Die Kunst am Hofe Rudolfs II.*, Hanau 1988.

FUKALA, Radek: *Jan Jiří Krnovský. Stavovské povstání a zápas s Habsburky*, České Budějovice 2005.

GINDELY, Anton: *Geschichte des dreißigjährigen Krieges*, I/1–3, Prag 1869–1878.

GMITEREK, Henryk: *Bracia Czescy a kalwini w Rzeczypospolitej. Połowa XVI–połowa XVII wieku. Studium porównawcze*, Lublin 1987.

GMITEREK, Henryk: *Związki intelektualne polsko-czeskie w okresie Odrodzenia (1526–1620)*, Lublin 1989.

GRACIOTTI, Sante (ed.): *Italia e Boemia nella cornice del Rinascimento europeo*, Firenze 1999.

HARDER, Hans-Bernd – ROTHE, Hans (eds.): *Die Bedeutung der humanistischen Topographien und Reisebeschreibungen in der Kultur der böhmischen Länder bis zur Zeit Balbíns*, Köln–Weimar–Wien 1993.

HARDER, Hans-Bernd – ROTHE, Hans (eds.): *Später Humanismus in der Krone Böhmen 1570–1620*, Dresden 1998.

HAUSENBLASOVÁ, Jaroslava: *Der Hof Kaiser Rudolfs II. Eine Edition der Hofstaatsverzeichnisse 1576–1612*, Prag 2002.

HAUSENBLASOVÁ, Jaroslava – ŠRONĚK, Michal: *Urbs aurea. Prague of Emperor Rudolf II*, Prague 1997.

HAUSENBLASOVÁ, Jaroslava – ŠRONĚK, Michal: *Gloria & Miseria 1618–1648. Prague during the Thirty Years War*, Praha 1998.

HRDLIČKA, Josef: *Hodovní stůl a dvorská společnost. Strava na raně novověkých aristokratických dvorech v českých zemích (1550–1650)*, České Budějovice 2000.

HREJSA, Ferdinand: *Česká konfesse, její vznik, podstata a dějiny*, Praha 1912.

HROCH, Miroslav – PETRÁŇ, Josef: *Das 17. Jahrhundert. Krise der feudalen Gesellschaft?*, Hamburg 1981.

HROCH, Miroslav – PETRÁŇ, Josef: *Die Länder der böhmischen Krone 1350–1650*, in: Handbuch der europäischen Wirtschafts- und Sozialgeschichte, III, Stuttgart 1987, p. 968–1005.

HRUBÁ, Michaela (ed.): *Víra nebo vlast? Exil v českých dějinách raného novověku*, Ústí nad Labem 2001.

HRUBÝ, František: *Die Wiedertäufer in Mähren*, Leipzig 1935.

JAKUBEC, Ondřej: *Kulturní prostředí a mecenát olomouckých biskupů potridentské doby*, Olomouc 2003.

JANÁČEK, Josef: *České dějiny. Doba předbělohorská 1526–1547*, I/1–2, Praha 1968–1984.

JANÁČEK, Josef: *Jan Blahoslav*, Praha 1966.

JANÁČEK, Josef: *Rudolf II. a jeho doba*, Praha 1987; 2nd and 3rd edition, Praha–Litomyšl 1997, 2003.

JANÁČEK, Josef: *Valdštejn a jeho doba*, Praha 1978, 2nd edition, 2003.

KAMENÍČEK, František: *Zemské sněmy a sjezdy moravské*, I–III, Brno 1900–1905.

KAVKA, František: *Bílá hora a české dějiny*, Praha 1962, 2nd edition, 2003.

KAVKA, František – Skýbová, Anna: *Husitský epilog na koncilu tridentském a původní koncepce habsburské rekatolizace Čech*, Praha 1969.

KLIK, Josef: *Národnostní poměry v Čechách od válek husitských do bitvy bělohorské*, Praha 1922.

KNOZ, Tomáš: *Državy Karla staršího ze Žerotína po Bílé hoře. Osoby, příběhy, struktury*, Brno 2001.

KNOZ, Tomáš: *Pobělohorské konfiskace. Moravský průběh, středoevropské souvislosti, obecné aspekty*, Brno 2006.

KOHLER, Alfred: *Ferdinand I. 1503–1564. Fürst, König und Kaiser*, München 2003.

KOLDINSKÁ, Marie: *Každodennost renesančního aristokrata*, Praha–Litomyšl 2001.

KOLDINSKÁ, Marie: *Kryštof Harant z Polžic a Bezdružic. Cesta intelektuála k popravišti*, Praha 2004.

KONEČNÝ, Lubomír (ed.): *Rudolf II, Prague and the World*, Prague 1998.

KRÁL, Pavel: *Mezi životem a smrtí. Testamenty české šlechty v letech 1550 až 1650*, České Budějovice 2002.

KRÁL, Pavel: *Smrt a pohřby české šlechty na počátku novověku*, České Budějovice 2004.

KRAMÁŘ, Vincenc: *Zpustošení Chrámu svatého Víta v roce 1619*, ed. Michal Šroněk, Praha 1998.

KROESS, Alois: *Geschichte der böhmischen Provinz der Gesellschaft Jesu*, I, Wien 1910.

KROFTA, Kamil: *Bílá hora*, Praha 1913.

KUČERA, Jan P.: *8. 11. 1620: Bílá hora – O potracení starobylé slávy české*, Praha 2003.

KYBALOVÁ, Ludmila: *Dějiny odívání – Renesance (15.–16. století)*, Praha 1996.

LAMBRECHT, Karen: *Hexenverfolgung und Zaubereiprozesse in den schlesischen Territorien*, Köln 1995.

LANGER, Andrea – Michels, Georg (eds.): *Metropolen und Kulturtransfer im 15./16. Jahrhundert. Prag–Krakau–Danzig–Wien*, Stuttgart 2001.

MACŮREK, Josef: *Čechové a Poláci v 2. polovině XVI. století*, Praha 1948.

MALÝ, Karel – PÁNEK, Jaroslav – JANIŠ, Dalibor (eds.): *Vladislavské zřízení zemské a počátky ústavního zřízení v českých zemích (1500–1619)*, Praha 2001.

MAŤA, Petr: *Svět české aristokracie (1500–1700)*, Praha 2004.

MÜLLER, Joseph Theodor: *Geschichte der Böhmischen Brüder*, I–III, Herrnhut 1922–1931.

ORZECHOWSKI, Kazimierz: *Ogólnśląskie zgromadzenia stanowe*, Warszawa–Wrocław 1979.

PÁNEK, Jaroslav: *Poslední Rožmberk. Životní příběh Petra Voka*, Praha 1996.

PÁNEK, Jaroslav: *Poslední Rožmberkové. Velmoži české renesance*, Praha 1989.

PÁNEK, Jaroslav: *Stavovská opozice a její zápas s Habsburky 1547–1577*, Praha 1982.

PÁNEK, Jaroslav: *Vilém z Rožmberka. Politik smíru*, Praha 1998.

PÁNEK, Jaroslav: *Výprava české šlechty do Itálie v letech 1551–1552*, Praha 1987; 2nd edition České Budějovice 2003.

PEKAŘ, Josef: *Bílá hora. Její příčiny a následky*, Praha 1921.

PEŠEK, Jiří: *Měšťanská vzdělanost a kultura v předbělohorských Čechách 1547–1620*, Praha 1993.

PETRÁŇ, Josef: *Poddaný lid v Čechách na prahu třicetileté války*, Praha 1964.

PETRÁŇ, Josef: *Staroměstská exekuce*, Praha 1972, 4th edition, 2004.

PETRÁŇ, Josef – Petráňová, Lydia: *The White Mountain as a symbol in modern Czech history*, in: Mikuláš Teich (ed.), Bohemia in History, Cambridge 1998, p. 143–163.

PLACHT, Otto: *České daně 1517–1652*, Praha 1924.

POLIŠENSKÝ, Josef: *Anglie a Bílá hora*, Praha 1949.

POLIŠENSKÝ, Josef: *Nizozemská politika a Bílá hora*, Praha 1958.

POLIŠENSKÝ, Josef: *Tragic Triangle. The Netherlands, Spain and Bohemia 1617–1621*, Praha 1991.

POLIŠENSKÝ, Josef: *The Thirty Years War*, London 1971.

POLIŠENSKÝ, Josef – KOLLMANN, Josef: *Wallenstein. Feldherr des Dreißigjährigen Krieges*, Köln–Weimar–Wien 1997.

POLIŠENSKÝ, Josef – SNIDER, Frederick: *War and Society in Europe*, 1618–1648, Cambridge 1978.

Prag um 1600. Kunst und Kultur am Hofe Rudolfs II., I–II, Freren 1988.

RATAJ, Tomáš: *České země ve stínu půlměsíce. Obraz Turka v raně novověké literatuře z českých zemí*, Praha 2002.

REJCHRTOVÁ, Noemi: *Václav Budovec z Budova*, Praha 1984.

UHLÍŘ, Dušan: *Černý den na Bílé hoře: 8. listopad 1620*, Brno 1998.

VÁLKA, Josef: *Česká společnost v 15.–18. století*, I–II, Brno 1972–1983.

VÁLKA, Josef: *Hospodářská politika feudálního velkostatku na předbělohorské Moravě*, Praha 1962.

VÁLKA, Josef: *Husitství na Moravě, náboženská snášenlivost, Jan Amos Komenský*, Brno 2005.

VÁLKA, Josef: *Morava reformace, renesance a baroka* (= Dějiny Moravy, II), Brno 1996.

VOCELKA, Karl: *Die politische Propaganda Kaiser Rudolfs II. (1576–1612)*, Wien 1981.

VOCELKA, Karl: *Rudolf II. und seine Zeit*, Wien–Köln–Graz 1985.

VOREL, Petr: *Česká a moravská aristokracie v polovině 16. století*, Pardubice 1997.

VOREL, Petr: *Páni z Pernštejna (Vzestup a pád rodu zubří hlavy v dějinách Čech a Moravy)*, Praha 1999.

VOREL, Petr: *Velké dějiny zemí Koruny české*, VII (1526–1618), Praha–Litomyšl 2005.

VOREL, Petr (ed.): *Stavovský odboj roku 1547 – první krize habsburské monarchie*, Pardubice–Praha 1999.

VYBÍRAL, Zdeněk: *Politická komunikace aristokratické společnosti v českých zemích na počátku novověku*, České Budějovice 2005.

WINKELBAUER, Thomas: *Ständefreiheit und Fürstenmacht. Länder und Untertanen des Hauses Habsburg im konfessionellen Zeitalter*, I–II, Wien 2003 (In: Österreichische Geschichte 1522–1699).

WOLF, Peter et al.: *Der Winterkönig. Friedrich V. – der letzte Kurfürst aus der Oberen Pfalz* (Katalog zur Bayerischen Landesausstellung – Amberg 2003), Augsburg 2003.

WOLKAN, Rudolf: *Geschichte der deutschen Litteratur in Böhmen bis zum Ausgange des XVI. Jahrhunderts*, Prag 1894.

ZEMAN, Jarold K.: *The Anabaptists and the Czech Brethren in Moravia (1526–1628)*, Hague–Paris 1969.

Divine protection of the Habsburg monarchy, a Baroque allegory. Rays of divine light from the Hebrew inscription Jehova in the heaven illuminate a crowned eagle, symbolizing the Habsburg ruler, aided by God (incsription *Adest Adjutor IEOVA* – Jehova's helper is present). On the chest, the eagle has the Austrian emblem and the Habsburg device AEIOU, which has different interpretations, e.g. *Aquila electa iuste omnia vincit* – the chosen eagle justly overcomes everything. The eagle soars above the earth, with the lands of the Habsburg monarchy highlighted, and fights off its enemies, the Turks and heretics, with bolts of lightning. A vista of Vienna is in the background. Engraving by Mathias Fuhrmann: *Alt und neues Oesterreich, oder compendieuse particular-historie*, 2. Teil, Vienna 1735

1 Constitutional and Social Changes
during the Thirty Years' War

The Battle of White Mountain put an end to the Bohemian Estates rebellion. The demoralized Estates army fell into disorder during the battle and lacked any will to protect the Prague town walls against the victorious armies. Frederick of the Palatinate left Prague the day after the battle, finding a temporary refuge in the Silesian town of Wrocław (Breslau). However, when he left for the Netherlands in December 1620, he left the Czech Lands for good. He was accompanied by some of the nobility resistance leaders, but most Estates politicians stayed in the Czech Lands hoping for only mild retaliation from the emperor. Nevertheless, the imperial army's entry to the town was followed by several days of looting and pillaging.

The victory of the Catholic armies on White Mountain was celebrated in Vienna, yet it also, for Emperor Ferdinand II and the Viennese Court, indicated the necessity of deciding the fate of the lost and regained lands. The first measures ensuing the suppression of the Estates Rebellion were intended to strengthen the ruler's power and to punish the Estates politicians. In 1621–1622, the imperial army gradually eliminated the remains of the Estates army's resistance and took control of the cities persisting in resisting their control. Ferdinand II entrusted the administration of the Kingdom of Bohemia to the ambitious Catholic politician and convert, Karl I, Prince of Liechtenstein, who thus became an authorized royal proconsul and, from 1622, a royal vice-regent. In Moravia, the ruler was represented by a proconsul and governor – the Bishop of Olomouc, Cardinal Franz of Dietrichstein.

In the spring of 1621, an investigation into and a great trial of the Estates politicians who had been active in the rebellion took place in Prague. First, the politicians who managed to emigrate in time were sentenced to death, the deprivation of honour and the confiscation of their entire property. The strict judgments indicated that the other Estates politicians, who had not been far-sighted enough to leave the country, could not hope for mercy. The final judgment was indeed merciless: over forty people were sentenced to death, as well as judgements of imprisonment and corporal punishment. Some punishments were, however, later reduced. On June 21, 1621, twenty-seven Estates opposition leaders were executed in the Old Town Square in Prague. The execution, staged as a monumental Baroque spectacle, was simultaneously to illustrate to the rest of Europe that Ferdinand II had a firm grip on power, and to intimidate local inhabitants. The choice of victims did not always reflect their real role in the rebellion, demonstrated by the large number of executed burghers, a total of 17, though the burgher Estate had played only a secondary role in the rebellion.

The punishments, however, did not end with executions. Both Bohemian and Moravian Estates were punished through harsh property confiscations. In 1622, Ferdinand II announced a general pardon, which indicated that he would abandon further punishments for the rebellion's participants, under condition that all the guilty appeared before special committees, which would determine property fines according to the extent of their guilt. However, since even paying taxes during the Estates' government was considered a crime, the property confiscations in the early 1620s affected the vast majority of noble families and royal cities. More than 150 people lost their entire property and over 500 noblemen suffered partial property confiscation. Royal towns were deprived of almost all estate property and confiscations also affected many individual burghers (among Prague towns, over 400 buildings were confiscated in the 1620s). The punishments in Moravia were less severe, the originally planned mass execution did not take place and the Estates leaders were merely imprisoned. Property confiscations, however, affected over 200 noblemen, most royal towns and many burghers. Both lands were subject to major property shifts as the confiscated property was distributed both among the Catholic nobility, which had been loyal to the Habsburgs during the rebellion, and among the foreign nobility in the imperial service, who settled in the Czech Lands during the Thirty Years' War.

Punishing individuals for their participation in the Estates Rebellion was only the first of many measures that the ruler used to pacify the rebellious Bohemian environment. The Habsburg plans to establish a new order were long-term and had a clear aim. Ferdinand II took advantage of the Estates Rebellion to implement radical changes in the Czech Lands' status. He decided to completely eliminate the Estates opposition, to establish a strong ruling position and to incorporate the Lands of the Bohemian Crown into the Habsburg monarchy much more firmly than ever before. This required the total and uncompromising defeat of the Estates opposition, ending the almost hundred-year struggle with the Habsburgs. After 1620, the Bohemian crown lands had to face a reality radically different from their earlier status. The Battle of White Mountain thus put a definite end to the Bohemian Estates' state that had been developing since the Middle Ages.

The new relationship between the King of Bohemia and the Estates was codified in the *Renewed Land Ordinances*, which were issued for the Bohemian Kingdom in 1627 and for the Margraviate of Moravia a year later. These provincial legal codes contained basic constitutional and penal norms. The Renewed Ordinances followed up the tradition of the old Bohemian and Moravian Land constitutions from the end of the 15th century. The Renewed Ordinance differed from the original ordinances in that they were issued without the Estates' co-operation, solely through the sovereign's authority. In the foreword to the Bohemian Renewed Ordinance, Ferdinand II applied the principle of collective guilt for the Estates Rebellion to the Kingdom of Bohemia. All legislation of this constitution, which increased the ruler's power and eliminated the political influence of the Estates, was justified as the collective punishment of the land's inhabitants. In the first article, Ferdinand II declared a hereditary accession to the Bohemian throne, thus depriving the Bohemian Estates of their right to elect freely their ruler; a right that was rather questionable, although it previously had been intermittently applied.

Many other of the Renewed Ordinance's provisions augmented the ruler's status and limited the powers of the Estates. The Estates structure of the Kingdom of Bohemia changed significantly as, after two hundred years, the Catholic clergy was elevated to become the first and most important Estate. On the other hand, the burgher Estate, which had never enjoyed many powers, was limited even further, so it was completely robbed of the possibility of participation in the political life of the Estates society. Diets, which had played an important role in the Estates' opposition's fight against the Habsburgs' power claims before the rebellion, were in the Renewed Ordinance granted the right to approve the ruler's tax demands, though their other rights were severely curtailed. The ruler strengthened his legislative power and the diets were left with only a passive role.

Another Renewed Ordinance provision, which bestowed on the ruler the right to grant citizenship and, as a result, also to accept new inhabitants and members of Estates, had a major impact on the formation of the new Estates society in Bohemia and Moravia. In the past, this right had belonged to the Estates. Ferdinand II, along with his son and successor (in 1637), Ferdinand III, used this provision when rewarding his loyal commanders and politicians from various countries who had settled in the Czech Lands during the Thirty Years' War.

The Renewed Ordinance considerably augmented the ruler's power in the Czech Lands. Formally, however, the status of the Bohemian state did not greatly change. The Czech Lands continued to be an independent administrative unit, ruled by the Habsburg in power as the King of Bohemia. The Habsburg monarchy remained a personal union, in which the ruler acted as the element connecting the individual states of this dominion. Neither did the inner organization of the Bohemian state formally change. The traditional structure of Land offices was preserved, although their assignment was fully in the ruler's hands with the Land officials directly responsible to him. Thus the offices, in which the Estates had held great influence before the rebellion, became purely royal institutions, and as such, were gradually subordinated to the central administration of the Habsburg monarchy.

The Renewed Ordinance also required a legislative confirmation of an important process, which was started in the Czech Lands after 1620: the conversion of the Czech Lands' inhabitants to Catholicism. The religious question had been crucial in the preceding power struggles between the Bohemian Estates and the rulers. Having crushed the rebellion, the court had to decide a course of action regarding creed. The first step was abolishing Rudolf II's Letter of Majesty from 1609, which granted freedom to worship to non-Catholics. This step was the first indication that major religious changes were underway in the Czech Lands. In 1622, after over a year of formulating a re-Catholicization policy, a decision on the blanket re-Catholicization of the Czech and Austrian lands was reached.

For the monarch and his closest circles, in which Jesuit representatives played an important role, the conversion of non-Catholic inhabitants to Catholicism was an important moral task and an act of personal devotion. Ferdinand II was strongly convinced of his duty to save the souls of his non-Catholic subjects. The depth of Ferdinand's faith and his Catholic zeal, however, do not suffice to explain the Czech Lands' re-Catholicization. The re-Catholicization policy was in perfect accord with his ideas of a centrally-ruled absolutist state, in which the ruler's religion was the only recognized creed. He initiated the re-Catholicization of the Austrian hereditary lands – Styria, Carinthia and Carniola – as early as at the end of the 16th century, while still the Archduke Ferdinand of Styria.

In the Czech Lands, the religious reasons for re-Catholicization, and the attempt to establish a uniform, centrally-ruled state with a strong ruler were accompanied by another practical reason. The rebellion of the Czech Lands' political representation put the Habsburg's hundred-year effort to build a large Central-European monarchy in great danger. The majority of inhabitants' different beliefs and their political manifestation played an important role in the rebellion. Therefore, spreading the ruler's creed in these lands was to remove forever the ancient discord between the Czech Lands and their Habsburg rulers. Non-Catholicism was to be proof of disloyalty towards the ruler, and thus a crime against the state. The rule, in force in the Holy Roman Empire from the mid-1500s, – *cuius regio, eius religio*: who rules the country, decides the creed – was thus introduced in the Czech Lands.

During the years immediately following the defeat of the Estates Rebellion, re-Catholicization was accompanied by excesses such as imperial troops' raids of non-Catholic towns, during which the inhabitants were violently forced to convert. Viewed from a long-term perspective, these acts were largely irrelevant, as forced conversions had only a temporary effect. The well-planned re-Catholicization process focused first on the intellectual and religious non-Catholic elites in the Czech Lands. The first to be persecuted was the Unity of Brethren, a domestic and relatively radical Protestant church. Then followed measures against the Anabaptists, who were expelled from Moravia in 1622. The so-called lower consistory, a body administering the matters of a major part of non-Catholic clergy in Bohemia, was also forced to cease its activities. As well as expelling Evangelic priests from Prague in 1621, the Lutheran clergy, which had originally been exempted from the previous provision due to the emperor's alliance with the Elector of Saxony, was driven out a year later. In 1622, the Prague Utraquist university was taken over by the Jesuits, resulting in the Catholicization of a non-Catholic school, which not only educated secular intellectuals and teachers for lower schools around the Kingdom of Bohemia, but which was also closely linked to many events and prominent personalities of the Estates rebellion.

Further re-Catholicization measures were aimed at the royal towns' population. They had a negative effect on the possibilities to self-sustainment of the non-Catholic burghers and curtailed their burgher rights. Although the Catholic faith was proclaimed the only permissible creed in Bohemia in 1624, the vast majority of the population remained loyal to their original non-Catholic creeds despite all that was attempted to sway them. There were two

JIŘÍ MIKULEC

main obstacles to the real conversion of the population. First was that a great number of the Evangelic nobility, which did not impose re-Catholicization on their demesnes, remained in the country, and second was the state's incapacity to enforce the laws.

The sovereign solved both problems in 1627. The Renewed Ordinance declared the Catholic faith to be the only permitted creed in the country. In the same year, Ferdinand II issued a crucial re-Catholicization edict, which ordered all non-Catholic noblemen to convert or emigrate. At the same time, "reformatory committees" were established, which, accompanied by troops, went from one region to another, rounding up non-Catholics of both the noble and the burgher Estates and, using violence, forced them to convert. This measure, which ensured the country's genuine conversion to Catholicism in 1627–1629, was accompanied by a large wave of emigration; the majority of aristocrats and royal town burghers left for neighbouring Saxony, though some headed for Silesia, Poland and the Slovak regions of northern Hungary. The country lost several hundred aristocrats, many burghers and even town and village serfs, who did not have the *ius emigrandi*, the right to emigrate. Among the emigrés were many outstanding scholars and intellectuals, such as Jan Amos Komenský (Comenius), a prominent thinker, teacher and scholar of European renown, who in 1628 went into exile in Poland.

Along with the losses caused by emigration, the re-Catholicization wave also resulted in unrest in the rural parts of the country in the late 1620s. Forced conversion, along with the tightening of serfdom and aggravating the social situation, led to several peasant rebellions in the landed estates in central and eastern Bohemia in 1627 and 1628. The villagers plundered chateaux and presbyteries, and chased away or killed Catholic missionaries. The situation required a severe crackdown by the imperial army.

The re-Catholicization efforts of the state and Catholic church were disrupted by the Thirty Years' War. In the autumn of 1631, the army of the emperor's former ally, John George, the Elector of Saxony, invaded Bohemia. Saxons fighting on the Swedish side, who in the early 1630s declared war on the emperor, took advantage of the weakened imperial army, which was reduced in numbers, and its experienced commander, Albrecht of Wallenstein, was relieved of command. The Saxon incursion culminated in a six-month occupation of Prague. Many emigrants returned with the Saxons, hoping for a permanent change of the situation. The Saxon army, however, only stayed for one winter and, in 1632 retreated without much resistance from the imperial army, which was then under Albrecht of Wallenstein's renewed command. This episode was followed by a thorough investigation and further property confiscations.

Albrecht of Wallenstein is associated with one of the major incidents of the Thirty Years' War. This originally Protestant aristocrat converted during the creed conflict and the rise of the Catholic side at the beginning of the 17th century. As a colonel of the Moravian Estates army, he deserted to the imperial side in 1619, when the Estates rebellion broke out. After crushing the rebellion his wealth increased thanks to confiscations and financial manipulations, and he became both the greatest war profiteer and a successful military leader. His first career peak – his appointment as the commander in chief of the imperial army in 1625 –

was followed by his successful campaign in the Danish War, which forced King Christian IV of Denmark to sign a peace treaty with the emperor in 1629. In 1630, however, Wallenstein was relieved of command after pressure from electors and imperial princes. He considered this a major injustice and probably started to negotiate with the Swedes regarding a potential alliance. In 1631, he was reinstated as the head of the army, in a short time had gathered sixty-thousand men and, in 1632, he clashed with the Swedes in an inconclusive battle near Lützen, in which the Swedish King Gustav Adolf was killed.

Wallenstein was nevertheless not trusted by the Viennese court and his military campaigns in Silesia and Germany in 1633 were considered hesitant and disadvantageous to the emperor. This distrust was exploited by his numerous enemies (among whom were the emperor's son Ferdinand III, Maxmilian I, Elector of Bavaria, Bohemian Supreme Chancellor Vilém Slavata, and many other influential courtiers and politicians). Numerous memoranda accusing Wallenstein of inability, incompetence and, ultimately, of treason were spread in Vienna. Weakened and seriously ill, Wallenstein had lost the capacity to judge the situation and, towards the end of 1633, he opposed the emperor's order to carry out a winter campaign to Bavaria; as a result he found himself in open conflict with the ruler. Ferdinand II relieved Wallenstein of his command and ordered that he be taken captive, or possibly eliminated. This was carried out on February 25, 1634 in Cheb, when a group of the generalissimo's former officers murdered those who remained loyal to him, and then Wallenstein himself.

The Czech Lands were considerably damaged as a consequence of the Thirty Years' War. They suffered from major changes in their constitutional character and in their status within the Habsburg monarchy, social changes caused by re-Catholicization, the emigration of thousands of inhabitants and property confiscations, to say nothing of the massive economic damage. First, the currency was devalued as a result of the Habsburg monarchy's high war expenses, though this was also an effect of the loose atmosphere of the first years following the Battle of White Mountain, which enabled unprecedented property and financial speculations, especially in minting. This period in the Holy Roman Empire is called *Kipper und Wipper* – devaluation, literally cutting the coins. In terms of societal impact, the most extensive and most destructive mintage speculation occurred in Bohemia.

In 1622, a mint consortium was formed (among its most prominent members were Karl I Prince of Liechtenstein, Albrecht of Wallenstein, as well as the Dutch merchant and banker Hans de Witte and Prague Jewish merchant Jacob Bassewi) and granted the right of coinage by the emperor, a monopoly to purchase unincuse silver and a pre-emptive right to all extracted silver. The consortium's eighteen months of activities resulted in its members' considerable enrichment, though also in a huge devaluation of coins, which led to state bankruptcy. At the end of 1623, the emperor lowered the nominal value of coins by up to 90 per cent. The impact on the country's economy and, importantly, on its inhabitants' property was naturally quite destructive.

More damage was inflicted upon the Czech Lands by the war. Particularly in the second half of the Thirty Years' War, the Czech Lands suffered from incursions and attacks by enemy armies, as well as from the imperial army's campaigns. Armies were fed to the detriment of the population, pillaging and raids by armed military or semi-military groups and extortion became part of everyday life in many towns and demesnes. Irrespective of the war's short-term economic boom, during the war, existing business relationships between the Czech Lands and the rest of the world were damaged or completely destroyed as a result of both plundering the neighbouring German lands and as a consequence of extreme uncertainty of travel. The economic situation of the non-privileged population in the Czech Lands was further affected by an excessive tax burden.

The Czech Lands' decline during the Thirty Years' War was also reflected in the demographic development. The population decrease started in the 1620s due to the religious emigration and in the following decades it was further deepened by the war, which brought with it the military draft, the loss of life in the war and, further, as a consequence of epidemics and local famines, all resulted in landed estates' depopulation. Many villages fell into ruin, town populations were decreasing.

In 1635, an attempt was made to stop the series of European wars. Negotiations and a peace treaty signing took place in Prague, partly thanks to its convenient location for the Habsburgs and German princes. The main goal of the treaty was to ensure peace between Ferdinand II and his former ally John George, Elector of Saxony, who had been joined by other German rulers. The Prague Peace, however, did not end the great war, as it proved unacceptable for France and Sweden. Nevertheless, it was important for the development of the Czech Lands, as it meant a definite annexation of Upper and Lower Lusatia, which had been part of the Lands of the Bohemian Crown since the 14th century, to Saxony, whose Elector kept them as a pledge from Ferdinand II to cover military expenses from 1621. Upper Palatinate, where the Bohemian Crown had had minor foreign fiefs since the Middle Ages, was ceded to Bavaria.

Enemy armies' incursions into the Czech Lands in the 1630s and 1640s were a consequence of military operations shifting to the Habsburg monarchy regions. After the Saxon incursion and occupation of Prague in 1631, the Swedish army invaded parts of Bohemia in 1639. The Swedes gained control of northern, central and eastern Bohemia, twice bombarded Prague, though they ultimately proved unable to take the town. During the year-long occupation of Bohemia, the Swedish regiments pillaged on a massive scale; according to estimates, they destroyed or severely damaged in the region six thousand towns, lesser towns and villages. In 1642, the Swedes came through Silesia, invaded northern Moravia and occupied Olomouc, the seat of the Land administration, as well as several other important towns, where they kept garrisons until the end of the Thirty Years' War. In 1643–1645, several Swedish campaigns took place in Moravia. After the imperial army's defeat in the battle of Jankov in south Bohemia in 1645, the Swedish army occupied a major part of south Moravia and attempted to conquer Brno. The three-month siege was, however, unsuccessful.

A last but still destructive military operation of the Thirty Years' War in the Czech Lands was an attempt by the Swedish army, under the command of general Königsmarck, to conquer Prague. During a sudden night attack in summer 1648, the Swedish army gained control of the left-bank half of Prague and for several months attempted to take the Old and

New Towns on the right bank of the Vltava river. The population of these towns, together with a rather small garrison, managed to defend their homes until November, when news of the Peace of Westphalia reached Prague. The Swedes, nevertheless, carried away vast amounts of money and works of art from the occupied Prague towns, as they had before from many conquered Bohemian, Moravian and Silesian towns. The looted treasures included Rudolf II's famous collections and Wallenstein palace's unique decoration.

For the Czech Lands, the main outcome of the Peace of Westphalia, which was signed in 1648, was international recognition of the interior political situation arising from the defeat of the Estates Rebellion. Section 2, article 5 of the peace treaty of Osnabrück sets January 1, 1624, as the binding date for settling all religious and political conditions in European countries. This peace treaty article completely buried the hopes of the Czech emigrants, who until the last moment had tried to gain Swedish support in an effort to return the Czech Lands to their pre-1620 state. The military and political situation in Europe, however, forced Swedish diplomats, along with representatives of other Protestant countries, to agree to 1624 and so to leave the Czech Lands in the Habsburgs' Catholic sphere. Comenius' numerous reproaches to the Swedish Chancellor Axel Oxenstierna could not change anything.

2 Post-War Consolidation and Reconstruction of the Czech Lands

Only after the end of the Thirty Years' War could the ruler complete all the processes which had been started in the Czech Lands in the 1620s, yet which could not be completed due to the war. Most importantly, it was the re-Catholicization, until now disrupted by incursions of the enemy Protestant armies, which encouraged emigrants to return to the country. The war-time atmosphere of general uncertainty and danger made the enforcement of legal matters more difficult. Even the Catholic church was facing a rather difficult situation as, within a short period of time, it had to take over the entire spiritual administration in the Czech Lands, which in Bohemia meant filling many hundreds of parishes with priests. Clergy were scarce and the Catholic administration was considerably disrupted.

The church did attempt to deal with these problems during the war – an archiepiscopal seminary for new priests was founded in Prague. The parish administration asked order members to participate and also invited those priests from German Catholic countries and from Poland who could communicate with the local population. Despite all these measures, a large number of parishes remained unfilled for a long time and the reconstruction of parish networks stretched far into the 18th century (as late as in 1713, only 70% of parishes were filled, compared to the beginning of the 17th century).

In the period following the Battle of White Mountain, the sovereign ceded part of the revenue from the salt tax to the Catholic church, thus granting it a financial basis for its existence. In Bohemia, the Catholic church administration was reorganized – in the early 1630s, vicarages were established as an intermediary administration unit between the archiepiscopal consistory and parish priests. After the war, the Prague Archdiocese, under whose original administration were almost the whole of Bohemia and Kłodzko County, was divided, which made church administration more difficult. A new bishopric was founded in the town of Litoměřice in 1655, and another in Hradec Králové in 1664. This era also witnessed the flourishing of religious orders on a scale unseen since the Hussite Wars. The boom of monasteries of old orders (namely Premonstratensians, Cistercians, Benedictines, Servites) was accompanied by the mass spread of new Counter-Reformation and reformed fractions of orders (Jesuits, Capuchins, Piarists, Carmelite brothers and sisters, Ursulines and others).

Although the official mission of the Czech Lands' re-Catholicization was to convert all Bohemian crown lands inhabitants, in reality the progress was uneven. Bohemia and Moravia were entirely converted to Catholicism, while Lutheran enclaves remained in Silesia. A large number of non-Catholics in several Silesian principalities survived the Thirty Years' War. Swedish support during the peace negotiations in Osnabrück, together with strong Saxon and Brandenburg support, ensured that the Silesian Protestants could adhere to the Augsburg creed (Lutheran denomination) and even establish new non-Catholic churches, known as "peace churches." However, various forms of the re-Catholicization pressure by the state and the Catholic church never really stopped; a considerable proportion of Silesian regions were eventually completely re-Catholicized. Silesian Protestants drew comfort from the fact that neighbouring Lusatia, with which Silesia had tight contacts, became totally absorbed into Lutheran Saxony.

The re-Catholicization pressure was revived again in the mid-17th century. From 1649, re-Catholicization patents were reissued and at the beginning of the 1650s, re-Catholicization committees were newly formed. The majority of non-Catholics were peasants, as well as in the subject towns and it was towards them that the re-Catholicization measures were aimed.

In 1651, the Catholic church and state administration carried out, independently of each other, censuses, recording both the Catholic and non-Catholic population, which increased the pressure on non-Catholics. Some peasants, particularly from the regions bordering Saxony, went into exile, while others stayed at home, formally converted to Catholicism but in secrecy remained non-Catholic; most Czech Protestants, however, converted to Catholicism. This was the result of not only long-term re-Catholicization pressure, but also due to generational change. People who grew up during and after the Thirty Years' War did not experience the relatively tolerant religious conditions in the Czech Lands of the pre-rebellion period and so found it easier than their ancestors to accept Catholicism.

Bohemian and Moravian conversion to Catholicism was completed in the second half of the 17th century, although missionary activities and the search for secret non-Catholics never truly stopped. Evidence of the Catholic genuineness of most of the Bohemian peasant population is the fact that during the series of social revolts across the country, which swept through most demesnes in Bohemia in 1680, there were no anti-Austrian or anti-church expressions.

At the beginning of the 18th century, religious freedoms for Silesian non-Catholics increased thanks to Swedish King Charles XII, who, during the Nordic War in 1706, invaded

Saxony, which belonged to the deposed Polish king and Elector of Saxony August II. To prevent a war with the Swedes, the Habsburg diplomats accepted the Swedish demand to restore the religious status guaranteed to Silesia by the Peace of Westphalia. In regions which were non-Catholic at the end of the Thirty Years' War, Protestants were given back their churches and schools. However, Lutherans had the right of private worship even in Catholic areas. The treaty signed by Emperor Joseph I and King Charles XII, called the Treaty of Altrandstädt, was concluded in September 1707. This treaty was the most extensive foreign intervention into the religious situation in the Czech Lands since the defeat of the Estates Rebellion and was also a turning point in Silesian re-Catholicization. Although the re-Catholicization processes in Silesian principalities did not entirely cease, the status of local non-Catholics, particularly those in Lower Silesia, was improved both legally and factually. Vicariously, this treaty was also important for Bohemian and Moravian non-Catholics, as it allowed for the establishment of more non-Catholic churches, some of which were located near Bohemian and Moravian borders and became the destination for secret visits of non-Catholics from these lands.

In the 1710s, after King and Emperor Charles VI's ascendance to the throne, the re-Catholicization pressure increased in reaction to secret non-Catholics, mainly from east Bohemia, finding support with the Kingdom of Prussia, which was established at the beginning of the 18th century and was becoming a dangerous rival to the Habsburg monarchy. Lutheran preachers were coming to the country and non-Catholic religious books were smuggled in. Prussia was willing to accept emigrants among Bohemian secret non-Catholics, which resulted in economic damage as it caused a decrease in the peasant population.

Non-Catholic peasants started to sympathize with Prussia on a large scale, which was extremely dangerous for the state. As in the first decades after the defeat of the Estates Rebellion at the beginning of the 18th century, non-Catholicism was considered a crime against the state. This time it was not because of the danger of an inner disintegration, as had been the case after 1620, but rather as an external threat.

The first important reactions to Prussian activities defending Bohemian non-Catholics were recorded in 1723, when emigrants brought a ten-article complaint by Bohemian secret non-Catholics regarding the local situation to Berlin. The letter also expressed their trust in the support and help of the King of Prussia. At this time, Bohemian religious emigrants started to arrive in Berlin, whose emigration importance increased in the early 1730s, when emigrés started to settle in the village of Rixdorf near Berlin. Offspring of these Bohemian emigrants are still to be found in the Berlin quarter of Neuköln.

The state re-Catholicization measures in the first half of the 18th century were mainly directed at the import of non-Catholic books and against Protestant preachers' activities in Bohemia. The first decree against them was issued in December 1717 and it triggered a new wave of re-Catholicization. In the 1720s, Emperor Charles VI issued several more strict decrees against the activities of foreign preachers and importers of non-Catholic books. The state measures also focused on potential recipients of the banned Protestant books: the domestic secret non-Catholics.

The re-Catholicization wave was not limited merely to legislative measures, it also included the active searching out of secret non-Catholics, confiscating their books, searching for and arresting Lutheran preachers. Re-Catholicization pressure and repression, however, mainly caused unrest in eastern Bohemia, the region with the most secret non-Catholics. In 1732, a rebellion in the Opočno demesne had to be suppressed by the army. The state and the church made their biggest re-Catholicization effort in the 1720s and early 1730s. In 1735, German non-Catholic princes (united in the "Corpus evangelicorum") intervened before Emperor Charles VI. The Protestant rulers from the Holy Roman Empire denounced the severe religious oppression of non-Catholics in the Czech Lands. The situation, however, did not begin to relent until after Charles VI's death, during the wars in the 1740s and 1750s, and it was only the enlightened philosophical environment that brought religious tolerance to the Czech Lands in 1781.

Another area where changes could not take place until the end of the war was the economy, whose recovery from the damage wrought by the war was very slow. The fastest to recover was trade with distant countries, followed by local trade and handicraft. Economic theories reached the Czech Lands as early as in the 1640s: Lower-Austrian Mautern's Pavel Hynek Morgentaller, who became a prominent Brno citizen in the mid-17th century, published his *Generales florentis et intereuntis rei publicae causae* (1649) in Vienna. It was the first comprehensive expression of economic thinking in the spirit of the West-European mercantilism, whose author lived his life in accordance with his theories and worked in the Czech Lands. Ten years later, land attorney-at-law and Moravian mercantilist, Šebestián Malivský of Malivy presented his proposal to establish a network of factories. His proposal was, however, too megalomaniac and unrealistic, although Malivský did establish and operate his own textile factory in Brno.

In 1666, a commercial board (Commerzkollegium), an office for the monitoring and support of economic life (particularly trade) in Czech and Austrian lands was established in the Habsburg monarchy. The board's mission was based on the thoughts of economist Johann Joachim Becher, a leading German mercantilist, and became the embodiment of this theory's spread into the monarchy's state economic policy. Becher's reform efforts, however, were not put into practice, the board's activities gradually became only formal and, in the late 1670s, it ceased to exist. Mercantilist economic theories nevertheless spread among governmental authorities and in 1699, the Bohemian vice-regency elaborated a report on the economic status of the Kingdom of Bohemia, which they presented to the emperor together with proposals for its advancement, focusing in particular on the improvement of trade and production. The report was written in the mercantilist spirit and concentrated primarily on the development of local production, mainly through factories.

The beginning of major manufacturing development in the Czech Lands dates to the first decades of the 18th century, when the Habsburg central administration followed mercantilist principles and made an effort to support these types of activities. The factory owners gained privileges and governmental interest-free loans for their activities, the government supported an influx of foreign experts (despite the strictly re-Catholicization practice, the authorities made an exception and tolerated non-Catholic experts). The state re-organized the customs code and consistently applied a protectionist policy, while limiting the medieval guild powers. In the Czech Lands, where the manufacturing was oriented mainly towards linen production, its large-scale spread and export growth was hampered due to the limited possibilities of long-distance trade and the great distance from ports. It was one of the reasons that in industrial production, the Czech Lands, and in a broad sense the entire Habsburg monarchy, fell behind the rapidly developing countries of Western Europe.

Major economic changes in agriculture, which had a great impact on the country's social situation, took place in the 17ᵗʰ century. Land owners embarked on entrepreneurial activities at their own expense, which became the management core of practically all estates. In the Czech Lands, farming enterprise landed estate, primarily based on unpaid subject labour, became a standard model of estate management.

The social situation in the country worsened considerably during the Thirty Years' War and the following years. The heavy burden of the subject labour and low social status were strengthened. Peasants were not allowed to marry, move house, study or learn a trade without their landlord's consent, various services in the lordly courts were introduced. They had to buy exclusively the products of their landlord's enterprises (beer, artisanal products), to use the landlord's mills, etc. The suzerains and their property interests, however, accounted only partially for the difficult countryside situation as the peasants were also burdened with heavy governmental taxation.

The changes in peasant status, standardized around the mid-17ᵗʰ century, had been set out almost a hundred years earlier. Land ordinances from the 16ᵗʰ century included the demesne's protection against the peasants' running away, and in the same century, suzerains' decrees, regulating life on the demesnes (these were known as peasant codes and judicial articles), started to introduce articles worsening the peasants' legal status. However, the landlords started to consistently enact these provisions, as their needs required, under the new social and economic conditions following the Battle of White Mountain. Moreover, the 17ᵗʰ century witnessed the rapid bureaucratization of demesnes and the growth of the administrative machinery: a large or small number of clerks, depending on the size of the estate, stood between the landlords and the peasants.

This serfdom status, in German called "Leibeigenschaft," did not mean their actual enslavement, as it is sometimes interpreted regarding the situation in Central Europe (the Central-European type of servitude). Peasants could, for instance, complain about their lords to governmental authorities and to the ruler, and they could even take their landlords to court. Although peasants did utilise these possibilities, only rarely could they actually successfully defy the monetary and social influence of their landlords. So they often turned instead to violent action. In the latter part of the 17ᵗʰ century and in the first half of the 18ᵗʰ century, demesnes were affected by a great many local unrests, revolts and rebellions.

In 1680, large-scale peasant protests, resulting from the petition movement, afflicted Bohemia. Emperor, Bohemian and Hungarian King Leopold I was staying in Prague, fleeing from the black death epidemics which were sweeping through the Austrian lands. Bohemian peasants – following the popular monarchist conviction of the just ruler and his bad advisors – started, on a mass scale, to bring petitions to Prague, in which they complained vociferously about their great burden of the subject labour. Out of fear of spreading the epidemic, they were soon denied entry to the town and the petition movement turned to unrest. Only a military intervention and subsequent death sentences managed to subdue the uprisings.

The peasant unrests in 1680 enabled the ruler to interfere with affairs between the landlords and peasants, which had been beyond his authority until this time. Leopold I issued a subject labour edict, which regulated the peasant burden and banned certain landlords' practices. Although this system could not significantly improve the Bohemian peasants' status, it had a great effect on the social system's development. It put an end to the old feudal practice of determining peasants' duties through an agreement with the landlord and, for the first time, introduced a general binding norm of peasant duties as a state act. The subject labour patent from 1680, which was also elaborated for Moravia and succeeded by several other decrees over the following decades, was the first of many state interventions regarding peasant status, which resulted in its radical change at the end of the 18th century.

The state interventions into the peasants status were begun in an effort to protect their capacity to contribute. The state clerks', clergy's and practical economists' opposition to the peasants' excessive exploitation was frequently motivated both morally (the inhuman treatment of peasants was denounced in Catholic moral theology) and economically. Advocates of mercantilist economic theory warned against an excessive peasant burden, which resulted in fleeing from demesnes and thus weakened the lords' economic power. They advocated a thesis that an impoverished and excessively bled country would not bring the landlords prosperity, and thus would subsequently affect the state, as the peasants' capacity to pay taxes would fall.

3 The Czech State as an Integral Part of the Habsburg Monarchy

The political, religious and social changes which occurred after the defeat of the Estates Rebellion in 1620 and during the Thirty Years' War, signalled the following centuries' development. The transformation of the Bohemian crown lands was immense and striking. As a result of the loss of Upper and Lower Lusatia, the Bohemian state's area was reduced. On the internal political scene, the country, which for centuries had witnessed conflicts between the Estates and the ruler's power, became a pacified country with suppressed Estates, yet it was a country which, despite its ties to the Habsburg monarchy, did not entirely lose its sovereignty. The lands, where in the 16th and early 17th centuries, various faiths existed side by side and where, before the Battle of White Mountain, a majority of its population professed non-Catholic beliefs, witnessed the forced creation of a unified Catholic environment.

The year 1620 was an important landmark not just in Czech history, but also throughout the entire Habsburg monarchy, as the defeat of the Bohemian Estates and the liquidation of the Czech Lands confederation enabled the Habsburgs to introduce a model based on a powerful monarch's rule, traditionally called royal (or Baroque) absolutism, to the entire monarchy, with the temporary exception of Hungary. Austrian Estates met the same end as the Bohemian ones: in Austria, the Estates' political influence was also essentially eliminated and Catholicism imposed.

The Peace of Westphalia weakened the Habsburg monarchy on the European political scene, while at the same time strengthening its internal political status. The Czech Lands were incorporated into the Habsburg monarchy system more firmly than ever before. At the same time, however, the ties between the Czech Lands were disrupted. Moravia, geographically closer to Vienna than Bohemia, resembled most closely the Austrian lands politically, economically and partly culturally, and its ties to Bohemia were becoming looser. The firmest link between the two lands – apart from the Czech language, which was used by the German population of Bohemia as well as Moravia – was the Bohemian Chancellery, which ultimately moved to Vienna in 1624. It was an important office, which represented the Czech Lands before the Viennese government and handled their agenda in the royal court. As each ruler's decree for the Czech Lands had to be countersigned by the supreme chancellor, this made the Bohemian Chancellery and its head the main bearer of Bohemian statehood in the post-White Mountain period. It was through the Bohemian Chancellery that the ruler and government communicated with the administrative bodies in the Bohemian crown lands: in Bohemia it was the Prague Vice-regency; in Moravia, the Royal Tribunal in Brno; in Silesia, the Supreme Office in Wrocław.

Silesia, quite different from Bohemia and Moravia, was granted a unique status after the defeat of the Estates Rebellion and the ensuing Thirty Years' War. This land, with its prevalent German-speaking population and bordered by influential German non-Catholic countries, remained a conglomerate of many small principalities, though still with a central Land administration. Politically, the Silesian Estates were obviously limited in their powers, but the Renewed Ordinance was not introduced here and the Silesian population maintained a limited possibility to profess the Lutheran creed even after the Thirty Years' War.

After the Thirty Years' War, political life in the Czech Lands was greatly dictated by the monarch. Aristocrats who wanted to assert themselves in high-level politics or diplomacy had to build their careers in the Viennese court. Bohemia played an important role in Habsburg court policy in 1657, when the King of Bohemia and Hungary Leopold I chose Prague as his diplomatic seat, which aimed to ensure that he gained the Imperial Crown. As the King of Bohemia and one of the Imperial Electors, Leopold I did not address the other Electors merely as a candidate for the throne, but also as their peer. He entrusted Bohemian politicians with these complicated negotiations and their diplomatic mission was successful: in summer 1658, Leopold I was elected Emperor. This election, however, was for many decades the last important foreign policy activity carried out from the Czech Lands.

Despite this, even after principal Habsburg political activities had moved to Vienna, the Czech Lands preserved its important role in the political life of the Habsburg monarchy. Czech aristocrats, as well as some ambitious representatives of the bureaucratic nobility, held important offices in the court, in the army or in the diplomatic service. Among them we find both members of old Bohemian and Moravian noble families (such as the Lobkowiczes, the Kaplířs of Sulevice, the Kinskýs, the Vratislavs of Mitrovice, the Kaunitzes, the Martinitzes, the Wallensteins, the Czernins and the Kolowrats) along with members of the "foreign" nobility, who had settled in the Czech Lands after the Estate Rebellion's defeat (namely the Rottals, the Gallases and the Schwarzenbergs).

Aristocrats from the Czech Lands who built up their careers in the royal service, and remained in the Viennese court, supported integration in the Habsburg monarchy and the convergence of the Bohemian political and cultural environment with the Austrian lands. In the court, they found themselves in a cultural environment oriented towards Italy. They married here and thus participated in the rise of the supranational aristocratic Baroque society within the monarchy. These noblemen, however, also remained linked to their lands and Estates, which enabled the court culture and political thought to spread throughout the monarchy's territories.

The Viennese court's relationship to the Bohemian environment, however, was somewhat ambiguous. During the Bohemian Estates Rebellion, the old notion of Bohemian Estates as unreliable Habsburg subjects had been reinforced. This view had two aspects – political and religious. Politically, Czechs were suspected of being potential traitors and an unreliable and fundamentally untrustworthy element. As regards denomination, Czechs were considered heretics. This stereotype prevailed in the thoughts of the Habsburg courtiers of other than Bohemian origin long after the defeat of the Estates Rebellion, though it no longer had a realistic basis. Such a view suited Austrian, German, Italian and Spanish politicians in Vienna as it could be easily used in court intrigues.

Ideas of potential Bohemian betrayal were bolstered by cases such as the Albrecht of Wallenstein affair in 1634, which stirred up thoughts about unreliability of the Czech Lands and their Estates representation. A similar reaction caused the fall of Václav Eusebius Lobkowicz forty years later. This prominent Bohemian nobleman built a successful career and became Emperor Leopold I's first minister. In 1674, he fell foul of the emperor, was expelled from court and interned in his chateau in Roudnice until his death. He fell victim not only to his ambitions and short-sighted political decisions, but also to court intrigue. Lobkowicz never betrayed the emperor, though this topic was hotly debated after his fall. Similar cases occurred in the 17th century: in 1680, at the time of great unrest in the Bohemian countryside, rumours of the connection between the rebellious peasants and the monarchy's greatest enemies appeared. The rumours had it that Bohemian peasants were receiving French gold and plotting with Turkish envoys. The state administration launched an investigation, which, however, could not and did not confirm such speculation.

The view of the Bohemian population as potential campaigners against the Habsburgs did not only appear in court and among state clerks in Vienna. As the Bohemian Estates

Rebellion from 1618–1620 was an important event in European history, it sometimes reflected the perception of the Bohemian population abroad. The Habsburg monarchy's enemies' plans sometimes contained notions of using these alleged Bohemian anti-Habsburg sentiments. Such ideas were generally based on poor knowledge of the Czech Lands and, occasionally, on naivety. In the early 1650s, these inaccurate ideas about the local environment even appeared among Bohemian emigrants in Komenský's circle. In 1654, six years after the Treaty of Westphalia finally buried their hopes for the over-turning of the situation in their old homeland, Komenský's friend Václav Sadovský of Sloupno, a religious emigrant and former officer in the Swedish army, made a vain attempt to win Oliver Cromwell over to the idea of an invasion of the Czech Lands. One of his arguments was that the Bohemian and Moravian population would spontaneously and enthusiastically join his army.

In the second half of the 17th century, the picture of Bohemians, Moravians and Silesians as potential rebels against the Habsburgs also prevailed among Leopold I's Hungarian opponents. In the second half of the 17th century, Hungary was an unstable region, with several anti-Habsburg rebellions taking place. Many Hungarian conspirators and rebels calculated the possibility of inciting a revolt among Bohemian and Moravian population and winning them to their side. Some of them went so far as to distribute anti-Habsburg flyers in the Czech Lands. In spite of all their efforts, they never succeeded in inciting any unrest against Vienna.

Though we can trace an interest in the state tradition, the country's history and its elevation, or at least in achieving a dignified position within the Habsburg monarchy, among the Bohemian nobility in the post-White Mountain period, this was not the case within Moravian nobility. In Moravia, it was the Royal Tribunal, part of the state administration, that advocated the interests of both the land and its inhabitants, rather than the aristocratic land administration. It was evident even concerning such important questions as the land's integrity, when the Tribunal, unlike the Estates institutions, actively railed against the attempt to change some of the Moravian estates into imperial principalities.

Internal political life in the Czech Lands throughout the second half of the 17th century did not have the dynamics and conflicting character typical of the times before the White Mountain. It was closely connected to the ruler and occurred largely within bounds determined by the ruler. Land offices, necessary for the Czech Lands' administration, were transformed into clearly royal institutions, while the Land Diets, which in the past had served as a tool for the Estates' opposition, obediently followed the ruler's demands. The Bohemian Land Diet held its most important position, although its role in the administration of the Czech Lands was rather small. It did sometimes disagree with the king's financial demands, but it could not give rise to any real opposition.

The diets were in charge of many areas of public life – security, economy, healthcare, religious life. Their main task was to approve taxes demanded by the ruler: the tax negotiations were long and difficult, even though in the Baroque absolutist environment, no direct confrontation with the ruler was possible. The diet's representatives could mainly influence the structure of taxes, the methods and dates of their collection, and were also in charge of the finance management.

Taxes in Bohemia and Moravia were principally based on land possession (the homestead system), in Silesia, the main tax was that of property. In the mid-17th century, the first provincial land registers were established. In Bohemia, it was a list of tax duties (*berní rula*); in Moravia, land registers (*lánové rejstříky*). Land taxes were occasionally complemented with indirect excise taxes, which were mainly paid by the unprivileged population, the subjects in the country as well as those in the towns, and the royal town burghers. In the 17th century, however, the state showed strong tendencies to include suzerain land and members of the higher strata of the society in their taxation.

In the 17th and 18th centuries, the tax burden in the Czech Lands was substantial, with the majority of the revenue going to covering the cost of the growing standing army and its immense military expenses in the second half of the 17th and in the 18th centuries. From 1655, the tax burden of Czech versus Austrian lands was 56 : 44, and this grew to 65 : 35 after 1682. Within the total levy from the Czech Lands, taxes from Bohemia made up about one half; from Moravia, one sixth; from Silesia, one third. At the beginning of the 18th century, the tax ratio further disadvantaged the Czech Lands.

The tax demands were a heavy burden, which slowed economic reconstruction in the aftermath of the Thirty Years' War. In exchange for the money and human resources which went into the Habsburg wars, the Czech Lands gained something very rare in the tumultuous Europe of the time – ninety years of uninterrupted peace. In the period from the end of the Thirty Years' War in 1648 to the beginning of the War of Habsburg Succession in the early 1740s, the Czech Lands were spared, with a few exceptions in the border regions, military campaigns.

In the 17th and 18th centuries, wars several times jeopardized the very existence of the Habsburg monarchy, but were only perceived from a distance in the Czech Lands. In autumn 1663, during the war with the Turks, the news spread that Turkish-Tartar troops had made three short incursions into Moravia, and panic swept through Prague. In 1683, when Vienna was besieged by the Turkish army, Moravia was better protected. The Moravian population was only reminded of war, this time the war for the very existence of the Habsburg monarchy, when Polish King John III Sobieski's armies passed through to the aid of besieged Vienna. The last military conflicts took place in south Moravia during Francis II Rákóczi's Hungarian uprising. There were local fights along the Moravian-Hungarian border and the occasional incursions by Hungarian rebels in 1703–1708. The uprising's elimination put an end to more than a hundred years of threat to south Moravia from both Turkish and Hungarian dangers. Silesia also experienced several military campaigns at the beginning of the 18th century, all related to the Great Northern War. It was only from newspapers that the Czech Lands' population was aware of the existence of the Habsburg wars, which were distant from their borders (mainly the War of the Spanish Succession and wars with the Turks in the Balkans), though they were ordered to pray for the success of the Habsburg weapons and were affected by an increase in imperial recruiting officers' activities.

At the beginning of the 18th century, political and economic life in the Czech Lands was strongly marked by the reform policy of Emperor Joseph I, who succeeded his father Leopold I to the throne in 1705. Joseph surrounded himself with pragmatic politicians and diplomats, who helped him in his efforts to implement administrative and financial reforms in the Habsburg lands, which were aimed at modernizing this dominion along the model presented by Western monarchies. Joseph I strengthened the role of the state bureaucracy, but he also considered the possibility of systemic changes across the entire Habsburg dominion, such as the idea to form a diet common to all Habsburg monarchy lands. He commenced reforming the tax system (an attempt to introduce an excise duty on a mass scale) and started to interfere more frequently in the economy of the lands in accordance with mercantilist principles. In the Czech Lands, a commercial committee, central and permanent agencies were formed, whose primary task it was to support interior and foreign trade. Joseph's short rule (he died in 1711), however, did not allow for the implementation of most of the reforms.

Of all reforms, it was the attempt to revise the Renewed Ordinance that affected the Czech Lands most. Its main goal was to simplify the legislature and make it more transparent, as over the almost hundred years of its existence, the Renewed Ordinance had been supplemented by numerous other laws, issued in the forms of rescripts, resolutions or declaratory provisions.

Committees were established to revise the Land ordinance and their activities reveal the efforts of the Bohemian nobility to at least partially mitigate the consequences of penalties imposed after the Battle of White Mountain. A preserved report elaborated by the Bohemian committee demonstrates their effort to omit all references to the 1618–1620 Estates Rebellion from the Renewed Ordinance. Another important feature of the revisions to the Bohemian and Moravian Renewed Ordinance was an emphasis on the specific character of the Lands of the Bohemian Crown, particularly with respect to the cohesiveness of Bohemia and Moravia. It also illustrated their efforts to emphasize and strengthen the Estates' privileges, naturally, while fully recognizing the ruler's power. The committees for the revision of Land ordinances worked intensively in 1709–1710. However, after Joseph I's death, they ceased to exist and did not reappear until the 1720s, and then only for a brief period. However, they failed to complete their task and the Renewed Ordinance remained in force in its original form from the first half of the 17th century until the 19th century.

Joseph I was the first King of Bohemia in the early modern era who was not crowned with the Crown of St Wenceslas. In the period before the Battle of White Mountain, coronation in the Prague's St Vitus Cathedral was a necessary condition for performing the royal duties. Coronations took place in Prague even after the Bohemian throne was declared hereditary – in 1627 Ferdinand III's coronation, in 1646 his oldest son Ferdinand IV's coronation and, after his sudden death, Ferdinand III's younger son Leopold I was crowned while his father was still alive. During his reign, in the second half of the 17th century, the coronation ritual in Bohemia lost its importance and attractiveness for the Habsburgs, as can be seen from the fact that none of Leopold's three wives was crowned with the Bohemian royal crown. Joseph I's coronation did not take place in Prague either, although his father ensured the Hungarian throne for him through a coronation with the Crown of St Stephen when Joseph was only nine years old. This shows the Habsburg's different approaches to the Czech Lands and to Hungary. While their position in the Czech Lands was quite firm in the second half of the 17th century, their status in Hungary, jeopardized by the Hungarian Estates' frequent uprisings and by the threat from the Ottoman Empire and its vassal state, Transylvania, was much shakier.

The coronation ceased to be a necessary condition for ruling over the Czech Lands and the Estates Tribute – a promise of hereditary subjection, although also a formal act, became more important. The title of the King of Bohemia was, however, internally still very important – for the Czech Lands (the Habsburgs ruled here as the Kings of Bohemia even during the Baroque absolutism), but also externally. The title of the King of Bohemia was the third in the Habsburg rulers' titles, following the titles of Roman Emperor and King of Hungary. This was connected to the electoral vote, which was important during the elections of Holy Roman kings and emperors. Joseph I took advantage of the title of the King of Bohemia to secure the King of Bohemia's permanent ambassador (part of what was known as the readmission of the Bohemian vote) at the Reichstag (Imperial Diet – parliament of the Holy Roman Empire), which met in Regensburg from 1663. It was merely a formality, yet it illustrates the importance of the Kingdom of Bohemia in Joseph's imperial policy. This act had only one effect for the Lands of the Bohemian Crown – they had to finance the emperor's ambassador to the Reichstag and one associate justice at the Imperial Chamber Court.

The lack of interest in the Bohemian coronation was also prevalent during the reign of Joseph's brother and successor Charles VI (r. 1711–1740). His Hungarian coronation took place a year after Joseph's death in 1712, while his coronation in Prague was not held until 1723, twelve years after his accession to the throne, and it was interpreted as the ruler's good will towards the Bohemian Estates.

Charles VI's rule was marked by a dynastic crisis. Neither Joseph I nor Charles had any living male descendants and there was a danger that the Habsburg monarchy would die out in the male line in the 17th century. This situation was to be solved by the "Pragmatic Sanction," a law which, among other things, ensured the succession by female family members of the Austrian Habsburgs if there were no male heirs. If there were no male descendants, succession was to pass to Charles VI's daughters, then to Joseph I's daughters and then to Leopold I's daughters. This provision became the legal grounds for the succession of Charles VI's daughter Maria Theresa as the head of the Austrian dominion after her father's death in 1740.

Aside from the above-mentioned female succession, the Pragmatic Sanction had another equally important function: ensuring the indivisibility of the Habsburg monarchy, which at the beginning of the 18th century represented a dynastic union of three state units – Austrian lands, the Lands of the Bohemian Crown and Hungary. In each of these units, the Habsburg ruler ruled as a hereditary sovereign, as the King of Bohemia in the Czech Lands. When this law was passed in 1713, Charles VI still had hopes of producing a male heir and so did not strive for its universal recognition. It was only in the 1720s that he had the Land Diets enact the Pragmatic Sanction and, at the same time, a complicated process for its international recognition was started. In 1720, the Diets of the Lands of the Bohemian Crown enacted the Pragmatic Sanction unanimously. The Pragmatic Sanction was an intervention into the constitutional status of the Bohemian state. Its provision regarding the indivisibility of the monarchy meant a demand for a certain level of integration of the Czech Lands into the Habsburg dominion and constituted conditions for further limitations to the Bohemian state's sovereignty, which commenced in Maria Theresa's reign.

4 Baroque Culture and Society in the Czech Lands

The second half of the 17th and the first half of the 18th centuries were marked by the rapid development of Baroque culture. The nobility built Baroque chateaux or rebuilt older palaces in this style, which meant commissions for visual artists, as well as for music composers and interpreters. Richly decorated gardens became a must for chateau complexes. Theatres were built in chateaux and prominent European opera and drama works made their way to the Czech Lands. Construction activities were not limited to the nobility, as burghers also rebuilt their houses and in many towns Baroque town halls were erected.

The Catholic church helped to spread Baroque culture still more, as it was one of the greatest commissioners of Baroque art works. Churches and monasteries were rebuilt, and Marian columns started to appear in the squares of Bohemian, Moravian and Silesian towns. The first was erected in Prague in 1650, initiated by Emperor Ferdinand III as thanks for defending the town against the Swedes in 1648 and to commemorate the end of the Thirty Years' War. It also became a symbol of the re-introduced Catholicism.

Baroque artists working in the Czech Lands were drawn partly from the local environment, though many had foreign experience. In the Baroque era, the first Moravian arts market was established and the first generations of Moravian artists appeared. Among the many outstanding local artists working in the Czech Lands, we should mention painters Karel Škréta (1610–1674), Petr Brandl (1668–1735), Václav Vavřinec Reiner (1689–1743), architect František Maxmilián Kaňka (1674–1766), music composers Adam Michna of Otradovice (1600–1676), Bohuslav Matěj Černohorský (1684–1742) or Jan Dismas Zelenka (1679–1745). Among the foreign artists who worked in Bohemia and Moravia were sculptor Matthias Bernard Braun (1684–1738) from Tyrol, members of the sculpting Brokoff family from Upper Hungary (in today's Slovakia), architect Jan Blažej Santini-Aichel (1677–1723) who was born in Italy, and architects from the Dientzenhofer family, who came from Bavaria. All these foreigners, finding a favourable artistic environment and a sufficient amount of commissions, settled in the Czech Lands permanently. Many artists working in the Czech Lands asserted themselves abroad, Jan Dismas Zelenka, for example, worked in the Elector of Saxony's court in Dresden, sculptor Ferdinand Maximilian Brokoff (1688–1731) designed churches in Wrocław and Vienna, while Czech painter and engraver Václav Hollar (1607–1677), who left the country for religious reasons, worked in England.

In connection to the development of Baroque art, the landscape of the Czech Lands started to change. Its appearance was marked with palace complexes, large structures marking pilgrimage sites, as well as different-sized chapels, crucifixes and statues. Baroque culture was multifaceted; it existed as high culture for social elites, for whom it was a distinctive feature, but also as mass culture intended for the widest population. It was not only limited to visual arts and music. Baroque asserted itself deeply in the lifestyle of the post-White Mountain generations. It inspired a new expression of piousness, which essentially spontaneously established itself in the Czech Lands. It was characterized by a remarkable symbiosis of sacred and profane motifs. In Baroque religious life, religious zeal, reminders of earthly vanity, expressions of ostentatious humbleness and an emphasis on quantity (the number of prayers recited, masses attended, hours spent at services and the like) naturally entwined with earthly self-indulgence, the sense of elevating one's importance and the need for representation. It is impossible to distinguish between religious and profane motifs in Baroque piety, its expression is theatrical, which is one of the defining characteristics of the Baroque. Therefore, any ceremony, religious or secular, became a natural and essential part of Baroque culture as it allowed for the cultivation of histrionics while taking advantage of the synthetic character of the Baroque, incorporating many different arts.

One of the most important profane Baroque ceremonies was the coronation of Charles VI and his wife Elisabeth Christine in 1723. During the sixty years without a coronation taking place in Prague (1656–1723), important festivals were represented by ceremonial entrances and enthroning of Prague archbishops. Similar ceremonies, though on a much smaller scale, took place in the demesnes to welcome lords or in the towns in connection with reinstating town councils, celebrations of the Habsburg army's victory or events in the ruler's family.

Many of these secular festivities also had a religious element, although there were also clearly religious festivities – processions, pilgrimages, public services organized by religious confraternities, and the luxurious funerals of prominent personalities. In Moravia, spectacular coronations of Marian images took place in the Hradisko Monastery near Olomouc (1732) and in St Thomas Monastery in Brno (1735). The peak of religious Baroque festivities in the Czech Lands were massive celebrations marking the canonization of the Czech Baroque saint, John of Nepomuk (or Nepomucene), were held in Prague in autumn 1729. This saint, whose mythical identity can be traced to the historic figure of the general vicar of the Prague archdiocese John of Pomuk, became the most famous personality of Baroque Bohemia. The Nepomucene cult of the first martyr of the Seal of the Confessional even gained popularity outside the Czech Lands and spread throughout the whole of Catholic Europe, as well as in the Catholic areas of Central and South America.

Baroque festivities overwhelmed one's senses with colours, splendour and monumentousness. They initiated the creation of new paintings, statues, special stage decorations – festival gateways, triumphal arches; for church funerals, castra doloris – the structures and decorations sheltering the catafalque, were built. Music was composed, speeches and sermons written for special occasions. The main goal of the decoration was to overwhelm and dazzle participants, to carry them away from real life. Everything was ephemeral and so every important Baroque festivity soon had its printed description, frequently accompanied with engravings.

Literature became an important part of Baroque culture as it developed. During the Baroque, much religious educational literature (postils, prayers, Scripture interpretations, hagiographic writing, historical works devoted to important pilgrimage sites) in Czech, German and Latin was written in the Czech Lands. Many of these works were exchanged for confiscated non-Catholic books, which missionaries sought out in rural areas. Religious lyric poetry and song lyrics in hymnbooks were also important. A second major literature area for the Baroque were historical texts, most usually interpretations of Bohemian and Moravian history from a patriotic Baroque standpoint, which frequently deliberately emphasized the Catholic past. Historiography, represented by Bohuslav Balbín (1621–1688), Tomáš Pešina of Čechorod (1629–1680), among other writers, was not merely a part of popular literature, expressing as it did more and more scientific tendencies. Most widely read was light reading for the general population, among them pulp literature and pedllers' songs

Another important aspect of Bohemian Baroque culture were also works by religious emigrants, among which the works of Jan Amos Komenský (Comenius) (1592–1670) stand out. His pansophism project represented a self-contained system based on theology, which was to lead to the "reform of human affairs." It was an attempt to link devout faith with perfect knowledge, which was to overcome the chaos brought to human life by war and social change in the first half of the 17th century. Komenský was one of the thinkers of the European horizon. He met René Descartes in person, though his objections to Cartesianism prevented him from being duly appreciated by the French philosopher.

Komenský's interests were numerous and varied, he engaged in political and diplomatic activities striving to change the political and religious situation in the Czech Lands during the Thirty Years' War. His failure to effect any real change, disappointment over the political situation, and a feeling of hopelessness lead Komenský in his declining years to mysticism, chiliastic feelings and prophesies, as well as publishing prophesies by his friend and Brethren priest Mikuláš Drabík.

His educational and didactic works, which won him European fame, belong within the context of Komenský's efforts to reform society. In education, he transgressed denominational and political borders, which separated him from the world of his religious and ideological opponents, from the Catholic church. Komenský did not hesitate to embrace the developed tradition of Jesuit language instruction, while on the other hand, his most famous textbook *Janua linguarum reserata* (The Gate of Languages Unlocked, 1631) was even used in Catholic countries. It was translated into many European languages and also republished by Bohemian and Moravian Jesuits.

Education in the Czech Lands had a rich tradition and a solid foundation from the past, yet after the defeat of the Estates Rebellion it was restructured. All schools were Catholicized, secondary schooling became the Jesuit domain, while lower schooling, despite initial disagreements and controversies with the Jesuit Order, was controlled by the Piarists. Basic literacy was not only commonplace in towns, but most of the peasant population could also read and write, which was reflected in the re-Catholicization struggle at the beginning of the 18th century, when non-Catholic literature printed abroad was sent to rural areas.

Many monasteries established and developed their own monastic schools and diocesan seminaries for clerical education, which followed the rules established by the Trident Council. Prague's university, which during the Estates Rebellion had been on the side of the Estates, provided its halls for their meetings, and whose rector, Doctor Jan Jessenius, was among the executed leaders of the rebellion, had to dismiss non-Catholic teachers and was handed over to Jesuit control. After years of controversies between the Society of Jesus and Prague Archbishop Harrach, who was the university chancellor by virtue of the power of his office, a united Charles-Ferdinand University was formed in Prague in 1654, which joined together the old university, founded in the mid-14th century by Emperor Charles IV, and the Jesuit Academy from the second half of the 16th century. Apart from the Prague university, there was also a Jesuit university in Olomouc (founded in 1573) and in Wrocław (founded by Leopold I in 1702). At the beginning of the 18th century, a technical training college was founded in Prague. In 1707, Joseph I agreed that Christian Joseph Willenberg could teach "engineering science" in Prague, but the school (a predecessor of the Czech Technical University) was not founded until ten years later, upon an Estates decree of November 1717.

The population structure and social development in the Czech Lands over the century following the Battle of White Mountain underwent extensive changes. Political and religious migration, war plundering and the epidemics of the Thirty Years' War considerably lessened – as in other Central European countries – the population figures. The balancing out of this demographic decrease was gradual and lengthy, as it was continuously hampered by military drafts and, most notably, plague epidemics, which affected the Czech Lands in 1680 and again in 1713–1714. Despite this, the decrease in population caused by the Thirty Years' War had been redressed by the end of the 17th century.

Social strata were also affected by major changes during the Thirty Years' War. Among the aristocracy, the development which started in the period before the Battle of White Mountain, when a considerable decrease in the lower nobility occurred, while the higher nobility increased in number, was accelerated. Higher nobility also controlled most of the landed estates in the country, of which a great proportion was owned by members of foreign families, who were granted the citizenship rights by the ruler during the Thirty Years' War. This mainly concerned the families who were enriched through participation in the plundering and through military enterprises, or those who profited from the property confiscations of the 1620s and 1630s.

Another stratum which underwent major changes was Catholic clergy after its prelates became most important among the Estates (1627–1628). There was an enormous increase in the number of clergy, of which the lower clergy was particularly highly sought after due to the great number of unoccupied parishes in Bohemia. The number of monks and nuns also increased and, as a result, the number of monasteries and convents multiplied in the

17th and 18th centuries. The clergy, in the Bohemian Diet represented mainly by Prague archbishops, was the only Estate that could, in the second half of the 17th century, notably stand up to some of the ruler's demands. Generally speaking, however, the Catholic church was gradually losing the battle with the Habsburg state and was more and more subjugated by the ruler and the state.

The burgher Estate was in decline after the Battle of White Mountain. Its political influence was completely eliminated and the presence of royal town representatives in the Land Diets was merely formal. Although the economic situation in the second half of the 17th century gradually improved, the traditional guild hampered more intensive industrial development. Despite this, even town environments played their role in the development of construction, as most of Bohemian towns acquired their Baroque appearance in this period. Prague, the most important Bohemian town, became a mere provincial town of the Habsburg monarchy when the Habsburgs permanently settled in Vienna. Nevertheless, it remained the seat of land administration and Land Diet. It also became an important residential town for nobility. Many a noble family had palaces in both Vienna and Prague.

In this period, the unprivileged village and small subject town population suffered from a heightened dependence on their suzerains, as well as from an increased burden of subject labour and contribution duties. However, this time also witnessed the beginning of state regulation of peasant status, which eventually, in the second half of the 18th century, led to the considerable alleviation of their burden. Despite all these social problems, Baroque culture, particularly its lowest popular component, flourished also in the rural areas and it has been preserved till today in folklore.

The Baroque period also brought about the first systematic social welfare measures. Most parsonages had their own hospitals for the poor and sick, and charitable activities were on the increase. Following the French models, the state also took care of its veterans and handicapped soldiers; in 1728, L'hotel des Invalides was founded near Prague's New Town, whose mighty 1730s structure was designed by Kilian Ignaz Dientzenhofer. From the second half of the 17th century, royal and subject towns also systematically dealt with the problem of begging and people on the fringes of society. Police codes, laying out in detail the conditions under which such individuals could stay and beg in town, were implemented. A great emphasis was placed on keeping records of beggars. Those without work who did not have a begging permit were locked up in coercive workhouses. The first such facility was founded in the 1670s in Prague's Old Town. Not only convicts, but also vagabonds and beggars, had to work in the spinning factory for wool, cotton and silk, which was linked with the penitentiary. Prague thus followed a common Western-European practice based on the mercantilist economic science. A different solution for the social problems of the lowest strata in society was public almshouses; the first in Prague was established in 1733.

In the early modern era, minorities, in particular the Jews and Roma, were pushed to the fringes of society. On the one hand, the Jews in the Czech Lands gained new privileges and experienced an economic boom in the 17th century, on the other hand the town population, where Jewish ghettoes existed, often expressed anti-Jewish sentiments. Uncontrolled and destructive anti-Jewish pogroms no longer occurred, although in the 17th and in the first half of the 18th centuries, riots took place in Prague, during which Jewish merchants' stores were destroyed. They were mainly expressions of the Prague population's oversensitivity to the Jewish artisans' competition and to the expansion of more and more small Jewish merchants beyond the ghetto borders. Anti-Jewish sentiments were even present in the Land Diets' agenda. Bohemian Estates tried to curtail the Jewish population and in the early 1680s, following the Viennese model, they attempted to expel them from Prague. It did not, however, happen. State regulative interventions and administrative measures aimed at limiting the Jewish population, were implemented. According to a 1681 decree, Jews should not be tolerated in places other than those where they had settled before 1657. In 1726, the government passed the Familiant Law, which set the number of Jewish families which could legally settle in the country.

The Roma status was much worse. The gypsy nomads committed petty offences against property and in the early modern society, their appearance, language, lifestyle and behaviour provoked the fear of the unknown. They were perceived as a multiple danger: they were accused of theft and in tense periods of spying for the Turks, of arson and of spreading epidemics. All this explains the anti-Roma patents, mostly issued in the first half of the 18th century. The wholesale persecution of Romas took the form of banishment from the Czech Lands and apprehended Roma were subject to many punishments, including capital punishment.

Higher social levels in the Czech Lands naturally sought their integration within the Habsburg dominion, defined their relationship to the state and searched for their new identity, and finding it in two types of patriotism, Baroque national patriotism and patriotism to the land. Land patriotism was based on citizenship, irrespective of language. It mainly concerned the nobility, which felt linked to the fate of the country in which they had settled, with its history and Land laws. At the same time, however, knowledge of the local language was of secondary importance. The mother tongues of the Czech Lands' nobility were both Czech and German, though a court career demanded knowledge of Italian, Latin and other languages. The nobility was also culturally cosmopolitan and Land patriotism was a tie to the country in which they resided and from which their income flowed.

Baroque national patriotism, on the other hand, was defined linguistically. Intellectuals from the clerical Estate, as well as many burghers, realized the decreasing importance of Czech in the everyday life of the Czech Lands, and tried to highlight the importance of this language as one of the symbols of the former sovereignty of the Bohemian state. They also, like Land patriots, felt the urge to defend the old Land rights and emphasized the Bohemian state's famous history. They maintained their loyalty to the Habsburg dynasty and to the Catholic church, though the main purpose of their historical works was a search for and praise of the Catholic traditions of the Czech Middle Ages.

Bibliography

BAHLCKE, Joachim (ed.): *Glaubensflüchtlinge. Ursachen, Formen und Auswirkungen frühneuzeitlicher Konfessionsmigration in Europa*, (=Religions- und Kulturgeschichte in Ostmittel- und Südosteuropa, Band 4), Berlin 2008.

BAHLCKE, Joachim – BÖMELBURG, Hans-Jürgen – KERSKEN, Norbert (eds.): *Ständefreiheit und Staatsgestaltung in Ostmitteleuropa. Übernationale Gemeinsamkeiten in der politischen Kultur vom 16.–18. Jahrhundert*, Leipzig 1996.

BAHLCKE, Joachim – STROHMEYER, Arno (eds.): *Konfessionalisierung in Ostmitteleuropa. Wirkungen des religiösen Wandels im 16. und 17. Jahrhundert in Staat, Gesellschaft und Kultur*, Stuttgart 1999.

BALCÁREK, Pavel: *Kardinál František Ditrichštejn 1570–1636. Gubernátor Moravy*, České Budějovice 2007.

BEIN, Werner: *Schlesien in der habsburgischen Politik. Ein Beitrag zur Entstehung des Dualismus im Alten Reich*, Sigmaringen 1994.

BIRELEY, Robert: *The Refashioning of Catholicism, 1450–1700. A Reassessment of the Counter Reformation*, Washington D.C. 1999.

BOBKOVÁ, Lenka: *Exulanti z Prahy a severozápadních Čech v Pirně v letech 1621–1639*, Praha 1999.

BOBKOVÁ-VALENTOVÁ, Kateřina: *Každodenní život učitele a žáka jezuitského gymnázia*, Praha 2006.

CATALANO, Alessandro: *La Boemia e la riconquista delle coscienze. Ernst Adalbert von Harrach e la controriforma in Europa centrale (1620–1667)*, Roma 2005.

CONRADS, Norbert: *Die Durchführung der Altranstädter Konvention in Schlesien 1707–1709*, Köln–Wien 1971.

ČECHURA, Jaroslav: *Selské rebelie roku 1680. Sociální konflikty v barokních Čechách a jejich každodenní souvislosti*, Praha 2001.

ČORNEJOVÁ, Ivana: *Kapitoly z dějin pražské univerzity 1622–1773*, Praha 1992.

ČORNEJOVÁ, Ivana (ed.): *Úloha církevních řádů při pobělohorské rekatolizaci*, Praha 2003.

ČORNEJOVÁ, Ivana – KAŠE, Jiří – MIKULEC, Jiří – VLNAS, Vít: *Velké dějiny zemí Koruny české*, VIII (1618–1683), Praha–Litomyšl 2008.

DEVENTER, Jörg: *Gegenreformation in Schlesien. Die habsburgische Rekatholisierungpolitik in Glogau und Schweidnitz 1526–1707*, Köln–Weimar–Wien 2003.

DOLEŽAL Daniel – Kühne, Hartmut (eds.): *Wallfahrten in der europäischen Kultur – Pilgrimage in European Culture*, Frankfurt am Main 2006.

DRABEK, Anna M.: *Die Juden in den Böhmischen Ländern zur Zeit des landesfürstlichen Absolutismus (Von der Schlacht am Weißen Berg bis zum Ausgang der Regierungszeit Maria Theresias)*, in: Bad Wiesseer Tagungen des Collegium Carolinum, München–Wien 1983, pp. 123–143.

EICKELS, Christine van: *Schlesien im böhmischen Ständesstaat. Voraussetzungen und Verlauf der böhmischen Revolution von 1618 in Schlesien*, Köln–Weimar–Wien 1994.

EVANS, Robert J. W.: *The Making of the Habsburg Monarchy 1550–1700. An Interpretation*, Oxford 1979.

FEJTOVÁ, Olga – LEDVINKA, Václav – PEŠEK, Jiří – VLNAS, Vít: *Barokní Praha – Barokní Čechie 1620–1740*, Praha 2004.

FORBELSKÝ, Josef: *Španělé, Říše a Čechy v 16. a 17. století*, Praha 2006.

FRANZL, Johann: *Ferdinand II. Kaiser im Zwiespalt der Zeit*, Graz–Wien–Köln 1978.

HANZAL, Jiří: *Cikáni na Moravě v 15. až 18. století. Dějiny etnika na okraji společnosti*, Praha 2004.

HASSENPFLUG, Eila: *Die böhmische Adelsnation als Repräsentantin des Königreichs Böhmen von der Inkraftsetzung der Verneuerten Landesordnung bis zum Regierungsantritt Maria Theresias*, Bohemia 15, 1974, pp. 71–90.

HEROLD, Vilém – Pánek, Jaroslav (eds.): *Baroko v Itálii – baroko v Čechách. Setkávání osobností, idejí a uměleckých forem*, Praha 2003.

HRUBÁ, Michaela (ed.): *Víra nebo vlast? Exil v českých dějinách raného novověku*, Ústí nad Labem 2001.

HAUSENBLASOVÁ, Jaroslava – ŠRONĚK, Michal: *Gloria & Miseria 1618–1648. Prague during the Thirty Years War*, Praha 1998.

HROCH, Miroslav – PETRÁŇ, Josef: *Das 17. Jahrhundert. Krise der feudalen Gesellschaft?*, Hamburg 1981.

JANÁČEK, Josef: *Valdštejn a jeho doba*, Praha 1978, 2nd edition, 2003.

JANÁK, Jan – HLEDÍKOVÁ, Zdeňka: *Dějiny správy v českých zemích do roku 1945*, Praha 1989.

KNOZ, Tomáš: *Državy Karla staršího ze Žerotína po Bílé hoře. Osoby, příběhy, struktury*, Brno 2001.

KNOZ, Tomáš: *Karel st. ze Žerotína. Don Quijote v labyrintu světa*, Praha 2008.

KNOZ, Tomáš: *Pobělohorské konfiskace. Moravský průběh, středoevropské souvislosti, obecné aspekty*, Brno 2006.

KUMPERA, Jan: *Jan Amos Komenský. Poutník na rozhraní věků*, Ostrava 1992.

KUMPERA, Jan – HEJNIC, Josef: *Poslední pokus českého exilu kolem Komenského o zvrat v zemích České koruny*, Brno–Uherský Brod 1988.

MANN, Golo: *Wallenstein*, I–II, Berlin 1989.

MAŤA, Petr: *Svět české aristokracie (1500–1700)*, Praha 2004.

MATĚJEK, František: *Morava za třicetileté války*, Praha 1992.

MIKULEC, Jiří: *Leopold I. Život a vláda barokního Habsburka*, Praha–Litomyšl 1997.

MIKULEC, Jiří: *Poddanská otázka v barokních Čechách*, Praha 1993.

MIKULEC, Jiří: *31. 7. 1627 – Rekatolizace šlechty v Čechách. Čí je země, toho je i náboženství*, Praha 2005.

PÁNEK, Jaroslav (ed.): *Comenius in World Science and Culture*, Praha 1991.

PÁNEK, Jaroslav: *Comenius. Teacher of Nations*, Košice–Praha 1991.

PETRÁŇ, Josef: *Staroměstská exekuce*, 3rd edition Praha 1996 (3. vyd.).

PETRÁŇ, Josef – Petráňová, Lydia: *The White Mountain as a symbol in modern Czech history*, in: Mikuláš Teich (ed.): *Bohemia in History*, Cambridge 1998, p. 143–163.

PETRY, Ludwig – Menzel, Joachim J.: *Geschichte Schlesiens*, II: *Die Habsburgerzeit 1526–1740*, Darmstadt 1973.

POLIŠENSKÝ, Josef: *The Thirty Years War*, London 1971.

POLIŠENSKÝ, Josef – KOLLMANN, Josef: *Wallenstein. Feldherr des Dreissigjährigen Krieges*, Köln 1997.

PREISS, Pavel: *František Antonín Špork a barokní kultura v Čechách*, Praha 2003.

RATAJ, Tomáš: *České země ve stínu půlměsíce. Obraz Turka v raně novověké literatuře z českých zemí*, Praha 2002.

REPGEN, Konrad (ed.): *Das Herrscherbild im 17. Jahrhundert*, Münster 1991.

SKUTIL, Jan (ed.): *Morava a Brno na sklonku třicetileté války*, Praha–Brno 1995.

ŠTĚŘÍKOVÁ, Edita: *Stručně o pobělohorských exulantech*, Praha 2005.

URBÁNEK, Vladimír: *Eschatologie, vědění a politika. Příspěvek k dějinám myšlení pobělohorského exilu*, České Budějovice 2008

URFUS, Valentin: *Císař Josef I. Nekorunovaný Habsburk na českém trůně*, Praha 2004.

URFUS, Valentin: *19. 4. 1713 – Pragmatická sankce. Rodný list podunajské monarchie*, Praha 2002.

VÁLKA, Josef: *Česká společnost v 15.–18. století*, II: *Bělohorská doba. Společnost a kultura "manýrismu"*, Praha 1983.

VÁLKA, Josef: *Morava reformace, renesance a baroka* (Dějiny Moravy II), Brno 1996.

VESELÁ-PRUDKOVÁ, Lenka: *Židé a česká společnost v zrcadle literatury. Od středověku k počátkům emancipace*, Praha 2003.

VLNAS, Vít: *Jan Nepomucký, česká legenda*, Praha 1993

VLNAS, Vít: *Princ Evžen Savojský. Život a sláva barokního válečníka*, Praha 2001.

WINKELBAUER, Thomas: *Fürst und Fürstendiener. Gundaker von Liechtenstein, ein österreichischer Aristokrat des konfesionellen Zeitalters*, Wien–München 1999.

WINKELBAUER, Thomas: *Ständefreiheit und Fürstenmacht. Länder und Untertanen des Hauses Habsburg im konfessionellen Zeitalter*, I–II, Wien 2003 (In: Österreichische Geschichte 1522–1699).

ZUBER, Rudolf: *Osudy moravské církve v 18. století*, I, Praha 1987; II, Olomouc 2003.

X. Enlightened Absolutism and the Birth of a Modern State (1740–1792)

Emperor Joseph II among his people. Emperor Joseph II (on horseback), clad in a simple uniform, free of lavishness, ornaments and symbols of ruler's position, talking with country people about their lives and problems. Copperplate, from *Leben und Geschichte Kaiser Joseph des Zweiten*, II, Amsterdam, 1790 (no pagination, between pages 34–35).

1 On the Way to the Centralized State

After the death of Emperor Charles VI, who died without a male heir, his oldest daughter Maria Theresa (r. 1740–1780) assumed power in the Habsburg hereditary lands in October 1740. Her marriage to Francis Stephen of Lorraine gave rise to the Habsburg-Lorraine dynasty, which ruled in the Habsburg monarchy until 1918. Maria Theresa formally named her husband co-regent, however, in reality he only had an advisory role, while Maria Theresa kept all power and decisions in her own hands. The young ruler, only twenty-three years old at the time of accession, was not prepared for her new duties, however, among her qualities were natural intelligence and sagacity, as well as diligence and a talent for surrounding herself with capable advisors and an ability to orient herself quickly in a new situation. The course of events soon allowed her to exhibit these qualities. The heritage she gained was not without problems, both internationally and internally. The first great danger she had to face was the threat of losing most of the inherited lands and their distribution among foreign powers. From the very beginning of her rule, this problem determined the course of the first half of her reign, which was marked by conflict.

The right of the new female ruler's accession in the hereditary lands of the Habsburg family was based on the Pragmatic Sanction from 1713, which established the indivisibility of the hereditary lands, as well as the succession rules in the Habsburg monarchy: if Habsburgs died out along the male line, the rule passed to the female offspring. Although the Pragmatic Sanction was recognized by most European governments as an internationally valid document, after Charles VI's death some powers challenged its validity and took advantage of diplomatic and legal disputes to present their claims to Habsburg lands.

These disputes led to the War of the Austrian Succession in 1740–1748, an umbrella term for many smaller conflicts that took place in the Czech Lands, Austria, Italy and the Austrian Netherlands (Belgium). The fights did not merely concern the Habsburg territories, but also the influence in the Holy Roman Empire, or, more specifically, the Imperial Crown, which was last held by Charles VI. The war most notably affected the Bohemian crown lands in which foreign powers were particularly interested at the outset of the war.

This resulted in the economic and political weakening of the old Czech state, which suffered major territorial losses as a consequence.

The Czech Lands, as well as Upper Austria and Tyrol, were claimed by Charles Albert, Elector of Bavaria, while August, Elector of Saxony, demanded Moravia and the King of Prussia, Friedrich II, was interested in the populated and economically prosperous Silesia and north-western parts of the Kingdom of Bohemia, which was to be partitioned. The Spanish Bourbons demanded the Habsburg territories in Italy, while France wanted the Austrian Netherlands and aspired to fill the imperial throne with its candidate – Charles Albert, Elector of Bavaria. This division of spheres of interest was a result of many treaties among the above-mentioned powers and of much international and domestic negotiation, which continued until November 1741. Of the entire heritage, Maria Theresa was thus to be left with only Hungary and the eastern part of the Austrian lands.

The young ruler, however, decided to defend not only the integrity of the Habsburg legacy, but also the Imperial Crown for her family and her offspring. This proved to be an arduous task. The Ottoman wars at the end of Charles VI's rule had emptied the state coffers, high taxes exhausted the population, which started to show considerable dissatisfaction with its new tax burden. And there were other problems – the defeat in the last war with the Ottoman Empire (1737–1739) demoralized the army, which lacked modern military equipment and training, as well as experienced commanders. In the multinational monarchy, Maria Theresa could not count on spontaneous and enthusiastic support from the Estates or the population. She only secured an unequivocal support from the Hungarian Kingdom in exchange for far-reaching political concessions to the Hungarian nobility. The Bohemian nobility at first assumed a neutral stance towards the ruler, which was probably caused by an awareness of the decline of Czech political influence in the court, and was waiting for further development of the war, which was not at first at all favourable for Maria Theresa.

Even before the powers agreed on partitioning the Habsburg lands, Friedrich II, King of Prussia, started a campaign in Silesia without formally declaring war. His main goal was to annex this part of the Kingdom of Bohemia to his dependencies. This was the beginning of the first war over Silesia (1740–1742 and 1744–1745), which became one of the conflicts of the War of the Austrian Succession. In a short period of time, Friedrich managed to subjugate most of Silesia, including its capital Wrocław (Breslau). This successful campaign was crowned in the following months with two victories over the Austrian army – in the battle of Molvice in Silesia (April 1741) and the battle of Chotusice in eastern Bohemia (May 1742).

Maria Theresa, who also had to face enemy armies on the western front, had no choice other than to accede to an accord with the King of Prussia, who, after the battle of Chotusice, also controlled north-eastern Bohemia. The separate peace negotiations were concluded on June 11, 1742 with the signing of a peace treaty in Wrocław. Its conditions were further confirmed by the Berlin peace treaty, signed on July 28, 1742. As a result of these agreements, Maria Theresa ceded almost all of Silesia and Kłodzko County (Glatz) to Prussia, while keeping only the Těšín (Cieszyn) duchy and parts of the Opava and Krnov duchies.

Three years after the battle of Chotusice, the ruler tried to regain the lost territories in an anti-Prussian offensive, but her armies were once again defeated. The new peace treaty with Prussia concluded in Dresden (December 25, 1745), only solidified the Prussian annexation of Silesia.

The Wrocław Peace of 1742 allowed Maria Theresa to concentrate on the defence of her heritage on the western front. While Friedrich II was defeating Maria Theresa in Silesia, Charles Albert, Elector of Bavaria, supported by French and Saxon armies invaded Bohemia and in November 1741, conquered Prague, where most of the Bohemian Estates recognized him as the King of Bohemia. He left the town in 1742 to be elected Holy Roman Emperor, leaving a garrison in Prague. It was at this time that the situation started to turn in Maria Theresa's favour. Her armies carried out a successful campaign in Bavaria and in 1743 managed to push the French-Bavarian armies out of Prague and then gradually out of the rest of Bohemia. In May 1743, Maria Theresa was crowned in Prague. In September 1745, upon the death of Charles Albert (Emperor Charles VII), this success was crowned with the election of her husband Francis Stephen of Lorraine as Roman Emperor.

The War of the Austrian Succession against France and Spain continued until 1748, but did not concern the Czech Lands. It was around this time that the Habsburg monarchy gained valuable allies in Holland and England and, as a result of the peace of Aachen in 1748, lost part of the Milan region, while regaining the Austrian Netherlands. Maria Theresa thus managed to defend almost her entire heritage, the only major loss being that of economically-developed Silesia, ceded to the King of Prussia. The Empress, however, had no intention of reconciling herself to this situation. After the Wars of the Austrian Succession, she put all her effort into perfecting her army and its financial and material provisions, as well as into the changes in the Austrian alliances, hoping to potentially regain the lost territories.

The result of this alliance reappraisal was what became known as a reversal of alliances: an alliance treaty between the Austrian and French governments from May 1, 1756 and Austrian alliance with Russia and Sweden concluded at the same time. The establishment of a new military coalition, however, compelled the King of Prussia to react quickly. At the end of summer 1756, Friedrich II reopened the conflict, which once again was to affect the Kingdom of Bohemia. It was the beginning of the Seven Years' War (1756–1763).

The Prussian army invaded Bohemia and, in October 1756, defeated the Austrian army at Lovosice and again in May 1757 at the battle of Štěrboholy near Prague. The war's turning point occurred after the battle of Kolín (June 18, 1757), in which Maria Theresa's army, under the command of Leopold Daun, defeated the Prussians. It was the Prussian army's first major defeat. For the Habsburg forces, however, it was a triumph and the imperial army's first crucial victory over Friedrich II. The battle also helped to liberate Prague from a month-long siege and gradually freed Bohemia from Friedrich's army. The Austrian army regained control of Silesian fortresses and in November 1757, reclaimed Wrocław. Despite this, the peace concluded in 1763 in Hubertsburg between Austria and Prussia, confirmed Friedrich II's possession of Silesia and Kłodzko to the same boundaries set out in the peace treaties of 1742 and 1745. The old Bohemian state thus lost these important regions.

In the mid-1760s a relatively long and, internationally quiet period for Maria Theresa's reign started, which meant she could focus on the consolidation and modernization of her lands. The military defeats in the first years of her rule, had taught her about the problems in her dependencies' administration.

Each of the Habsburg dominion lands had its specific historical ordinance. Their political, economic and judicial administration was in the hands of the Land Estates, particularly of the nobility. They did not always have to accede to all the ruler's demands, nor always ensured proper tax payment to the monarchy's common treasury. Moreover, those who held positions in Land offices had gained them thanks to their origin and social contacts, rather than due to their qualification. On the level of central institutions, there were frequent arguments between officers representing individual lands, such as Bohemian and Austrian Chancellery. These arguments hampered decision-making regarding the monarchy's domestic matters and, as the government and central bodies perceived it, they protracted the resolution of difficult political situations.

Maria Theresa thus decided to transform this complex multinational dominion into a compact state. It was to be a state unified on legal, ideological and, later, linguistic levels, an economically and politically strong state, managed centrally and efficiently by qualified people. The first stage of this programme was the formation of a new administration. In reality, it meant reducing the Estates' influence on the state administration, the transformation of the traditional Land offices into state institutions and forming a qualified bureaucratic machinery.

Maria Theresa did not elaborate and implement these changes alone. Her most important advisors and helpers in the monarchy's reorganization were two ministers – first, the Silesian nobleman Count Friedrich Wilhelm Haugwitz, and later, the Moravian aristocrat Count Wenzl Anton Kaunitz. From 1765 her advisers were joined by Joseph II, Maria Theresa's oldest son, who became Roman Emperor and his mother's co-regent in the Habsburg lands after the death of Francis Stephen of Lorraine.

The most urgent matter regarding the consolidation of the monarchy and its army was the improvement of state finances. This was achieved through the decennial recess from 1748, initiated by Haugwitz, which forced the Czech and Austrian Diets to approve higher taxes a decade in advance. The Land Estates thus lost their means of coercing the ruler: the yearly approval of taxes. Moreover, the administration of military and financial matters was removed from the authority of the Land government (in the Czech Lands, the royal vice-regency) and entrusted to deputations, new institutions subordinate to the government.

Deputations themselves, however, did not entail a renunciation of the traditional Land system, as they only assumed control over part of the Estates' agenda. That changed a year later (1749), when the Viennese government dissolved the royal vice-regency in Bohemia and the Estates Land government in Moravia, and these offices' entire remit was transferred to the deputations, which were renamed royal representations and chambers. In 1763, these offices were renamed again, and were now called royal gubernia. They were presided over by the highest Estate clerk, despite the nominal attribute "highest," the performance of his function, along with his entire office, were subordinate to the central Viennese institutions and formed a firm link in the chain of the state – no longer Estate land – administration. The bringing of the Land institutions under state control went hand in hand with that of their subordinate regional offices (1748–1751). The original two Estates' governors, settled in the region and subsidized by the Estates, were replaced by a single one, paid by the state.

Bringing the Land administration under state control took place at the same time as the reorganization of offices representing individual lands in the court and in the central administration. The special court chancelleries for Bohemian and Austrian matters were dissolved in 1749. The political and financial agenda was taken over by a single state institution, *directorium in publicis et cameralibus*, which was transformed into the new United Bohemian and Austrian Court Chancellery in 1762. This central body's sphere of influence was restricted by the state council, which was formed in 1760 and presided over by Count Kaunitz. This institution was a direct advisory board of the ruler in the most important matters concerning state reform, its centralization and modernization.

The land and Estate administration also lost power in the justice system, as it was removed from the jurisdiction of court chancelleries and became a purely state and professional institution, the Supreme Court of Justice (Oberste Justitzstelle), seated in Vienna. This was an important step towards bringing justice under state control and towards the unification and reformation of the legal system in the spirit of a modern civic society. In the 1780s, the original courts (Land, chamber, appellate and courtly) were dissolved and replaced by a new Land court as a first-instance court for the nobility. The second instance was the appellate court, which was the appellate institution for all courts in the land. The Supreme Court of Justice was the third and highest instance. All of these were state courts and their offices were held by competent clerks who had received a legal education. The state also oversaw local courts and all activities of the town administration, as well as suzerain trials over their subjects, which put an end to the uncontrolled dominance of the nobility over their subjects.

The administrative reorganization and centralization under Maria Theresa concerned only Czech and Austrian lands, not the Hungarian part of the monarchy. Hungary, which obtained many privileges for its help in the War of Austrian Succession, was, until the reign of Joseph II, spared any centralization measures. This ensured different development patterns in the two parts of the monarchy and was the next step in the Austro-Hungarian dualism which developed in the second half of the 19th century. Centralization reforms also affected the administrative integrity of the Czech Lands. Bohemia, Moravia and the remains of Silesia became normal territorially administrative provinces of the Austrian monarchy, almost entirely independent of each other, and through their own offices and courts were directly connected to the Viennese central institutions. All these measures greatly interfered with the traditional Land system. Institutions reflecting the specific character of the Czech state were dissolved, the Land Estates' influence on the Land's administration was reduced and their right to priority in the official functions ceased to be automatic.

Only a few of the original Land clerk titles were preserved, all of which were connected to positions in the state administration and thus gave the impression of an ideal link between both administrative systems – the historical Land Estates and the centralized state. For example, the Supreme Burgrave of Prague was the president of the gubernium, while the Supreme Steward was the chairman of the appellate court. The Land offices were formally held by people who represented the new state administration.

The Land Diet gathered regularly, but its already weak powers were further limited. In the newly organized state, the diet appeared to be a relic of the past and the government strove to integrate this Estate body into the new system. The diet's right to approve taxes became merely formal and, at the end of Joseph II's rule, it was to cease altogether under the new tax and urbarial reform. The Estates retained the right to allocate and collect taxes (under the supervision of the state institutions, naturally), but they were usually not asked for their opinion regarding administrative, legislative, social and economic reforms concerning, among other things, noble privileges and peasant matters. When they were asked for their opinion, the question was of "how," not "whether."

The Kingdom of Bohemia and Czech statehood did not cease to exist as a result of the centralization reforms – neither on legal and historical levels within the Habsburg monarchy itself, nor on the international scene. Although the Habsburg monarchy, which had no official name at the time, was called the Austrian monarchy in the course of normal political communication, we would not be able to find it under this name in the foreign encyclopaedic or scientific geographic literature of the period. This literature only recognized historical state units, such as the Kingdom of Bohemia, which were a part of the Habsburg dominion and, with its other parts (Archduchy of Austria, Kingdom of Hungary, etc.) were connected through the person of the ruler.

The restriction of the Land Estates bodies' influence; their blending into the newly established centralized state administration; did not deprive the Czech Lands' population of their role in the administration of their own affaires. The remains of the old Estates system, whose roots dated back to the Middle Ages, had to give way to the new concept of the state administration, as demanded by the Enlightenment. The modern administration was in the hands of highly competent state clerks, who were supposed not only to meet the demands of the superior bodies, but whose primary function was to resolve the problems and requests of all citizens without bias, in an obliging, loyal and rational manner.

The Theresian and, particularly, the ensuing Josephine state gradually created an efficient bureaucratic machinery, which only employed qualified people, irrespective of their national or social origin. The entire state population had the same access to administrative positions, which earlier had been reserved for the privileged Estates, particularly the aristocracy, and thus gained a certain share in the state administration. For example, in the Prague gubernium and its subordinate regional offices in Bohemia at the end of the 18th century, two-thirds of officials did not hold a noble title, but were the sons of artisans and merchants. The remaining third was primarily represented by the new bureaucratic nobility. Personal abilities and education, which was particularly important, became the only criteria for being hired into the state service. From 1750, legal education, possibly complemented with knowledge of technical or economic fields, was recommended as suitable education for clerks. Career progression depended solely on the education, work experience and abilities of each clerk, not on his social status. What had been impossible at the beginning of Maria Theresa's rule; that higher offices would be held by people of other than noble origin; was not unusual during the reign of her son Joseph II. In the 1780s, an educated person not of noble origin could, in five years, achieve such a position and advance up the career ladder that would earlier have taken him over twenty years, had he ever succeeded, and he could get ahead of a less educated nobleman in terms of career progression.

This new concept of state machinery was due not only to the utilitarian goals of the government, but it also reflected the enlightenment view of the equality of people, education and a rational attitude towards the world. Qualified bureaucracy and a centralized and modernized state administration was to serve higher purposes than merely the simplification and streamlining of state administration. The clerks had a much more serious task – the final implementation of the reforms which impacted on many other state sectors and the life of its inhabitants. These reforms were carried out in the spirit of the Enlightenment and their goal was to strengthen the state economy and, principally, to help transform the remainder of the old society, based on the Estates corporate principles, into a modern civic society.

At the outset of the Theresian reformation process, it was undoubtedly necessary to modernize both state and society, yet some of the reforms lagged behind social development. This was mainly the case in regards to the status of the subject peasants, who were burdened by heavy labour duties, obligatory purchase of their landlord's goods and bound to their landlord and soil in many ways which restricted their personal freedom. The state interfered with the landlord-peasant relationship as early as the end of the 17th century and, in the first half of the 18th century, the state started to develop protective measures against the excesses that many landlords committed against their subjects. The Theresian state attempted to continue this trend (through a land register reform and a court of peasant complaints, established in 1748, or peasants' compensations for divested rural land in the 1750s).

As a result of the economic difficulties after the Seven Years' War, as well as due to the physiocratic economic sciences and the growing dissatisfaction in the rural areas, the state was forced to initiate large-scale reforms. Among them was the alteration of the peasants' urbarial duties, for which a committee was established at the beginning of 1775. At that time, a huge peasant rebellion started in eastern Bohemia, which was sparked by the peasants' exaggerated hopes and expectations. In March 1775, bands of peasants streamed towards Prague, determined to force the Prague offices to implement radical urbarial reform. During this campaign, many landlord offices and parsonages were looted and the rebels were ultimately suppressed by the army.

In reaction to these well-organized disturbances, which culminated in peasant strikes in many estates at the end of the spring and in summer, Maria Theresa issued a subject labour patent regulating labour duties (published in Bohemia in 1775, in Moravia in 1776). The patent, which determined subject labour duties based on a new peasants' tax appraisal and led to their mitigation, was, however, met with disappointment in rural areas as the peasants had expected much more. Apart from this patent, in the Bohemian landed estates the government promoted what became known as raabization, that is a transformation of the subject labour into a monetary form, although this method was limited to estates owned by the state (such as former Jesuit estates) and to the estates of the nobility which voluntarily accepted it. Unfortunately, neither the Theresian urbarial reform nor the raabization in the 1770s solved the crisis in the peasants' economic and social status. Its real solution, based on a far-reaching reform of the landlord-peasant relationships, did not come until Joseph II's radical reforms.

2 Enlightened Absolutism Reforms

The expression "enlightened absolutism" was debuted in the 19th century as a name for a certain type of government. As early as the 18th century, however, there was a name for the intentional linking of monarchical political power to Enlightenment principles and thought – enlightened monarchy. This connection was evident in many social and state changes, which were based on universal Enlightenment ideals of freedom, reason and education. Maria Theresa's and especially her son Joseph II's reign became a synonym for this regime in Habsburg monarchy lands.

Maria Theresa was not a keen supporter of the works by Western-European, and particularly French philosophers, however, she listened to her advisors, who adjusted these modern philosophical and economic theories to the needs of the Habsburg monarchy. Her son, Joseph II, on the other hand, was a fervent reader of enlightenment literature and during his journeys around Europe, two of which were to France, he did not hesitate to meet with representatives of modern philosophy and science. He himself followed the principles which, according the theorists of the Enlightenment, were typical for a "king-philosopher."

Included among these qualities were a rational attitude to the world, the favouring of all that was useful and service to society. Joseph II, like other enlightened rulers, considered himself the first clerk or servant of the state. Complicated court ceremonies, typical for rulers of the Baroque period, were on the decline during Maria Theresa's reign and her son almost dissolved the court as a useless and unnecessarily expensive anachronism. Typical for Joseph II, the enlightened ruler, was simplicity and informality in the ruler's representation and behaviour. It was a symbol of his civic solidarity with the state's population and, at the same time, an example of the economic measures which were to be followed.

The goal of Joseph II's enlightened state was to achieve "general welfare," happiness for the entire society. To fulfil this goal, it was necessary that the state functioned rationally and unmistakably, and that all its segments worked in perfect harmony. This harmonic organization of the state had its metaphors – the state administration and society were supposed to function as a precise machine or the perfect system of the human body. To ensure this perfect functioning, both ruler and subjects had to participate. The subjects were ascribed an active role in public life and were supposed to put state interests above private ones. In other words, each individual, as well as the whole of society, were to unify, bringing the various parts together to act as a whole.

MARTINA ONDO GREČENKOVÁ

The state thus strove for educated, healthy and independent inhabitants who would not only guarantee its smooth functioning, but also contribute to its wealth and power. This was to be achieved through the modernization of all spheres of state life – education, justice, economy, religion – which was to ensure a gradual emancipation of society from its ties to the old system and to lay the foundation for a new society.

Emperor Joseph II issued over six thousand decrees over his rule which lasted only ten years (1780–1790). Although he initiated many of these changes, several other people, both from his circles and among Maria Theresa's confidants, helped to realize the reform programme of the government. Among them were the previously mentioned Count Wenzl Anton Kaunitz; the Empress's personal physician Gerhard van Swieten, who prepared the education system reforms; the economist Count Charles Zinzendorf, who was in charge of the Josephine land register and of tax and urbarial reforms; Leopold Hay, Bishop of Hradec Králové, who helped to disseminate Enlightenment and toleration ideas in the church and among believers; and university professors Karel Antonín Martini and Josef Sonnenfels, theoreticians of the enlightened absolutism of the Austrian type.

Besides competent clerks, the state also needed well-educated, rationally thinking and responsible citizens. Education was one of the main demands of the Enlightenment philosophers and its spread among the wider population became an essential precondition for the change in people's thinking and so the modernization of the entire society. This explains why the Austrian government placed such a great emphasis on the reform of elementary education, which concerned the widest population. In 1774, Maria Theresa introduced obligatory school attendance for all children aged six to twelve. She put all schools, which had been administered by churches or local communities, under state control and unified them, establishing a three-level system of elementary education. Children from the country attended what were termed trivial schools, teaching practical subjects – reading, writing and counting – which were to ensure the population's literacy. The main schools were located in larger towns. They represented a higher level of state schools and also taught Latin, geography, history and several vocational subjects. "Normal," or "model," schools, established in the Land capitals, were the highest level of these new state schools. Normal schools included a special preparatory programme for the prospective teachers of the lower-grade schools. These schools had a unified curriculum, which ensured that a future citizen, as well as a teacher, was educated not only in the spirit of the Enlightenment, but also in the spirit of affiliation to the unified Central-European state – the Habsburg monarchy.

After the Jesuit order's dissolution in 1773, grammar schools called *Gymnasium* also became state controlled. Their curricula were unified and adjusted to suit the new ideas on the education of the citizen. Universities were also state controlled, with their staff consisting of an increasing number of secular teachers. Changes were applied to their specialization and curricula, which included Enlightenment sciences, such as natural right theory, later the Enlightenment science of the state (statistics) and another subject concerning administration, finances and economics (political science). This latter subject primarily promoted the teaching of Austrian Enlightenment philosophers concerned with society and the state, but also presented the ideas of Western Enlightenment philosophers. History, geography and natural sciences also found their way onto university curricula, and, in the spirit of the Enlightenment, a stronger emphasis was placed on practical subjects. In the 1770s and 1780s, the university education provided by the Prague university included economics and, after the original Estates engineering schools were merged with it, it also offered technical sciences. A university thus became a state institution educating the qualified employees for various spheres of the state administration.

A literate and well-educated citizen of the monarchy could not be a fully-fledged and independent state citizen unless the government implemented other reforms adjusting his status in the state and society. That was the goal of legal reforms, emphasized by both Maria Theresa and Joseph II. From 1753, the government gradually tried to unify the legal system in the Czech and Austrian lands, making it transparent and stripping it of the traditional discrepancies between the rights of the nobility, royal town inhabitants and peasants. This effort resulted in several codes – Maria Theresa's Penal Code from 1769, the first part of the general Civil Code (1786) and Joseph II's Penal Code (1787). They were later followed by the general Civil Code from 1811, which was used in the Habsburg monarchy throughout the 19th century.

The main goal of these codes was the gradual formation of a unified law, applicable to the members of all Estates, the modernization of trials, a reappraisal of the role of punishments and their humanization, and state regulation of both respect for and enforcement of the law. In the 1770s, torture as an instrument for obtaining confessions disappeared from court procedures. Sentences were no longer considered a certain type of social "revenge" on the culprit, but started to play an educational role and their forms were to be useful for the society. Although cruel forms of punishments did not entirely disappear, enlightened lawyers tried to make sure that punishments fit the crime and that the existing ambiguity and arbitrariness in the penal agenda were removed. The question of guilt was gradually reassessed, trials defined more precisely, more attention was paid to evidence and the circumstances of the crime, and the health (that is mental state) of the accused were taken into consideration. In the 1780s, capital punishment was temporarily abolished and living conditions in prison were improved. In 1781, an important change in the legal status of the state population occurred – equality before the law was declared, irrespective of Estates or other privileges. This equality was mainly enforced by the court of higher instance, the appellate court (the court of appeal for the land, community and suzerain courts), which did not distinguish between a nobleman and a peasant, considering all citizens of the state equal.

The transformation of a peasant into a citizen required several more changes in the sphere of social intellectual and economic emancipation. Freedom of speech and freedom of religion were the first steps. In 1781, censorship was loosened to the extent that citizens could comment on domestic political matters, including the ruler. In October 1781, Emperor Joseph II issued the Toleration Patent, which granted freedom of religion to other, non-Catholic, denominations: Orthodox, Calvinist and Lutheran. Although these creeds were

MARTINA ONDO GREČENKOVÁ

tolerated rather than promoted, the era of state-promoted re-Catholicization was definitely over. People professing the tolerated beliefs could not only practice their religion freely and publicly, but also had the same rights and opportunities for employment in the state services or to study and teach at university. In the 1780s, these rights and possibilities were also applied to the Jews, who became equal citizens of the state.

Another important step in this emancipation process was the Serfdom Patent of November 1, 1781. At that time many peasants were still personally bound to their landlords and could not marry, study or leave the estate without their permission. The patent abolished these restrictions, granting the peasants personal freedom and ranking them among other equal citizens. The state also limited the landlord's punitive power over the peasants and gave peasants the right to complain and file a lawsuit against their landlords. Some peasant obligations towards landlords were preserved, among them the subject labour and the duty to pay peasant duties and rents.

The enlightened state, which drew from physiocratic principles and which considered the work of the peasants its main source of wealth, ensured the best conditions for their development. These included personal freedom and greater legal rights, as well as economic liberation, such as lowering the peasants' tax burden demanded by the state and relieving them of burdens required by their landlords. The government therefore paid great attention to the tax system reforms and to the problems of the subject labour and other peasant duties.

The tax reform was to replace the existing duties with a universal land tax, which was to be paid by all the population. This was even to affect those who had been exempted from taxes: aristocracy and the church. In 1748–1756, Maria Theresa ordered the creation of new registers not only of peasant land (rustical), but also of landlords' income and property (dominical). This Theresian land register taxed landlords' incomes, although still less than the income of the peasant farmsteads, who had to pay up to 40% of their income to the state treasury.

Joseph II tried to change this by introducing a unified land tax, the same for the peasants and for the landlords. It was a modern and courageous political deed inspired by, among others, the French physiocrats. At that time other European powers also tried to implement similar measures, with varying degrees of success. In France, the failure to do so contributed to the course of events leading to the French Revolution.

To be able to determine a universal state tax and to adjust the peasants' duties towards their landlords, it was necessary to establish the exact area of the taxable land. In 1785–1789, a Josephine land register was elaborated, listing entire dominical and rustical land in the monarchy, with cadastral municipalities representing territorial units for the purpose of taxation. Tax duties were further determined according to the land's gross yield, which took into account the types of plantation and the different expenses necessary for producing the yield. Taxation was thus based on real economic conditions and the new tax schedule lowered the tax duty of the peasants and increased the landlords' taxation. The landlords lost their influence over collecting taxes, which was entrusted to educated state clerks.

If the peasant was to keep 70% of the gross output, the state was to receive on average 12.2% of the output, with 17.8% left for the peasant urbarial duties to landlords. Their adjustment was based on the replacement of the subject labour and existing taxes in kind by a fixed financial amount, which was a common practice with the chamber estates. The subject labour on landlords' estates, which was somewhat mitigated after the peasant rebellion in 1775 by Maria Theresa's Subject Labour Patent, was to be finally abolished.

The reform announced in the tax and urbarial patents of February 1789 came into force on November 1, 1789, with a one-year transitional period, during which the peasants were to perform the subject labour, but that they would be paid for this. Unfortunately, before this transitional period had elapsed, Joseph II died and the political changes which were implemented after his death put an end to this important reform. The peasants had to wait until 1848 for the subject labour to be abolished.

The state had other means of taking care of each citizen's personal and economic development. Following populationist theories, according to which the greater the state's population, the more powerful it is, the state took care of its inhabitants' health through health education, urban sanitation measures, the newly established position of "official" regional physician – educated doctors and medical workers – and by promoting vaccination. In connection with this, the state also introduced regular censuses in 1753. These state efforts bore their fruit and, in the last quarter of the 18th century, the population of the Czech Lands had grown by 22% to about 5 million people.

In the economic sphere, the state tried to remove all obstacles and limitations to production and trade, it abolished medieval guilds and customs barriers between the monarchy's provinces, introduced uniform units of size and weight, unified the currency and built an extensive road network. Royal economic societies, established in Prague, Brno and Opava in 1769, were to help promote new agricultural, cultivation and breeding practices among the peasant population and to support the newly established economic schools, along with research in agriculture and engineering.

The state involved not only teachers, university professors and state clerks in its educational activities, but it also tried to include the church, which was put under state control. Papal bulls could only be published with the consent of the government, which started a campaign against superstitions, and the various benefactions and bequests that the citizens donated to the church. It restricted recruitment to monastic orders, taxed the church and supervised the administration of its property. During Emperor Joseph II's reign, the government had gone so far as to dissolve those monasteries which had not engaged in activities beneficial to either state or citizen – not education, healthcare nor charity.

On the other hand, using the finances from the dissolved monasteries, the government founded new countryside parsonages and educated the priests who were to work there. These priests were educated in the newly established state seminaries in the Josephine spirit: according to the enlightened social and state opinions and reforms, which had been implemented by Joseph II's government. They were well-educated, paid by the state, and in addition to their religious duties, they were also in charge of administrative and educational activities. They administered population registries, executed medical supervision, and informed their parishioners of the content and purpose of state decrees, and about their duties, possibilities and rights. Their pastoral activities were to focus on cultivating the love for one's neighbour and on teaching people the qualities of an enlightened state's citizen, a more rational view of the world and participation in public affairs, and putting the common interest of all, the "general welfare," over one's personal goals and ambitions.

The Enlightenment state reforms, particularly the changes introduced by Emperor Joseph II, did not meet with a universally positive response. However, the enlightened elites, some Enlightenment representatives from nobility and church, members of non-Catholic denominations and the rural population welcomed most of the important reforms, or at least those that directly concerned them, with enthusiasm. The nobility, on the other hand, refused to accept the loss of its political position, privileges and powers over the peasants, and did not intend to relinquish their existing estates management practices. Most religious dignitaries found it difficult to respect state intervention in the life of the church and its institutions, and many Catholic believers had problems tolerating other creeds. On the other hand, the Enlightenment reforms were hampered by the fact that they were implemented very quickly and in an authoritative manner. This state modernization along Enlightenment rational ideas sometimes went too far. This was the case of Joseph II's decrees, which, for economic and utilitarian reasons, banned burying the deceased in coffins, restricted the number of candles used during religious services, cancelled many holidays, pilgrimages and processions, all of which naturally caused indignation throughout the population, including those who otherwise welcomed the Enlightenment governmental reforms.

While Joseph II's accession was accepted with enthusiasm and expectation, the end of his rule was marked by a shift in "public" opinion. Enthusiasm and expectations were replaced by denial and criticism, sometimes in the form pamphlets and slander. This was partly due to the unpopular and costly war with the Ottoman Empire, which Joseph II started towards the end of his rule. The Emperor had to rescind most of his reforms before his death (February 20, 1790). His brother and successor, Emperor Leopold II (r. 1790–1792) came under a heavy pressure by the Estates, which in the early 1790s opposed the Josephine reforms at the Bohemian Diet. Leopold II had to revoke some of his predecessor's decrees, such as the important tax and urbarial patent from 1789, which was to abolish the subject labour.

Despite this, Emperor Leopold II managed to preserve the most important reforms from his mother's and brother's legacies – the Toleration Patent and the Serfdom Patent, modern education and justice, as well as an efficient and competent administration. People soon forgot about Joseph II's interventions into folk customs and religious traditions, and the rural population remembered the Emperor as a great friend and champion of the people, so gradually giving rise to the legend of the "good", "peasant" or "people's" Emperor Joseph II.

Marie Theresa's and Joseph II's reforms played an important role in the transformation of the old society into a civic society, initiated economic development and education progress and, in many ways, laid the foundations for a modern state. It was the enlightened reforms that transformed the peasant into a citizen with defined rights, a citizen guided by his own judgement.

3 Czech Enlightenment and the Beginning of the Civic Society

Unlike Western Europe, where we find the beginnings of the Enlightenment at the end of the 17th century, in the Czech Lands we can speak of the Enlightenment no earlier than in the mid-18th century. It reached its peak in the 1780s, during Joseph II's reign, which was characterized by intellectual life and loosening censorship. This period's Enlightenment in the Habsburg monarchy is also sometimes called the Josephinism, thanks to its unique character acquired through the reform policy of the Josephine government. Unlike Western Europe, the Enlightenment in the Czech Lands lasted deep into the mid-19th century (such as in Bernard Bolzano's work) and gradually faded away in the thoughts of some authors over the following generations (among them historian František Palacký). In the Czech Lands, Enlightenment includes two interconnected streams of this movement: a territorially Bohemian Enlightenment, that is the Enlightenment in the Czech Lands on the one hand, and Czech language Enlightenment, Czech Enlightenment proper, on the other.

Among the supporters of the Enlightenment as interpreted in the Czech Lands were scientists, journalists, along with state clerks and a segment of the nobility who lived in the Czech Lands and considered them their home. They understood the idea of "homeland" as a territory on which they could claim their civil rights, publicly express their opinions, live in safety and enjoy their property. They identified primarily with Josephinism and purchased both domestic and foreign Enlightenment literature, acquainting themselves with its ideas. Some maintained extensive correspondence with representatives of the European Enlightenment, as well as with their local colleagues. In the noble salons and in Masonic lodges, they discussed current problems, literature and philosophy. They also contributed to the cultural life of the period, supported music and theatre, and some were even artists.

Two Prague noble salons became important centres of enlightened life and communication in the 1770s and 1780s. They were organized by high state clerks, presidents of gubernia – Count Charles Egon Fürstenberg and Count Francis Anthony Nostitz. Count Nostitz, a supporter of science and culture, commissioned the construction of a large and modern theatre in Prague in 1787, where two of Mozart's operas, *Don Giovanni* in 1787 and *La clemenza di Tito* four years later, were premiered. In Prague there were several active Masonic lodges, which, in the second half of the 18th century, merged into three Masonic lodges, connected with Masonic institutions in other lands of both the Habsburg monarchy and abroad. Their members were recruited mainly from among the enlightened state clerks and army officers and focused on charity. Similar societies were also active in Moravia. Among important Enlightenment centres were the Dietrichstein salon in Mikulov and the Mittrowsky salon in Brno, where Masonic lodges were also active.

276

A Europe-wide Enlightenment trend inspired by freedom was a development of academies, whose main goal was to cultivate science in a more independent and critical manner than at universities, spread through the Czech Lands, where universities, particularly in the Josephine era, ceased to play the role of both educational and research centres, focusing instead on educating potential employees for various state administration departments. In 1746, the first predecessor of modern academies, known as the Society of Unknown Scholars (Societas incognitorum) was established in Olomouc, while in 1753–1761 Prague had its own scientific club, chaired by mathematician Josef Stepling. These societies, however, were not proper institutions. A real scientific institution started to take shape in 1775 thanks to the enlightened thinker Ignác Antonín Born. This Private Society in the Czech Lands for the Development of Mathematics, Patriotic History and Natural Sciences was transformed into the Bohemian Society of Sciences in 1784. In 1790, it achieved official governmental recognition, which led to the change of its name to the Royal Bohemian Society of Sciences, a predecessor of today's Academy of Sciences of the Czech Republic.

From 1775, the Society of Sciences published its own academic journal, the German-language Treatises (*Abhandlungen*), which presented the results of their members' research, as well as articles by foreign contributors. It also announced scientific competitions and supported exploratory expeditions. Its members were the most prominent scientists in the Czech Lands, such as mathematicians Josef Stepling and Jan Tesánek, who presented Isaak Newton's work to the Czech community, astronomer Antonín Strnad, who introduced regular meteorological observations, along with mathematician, physicists and engineer František Josef Gerstner.

Unlike the Western European academies, which focused mainly on natural sciences, the Bohemian Society of Sciences also pursued historical research. The Enlightenment imperative of critical and experimental knowledge was always connected to the patriotic interest of the native land. The Enlightenment scientists engaged in a critical reappraisal of Bohemian history, Bohemian monuments, numismatics and literature. They emphasized a nationalist approach to legends, both religious and concerning Czech mythology. In academic society, the field of historiography was represented by historian Gelasius Dobner, the cultural and numismatist historian Mikuláš Adaukt Voigt, historian František Martin Pelcl, philologist and historian Josef Dobrovský, and statistician Josef Antonín Riegger. Among their collaborators were university professor Ignác Cornova and arts historian Jan Bohumír Dlabač.

Enlightenment literature and science were presented to the general public by the professor of "belles sciences," Karel Jindřich Seibt, and the professor of the engineering school, František Antonín Leonard Herget. The Bohemian Enlightenment and the Bohemian Enlightenment science were linguistically mostly German, and so were not available to most of the Czech speaking population. Czech translations of Western European Enlightenment thinkers – Voltaire, Rousseau or Diderot – were not available and their ideas were not even disseminated in abridged versions, in the form of abstracts or paraphrases. On the other hand, there was a particular form of Czech language Enlightenment for educating the lower levels of the population, who could only speak Czech. This Enlightenment utilized various forms of literary production read by the Czech rural population, such as books of prayers and hymnals, popular educational books and chronicles, along with popular literature and plays. It filled the existing literary forms with new content to ensure that its production spread the Josephine enlightened principles in ways accessible to commoners.

Enlightenment ideas were spread among the general population by the better educated people among the rural population – such as peasant mayor František J. Vavák – and representatives of the Czech intelligentsia, such as František Faustin Procházka or Václav Matěj Kramerius. The journalist Kramerius started introducing essential precepts of the Enlightenment and Josephinism (tolerance, a new concept of relations between an individual and society, new information regarding science and agriculture, and also the intentions of the enlightened government) to the country population through popular brochures of *The Toleration Calendars* and other educational publications. The most important deed of this kind was Kramerius' *Joseph's Book* from 1784, written in the form of a biblical text, prophesies, contemplations and prayers. This approach was paradoxical from an Enlightenment perspective, but it was both familiar and accessible to the commoner. *Joseph's Book* told of the life and deeds of Joseph II and aimed to explain the importance of the Emperor's reforms, particularly those concerning the church and religious life.

Kramerius gradually linked his activities relating to the Czech-language Enlightenment with an effort to revive the Czech language, which almost disappeared from administration and higher education in the second half of the 18th century. He played an active part in the initial stages of the movement, which reached its peak in the middle of the 19th century and was later called the Czech National Revival. Its rise was connected to a Czech language programme, which was characterized by publishing apologies of the language, significant Czech literary works and philological research.

As an editor and later publisher of a Czech newspaper – Kramerius' Imperial Royal Prague Postal Newspaper *(Krameriusovy cís. král. pražské poštovské noviny)*, Kramerius founded a Czech publishing house and a bookstore called the Czech Expedition in Prague in 1790. At the end of the 18th century, this company published Czech texts and disseminated books, both educational and fictional, written in Czech. Kramerius also focused on the systematic publishing of significant Czech literary works, particularly those from the Veleslavín times (16th century), whose linguistic qualities were taken as a model for revivalist Czech. The Czech Expedition was popular among its commoner readers, as well as among the Czech Enlightenment and revivalist elites. It also became the centre of the activities of a group of Czech Enlightenment journalists thus creating the basis for the budding revival movement.

Among the prominent personalities co-operating with the Czech Expedition were Czech scientists František Martin Pelcl and Josef Dobrovský, young writers Antonín Jaroslav Puchmajer, Šebestián Hněvkovský, brothers Vojtěch and Jan Nejedlý, revivalist playwrights Václav and Karel Ignác Thám and many others. From the 1780s, a Czech theatre called the Shack (*Bouda*) presented Czech translations of German plays alongside original Czech plays, whose main themes were Czech history and mythology. Czech theatre thus contributed to the development of the Czech language, as well as Czech patriotism, which differed from enlightened Land patriotism in its emphasis on the specific national features of the Czech state, especially its linguistic and cultural Czech identity.

The developing national programme was also joined by Czech Enlightenment scientists. Historian František Martin Pelcl, an author of several works on Bohemian history, written in German, was the first Bohemian scientist to publish a work in Czech, a language the learned Enlightenment circles considered merely a commoner language. In 1791–1796, he published *A New Bohemian Chronicle* in several volumes, depicting Bohemian/Czech national history from the earliest times to the Hussite movement. This deed promoted Czech language to a language of science. Pelcl's friend, the prominent Czech Enlightenment thinker and founder of Slavic studies, Josef Dobrovský, did not write in Czech, although he devoted many of his books to Czech language and literature from both theoretical and cultural-history standpoints. As well as a German-Czech dictionary, a Czech grammar book and many other works, in 1792 he published an important work titled The History of the Czech Language and Literature (*Geschichte der böhmischen Sprache und Literatur*). Based on his analysis of the development of the language and literature, he highlighted the cultural development and specific features of the Czech nation.

These early revivalist efforts did not remain restricted to the circle of Czech Expedition collaborators and their primarily lower-strata readers. On the occasion of Leopold II's coronation as the King of Bohemia in 1791, they won a wider audience and to some extent even asserted themselves on the political scene. This event was accompanied by a great campaign for the rights of the Czech language and Czech nation, lead mainly by Kramerius in the Czech newspapers and brochures, and supported by scientists throughout scientific society and also by some Estates members in their demands addressed to the Emperor. The most important public expression of this kind was the speech delivered by Josef Dobrovský at the session of the Royal Bohemian Society of Sciences before Emperor Leopold II. His speech *On Constant Loyalty, which the Slavic Nation of the Austrian House Has Demonstrated the Whole Time* recalled the merits of Czechs and their importance for the Habsburg dynasty, and emphasized the usefulness of Czech for the monarchy's administration and the harmfulness of its suppression by the state. One of the campaign results was the establishment of the Department of Czech Language at the Prague university, which was chaired by F. M. Pelcl. On the occasion of the inauguration of instruction in 1793, he delivered a speech on the usefulness of the Czech language, not only for the Czech Lands' population, but also for the state interests of the Habsburg monarchy.

Pelcl's lecture and its message matched Josef Dobrovský's speech, as well as the opinions of other Enlightenment thinkers focussed on Czech patriotism. Both speeches indicated the programme of the Czech patriotic movement within the Habsburg monarchy, which connected Czech patriotism to Austrian imperial patriotism and to the attitudes of enlightened cosmopolitanism.

Bibliography

BEALES, Derek: *Enlightenment and Reform in Eighteenth-Century Europe*, London 2005.

BEALES, Derek: *Joseph II.:In the shadow of Maria Theresa, 1741–1780*, Cambridge 1987.

BĚLINA, Pavel – KAŠE, Jiří – KUČERA, Jan P.: *Velké dějiny zemí Koruny české*, X *(1740–1792)*, Praha–Litomyšl 2001.

BLUCHE, François: *Le Despotisme éclairé*, Paris 2000.

DICKSON, P. G. M.: *Finance and government under Maria Theresia*, Oxford 1987.

FEJTÖ, François: *Joseph II, un Habsbourg révolutionnaire*, Paris, 1982.

GERSHOY, Leo: *From despotism to revolution, 1763–1789*, New York–Evanston–London 1944.

HASQUIN, Hervé: *Joseph II, catholique anticlérical et réformateur impatient*, Bruxelles 2007.

KLINGENSTEIN, Grete: *Der Aufstieg des Hauses Kaunitz. Studien zur Herkunft und Bildung des Staatskanzlers Wenzel Anton*, Göttingen 1975.

KOČÍ, Josef: *České národní obrození*, Praha 1978.

KROUPA, Jiří: *Alchymie štěstí. Pozdní osvícenství a moravská společnost*, Brno–Kroměříž 1985 (2nd edition 2006).

KUTNAR, František: *Sociálně myšlenková tvářnost obrozenského lidu. Trojí pohled na český obrozenský lid jako příspěvek k jeho dějinám*, Praha 1948.

KUTNAR, František: *Obrozenské vlastenectví a nacionalismus. Příspěvek k národnímu a společenskému obsahu češství doby obrozenské* (Martin Kučera ed.), Praha 2003.

LEBEAU, Christine: *Aristocrates et grands commis à la Cour de Vienne (1748–1791), le mod le français*, Paris 1996.

MAGENSCHAB, Hans: *Josef II. Revolutionär von Gottes Gnaden*, Graz–Wien–Köln 1979.

MAUR, Eduard: *12. 5. 1743. Marie Terezie. Korunovace na usmířenou*, Praha 2003.

MELMUKOVÁ, Eva: *Patent zvaný toleranční*, Praha 1999.

MIKOLETZKY, L.: *Kaiser Joseph II., Herrscher zwischen den Zeiten*, Frankfurt–Götingen–Zürich 1979.

NEŠPOR, Zdeněk R.: *Náboženství na prahu nové doby. Česká lidová zbožnost 18. a 19. století*, Ústí nad Labem 2006.

NOVOTNÝ, Jan: *Matěj Václav Kramerius*, Praha 1973.

PADOVER, Saul – K.: *The Revolutionary Emperor: Joseph II. of Austria*, London 1967.

PETRÁŇ, Josef: *Kalendář. Velký stavovský ples v Nosticově Národním divadle v Praze dne 12. září 1791*, Praha 1988.

PETRÁŇ, Josef: *Nevolnické povstání 1775*, Praha 1973.

PETRÁŇ, Josef et al.: *Počátky českého národního obrození. Společnost a kultura v 70. až 90. letech 18. století*, Praha 1990.

RIEGER, Bohuš: *Zřízení krajské v Čechách*, II, Ústrojí správy krajské v letech 1740–1792, Praha 1893.

ROZDOLSKI, Roman: *Die grosse Steuer- und Agrarreform Josephs II.*, Warszawa 1961.

SLAVÍK, Bedřich: *Od Dobnera k Dobrovskému*, Praha 1975.

STELLNER, František: *Sedmiletá válka v Evropě*, Praha 2000.

SZABO, A. J. – SZÁNTAY, Antal – TÓTH, István György (eds.): *Politics and Culture in the Age of Joseph II*, Budapest, 2005.

TANTNER, Anton: *Ordnung der Häuser, Beschreibung der Seelen. Hausnummerierung und Seelenkonskription in der Habsburgermonarchie*, Innsbruck–Wien–Bozen 2007.

TAPIÉ, Victor-Lucien: *L'Europe de Marie-Thérèse. Du baroque aux Lumières*, Paris 1973.

TINKOVÁ, Daniela: *Hřích, zločin, šílenství v čase odkouzlování světa*, Praha 2004.

WANDRUSZKA, Adam: *Leopold II., Erzherzog von Österreich, Grossherzog von Toskana, König von Ungarn und Böhmen, Römischer Kaiser*, Wien–München 1963.

WINTER, Eduard: *Barock, Absolutismus und Aufklärung in der Donaumonarchie*, Wien 1971.

WINTER, Eduard: *Josefinismus a jeho dějiny. Příspěvky k duchovním dějinám Čech a Moravy, 1740–1848*, Praha 1945.

MARTINA ONDO GREČENKOVÁ

XI. The Birth of the Modern Czech Nation (1792–1848)

Rise of modern age: The bustle at the České Budějovice – Linz horse-drawn railway line in the late 1830s. This railway line, built by a private joint stock company, in which Rotschild's capital eventually prevailed, was opened for public operation on August 1, 1832. With its almost 130 km of rails, it was the longest public horse-drawn railway line in Europe. It served as a carrier of people and goods until 1872, when it was transformed into a steam-engine line.

1 On the Threshold of a New Era in Czech History

For over a hundred years, Czech historians have pondered on how to grasp the period in Czech history commencing with the Josephine reforms and ending with the revolution of 1848/1849. They have not reached a universally agreed concept and it does not seem likely one will be found in the foreseeable future. This is mainly due to the fact that this is a very complex period, full of contrasts and changes that occurred outside the political sphere, with its exhaustively elaborate research methodology, but rather in the sphere of social consciousness and sub-consciousness, whose research has been considered the realm of other scientific fields or which has been spontaneously seized by artists, and even then primarily by novelists and journalists. A historian is challenged with several important facts, whose interpretation considerably influences the method of exposition, the work's organization and the terminology chosen.

First, the subject of historical research is undergoing radical change: the current concept of the history of the Bohemian Kingdom (sometimes only Austrian) state and the history of the Bohemian crown lands is mostly transformed into a concept of ethnic history: history of only one, Czech national society, later the Czech nation on the territory of the Czech Lands. Naturally, the Bohemian Kingdom had never faded from reality and the consciousness of the inhabitants of Bohemia and Central Europe, but its external attributes were considerably reduced as a result of Theresian and Josephine centralization and unification. Moreover, in the period of bureaucratic absolutism following 1792, high politics became the exclusive domain of a very narrow ruling class and it was rarely pursued in Prague or Brno. This fact also results in the initial non-existence of "Czech" – that is Czech burgher's – politics. This also explains why the most successful and productive concept of Czech historical interpretation has been the "National Revivalist" concept, which ascribes the most important active role to the ethnically Czech intellectual elites, largely linked through cultural, or linguistic, literary and historiographical work. The transfer to this nationalist and literary-science principle of historical interpretation has caused other ethnicities and diasporas living in the Czech Lands (such as Germans or Jews) to remain of marginal interest; as was the case of the nobility, those who elected to live without aligning themselves to any particular nationality and those who remained indifferent Austrians; as they did not fit in this narrowed history concept.

The non-existence of a systematically developed social history of this era has, until recently, played into the hands of historical simplification and narrowing. Another factor complicating the conceptual understanding of this era's history is that, due to the administrative integration of the so-called hereditary German lands, and as a result of the notable administrative separation of Bohemia from Moravia and Silesia, and given the proportionally different national composition of Moravia, Bohemian-Moravian dualism was deepened. Due to all the above-mentioned facts, the social and national processes in the 19th century were delayed in Moravia in comparison to Bohemia.

In this period, not only the Kingdom of Bohemia and Czech society, but also their Central-European roots underwent an immense transformation. The Holy Roman Empire of the German Nation, which had dissolved during the Napoleonic Wars, was replaced by a very loose union called German Confederation (*Deutscher Bund*), in which the western territories of the newly established Austrian Empire played the most important role. The Czech Lands retained their position of the Habsburg monarchy's most developed, both demographically and economically, and most important territory; though as the individual and administratively separate lands of Bohemia and Moravia with Silesia, rather than as a unified state. In this context, we must also note the fact that from 1848/1849, an important socio-economic transformation of the inhabitants in the Czech Lands' status was gradually taking place.

All these constitutional, socio-economic, cultural and psychological changes provide a historian with immensely interesting material, for which it is, however, rather difficult to find a unifying line of interpretation. This interpretation is thus a compromise between the history of lands (Bohemia, Moravia and Silesia) and the history of their ethnicities (Czechs, Germans and Jews), as well as a compromise between history presented chronologically and structural history, where the unifying element – naturally, apart from the Czech Lands' territory, which had little changed over the centuries – is primarily the current main bearer of Czech statehood: the modern Czech nation, which was only shaped in the period of the late 18th century to the mid-19th century.

2 General Development Features

Czech Lands as part of the Habsburg monarchy experienced two contradictory periods between 1792 and 1848. The first two decades were filled with conflict, fighting either alone or allied to other forces against revolutionary and, later, Napoleonic France, while for more than thirty years after 1815, the Czech Lands, like the rest of the Austrian Empire, lived in unusual Biedermeier peace and quiet. The form of government, absolutism, remained as in the previous period, the only difference being Emperor Francis II's (from 1804 Austrian Emperor Francis I) abandoning any further reform efforts due to the influence of events in France and pressure from the unfavourable development of anti-French wars. Despite this, most of the Theresian and Josephine reforms were not abolished. Instead, they were revised and supplemented by new decrees whose primary aim was the prevention of inciting the populace.

The Habsburg monarchy in Francis' times was a patriarchal empire, where the strictly administered bureaucracy gradually took over the most important administrative and economic roles, which had originally been in the hands of Estate corporations and patrimonial offices. Even in Austria, basic period trends leading to the introduction of personal liberties, civil equality before the Court (from 1812) and tax equality of inhabitants ensured by the new fiscal system in 1817, were gradually implemented. These liberal principles were, however, simultaneously limited by laws, schooling and edification from the pulpit, so that the newly acquired individual liberties were not "misused" as in the French revolutionary experience. The new citizen, or rather burgher – since a majority of the country population was still tied to the land, landlords and the Catholic Church through urbarial and other duties, and also to their life and vocational obligations through labour and guild orders – was formally freer, yet he was still under the permanent control of the newly established and restructured state bureaucratic authorities (particularly the police and censorship).

The right of formal civil equalities along with the omnipresence of the supervising and omnipotent state official was formalised in the new General Civil Code (*Allgemeines bürgerliches Gesetzbuch*) in 1811. This Code was conceived as a compromise between the values and authorities of the new and old ideologies as it introduced civil equality before the Court and civil marital agreement, yet it froze the feudal divided estate ownership, the existence of the noble fideicommis (majorat) and preserved the obvious patriarchy in all family matters. In other spheres of human endeavour, it did not mitigate the real differences between the nobleman and the commoner. During the largely unsuccessful wars with France, the authority of the police along with stricter censorship and surveillance of population movement and behaviour were considerably strengthened. Wars with France depleted state finances and worsened the material status of the common people. The state and ruler's prestige suffered greatly when the empire's inhabitants witnessed the destructive campaigns of foreign armies and the Austrian army's crushing defeats (as on December 2, 1805, in the Battle of the Three Emperors near the Moravian town of Slavkov (Austerlitz)) or the devastating collapse of the state finances in February 1811, when paper currency was devalued to a fifth of its original value.

Political and economic stabilization did not occur until after the Congress of Vienna, in 1815, which secured the state and political situation in Central Europe for several decades and, in the spirit of counter-revolutionary conservatism, strengthened the role of the Habsburg monarchy in the struggle against liberalism and nationalism. The Austrian Empire could be satisfied with the results of the Congress of Vienna. Though several remote territories were irretrievably lost, new ones were gained (particularly those in northern Italy and on the Adriatic coast) and the heart of the empire was secured to the modern concept of a state territorial unit. In place of the Holy Roman Empire of the German Nation, the German Confederation was established under Austrian chairmanship, although it was burdened by the Prussian-Austrian power dualism, with Emperor Francis I ruling over the empire until the beginning of 1835. Then he was succeeded to the throne by his oldest son, the intellectually challenged Emperor Ferdinand I. For almost forty years, since 1809, foreign affairs were governed by Prince Metternich, a convinced conservative monarchist. In 1819, he used the murder of writer August Kotzebue by a German university student to repress the liberal and nationalist movement in Austrian and German universities and to strengthen press censorship. Through a system of "Holy Alliance," he then oversaw, largely successfully, abidance of the state order established by the Congress of Vienna until almost mid-19th century.

With Austrian Emperor Ferdinand I's accession to the throne, the Habsburg absolute monarchy plunged into clear internal dynastic crisis. State conference, represented by Prince Metternich and Count of Kolowrat, directed the administration of the empire, and diligent bureaucrats kept the state machine running, while Ferdinand's coronations were to provide a feeling of peace and certainty for monarchist inhabitants. Only a few realized the sharp contradiction between the idea of an absolute monarchy and its external personification by the incompetent emperor, who had to face a deep internal crisis infecting the whole empire in the late 1840s.

3 Czech Lands as Part of the Habsburg Monarchy

The Kingdom of Bohemia, the Margraviate of Moravia and the Duchy of Silesia formed a specific and distinct group of countries within the Habsburg monarchy. Around 1815, the population was estimated to be around 5 million, of which two thirds considered Czech their mother tongue. The majority of the population lived in the countryside and their main source of living came from agricultural activities (farming, forestry and fish farming). About 15% of the population lived in royal and subject towns and worked in trades, commerce and farming, since a majority of Bohemian royal towns owned large estates and subject towns were integrated into the economy of the local demesne. The Jewish population was estimated at 80 thousand. The higher clergy and nobility accounted for no more than 0.2% of the population, however, the combination of their social influence and landed property (they owned over one third of the best quality agricultural and forest land) ensured their exceptional status beyond merely the food market. The political nation consisted of higher clergy, aristocracy and lower nobility, the Estates, which represented the bilingual inhabitants before the monarch. During coronation ceremonies of 1791, 1792 and 1836, the Bohemian Estates reminded the monarch of their special status within the monarchy. However, the Kingdom of Bohemia's position was seriously weakened after the dissolution of the Holy Roman Empire in 1806, when it lost the possibility of the external modest political representation, most notably in electing the Roman king and also in sending Bohemian representatives to the Reichstag in Regensburg (Imperial Diet) and the Imperial Chamber Court in Wetzlar. After 1815, the historic and political individuality of the Kingdom of Bohemia was only formally represented in the newly created German Confederation. It seemed that the idea of centralization had won a convincing victory over the Estates' political and cultural past, particularly relating to the Kingdom of Bohemia.

286

Even in the Bohemian and Moravian Diets and their Land committees – the highest territorial legislative institutions – incessant confrontations of the governmental absolutist-centralized and the Estates' Land principles were appearing. During the preceding Theresian-Josephine period, the importance of Land Diets was markedly diminished, not even being assembled to approve Land taxes and state contributions during the reign of Emperor Joseph II. Gubernia (Bohemian Gubernium and Moravian-Silesian Gubernium) gained considerable superiority over the diets, although each of these institutions were directed by the same official, who served concurrently at the Estates and Land levels. The President of the Bohemian Gubernium presided over the Bohemian Diet as the Supreme Burgrave of Prague, while the President of the Moravian-Silesian Gubernium was also the Land Commissioner and thus also the head of the Moravian Diet. Gubernia were directly subordinate to the central administration in Vienna.

Bohemia on the one hand and Moravia and Silesia on the other became administratively independent of each other thanks to direct communication with the Viennese centre. Their last administrative bond, their common appellations and the Mint, were loosened during Emperor Joseph II's reign, by which time the Estates had lost their influence in the district offices and even earlier in land financial and judicial institutions. Nevertheless, they retained their exclusive political, tax and police power over their latifundia. Emperor Leopold II returned the Bohemian and Moravian Estates almost all of the rights, prerogatives and privileges they had in the pre-Josephine times, including the option of using both Land languages in administration. His successor, Emperor Francis I, preserved the Estates' rights in legislative acts concerning the lands, specifically the right of audience before and after issuing decrees and rescripts, the right to challenge imperial propositions, the right to attend to the monarch's claims concerning primarily the financial and military obligations of the land towards the sovereign. The Estates were also regularly asked for their opinion on matters concerning the development of the Catholic faith, land privileges, the sale of landed estates enlisted in the Land Rolls and vassal matters. Leopold II renewed the Estates' Land committees as well as the land accounting office and a committee for inheritance tax and the amendment of the land tax. The Estates were once again granted the right to nominate for some endowment positions, to hire land Estates officials and to self-administer the "domestic" fund, which became the main financial source for maintaining land educational and charity establishments, for keeping the rivers navigable and for road construction.

The structure of the Land Diets was determined by old territorial constitutions from 1627–1628 and was tied to the Land right of citizenship and the ownership of landed estates listed in the Land Rolls. Only the Land Estates belonging to the curia of prelates, lords and knights had the right to vote in the Land Diet. Royal towns had only one vote, reflecting the fact that the town administration had been bureaucratized since Josephine times, and it was always a vote to support governmental propositions. In the first half of the 19th century, two matters were handled by the Land Diets: firstly, they discussed the monarch's proposals, which was the routine annual and mainly financial agenda, over which the Estates could not exert any political influence and in which they usually obligingly approved the king's position; secondly, the Supreme Burgrave or the Land Commissioner summoned the Estates once a year to manage those duties unique to the Land and Estates' Diets. These Estates Diets provided room for more political initiative than the formal postulate sessions. Yet it was not until the 1840s that the Land Diets became the sites of political battles between the Estates opposition and the central government.

In the entire period of 1791–1847, the Bohemian Diet and the Moravian Diet were politically active only twice: in the early 1790s and in the 1840s. The first action was initiated by Emperor Leopold II himself when he asked the Estates to formulate their demands towards the monarch, after the death of Joseph II. In their "desideria" (demands) the Estates expressed their wish to regain their former participation in legislation and required guarantees that the old Land structure would not be changed without their consent. The emperor met these demands primarily because they did not imply the reinstatement of an independent and sovereign historic Bohemian state, but only "the recovery of the historical Estates' privileges."

After this easy "victory," the Land Estates lapsed into political lethargy, which was clearly illustrated in the first decades of the 19th century by their scarce attendance at regular Land Diets and their docile approval of all the sovereign's propositions. During war years and times of the economic uncertainty, the Bohemian and Moravian nobility sympathized with the monarch and did not engage in any opposition activities. It was not until the 1830s and 1840s that the Bohemian Estates, more than their Moravian counterparts, began to remember their "ancient rights;" they started to critically examine the decrees and requests issued by the Viennese court as to whether they did or did not contradict the Land constitution. In their *Reasoning about the legal continuity of the constitutional rights and freedoms of the Bohemian Estates* of 1847, their primary demand was for the consistent respect of their privileges by the central Viennese administration, as they had discovered that they had, in fact, been stripped of many rights. It was typical that the leading aristocrats invited Land historiographer František Palacký to develop this Estates' platform, as at the time, Palacký was the only person able to analyze the Bohemian state's legal history and its Estates institutions from the Renewed Land Ordinance to the current day.

This defence of the Estates' rights and the distinctiveness of the Kingdom of Bohemia, which was as a petition dispatched to Vienna (never to see a reply), surprisingly became the basis of the Czech burghers' politics almost twenty years later. The restoration of the Kingdom of Bohemia's rights remained its fundamental agenda. The content of the Estates' state platform was later duly nationalized when the Estates' role as a political and social institute and a political power was eliminated through the revolution that abolished serfdom and the patrimonial system, and through the bureaucratization of the state apparatus.

The aristocratic opposition had ensured that the problem of wider representation for the population in the Land Diets was not addressed until the revolution of 1848. Before then, the Bohemian and Moravian Estates Diets represented neither wider society strata nor Land nations. They remained mere isolated "historical Estates," which could not divest themselves of aristocratic prejudices and did not intend to overcome their somewhat narrow political and economic interests. It was the liberal Czech townspeople who assumed the defence of the land's interests and, eventually, of the nation against the Viennese centralization.

4 The Beginning of Industrialization

From the 1770s, the Czech Lands were part of a uniform economic and customs area of the non-Hungarian part of the Habsburg monarchy. Their agricultural and proto-industrial potential ranked them, alongside the North-Italian provinces and Lower Austria with Vienna, among the most developed economic regions of the empire. This unified customs environment, along with prohibitive protectionism against foreign products, granted domestic producers protection from foreign competition, most notably from German and West European countries. By the mid-19th century, about 19% of the empire's population lived in the Czech Lands, which contributed 28% to the total industrial production of the empire. Of the main non-agricultural fields, 75% of woolen cloth production, 42% of the cotton production, 38% of the linen production, 69% of the glassmaking, 50% of brewing and distillery, and 33% of paper industry production were concentrated in the Czech Lands. The Czech Lands also produced two thirds of the sugar and one quarter of the iron production of the monarchy, and three quarters of the coal in the western part of the country. In 1846, 64% of the reliable steam engines in the entire western part of the monarchy were in operation in Bohemia, Moravia and Silesia. The economic importance of the Czech Lands within the Habsburg monarchy rose steadily thanks to rationalization in agriculture and forestry, as a result of a gradual assertion of new industrial plants, and the rapid construction of the road and railway networks.

Considerable fragmentation of the internal market was one of the negative factors influencing the development of the Czech Lands as it did not provide conditions for the transition from the natural and limited market production to wider, business-oriented goods production. Two of the exceptions were linen and factory glass production, which depended on the sales in foreign markets. The long wars with France, an unfavourable inland location, the lack of any important international trade routes, an insufficiently developed and integrated internal market and a lack of navigable rivers all had a negative effect on the development trade and capital accumulation. Rivers, moreover, considerably contributed to the varied business orientations of individual lands. Trade from Bohemia was oriented north-westwards – along the Elbe (*Labe*) to Saxony and beyond to Hamburg and the North Sea, while Moravia inclined economically to Lower Austria and Vienna, and most of the goods exported from Silesia were transported by ships along the Oder (*Odra*) to Prussia and the Baltic.

The market and industrialization processes in the Czech Lands were preconditioned by the economic and social reforms of enlightened monarchs, which followed up the previous mercantilist state efforts to increase the population, more rapid development of goods production and trade to achieve higher tax yield and economic self-sufficiency. Population growth and an increase in primary education, the social rise of many low-born people, the liberation of Jews from town ghettoes, a tolerance towards other faiths and the large-scale use in the workforce of women and children beyond domestic labour also had an economic dimension. After Joseph II's reforms, aristocratic, church and town landed properties and peasant enterprises showed a higher motivation towards increasing revenues and the appearance of surplus foods in the market. The Royal Chamber's demesnes and former monastic landed estates were subdivided and the subject labour on these and some other manors was replaced by monetary taxes. According to estimates, by around 1800 the subject labour was abolished in one third of Bohemian landed estates and, in another third, it was partially replaced by other forms of rent.

After Joseph II's reforms and during the Napoleonic wars a gradual transfer of ownership of estates listed in the Land Rolls was also taking place. At the beginning of the 19th century, a quarter of these estates, although only one tenth of total land area, were in the hands of commoners (civil landowners). Nevertheless, food market conditions in the Czech Lands were still principally determined by aristocratic demesnes, which were distinguished, in comparison to other Habsburg territories, by the unusually high concentration of land in consolidated landed estates. Many subject towns became centres of noble landowners' entrepreneurship as part of agricultural and food production, while many Bohemian and Moravian royal and mining towns with traditional guild production stagnated. Due to this socio-economic situation, Bohemian and Moravian townspeople did not become the bearers of economic progress, the movers of industrialization or the initiators of new entrepreneurial forms in the 19th century, it was rather the nobility, which embarked on enterprises outside their agricultural and forestry production. Their economic domain were principally the fields connected with: 1) an immediate use of the landed property, such as accessing cheap fuel sources from the vegetation of large forests or mineral mining for their own ironworks, glassworks and porcelain factories, 2) exercising their feudal monopoly in the market, such as exploiting the right to make and sell alcoholic beverages and the milling right in beer brewing, distillery and millinery, 3) a further industrial use of their own agricultural resources for woolen cloth production or wood processing, and 4) partial use of the subject labour system in non-agricultural production.

Industrial entrepreneurship in the field of agricultural industry remained a secondary source of the nobility's income. Its main facet continued to be profit from farming enterprises, through forestry and corn growing, and later also from breeding sheep for fleece and

Demographic growth in the Czech Lands in 1754–1850

Year	1754	1772	1792	1815	1850
population (in mil.)	3.0	3.7	4.5	4.8	6.8
Period		1754–1772	1772–1792	1792–1815	1815–1850
annual growth (in thous.)		39	40	13	57

from feudal rent. Despite this, the importance of the processing industry in the food production (mainly in beer brewing, distillery and sugar production) continued growing rapidly.

In 1790–1830, the percentage of arable soil increased by 20%, which was achieved through using fallow land and through pond desiccation rather than through extensive enlargement of the cultivated area. The traditional three-field crop rotation was gradually replaced by a diversified farming system, due in part to the introduction of two crops – potatoes and clover. Clover asserted itself mainly in landed estates' farming, while potatoes spread throughout peasants' farms and became an important element in the diet of the poorer strata of the rural population. The transition to indoor livestock farming was another step towards intensification, while in the mountainous demesnes, sheep husbandry for fleece was on the rise.

The almost quarter century long Napoleonic wars influenced the Czech Lands' economy in many, and often contradictory, ways. The extraordinary entrepreneurial boom, based mainly on war supplies, created conditions for accelerating capital sources and, together with the marked change in entrepreneurial approaches, opened the way to a wider use of goods production and the ensuing industrialization of some of the boom fields. It was not until this time that another essential precondition for industrial production came to the fore – the emancipation of numerous landless people and the farm holders not able to be self-sufficient from the urbarial dependence. Through gradual social mobilization, these strata started to be a prospective source of labour both for the rising factory industry and for the farming enterprises managed in the capitalist spirit.

Artisanal and beginning industrial production were influenced not only by wars, but also by the continental blockade, which made trade with England impossible in 1806–1814. The continental blockade had two impacts. On the one hand, it contributed to a considerable boom in economic activity and on the other hand, it damaged many export branches (such as glassmaking or linen production) as many foreign and overseas markets were closed. The continental blockade removed the competition from most of the traditional and non-traditional production (that was the case of mainly cotton and woolen cloth production, which supplied the sizeable army orders, and food industry) and these branches started to quickly prosper. The limited import of colonial goods also motivated domestic effort to produce substitutes. While some of them did not assert themselves (such as making sugar from maple sap), others found their place in the market production of the Czech Lands and because their low price made them much sought-after contributions to the diet. That was the case of making sugar from the sugar beet and coffee substitutes made from chicory.

Another economic consequence of wars with France was the depletion of the state treasury. In the long term, the state was not able to balance the budget deficit with loans and ran into debt, also through emissions of unsecured banknotes. The state finances were to be rehabilitated by a state bankruptcy announced at the beginning of 1811, during which the value of the banknotes in circulation was lowered to a fifth of their value. The state bankruptcy severely affected wide strata of the population as price levels remained the same. Financial deficiency had a negative impact on purchasing power, limited the creation of natural domestic capital resources, emphasized the traditional aversion to investing into the industry and inhibited all economic activities. The state bankruptcy, however, did not stop inflation and despite the short-term benefit, the Austrian state struggled with debt and inflation also in the ensuing decades.

The short-term entrepreneurial euphoria during the coalition wars caused major property shifts. Some merchants, who got rich thanks to arranging military supplies (Jakub Wimmer in Prague or Jakub A. Veith in České Budějovice) ranked among the richest people in the country. Despite the general growth of entrepreneurial activities in non-agricultural branches and the increase of personal property of several individuals, the landed property, completed with a noble title, remained the basis of economic certainty and guaranteed prestige in the society. That was why Christian and Jewish civil businessmen preferred to invest their capital into landed estates and unproductive representation rather than into the expansion of industrial branches.

The state liberalization efforts in the economic sphere can be characterized as inconsistent. They were limited only to creating a basic, although very strict legal framework for the new sphere of business. Its practical impact was restricted by different interests of the state and suzerain administration, guild and non-guild free production and tax and customs policy. It was only the recovery of the state economy in the 1830s and 1840s and the growing financial problems of the Austrian Empire that necessitated changes in the state policy in the spirit of a limited economic liberalism. The discrepancy between the moderate economic liberalism and state political conservatism, which was afraid of the social consequences of the technological and economic innovations, was still apparent.

The production of textiles remained the most important branch of the artisanal, manufactory and later also factory production. In the Czech Lands proper, over half a million people worked in this field. Within this branch, it was linen production that kept the most important position. Hundreds of thousands of people from less fertile mountain and mountain foothill regions of north and north-eastern Bohemia, north Moravia and Silesia engaged in domestic flax spinning and weaving. These two activities created supplementary income for the agriculturally self-insufficient farmsteads in the infertile foothill regions deep into the 19th century. The linen production was usually organized in such a way that the entrepreneur supplied the raw material to the domestic workers and collected ready products (so-called "factor system"). Only during the ensuing linen finishing, namely during its bleaching, was the production concentrated in bleacheries.

Unlike linen production, wool processing and woolen cloth production, was centered in traditional towns of this specialized artisanal production (for instance in Brno, also called the Austrian Manchester, Liberec or Jihlava). In this branch, supplying the army was the most important impulse for manufactory business. At the beginning of the 1840s, woolen cloth production represented about a half of the entire textile production in the Czech Lands. Also in this branch, the mechanization of the production processes progressed fast (mainly machine spinning, while weaving wool fabrics kept its hand-made guild techniques for a long time).

Before the end of the 18th century, a new branch dependent on overseas import, cotton processing, began to assert itself. After 1820, the processing of cotton became the most progressive branch of the textile production, because it was the first to implement machine production (mainly in spinning and fabric printing). Like linen production, cotton processing was also concentrated in the border regions of north and north-eastern Bohemia, which were settled by German inhabitants, in the valleys of mountain rivers, which supplied the much needed energy, and later (particularly in connection with introducing steam engines) also in the suburbs of larger towns (Prague, Liberec, Mladá Boleslav).

Apart from textiles, glass was the most important export article of the Czech Lands. It was produced mostly in the Bohemian Forest (*Šumava*), Lužice Mountains (*Lužické hory*) and Jizera Mountains (*Jizerské hory*) wooded regions and around the upper reaches of the river Sázava. Also charcoal iron production was important. It was produced in the noble estates and its technology was based on cheap wood and local poor-quality deposits of iron ore. It developed mainly in the central-Bohemian Brdy area (between the towns of Beroun, Příbram and Rokycany) and on the Bohemian-Moravian borderland of Žďár Hills (*Žďárské vrchy*). In Moravia, it was around the town of Blansko and in the Bruntál region. In the 1830s, forty-seven ironworks were in operation in the Czech Lands, owned by the noble families of Fürstenberg, Colloredo-Mansfeld, Kolowrat, Vrbna, Metternich, Nostitz, Stadion and Salm. The opening of the first coke blast furnace in Vítkovice in the Moravian-Silesian borderland in 1836 was a real breakthrough in the traditional charcoal iron ore processing. The company was then owned by the Archbishop of Olomouc and in 1841 it was transferred to the hands of the Viennese Rothschild family and became the basis of their iron and coal empire in north Moravia.

The process of industrialization of the Czech Lands was slow and complicated until the 1830s. The causes of this delay relative to the German states and Western Europe can be found in the capital weakness of the burghers, in the high subject labour and tax exploitation of the rural population, in the drain of a considerable amount of profit from the long-distance trade abroad, in unsecure economic situation during the coalition wars and in the social elites' lack of assertive business mentality.

Another important barrier was the lack of cheap loans. More prominent bankers in Prague (for instance Lämmel, Fiedler or Zdekauer) were not very active in loan support for the industrial enterprises. In the first half of the 19th century, they focused mainly on financing the state commissions and on government bonds operations. Only in the 1820s, the first financial enterprises of a new type were established in the Czech Lands. They were savings companies and insurance companies (Bohemian Savings Bank in Prague in 1825, The First Bohemian Mutual Insurance Company in Prague in 1827 and Moravian-Silesian Mutual Insurance Company in Brno in 1830). They were mostly founded by rich landed aristocracy. The full development of industrialization and urbanization, however, had to wait for releasing of most of the Czech Lands' population from subject duties in 1848 and for a total transformation of the state economic policy after 1850.

In the first three decades of the 19th century, machinery was used only as a supplement in some isolated operations, such as cotton spinning. In the Czech Lands, virtually their only source of energy was water power. From around 1830, machinery started to be used on a larger scale in the production or textiles, particularly in spinning and wool fabric printing and partly also in the food industry (mainly in sugar production). The unprecedented spread of mobile and stationary steam engines was brought about by the railway in the 1840s and glance coal and lignite mining, mainly in the Ostrava, Kladno and Teplice regions. The steam engine enabled the move of industrial factories from the water power sources to the towns. Stationary and mobile steam engines were at first imported from England and from the 1830s, they were produced in Luz's machine works in Brno. Mobile steam engines, that is locomotives were produced exclusively in Vienna and Wiener Neustadt. The first Bohemian and Moravian machine works were transformed from mechanic workshops attached to textile companies, particularly in the Liberec, Jablonec and Prague areas. They were founded mostly by naturalized Englishmen (such as Robert Evans or Joseph J. Ruston).

In the second quarter of the 19th century, a boom in the food industry occurred. Although many distilleries, oil production companies and breweries still used simple artisanal technologies, new companies managed in modern ways began to appear. In 1842, the Burgher Brewery, a joint-stock company, in Plzeň (Pilsen) was founded and it used the advanced technology of bottom fermentation. Its main product was light lager with distinct hoppy taste. This type of lager of the "Pilsen type" (so-called Pils) gave its name to the most widespread type of beer in the world.

Before the mid-19th century, radical changes in the transportation of people and goods occurred in the Czech Lands. From the end of the 18th century, so-called imperial roads with firm and sufficiently wide surfaces, side ditches and fruit tree or ornamental tree alleys were constructed. The basic network of quality roads, which were used also by so-called postal expresses from 1823, was completed at the end of the 1840s. The contemporary road network of the Czech Lands is based on this network.

The first railway, or horse-drawn railway line, was constructed in 1832 between České Budějovice and Linz in the area where the mercantilists had planned a canal connecting the Vltava and the Danube (Dunaj). It was used primarily for transport Salzburg salt to Bohemia and for passenger transport and it was in fact the first long-distance public railway on the continent. The second, economically much less successful horse-drawn railway was built also in the early 1830s between Prague and Lány (originally it was to stretch to Plzeň and České Budějovice). Its economic importance increased after the discovery of high-quality coal near Kladno in the 1840s.

In 1836, Rothschild's Viennese bank was granted the imperial privilege to build the steam engine railway from Vienna to the salt mines in Galicia along with routes to Brno, Olomouc and Opava. The first section (to Brno) of this Emperor Ferdinand's Northern Railway was inaugurated on July 7, 1839. The railway was further built from Břeclav to Přerov, from Přerov to Olomouc and from Hrušov (today Ostrava main station) to Opava (and further to the Prussian border) and to Cracow. This railway was connected with the Northern State Railway in Olomouc, whose connection to Prague was completed in August 1845 and to the Saxon border near Děčín in April 1851. The modern railway connection became one of the prerequisites of the rapid disintegration of the late feudal barter trade and was a break-through into the closed small market regions. This long-term trend was completed in the second half of the 19th century by a gradual implementation of a unified market.

The advantages of the steam engine for shipping were first appreciated in Bohemia in 1841, when the first steamboat "Bohemia" was floated in Prague-Karlín. It was built by Joseph J. Ruston and operated between Prague-Karlín (or Obříství near Mělník) and Dresden by another naturalized Englishman, John Andrews. In 1847, Prague was telegraphically linked with Vienna.

The Czech Lands' industrialization had its territorial, social and national dimensions. The iron and agricultural production was controlled mainly by noble farming enterprises and later larger farmsteads from the fertile Bohemian interior. Most of the technologically demanding industries of the budding industrial and transportation base were founded and operated by foreigners, who came from German states and from England (Robert Evans, Joseph J. Ruston, John Andrews). Prague banks and forwarding companies, textile factories and print-works were mostly owned by Jewish businessmen (the Porges of Portheim, Zdekauers, Fiedlers, Lämmels). The rise of textile factories, bleacheries, glassworks, porcelain plants, potash production in the foothills and finally also mass coal mining in the borderlands inhabited by German population was mostly caused by unique natural and climate conditions. The relative overpopulation of the infertile mountain and foothills areas forced their skilled inhabitants to look for subsistence in non-agricultural branches or to seasonal search for work in other parts of the monarchy or abroad. The fertile Bohemian and Moravian interior had the character of a country's granary, where mainly food processing industry started to assert itself. The German-speaking population from border regions thus had a technological head start before the main wave of industrialization. This state of affairs was to a large extent caused by the character and orientation of the proto-industrial and beginning industrial production in the Czech Lands.

5 Rise of Czech National Movement

The formation of a modern Czech nation was part of a wider European process of emancipation. Like the Poles, Hungarians, Irish, Norwegians, Finns and Slovaks, Czechs embarked on a mission to uplift national cultural and social life at the end of the 18th century and, later, for the advancement of political culture and constitutional status to the level of more developed European countries. Czech ethnic status at the turn of the 18th and 19th centuries could be characterized as a position of a non-ruling nation or ethnic group, which did not equal the state community. This ethnic communality was jeopardized in three ways: it lost the language as a means of communication in the higher spheres of intellectual activity; as a result of the Josephine centralization and the disintegration of the Holy Empire of the German Nation, the local population lost sight of almost all exterior attributes of the Czech statehood; and finally, the society in Bohemia was, for the first time in history, suffering from a serious identity crisis, stemming from more than merely these changes.

In the context of demographic and socio-economic changes, the process of ethnic majoritarianism, or minoritarianism, commenced in Bohemia and Moravia and resulted in a temporary replacement of the originally dominant German language and culture with Czech language and culture at the turn of the 18th and 19th centuries. These ethnic shifts were expressed mainly in a national identification. The non-ruling nations of Central Europe experienced a national "awakening" or a national emancipation. Their new identities, based on ethnicity, competed with older identities based on regions, Estates, creed, state or dynasty. This advancement of the ethnic-national identity took place in central and south-eastern Europe throughout the 19th century. At the beginning of the 19th century, only a very few nation-conscious Czechs and Germans in the Czech Lands were found, while the majority of the kingdom's population considered themselves citizens of the Czech Lands (the so-called *Böhme(n)*), however, at the end of the century, most of the population defined themselves along national or ethnic lines. Another factor, which played an important role in the rise of the new Czech identity, was territory. From the very beginning, the Czech national movement was established as an organized and purposeful occupation only in Bohemia. The Czech-speaking ethnic sector in Moravia was "merely a declared part of the Czech national programme," but it did not play an important role in it at the beginning.

The Czech emancipation movement went through three stages between 1780–1848, which can be characterized as (1) the stage of scientific interest in the ethnic group, its past, language, customs, social conditions and so on in the spirit of enlightened patriotism. This stage occurred approximately between 1780 and 1810; (2) the stage of the national agitation, which was sparked thanks to the decision by a part of the Czech ethnic community to win all ethnic Czechs over to the idea of being part of a single nation and for a maximum degree of cultural emancipation; this stage took place approximately from 1810 to 1830; (3) the stage when a broad spectrum of the population identified with the idea of belonging to a nation which represented specific values, and when the national movement reached its mass and irreversible character; this occurred in the period after 1830 and mainly after the 1848 revolution.

The first stage of the Czech national movement took advantage of the social loosening brought about by the Theresian and Josephine reforms. Education reforms and lighter censorship increased the population's literacy and knowledgeability, thus indirectly influencing the growing demand for printed texts. The spirit of the Enlightenment, striving for a general advancement of the wider population's standard of living, spread not only among the laymen and to the university, but also found its way to the burgher circles and lower Catholic clergy, whose representatives became the most enthusiastic exponents of Czech patriotic and cultural endeavours after 1800. The Josephine efforts to unify administration confirmed German as the state language of communication, yet in the spirit of the enlightened patriotism, they also brought about defensive reactions leading to the examination and preservation of the majority language in the land, which was Czech. From 1792, Czech language and literature were taught at the university in Prague. Another factor that contributed to the development of Czech cultural communication was Czech theatre (from 1785) and the large-scale publishing of books and newspapers printed in Czech.

The Czech-German relationship gradually developed into social conflict even though the Czech ethnic identity was not, until the end of the 18th century, based singularly on an awareness of a difference from or an aversion to the local Germans. According to M. Hroch, in the second half of the 18th century, the Czech ethnic group was conscious of itself and defined itself primarily in opposition "to enemy and ethnically foreign aliens coming mainly from Prussia, but also to the patrimonial state administration in German." The relation of German ethnicity to the Czech one had been marked by distinct expressions of superiority by the ruling elites towards a subjected ethnic group, on both social and Estates levels. These expressions of superiority were not merely verbal, but were also reflected in religion, that is the only sphere of interest in which members of the Czech ethnic group could appear equal with the ethnic Germans. At the time, there were no real Czech-German enmities that were openly and publicly displayed, in addition, the dissatisfaction of the Czechs was one-sided and was not perceived by the Germans as either generally alarming or politically relevant. Due to further bureaucratization, the intensity of contact between the growing Czech ethnic group with the institutions administered in German increased, with ethnic differences gradually expanding into the sphere of relations and discrepancies, and started to lose their earlier character of random experience. It became socially serious when a Czech applicant with equal intellectual and language qualities had no chance to succeed in the competition for social and professional advance.

Historians do not normally answer the question of why national agitation started and what led a particular segment of intellectuals to disseminating nationalist ideas, to agitating for a national language and for the nation, as the field's methodology is insufficient for such socio-psychological problems. Thanks to sociology and historical anthropology, however, it can be stated that one of the things that defines humans has always been man's need to identify himself with behaviour models of his social environment and to protect this environment perceived as identity. The national community became the best form of mutual defence and also a means of expansion outside this group.

The second phase of the Czech emancipation process commenced with Kramerius' publishing activities and Jungmann's scholarly polemics. Václav Matěj Kramerius (1753–1808) contributed three innovations to patriotic communication: emancipation from the noble environment, the purposeful cultivation of social communication through so-called collectors (in fact, he introduced patriotic work for commission) and connecting the Czech ethnic group with the world of power politics; with events which directly concerned this ethnic group. In the words of modern sociology: Václav Matěj Kramerius, or rather his Czech publishing activities, broke through the information barrier around the Czech ethnic group and brought patriotic activities to the higher levels of the value ladder.

Josef Jungmann (1773–1847) was a representative of the Czech commoner community, which for the first time assumed the leadership of the national movement. The existing noble-patriotic and burgher-enlightened character of the cultural movement, however, continued. Josef Jungmann with his contemplation on the Czech language from 1806 and his polemic against the private person who called himself Bohemarius (secondary school teacher Alois Uhl) from 1814, which was a polemic against a member of his own circle, for the first time, publicly attacked the official language doctrine of the Austrian state and so shifted the goals of the Czech emancipation movement onto a national and social level. Jungmann considered a person a true Czech only if he regularly used the Czech language. In his polemics, Josef Jungmann for the first time publicly denounced the opponents of the national goals, claiming that if Czechs gave up their nationality and became Germanized, they would not differ from "other deplorable half-castes without a character, virtue..."

They were Czech commoner intellectuals who gradually became the bearer of this new, national type of patriotism. Their efforts were not yet institutionalized, and thus lacked institutionalized communication. In connection with Jungmann's polemics, the feeling of the social inferiority started, for the first time, to blend or resonate with belonging to the linguistically-defined Czech nation or Czech ethnic group, which was in an inferior position compared to the German-speaking bureaucracy, hence the conviction that "should a social emancipation of the Czech people occur, it must happen through their language's equalization in the Czech Lands," but also through a shift in attitude by Czechs to their mother tongue. Another important factor, which spurred patriotic activity, was the fact that the newly acquired notions of homeland, patriotism and nation coincided with the same notions used by the official Austrian propaganda in the war years. Although the content of these notions was different, this coincidence enabled the patriotic commoner intellectuals to transform official patriotic agitation into proclamations which emphasized only the national interests.

In this second stage of national agitation we cannot speak about an organized Czech national movement, although the appropriate intellectual and social conditions were being created. Enforcing the Czech national identity was, at that time, not a must, rather merely one possibility. There were other alternatives: a development towards Land identity, which would have meant a bilingual Land-based nation (in the sense of Bolzano's alternative project of bilingual Bohemism) or a national-state understanding of an Austrian identity or a German identity.

In this context, Bohemism can be considered a parallel, yet finally an unsuccessful integration model in the Kingdom of Bohemia and the Czech Lands, which strove to overcome national interests, as well as the discrepancies between Czechs and Germans, in favour of a supranational Land patriotism. This Bohemistic concept was based on a fundamental equality of the Bohemian population of the Slavic and Germanic tribes, in the sense of their general equality, which included linguistic equality. Bohemism was verbally shaped primarily in 1815–1848, during the most intensive cultural emancipation effort of the Czech nation, which caused defensive reactions among Germans living in the Czech Lands. Against the nationalist conflict, which started to appear more intensively in the Czech Lands, the supporters and proponents of Bohemism presented the concept of a gradual overcoming of rapid national polarization mainly through unselfish Land patriotism. Historiography explains the rise of Bohemism as a reaction to the centralist tendencies of the enlightened state in the last third of the 18ᵗʰ century and as a natural consequence of the gradual decline of Latin as the language of the educated elite and bureaucrats, and its replacement with German. Bohemism thus came to life at a time when the language of the culture became separate from the real ethnic linguistic situation based on national consciousness. The increasingly manifest national polarization occurred in the Czech Lands in this insecure time of the Napoleonic wars and was influenced by German Romanticism. Bohemism thus appeared as an anachronistic and, to some extent, utopian cultural and social alternative in reaction to the evident national separation of Jungmann's circle and to the political indifference and helplessness of the Viennese centre and its aristocratic elites.

The religious philosopher and logician Bernard Bolzano (1781–1848) is considered to be the most important proponent of Bohemism. In his exhortations, he tried to prevent the pending ethnic conflicts in the Czech Lands through his appeals against placing one's own national tribe over other population groups in the country. His programme of "ethnic love for the neighbour" and intellectual and material support for the virtue and welfare of all citizens was probably most influential in the 1820s and 1830s. This Bolzanoesque patriotic-Christian spirit was the foundation of the newly established Patriotic Museum in Prague and its two journals, which were to serve the entire cultural and historical environment of the Czech Lands. Bohemistic thought, promoted by enthusiasts among the cultural and social elite, with its supranational and, to some extent, even Estate orientation (such as Karl Egon Ebert or Count Josef Matyáš Thun) and its cultural works could assert itself only before the 1848 revolution. It was followed by rapid political and cultural alienation in which the bilingual Bohemistic social concept succumbed to ethnocentric and nationalistic tendencies. National identity thus became the main expression of collective identity at a time when the Estates principles were dying away.

While the first fifteen years of the 19ᵗʰ century (1800–1815) were a period where alternative possibilities for the formation of the Czech nation had been created, and the national movement was not irreversible, in the following fifteen years, the foundations for a successful start of a mass Czech national movement were laid. National agitation moved from the sphere of proclamations, desires and dreams to the sphere of reality. Patriots were forced to move on to activities which jeopardized all, including their moral and existential values. From the 1830s, national agitation could fall back on the strong organizational platform of the literary foundation, Matice česká, on several journals and a growing social communication among patriots. Thanks to all of these factors, Czech national identity became the best long-term alternative. The "national" history written by František Palacký became a basic argument for the existence of a nation. The process of the formation of the modern Czech nation was then an irreversible process.

Until nearly the end of the first decade of the 19ᵗʰ century, patriotic activity was an academic matter for a small group of patriots, hence the literary character of Czech patriotism. This was essentially the only allowed form of communication, as the current political circumstances did not allow the formation of any political clubs or societies. Social gatherings, however, were conducted, although not in the name of political conversation and political or party activities, but rather for charity, philanthropy, entertainment (such as Czech national balls) or in support of the domestic business spirit. In these clubs, although they had originally been built around Estates, rather than on liberal or majority principles, it was possible to indulge in liberal political behaviour, for instance when voting for statuses, accepting new members or when deciding the club's finances. The nobility spontaneously left these liberally administered clubs – including the Union for the Promotion of Industry in the Czech Lands – at the beginning of the 1840s. Clubs based on liberal majority principles, or gradually transformed according to these principles, then quickly succumbed to the "laws of nature," to quote Josef Wenzig in the 1840s and František Palacký in the 1860s and were soon nationalized by the will of the majority – first in one or several sections and, later, throughout the entire club.

From the 1830s new collective identities were formed and the (often) merely abstract ideas regarding nation started to acquire concrete shapes. This process evinces, in both a conscious and instinctively verbalized way, and in a verbally symbolic way, both individual and collective attitudes. Sociologists call it a discursive creation or cementing. Part of this discourse is usually one's identification in opposition to the other. At the end of the 1830s and at the beginning of the 1840s, public debates became strikingly politicized. These intellectual battles took place in newspaper and pamphlet polemics. In the German environment, they were written mainly by the young or the younger member of the national liberal movement Young Germany. The Young Germans attacked many phenomena of the "imperfect" non-liberal social reality (the alliance of the altar and the throne, the non-liberal social environment, badly administered finances or the underdeveloped schools).

Liberal German journalists' harsh attacks did not spare the expressions of the Czech national movement. However, it was a slanted discourse as it took place in a non-liberal environment. Its initiators, who strove for a public and free discussion concerning public matters, were sometimes subjected to the repressive state policy. The discussion was encouraged by German liberal emigrants in brochures which were printed mainly in Leipzig and secretly, or even illegally, imported into the Habsburg monarchy. In the 1830s and 1840s, these skirmishes resulted in bitterness, suspiciousness and accusations of pan-Germanism on the one hand, and of pan-Slavism among the Czech intellectual elites on the other. The fear of the other, including the use of slander, such as Czech denunciation to Russia, contributed to the rapid and mutual distancing and lack of communication. The Young Germans especially considered the Czech national emancipation a surprising obstacle to the realization of their own political plans for the near future, one of which was undoubtedly the political unification of Germany. This process of the mutual intellectual distancing of the social elites could not be stopped in the 1840s. The ammunition for the national political argument was ready, and neither party was willing to withdraw. This was the environment in which a major political blow occurred in spring 1848, which made all the thus-far verbalized suspicions concrete and politically real.

For the Czech ethnic group, the period after the Napoleonic wars and, in particular after 1830, was decisive as it proved the turning point in Czech ethnic emancipation. The gradual separation from the German cultural circle and its intellectual discourse became irreversible. As well as defining themselves in opposition to the German world in the 1840s, thanks to Karel Havlíček, the nation found a concrete place in the Slavic element and dropped its pan-Slavic illusions.

In 1848, these intellectual skirmishes and mutual suspicions were augmented by a political trauma expressed in the fear of the future, which each party envisaged quite differently. Czechs wanted to remain part of Austria, which was to be transformed to fit the Czech national programme, while Germans dreamed of a (great) German unification, which would also include Czech and Alpine lands. Both concepts concerning the near political future were – as became evident in the events of 1848 and 1849 – entirely contradictory. The consequences of this cultural and, eventually, political break-up of society showed up in different levels – from the separation of families to a national split.

The verbal intellectual disintegration of the early 1840s was followed by a highly explosive political break-up during the 1848 revolution, which turned into a permanent constitutional and nationalist fight after constitutionality was renewed and as a result of the political liberalization in the 1860s. It was Czechs who were always more proactive because they wanted to change the unsatisfactory state of affairs. The revolution also put an end to most Utraquist efforts connected to the Land patriotic concept of Bohemism as the originally ambitious conciliatory projects, such as Glaser's magazine *Ost und West* or, later, Pinkas' review *Union*, went out of print due to a lack of readers. The non-nationalist possibilities of development were no longer conceivable, something confirmed and accelerated by the 1848 revolution. Bohemism as a possible supranational identification concept gradually disappeared and, with it, its main proponents – both the Land nobility and Czech-German intellectuals ended up socially on the defensive. From the 1860s, the concept of national identity was victorious on both the Czech and the German sides.

The advancement of the Czech language and the Czech ethnic group continued in a liberal environment to an unabated extent throughout the entire second half of the 19th century, although the attractiveness and prestige of the German language and education as a means of social mobility was still considerable. Before the end of the 19th century, the Czechs in the Czech Lands essentially attained their national goals. They revived the language, advanced literary and artistic activities, formed their own political representation with a defining political culture, nationalized education, self-government and some business branches. They became a nation with a complete interior social structure and with a complete socially structured political representation. While, at the beginning of the 19th century, nationally conscious individuals formed only a tiny minority, at the end of the century, almost all the population identified with only national categories. In gaining the attributes of a standard European nation, the Czechs paid a standard price: the complete intellectual and later real political break-up with the other – German – society in Bohemia, and eventually also in Moravia.

6 Spiritual Background.
Bohemian and Moravian Revivalist Culture

The most essential spiritual social basis in the Czech Lands of the end of the 18th and the first half of the 19th centuries was that of everyday piety, which kept the majority of the society in a humble acceptance of their earthly reality. Intensive Baroque piety was replaced by reformed and enlightened Catholicism, strengthening the state power, which abandoned the Baroque exultation with its considerable emotional animation and preferred a more sober piety, without superstitious practices and religious pressure. Religion became an important state asset especially in education, edification and charity. Religious communities and renewed religious confraternities were also to help in dealing with the problem of the poor. The reform carried out in the spirit of a tolerant Christian humanism also strengthened state supervision of the church and tried to make it an important supplementary means of state administration, for example, it was to be in charge of the parish registers.

Under the rule of Francis I, the revival of conservative Catholicism prevailed. An emphasis on enlivening Catholicism, which was facing mild competition from the tolerated creeds, on the fortification of the population's morality, as well as on consolidating the lower clergy's discipline, was placed not only in the insecure war years, but mainly, as in the case of Bernard Bolzano, at a time of implementing anti-liberal (so-called "Karlovy Vary") resolutions. Religion, and Catholicism in particular, were both the proclaimed and genuine fundamental spiritual basis of the Austrian Empire. The idea that somebody for whom faith was a foreign or unknown concept would live in the empire was unacceptable.

What could be different, though, was the manner of the faith and an individual's inner attitude to God. All permitted creeds contained four similar pillars: love of God, love for your neighbour, humility in the face of divine provident creation, and hope for posthumous salvation. These pillars of religious feelings and behaviour were also included in official governmental policy, which even encouraged a certain degree of deification of the ruler. To the monarchy were attributed divine qualities of an infallible government and this faith ensured that the monarchy's foundations were unshakeable, even after the accession of the new ruler, Ferdinand I, who was incapable of ruling. From October 13, 1781, in what were known as the German-Galician provinces of the Habsburg monarchy, prevailed a proclaimed religious tolerance based on an individual's full inner freedom. The population was divided along religious lines into Catholics, non-Catholics, Jews and sectarians.

The majority creed in the Czech Lands was Catholicim. Several dozen Lutheran and Calvinian parishes, financially supported from abroad, were tolerated. Non-Catholic churches, followers of the Augsburg and Helvetic confessions, had been tolerated since Joseph's times. They had the right to establish a chapel and a school for 100 families or 500 believers and perform burials according to their rites; their priests could serve the Eucharist and administer the last rites; non-Catholic parishes could keep a minister and a teacher, though these had to receive accreditation from the political administrative institutions. Non-Catholics could perform, with certain limitations, public offices, become Masters and acquire real estate.

On the other hand, they were restricted in the design of their shrines (they could not have towers or bells and direct street access). The Catholic parish priest could collect fees for performing religious services (such as marriages and burials), including from non-Catholics and, unlike their evangelic counterpart, he was in charge of administering parish registers and other important religious books. All mixed marriages had to be married by a Catholic priest and a Protestant pastor was invited as a mere witness. Children from these mixed marriages had to automatically follow the father's creed if it was Catholic. Otherwise, only the sons followed the father's creed, while the daughters became Catholic.

Tolerance was far from equality, and these everyday restrictions for non-Catholics and their priests were understood to be an effort to prevent the natural spreading of non-Catholic parishes. Religious tension in the pre-March society was caused mainly by the fact that the above-mentioned rules were not always obeyed by the Catholic clergy as they were interpreted and applied arbitrarily. The disputes were caused mainly by measures such as the following: before marrying a Catholic bride, a non-Catholic bridegroom was forced to sign a commitment that they will bring their children up as Catholics (as was the case of František Palacký) or a Catholic's conversion to Protestantism could only happen after six weeks of Catholic parson's persuasions. So there was an area of concrete expressions of inequality exceeding the Toleration Patent's scope. In the late 1840s, they were sharply criticized by the more courageous Protestant priests.

The Jewish population's status in the pre-March period can be characterized as tolerated by the state. Jews were not considered full-fledged citizens and were far from complete religious and social emancipation. The written norms from the end of the 18th century were gradually evened out, particularly in the Czech Lands, thanks to the real economic and material status of the Jews. Their influence on the country's economic performance, expressed in the considerable ownership of industrial, merchant and banking companies, as well as having money at their disposal, boosted their confidence and hope in the future. Riches opened many a forbidden gate, as was the example of Rotschild's purchase of Moravian and Silesian landed estates enlisted in the Land Rolls against the Estates' will. The Jewry residing in the Czech Lands, 50,000 people out of a total 460,000 in the entire empire, was probably the richest in the Habsburg monarchy. At the time, it was not a problem for rich Jews to pay the Jewish tax or, through exceptional fertility, to refute the familiant law, regulating the number of Jewish families. Jewish access to the highest education, even though only at the faculties of medicine or law, and to business, trade, lower officer ranks in the army, court justice and even to noble titles (the Hoeningsberg and Leammel families) partially removed the social barriers which separated Jews from Christians. Some things had still to be achieved: an unconditional (that is, without baptising the Jews) access to work in state administration, enlisting their property in their name in the Land Rolls, free access to all crafts and the removal of administrative property barriers for gaining approval to marry. However, even in these cases, the revolution in the mid-19th century brought about a partial fulfilment of these emancipation demands, and the December Constitution of 1867 ensured their full equality. After this date, the inner social and mental emancipation of the Jewry was no longer a state task. Despite religious tolerance in pre-March times, we can find much potential for conflict in internal human sentiments, which contributed to revolutionary ferment in 1848.

Linguistic and cultural equality was also a necessary condition for social and political equality. In this sense, all Czech cultural, scientific and organizational activities had their own – mostly hidden – political dimension. It was Czechs who had to modernize their own language after 1800 to adapt it to general progress, in order not to lose the chance for social advancement or participation in the production and technological progress. Without this, they ran the danger of retaining a secondary social and economic status and, in the end, assimilation with a more developed ethnic group. New intellectual movements and technological progress came mainly from the German world and, through it, they were implemented in the Czech Lands. The linguistic and literary modernization was essentially a question of the survival of the Czech ethnic group and its transformation as a national community for a new era. The revival of the language in 1792–1848, based on scientific principles, was linked to a range of prominent Czech scholars and artists; among the most notable were Josef Dobrovský, Václav Thám, Antonín Jaroslav Puchmajer, Jan Nejedlý, Josef Jungmann, Václav Hanka, the Presl brothers and one of the founders of Czech Slavic studies (along with Dobrovský) – Pavel Josef Šafařík. Among the contributors to modern Czech literature were playwrights Karel Ignác Thám, Václav Kliment Klicpera and Josef Kajetán Tyl, poets Ján Kollár, František Ladislav Čelakovský and Karel Jaromír Erben with their lyric epics, and undoubtedly the biggest romantic talent of the period – poet Karel Hynek Mácha. Fiction was still waiting for its masterpieces from the pen of Božena Němcová.

The first Czech newspapers published by Václav Matěj Kramerius appeared as early as in the Josephine period. Thanks to their writing's clear style and slightly simplified language, they gained mass popularity among their readers. In 1791, the Department of Czech Language and Literature was founded at the Charles-Ferdinand University and, in 1805, the first Czech-German-Latin dictionary was published. At a period when aesthetics and poetics were the foundations of philosophical education, the rise of Czech lyrical works published in Puchmajer's collections had a great impact on national confidence. The hardworking linguist and teacher, Josef Jungmann (1773–1847), who, unlike Josef Dobrovský (1753–1829), wrote primarily in Czech, elaborated the Czech vocabulary, which could describe an ever-more complex living and spiritual reality. This achievement was possible thanks to his successful translations of works by famous world authors and a careful dictionary work, which was based on an analogy with and borrowings from other Slavic languages

Czech cultural and scientific life in the second decade of the 19th century was getting firmer organizational contours. Several events brought Czech cultural life and scientific activities to a new stage. Among them were the establishment of the Utraquist Patriotic Museum (1818), the discovery of the *Manuscripts* in 1817–1818, the founding of several Czech social magazines, the activities of the theatre organizer Jan Nepomuk Štěpánek (1783–1844), the founding of Czech reader societies and, last but not least, František Palacký's arrival in Prague. Palacký's contacts in the highest society and his organizational talent led to founding a museum journal in 1827, which was originally published in both Land languages. The German journal foundered for a lack of readers, while the Czech version survived as it was taken over by the newly established literary foundation, Matice česká. This patriotic organization, which primarily focused on publishing Czech books, became the first official guardian of Czech cultural interests. Books published by Matice česká (particularly Šafařík's *Slavic Antiquities* in 1837 and Jungmann's *Czech-German Dictionary* in 1839) were scientific works, which contributed to the formation of the Czech national conscience. The Czech encyclopaedia project, however, did not succeed at this stage, because Czech terminology did not exist for many non-humanity fields nor for practical crafts, and there were not enough experts. This lack was eliminated in the 1830s and 1840s by a lexicographical work by natural scientist brothers Jan Svatopluk and Karel Bořivoj Presl. The necessity of reviving the language became more urgent as a result of the modernization pressure on Czech society, which quickly adopted the newest scientific information, and technical and technological innovations. Among the successful activities in the field of non-spiritual creation were also entrepreneurial initiatives of the young Czech technical elites, who were educated at the Prague's Estates industrial school and who, from the late 1830s, participated in the national movement and in the Union for the Promotion of Industry in the Czech Lands.

Writing the country's history in the national spirit as well as organizing Czech scientific and cultural life around the Patriotic Museum and Matice česká was a major achievement for the Protestant, František Palacký (1798–1876). It was no accident that scientific historiography was established in the middle of the process forming a modern nation, when the modern existence of the nation needed to be interpreted as a continual historical process. The process of a modern nation formation was accelerated through the knowledge of its past which became a "generally accepted authority" and one of the main arguments for the present. The time-honoured existence of a nation and the discovery of the qualities of a historical or a state-defined nation was the gravest argument for promoting other Czech national demands. Thanks to Palacký's intellectual activities, Czech history ceased to be part of the history of the Holy Roman Empire, that is part of the German nation, and became a full-fledged history of the historical Czech nation, which as in the past now fought for its existence against the German element. From here, it was just a step to the national history's gradually becoming part of family upbringing, school curricula and fiction. New generations were then brought up in the spirit of the national history and national myths. These generations had no doubts about the existence of their own nation. National and historical awareness were boosted by the ingenious fakes of two manuscripts (*The Dvůr Králové Manuscript* and *Zelená hora Manuscript*), which were "discovered" at the end of the second decade of the 19th century, in the period that was decisive for the reversibility or irreversibility of the process of the Czech nation's formation. An important role in Czech society was also played by the visualization and fictionalization of the newly discovered national history (including the visualization and fictionalization of the texts which were later labelled fakes) through visual arts and fiction. History and national history in particular helped Czechs to fight for historical statehood, which after 1860 became the subject of fierce political debate in the name of the state right. Using historical topics in fiction was nothing new, even long before March 1848. The main difference, however, occurred after Palacký's achievements and after the acceptance of his Bohemian national history concept by the wider Czech intellectual elite. While in the 1820s and 1830s, it was mainly German poets and playwrights from German states, as well as those from the Czech Lands, who fictionalized and dramatized topics from Czech history, among them Clemens Brentano, Karl Egon Ebert, Moritz Hartmann and Uffo Horn. Later, in the 1840s, when Germans from the Czech Lands realized the separation of the Bohemian history from the context of the Holy Roman Empire and recognized the clearly national drift of Czechs, they deserted these historical topics and never returned to them. Bohemian history topics then became the exclusive domain of Czech culture.

Cultural and intellectual development in Moravia, unlike that in Bohemia, retained its patriotic German-language character for much longer. The general culture in Moravia was spread thanks to Cristian Carl Andrée and Karl Josef Jurende, who published the educational magazines *Patriotisches Tagesblatt* and *Jurende's vaterländischer Pilger*. Jurende's magazines and calendars in particular became almost an encyclopaedia of current human knowledge and also contained contributions to Moravian homeland study. Truly Czech national awareness began to wake in Moravia in the late 1820s. Moravia retained its specific cultural character deep into the 19th century. A Czech or Czech-Prague, that is a Jungmannean, concept of the language revival and Palacký's interpretation of national history were always accepted with a slight time, intellectual and argument delay here, which can be explained by an inward link to the Catholic environment and the Cyril-Methodius tradition, a different national structure in the Moravian towns' elites and the existence of two Moravian cultural centres.

While Bohemia had had its natural political and cultural centre in Prague since the Middle Ages, Moravia suffered from a remarkable dichotomy. Olomouc, in the north, with its long intellectual and cultural tradition, which in the 1870s had become the seat of the Archbishopric and, in 1827, university education was renewed here, while the more populous Land capital Brno, in the south, was an early pioneer in proto-industrialization, industrialization and technical education in the entire Habsburg monarchy. The Estates Francis Museum was relocated here in 1818, although it did not make any nation-oriented efforts, which were concentrated mainly in clerical seminaries. Moravian journalist and, later, deputy Jan Ohéral (1810–1868) considered Brno the capital of the land, although "in the heads of Moravians it was Olomouc that ruled." These two largest Moravian cities remained nationally hetero-geneous and bilingual throughout the 19th century. Until the dissolution of the monarchy, the town halls were controlled by the monarchists and then liberal German burghers. Czech patriotic circles often considered Brno a mere suburb of Vienna. Economically, it definitely came under the southern imperial centre, with which it was connected by a railway from July 1839, while it had to wait for a similar connection to Prague for another ten years.

This nationally mixed Czech-German environment provided a background for the devel-opment of Czech national awareness in the 1830s and 1840s, when Czech journals, as well as Czech scientific and literary works, were published. "Czech Moravia was woken up" first by patriots from Bohemia. Among them in particular František Matouš Klácel (1808–1882), František Cyril Kampelík (1805–1872) and Alois Vojtěch Šembera (1807–1882). They all worked as teachers and organized Czech national life (F. M. Klácel at the Brno Faculty of Arts, F. C. Kampelík in the clerical seminary in Brno and A. V. Šembera at the Department of Czech Language and Literature at Olomouc University, which was relocated to Brno in the 1840s). They became the "apostles" of cultural patriotism. Although Klácel's, Kampelík's and Šembera's work in Moravia was isolated, they represented one of the sources of the local national conscience. They all brought the national idea, which they had become acquainted with during their studies in Bohemia, to Moravia.

The development of national consciousness in Moravia required more than the effort of a few Czechs; a wider intellectual background was seriously needed. It was necessary to educate revivalists from Moravia, who would then spread the national consciousness throughout the Moravian countryside. The Czech national movement found these people among Moravian Catholic priests, educated mainly by František Sušil (1804–1868). A priest and collector of folk songs, F. Sušil spread national awareness in the conservative rural circles. He and his followers, however, represented the second, although main and specific national stream in Moravia, which came to be named after the missionaries Cyril and Methodius. It was formed thanks to a unique symbiosis of Czech national awareness (Sušil was unshakeably convinced that Moravians and Czechs should form a single nation), old Moravian Land patriotism promoted by the Land historiographer Antonín Boček (1802–1847), despite the occasional faking of history, and the omnipresent popular Catholic religiousness. The symbol that could unite the three central elements was the legendary pair of Slavic missionaries – Cyril and Methodius. The work of Sušil's followers and their organizational base – The Legacy of Ss Cyril and Methodius – occurred in the years after the mid-19th century. After that, Czech national consciousness in Moravia ceased to be, as had been the case of Bohemia thirty years earlier, a matter of a few intellectuals from Brno and Olomouc and started to spread around the Moravian countryside. Although society in Moravia was increasingly polarized into Czech and German parts, a majority of the Moravian population was indifferent to the national movement.

Bibliography

AGNEW, Hugh L.: *Origins of the Czech National Renascence*, Pittsburgh 1993.
BERÉNGER, Jean: *A History of the Habsburg Empire II, 1700–1918*, London 1997.
BIRKE, Ernst: *Frankreich und Ostmitteleuropa im 19. Jahrhundert. Beiträge zur Politik und Geschichte*, Köln–Graz 1960.
BIRKE, Ernst – OBERNDORFFER, Kurt (eds.): *Das böhmische Staatsrecht in der deutsch-tschechischen Auseinandersetzungen des 19. und 20. Jahrhunderts*, Marburg/Lahn 1960.
BOHMANN, Alfred: *Bevölkerungsbewegungen in Böhmen 1847–1947 mit besonderer Berücksichtigung der Entwicklung der nationalen Verhältnisse*, München 1958.
Böhmen im 19. Jahrhundert. Vom Klassizismus zur Moderne, ed. Ferdinand Seibt, München–Berlin–Frankfurt am Main 1995.
BOLDT, Frank: *Kultur und Staatlichkeit. Zur Genesis der modernen politischen Kultur in den böhmischen Ländern im Widerspiel von kulturellem und politischem Bewußtsein bei den böhmischen Tschechen und Deutschen*, Prag 1996.

BRANDL, Vincenc: *Josef Dobrovský*, Brno 1883.

Deutsche Geschichte im Osten Europas. Böhmen und Mähren, ed. Friedrich Prinz, Berlin 1993

Frankreich und die böhmischen Länder im 19. und 20. Jahrhundert. Beiträge zum französischen Einfluss in Ostmitteleuropa, ed. Ferdinand Seibt and Michael Neumüller, München 1990.

GOOD, David G.: *The Economic Rise of the Habsburg Empire 1750–1914*, Berkeley 1984.

HAMANN, Brigitte: *Die Habsburger*, Wien 1988.

HLAVAČKA, Milan: *Dějiny dopravy v období průmyslové revoluce*, Praha 1990.

HLAVAČKA, Milan: *Das böhmische Staatsrecht in der historischen Retroperspektive der letzten Jahrhunderte*, Etudes Danubiennes 10, 1994, pp. 77–94.

HROCH, Miroslav: *Europa der Nationen. Die moderne Nationsbildung im europäischen Vergleich*, Göttingen, 2005.

HROCH, Miroslav: *Na prahu národní existence. Touha a skutečnost*, Praha 1999.

HROCH, Miroslav: *V národním zájmu. Požadavky a cíle evropských národních hnutí devatenáctého století ve srovnávací perspektivě*, Praha 1999.

HROCH, Miroslav: *Social Preconditions of National Revival in Europe. A Comparative Analysis of the Social Composition of Patriotic Groups among the Smaller European Nations*, Cambridge 1985.

Intelectual and Social Development in the Habsburg Empire from Maria Theresia to World War I. Essays dedicated to Robert A. Kann. Ed. by Stanley B. Winters and Joseph Held. New York–London 1975.

JANÁK, Jan: *Dějiny Moravy III/1: Hospodářský rozmach Moravy 1740–1918*, Brno 1999.

JELAVICH, Barbara: *The Habsburg Empire in European Affairs 1814–1918*, Chicago 1969.

KANN, Robert A.: *Das Nationalitätenproblem in der Habsburgermonarchie*, I–II, Graz–Köln 1964.

KANN, Robert A.: *Werden und Zerfall des Habsburgerreiches*, Graz–Wien–Köln 1962.

KLÍMA, Arnošt: *Economy, Industry and Society in Bohemia in the 17th–19th Century*, Prague 1991.

KOČÍ, Josef: *České národní obrození*, Praha 1978.

KOHN, Hans: *Pan-Slavism: Its History and Ideology*, New York 1960.

KOMLOS, John: *The Habsburg Monarchy as a Customs Union. Economic Development in Austria-Hungary in the Nineteenth Century*, Princeton 1983.

KOŘALKA, Jiří: *František Palacký (1798–1876), der Historiker der Tschechen im österreichischen Vielvölkerstaat*, Wien 2007.

KOŘALKA, Jiří: *Tschechen im Habsburgerreich und in Europa 1815–1914. Sozialgeschichtliche Zusammenhänge der neuzeitlichen Nationsbildung und der Nationalitätenfrage in den böhmischen Ländern*, Wien–München 1991.

KROUPA, Jiří: *Alchymie štěstí. Pozdní osvícenství a moravská společnost*, Brno 1987.

KŘEN, Jan: *Konfliktgemeinschaft. Tschechen und Deutsche 1780–1918*, München 1996.

KUTNAR, František: *Obrozenecké vlastenectví a nacionalismus. Příspěvek k národnímu a společenskému obsahu češství doby obrozenecké*, Praha 2003.

LNĚNIČKOVÁ, Jitka: *České země v době předbřeznové, 1792–1848*, Praha 1999.

LORENZOVÁ, Helena: *Hra na krásný život. Estetika v českých zemích mezi léty 1760–1860*, Praha 2005.

LUTZ, Heinrich – RUMPLER, Helmut (eds.): *Österreich und deutsche Frage im 19. und 20. Jahrhundert. Probleme der politisch-staatlichen und soziokulturellen Differenzierung im deutschen Mitteleuropa*, München 1982.

MACARTNEY, Carlile A.: *The Habsburg Empire 1790–1918*, London–New York 1968–1969; 2nd edition 1971.

MACARTNEY, Carlile Aylmer: *The House of Austria: The Later Phase 1790–1918*, Edinburgh 1978.

MACURA, Vladimír: *Znamení zrodu. České obrození jako kulturní typ*, Praha 1983.

MACHAČOVÁ, Jana – MATĚJČEK, Jiří: *Nástin sociálního vývoje českých zemí 1781–1914*, Opava 2002.

MAJER, Jiří: *Kašpar Šternberk*, Praha 1997.

MAREK, Jaroslav: *Česká moderní kultura*, Praha 1998.

MAY, Arthur J.: *The Age of Metternich, 1814–1848*, New York–Chicago–San Francisco–Toronto–London 1963.

MELVILLE, Ralph: *Adel und Revolution in Böhmen. Strukturwandel von Herrschaft und Gesellschaft in Österreich um die Mitte des 19. Jahrhunderts*, Mainz 1998.

MOMMSEN, Hans – KOŘALKA, Jiří (eds.): *Ungleiche Nachbarn. Demokratische und nationale Emanzipation bei Deutschen, Tschechen und Slowaken (1815–1914)*, Essen 1993.

OKÁČ, Antonín: *Český sněm a vláda před březnem 1848. Kapitoly o jejich ústavních sporech*, Praha 1947.

OKEY, Robin: *The Habsburg Monarchy c. 1765–1918. From Enlightenment to Eclipse*, London 2001.

PURŠ, Jaroslav: *Průmyslová revoluce v českých zemích*, Praha 1960.

ŘEPA, Milan: *Moravané nebo Češi? (Vývoj národního vědomí na Moravě v 19. století)*, Brno 2001.

RUMPLER, Helmut: *Die österreichische Geschichte 1804–1914. Eine Chance für Mitteleuropa. Bürgerliche Emanzipation und Staatsverfall in der Habsburgermonarchie*, Wien 1997.

SANDGRUBER, Roman: *Österreichische Agrarstatistik 1750–1918*, Wien 1978.

SKED, Alan: *The Decline and Fall of the Habsburg Empire 1815–1918*, London–New York 1989.

ŠOLLE, Zdeněk: *Století české politiky*, Praha 1998.

ŠTAIF, Jiří: *Obezřetné elity: Česká společnost mezi tradicí a revolucí 1830–1851*, Praha 2005.

ŠVANKMAJER, Milan: *Čechy na sklonku napoleonských válek 1810–1815*, Praha 2004.

STECKL, Hannes: *Österreichs Aristokratie im Vormärz. Herrschaftsstil und Lebensformen der Fürstenhause Liechtenstein und Schwarzenberg*, Wien 1973.

TAPIÉ, Victor-Lucien: *The Rise and Fall of Habsburg Monarchy*, London 1971.

TAYLOR, A. J. P.: *The Habsburg Monarchy 1809–1918. A History of the Austrian Empire and Austria-Hungary*, London 1947; 2nd edition 1969.

The Czech Renascence of the Nineteenth Century. Essays Presented to Otakar Odložilík in Honour of His Seventieth Birthday. Ed. by Peter Brook a H. Gordon Skilling, Toronto and Buffalo 1970.

TIMMERMANN, Heiner (ed.): *Die Entstehung der Nationalbewegung in Europa 1750–1849*, Berlin 1993.

URBAN, Otto: *České a československé dějiny do roku 1918*, Praha 1991.

URBAN, Otto: *Kapitalismus a česká společnost. K otázkám formování české společnosti v 19. století*, Praha 1978.

WINTER, Eduard: *Romantismus, Restauration und Frühliberalismus im österreichischen Vormärz*, Wien 1968.

XII. Czechs during the Revolution and Neo-absolutism (1848–1860)

Mythologized revolution: A scene from the fighting during the Prague June uprising in 1848. Fighting between rebels and army outside the Charles Bridge Old-Town tower.

1 The Rise of the Nations in the Habsburg Monarchy and its Consequences

After Napoleon's defeat, the Habsburg monarchy had become, together with Russia and Prussia, the guardian of the European conservative order. No constitutional experiments were allowed in the monarchy and the government ruled on mechanically, as though by sheer force of habit, yet in an altogether absolutist manner. The liberal-leaning burghers had little influence over public matters. Among the main demands of the German societies in Austria was the mitigation of Viennese centralism. Many burghers and aristocrats also publicly called for the abolishment of the economically inefficient subject labour. Nationalist sentiment began to awaken in the Hungarian, south-Slavic and Bohemian-Moravian parts of the Habsburg monarchy, although they still lacked wider social support. In the early 1840s, Hungarian became an official language of the Hungarian Diet, alongside Latin. A movement striving to make Czech equal to German in both offices and higher education was getting stronger and there was also an effort to accentuate Bohemian statehood on the outside. Most of the vast empire's rural population, however, did not show any interest in politics and trusted implicitly the emperor and his clerks.

News of revolutionary events in Italy and France reached Vienna at the beginning of March 1848. On March 13, 1848, clashes between the town's population and the army claimed several lives. The revolutionary atmosphere in the capital forced the emperor to dismiss Chancellor Metternich, to establish new ministries and to promise to formulate a new constitution, to summon the Reichstag (Imperial Diet) and to resolve the subject labour problem. At the same time, press censorship was abolished and civil freedoms introduced. The Hungarian part of the empire, where a Hungarian government was formed with the emperor's permission, gained relative independence, while liberal and nationalist forces became active in the empire's other national societies. Revolution triumphed quickly and unexpectedly. The Habsburg monarchy, however, fell into a deep power and constitutional crisis as its integrity was violated in many ways.

The general enthusiasm which accompanied the newly won civil freedoms cooled to some extent when, in late April, the Viennese government passed a new constitution, valid for all territories but Hungary. This constitution, issued by imperial decree or "octroi," hence called octroyed, placed executive power in the hands of the ruler and ministers, who were responsible to the Reichstag. The Reichstag, the supreme legislative body, had two chambers. The House of Lords, with members appointed by the ruler, and the House of Deputies, with members decided according to election results, in which only wealthy citizens had the right to vote. Nevertheless, Viennese democrats, led by students who disagreed with this constitution, rebelled in May 1848, thus forcing the emperor to withdraw the constitution. The constitution was to be drafted by a one-chamber Reichstag, to be elected from the broader spectrum of men who had now been granted the right to participate. The second Viennese revolution achieved an important success. On May 17, 1848 the emperor fled the town for Innsbruck, where he stayed until August, and the Viennese government agreed that Austrian deputies should participate in the Frankfurt Diet, which focussed on the question of German unification and the potential annexation of the western segment of the Habsburg monarchy to the future united Germany.

Events in Prague were not as sweeping as those in Vienna. Spurred by radical democrats, Prague's burghers met on March 11, 1848 in the New Town's St Wenceslas Spa restaurant to compile a petition of liberal, national and constitutional demands that was to be signed by Prague's citizens and then taken to the emperor in Vienna. The Czech liberal burghers and the newly established St Wenceslas Committee did not want the Czech Lands to merge with the centrally administered empire, and they demanded more extensive autonomous administration within a federalized constitutional monarchy. In their other demands, such as abolishing the subject labour and serfdom, the Czech political spokesmen were in accord with the requirements of the Viennese revolution.

The emperor and his clerks were at first hesitant, however, in the Rescript, their reply to the second Prague petition from April 8, 1848, they accepted almost all the petition's demands. The Rescript proclaimed the equality of Czech and German in offices and promised to establish a Land government in Bohemia, and to summon the Land Diet, not based on Estates, but rather on the results of regular elections. The constitutional status of the Czech Lands within Austria was to be determined by the constitutional Reichstag. Land elections were organized by the National Committee, which came to life when prominent burghers and aristocrats joined the St Wenceslas Committee. The imperial rescript, which German historiography calls the Czech Charter, largely acceded to the Czech demands. Their demand for more control over the lands of the Bohemian Crown was, however, delegated to the future Reichstag as it was opposed by the Bohemian Germans and also, from mid-April 1848, by the Moravian Diet.

In the first revolutionary weeks, the German speaking population acted in accordance with the Czechs in an effort to attain some basic liberal demands (a new constitution, elections to the Reichstag and civil liberties). The mutual relationship between the German and Czech populations declined in April and May, 1848 when the Czechs, represented by František Palacký, refused to participate in German unification and boycotted the elections to the Frankfurt parliament. The new Czech representation, led by František Palacký,

František Augustine Brauner and František Ladislav Rieger, strove for the formation of a strong, federalized Austria and disagreed with the dissolution of the Czech Lands and Austria as a part of the German unification process. The Bohemian, Moravian and Silesian Germans, however, welcomed the possibility the revolution presented for the fast political unification of Germany, including the Czech Lands, and sent their representatives to the Frankfurt parliament.

Czech-German coexistence became even more complicated when a Slav congress, attended mainly by representatives of the Slavs living in the Habsburg monarchy, convened in Prague. The German population, among others, saw this as the counterbalance to the Frankfurt parliament. The Slav congress suffered from factionalism and in the course of its short convention only managed to draft *A Manifesto to the European Peoples*. The congress was an expression of Austroslavic sentiments among Slavs in the Habsburg monarchy. Austroslavism as a political viewpoint was shaped in the revolutionary year of 1848 and its central tenet was the conviction that the Slavs were the most numerous "nation" and the main pillar of the Habsburg monarchy. Austroslavic leanings can be traced back to the end of the 18th century, such as in Josef Dobrovský's speech before Emperor Leopold II in September 1791, or in the works of Count Leo Thun or Karel Havlíček from the pre-March period, where they recommended a more extensive cultural and economic co-operation among the Habsburg monarchy Slavs. In the revolutionary years of 1848–1849, Austroslavism, however, acquired its political dimension thanks to František Palacký, who linked the idea of closer Slavic co-operation to the federalist reconstruction of the monarchy in several documents (including *A Letter to Frankfurt*, published on April 11, 1848, in which he refused to participate in the Frankfurt unification parliament) and in his constitution draft. Later, particularly after the Austro-Hungarian Compromise, the Austroslavic idea started to fade away.

During the Slav congress, clashes between the army and radical Prague citizens, mainly students, erupted. Barricades appeared in Prague streets. The fiercest fighting took place on June 12–14 in Prague's Old and New Towns. These Prague Pentecost Riots were suppressed by the army of Prince Alfred Windischgrätz, the Land military commander, in under five days. The fights claimed several dozen lives and destroyed many buildings. General Windischgrätz then declared a state of siege. The National Committee and the Slav congress were dissolved, the Bohemian Diet was not summoned. The radicals' defeat prevented the Bohemian Kingdom from following the steps of the Hungarian revolution and demanding more extensive administrative independence for the country at the upcoming Land Diet. Because of Windischgrätz's soldiers and the Viennese government, the Bohemian Diet and the Bohemian Land government never convened during the revolution. The Reichstag thus remained the only legal political platform of Czech liberals. At the Reichstag, Czech deputies belonged the right wing, which pushed through the serfdom solution in the form of financial compensation and then ruled against co-operation with the Hungarian Diet.

The German press presented the Prague events as a Slavic conspiracy, which helped trigger the start of escalating tension between Czechs and Germans, particularly in Bohemia; the Czech representatives hated the Germans for their participation in the Frankfurt parliament and the German representatives despised the Czechs for summoning the Slav congress. This period was the source of strong mutual animosity between Czechs and Germans, which sprang from a fear that Austria's and Czech lands' constitutional future would be decided against the will of the opposite nation. The June armed uprising thwarted any of the liberal citizens' hopes for a common advance and a reasonable agreement. The counter-revolutionary powers, led by General Windischgrätz, achieved their first victory over the revolution.

In Hungary, the Land Diet was transformed into an Imperial Diet, which through the "April Laws" made a decision on the rather difficult questions of freeing the peasants, abolishing the tithe, introducing religious equality and regarding the new comitatus (county) administration. On April 10, 1848 the Diet was closed and left Prešpurk (now Bratislava) for good. The old Hungarian Kingdom was dead, and the new one had just been born from the constitution approved by the emperor. Deputies and ministers moved to Pest, where a new Hungarian Diet was opened on July 5, 1848. The Hungarians had gained exactly what other politically awakening national communities were demanding. Croat, Serbs, Slovaks and Romanians were calling for their political rights, threatening secession if their demands were not met. As a move against the overtly-independent Hungarian government, Vienna appointed Josips Jelačić, an unknown officer, to the position of the Croat Ban (Governor). When Jelačić refused to implement the April Laws in Croatia, the country verged on war. The Hungarian government started to build their own army, military administration and finances. This and the lynching of General Franz Lamberg, who was sent to Pest by the Viennese government, were the final steps in the rupture between the Hungarian government and Vienna. Lájos Batthyány's government resigned and a new one was assembled by Lájos Kossuth. Ban Jelačić and his Croat army crossed the river Dráva in mid-September; but his offensive was fought off by the hastily formed Hungarian army.

In June and July 1848, elections for the Reichstag took place. It was the first time in the history of the Habsburg monarchy that an assembly was formed not according to the Estates privileges, but based on free political elections. Liberals won in the towns, conservative candidates in the countryside, while the radicals suffered a crushing defeat. Elections in the monarchy's lands were based not on political, but on nationalist principle. This essential nationalist principle, which was of cardinal importance for the Habsburg monarchy in the ensuing decades, was here demonstrated for the first time.

The Reichstag, composed along national, rather than political, lines first met in the second half of July, 1848. After procedural matters, it progressed to the election of the constitutional committee, which was to draft a liberal constitution. Czech deputies František Palacký and František Ladislav Rieger were particularly active in working on the constitution. On July 26, Silesian deputy Hans Kudlich presented his proposal for the abolition of serfdom and subject labour. After heated debate, the deputies recognized the legitimacy of his proposal: the unfree peasant tied to the land could not enjoy constitutional liberties. After a lengthy and emotionally charged discussion, the Reichstag, with a narrow Slavic conservative majority, decided to abolish serfdom in exchange for a moderate, two-thirds compensation. The emperor, who returned from Innsbruck to Vienna in August, sanctioned abolishing serfdom and subject labour on September 7, 1848. This Viennese Reichstag ruling was successfully implemented in the early 1850s. The peasant thus became the first victor of the revolution. Having paid compensation, he could freely use the land he worked. The revolution in the town helped the countryside to resolve its social problem. The result, however, was the peasantry losing any interest in continuing the revolution.

Events in Hungary were the trigger for another riot organized by radicals in Vienna. The Hungarian Diet was preparing to draft a new constitution for the eastern part of the empire, including the south-Slavic and Romanian population, which would change considerably the existing constitutional framework of the monarchy. Croats, led by Josip Jelačić, who strove for a renewal of the ancient Croat Kingdom, rose against the formation of greater Hungary. The Viennese government decided to support Jelačić against the Hungarian government in Pest and sent military troops to his aid. Viennese democrats, who sympathized with the Hungarian revolution did not, however, allow the soldiers to leave for the Hungarian battle-field. Petty skirmishes with the departing soldiers grew into an uprising, which ended in bloodshed when suppressed by the combined power of Windischgrätz and Jelačić. Martial law was imposed on Vienna. Austrian Emperor Ferdinand I, who had returned to the town in August, found refuge in the Olomouc fortress. He dissolved the Reichstag in Vienna and summoned it in the Moravian town of Kroměříž (Kremsier). The defeat of the radical democratic forces in Vienna once again sent the revolution spinning downward.

The deputies convened again in the Kroměříž archiepiscopal chateau at the end of November to continue their work on the imperial constitution. Despite numerous disputes between the Slavic and German deputies concerning the future constitutional character of the empire, work progressed successfully and the constitution was to be ceremonially adopted at the beginning of March 1849. During work on the constitution, several serious problems appeared for the first time in the history of the Habsburg monarchy which were to accompany the empire to its end. First was the problem of the future constitutional empire's structure, as it was not easy to bring the principle of the lands' historical personalities together, while respecting the desires of the new national political elites. Kroměříž also saw the end of František Palacký's proposal; both future-oriented and, for his contemporaries, absolutely unacceptable; which over-rode the traditionally defined historical-political natures and replaced them with an ethnic administrative principle. In the end, the deputies were willing to respect the special status of Hungary and individual historical units to ensure that the final proposal could be realized using existing administrative means. Thus Moravian deputy Kajetán Mayer's proposal, confirming the existing development in that it preserved the individual historical lands, whose administration on the regional level was to be organized according the to the national principle, was adopted. As well as Land Diets, Regional Minor Diets were also to be formed, which would – for the first time – more distinctly reflect the ethnic structure of the territory on the political level. Equally delicate and sensitive was the constitutional confirmation of the emperor's power. Rieger's original proposal that the new constitution's first article opened in a manner similar to the

American constitution: that all power comes from the people and is executed by elected representatives, was not accepted due to pressure from the court, backed by an agreement from opportunistic deputies. The emperor was to remain untouchable and answerable to nobody during the existence of the empire and all future constitutions were to implicitly accept the principle of his only partially limited rule granted by divine right.

The new constitution was to be adopted during the Reichstag's plenary session, which was to be symbolically held on the day of the revolution's first anniversary. Austria was to become a constitutional monarchy with a two-chamber parliament. The constitution was to contain an extensive list of civil rights and freedoms. Its adoption by the Reichstag, however, did not take place due to a major change on the throne that occurred at the beginning of December 1848. The mentally ill Emperor Ferdinand I, compromised by the revolution, was replaced by the 18-year-old and very conservative Francis Joseph I, who decided to reform the old order in his empire and the powerful position of the Habsburg monarchy in Central Europe with the help of Prince Felix Schwarzenberg's new government. The government secretly drafted its own imperial constitution and did not allow the Reichstag to finish its liberal one. On March 7, 1849 the Reichstag in Kroměříž was dissolved by the army.

Most deputies left for their homes, as the Emperor wished in his manifesto, an action which closed one of the most remarkable periods of modern Habsburg history. Most of the parliament's conservative wing joined the new regime. The radicals, including Hans Kudlich, involved in the October Vienna events, chose emigration. The victorious counter-revolution acted very skillfully. The dissolution of the Kroměříž assembly was accompanied by explicit assurances to the rural population that the Reichstag's decision regarding the compensation for the subject labour and the abolishment of serfdom would take place as soon as possible. The urban population stayed calm because most of the liberal achievements of the revolution were confirmed in the "octroyed" constitution of March 4, 1849, approved by the ruler.

This new, so-called Stadion's constitution, whose force was suspended after fights in northern Italy and Hungary, had a calming effect on the wealthy population, who desired a speedy end to the period of revolutionary uncertainty. It was to be empire-wide with a strong ruler at the head. The emperor's sovereignty was strengthened by his veto power and by the House of Lords with veto power and extemporaneous sections. Apart from the Reichstag, it also listed the Reichsrat (Imperial Council) as the monarch's advisory board and mentioned the equality of all "peoples," known as the Volksstämme, in the empire. Throughout the existence of the Habsburg monarchy the emperor remained the untouchable head of the empire, answerable to no one. All future constitutions tacitly accepted the principle of the partially limited self-government of the emperor installed by divine right. The Stadion's octroyed constitution was formally adopted, but because of the continuing wars it never came into effect. Only a few contemporaries, such as journalist Karel Havlíček, understood that it was merely a well-planned tactical move of the burgeoning counter-revolution, rather than a serious attempt to implement constitutionalism and that the short constitutional period, in fact without a constitution, was over.

318

In spring 1849, Marshal Jan Josef Václav Radecký defeated the army of the Sardinian king in Lombardy and gradually managed to re-annex northern Italy into the Habsburg monarchy. Most Austrian deputies left the Frankfurt parliament after the decision to offer the Holy Roman Crown to Prussian King Frederick William IV was made. Everything seemed to return to their pre-revolutionary state. To make sure that the revolution was over in the Habsburg monarchy, the Hungarian revolutionary army had to be defeated, which was achieved by the Austrian and Russian armies in August 1849. With the help of military terror, Hungary was annexed to the centrally administered monarchy. The emperor was gradually returning to the absolute government.

The revolution in Austria was crushed by the army. Unlike Western European countries, the Habsburg monarchy did not become a constitutional monarchy. The Czech Lands remained part of a large centralized empire. Their distinctiveness was, in the coming decade, even more suppressed than at the time of Franciscan-Metternich absolutism. Despite this, the revolution had left a permanent trace. Serfdom was abolished and the rural population was released from feudal burdens, including the subject labour. The peasant became the real owner of the land he worked. The landlords, particularly the nobility, lost their privileges and the manorial administrative system was replaced by a system of state administration, including the consistent equality of citizens before the law. Jewish emancipation enabled their full integration into the society and accelerated their assimilation both culturally and nationally. In the economic sphere, the guilds were dissolved, the customs borders between the Austrian and Hungarian parts of the monarchy were abolished and the implemented liberal (free) economic policy had opened the way for the capitalist transformation of the economy and the whole of society.

2 The Birth of Czech Political Representation

The years 1848 and 1849 were a true milestone in the history of the Czech Lands. The population was confronted with many novelties, among them the constitution, elections to Land Diets, the Frankfurt National Assembly and the Viennese Reichstag, which were preceded, for the first time in history, by drawing up lists of candidates, political agitation and heated debates; for the first time, rules of procedure in elections were tried; for the first time there was a need for the political "education" of the general population; for the first time, political programmes were presented at public gatherings; for the first time, the elected deputies discussed the standing rules of the chamber, including the language of debates, chamber protocols and determining the method of voting to indisputably push through the decision-making principle by majority. For the first time, chamber debate duels were held, in which not only preparedness and higher intellect, but also the ability to accommodate the mentality, attitudes and, last but not least, the nationalist sentiments of the voters were to determine the winner. In 1848, for the first time in the Czech Lands, we observe the phenomenon of public opinion in conflict with the "divine" authority of the emperor. For the first time in the history of the Czech Lands, the deputies could not only make laws, but through their behaviour and actions could also lay out the foundations of the political culture.

The years 1848 and 1849 are inseparably linked to the abolishment of serfdom and the patrimonial system, which was replaced by state bureaucratic administration, a liberal economic system and the rise of political journalism, and the major alienation between Czechs and Germans due to different ideas concerning the constitutional and national future. The mid-19th century revolution used to be labelled as incomplete, half-hearted and even defeated. While it is true that its aims were not achieved, what survived the revolution and mainly what was started can be called impressive, as Central-European nations still draw from this intellectual, political and practical heritage.

The mid-19th century revolution began the political refinement process of Czech and German society in the Czech Lands. The main political current of the time was liberalism, which furthered and promoted constitutionalism. Its bearer was the first Czech political burgher representation, inseparably linked with František Palacký, František Ladislav Rieger, František Augustin Brauner, Alois Pravoslav Trojan, Adolf Maria Pinkas and Karel Havlíček Borovský. Their political platform was the semi-legal St Wenceslas Committee, later thanks to the decree from the ruler of April 8, 1848, the legal National Committee and finally, after the June Prague riots, the Viennese and Kroměříž Reichstags. During the revolution, a new Bohemian Diet was not constituted, which Czech liberals considered the greatest political tragedy of the revolutionary year. In Moravia, on the other hand, the old Estates Diet was transformed into a regular Land Diet after the May elections, in which about 20 per cent of the mandates were held by peasants. This "peasant" Moravian Diet was the first in the empire to suspend subject labour. An expanded Silesian Diet convened in Opava. The Reichstag in Vienna was dominated by the future middle class, and was made up of clerks, clergy, writers, doctors, professor, brewers and millers.

The diet and parliamentary argumentation and tense political fights endowed prominent political authorities with moral credit. In the Czech Lands, this was represented by Palacký, Rieger and Brauner, along with the first elected Prague mayor and the second president of the Reichstag, Antonín Strobach, Moravians Alois Pražák and Josef Feifalík, and their German opponents Ludwig von Löhner, Hans Kudlich and the centrist Kajetán Mayer, whose draft of the imperial constitution was ultimately more acceptable for the deputies than Palacký's clearly ethnocentric and autonomist concept of empire administration. The Reichstag saw political fights over each section of the future constitution between the Slavic right and the German left, and occasionally even general moves against imperial authoritarianism. The priority of nationalist attitudes clearly prevailed over generally liberal proclamations. At the end of 1848, the first deputy clubs were spontaneously formed and demonstrated a high degree of inner discipline, and the majority of ethnically Czech and Moravian deputies joined the Slavic club of the Reichstag.

Another political current, which did not become manifest until the revolution, was political radicalism, which, with little exaggeration, can be called democratic. The radical democratic opinions and activities are linked primarily to the Prague June riots of 1848 and the "May Conspiracy" of the following year. The conspiracy, which was uncovered by the police during the night of May 9/10, 1849, was organized by young people attracted by the revolutionary visionarism of Russian Mikhail Alexandrovich Bakunin. Among them were the young student Josef Václav Frič, later the most famous Czech emigré, writer Karel Sabina, Smetana's librettist and later the most famous Czech informer in the 19th century, and the future first chairman of the National Liberal Party (Young Czech) (*Národní strana svobodomyslná*) Karel Sladkovský. These radicals genuinely believed that after the dissolution of the Kroměříž parliament at the beginning of March 1849, the revolution went into decline and that the town society had started to succumb to political apathy and too soon yielded to the renewing forces of order and reaction. The police raids and adamant sentences handed down to the conspirators had one common goal: to stifle at the very beginning any conspiracy movements aiming to push through the republican ideals and to deter most of the Czech and German radical society members.

The radical democrats' zeal for a revolutionary act sharply contrasted with the political opportunism of older generations, and they felt that the new national leaders did not speak for them. They instinctively hated these men instead, as was the case of the 18-year-old Josef Václav Frič and the 50-year-old František Palacký, or the journalists and writers Karel Sabina and Karel Havlíček. Everybody learned their own political lesson in the revolutionary years. Among conservatives, dislike for moving masses, barricades and opening politics to the unprivileged classes became stronger. The liberal wanted at all costs to maintain a legal political foundation, guaranteed by the constitution and the emperor, and to place political rights only in the hands of wealthy citizens. The radical dreamed of equal chances for all and of the rapid transformation of society. In revolutionary times, these ideas met and clashed on everyday basis.

The majority finally prevailed in the voices of conservative and liberal citizens. The radicals ended up a minority and became intellectually defensive. They could not push through their ideas for an ideal society in a peaceful and parliamentary manner, they therefore resorted to another method – labelled subversive, revolutionary, conspiring and carbonari. Through their impetuous action, the "little party of café politicians," the radicals, as talented journalist Karel Havlíček suspected, provided a pretext for the Viennese government to further limit liberal freedoms, brought about by the fading revolution and guaranteed by the octroyed constitution from March 4, 1849.

The May Conspiracy provided a suitable pretext for the government to set an example in the punishment of the radicals to deter the rest of the liberal population. In the 1850s, the desired political silence fell upon the Czech Lands. Although the May uprising did not really take place, today we can notice one important fact – for the last time in the Bohemian history Czechs and Germans co-operated in its preparations to achieve the unclear at the time, but still attractive, republican ideal.

3 Two Faces of the Neo-absolutism

The new absolutism of the 1850s differed from the old, pre-March version associated with Metternich. It only partially conserved society and the only similarity with the pre-March period was the appearance – a formally absolute government over a voluntarily or forcibly apolitical society. In other respects, even in those concerning the political repression, it was very dynamic and energetic. It did not go against the "modernization" consequences of the revolution. The compensation for subject labour and the formation of a new administrative system on the lowest level, which replaced the former patrimonial system, soon ended in success. In its initial stages, the new regime intended to make use of strong communities, as was demonstrated in March 1849 in Stadion's law concerning local self-government. State bureaucracy, which the nobility considered the second real winner of the revolution, next to the peasantry, dominated both the sphere of genuine power and many other spheres in social life.

The political system of an absolute monarchy was visibly renewed through the "New Year's Eve's Patent" from the end of 1851. The sovereign status of the young emperor was ensured not only by the formal withdrawal of the March octroyed constitution and the shift of responsibilities from parliamentary ministers to the ruler, but also by the unexpected death of the outspoken Prime Minister, Prince Felix Schwarzenberg, in April 1852. Francis Joseph I started ignoring the opinions of even the "older" noblemen and bureaucrats, and, vehemently supported by his mother Archduchess Sophia, he believed in his absolute powers and the favour of divine Providence. This short absolute and seemingly very successful period in the emperor's life was symbolically framed by an unsuccessful assassination attempt by a Hungarian patriot and by his marriage to the intelligent and indomitable Elizabeth of Bavaria. Although blood connection between the Habsburgs and Wittelsbachs brought peace to the Habsburg-Lorraine house for a few years after Crown Prince Rudolf was born, it did not bring peace to the emperor's mind and soul. His wife Elizabeth could not bear the burden of the imperial majesty.

In the meantime, hard-working and self-confident bureaucrats, such as Franz Stadion, Alexander Bach, Karl Ludwig Bruck, Leo Thun, Josef Alexandr Helfert and Karl Kübeck, thoroughly reformed the empire's domestic system, including the police, the army, education and the entire economy. Apart from the "municipal" police, a mobile gendarmerie was formed, lead by the two-metre-tall General Superintendent Johann von Kempen, to ensure "safety in the countryside." Secondary and higher education was reformed along the lines of the Prussian model. The relationship between the throne and the Catholic church was also redefined. The ruler and the Minister for Cult and Education, Count Leo Thun-Hohenstein, met the demands of the Catholic clergy and abolished the Josephine *placetum regium*, which restrained the uncontrolled contact between the church and the public, returned marriage administration to religious control and subordinated schools to intensive religious oversight. The new Viennese Cardinal, Othmar von Rauscher, negotiated a "concordat" with the papal curia, which was published in an imperial patent on November 23, 1855, and which legally secured the above-mentioned, to the dislike of the liberal townspeople. The concordat was a triumph of clerical and conservative forces. Society found itself under double control: its acts were guarded by Bach's and Kempen's police and the gendarmerie, while its ideas were guarded by the clergy through their pulpits, confessions and catechism.

One of the weaknesses of neo-absolutism was finance. Even Finance Minister Karl Ludwig von Bruck's daring juggling of the state budget eventually failed. In the mid 1850s, due to costly domestic administration reforms, ambitious construction of the railway and telegraph along with rash foreign-policy decisions, the state treasury faced bankruptcy several times, though this was averted by public loans from the loyal population.

The initial foreign-politics triumphs, manifested in November 1850 through the "Olomouc humiliation of Prussia" and by the formal return of Austria to the head of the German Confederation, were completely devalued by the Austrian "ungrateful" attitude towards Russia during the Crimean War. International isolation was evident for the first time during the fateful Austro-Sardinian conflict in 1859. Austrian diplomacy did not suspect that Sardinia's build up of arms was an attempt to provoke Austria to wage war. In April 1859, Austria issued an ultimatum, which demanded an immediate cease to militarization. Sardinia did not comply and the self-confident Austrian army crossed the border, convinced of an easy victory on the Lombardy battlefield, as in the times of the recently deceased Marshal Radecký. As Emperor Francis Joseph I was formally the attacker, he could not claim support from the German Confederation countries. On the other hand, Sardinian King Victor Emmanuel II secured the help of the French Emperor Napoleon III in advance. The penultimate offensive on the Apennine Peninsula ended in fiasco for the Habsburg monarchy. After a battle without a winner near Magenta, north of Milan, on June 4, the Austrian army suffered an outright defeat in a gory battle near Solferino on June 24, 1859. Emperor Francis Joseph I willingly agreed to French mediation and, on July 11, 1859 signed a truce in Villafranca, which was ratified in Zurich. The Habsburg monarchy thus lost not only Lombardy, but also its apparent domestic peace. It was the beginning of a revolutionary top-down period, in which not only the economy, but also the entire political system, was to be liberalized.

In the period of Bach absolutism, Czech liberal politics lost its legal platform. The liberal opposition press was silenced and all political and cultural activities were systematically repressed through informing, censorship and denunciation. The Ministry of the Interior, presided over by Alexander Bach, was a perfect centralized machine, which relied on "Germanness." The emphasis on the empire's political and ideological unity caused a fear of Germanization among the non-German peoples. One exception were the educational reforms brought in by Minister Count Leo Thun, who increased the number of Czech general secondary schools – *Gymnasia*, "Real" *Gymnasia* and business academies in Bohemia and Moravia. The result of political inactivity was the rapid break-up of the national movement and a drop in Czech political self-confidence.

Most Czech liberals, if they did not join the governmental services as did those like František Augustin Brauner and Václav Vladivoj Tomek, withdrew from political life and chose emigration, as did František Ladislav Rieger, or a return to their professional activities. The only person who did not withdraw from his political and moral principles and who, even after the unsuccessful May Conspiracy, did not lose political optimism was journalist Karel Havlíček Borovský. His National Newspaper (*Národní noviny*), which had a considerable effect on public opinion in Bohemia, persistently took issue with the government, mainly in questions of domestic administration, educational and ecclesiastical policies. At the end of 1849, at the time Bach's ministry issued centralized Land ordinances, František Palacký published his article *On the centralization and national equality in Austria* in the National Newspaper. The article contained a proposal for a radical revision of the octroyed constitution, promoting his earlier concept of ethnic federalism. The article's publication was immediately followed by the newspaper's ban. After many attacks against him, František Palacký gave up all political activities in January 1850.

Apart from Havlíček's and Palacký's national liberal movement, a group of moderate Austria-oriented Prague liberals around Adolf Maria Pinkas and Anton Springer rose to prominence in May 1849. They started to publish a German magazine *Union*, which intentionally went against Palacký's ethno-federalist break-up of the Austrian empire. The Union was based on the March octroyed constitution and strove for co-operation with the government. However, even this liberal platform was unacceptable for the ruling faction and *Union* soon went out of publication. Only the conservative "Thun platform" (named after the Minister of Cult and Education, Czech aristocrat Leo Thun) was tolerated, which, managed by Václav Vladivoj Tomek and Hermenegild and Josef Jireček and in co-operation with its Prague supporters Pavel Josef Šafařík, František Ladislav Čelakovský and Karel Jaromír Erben, published the Viennese Daily *(Vídeňský denník)*. This national right wing co-operated with the government on deadening the overtly liberal movement, participated in the removal of František Palacký from the board of the Patriotic Museum and tacitly approved the excommunication of Augustin Smetana, the former liberal dean of Prague's Faculty of Arts, from the Catholic church.

All political activities ceased in 1851 when a Vienna-oriented party won the Prague local elections, although it gained three times fewer votes, and when Havlíček's last attempt to renew political journalism outside Prague failed. His new newspaper, the weekly Slav *(Slovan)*, published from May 1850 in Kutná Hora, was banned in August 1851 after two warnings from the government. By this time, most periodicals had lost their political content. Karel Havlíček, indicted for his journalist activities, managed to defend himself twice in court. He was, nevertheless, secretly deported to the Tyrol town of Brixen in December 1851. Havlíček's internment symbolically lead to the silencing of Czech liberals for many years.

4 Neo-absolutist Economic Policy

The transformation of the monarchy's economic and business climate in the 1850s was deep. Although the last epicentres of the revolution were stifled by the army in summer 1849, the process of economic development did not stop. On the contrary, the political reaction, which quickly reinforced its foreign and domestic status, paid great attention to economic questions. The loosening of various administrative and regulatory anachronisms from the pre-March era paved the way for rapid capitalist industrialization. Political reaction implemented these measures without making any political concessions to the defeated opponent, knowing that active reform of the economic policy would, to some extent, blunt the demands for political power raised by the liberal urban population.

The feverish reform of economic policy under neo-absolutism had grand political goals. Economic prosperity was to contribute to further the domestic integration of the huge territory. First, the special political and economic status of Hungary was to be eliminated while strengthening Austrian positions in the German and north-Italian area and in the Balkans. In a short period of time, "the grave-diggers of the revolution" dealt with and managed to solve the social problems in the countryside and, in the spirit of the period, liberal economic theories abolished domestic customs borders, and loosened trade, customs and business policy. They created a qualitatively new banking and loans system, a necessary condition for getting sweeping business activities under way.

The lack of cheap business loans was, before 1848, an object of criticism in trade and business circles, and it was also one of the causes of the relatively slow pace of industrialization and urbanization. To change this situation more radically, to transform existing banks into real financial institutions supporting business activities, it was necessary that they ceased to be mere state creditors and, at the same time, that they spread their activities from the empire's centre to other provinces. If the ambitious post-revolution state wanted to fulfil its domestic and foreign goals, it had to intentionally mobilize individual forces and offer them legal protection. That, however, meant that it gradually lost track of financial, economic and – eventually – social processes in society, thanks to which it could focus on domestic administration reforms and demanding foreign ambitions.

The first breakthrough in the pre-March banking and financial system was establishing the Lower-Austria Discount Bank in autumn 1853. A truly generous capitalist banking enterprise, which was to procure and accumulate business capital, was the establishment of the Credit Institute in Vienna (Österreichische Credit-Anstalt für Handel und Gewerbe) in November 1855. The Credit Institute was organized along similar lines to French and German institutions as a joint-stock company, and had an extensive capital of 60 million gulden of the day's currency. The founding members were Viennese bankers and entrepreneurs, as well as Czech aristocrats, who gained huge sums of money as compensations for subject labour. The Credit Institute was truly the first Austrian bank, which got rid of the traditionally reserved attitude of industrial, transportation, business and agricultural enterprises and started to actively intervene in the empire's economic life. In the mid-1850s, the Austrian business world believed that the key to cheap loans had been found.

Along with creating a modern credit system and developing joint-stock businesses, the neo-absolute state adopted many other economic measures, mainly through the Ministry of Finance, presided over by the German Protestant Karl Ludwig von Bruck, which facilitated many kinds of business activities. At the very beginning of the 1850s, internal

Hungarian-Austrian customs borders were abolished, business and trade chambers as semi-official professional organizations of entrepreneurs and traders were established in all regions and had a major influence on creating economic legislation. At the same time, the state railways and mining property in Banat and north Moravia were sold and preparations for publishing a new trade code, which replaced all existing economic rules and laws, commenced.

The new Trade Code of 1859 was a total revolution in the world of small and medium enterprises. It heralded an era of real economic liberalism, with all its pros and cons. Everybody who paid the trade tax had access to all trades. Everybody was also guaranteed freedom of production and sales and the possibility to employ a work force and to accumulate capital without any limitations. The state confined itself to being the issuer of trade licences. It did not control entrepreneurial activities of individuals and companies, and it also disregarded relationships in the job market. The state was not yet interested in the social dimension of capitalist enterprises, nor could it yet comprehend such a concept. The social question came to the fore much later – in the mid-1880s – during a completely different political and economic situation.

The new Business Code of 1862, like the Trade Code, promulgated unlimited entrepreneurial freedom. The business protectionism of the domestic market was replaced by moderately regulated liberalism. The result of these radical business-political measures, including the loosening of market relations in the rural areas in the 1860s, was a completely transformed business climate, particularly in the western part of the empire. The "release" of the peasantry and a formation of a new state administration at the lowest levels were unprecedented and financially extremely demanding operations. They considerably contributed to the formation of the general social and economic environment. The entrepreneurial lethargy of the pre-March era was replaced, particularly in the mid-1850s, by feverish capitalist activities. The 1850s witnessed realignment with what had been neglected in the pre-March period. However, the difference between this time and the following, truly liberal, decade lay in the fact that the legal economic foundation of the new society in the neo-absolutist period was formed in a deep political silence, without the co-operation of those social strata that were directly affected by the reforms.

The Czech Lands profited considerably from the transformed economic and business climate. The wealthy burghers and in particular the nobility, who gained large sums of money in compensation for subject labour and serfdom, cast aside their previous entrepreneurial hesitations and plunged into the often risky establishment of industrial and transport joint-stock companies. For the first time, large and small entrepreneurs gained influential professional representation in business and trade chambers and their decisions were respected by all, including the central government. It was the time of the first major boom of coal mining in the north of Bohemia, the Kladno and Brno regions, and in north Moravia. The 1850s witnessed the modernization of mining technologies and these regions' connections to river ports and to large cities through a network of "coal railways." In the 1850s, the longer Prague-Dresden, Pardubice-Liberec and Czech Western Railroads (from

Prague to Plzeň and further to the Bavarian border) were constructed, as well as the shorter Kladno-Kralupy, Teplice-Ústí nad Labem, Rosice-Brno coal railways and a thick network of Ostrava mining railways. For many years, these railways solved the energy crisis caused in the preceding decades by the felling of woods around large Bohemian and Moravian towns. Large metallurgical companies and ironworks were established in the vicinity of the mines (notably the Prague Iron Company in Kladno and the Mining and Metallurgical Company in the Ostrava region), which used modern technologies (coking and puddling).

The construction of the railway system and the influx of the rural population into the cities and new industrial areas around Prague, Liberec, Teplice, Plzeň, Brno and Ostrava were accompanied by a boom in the construction industry, textile production, machinery production and agricultural industry. This period saw the transformation of the Czech Lands into the energy, iron, machinery and food base of the Habsburg monarchy.

Bibliography

1848/49. Revolutionen in Ostmitteleuropa, München 1996.
BRANDT, Harm-Hinrich: *Der österreichische Neoabsolutismus. Staatsfinanzen und Politik 1848–1860*, I–II, Göttingen 1978.
ČERNÝ, Jan M.: *Boj za právo*. Sborník aktů politických u věcech státu a národa českého od roku 1848, I–II, Praha 1893; 2nd edition Praha 2007.
Český liberalismus. Texty a osobnosti, eds. Milan Znoj, Jan Havránek, Martin Sekera, Praha 1995.
HLAVAČKA, Milan: *Böhmen und die Habsburgermonarchie im Revolutionsjahr 1848/1849*, in: 1848 – Revolution in Europa. Verlauf, politische Programme, Folgen und Wirkungen, ed. Heiner Timmermann, Berlin 1998, pp. 199–208.
KAZBUNDA, Karel: *České hnutí roku 1848*, Praha 1929.
KISZLING, Rudolf: *Die Revolution im Kaisertum Österreich 1848–1849*, I–II, Wien 1948.
KLÍMA, Arnošt: *Češi a Němci v revoluci 1848–1849*, Praha, 1988, 2nd edition 1994.
KLÍMA, Arnošt: *Revoluce 1848 v českých zemích*, Praha 1974.
KOLEJKA, Josef: *Národy habsburské monarchie v revoluci 1848–1849*, Praha 1989.
KOLMER, Gustav: *Parlament und Verfassung in Oesterreich I–VIII*, Wien–Leipzig 1902–1906.
KOŘALKA, Jiří: *Prag – Frankfurt im Frühjahr 1848. Österreich zwischen Grossdeutschtum und Austroslawismus*, in: Heinrich Lutz – Helmut Rumpler (eds.), Österreich und die deutsche Frage im 19. Jahrhundert. Probleme der politisch-staatlichen und soziokulturellen Differenzierung im deutschen Mitteleuropa, Wien 1982, pp. 117–139.
KOŘALKA, Jiří: *Tschechen im Habsburgerreich und in Europa 1815–1914. Sozialgeschichtliche Zusammenhänge der neuzeitlichen Nationsbildung und der Nationalitätenfrage in den böhmischen Ländern*, Wien–München 1991.
KŘEN, Jan: *Konfliktgemeinschaft. Tschechen und Deutsche 1780–1918*, München 1996.
MACURA, Vladimír: *Znamení zrodu. České obrození jako kulturní typ*, Praha 1983.
MATTUSCH, Rudolf: *Geistige und soziale Voraussetzungen der nationalen Wiedergeburt in Böhmen vor 1848*, Bohemia. Jahrbuch des Collegium Carolinum 14, 1973, pp. 155–178.
MELVILLE, Ralph: *Adel und Revolution in Böhmen. Strukturwandel von Herrschaft und Gesellschaft in Österreich um die Mitte des 19. Jahrhunderts*, Mainz 1998.
PECH, Stanley Z.: *The Czech Revolution of 1848*, Chapel Hill, North Carolina 1969.
POLIŠENSKÝ, Josef: *Aristocrats and the Crowd in the Year 1848*, New York 1980.
POLIŠENSKÝ, Josef: *Revoluce a kontrarevoluce v Rakousku*, Praha 1975.
PRINZ, Friedrich: *Prag und Wien 1848. Probleme der nationalen und sozialen Revolution im Spiegel der Wiener Ministerratsprotokolle*, München 1968.
PRINZ, Friedrich: *Die Sudetendeutschen im Frankfurter Parlament*, München 1963.
REDLICH, Josef: *Kaiser Franz Joseph von Österreich*, Berlin 1929.

REDLICH, Josef: *Das österreichische Staats- und Reichsproblem. Geschichtliche Darstellung der inneren Politik der habsburgischen Monarchie von 1848 bis zum Untergang des Reiches*, I–II, Wien 1920–1926.

ROUBÍK, František: *Český rok 1848*, Praha 1948.

SAK, Robert: *Rieger: Příběh Čecha devatenáctého věku*, Semily 1993.

ŠTAIF, Jiří: *Revoluční léta 1848 a 1849 a české země*, Praha 1990.

TIMMERMANN, Heiner (ed.): *Die Entstehung der Nationalbewegung in Europa 1750–1849*, Berlin 1993.

TIMMERMANN, Heiner (ed.): *1848: Revolution in Europa. Verlauf, politische Programme, Folgen und Wirkungen*, Berlin 1999.

TOBOLKA, Zdeněk Václav: *Počátky konstitučního života v Čechách*, Praha 1898.

TOUŽIMSKÝ, Josef J.: *Na úsvitě nové doby. Dějiny roku 1848 v zemích českých*, Praha 1898.

TRAPL, Miloslav: *České národní obrození na Moravě v době předbřeznové a v revolučních letech 1848–1849*, Brno 1977.

URBAN, Otto: *Die tschechische Gesellschaft 1848–1918*, I–II, Wien–Köln–Weimar 1994.

WINTER, Eduard: *Revolution, Neoabsolutismus und Liberalismus in der Donaumonarchie*, Wien 1969.

ŽÁČEK, Václav: *Slovanský sjezd v Praze v roce 1848*, Praha 1958.

MILAN HLAVAČKA

XIII. The Definition of Czech National Society during the Period of Liberalism and Nationalism (1860–1914)

Textile factories of Mauthner company in Náchod in the 1890s. Woolen cloth production and later linen production were traditional branches of artisanal and factory production in the Czech Lands in the Middle Ages and Early Modern Era. From the 19th century it became one of the main industrial branches.

1 The Renewal of Constitutional Life and Struggles for State Rights

The neo-absolute regime's gradual thawing following the Austrian army's defeat in the war with Sardinia and France in 1859 was an impulse for reviving the political activities of the people living under the Habsburg monarchy. The first expression of the regime's gradual transformation was the summoning of the extended Reichsrat by Emperor Francis Joseph I in March 1860. The Reichsrat, composed of representatives of the bureaucracy, aristocracy and burghers, was to evaluate financial propositions necessary for the stabilization of the state economy affected by the war. The Reichsrators mostly criticized the existing absolute system and concluded that the empire's domestic situation had to be reformed.

The Czechs did not have their representatives in the Reichsrat, though even the Czech nation's leaders considered further developmental prospects of the monarchy and their nation. Among the Czech political representation were personalities who enjoyed great authority: in Bohemia, historian František Palacký and lawyer František Ladislav Rieger; in Moravia, attorney-at-law Alois Pražák. Rieger was at the centre of the National Party's gradual formation, organized on a liberal basis, which soon established itself as a recognized voice of the entire nation.

Rieger was aware of the need to unify the national forces around a common political agenda. He initiated the foundation of a political newspaper, published in Czech, which was to help spread national ideologies. In June 1860, he presented a memorandum to the emperor asking for a press licence. He demanded national and linguistic equality for the Czech nation, in which he included the Slovaks. In the accord with the natural right, Rieger demanded a political representation for the Czechoslovak nation. He also insisted on the principle of national equality in secondary education, asked for understanding regarding Czech cultural institutions (the National Theatre, the Museum of the Kingdom of Bohemia and Matice česká publishing house) and for the proper place of the Czech language in courts and state offices. The National Paper *(Národní listy)* came into publication in 1861, and under editor Julius Grégr, it became the best and most influential Czech newspaper for decades.

The Reichsrat's uniform opinion concerning the necessity of introducing a constitutional system to the monarchy moved Emperor Francis Joseph I to issue the "October Diploma" on October 20, 1860, which promised the summoning of both Land Diets and the Reichstag. As a concession to the Hungarian opposition it renewed the Hungarian Court Councilor's office, with the councilor becoming a member of the government. It also abolished the Ministries of the Interior, Justice, and Cult and Education. Their agenda was transferred to a new state ministry, presided over by Agenor Gołuchowski, who was charged with drafting Land ordinances for all the lands. Czechs welcomed the October Diploma as they were satisfied by the promise that the historical traditions of individual nations and lands would be taken into account. However, the opposition, consisting of various ideological streams, criticized it. The Hungarian nobility demanded full autonomy, while the Viennese burghers requested a liberal constitution.

The German liberals' opposition bore fruit – Gołuchowski was dismissed and replaced by Anton Schmerling, whose main task was fulfilling the October Diploma. Following his proposal, the emperor issued a set of election rules for Land Diets and the Reichsrat, which formed the "February Patent". The Reichsrat was now bicameral, consisting of the House of Lords and House of Deputies. Membership in the House of Lords was granted by the emperor to the archdukes of the ruling house, leading church dignitaries, as a hereditary right to high aristocracy members, and as life peerages to "excellent men of merit for the state, church, science and arts."Members of the House of Deputies were elected by Land Diets. The House of Deputies was to have 343 member, of whom 203 were from the western (later Cisletihan) part of the monarchy.

All Land councils were formed on a uniform basis. Schmerling divided voters into three election curiae (landowners, countryside community, town community). Suffrage was limited by property and literacy criteria to a narrow stratum of the male population. Electoral districts were constructed in favour of the German population. In the Bohemian and Moravian Diets, the landowners held the key position, as neither Czech nor German citizens' deputies could gain a majority by themselves. This was the main intention of Schmerling's election system, as in an environment of several dozens or hundreds of traditionally loyal noble voters, it was not difficult to win over the landowners' curia. In Bohemia, this system worked almost perfectly as landowners voted in a single electoral district, so the majority of a single vote would be decisive. As a result, the Czech complaints mainly concerned the system, because the Czech nation, which had a majority in Bohemia and Moravia, was often doomed to minority status in the Diet.

Business and trade chambers gained not only economic autonomous rights, but also the right to participate in Land Diets. The German industrial bourgeoisie controlled all chambers in Bohemia until 1883–1884, when Taaffe's government changed the election system, which provided the opportunity for a Czech victory in the business and trade chambers in České Budějovice, Plzeň and Prague, while the chambers in Cheb and Liberec remained under German control. In Moravia, however, Czechs did not manage to assert themselves in these self-governing institutions.

The structure of Czech political representation, and principally the question of engaging the nobility in the struggle for national rights, played an important role in the negotiations concerning the favourable legal status of the Czech nation in the Habsburg monarchy, as Schmerling's system granted the nobility the crucial position. Leading burgher politicians realized this and sought to engage the Czech Lands' nobility in nationally-motivated activities. In 1861, Rieger agreed with the leader of Czech historical nobility, Jindřich Jaroslav Clam-Martinitz, on co-operation based on the theory of Bohemian state law. It was centred around the claim that the historical Bohemian Kingdom had never ceased to exist and that its fate should be determined in a mutual accord by the ruler and elected representatives of the Czech political nation. The Czech historical nobility, however, limited its efforts to the struggle for the rights of the Bohemian Kingdom (that is, only Bohemia). Czech burgher politicians, on the other hand, emphasized that the Bohemian Kingdom, called the Bohemian Crown, always consisted of Bohemia, Moravia and Silesia. Both parties took the Hungarian nobility as their model, as it based its politics on the historical rights of the Hungarian Kingdom.

The attempt to involve the nobility in the struggle for national rights failed despite some aristocrats holding prestigious posts (for instance, Clam-Martinitz was elected the head of the committee for the Museum of the Kingdom of Bohemia, while Karel Schwarzenberg became the vice-chairman). Seeking support among conservative wings of the monarchy drove the policy of the National Party (*Národní strana*) to a more conservative position. The Bohemian historical nobility was conciliatory to the Czech national efforts, but in the second half of the 19th century it remained anational, tied rather to German culture. The nobility's support of the Czech national efforts thus had clear limitations.

In May 1861, elections to Land Diets took place. In Bohemia, the National Party's candidates won in Czech electoral districts, while the Liberal Party's (*Liberální strana*) representatives won in the German districts. The situation in Moravia was similar, although the Czech National Party was much less consolidated here due to a lesser degree of national consciousness of the local Czech-speaking population. The federalist-oriented nobility co-operated with the Czech National Party in both Diets while the German Liberal Party found an ally among the nobility "loyal to the constitution," headed by Karl Auersperg. Political life in the Czech Lands was thus controlled by both national parties and their noble allies.

The Land Diets were summoned at the beginning of April 1861 with one task on their agenda – to elect deputies to the Reichsrat. The National Party considered boycotting the Reichsrat as it was, in the view of its members, a foreign body which interfered with the historical rights of the Kingdom of Bohemia. In the end, even the Czechs reluctantly decided to send their deputies to the Vienna parliament. The Czech nation was represented by twenty deputies from Bohemia and four from Moravia, while Silesia was represented only by Germans. Only one Czech was appointed to the House of Lords – František Palacký.

Czech political representation consisted mainly of burghers, most of them lawyers, followed by university and secondary-school teachers and Catholic clergy. The Czech entrepreneurs' representation was not particularly numerous, yet nor was it marginal. Middle peasant class representation was higher in Moravia, although in Bohemia the number of peasant representatives rose sharply from the late 1880s.

The Reichsrat was summoned at the beginning of May 1861. The proposed bills had to win approval in both houses and the ruler, who held the power of veto. It was the ruler who dissolved and summoned the Reichsrat. The newly formed parliamentary system was shaken from the very beginning, as the deputies for the Hungarian Kingdom, Croatia and the Venice region did not attend it. The Vienna parliament thus remained limited to the representatives of non-Hungarian lands. Even then, not all the deputies present at the Reichsrat were satisfied with the existing political situation. The Czechs and Poles demanded a federative reconstruction of the monarchy on a historical basis, while the German majority in the House of Deputies insisted on a centralist system. The Czechs were unhappy that they could not push through their ideas on the reform of the monarchy and so they decided to follow the Hungarian tactics of boycotting the parliament, which they gradually left over 1863 and 1864. Their abandoning of the Reichsrat was not a denial of the very existence of the monarchy, it was a mere protest against its centralist arrangement.

Decisive political power was, from the central to the municipal level, in the hands of bureaucracy, although representatives of the Czech nation gradually asserted themselves on the local level. In 1861, Czechs gained control over Prague and within several years the Czech majority also asserted itself in all towns in the Czech areas (the only Bohemian exception was the town of České Budějovice). In Moravia, winning power was more difficult for the Czech administration; in many cases it took until the 1890s for Czechs to dominate the local town-halls and larger towns (Brno, Olomouc, Moravská Ostrava) remained in German hands until 1918. The towns under the Czech administration helped develop Czech social and cultural life for decades. District councils, which existed in Bohemia from 1864, had a similar role. The Germans in Moravia realized this and several times managed to prevent the establishment of the district councils in Moravia as they were afraid of strengthening the Czech positions.

The rising consciousness of the Czech national society was boosted by the establishment and development of a dense network of national clubs in all areas of public life and in all municipalities and districts. Around the country, singing, theatre, social and entertainment clubs sprang up. The Sokol (Falcon) sports organisation, established in 1862, became the Czech Lands' largest mass-scale organization, as it linked physical activities with national educational goals. At the beginning of the 1870s, over 10,000 members gathered in the fifty sports clubs in Bohemia, Moravia and Lower Austria. At the end of the 19th century, the 466 Sokol sports clubs had over 44,000 members, although Sokol's ambition to become an exclusive representative of the nation-wide interests in sports was thwarted by the establishment of the Catholic national sports organization called Orel (Eagle) and the rise of working-class sports clubs.

Unity within the National Party was, however, only exterior in the early 1860s. The main catalyst for ideological differentiation inside the National Party was a differing opinion of the Polish January Uprising in 1863. In opposition to the existing ("Old Czech") leaders of the

National Party, a radical ("Young Czech") wing crystallized. The Young Czechs disapproved of the alliance with the Czech nobility; they denounced the surviving aristocratic privileges and promoted the consistent separation of the state and church. The one thing they had in common with the Old Czechs was the opposition to the centralism in Cisleithania. Their criticism was only to influence the policy of the National Party; they did not seek a formal independence. As a result, the Old Czechs lost their influence in the editorial board of the *National Paper* and had to develop their own, less successful, journalist enterprises.

In 1865, František Palacký deliberated on the settlement of state issues in the monarchy in his series of articles titled *The Idea of the Austrian State,* published in the pages of the Old-Czech paper Nation *(Národ).* He proposed a solution to the language problems in the monarchy through establishing assemblies for groups of lands, in which the representatives of individual nations discussed common matters. These general assemblies were to replace the Reichsrat. Palacký rejected Schmerling's centralism and strongly warned against dividing the monarchy into German and Hungarian parts.

In 1865, Schmerling was dismissed in light of the lasting Hungarian opposition and was replaced by Bohemian aristocrat Richard Belcredi. Belcredi's imperial patent of September 1865 suspended the February Patent, which granted him more freedom in negotiating with Hungarians and Croats. Unfortunately, his moderately federalist course was unsuccessful.

Austrian domestic policy was significantly affected by the Habsburg dynasty's foreign policy which strove to maintain its power in the German Confederation. Austrian diplomacy first failed with its proposal for a reform of a federal arrangement at the German Congress of Princes in 1863 and was later drawn into a war against Denmark over Schleswig and Holstein. The quarrel over the administration of these two duchies led to aggravated tension between the German powers. The question of dominance in the German Confederation was to be decided by military means. The short Austro-Prussian war revealed Austrian diplomacy's inability as well as technical underdevelopment of the imperial army and the worse quality of its commanders. Archduke Albrecht's victories over Italy on the south front did not help Austria much as, in the main battlefield in Bohemia, the Austrian army suffered a crushing defeat in the battle of Sadová on July 3, 1866. Only the political foresight of the Prussian Prime Minister Otto Bismarck spared Austria a major disaster, as he did not strive to humiliate the Habsburg monarchy. In the Peace of Prague of July 23, 1866, Austria agreed to the dissolution of the German Confederation and promised not to interfere with further arrangements in the rising Germany. The loss of the Venice region, which was annexed to the Italian Kingdom, was even more painful.

After this unsuccessful war, the highest Viennese circles came to the conclusion that it was necessary to reach an agreement with the Hungarian opposition's representatives. Former Saxon Prime Minister Friedrich Ferdinand Beust became the emperor's new advisor and he quickly forged an agreement with Hungarian leaders Gyula Andrássy and Ferenc Deák. It was based on accepting the Hungarian interpretation of the legal continuity within the Hungarian Kingdom. Francis Joseph I appointed a Hungarian government, led by G. Andrássy on February 18, 1867. The compensatory agreements were approved by the

Hungarian Diet in May 1867, and soon after confirmed by the ruler during his coronation as the King of Hungary. The Austrian empire was thus reformed into a dual Austro-Hungarian monarchy.

The dual arrangements were initially merely an agreement between the crown and the political representation of the Hungarian Kingdom. They were to be approved by the Reichsrat, which first met in Vienna on May 20, 1867. The German liberal majority took advantage of the situation and, with the help of Poles, pushed through a recognition of basic constitution principles and essential democratic freedoms, which were later confirmed in the "December Constitution" of December 21, 1867.

The new political system was based on limiting the ruler's decision-making power by requiring counter-signatures by the pertinent ministers, a new club law and the law of assembly; six basic constitutional laws; a law concerning the Reichsrat, which transformed it into a true co-decision-making body; a law concerning general civic rights, guaranteeing the citizens equality before the law (including national equality); a law concerning the Imperial Court, which was to deal with disputes between institutions and with citizens' complaints concerning constitutional rights prejudices; a law concerning judicial power, which ensured the independence of courts; a law concerning the performance of governmental and executive power, which bound the emperor and other executive power representatives to rule in accordance with the passed laws.

"The Kingdoms and Lands represented in the Reichsrat"(Cisleithania, which constituted territories to the west of the river Leitha) and the Hungarian crown lands (Transleithania) shared a ruler; and foreign matters were also dealt with in common, including the diplomatic and business representation abroad, most military matters and financial matters concerning the trans-national expenditures of the entire monarchy. Legislation concerning common matters was implemented by special delegations from both the Reichsrat and the Hungarian Diet, which met alternately in Vienna and Pest once a year. Shared ministries of foreign affairs, defence and finances were established. The relationship between the two territories was based on equality. The domestic affairs of both halves of the empire were under the jurisdiction of sovereign parliaments and governments. The Habsburg monarchy reconstruction was completed on December 30, 1867 by appointing a government responsible for non-Hungarian territories, presided over by Karl Auersperg and consisting of many influential personalities of the German Liberal Party.

While German politicians from the Czech Lands supported the Austro-Hungarian Compromise, the Czech National Party assumed a negative attitude towards it. Its members demanded that the compromise be approved by the Bohemian and Moravian Diets as, according to them, the sovereignty of the Bohemian Crown was hampered by the compromise. Both Diets, in which the coalition of Czech national deputies and historical nobility had a majority in December 1867, refused to send their representatives to the Reichsrat, which debated the compromise agreements. Beust dissolved both Land Diets and a majority in favour of the government was reached through an unprecedented pressure on the landowner curia, which eventually sent their Bohemian and Moravian representatives to the Reichsrat.

The Czech representatives tried to find an ally in their struggle against dualism. In May and June 1867, they went on a telling visit to Russia, however this only further increased German accusations of Pan-Slavism. More serious were contacts with France, which culminated in July, 1869, in F. L. Rieger's audience with Emperor Napoleon III, to whom Rieger presented a memorandum containing Czech political goals. Czech representatives also made several attempts – with little success – to form a coalition of autonomist forces in Cisleithania.

The idea to organize mass manifestations supporting the Czech national agenda was more successful. The first rally took place at the foot of Říp hill on May 10, 1868. These gatherings organized by the Young Czechs, though frequently not officially sanctioned, voiced national, (generally) democratic and social demands. This rally movement significantly contributed to the nationalization of other Czech social strata and increased interest in politics. In 1868–1871, it spread in several waves throughout Bohemia and Moravia and even affected Silesia. There were a total of 140 rallies, in which about a million and a half people participated, according to the Czech press estimates. In Moravia, this movement was more conservative, and frequently demonstrated a clerical element.

The political agenda of this rapidly developing popular movement was formulated in declarations of August 1868, which the Czech national deputies presented in the Diets in Prague and Brno to explain why they would send their representatives to neither the Reichsrat nor the Land Diets. They refused to recognize the December Constitution and Austro-Hungarian Compromise, arguing that they had been enacted by a parliament representing a new constitutional subject, whose legitimacy they denied. The Czech deputies were willing to limit the historical rights of the Kingdom of Bohemia only in favour of a Reichsrat, which would represent the entire empire. The new agreement between the justly elected council and the ruler would have to be confirmed by Francis Joseph I's coronation as the King of Bohemia.

The emperor strove for the gradual reconciliation of all his empire's peoples, including the Czech nation, and so appointed Karl Hohenwart's conservative government to carry out negotiations concerning a Czech-Austrian compromise. Confidential discussions with the Czech constitutional opposition continued from February to August 1871. An agreement concerning the compromise was reached and further steps agreed upon. The first outcome of this agreement was the imperial rescript of September 12, 1871, in which the emperor committed to his coronation as the King of Bohemia and invited the Bohemian Diet to consider carefully the Kingdom of Bohemia's constitutional situation. Soon after, the German liberal deputies, who were a minority, left the Diet. On October 10, 1871, the federalist majority passed a set of 18 fundamental articles which defined the constitutional status of Bohemia within the monarchy, new election rules and a law protecting nationalities, which was to guarantee national equality in Bohemia. It determined that individual administrative and electoral districts were to be constituted as nationally homogeneous, German and Czech were to be official languages of the state offices in Bohemia and their clerks were to master both languages.

In fact, fundamental articles were Czech recognition of Austro-Hungarian dualism. Matters not considered imperial were to be in the competence of the Reichstag and the Bohemian Land government, led by a Czech court chancellor. The Bohemian Diet's prospect of a reform of the monarchy's constitutional situation was in sharp opposition to the interests of the Austro-German, Hungarian and Imperial-German politicians. Both chancellor Beust and the Hungarian Prime Minister Andrássy opposed the fundamental articles at the assembly of imperial and Cisletihan ministers held on October 20, 1871. In the end, even the emperor supported a reply to the Bohemian Diet, which emphasized the force of the existing constitutional situation and required that any proposed changes be submitted to the Reichsrat for approval. Soon after, Hohenwart's government, which had sealed its own fate with the success of the Czech compromise, resigned.

Prince Adolf Auersperg's new government set as its goal to push through a constitution and crush the Czech opposition. The central parliament's status was strengthened by introducing direct elections to the Reichsrat in 1873, which deprived the Land Diets of their privilege of sending representatives. Auersperg's government followed a harsh course in dealing with the Czech national movement, particularly in Moravia. The state offices often closed down the Czech savings banks in Moravia for an alleged breach of by-laws, which markedly weakened the local Czech bourgeoisie's positions. The National Party's leadership understood that they must not give up any platform on which its deputies could defend Czech political and economic interests. In November, 1873, they attended the Moravian Diet and, at the beginning of 1874, also the Reichsrat, although they held only a minority in both.

The question of whether to send deputies to the Bohemian and Imperial Diets caused a major political commotion inside the National Party. Rieger and Palacký's Old Czech leadership insisted on a consistent boycott of the Diet and parliament as they believed that it would force the Viennese court to start new negotiations. The more agile Young Czechs did not believe in the success of these tactics and recommended a more active policy. This schism escalated when seven Young Czech deputies attended the Bohemian Diet in September, 1874. After Christmas, 1874, the Young Czechs established an independent National Liberal Party (*Národní strana svobodomyslná*) in Prague, whose main goal was a struggle against passive resistance. Both parties repeatedly offended each other for several years, yet there were no tangible results effecting the Czech nation's status.

An overall tiredness caused by the fruitless Old Czechs' passivity and Young Czechs' parliamentary activity brought both parties closer together. In a common statement from March 30, 1878, Old Czechs and Young Czechs abandoned the essential constitutional standpoint and admitted that they might go to Vienna if most Czech deputies would consider it a beneficial step. In 1878, the formation of a common Constitutional Club of Czech deputies was announced. It was to make decisions concerning important questions of the state law, self-government and nationality. In 1878, 69 Old-Czech and 14 Young-Czech deputies returned to the Bohemian Diet.

2 Czechs and Germans – National Struggle's Aggravation

At the end of the 1870s and as a result of the Balkan war, a change in the political situation was drawing near. The Berlin congress' decision to allow the Habsburg monarchy to occupy Bosnia and Herzegovina destroyed the unity of the German liberals in power. Most members of the Liberal Party opposed the occupation for the fear of strengthening the empire's Slavic population. As a result, Auersperg's government lost its majority in the parliament and the Prime Minister resigned on October 4, 1878. The distribution of political power started to change as the autonomous circles loyally supported the emperor's policy in the Balkans. Eduard Taaffe, the emperor's favourite, was asked to reverse the situation by forcing the Czech constitutional opposition to stop boycotting the Reichsrat.

The Czech deputies' attendance at the Reichsrat was due to relatively favourable results of the June 1879 parliamentary elections, which thanks to Taaffe's effort weakened the position of the German party "loyal to the constitution" and suggested that autonomist forces might gain a majority in the House of Deputies. At the beginning of August 1879, Taaffe, Rieger and Pražák met in Vienna to discuss the situation's potential development. Taaffe promised a revision of the election rules for the Bohemian Diet, language equality in the Czech Lands, the establishment of a Czech university and accepting the constitutional objections by the emperor. Alois Pražák was appointed a minister in Taaffe's government and Czechs returned to the Vienna parliament.

The Czech deputies club only slowly managed to push through some of the national-political agenda due to the rivalry of various national and political factions. The Czech politicians' first success was Stremayr's language decree for Bohemia and Moravia in April 1880, which made Czech equal to German in external service communication (in contact with parties), while all documents used internally were kept in German. With the help of Taaffe's administration, the coalition of the National Party and the Conservative Landlords (*konzervativní velkostatek*) assumed control of the Bohemian Diet in 1883. Its representatives had to promise that the new Diet's majority would not misuse its status to repress Germans and they would support the government. The Moravian Czech element's weakness was manifested in the fact that only some of the Czech political gains concerned Moravian territory.

The greatest Czech success was the division of Charles-Ferdinand University in Prague. Lectures in Czech were held at the university from the early 1860s, when several Czech professors were appointed. In 1870, the ratio of Czech students at Charles-Ferdinand University and at the Technical University in Prague was larger than the percentage of the Czech population, which explains why Bohemian Germans agreed, relatively voluntarily, to the division of Charles-Ferdinand University into two universities with equal rights – Czech and German, which was enacted in February 1882. This attracted a young generation of university professors and researchers, who were open to the results of European science, and thanks to whom the scientific atmosphere at the university quickly approached the European standard. At the turn of the 19th and 20th centuries, the Czech university with its 3,000 students had surpassed its German parallel by two-and-a-half times and this ratio gradually increased.

The situation was similar in technical education. Prague's Technical University was split into Czech and German institutes in 1868/1869 with the quality of the Czech institute not lagging behind the German in the least. The original Utraquist Technical University in Brno (founded in 1849) was transformed in the 1850s into a linguistically German institute. It was only in 1899 that the Czech Technical University was established in the town, although it struggled with insufficient equipment. Moravian Czechs' efforts to establish a second Czech university in Brno were unsuccessful as the local German community was afraid of the Czech element's strengthening influence, particularly in Brno.

The second industrial revolution, which was already underway, was accompanied by an influx of the rural population to large towns, which changed their national character. This process was obvious as early as in the early 1860s. Prague was a typical example – the Czech suburbs grew much faster than the German inner town. The town centre preserved its predominantly German character to the end of the 1850s, which was important for the Prague Germans' consciousness. In the last quarter of the 19th century, the Prague German minority grew smaller (not only in relative numbers, but also in the absolutes – in 1880, there were 33,160 Germans, which constituted 19.16% of the population, while in 1910 their number stood at only 18,753, 8.48 %). This development was caused by assimilation and the trend in a certain part of the German speaking population (frequently of Jewish origin) towards adopting Czech nationality, which the German immigration from other parts of the country could not even out.

Important changes in the national structure also occurred in the western part of the North-Bohemian brown-coal fields, whose developing mining industry attracted economic immigrants from the Czech interior. Czechs formed their own social structure in this originally German area. Czech miners were followed by innkeepers, traders, teachers, lawyers and other professionals. This sudden change in the nationalist structure of the north-western Bohemia caused a major anxiety among the German population. This migration gradually ceased in the 1890s as a result of a continuing industrial development of the Bohemian interior and the Czech-German border became reasonably stabilized. The influx of the Czech rural population to towns in the interior continued to change their character. For instance, in 1910, the linguistically originally-German town of České Budějovice became a town with a 40% German minority.

Similar development also occurred in Moravia, where the German burghers' positions were even stronger than in Bohemia. German towns, however, often lacked a rural German background. The Czech element was thus mainly strengthened in the linguistically mixed areas of Moravia, while the German districts preserved the German element's unshaken position. In Brno, the local Germans even managed to strengthen their position.

From the national point of view, the Czech university in Prague played an important role in the education of the Czech intelligentsia as it attracted also Moravian graduates from Czech Gymnasia (general secondary schools) and gradually changed their existing educational orientation towards Vienna. These students did not find it difficult to link their provincial Moravianism with the national Czechness. Educated Moravia then became an organic part of the Czech national community. Despite this, even in the 1880s, the majority of Czech-speaking Moravians remained indifferent to the national consciousness. In the less developed parts of Moravia (Moravian Slovakia, Wallachia), national consciousness became established thanks to national journalism as late as in the 1890s.

The position of the Czech community in Vienna was rather distinctive. The monarchy's capital acted as a strong migration magnet for Czechs, and immigration, especially among the lower strata, reached its peak before the end of the 19th century. According to the 1910 census, 340,000 Czechs lived in Vienna and they were subjected to strong assimilation pressure. Official Czech politics could not ensure sufficient protection to the Viennese Czechs.

German liberals considered the strengthening of Czech political influence at the beginning of Taaffe's government intolerable for Austrian Germans. The Czech successes caused a defensive reaction among the Germans in the Czech Lands. Although the German positions in education were still far better than the Czech, Germans felt they were losing their footing. In 1880, the German Educational Club (Deutscher Schulverein) was founded to take care of German education, particularly in nationally mixed areas. Clubs focusing on regions were gradually established on both German and Czech sides to ensure the maintenance of "national domain." Economic nationalism also became more noticeable, contributing to the loosening of the ties between both communities. The belligerent nationalism promoted among the petty bourgeoisie was demonstrated through fierceness, noise and aggression.

These sentiments were reflected in the German national Linz programme of 1882, which set out social and economic demands along with a call for German Austria. It requested the separation of Dalmatia, Galicia and Bukovina from the Czech and German-Austrian lands. In the rest of the Cisleithania, German was to be recognized as the state language and its status in public life was to be strengthened. The Linz programme was perceived as extreme in the liberal atmosphere, but it still contributed to the general nationalization of German politics. German liberals, for example, several times vainly sought to promote German as the state language in Cisleithania through the Reichsrat.

The national competition did not have only negative effects, but also brought some positive consequences, particularly in the growth of general education as both Czechs and Germans paid great attention to it. Czechs surpassed all other Habsburg monarchy nations, including Austrian Germans, in elementary education. According to statistics from 1900, only 4.3% of Czech-speaking Austrian citizens over 6 years of age were illiterate, while among Germans, this figure stood at 6.8% and the Austrian average was 29.5%. In comparison with other countries, Czech society was among the most literate in Europe and was close to the general education standard of northern Europe's Protestant countries. This development was due to the fact that the leading personalities of the Czech national movement considered the education of broad national social classes one of its priorities. They based this idea not only on the old tradition of education in the Czech Lands and the deeply rooted habit of reading in Czech families, but they also took advantage of the positive aspects of the Austrian educational system.

While Czech elementary education could draw from long traditions, the development of secondary education in Czech occurred in the second half of the 19th century. Czech Gymnasia did not start developing until the 1860s – in 1866, there were only 10 Czech Gymnasia and "Real" Gymnasia, but in 1873 this number stood at 26; their number grew to 41 by 1894 and to 68 before the First World War. The number of Czech Real Gymnasia also grew between 1873 and 1914 from 14 to 43. The densest network of Czech secondary schools was in Bohemia, with fewer in Moravia, but the most difficult situation in establishing Czech secondary education was in Austrian Silesia. Particularly important was the establishment of two Czech Gymnasia in Brno and Olomouc, which from 1867 educated the youth of Moravia in the national spirit.

Many of these institutions were established by town councils and other non-state corporations and only gradually did the Austrian state take them under its control. Particularly in the 1880s, bringing Czech schools under state control was considered an important (though under-estimated) success of Rieger's pro-governmental policy. Czechs also pioneered education for women. In 1890, a private Czech Gymnasium for girls called Minerva was established, and was the very first institution of its kind in Austria. In 1914, there were five Czech Gymnasia for girls. Czechs were equally active when establishing technical and other specialized secondary schools.

The growth of the Czech intellectual stratum brought about the inevitable differentiation of opinions and the bolstering of critical thinking. In 1886 in the pages of the *Athenaeum* journal, philologist Jan Gebauer raised the question of the genuineness of the Manuscripts (Zelená Hora and Dvůr Králové Manuscripts), which had long been among the central components of the nationally oriented interpretation of Czech history. Gebauer was supported by the younger generation of Charles-Ferdinand University professors, among whom sociologist Tomáš Masaryk excelled. It was Masaryk who expressed his distrust for the genuineness of the Manuscripts and criticized the authoritarianism of Czech public life, which under the guise of patriotism assumed the right to decide internal matters of science. The unleashed scientific dispute was exploited as a political issue of primary importance by both the Young and Old Czech journalists and their opponents were branded traitors to the nationalist idea. Their professional arguments gradually proved convincing and their challenging the untouchable authorities heralded changes to the political field.

From the mid-1880s, dissatisfaction with the political situation was growing on both the Czech and German political sides. The Czech public, stirred up by the Young-Czech *National Paper*, expressed its discontent with the parliamentary tactics of its deputies and, especially, with their results. Taaffe's government was not as open to the Czech demands as had been the administration at the beginning of the 1880s. The Old-Czech politicians were caught in a "constitutional trap," as for many years they had proclaimed the Bohemian Crown's state rights as their main political goal. From this point of view, even the indisputable successes of Czech politics (particularly the development of secondary education) appeared to be only minor gains. Thanks to a much thicker network of its political clubs, the Young Czechs managed to react to this dissatisfaction better than the Old Czechs. At the beginning of 1888, the Young Czechs founded a separate deputy club at the Reichsrat and in the Bohemian parliamentary elections in July 1889, they defeated the Old Czechs in the rural electoral districts, which greatly curtailed the Old-Czech prevalence in the Czech politics.

In their political struggle, the Young Czechs also took advantage of the better quality of their journalism, which became the most important instrument of national agitation. The *National Paper* was seen as a leader among Czech newspapers; it had the best editorial board, the widest network of contributors, and took advantage of the organizational talent of its owner Julius Grégr. Old Czech journalism (dailies The Nation *(Národ)*, Progress *(Pokrok)*, Voice of the Nation *(Hlas národa)* and the German Politics *(Politik)*) was overshadowed by the *National Paper*, even during the time of the National Party's political dominance. The Old-Czech National Politics *(Národní politika)*, with its focus on general readership was more successful and, in the 1890s, was the most widely read Czech daily with a circulation of 32,000. Czech journalism in Moravia was principally represented by the Old-Czech Moravian Eagle *(Moravská orlice)*, although it had to fight material difficulties and the lower interest of the local population in the nationally-oriented press. From 1890s, People's Newspaper *(Lidové noviny)*, owned by Young-Czech leader Adolf Stránský, started to assert itself. An important role was also played by Czech regional journalism, which overshadowed the German equivalent by sheer force of numbers. At the turn of the 19th and 20th centuries, there was a wide variety of Czech dailies of various political orientations, in which the new political parties on the rise were represented by the social-democratic People's Right *(Právo lidu)* and the agrarian paper The Countryside *(Venkov)*.

The Czech question became the largest national conflict in the monarchy in the late 1880s, particularly after the German opposition left the Bohemian Diet in 1886. Taaffe's government tried to act as a mediator in the reconciliation of both parties. In 1890, discussions on the Czech-German compromise took place among the politicians from the Czech National Party, the German Liberal Party, the Czech Conservative and Landlords Constitutionalist Party (*konzervativní a ústavověrný velkostatek*) politicians in Vienna. Their result, the "Points Agreements" (*Punktace*), principally demanded the division of the Land school board and agricultural council into two sections, newly defined judicial circuits for the district and regional courts, which were concessions to the long-term German effort for the creation of a linguistically enclosed territory.

The further fate of the Points Agreement was determined by several facts: a protest by the uninvited Young Czechs, whom the emperor considered an unconstructive element, premature expressions of victory by German liberals and the tactless preferential fulfilling of the points that were advantageous for the Czech Germans. The Young Czechs accused the agreements' authors of replacing historical right with a nationalist right and creating a dual territory with dual law, which jeopardized the unity of the country. They resolutely rejected Points Agreements. Discussion on the individual parts of the Viennese agreements in the Bohemian Diet of 1890 clearly showed that a majority of the public supported the thus-far minority Young Czechs. The Old-Czech parliamentary club grew smaller and, in January 1891, the Young Czechs gained a majority among the Czech deputies in the Bohemian Diet.

The end of the National Party's hegemony in Czech politics came with the parliamentary elections in 1891, in which the National Liberal Party's (*Národní strana svobodomyslná*) candidates triumphed. The Young Czech Party was in fact a conglomerate of socially and politically heterogeneous forces, which were united in their opposition to the Old-Czech politics and Taaffe's government. In April 1891, the Young Czechs submitted their constitutional protest to the parliament in Vienna. They demanded that the Czech Lands be united in a special constitutional unit with a status similar to that of the Hungarian Crown. This standpoint, however, did not have a chance to gain broader support in the parliament and drove Czech politics into external isolation. As the Young Czechs based their politics on defending the Czech state, they consistently had to resort to opposition tactics. The Old Czechs' defeat and the ensuing disintegration of the pro-governmental majority started a period of political instability in Cisleithania.

From the end of the 1880s and with the gradual expansion of suffrage, political movements that sought popular support became important. Among the most significant were the Christian-social movement, which gained great popularity in the Alpine lands and especially the social-democratic movement which, thanks to its internationally oriented ideology, was unique in seeking the creation of a local network of centrally controlled organizations in all parts of the monarchy.

Social Democrats were particularly important in the Czech Lands as they were supported by the growing labour movement. The beginnings of this movement's wider development date back to the 1860s, when workers' self-help and educational clubs were established in the industrial centres (Prague, Brno, Liberec), often supervised by petty-bourgeoisie activists. Czech workers' emancipation was manifested in the foundation of the Czech-Slavic Social Democratic Workers' Party (*Českoslovanská sociálně demokratická strana dělnická*) at a congress in Prague-Břevnov in April 1878. In the 1880s, social-democratic organizations were, even in the Czech Lands, destroyed by Taaffe's repressive policy directed against anarchist expressions. The end of the 1880s, however, witnessed the rise of social-democratic organizations in the Czech Lands with Austria-wide leadership headed by Viktor Adler. The social-democratic movement won workers by emphasizing their demand for social equality and their fight for the workers' political rights.

A great discussion was stirred up in the mid-1890s by T. G. Masaryk's three central works: *The Czech Question, Our Current Crisis* and *Jan Hus.* Masaryk criticized the current fruitless Czech constitutional radicalism as represented by the Young Czechs' radical wing and led by Eduard Grégr. Masaryk agreed with Palacký that the Czech nation could not achieve political independence without major political turbulence in Europe or the fall of the monarchy. He criticized political maximalism with its unwillingness to make concessions concerning state rights and accused it of a demobilizing inclination to passiveness and excessive reliance on help from outside. He advocated positive politics based on piecemeal constructive work. Czechs were to assert themselves through their own physical activity in all areas and by learning the principles of modern democracy. The Czech question was not merely a problem of state rights or national politics, but rather a complex of social, cultural,

344

ideological and economic problems, whose common denominator was an effort to democratize society in the Czech Lands.

Czech Moravia remained in the shadow of events in Bohemia. The open schism between the conservative and liberal streams in Moravia occurred as late as in the early 1890s. The Old-Czech National Party was forced to concede the leadership of Moravian Czech politics to the Young-Czech oriented People's Party (*Lidová strana*), although the Old Czechs preserved several representative posts. The coming to power of the Moravian liberals led to the separation of a clerical movement and the foundation of the Catholic National Party (*Katolická strana národní*). For a long time, Czech political parties in Moravia strove in vain to ensure that the majority Czech population also had a majority in the Moravian Diet and a corresponding status in the land's administration. In reality, however, the most important posts in the legislature (Land Diet), administration (vice-regent, Land governor, head of the Land financial office, officers of the Land school board, administrators of post offices and state railway) and in the judiciary (the president of the Supreme Land Court) were controlled by Germans.

A similarly dismal situation from the Czech national movement point of view was in the smallest of the Czech Lands – in Silesia, where the German population had a slight majority over the Polish and Czech minorities. However, the Silesian Diet was, from 1861 to the First World War, entirely under the control of the German political representation. Similarly, the land's administration was entirely in German hands. Czechs and Poles gained symbolic representation in the Diet's leadership as late as in the 1890s. The Slavic population could not assert itself more widely not only due to the disadvantageous election system, but also because of the mutual rivalry between Czech and Polish politicians. The Czech political elite considered the Silesian Czechs a fully-fledged part of the national organism, yet they tried to improve their national positions primarily in Bohemia and Moravia.

In 1895, Galician governor Kazimierz Badeni was appointed the Cisleithan Prime Minister. One of the main tasks of Badeni's government was the solution of the national question, which was particularly difficult in the Czech Lands. The second problem was the calls of the masses for the democratization of the election rules. Badeni tried to mitigate public dissatisfaction by establishing the "fifth curia," in which all male inhabitants could, in 1897 and for the first time, elect a total of 72 deputies. This increased the number of mandates in the House of Deputies and helped the Social Democrats be elected into the parliament; however, it did not change the principle of the curia-based election system.

Badeni made contact with some Young-Czech politicians and, after consulting them, issued a language decree in April 1897, which within five years went so far as to introduce Czech to the internal office dealings in Bohemia and Moravia. This won the Czech deputies' support for the government. As this step, however, had not been agreed upon with the German politicians, Badeni's linguistic decrees caused a deep domestic crisis. The Czech Germans protested that the presumptive knowledge of both land languages (even in the purely German areas) by the judges and officers would hamper the Germans' dominance in public administration. A broad spectrum of the German population in the Czech and

Alpine lands opposed Badeni. In autumn 1897, the German obstruction in the parliament, accompanied by tumultuous demonstrations in the streets of Vienna, led to the fall of Badeni's government.

The ethnic unrest partly paralyzed political life in Austria. To solve the nationalist disputes, the former Bohemian governor Franz Thun was appointed the head of the Austrian government in March 1898. Young Czech Josef Kaizl became the cabinet's soul and the Minister of Finance and he was convinced that Czechs should enact "purely Austrian politics," as "our safest shelter is in a strong and just Austria." Nevertheless, Thun's government also failed to break the German stonewalling and had to rule Austria through imperial decrees. Thun was eventually dismissed and the offices in the Czech Lands were to follow Stremayr's linguistic decrees. In reality, however, Czech was maintained to some extent in the internal service. The apparent German victory had a negative impact on the overall political atmosphere in the monarchy.

The German party's success resulted in a Czech stonewall. Austria thus had to be ruled according to Section 14 of the Austrian constitution, which endowed the government with special rights. The German parties' politicians against the state rights cast doubt upon relying on the possibility that Cisleithania could be ruled in a parliamentary manner. Earlier, there had been a certain identification on the side of Austrian Germans with the state needs concerning matters such as the budget or the army, and the Austrian government could count on their support. Now the Germans did not hesitate to obstruct the government if it went against their national interests and thus to jeopardize the basic functioning of the state mechanism.

As a result, the Cisleithan administration was placed in the hands of bureaucracy, standing above the parties, parliament and nations. Prime Minister Ernst Koerber tried to mitigate the political tension through state support for some economic projects, such as the regulation of the river Labe (the Elbe) and the construction of railways. Koerber inspired new negotiations concerning the Czech-German compromise, but it was a vain effort. As he had failed to settle the nationalist conflicts within the monarchy, he was replaced on January 1, 1905, by Paul Gautsch, whose government managed to successfully end the several-year-long discussions of Czech and German politicians in Moravia. The "Moravian Pact" of 1905 contained four laws reforming the Diet election rules, settling, among other things, the situation in education and the language question in the self-governing offices. In reality, Czech and German election cadastres were introduced for elections to the Land Diet. This agreement inspired similar compromises in Bukovina (1910) and Galicia (1914).

The question of universal suffrage came into public focus at the beginning of the 20th century. After massive demonstrations in Prague and Vienna in autumn 1905, Gautsch presented a radical proposal for suffrage reform, which, however, failed due to the problem of the national division across electoral districts. Gautsch was replaced by another bureaucrat Max Wladimir Beck, a close collaborator of the successor to the throne, Francis Ferdinand. Beck managed to win the Reichsrat's support for the abolishment the curia election system and the introduction of universal suffrage to the House of Deputies.

346

The new election rules were applied to the elections of 1907 and 1911. The 1907 elections brought a defeat of the nationalist wing on both the German and Czech political sides. Popular political parties, which were founded in the Czech environment from the 1890s, came to the fore. The most successful of these in terms of number of mandates – the Czech Agrarian Party (*Česká strana agrární*) (founded in 1899) – was among those active both in Bohemia and Moravia. It followed the Czech peasantry tradition of strong professional organizations, which were emancipated from the influence of the liberal and clerical parties in the 1890s. The party primarily advocated the interests of the middle-class Czech peasantry. Antonín Švehla, a talented politician, became its leader at the beginning of the 20th century.

The Czech National Socialist Party (*Česká strana národně sociální*) was founded in 1898 as a party for the nationally-oriented workers and in opposition to international social democracy. Gradually, it became the party of lesser burghers and intelligentsia. The Catholic stream of Czech politics was weaker in Bohemia than in Moravia, where the Catholic National Party (*Katolická strana národní*) and Christian-Socialist Party (*Křesťansko-sociální strana*) co-operated and complemented each other as they were oriented towards different social strata. In Bohemia several small parties were founded, which advocated Czech state rights, and amog them the Czech State Right Progressive Party (*Česká strana státoprávně pokroková*) demanded complete independence, one not explicitly tied to the existence of the Habsburg monarchy.

The party with the strongest support in the Czech Lands before the First World War was the Czech-Slavic Social Democratic Workers' Party. It gained 38% of votes in the 1907 elections. It had most numerous and best organized membership, and was supported by the trade unions, in which the social democrats completely surpassed national and Christian socialist organizations. The party advocated the ideas of international socialism, yet it became independent of the Austria-wide social democratic leadership in Vienna. Disputes concerning the trade union movement's character led to the foundation of the centralist Czech Social Democratic Workers' Party (*Česká sociálně demokratická strana dělnická*) in Austria in 1910, which was oriented towards and financially supported by Vienna.

In Bohemia, the national question remained the most delicate problem. Czech and German politicians were pushed into co-operation by the government. In 1910, negotiations started in the Bohemian Diet committees. These negotiations failed, as the Czechs rejected the German proposal for a two-language status for Prague. The difficult financial situation in the Kingdom of Bohemia, caused by bad management, had to be solved through governmental intervention. In 1913, the St Anne Patents, which suspended the Czech Land Constitution and its Land autonomy without the emperor's daring to octroi a new constitution based on the agreements reached. During the last compromise discussions, an agreement was within reach. It seems as though the Czech and German political representation did not have the genuine will to reach an agreement as in the time of general doubts concerning the ability of the Habsburg monarchy's political system to function, they did not have the courage to take this fundamental political step. It is also doubtful whether the concluded compromise agreements would help to calm the nationalist situation as they were aimed at settling the situation within one land only, never to reconcile nations.

Before the First World War, Czech society had an almost complete structure of a modern capitalist society with a well-developed structure of political parties, clubs and social organizations. Czech national society was characterized by an extensive system of self-help clubs and political, economic and cultural organizations. Czechs could take advantage of state institutions in these areas without being responsible for the Austro Hungarian state. Czechs created their national society in the opposition to the Austrian state, which from the beginning of the 20th century was losing popularity in Czech society. The Czech nation had its own representation in some international organizations; and the Czech Olympic Committee representation participated in the Olympic Games independently. The national society's high consciousness was in a contrast to the relatively slight achievements of the Czech politicians. However, not even the failure to push through the monarchy's federalization gave rise to the idea of an independent Czech state. The discrepancy between the overall development of Czech society and its constitutional insignificance became one of the most serious domestic problems of the Habsburg monarchy. Before 1914, Czechs had the status of a state nation without its own state.

3 The Economic Rise of the Czech Lands

The economic capacity of the Danubian monarchy unquestionably ranked it among leading European countries. It generated one tenth of the entire continent's gross domestic product in 1913, approximately equal to the share of France. Only Russia and Germany (both countries accounted for about one fifth of European production) and Great Britain (about 17%) were economically ahead of the Habsburg monarchy. In per capita GDP, however, Austria-Hungary lagged behind the most developed west-European countries. The data for the Habsburg monarchy as a whole was lowered because, as well as the developed regions of Cisleithania ("Austria"), which included the industrially developed Czech and Austrian lands, it also contained Transleithania ("Hungary"), which was prevalently agricultural with poorly developed industry playing only a marginal role.

Economically, both parts of the empire were each others' main business partners. Transleithania principally exported agricultural products (crops, flour, animals, food and beverages) to Cisleithania, while Cisleithania exported mainly fuel, textiles, chemicals, machinery and other industrial products to Transleithania. With little exaggeration, the monarchy is sometimes called a marriage of "wheat and textiles."

Beyond the afore-mentioned differences between the western and eastern parts of the monarchy, there were also considerable differences within the more developed Cisleithania, where the Czech Lands held an essential and indispensable economic position. In 1913, their population was approximately 10 million, more than a third of the Cisleithan population. Within their territory were 52% of industrial and trade companies, which employed 57% of all the people working in industry in the entire Cisleithania.

PAVEL CIBULKA — JAN HÁJEK — MARTIN KUČERA

The Czech Lands thus produced almost a half of the Cisleithan national income (in 1910, this figure stood at around 45%). The Czech Lands held a dominant position in fuel resources (coal mining), porcelain production, textile industry and sugar production – the empire's most important export commodity.

Agricultural production also played a considerable role in the growing economic importance of the Czech Lands, despite the fact that the percentage of the populace engaged in farming in Bohemia dropped from three quarters in the mid-19th century to mere one third in 1910. From the 1880s, grain production developed intensively. The gradual specialization of agricultural companies and industrial crops, particularly sugar beet and – in less fertile areas – potatoes, were also important. The food industry, the sugar, distilling, brewing and malting industries in particular, thrived thanks to these crops. The Czech Land's share in Cisleithan animal husbandry was smaller – amounting to only about one third.

The significant economic position of the Czech Lands within Austria-Hungary can be attributed to all three main ethnic groups living in the territory together for centuries – the Czech majority (almost 7 million in 1900), the Germans settled in the Czech Lands (approximately 3 million) and the citizens of Jewish origin, who all gradually became assimilated with one or the other linguistic group. Originally, they mostly belonged among the German-speaking population, however around 1900, most Jews in the Bohemia inclined to the Czech nationality.

Abolishing the remaining patrimonial relationships in the revolutionary years of 1848–1849 removed the last obstacles to entrepreneurial activities. Economic development in the Habsburg monarchy in the second half of the 19th century was boosted by the reforms of the 1850s and early 1860s, the most important of which was the foundation of a special central Ministry of Trade, and the newly established institutions – business and trade chambers, which were to protect entrepreneurial activities in the regions. The promulgation of

The share of the economically most developed regions of the monarchy - the Czech Lands and Lower Austria - in the Cisleithan industrial production in 1880 (as a percentage)

industry	Czech Lands	Lower Austria	other Cisleithania
glass, stone and earth industry	80.4	10.9	8.7
textile industry	78.2	11.3	10.5
food industry	65.6	16.5	17.9
machinery industry	50.5	34.2	15.3
leather industry	42.8	42.2	15.0
iron industry	46.1	11.1	42.8
chemical industry	37.7	42.8	19.5
paper industry	28.8	36.2	35.0
clothing industry	27.5	69.7	2.8
timber industry	26.4	24.7	48.9
graphic industry	11.1	88.9	0.0
total Cisleithan industry	63.8	19.8	16.4

the Trade Act in 1859 ensured open competition in industrial business activities, while the Business Code of 1862 was of a similar importance for commerce. One of the examples of the state support for a liberal economy was the privatization of a major part of the railway system and in further subsidies for its construction. The entire 1860s and the early 1870s are characterized by an immense growth of industrial production. The third quarter of the 19th century can be considered a period of expansion and completion of the industrial revolution in the Czech Lands.

Alongside the development of industrial companies, the beginning of the modern banking industry also dates from this period. The first commercial banks were founded in Prague, Brno and several larger towns of the Bohemian borderland (among the biggest German banks were Böhmische Eskomptebank and Böhmische Union-Bank in Prague). In the Czech Lands – and particularly in the Czech nationalist environment – self-help credit coops (mutual savings banks) played an important role. The first of these were established in the late 1850s and over the course of the following fifteen years their number grew to several hundred. This was also part of the impetus that saw the establishment of the largest Czech national financial institution – the Trade Bank in Prague.

New forms of entrepreneurships were also spreading. Between 1867 and 1873, the Austrian government issued over a thousand licences for joint-stock companies, of which 682 actually came to existence. Of these, about 40% were based in Vienna, almost half of them in the Czech Lands, and only the remaining 10% in the other Cisleithan regions. This period is justly known as the "foundation period" (*"Gründerzeit"*).

The Vienna stock market crash in May 1873 put an end to this dynamic period. It was followed by a deep financial and economic crisis. It had a devastating effect most particularly on the banking industry. Over a period of several years, in both Bohemia and the economically decisive Vienna, a full four fifths of all banks founded before 1873 went bankrupt. In terms of industrial production, the crisis mainly affected the textile and food industries – the two dominant branches in the Czech Lands. In 1880, the textile industry accounted for 41.5%, the food industry for 33.5%, means of production for 16% and other branches 9% of the total industrial production in Bohemia. Sugar production was decimated again in the mid-1880s during a sugar crisis.

To a lesser extent, the crisis also affected coal mining and metallurgical and iron production. These branches were saved mainly by new technologies, particularly the acid Bessemer process in steel production and the Thomas (basic Bessemer) process in the processing of lower quality Czech ores. Another positive factor was the continuing construction of the railways. While in the mid-19th century, about 800 km of railway had been built; in 1860, it was about 1300 km; in 1870 approximately 2800 km; and in 1880 as much as 5000 km. The building of the rail network between major population centres was essentially completed in the second half of the 1870s. In the following years, it grew denser and was supplemented by local railways.

Most branches of industry managed to overcome the immediate consequences of the 1873 crisis as early as the late 1870s. One of the long-term effects was, however, the public's general distrust of new forms of business activities, particularly in banks and joint-stock companies. This lasted until the 1890s and greatly hampered production and investment activities. In this context, this period, which lasted almost a quarter of a century, is sometimes called "the great depression." It was not until the second half of the 1890s that signs of a new economic boom began to appear in Cisleithania. The number of commercial banks as well as their share capital grew. Banks started to invest in industry and, as a result, they participated more intensively in managing industrial companies.

This trend was most apparent in the decade prior to the First World War. After overcoming a brief crisis in the first years of the 20th century, this was the period of a boom in industrial production and general economic prosperity. It was mainly due to rapid technical development, which brought about many technological changes in a number of industrial fields. One of the most important was the gradual introduction of electricity to production, urban transport, street lightning and households. In machine production, it was the use of stainless and high-speed steel. Farming was also on the economic rise, using artificial fertilizers, melioration, improved animal husbandry and a slight increase of grain prices. The pre-war decade is sometimes called "the second foundation period."

From the end of the 19th century, the Czech Lands developed considerably faster than the monarchy as a whole, even faster than the previously better developed Lower Austria and Vienna. The exceptionally successful development of the Czech Lands was mainly due to there being sufficient energy resources (black and brown coal reserves), agricultural intensification and the expansion of rail transport connected to the construction of an extensive network of local railways. Hundreds of years of glassmaking tradition and the textile industry had a positive effect. Some new fields became important in the Czech Lands' industrial production. Among the progressive and rapidly developing companies, we should mention Prague's electrical companies Kolben and Křižík, machine-building plants including Prague's Ringhofer, which produced train cars, and Plzeň's Škoda, which gradually transferred its production from general machinery to armament production, car producers Laurin & Klement, and, in the field of chemical production, the Association for Chemical and Metallurgical Production in Ústí nad Labem. Rapid urbanization was another factor in the Czech Lands' economic growth. The construction of entirely new town districts, town commissions (sewerage, water piping, gasworks, lightning, the consolidation of waterfront roads) and the further development of infrastructure contributed to a great expansion in construction trades.

The dynamic of the Czech Lands' economic development was undoubtedly influenced also by close ties between its two important industrial regions (northern Bohemia and the Ostrava region) and two developed areas in Germany (Saxony and Upper Silesia). On the other hand, the fact that many large companies had their seats in Austria, most particularly in Vienna, was a negative factor, as it was to there that they returned their profit. The capital city thus received huge sums of money, while the social wealth, produced in the Czech Lands, could only partially be used by the local population.

Although the Czech national bourgeoisie's industrial position was considerably strengthened in the two pre-war decades, its status was still less than that of the local Germans.

The German-Austrian capital in the Czech Lands controlled most large and medium-sized companies, mainly in the crucial industrial fields: coal mining, metallurgy, textiles, chemistry and glassmaking. The position of the capital of German speaking business circles as a whole was frequently maintained by state economic interventions and thanks to the gradually arising monopolies. Again, it was the great capital of Vienna that profited most.

The economic foundation of the Czech nation was based mainly on small and medium-sized companies, in handicrafts, retail and services. Czech entrepreneurs built up prominent positions in the food industry, particularly the sugar production, brewing, malting and distilling industries. Several important electric and engineering companies were also in Czech hands. The specialized production of farming machinery and machinery for the food industry became the true domain of Czech entrepreneurs. From the end of the 19th century, Czechs also began to assert themselves in branches which had until then been exclusively German – the textile and chemical industries and the production of applied ceramics. Despite all this, the fields of agriculture and production closely linked to it remained the main pillar of the Czech economy. Agrarian bourgeoisie from central Bohemia, the Labe region, Haná and south Moravia were the most numerous and economically dynamic group of Czech entrepreneurial circles.

Czechs gradually achieved much more important positions in banking and other monetary fields than in industry. With the beginning of a new phase in the development of the economy, it was a sphere which gradually gained much greater importance. Despite its late start in business activities, Czech society started to be interested in these progressive and influential economic fields and then began to assert itself. Thanks to its more rapid economic growth at the end of the 19th and the beginning of the 20th century, the capital accumulation in the Czech Lands increased markedly. The percentage of the banks' share capital in the Czech Lands between 1881 and 1913 grew from one fifteenth to an almost one quarter of the share capital of the entire Cisleithania. Prague became the second most important financial centre of the western part of the monarchy. This growth was essentially thanks to Czech financial institutions. For instance, over the fifteen pre-war years (1898–1913) the share capital of the ethnically Czech commercial banks grew ten times, while the assets of the local German banks in the same period grew by less than three times. The ethnically Czech banks thus started to dominate their local German partners, which had been dominant before the end of the 19th century. The rise of a Czech financial capital at the beginning of the 20th century was unprecedented even at a European scale.

Though throughout most of the 19th century, ethnically Czech businesses had to fight a chronic lack of investment capital (hence the great expansion and importance of the self-help credit co-operatives), the decade before the war was marked by the opposite extreme – the relative surplus of Czech financial capital. As it was impossible to use within the local market, which was mostly controlled by older and more developed Viennese and domestic German financial institutions, it had to be invested outside the Czech Lands. The economic expansion of Czech entrepreneurial circles was principally directed towards the less developed southern and eastern parts of Cisleithania (Slovenia and Galicia) and to the

PAVEL CIBULKA — JAN HÁJEK — MARTIN KUČERA

Slavic Transleithan regions (Croatia, Slovakia). Beyond the monarchy's borders, its targets were mainly Russia and the Balkans. However, here it was met with keen competition from the rapacious capital of the German Empire.

When entering new markets, Czech entrepreneurs took advantage of the idea of Slavic solidarity and the declared need for economic unity of Slavs against German expansionism. To achieve these goals, Czech political and economic circles took advantage of the "Neo-Slavic Congress" in Prague in 1908. The economic exhibition by the Prague business and trade chamber, which took place in Prague at the same time, enhanced the congress' participants' admiration of Czech economic development and promoted Czechs to the position of the most economically developed Slavic nation. "We are obliged … to exert an effort so that each Slavic nation achieves the same level of culture and development as the Czech nation," said one of the delegates.

Economic prosperity in the pre-war decades had many consequences. Thanks to a long stagnation of some traditional production fields (especially the textile industry, concentrated primarily in the borderlands settled by Germans) and the development of engineering and many new fields (including the electrical, chemical and automotive industries), there was a gradual shift, starting at the end of the 19th century, with industrial production moving into new economic centres situated mostly in the ethnically-Czech interior of the Czech Lands. The Czech population started to leave the countryside, moved to large towns and changed their ethnic structure. Czechs even started to move to some areas with an originally large percentage of German population, such as the industrial Ore Mountain basin. The economic importance of ethnically Czech areas in the interior grew while simultaneously boosting the economic self-confidence of Czechs. The increasing emancipation thus crowned the formation and maturing of a modern Czech nation, which took place in a historical succession of three inseparable parts – first language and cultural emancipation, then political equality and now the economic "equality" of Czechs.

One of the means of economic emancipation was exploiting economic nationalism. It was an instrument used not only by Czechs, but it was also used (alongside other nationalities of Austria-Hungary) by Germans settled in the Czech Lands. They believed that the gradual economic rise of Czechs and the transformation in the balance of economic strength of both ethnicities would jeopardize their future. While the originally self-preservation character of economic nationalism in the Czech environment was becoming ever more expansive, it was exactly the reverse for the local Germans. At the turn of the 19th and 20th centuries, economic life in the Czech Lands, and in fact throughout society, was influenced by various expressions of economic nationalism, when economic achievements of one ethnicity were perceived as a weapon against the economy (and often even the existence) of the other. With little exaggeration, we can even say that the aggravated sentiments of the Czech-German linguistic quarrels and controversies of the second half of the 1890s had been transferred to the economic sphere.

The positive development of the Czech Lands' economy, however, was not always reflected in their infrastructure nor on their social level. Workers' wages in Bohemia, Moravia and Silesia were well below the wages in Austrian lands – in Vienna, Lower and Upper Austria and Styria, while artisans and businessmen also earned less. Small and medium entrepreneurs were harmed by the dictates of large Austro-Hungarian cartels. A more progressive economic development of the Czech Lands was also impeded by high taxation, which disproportionately burdened some of the modern forms of businesses, such as joint-stock companies. Approximately half of the income from taxes, fees and state monopolies flowed into the state treasury from the Czech Lands. Particularly heavy was the burden of indirect consumer taxes, of which the Czech Lands paid more than 63% of the entire Cisleithan revenue in 1909.

We can say that the Czech Lands provided over half of the Austrian state's income. Ethnic Czechs, who inhabited a large part of these lands, were nonetheless kept in an unequal position. This fact, hand in hand with the growing consciousness of its own economic force, sparked indignation among Czech business circles. Their negative attitude was not aimed against the empire itself: they considered the existence of Austria-Hungary necessary and were aware of its many economic advantages. They especially appreciated the benefits a large domestic market provided for the Czech Lands' industrial production. Their main complaints were against the constitutional structure of the state. Although Czech economic representatives were gradually invited into Austria-wide economic institutions, they believed that they had not been given sufficient room and that their economic importance was not reflected in their share of political power and the economic advantages tied to it. Calls for change were becoming both stronger and more frequent.

4 Culture in the Czech Lands in the Second Half of the 19th Century and at the Beginning of the 20th Century

The cultural-historical development of the Czech Lands in the second half of the 19th century and in the period commonly referred to as the "fin-de-siècle" was defined by two key historical events – on the one hand, the sweeping defeat of the revolutionary democratic attempts on Habsburg monarchy territory and the rise of an unconstitutional regime, and on the other, Austria-Hungary's break-up as a result of destructive international political and social leanings, which were partly caused and party merely accelerated by the First World War. These two milestones marked a relatively short historical epoch, which played a particularly important role in the cultural development of Europe and the Czech Lands. The beginning of this period was characterized by subsiding romanticism in art, but also to an extent in science, and the first results of systematically polished critical realism, while its end witnessed the rise of the avant-garde movement, which shook the existing paradigms of European art.

The social effect of culture in an era of industrial civilization stopped being limited merely to artistic and literary values, scientific theories and discoveries or to the influence of religious movements and churches. Particularly after the revolutionary events of

PAVEL CIBULKA — JAN HÁJEK — MARTIN KUČERA

1848–1849, culture came under influence of social and political mass movements, even political parties' ideologies. Cultural activities became an inseparable part of social movements. The producers of cultural values and cultural organizations grew and spread through social strata and environments previously unaffected by cultural activities and, at the same time, the numbers of the recipients of cultural values grew. This general trend had both social and national dimensions. Culture was also becoming more prominent in the nations of northern, central, eastern and south-eastern Europe, which had for centuries been either on the periphery of cultural development or deprived of their rights. Public life was enriched by the progressive reception of cultural deeds, products and values by general society and most individuals.

For the above reasons, erudition, literacy levels, school systems, upbringing and education were dominant factors in the development of any national culture. With the growing demand for qualified workers, from trainees to university graduates, the education and specialization requirements increased as a result of the growing importance of science and technology in industrial civilization. The second half of the 19th century can be referred to as the epoch of an extraordinary boom in education, which became a profitable business in the capitalist era. The transformation of cultural values into goods had serious cultural consequences. It led to a special kind of cultural market: the cultural values were transformed into consumer products and the recipient became a consumer. The first consequence of this process was the growing distance between the producers of cultural values and the market cycle of cultural goods. A creative person, an artist or scientist, could no longer decide or influence how they were consumed. This task was gradually transferred to many go-be-tweens: institutions (mainly in science), directly subordinated to state supervision; media (mass press) as a manipulator of public opinion; people engaged in the trade of cultural products (managers); cultural entrepreneurs and companies. The second consequence was inevitably an interest in cultural goods of low quality. Alongside educational tendencies in popular edification, there was an increasing tendency towards mass-consumption, triviality, trash, bestsellers and snobbery resulting from fashion or prosperity, which were denounced by the avant-garde. Cultural goods headed towards mass consumption and their producers and sellers assumed the role of disseminators and promoters and determined the fashion of its consumption. The third consequence was due to the democratization of cultural goods consumption, and was inherent in the general spread of industrial goods production. The last and very inspiring consequence was the fact that Modernists and the following avant-garde artists rejected trash art and pseudo-values and mercilessly destroyed them.

Market influence on the production of the cultural goods affected cultural activities in two ways. First, it engaged all cultural activities in goods exchange and thus equalized them, so they stopped being isolated and exclusive acts. The cultural goods market surpassed the limits of nations and states. Although the 19th century was strongly marked by nationalism, it created the conditions necessary for global cultural movements, and the cultural expressions of individual nations professed general ideals of humanity and social justice. This development was due to the fact that the material conditions of people's lives to some extent levelled out and averaged, the distances between countries and continents shrank, migration increased, population stratification changed considerably and the relationships and ties between people multiplied. All these factors removed the barriers of the territorially defined cultural activities. National cultures accepting foreign cultural values were often closely linked to the pressure of state ideologies; culture progressed most when the current cultural trends were implemented in an environment with an advanced and conscious understanding of one's traditions.

Czech culture was, in the second half of the 19th century, closely linked to the rest of Europe although for a long time it lagged behind the continent's west, which was due to the peripheral position of central European countries and the inequality of the nation and the historical Bohemian Kingdom in the Habsburg monarchy from the time of the Renewed Land Ordinance of 1627. The cultural movement programmes, which gradually appeared after the Napoleonic wars, had a markedly nationalist orientation; culture was perceived almost exclusively as national culture. It was referred to national literature, national music, national visual arts, and also national education. German cultural activities in the Czech Lands were also slightly behind Western Europe, although after 1860 they were more closely tied to the Viennese centre, from which they could draw inspiration relatively rapidly – particularly in theatre, music, literature and philosophy. The German population did not escape the cultural nationalization and, after the establishment of a unified German Empire, its spiritual orientation towards the empire and, occasionally, even dependence on its events grew. The conditions for the conception of the avant-garde were more difficult due to the peripheral position of the Czech Lands, both in the ethnically Czech and German environments, when compared to Vienna, Berlin and even Budapest or Cracow. Despite all the differences between the national and political goals of the Czech and German populations in the Czech Lands, the stages of the industrial, socio-political and cultural development of both nations were essentially the same. The cultural sphere can be divided into three stages: a) a period of tasks for national self-preservation and the national rise with its fading romantic elements and the first signs of realism prior to the beginning of the 1870s; b) the period of the burgher society of the Czech Lands coming to terms with the world and the 1890s Modernist movement to the end of the 19th century; c) the years of the rising avant-garde as an impetus for further development, which was interrupted by the First World War. Czech and German ethnic groups developed in parallel rather than in mutual co-existence, although individuals maintained mutual relationships irrespective of the situation, the cultures inspired each other both positively and negatively with the Czech and German avant-garde even permeating each other. Before the war, the avant-garde exponents helped to address nationalist discrepancies through co-operation, but the war again brought things to a head.

The German population's culture in the Czech Lands, with the exception of important enclaves in Prague and Brno, developed in a less revolutionary manner in comparison to Czech culture. Germans entered the modern era with the advantage of their nationality and strong support from Vienna though they mainly lived in the borderlands. The narrowed social base of their cultural rise was demonstrated most obviously in the lifestyle of the average

PAVEL CIBULKA — JAN HÁJEK — MARTIN KUČERA

Czech-German borderland inhabitants, primarily at a rural level. Financial institutions in the Czech Lands, which were almost exclusively in German hands until 1873, went into decline after the crisis, while the Czech capital was increasing and its growth was directly reflected in culture. Moreover, after the establishment of a unified Germany, Germans in the Czech Lands in general, and particularly in the increasingly poor borderlands, accepted the culturally-weak productive ideology of the nationalist Germans and creative values appeared only where this ideology was overcome (in large, linguistically heterogeneous agglomerations and in avant-garde communities).

The status of the Jewish population was quite specific. Its members either became culturally integrated in the predominant (Czech or German) environment or, on the contrary, created conditions for differentiation. This culturally inspirational population segment deserves to be treated separately.

Cultural Development Before the 1870s

The neo-absolutist period and the following decades of renewed constitutionality were characterized by a process of steady economic growth across the Habsburg monarchy's society, and its western half in particular. This proved to be the essential impetus for the change of culture in general. In the mid-19th century, people lived in late Biedermeier ambience, with a low level of general education demonstrated mainly in a high illiteracy rate (especially in the rural population), with little sanitation and completely insufficient healthcare. The beginning of the 1870s, however, were marked by a fundamental shift in attitudes to education, even among the lower social classes (workers, peasants, traders), a revived interest in public matters and rising living standards in Cisleithania. This was almost exclusively in its most developed regions – in Austrian and Czech lands.

While Biedermeier, prevalent among the still somewhat socially self-conscious burghers, imitated the noble lifestyle, at the end of the 1860s and the beginning of the 1870s, the modern bourgeoisie gained self-awareness, the monarchy's lifestyle gradually rationalized and the cultural situation democratized. Liberalism attracted the wider public to participate in social and cultural activities. Until the Viennese Stock Exchange Crash in 1873, German entrepreneurs in the Czech Lands experienced the steepest rise. Together with Viennese liberals, they collaborated in enacting parliamentarianism, that is a higher form of democracy within the monarchy. While the 1850s were marked by German legal centralism, the 1860s saw the implementation of national liberalization, which had serious consequences, most notably for Czech culture and learning.

Despite the neo-absolutist era's restrictive measures, which mainly affected journalism, theatre and literature, in the latter part of the 19th century, the role of literature steadily rose as it helped to form the ideological orientation and national life of Czech society, and the importance of general knowledge and purview of the current problems also increased. While Hegel's revolutionary democratic philosophy, which inspired mainly aesthetics and psychology although bearing few ideological results, was replaced in the 1850s by Herbartianism in the monarchy, in the period of renewed constitutionality, the situation in the Prague university – in the main centre of domestic science – started to improve (for example, in 1862, Josef Dastich started his Czech lectures on philosophy). However, even the neo-absolutist era handed down some positive aspects to the subsequent constitutional period; primarily a well-reformed secondary education, whose system of "classical" and "real" Gymnasia (general secondary schools) was used in the Czech Lands until the mid-1920s. In the 1860s, the emancipation process in Czech education and expansion of the intellectual level of the Czech nation commenced. All this was reflected in the high number of linguistically Czech schools and their work with all social classes and groups.

German society in the Czech Lands was in a completely different situation. With only a little simplification, we can say that after the defeat of the 1848–1849 movements, the German nation was the ruling nation in the Habsburg monarchy. It almost entirely controlled state administration, military matters, and finances, as well as industrial production and business; only in agriculture did the situation differ. Nevertheless, even Germans, at least the revolutionary democratic ones, were among the defeated in 1849 as their programme of German unification with a democratic basis crashed. From that time, the German opinion in the Habsburg empire was split: on the one hand, there were democratic Germans who supported the existing state system and were connected to the House of Habsburg, and on the other, there were radical, nationalist and democratic Germans in opposition to the Habsburgs, who hoped that their nationalist ambitions would be realized in the Prussian royal dynasty of Hohenzollerns and in their efforts to unify Germany from above. Until the establishment of the German Empire, this part of the German population fulfilled their progressive political and cultural role as they were the bearers of liberal and radical democracy. They were the genesis of most cultural values, both artistic and scientific. In the Czech Lands, they were mainly concentrated in Prague with its rich club life, theatres, university, technical university and scientific institutions; to some extent the same applied to Brno.

Only in the 1870s did the Bohemian Germans split into radical nationalists, ideologically inclining to more aggressive forms of German-wide chauvinism and beginning to stagnate culturally, and democrats, whose activities inspired other Cisleithan nations. The most prominent personality of German literature in the Czech Lands in this period was, paradoxically, Adalbert Stifter, linked with Vienna and one of the most steadfast Austrians among the monarchy's German writers. In his works, this artist with his ties the Bohemian Forest, managed to link political conservatism with the period's humanist ideals. In other artistic fields, Germans surpassed Czechs – visual artists, actors and musicians met with positive response among the wealthy German burghers, who provided enough demand for these artists to continue. German science also held a clearly leading position. However, in education, there was a discrepancy between the developed German population in urban areas and the rural population living in the borderlands, working on infertile mountain soil and generally illiterate.

From the 1840s, there was a movement among the Jewish population to become an independent cultural element within the monarchy. The Jews participated in the revolutionary democratic movement, as well as in the conservative opposition to it, however, they were content with the preservation of the unity of the Austrian dual state. The Frankfurt programme meant the danger of greater-German nationalism, often intolerant of other ethnic groups. Jewish self-confidence grew in the 1850s, but their coveted goal – full civic equality – was not achieved until the December Law of 1867. Jewish emancipation could socially rely on the positions of Jewish financial, business and industrial capital, thanks to which it gained a society-wide importance. In the 1860s, the idea of assimilation prevailed among the monarchy's Jewish inhabitants. The ghettoes were almost forgotten and the solution of the "Jewish question" seemed to rest on accepting the external features of the nationality in whose territory the Jews lived and worked – mainly the language, sometimes the religion. This aculturalist or assimilation contact, which was beneficial for both sides, gave rise to artistic and scientific values created by Jews who accepted either Czech or German nationality. The Jews in cities were generally well educated, while rural Jews – particularly in Moravia – did not share such a high cultural potential unless they had access to good quality Jewish schools. The democratization and unification of education in Cisleithania eventually also brought advantages to the Jewish population.

Cultural Development Before the Turn of the 19th and 20th Centuries

In the last three decades of the 19th century, when the industrialization and urbanization of the western part of the Habsburg monarchy reached its peak and in an atmosphere of economic liberalism, the Czech and Austrian lands as a whole experienced an unprecedented economic rise. Unfortunately, inequality in the economic, political and cultural development of different parts of the multinational monarchy were difficult to overcome, especially with the accompanying national discrepancies of a socio-psychological, political and power-politics character. However, before the end of the 19th century, urban areas were modernized and brought up date with European trends, the living standard in the Lower-Austrian, Bohemian and Moravian countryside increased and the entire society engaged in cultural activities, albeit differentiated according to education, social status and wealth.

As lifestyle was gradually rationalized, sanitation measures followed the expansion of medical sciences and the increasing quality of public healthcare, modern agglomerations acquired sewerage systems, public refuse incinerating plants were built and dumps founded, towns ensured gas distribution, the appearance of towns and rich villages radically changed. Old fortifications were demolished in many towns, apartment and municipal buildings were erected, larger communities acquired public lighting, the open countryside gave way to human work, new machines appeared everywhere. Railways made previously important towns insignificant, while making others important hubs. The road network grew thicker and, at the end of the century, the first cars appeared. Declining small trades were gradually replaced by a network of department stores and town markets, where the food was cheaper than in small shops.

The politicization of life was on the increase, expanding education and political differentiation augmented social discrepancies. The press became the "seventh power." Public libraries, reading rooms and educational institutions for everyone – including many new museums – supplemented the well thought-out education system in an effort to limit illiteracy. This marked trend was most obvious in the economically and socially developed regions, such as in the ethnically Czech inland of the Czech Lands and in some areas of the Austrian lands. The achievements of science and engineering, linked to technologically developed industrial production, permeated everyday life. By the turn of the centuries, Austria-Hungary in its most developed parts, the Czech Lands among them, equalled European countries and made up for a certain developmental delay, whose rudiments can be traced back to the 17th century and the Thirty Years' War, and which were carried through to the following centuries.

After the disappointment caused by the failure of the Fundamental Articles and overcoming the shock of economic crisis, the Czech nation underwent the steepest rise of all monarchy's nations. It was already sufficiently emancipated in the cultural, national and social spheres, but lacked its own capital, and hence the crisis did not throw the Czechs into as destructive a recession as it did the Bohemian Germans. Czechs used Taaffe's regime to profit from their participation in the "Iron Ring of the Right" through establishing industrial companies (at this time mainly in the consumer goods industry), ensuring the functioning of their own financial institutions (the Trade Bank) and the intensification of agricultural production, which, as they rightly suspected, was an opportunity to overcome the protracted agrarian crisis. The successful accumulation and investment of domestic capital had a positive impact on Czech cultural activities. The 1870s started the period of creating "national" artistic archetypes: national opera and music (Bedřich Smetana), national sculpture (Josef Václav Myslbek), national painting (Josef Mánes and Mikoláš Aleš), national historical novels (Václav Beneš Třebízský and Alois Jirásek) and also national poetry (Jan Neruda).

The opening of the National Theatre was an exceptional event for the Czech nation. It was the culmination of several previous generations' efforts to concentrate the best representatives of Czech drama, music and the budding ballet theatre into one respectable building, which could compete with the largest theatrical groups in Europe and which would predominantly stage Czech-language performances. The fire of August 12, 1881 led to a nation-wide collection and, so, the theatre could be reopened within a very short time – on November 18, 1883. The activities accompanying its organization reflected a period political struggles, but in general it was the culmination of the national-revivalist efforts of the entire epoch. The construction of the theatre brought artists, actors, writers, masters of artistic crafts together alongside Czech industrial entrepreneurs and it was an event of great symbolic value. Even the external appearance of the building was planned as unique and when completed it truly was. The decorative work employed Czech visual artists thus increasing their prestige across the nation.

The tendency to emphasize ethnicity was particularly well reflected in architecture. The first Czech architectural works were created as soon as there were people to finance them and demand arose. The arcades of the Vyšehrad cemetery (Viktor Barvitius), the buildings of the National Theatre (Josef Zítek), the National Museum (Josef Schulz) and later the

PAVEL CIBULKA — JAN HÁJEK — MARTIN KUČERA

respectable Rudolfinum (Josef Zítek, Josef Schulz) rank among the top exemplars of European Neo-Renaissance Palladianism, while Antonín Wiehl and, after him, Jan Zeyer designed purely Czech Neo-Renaissance buildings of an urban, residential type. Czech literature of the last decades of the 19th century can boast works of eternal value created by three literary generations – mainly the generation of Jan Neruda, then of Jaroslav Vrchlický, Julius Zeyer, Josef Václav Sládek and Svatopluk Čech and, last but not least, of "Czech Modernism." The successful development of literature was closely linked to society's general upswing.

In 1870–1900, Czech music quickly reached a gold-standard level thanks to its most prominent representatives. It did not reflect the first avant-garde tendencies, due to a certain conservatism in the local public, which was attached to the national binding model of Bedřich Smetana's operas and symphonic poems. It came to terms with the compositional innovations of the best representatives of a younger generation only shortly before the First World War. In this respect, Vienna and Budapest were where music's avant-garde revolts appeared ten or more years earlier than in the Czech environment. Before end of the 19th century, Czech music outgrew its hitherto developmental handicap and, in quality and quantity, in composition and interpretation, it could start focusing on the important tasks laid out by its international context. First it was the conclusion of Bedřich Smetana's life-long striving for original Czech music expression. Most of his best works were composed after he lost his hearing; moreover, in his last compositions he anticipated the 20th-century developmental trends which were so ungraspable for his contemporaries. The second part of the 19th century is also closely linked to the work of the second genius of the Czech music – Antonín Dvořák. Unlike Smetana, Dvořák was a spontaneous musician who introduced to Czech music a sense of the natural beauty of sound and became one of the masters of instrumentation. He focused on areas which Smetana had neglected – chamber, symphonic, orchestral, oratorial and church music and his role in them was that of a founder. He focused on classicism enriched by Neo-Romantic orchestration and softness. Of Dvořák's work, his symphonies were particularly important and among them is his most popular: Symphony No. 9 *From the New World* (1893). The youngest of the founding Czech composers – Zdeněk Fibich – was linked to musical Romanticism. As the choirmaster and conductor of the Provisional Theatre and, later, the operatic dramatic advisor for the National Theatre and a teacher, Fibich was one of the best educated Czech composers. Among Fibich's best works were nine melodramas; he is internationally considered the most important composer of melodramas.

The 1890s were the peak of national life begun over the previous decades and reflected a successful end of the "first industrialization," which in culture and lifestyle brought tangible achievements and provided new methods of subsistence for intellectuals (also thanks to the extraordinary boom of Czech periodicals). This stimulated a previously unsuspected need for university education. The favourable situation created conditions for a further cultural boom and approach to world – in the 1890s, Czech literary, artistic and musical Modernism came to life. The *Manifesto of Czech Modernism* (1895) and the rise of poetic symbolism (Otokar Březina), impressionism (Antonín Sova) and critical realism (Josef Svatopluk Machar), the foundation of the Modern Review *(Moderní revue)* as the mouthpiece of decadence, the *Almanac of the Art Nouveau* as an anarchist revolt of the creative individual (Stanislav Kostka Neumann), Czech Catholic Modernism as a union seeking to reform Catholicism and excellent artistic criticism (Sigismund Ludvík Bouška among others) and the birth of Czech criticism (František Xaver Šalda); these were all intellectual deeds which rescued Czech literature from the grip of provincialism. A similar role was played by impressionism and symbolism in painting (Antonín Slavíček, Max Švabinský) and in sculpture (František Bílek) and modernism in music, where the legacy of the founders – Smetana, Dvořák and Fibich – was continued and developed along original lines by five personalities of European creative significance (mainly the burly avant-garde figure of Leoš Janáček, but also Josef Bohuslav Foerster, Vítězslav Novák, Josef Suk and Otakar Ostrčil). In musical interpretation, the long Czech musical tradition reached its peak in the Czech Quartet, a world quality chamber ensemble. The slow development in comparison to Western Europe was most marked in visual arts and theatre, while new technical types of visual arts – photography and film – took root in the Czech Lands relatively quickly.

The re-establishment of the Czech university in Prague in the 1882–1883 academic year became a landmark in the post-1870 history of Czech education. In the 1870s, the number of Czech lectures at the Charles-Ferdinand University, which was linguistically still formally centralized, was growing. The lectures were delivered by scholars from the younger generation who were open to Europe. They were offered in all faculties, including the theological. Among the lecturers at the Faculty of Law were, for instance, Antonín Randa and Emil Ott who were the authors of Czech legal terminology; the number of Czechs was also increasing in the Medical Faculty (internist Jan Bohumil Eiselt and others). At the Faculty of Arts, Czech science was represented by several natural scientists, as well as prominent Herbartianism proponents, Josef Durdík in the Philosophical Seminary and Gustav Adolf Lindner in pedagogical studies, along with Miroslav Tyrš, the pioneer of the Raphaelite aesthetic ideal, which influenced the National Theatre artistic generation, and organizer of Czech physical culture. Among prominent personalities in the Faculty of Arts were the excellent linguist Jan Gebauer and historians Jaroslav Goll and Antonín Rezek, founders of the Czech Historical Journal *(Český časopis historický)* (1895), a journal specializing in historical sciences in the Czech Lands. They, together with aesthetician Otakar Hostinský, belonged to the circle of friends of the Czech philosopher who had graduated in Vienna, Tomáš Garrigue Masaryk, an adherent of Brentan's school with an interest in sociology, ethics and later the philosophy of politics. They all met on the ground of the re-established Czech university and engaged in various, often personal, battles over the character of Czech scientific knowledge, over the meaning of history and historical learning.

In 1886, the public was shaken by an affair, in which contributions to Masaryk's *Athenaeum* review written by members of the newly constituted "realistic" group of Czech scientists proved the revivalist "discoveries," the allegedly medieval *Dvůr Králové and Zelená hora Manuscritps* to be forgeries. The "Czech Ossian" fell through and this fall of the fakes was variously perceived by the emancipating Czech nation. The nation had not gained its self-confidence, only acquired in the modernism stage of the 1890s and through the pre-war avant-garde. Moreover, as Albert Vyskočil rightly pointed out, the manuscripts had significant artistic value and influence, comparable to Mácha's *May*. Domestic science had to convince the nation that it could withstand confrontation from international science. Czech science in the 1880s had to fulfil a demythicizing role in establishing modern Czech scientific schools on this newly purified basis.

One of Czech education's major achievements was the success of Josef Hlávka, the most prominent Czech patron, architect and entrepreneur in the building industry, who managed to convince the government and the court that the emperor should provide auspices to the foundation of the Emperor Francis Joseph's Czech Academy for Sciences, Literature and Arts. It came to fruition in January 1890. The Academy was to cultivate all scientific and artistic disciplines in the Czech language, thus contributing to the self-sufficiency of Czech education. It was fundamentally a symbolic success, yet it came at the right time. It truly aided in boosting the Czech cultural character and, as a result, essentially all cultural fields in the Czech Lands developed as nationally Czech before the end of the 19th century. Some managed to enter the international context through the works of their representatives – literary theorist František Xaver Šalda, historian Josef Pekař, linguist Josef Zubatý, orientalist Rudolf Dvořák and literary historian Jaroslav Vlček as well as excellent lawyers, doctors, biologists and natural scientists. The Czech nation also had remarkable achievements in technical fields, which was demonstrated by the Czech Technical University in Prague (which became independent in 1869), as well as by the foundation of a second technical university in Brno in 1899. It came as no surprise that Czechs demanded a second Czech university, located in Moravia, though for nationalist-political reasons (opposition by Austrian, Bohemian and Moravian Germans) their demand was rejected.

Thanks to a general growth in the national economy, the population's social mobility, as well as the rising living and cultural standards, a network of Czech secondary and technical schools of all specializations was gradually created and consistently perfected. These institutions, founded on the basis of Cisleithan education legislation, produced well-prepared potential university students and credible experts, including artisans. The general education level was rather high. Among the monarchy's ethnicities, Czechs excelled not only in the level of achieved education, but also in its quality. Before the turn of the 19th and 20th centuries, illiteracy among the Czech nationality professional population in towns and, to a degree, in the developed countryside (the Labe region, Jizera region and Haná in Moravia) was eliminated. The Czechs thus gained prominence in education quality.

The German population, mainly inhabiting the borderlands and the less fertile interior enclaves the Bohemian-Moravian Highlands, České Budějovice region, the Giant Mountains foothills, suffered from the 1873 crisis and its consequences, as well as from the ensuing protracted agrarian crisis. Bohemian-German capital was concentrated exclusively in urban centres (Prague, Liberec, Ústí nad Labem, Karlovy Vary, Plzeň, Brno, Olomouc, Ostrava, Jihlava and, to a degree, České Budějovice) and linked to German-Empire or Viennese capital – particularly among the German-Jewish entrepreneurs – and it did not have enough money for the financial rehabilitation of the farmers and west-Bohemian miners who were increasinlgly impoverished. The growing anti-Czech animosity was mainly due to the awareness of the borderland German population's growing poverty. In the consumer goods industry, Czech capital started to outstrip the German at the end of the 19th century. The educational, cultural and living standards of the rural population was incomparable; Czech peasants ranked among the highest in the world in sanitation, agricultural engineering, literacy, and so on, while the German borderland was 60% illiterate. German culture was therefore concentrated exclusively in the above-mentioned centres, and was successful principally in Prague and Brno – a Moravian metropolis linked to Vienna through German theatrical culture. This also explains why literary German nationalists, intolerant and non-democratic, recruited from the borderlands rather than from Prague and Brno.

Prague provided Germans with a great material, financial and institutional background, which undoubtedly had a positive effect on culture. German visual artists graduated from the Academy of Fine Arts as well as from the School of Decorative Arts, German musicians – both composers and interpreters (pianist Romeo Finke and others) – from Prague's conservatory. From 1891, the Society for the Development of German Science, Literature and Art had its seat in Prague, as a counterpoise to the Czech Academy. Prague's German university, generously subsidized by the state, played an important role among the monarchy's universities. It was smaller than the Czech one, but created a rather expansive model of German "national" science, mainly in medicine, comparative linguistics, oriental studies, art history and theory, physics and mathematics, political disciplines, national economics and, particularly remarkably, in philosophy. German philosophy of language (Alexius von Meinong) or experimental psychology (Christian von Ehrenfels) became recognized disciplines. Technicians in both Bohemian and Moravian German polytechnic schools did not lag behind Europe either (Brno's inventor Viktor Kaplan). The national concept, on the other hand, hampered broader advancement in the historical and literary-historical learning. Yet Ernst Mach, one of the initiators of relativism in philosophy and physics, and Eugen von Böhm-Bawerk in economic theory, represented one of the peaks of Bohemian-German science.

The establishment of a central German theatre in the country, the Neues Deutsches Theater (1885), and most notably its operatic dramatics were of special importance. Angelo Neumann, the founder and first director of the German theatre, and one of the leading consummators of Wagner's programme of musical-dramatic theatre reform, brought his Bayreuth experience to Prague. Gustav Mahler, a conductor and composer of revolutionary importance and one of the promoters of Czech music in the German environment, began his starry career under Neumann's leadership. The musical culture of Germans in Bohemia, more markedly than in Moravia, mingled in an amiable way with Czech music.

German literature in the Czech Lands was quite specific. Before the turn of the centuries it developed in realistic (Marie von Ebner-Eschenbach, Friedrich von Saar) and Neo-Romantic directions. Neo-Romantic authors mainly came from Prague's multi-national environment, and were influenced by the Slavic element and created conditions for a further extraordinary boom in Bohemian-German Prague literature. The German group (Gustav

Meyring, German Moravian Alfred Kubin), however, differed from the German-Jewish group (Hugo Salus, the musically-oriented Adler family), which was less distant from the Czech ethnical group's interests and was closer to the efforts to reform the Habsburg monarchy. Austrian Neo-Romanticism, which also found expression in painting (the Laukotas salon), was inspired by Salzburg's writer, playwright and theoretician, the Czechophile Hermann Bahr. It was conceived as part of Austrian-German Modernism, which was the direct predecessor to the avant-garde.

It the 1890s, it was already clear that Jewish cultural activities in the Czech Lands to some extent represented an independent chapter of cultural life. The effort to distinguish themselves was manifested only in the works of some representatives of the creative intelligentsia of Jewish origin, while a majority preferred the idea of assimilation – either with the Czech nation (Julius Zeyer) or the German nation (Gustav Mahler). The Jewish intellectual and artistic potential enriched Prague's and Brno's cultural scenes both in science and arts; however culturally active Jews were also to be found in Ostrava, Liberec or Plzeň (German), Hradec Králové, Pardubice and Mladá Boleslav (Czech) and sporadically in other places. They worked at universities, secondary and elementary schools, on the editorial boards of newspapers and magazines, in the machinery of political parties, but they were most influential in the German university and in Prague's literary, artistic and musical life. Although they accepted Czech or German nationality, they enriched their cultural works with the motif of uprootedness, the Wandering Jew, nostalgia, homesickness and missing identity, they were influenced by the mystical atmosphere of the Jewish Quarter, introducing those elements of the artistic works' structure which became fully established in the pre-war avant-garde.

Cultural Development on the Eve of the First World War

The conditions of Cisleithan civilization changed sharply over the years immediately before the First World War. Symbolically, this was demonstrated by the originally provincial town of Prague becoming a European metropolis. Industrialization entered its second phase, in which the leading role was assumed by financial capital. The material background of the cultural movement could only be purposefully developed by those countries with capital. From 1903 in the Czech Lands, the Trade Bank (a Czech bank) assumed a premier and unrivalled position in Bohemia and Moravia, with a branch office in Vienna and Chernivtsi (in German Czernowitz, in Czech Černovice), the Bukovina capital on the very eastern edge of the Habsburg monarchy, and played a decisive role. The so-called second industrialization made an impression with its rapid and visible results, as combustion engines and electric motors introduced new elements of civilization. Automotive transport expanded, the military was modernized, all of the globe's developed regions had adopted the practices of industrial mass production. Mass production was the only way to satisfy the fast-growing demands of industry, agriculture, the military, daily consumption and high-end commercialism. On the one hand, society was growing relatively rich, on the other, social differences deepened. Electric motors supplied energy to trades, power plants were built, the river depths changed and their flows regulated. Fields and their environs were changing in the face of irrigation and drainage. Intensive agricultural production made use of mechanization and chemistry, towns were gradually electrified, old town quarters demolished, giving way to new construction.

The appearance of neighbourhoods underwent great changes, which had some negative aspects, yet there was a growing need for applied and industrial art; books as well as glass window panes became artistic artefacts. European lifestyle was subjected to a unified decorative ornamental style – Art Nouveau. Art Nouveau varied according to place and application; nevertheless, it was the last movement to provide a rational unity of expression to the world of industrial civilization, often inspired by the re-discovered Orient as a world of new beauty. Hygiene became a daily requirement, so town water supply networks were introduced on a massive scale. The distances between countries grew shorter, time became relative. Natural and technical sciences developed in huge leaps and the world was dominated by industry and technology. Society was individualized and split, actual producers became an unignorable collective power. Discrepancies within societies grew larger and gravely serious, then led to a world war. The years before the war, however, were by no means idyllic; poverty was not disappearing, but being pushed to the margins – to the peripheries of the flourishing urban agglomerations.

In connection with European development, the Czech national environment underwent essential shifts, enhancing the previous growth conditions. After 1903, Czech economic growth surpassed Bohemian-German growth in all ways. Czechs held fewer large companies than Germans, yet they owned a large number of medium-size and prospering small companies, and they had their own banks (not only the Trade Bank, but also the Industrial Bank, Union Bank, Agrarian Bank and others). The Czech nation also became self-sufficient, competitive and export-oriented in agriculture. Czechs entered foreign markets and the international financial world.

By 1914, illiteracy had been almost entirely eliminated in the Czech environment and Czech education was on the rise. One of the main achievement was the fast educational upswing of the Czech countryside, though no less important was the development of Czech self-government – on all levels from province to community, which usually made qualified decisions. Although food was not cheap, only the poorest, least qualified and mostly illiterate people suffered from hunger. The unemployment rate was low and wages gradually grew. The Modernism of the 1890s and the rapid adoption of the Art-Nouveau lifestyle by Czech society led directly to an improvement of conditions among the young artistic generation who had few difficulties accepting the international impulses of the first (pre-war) avant-garde. Despite the intensification of Czech-German national discrepancies in everyday life and in politics, Czechs, Germans and Jews successfully co-operated in the avant-garde environment. Their social background developed and matured, political life became richly differentiated and acquired noticeable democratization features. All this created the positive conditions for multi-layered cultural activities.

Before the First World War, Czechs followed contemporary European movements in all spheres of public activities and managed not only to apply them, but also to contribute to their development in an original way. In literature, the Czech pre-war avant-garde was represented by two generations, the second appearing shortly after the first: the generation of "anarchist rebels," which took up the baton from Czech Modernism at the turn of the century and advanced its inspirations to the first anti-illusory tones in Czech lyric poetry, fiction and drama (Petr Bezruč, Karel Toman, Viktor Dyk, Fráňa Šrámek, and František Gellner among others). While the "rebels" seemed to some extent to be the followers of an individual revolt and synthesists of modern literary impulses, the generation of the Čapek brothers, Karel and Josef, was linked to the latest impulses of the Western-European avant-garde, mainly Cubist and Expressionist, but also Neo-Classical, Neo-Romantic and, to a lesser extent, Futurist. It entered the artistic peace as a destructive element, as a seeming destroyer of the 1890s' Modernist achievements, even though without them it could not have been born. Thanks to this atmosphere, formed by Modernism through its many struggles, a few years before the war, the Czech avant-garde could achieve world-class standards of intensity and originality in the history of Czech culture.

In Czech architecture, two basic impulses influenced avant-garde tendencies which asserted themselves from the beginning of Cubism in 1910: first, the influence of the school of Viennese Modernism, founded and shaped by Otto Wagner; second, the model of the national school of architectural Modernism, whose founder and soul was the versatile Jan Kotěra. Kotěra laid the foundations of Czech Cubist architecture. Cubism in Czech architecture was prominent until the 1920s (and in stage design until the 1930s) as one of the purest expressions of the Czech architectural avant-garde. Avant-garde Czech sculpture before the war was influenced by large exhibitions of works by August Rodin and Émile-Antoine Bourdelle which had been held in Prague. The French masters influenced European-style sculptors – Jan Štursa, Josef Mařatka and Otto Gutfreund, the most avant-garde of them all, whose works reflect Cubism, Cubo-Futurism and Cubo-Expressionism.

The Norwegian expressionist Edvard Munch's exhibition, held in Prague in 1905, sent the painting avant-garde in the Czech Lands on a difficult journey of seeking its own goals, specific to its own needs. In 1907, an exhibition of the painters group The Eight (*Osma*) was organized. Its programme was prevalently Expressionist and transgressed the narrowly defined limits of national art as the group consisted of Czech painters (Emil Filla, Bohumil Kubišta, Vincenc Beneš, Otakar Kubín, Antonín Procházka, Emil Artur Pittermann-Longen and Linka Scheithauerová) as well as Germans (Willy Nowak, Friedrich Feigl, Max Horb), who claimed, however, to be Bohemian-Germans. The members of The Eight were soon affected by Cubism, which they employed in a specific manner, initiating Czech Cubo-Expressionism. Echoes of Futurism and Cubo-Futurism also reached Bohemia before the war. Some Czech avant-garde painters followed Orphism and, rarely, abstraction (František Kupka and Vojtěch Preissing, among others), others discovered Fauvism or post-Art-Nouveau Neo-Symbolism and later neo-classicism (Jan Zrzavý). The existing centre of Modernist artistic efforts – the Mánes Association of Fine Artists – became the avant-garde's opponent when, in 1911, a wing of young Cubists left and established the Group of Fine Artists (Bohumil Kubišta, Emil Filla, Vincenc Beneš, Otakar Kubín, Antonín Procházka, with them Josef Čapek, Václav Špála,

Ladislav Šíma, Otto Gutfreund, architects Josef Gočár, Pavel Janák and others). The Sursum association (1910–1912) expounded late decadent Neo-Symbolism and Spiritualism. Its members included Jan Zrzavý, sculptor Jaroslav Horejc, graphic artists František Kobliha, Josef Váchal and others. A degree of counterbalance to these groups before the war was provided by the work of artists who purposefully and originally developed the legacy of Modernism (Ludvík Kuba, Jan Preisler, Karel Myslbek, Herbert Masaryk, Václav Rabas and others).

The musical avant-garde before the First World War followed the direction set by its five modern initiators, of which two composers, Leoš Janáček and Otakar Ostrčil, were the direct predecessors of the Czech musical avant-garde, which asserted itself only after the establishment of an independent Czechoslovakia. Janáček's work won world renown. Other avant-garde composers who later became world-famous, Bohuslav Martinů and Ervín Schulhoff, started their careers before the war. Modernism in drama and theatre had many features. First, the head of the National Theatre's drama section, Jaroslav Kvapil, drew inspiration from European theatre and especially the Moscow Art Theatre and created a directorial style which was suitable for the artistic needs of the time. His conceptual directing style brought to the Czech stage the principles of psychoanalysis, impressionism and Art-Nouveau symbolism. He laid the foundations of modern Czech dramatic acting (Eduard Vojan, Hana Kvapilová, Marie Hübnerová). Karel Kovařovic's era in the National Theatre opera played the same role as Kvapil's era in drama. Kovařovic was the first Czech virtuoso conductor, whose demanding interpretation style was inspired by Hans von Bülow, and he built the ensemble to the rules set by Gustav Mahler. It was clear that Prague's Czech opera was directed by a personality of international standard. The orchestra members revolted against him at the very beginning of his engagement for alleged despotism and, in 1901, established an independent orchestra – the Czech Philharmonic Orchestra. Kovařovic ignored the period prejudices, something demonstrated by his intensive co-operation with the Czech Philharmonic Orchestra as conductor (from the beginning of the 20th century, the largest Czech symphonic ensemble; the second largest was the Orchestral Association in Brno), as well as by his collaboration with Neues Deutsches Theater. Among opera singers, there were world-class soloists (Ema Destinnová, Karel Burian, Otakar Mařák).

The promotion of the Czech theatrical avant-garde forms a special chapter in the nation's cultural history. The European avant-garde was, before the First World War, linked to stage expressionism, promoted in Berlin by indefatigable experimenter Max Reinhardt, and the first important Czech directors of the new orientation (František Zavřel, Sr., Karel Hugo Hilar, Jan Bor, Karel Dostal) were his students. The Czech theatrical avant-garde was based in the City Theatre in Prague's Vinohrady. Meanwhile, ballet was only at the outset of its modern development. Theatrical life was significantly complemented by cabarets, in which many actors, including Emil Artur and Xena Longen, Jaroslav Hašek, Eduard Bass, Karel Hašler, Vlasta Burian, Ferenc Futurista, started their career. The artistic avant-garde affected the audiences only a little, though its importance for cultural development is fundamental as its oppositionist, socially-critical and even destructive content could only address a minority of the public's cultural perspective.

The First World War disrupted the development of Czech national society, so promising in so many respects. The positive trends, however, could not be stopped, although rather than in new growth, they were manifested in the universal employment of the wide-scale education growth of the Czech nation. According to statistics of the period, Czechs ranked first in the monarchy and among the highest across Europe in literacy rates – and it should be added, also in the quality and intensity of education achieved. This is revealed when comparing peasants from comparable fertile regions of Austria-Hungary: peasants from Lower Austria were one hundred per cent literate, yet in questionnaires they admitted no interest in reading, not to mention creative cultural activities, only 51% of peasants from the Hungarian lowlands were fully literate and in the Cracow regions, this level was even lower. Czech peasants from the Elbe, Jizera or Moravian Haná regions were not only fully literate, but also showed an interest in reading, often on a daily basis or as active members of readers' clubs, amateur dramatic societies and village music bands. They subscribed to newspapers and before 1914 there was an increasing trend towards attending secondary economic schools. The same can be claimed of the qualified workers. The specialized workers in factories were required to hold a certificate of apprenticeship, as well as being middle school graduates, which were generally of high-quality. They attended excellent follow-on schools and often (around 20%) also lower engineering schools; they were keen on reading and worked in various political and non-political cultural corporations.

The quality of the Czech intelligentsia which graduated from secondary schools and universities created a favourable climate for further improvements in Czech education system standards. Before 1914, the number of Czech schools grew, albeit slightly, and all specialized and scientific fields (social sciences, natural sciences, technical) experienced an intellectual boom. Because the Prague Czech university, the Prague and Brno Czech technical universities had lower financial state and Land subsidies than similar German institutions, which barely co-operated with their Czech counterparts, it was a major achievement of the growing Czech education and its effort to eliminate its historical delay. This national development tendency worried the Germans of the Czech Lands. Czech intellectual expansion can be documented through several examples. What is particularly remarkable is that the Czech intelligentsia managed to assert itself everywhere it settled in the world, including Paris, but particularly in the countries of eastern and south-eastern Europe, where there was enough room for its activity. Educated Czechs considerably influenced the cultural development of Bulgaria, Croatia and Slovenia, musicians and visual artists played their role in uplifting cultural life in Russia, along with scientists and engineers, teachers and doctors. Last but not least, the graduates from the Czech medical school were called for in Europe, with their contribution particularly noticeable during both Balkan Wars (1912–1913), when expeditions of young surgeons, who had studied under professors Otakar Kukula and Rudolf Jedlička, helped in Serbia, Montenegro and Bulgaria. They all contributed to the high quality of Czech war surgery. Social sciences were dominated by the schools of historians Josef Pekař, Josef Šusta and Václav Novotný, literary historian Jaroslav Vlček, philosopher T. G. Masaryk, pedagogue František Drtina, Indo-Europeanist Josef Zubatý and Germanist Arnošt

Vilém Kraus. These are all good examples of the variety within Czech education. Before 1914, Czech education and culture reached a European level in almost every sphere and, in the radically changed conditions after 1918, they could build upon these achievements.

German cultural activities in the Czech Lands can be divided, like Czech ones, to a commercial stream of popular entertainment, which was most burdened with nationalist prejudices, a traditional stream, whose adherents from the borderlands often demonstrated ethnically malicious traits, and an avant-garde stream, frequently by Germans of Jewish origin. This movement was close to the Czech avant-garde efforts, as they shared the desire for international recognition. Jewish avant-garde followers also turned away with abomination from pan-Germanism with its anti-Semitic, racially-charged content. The Bohemian-German avant-garde also asserted itself in all fields, although it had a weaker social background than the Czech avant-garde, but it could rely on certain support from Vienna (the relationship of painters Gustav Klimt and Egon Schiele is one example) as well as the avant-garde in Berlin and Munich. The literary avant-garde was linked mainly to Prague, as the largest number of Jews establishing themselves in the German literary scene, lived in this town. Prague's German literature, ethnically neutral, became a Jewish, rather than German phenomenon, although the avant-garde is characterized by a syncretism of influences, including ethnic. Ethnically German authors also had extraordinary talents in their midst – Rainer Maria Rilke, Robert Musil, Paul Leppin and Robert Michel.

Fine arts were characterized by a symbiosis of the Czech and German avant-gardes with Czechophile Willy Nowak at its head. The Jewish element also played an important role in German fine arts. German sculptors studied under Josef Václav Mysbek at the Academy of Fine Arts, where painters had three German professors. At the School of Decorative Arts, Germans attended classes given by František Schmoranz, the Jarosch brothers and Jakub Schikaneder, and at the conservatory, master classes with Vítězslav Novák (Fidelio Finke). Before the war, Jews contributed to German music and theatre. In the Neues Deutsches Theater, the prominent conductor and composer Alexander von Zemlinsky, a brother-in-law of Vienna's avant-garde composer Arnold Schönberg, was a leading personality. Zemlinsky, being a friend of Kovařovic, systematically co-operated with Czech musical culture and helped its flowering, for instance as a conductor of the Czech Philharmonic Orchestra. German theatrical culture in the Czech Lands, not only in Prague, but also in Brno, Ostrava or Liberec, was influenced by a mostly Jewish group called Young Vienna. Avant-garde expressions were based on Viennese Art Nouveau and inclined to draw inspiration from Austrian Neo-Romanticism, German Expressionism and neo-classicism and, later, from French Cubism, Fauvism, Orphism and Italian-Russian Futurism.

Many Czech musicians worked in the German environment – either in Vienna (Oskar Nedbal, František Ondrříček, Josef Bohuslav Foerster) or in Germany (František Neumann and many others), winning their sympathy for Czech culture, with one of the leading minds of global Neo-Romanticism, Richard Strauss, esteeming the musicality of Czechs. Nowak contributed to the spread of Czech visual arts to the European market; in Vienna, one of the architectural reformers of the 20th century, Brno's German Adolf Loos, was on friendly terms with the local Czechs, which was not such a surprise when we recall that he did, after all, speak Czech. This co-operation within the avant-garde movement helped promote the "Czech question" on the international scene.

The Jewish contribution to the Czech-German avant-garde before the First World War was of great importance. The Jews were fully emancipated and they mostly adopted Czech and German assimilation programmes and participated in cultural activities as equals. At the end of the first decade of the 20th century, the foundations were laid, thanks to Martin Buber's lectures, for the acceptance of Zionism by a part of the Czech Lands' Jewish population. Although before 1914, only a small percentage of the mostly German-speaking Jews from the Czech Lands supported Zionism, they were, in the main, influential and very creative intellectuals (Max Brod, Felix Weltsch, Hugo Bergmann, Franz Kohn, Chasid Jiří Mordechaj Langer among others). We can observe the merging of cultures in their activities: Brod's promotion of works by Leoš Janáček and Jaroslav Hašek played an important role. Among Jews assimilated in the Czech environment, we should mention poet František Gellner, novelist and playwright František Langer, Germanist Arnošt Vilém Kraus, poet, translator and Germanist Otokar Fischer, sculptor Otto Gutfreund, painter Hanuš Schwaiger, painter and actor Emil Artur Longen, singer Emil Pollert, philosopher Jindřich Kohn and many others. The Jews assimilated in the German milieu formed a particularly large cultural enclave, with some (painter Friedrich-Bedřich Feigl and composer Erwein-Ervín Schulhoff) professing both nationalities, but neither those who adhered to German nationality were ethnically entirely separatist and they promoted values of Czech art (composers Gustav Mahler and Hans Krása, writers Franz Kafka, Franz Werfel, Karl Kraus, painter Hugo Steiner-Prag and many others). Generally speaking, the Jewish cultural zone in the Czech Lands was one of the most democratic and humanist cultural streams in the region, whose extensive work greatly contributed to its opening to the world, which was evident even in the inter-war period.

Poles, who mainly inhabited the Těšín (Ciezsyn in Polish) region were an interesting element in the Czech Lands' cultural life. In the ethnically mixed environment with the linguistically dominant Germans and Czechs, it took the entire 19th century before they achieved conscious cultural emancipation. Even before the First World War, their literary work was scarce and the Poles only slowly increased their education. The Těšín region's literature appeared as late as the 1850s thanks to the local Polish revivalist, writer and journalist, Pawel Stalmach. The Těšín Poles distanced themselves from Cracow's cultural centre, which was in many ways on par with Western Europe. As a result, the Polish avant-garde affected the Czechs much more than the Těšín Poles. The Poles from the north of the Czech Lands were a typical cultural periphery, whose development did not interest Czechs and who paid much more attention to the support of the national emancipation of the Slavic inhabitants of Upper and Lower Lusatia in Germany. Among those who contributed to its success were the publisher of the Slavic Overview *(Slovanský přehled)*, Adolf Černý (Jan Rokyta) as well as ethnomusicologist and painter Ludvík Kuba and young Slavists, brothers František and Josef Páta. The small Roma population was on the fringes of the Czech Lands' cultural development. 98% of Roma were illiterate; they led a nomadic lifestyle and their cultural life was based on fragments of their own folk traditions. Despite this, the process of their assimilation began in the second half of the 19th century. Some Roma, especially in Moravia and the Czech-German borderlands, settled on the outskirts of villages, their children went to school, although irregularly, and the adults worked most commonly as blacksmiths or tinsmiths.

The former "secondary lands" of the Bohemian Crown – Moravia and Silesia (Opava region) – retained their specific character within the cultural life of the Czech Lands. Moravia was much more religious than Bohemia and had more lively folk customs, with folk elements permeating all cultural fields, as well as Moravian lifestyle and household equipment. As part of the Modernism and avant-garde, a unique symbiosis of regional folklorism, in the past represented by František Sušil and Pavel Křížkovský, with modern art influences arose, such as in the novels and dramatic works of Vilém Mrštík and in the poetic and mystical legacy of Otokar Březina, leading representatives of Czech Modernism, in the artistic work of Antonín Procházka and Otakar Kubín, in the publishing activities and translation works of Josef Florian, in the poetic work of Jakub Deml or graphic artist and poet Bohuslav Reynek and especially in the brilliant music of Leoš Janáček and the original architecture of Dušan Jurkovič, a Hungarian Slovak by origin. Generally speaking, cultural activities in Moravia were concentrated across a wide range of corporations and clubs, of which most notably the Club for the Czech Theatre and the Orchestra Club in Brno, the Moravian Circle of Writers and Hodonín's Association of Moravian Fine Artists achieved importance which surpassed the regional borders. We should not forget the importance of Janáček's pedagogical work, which supplied a range of young and talented Moravian musicians, composers and performers.

In comparison to Moravia, Silesia was disadvantaged by the fact that most capital was not in the hands of the minority Czech population, nor the German inhabitants, but held by the nobility and Jewish financiers. Despite this, Silesian culture developed in the second half of the 19th century, though, with a few exceptions, it did not spread beyond the region's borders. The largest Silesian contribution to national culture was the poetic work of Petr Bezruč, who drew inspiration from Silesian sources. As to ethnicity, Moravia and Silesia were less defined than Bohemia, due to a larger spread of German population in the territory and the smaller Jewish contribution to culture (Adolf and Jaroslav Stránský with their *People's Newspaper* excelled among those who assimilated). The local Germans also had several prominent individuals in their midst – architects Adolf Loos from Brno, Josef Maria Olbrich from Opava and composers Josef Gustav Mraczek and Ernst Křenek. Writer Robert Musil was also linked to Moravia; the founder of psychoanalysis, Sigmund Freud was born here. Stephan Zweig and Oskar Kokoschka had their Moravian roots.

From the beginning of national emancipation to the First World War, both Czechs and Germans underwent great dynamic and dramatic development. The Czechs had to prove that they were fully-fledged members of the family of cultural and creative nations. While at the beginning of the 19th century there were no signs that they would convince Europe of this (indeed, works of the most prominent minds of the "revivalist era," Josef Dobrovský, František Palacký, Jan Evangelista Purkyně and Pavel Josef Šafařík were written partly in German), at the beginning of the following century, Czechs were counted among the most progressive cultural streams on the planet – the first (pre-war) avant-garde. This progress was enabled only thanks to steep economic and social growth and, consequently, education. Czechs had to become fundamentally emancipated from German economic and financial superiority, and create their own, independent sources of national growth. From 1848 and the controversy over Czech representation at the Frankfurt assembly, it was clear that the developmental rhythms of both nations were parting. Their paths increasingly diverged with the success of the unification efforts of the German Empire. Bismarck's Germany's rapid development into a world power, along with the subsequent economic and cultural boom, was naturally attractive for Germans in the Czech and Austrian lands. The German "national state" became an ideal to which they pinned their hopes. This nationalist aspect was, in large cities such as Prague and Brno, weakened by the culturally and politically active Jews, for whom Germany represented Prussian militarism and aggressive forms of anti-Semitism and whose assimilation was directed partly to Austria and partly to the Czech nation. They acted as intermediaries between the Czech and German cultural zones.

Czech successes in European competition was due to their long-term effort to overcome the situation in which the demands of Czech society for state and ethnic equality were not met. The speed of growth in the second half of the 19th century and at the beginning of the 20th century was unprecedented in Czech history. More had happened in the course of several decades than over the previous centuries and Czech achievements were often internationally recognized. The tumultuous epoch of cultural development proved Czech creativity not only in literature, music, fine arts and theatre, but also in the general level of education, entrepreneurism and openness to the surrounding world. All this created conditions for the coming assertion of Czechs as one of nation-states and co-creators of central Europe's new map.

Bibliography

19. století v nás. Modely, instituce a reprezentace, které přetrvaly, Milan Řepa (ed.), Praha 2008.

ABLEITINGER, Alfred: *Ernst von Koerber und das Verfassungsproblem im Jahre 1900*, Wien–Köln–Graz 1973.

BELLER, Steven: *Francis Joseph*, London 1996.

BERÉNGER, Jean: *A History of the Habsburg Empire II, 1700–1918*, London 1997.

BIRKE, Ernst – OBERNDORFFER, Kurt (eds.): *Das böhmische Staatsrecht in der deutsch-tschechischen Auseinandersetzungen des 19. und 20. Jahrhunderts*, Marburg/Lahn 1960.

BLED, Jean-Paul: *François Joseph*, Paris 1994.

BOHMANN, Alfred: *Bevölkerungsbewegungen in Böhmen 1847–1947 mit besonderer Berücksichtigung der Entwicklung der nationalen Verhältnisse*, München 1958.

Böhmen im 19. Jahrhundert. Vom Klassizismus zur Moderne, Ferdinand Seibt (ed.), München–Berlin–Frankfurt am Main 1995.

BRADLEY, John F. N.: *Czech nationalism in the nineteenth century*, New York 1984.

BROUSEK, Karl M.: *Die Großindustrie Böhmens 1848–1918*, München 1987.

BURGER, Hannelore: *Sprachenrecht und Sprachengerechtigkeit im österreichischen Unterrichtswesen 1867–1918*, Wien 1995.

Český liberalismus. Texty a osobnosti, Milan Znoj, Jan Havránek, Martin Sekera (eds.), Praha 1995.

COHEN, Gary B.: *The Politics of Ethnic Survival Germans in Prague 1861–1914*, New Jersey 1981.

CYSARZ, Herbert: *Prag im deutschen Geistesleben*, Mannheim–Sandhofen 1961.

The Czech Renascence of the Nineteenth Century. Essays Presented to Otakar Odložilík in Honour of His Seventieth Birthday. Peter Brook a H. Gordon Skilling (eds.), Toronto and Buffalo 1970.

Die deutsche Schule in den Sudetenländern. Form und Inhalt des Bildungswesens, Theo Keil (ed.), München 1967.

DOUBEK, Vratislav: *Česká politika a Rusko (1848–1914)*, Praha 2005.

EFMERTOVÁ, Marcela C.: *České země v letech 1848–1918*, Praha 1998.

FASORA, Lukáš – HANUŠ, Jiří – MALÍŘ, Jiří (eds.): *Člověk na Moravě 19. století*, 2nd edition Brno 2008.

FASORA, Lukáš – HANUŠ, Jiří – MALÍŘ, Jiří (eds.): *Moravské vyrovnání z roku 1905 – Der Mährische Ausgleich von 1905*, Brno 2006.

FASORA, Lukáš – HANUŠ, Jiří – MALÍŘ, Jiří (eds.): *Občanské elity a obecní samospráva 1848–1948*, Brno 2006.

FIALOVÁ-FÜRSTOVÁ, Ingeborg: *Mährische deutschsprachige Literatur*, Olomouc 1999.

FLEISCHER, Manfred: *Die politische Rolle der Deutschen aus der böhmischen Ländern in Wien 1804–1918. Studien zur Migration und zum Wirken politisch-administrativen Eliten*, Frankfurt am Main 1999.

FRANKL, Michal: „*Emancipace od židů". Český antisemitismus na konci 19. století*, Praha–Litomyšl 2007.

FUCHS, Albert: *Geistige Strömungen in Österreich (1867–1918)*, Wien 1949, 2nd edition 1978.

GARVER, Bruce M: *The Young Czech Party 1874–1901 and the Emergence of a Multi-Party System*, New Haven–London 1978.

GLASSL, Horst: *Der mährische Ausgleich*, München 1967.

GLETTLER, Monika: *Die Wiener Tschechen um 1900. Strukturanalyse einer nationalen Minderheit in der Großstadt*, München–Wien 1972.

GOOD, David G.: *The Economic Rise of the Habsburg Empire 1750–1914*, Berkeley 1984.

Grossbritanien, die USA und die böhmischen Länder 1848–1938, Eva Schmidt-Hartmann, Stanley B. Winters (eds.), München 1991.

Die Habsburgermonarchie 1848–1918, Adam Wandruszka, Peter Urbanitsch (eds.). *Bd. I. Die wirtschaftliche Entwicklung*, Wien 1973; *Bd. II. Verwaltung und Rechtswesen*, Wien 1975, 2003; *Bd. III/1,2. Die Völker des Reiches*, Wien 1980; *Bd. IV. Die Konfessionen*, Wien 1985, 1995; *V. Die Bewaffnete Macht*, Wien 1987; *Bd. VI/1,2. Die Habsburgermonarchie im System der Internationalen Beziehungen*, Wien 1989, 1993; *Bd. VII/1,2. Verfassung und Parlamentarismus*, Wien 2000; *Bd. VIII/1,2. Politische Öffentlichkeit und Zivilgesellschaft*, Wien 2006.

HÁJEK, Jan: *180 let českého spořitelnictví – 180 Years of the Czech Saving System – 180 Jahre des tschechischen Sparkassenwesens. Česká spořitelna 1825–2005*, Praha 2005.

Hájek, Jan – KUBŮ, Eduard – JANČÍK, Drahomír (eds.): *O hospodářskou národní državu. Úvahy a stati o moderním českém a německém hospodářském nacionalismu v českých zemích.* Praha 2008.

HÁJEK, Jan – Lacina, Vlastimil: *Od úvěrních družstev k bankovním koncernům*, Praha 1999.

Handbuch der Geschichte der böhmischen Länder, III. Die Böhmischen Länder im Habsburgerreich 1848–1919. Bürgerlicher Nationalismus und Ausbildung einer Industriegesellschaft, Stuttgart 1968.

HEUMOS, Peter: *Agrarische Interessen und nationale Politik in Böhmen 1848–1889. Sozialökonomische und organisatorische Entstehungsbedingungen der tschechischen Bauernbewegung*, Wiesbaden 1979.

HLAVAČKA, Milan: *Dějiny dopravy v českých zemích v období průmyslové revoluce*, Praha 1990.

HLAVAČKA, Milan: *Zlatý věk české samosprávy*, Praha 2006.

HOFFMANN, Roland J.: *T. G. Masaryk und die tschechische Frage*, München 1988.

HROCH, Miroslav: *Social Preconditions of National Revival in Europe. A Comparative Analysis of the Social Composition of Patriotic Groups among the Smaller European Nations*, Cambridge 1985.

Huerta, Thomas F.: *Economic Growth and Economic Policy in a Multinational Setting. The Habsburg Monarchy, 1841–1865*, New York 1977.

HYE, Hans Peter: *Das politische System in der Habsburgermonarchie. Konstitutionalismus, Parlamentarismus und politische Partizipation*, Prag 1998.

Intelectual and Social Development in the Habsburg Empire from Maria Theresia to World War I. Essays dedicated to Robert A. Kann. Stanley B. Winters and Joseph Held (eds.), New York–London 1975.

JAKUBEC, Ivan – JINDRA, Zdeněk (eds.): *Dějiny hospodářství českých zemí od počátku industrializace do konce habsburské monarchie*, Praha 2006.

JANÁK, Jan: Dějiny Moravy III/1: *Hospodářský rozmach Moravy 1740–1918*, Brno 1999.

PAVEL CIBULKA — JAN HÁJEK — MARTIN KUČERA

JELAVICH, Barbara: *The Habsburg Empire in European Affairs 1814–1918*, Chicago 1969.

JOHNSTON, Wiliam M.: *Österreichische Kultur und Geistesgeschichte*, Wien–Köln–Graz 1974.

KAMMERHOFER, Leopold (ed.): *Studien zum Deutschliberalismus in Zisleithanien 1873–1879. Herrschaftsfundierung und Organisationsformen des politischen Liberalismus*, Wien 1992.

KANN, Robert A.: *Das Nationalitätenproblem in der Habsburgermonarchie*, I–II, Graz–Köln 1964.

KANN, Robert A.: *Werden und Zerfall des Habsburgerreiches*, Graz–Wien–Köln 1962.

KÁRNÍK, Zdeněk (ed.): *Sborník k problematice multietnicity. České země jako multietnická společnost: Češi, Němci a Židé ve společenském životě českých zemích 1848–1918*, Praha 1996.

KAZBUNDA, Karel: *Otázka česko-německá v předvečer Velké války. Zrušení ústavnosti země České tzv. annenskými patenty z 26. července 1913*, Zdeněk Kárník (ed.), Praha 1995.

KIEVAL, Hillel J.: *The Making of Czech Jewry. National Conflict and Jewish Society in Bohemia, 1870 to 1918*, New York 1988.

KIMBALL, Stanley B.: *Czech Nationalism. A Study of the National Theatre Movement 1845–1883*, Urbana 1964.

KLADIWA, Pavel: *Lesk a bída obecních samospráv Moravy a Slezska 1850–1914, I. Vývoj legislativy*, Ostrava 2007.

KLADIWA, Pavel – POKLUDOVÁ, Andrea – KAFKOVÁ, Renata: *Lesk a bída obecních samospráv Moravy a Slezska 1850–1914, II/1. Muži z radnice*, Ostrava 2008.

KOLMER, Gustav: *Parlament und Verfassung in Oesterreich*, I–VIII, Wien–Leipzig 1902–1914; Graz 1972–1980.

KOMLOS, John: *The Habsburg Monarchy as a Customs Union. Economic Development in Austria-Hungary in the Nineteenth Century*, Princeton 1983.

KOŘALKA, Jiří: *František Palacký (1798–1876), der Historiker der Tschechen im österreichischen Vielvölkerstaat*, Wien 2007.

KOŘALKA, Jiří: *Tschechen im Habsburgerreich und in Europa 1815–1914. Sozialgeschichtliche Zusammenhänge der neuzeitlichen Nationsbildung und der Nationalitätenfrage in den böhmischen Ländern*, Wien–München 1991.

KŘEN, Jan: *Konfliktgemeinschaft. Tschechen und Deutsche 1780–1918*, München 1996.

KUČERA, Martin: *Rakouský občan Josef Pekař*, Praha 2005.

LACINA, Vlastislav: *Hospodářství českých zemí 1880–1914*, Praha 1990.

LENDEROVÁ, Milena: *K hříchu i modlitbě. Žena v minulém století*, Praha 1999.

LENDEROVÁ, Milena – RÝDL, Karel: *Radostné dětství? Dítě v Čechách devatenáctého století*, Praha–Litomyšl 2006.

LÖW, Raimund: *Der Zerfall der „Kleinen Internationale". Nationalitätenkonflikte in der Arbeiterbewegung des alten Österreichs (1889–1914)*, Wien 1984.

LUTZ, Heinrich – RUMPLER, Helmut (eds.): *Österreich und deutsche Frage im 19. und 20. Jahrhundert. Probleme der politisch-staatlichen und soziokulturellen Differenzierung im deutschen Mitteleuropa*, München 1982.

MACARTNEY, Carlile A.: *The Habsburg Empire 1790–1918, London–New York 1968–1969, 1971.*

MALÍŘ, Jiří: *Od spolků k moderním politickým stranám. Vývoj politických stran na Moravě v letech 1848–1914*, Brno 1996.

MAREK, Jaroslav: *Česká moderní kultura*, Praha 1998.

MAREK, Pavel: *Český katolicismus 1890–1914. Kapitoly z dějin českého katolického tábora na přelomu 19. a 20. století*, Olomouc 2003.

T. G. Masaryk 1850–1937. I. Thinker and Politician. Stanley B. Winters (ed.). II. Thinker and Critic. Ed. by Harry Hanak, London 1989–1990.

MATIS, Herbert: *Österreichs Wirtschaft 1848–1913. Konjunkturelle Dynamik und gesellschaftlicher Wandel im Zeitalter Franz Josefs I.*, Berlin–München 1972.

MOLISCH, Paul: *Geschichte der deutschnationalen Bewegung in Österreich von ihren Anfängen bis zum Zerfall der Monarchie*, Jena 1926.

MOLISCH, Paul: *Politische Geschichte der deutschen Hochschulen in Österreich von 1848 bis 1918*, Wien–Leipzig 1939.

MOMMSEN, Hans: *Die Sozialdemokratie und die Nationalitätenfrage im habsburgischen Vielvölkerstaat, I. Das Ringen um die supranationale Integration der zisleithanischen Arbeiterbewegung (1867–1907)*, Wien 1963.

MOMMSEN, Hans – KOŘALKA, Jiří (eds.): *Ungleiche Nachbarn. Demokratische und nationale Emanzipation bei Deutschen, Tschechen und Slowaken (1815–1914)*, Essen 1993.

MÜHLBERGER, Josef: *Der Deutsche Beitrag Böhmens und Mährens zur Weltliteratur 1830–1930*, München 1968.

MÜHLBERGER, Josef: *Dějiny německé literatury v Čechách 1900–1939*, Ústí nad Labem 2006.

OKEY, Robin: *The Habsburg Monarchy c. 1765–1918. From Enlightenment to Eclipse*, London 2001.

Der österreichisch-ungarische Ausgleich 1867, ed. Anton Vantuch, Ľudovít Holotík, Bratislava 1971.

Der österreichisch-ungarische Ausgleich von 1867. Seine Grundlagen und Auswirkungen, ed. Theodor Mayer, München 1968.

Der österreichisch-ungarische Ausgleich von 1867. Vorgeschiche und Wirkungen, Peter Berger (ed.), Wien–München 1967.

PEŠEK, Jiří: *Od aglomerace k městu. Praha a středoevropské metropole 1850–1920*, Praha 1999.

Přehled československých dějin, II/1–2 (1848–1918), Praha 1960.

PRINZ, Friedrich: *Geschichte Böhmens 1848–1948*, Frankfurt am Main–Berlin 1991.

PUTNA, Martin C.: *Česká katolická literatura 1848–1918*, Praha 1998.

REDLICH, Josef: *Das österreichische Staats- und Reichsproblem. Geschichtliche Darstellung der inneren Politik der habsburgischen Monarchie von 1848 bis zum Untergang des Reiches*, I–II, Wien 1920–1926.

ŘEPA, Milan: *Moravané nebo Češi? Vývoj národního vědomí na Moravě v 19. století*, Brno 2001.

ROSENHEIM, Richard: *Die Geschichte der deutschen Bühnen in Prag, 1883–1918*, Prag 1938.

RUDOLPH, Richard L.: *Banking and Industrialization in Austria-Hungary. The role of banks in the industrialization of the Czech Crownlands, 1873–1914*, Cambridge–London–New York–Melbourne 1976.

RUMPLER, Helmut: *Die österreichische Geschichte 1804–1914. Eine Chance für Mitteleuropa. Bürgerliche Emanzipation und Staatsverfall in der Habsburgermonarchie*, Wien 1997.

SAK, Robert: *Rieger. Konzervativec nebo liberál*, Semily 1993.

SANDGRUBER, Roman: *Österreichische Agrarstatistik 1750–1918*, Wien 1978.

SCHAMSCHULA, Walter: *Geschichte der tschechischen Literatur, II. Von der Romantik bis zum ersten Weltkrieg*, Köln–Weimar–Wien 1996.

SCHARF, Christian: *Ausgleichspolitik und Pressekampf in der Ära Hohenwart*, München 1996.

SCHMID-EGGER, Barbara: *Klerus und Politik im Böhmen um 1900*, München 1974.

SEWERING-WOLLANEK, Marlies: *Brot oder Nationalität? Nordwestböhmische Arbeiterbewegung im Brennpunkt der Nationalitätenkonflikte (1889–1911)*, Marburg 1994.

SKED, Alan: *The Decline and Fall of the Habsburg Empire 1815–1918*, London–New York 1989.

SKILLING, Hubert G.: *T. G. Masaryk against the current, 1882–1914*, Basingstoke 1994.

ŠOLLE, Zdeněk: *Století české politiky*, Praha 1998.

SOUBIGOU, Alain: *Thomas Masaryk*, Paris 2002.

SOUKUPOVÁ, Helena: *Česká společnost před sto lety. Identita, stereotyp, mýtus*, Praha 2000.

Spor o smysl českých dějin, 1895–1938, Miloš Havelka (ed.), Praha 1995.

STÖLZL, Christoph: *Kafkas böses Böhmen. Zur Sozialgeschichte eines Prager Juden*, München 1970.

SUTTER, Berthold: *Die Badenischen Sprachverordnungen von 1897*, I–II, Köln–Graz 1960–1965.

SZPORLUK, Roman: *The Political Thought of Thomas G. Masaryk*, New York 1981.

TAPIÉ, Victor-Lucien: *The Rise and Fall of Habsburg Monarchy*, London 1971.

THER, Philipp: *Národní divadlo v kontextu evropských operních dějin. Od založení do první světové války*, Praha 2008.

Die Teilung der Prager Universität 1882 und die intellektuelle Desintegration in den böhmischen Ländern, ed. Ferdinand Seibt, München 1984.

TOBOLKA, Zdeněk V.: *Politické dějiny československého národa od r. 1848 až do dnešní doby*, I–IV, Praha 1932–1937.

TOMEK, Václav: *Český anarchismus a jeho publicistika 1880–1925*, Praha 2002.

URBAN, Otto: *Kapitalismus a česká společnost. K otázkám formování české společnosti v 19. století*, Praha 1978.

URBAN, Otto: *Die tschechische Gesellschaft 1848–1918*, I–II, Wien–Köln–Weimar 1994.

VOJTĚCH, Tomáš: *Mladočeši a boj o politickou moc v Čechách*, Praha 1980.

VOŠAHLÍKOVÁ, Pavla: *Jak se žilo za časů Františka Josefa I.*, Praha 1996.

VYBÍRAL, Jindřich: *Česká architektura na prahu moderní doby. Devatenáct esejů o devatenáctém století*, Praha 2002.

VYŠNÝ, Paul: *Neo-Slavism and the Czechs 1898–1914*, Cambridge 1977.

Weg – Leistung – Schicksal. Geschichte der sudetendeutschen Arbeiterbewegung, Stuttgart 1972.

Wien, Prag, Budapest. Blütezeit der Habsburgermetropolen. Urbanisierung, Kommunalpolitik, gesellschaftliche Konflikte (1867–1918), Wien 1996.

ZACEK, Joseph F.: *Palacký. The Historian as Scholar and Nationalist*, The Hague–Paris 1970.

ZATLOUKAL, Pavel: *Historismus – architektura 19. století*, Olomouc 1986.

XIV. The Czech Lands
during the First World War (1914–1918)

The medium state emblem of Austria-Hungary from 1915. The emblem contains parts of the empire including the Czech Lands' emblems (two-tailed lion – Bohemia, checkered eagle – Moravia)

1 Reaction to the Start of the War

Around the turn of the 19th and 20th centuries, in spite of the ever-expanding indications of international tension, no one in the Czech Lands thought that a global war was imminent, the course and fallout of which would have a profound effect on all social strata and inhabitants of the Austro-Hungarian empire, and which would fundamentally change the map of central Europe. Even during the first days after Austria-Hungary declared war on Serbia on July 28, 1914, the majority of people were convinced that it was just another in a long line of local conflicts to which the public had become accustomed over the preceding years. The course of events to come was, however, quite different. Over a period of several weeks, large military blocks formed around two previously existing superpower coalitions, the Entente and the Triple Alliance. Tsarist Russia came to the support of Serbia, while Austria-Hungary was supported by the Kaiser's Germany and also Turkey. After Russia entered the war, other Entente countries, France and Great Britain, did not remain aside; they were at least formally joined by Belgium, which had been attacked and occupied by Germany, and Montenegro was also drawn into the war on the side of Entente. The fighting spread beyond Europe. At the outset, Italy remained cautious, but then later left the Triple Alliance and in May 1915, joined the war against Austria-Hungary and Germany. The conflict had evolved into a world war.

The first wartime operations began at the end of 1914 on several European fronts: the Serbian, western (in France) and eastern (in Russia). Later they were joined by the Italian and less significant Romanian fronts. Europe remained the main battleground throughout "the Great War." From the very beginning of the war, the Central Powers, Germany and Austria-Hungary, undertook a series of extensive offensive actions in their enemy's territories. They did not, however, achieve the expected quick victory. The advancement of their troops was stopped, and the war became a drawn-out trench war, which quickly exhausted the material and human resources of the combating states. Over 70 million men were eventually mobilized and the Great War claimed up to 10 million human casualties in its four years.

The development of the situation during the summer and autumn of 1914 was a surprise for the great majority of inhabitants of the Habsburg monarchy. Reaction to the declaration of war differed across various ethnic environments. Germans living in the Czech and Alpine (Austrian) lands welcomed the steps of the militant left wing of the Vienna government, whose most prominent representatives were General Conrad von Hötzendorf, Chief of Staff of the Austrian army, and the Prime Minister, Count Karl Stürgkh. The German population, fully expecting a smooth path to victory, expected not only an expansion of German influence in international politics, but also a confirmation of the dominance of the German race within the Habsburg monarchy. To them, the war represented the prospect of creating a "German Central Europe."

While the Czech Lands' German population allowed themselves to be carried away by a wave of enthusiasm for the war, the outbreak of war was quite literally a shock for the Czech nation, which was opposed to a war against Slavic Serbia and, later, Russia. However, there were only limited opportunities to demonstrate their stance. The Czech political representation completely disappointed its people in this. The rapid change to a wartime military-bureaucratic regime and the repressive measures that accompanied it evoked feelings of dejection, hopelessness and resignation in the Czech milieu. Spontaneous, though mostly merely demonstrative, expressions of resistance or reluctance to meet state regulations were quickly suppressed by fierce actions from both the civil and military authorities. Starting with the provocation of singing Czech patriotic songs, efforts to avoid mobilization, these expressions went as far as desertion from the front-line and the formation of military units fighting on the side of the Entente against the Central Powers. At first it was only a few individuals, but from April, 1915, larger units comprised largely of Czech soldiers began to surrender, especially to Russian forces.

Not mere expressions of resistance to the war, these acts reflected the emotional and political divergence of the Czech nation with the Habsburg monarchy, and were contributed to by a slew of factors in both the rear and front lines, sometimes directly but often only indirectly related to the military conflict. The disproportionate spread and protraction of the military conflict, and the advances in weapons technology led to immense human and material losses, which imposed great demands on the warring nations' economies and the Vienna government was forced to take extraordinary measures. Manufacturing was subordinated to the needs of war. This resulted in a shortage of raw materials not only for the military, but also and most especially for civil manufacturing, and caused problems in the supplying of essential goods to the population.

The shortage of foodstuffs was especially burdensome. The war blockade caused the monarchy to rely only on its own agricultural production, which was declining due to the shrinking work force caused by the mobilization of men to the front lines, and also due to a reduction in investments into agriculture. In an effort to solve problems provisioning the front lines, the government put a mandatory purchase of grain, potatoes and meat into place, establishing a Wartime Grain Institute and Purchasing Centre for Livestock. The purchase was often accomplished with the active assistance of troops or the police. Even so, provisioning continued to worsen. Starting in the spring of 1915, a rationing system of foodstuffs, coal, textiles and other essentials was put into place. The general shortages caused the black market to come to life, profiting a number of speculators.

The cause of the inward divergence of the Czech nation with the monarchy was not just the material deprivation caused by the war. The changed political situation had a much more serious effect. All of the often hard-won elements of the parliamentary system that had existed to that time were abolished, and the political rights and freedom of citizens were limited. The Reichsrat operations and Land Diets were suspended (where they still existed), political parties were banned, the freedom to assemble was limited, the press was subjected to extreme censorship, and many Czech politicians were subject to persecution. Civil authorities were taken over by the high military command, forming a hitherto unknown form of military-bureaucratic dictatorship. Its goal was not only to prohibit all expressions of resistance to the war effort, but also to signify the beginning of the long-held intention of nationalistic German-Austrian circles to destroy any formal residual elements of Bohemian state law. The terms Austria and Austrian Lands began to appear in the official names of the monarchy's western parts in place of the names *The Kingdom and Lands Represented in the Reichsrat* or *Cisleithania*. Vienna legal and political theorists began to discuss the transformation of the Czech Lands into a part of a unified German Central Europe, and was openly expressed by the so-called Easter Programme, published in Vienna in July, 1915. According to this, a large part of Cisleithania formed the German state. The Czech Lands would be divided into German districts and districts with mixed languages and the entire empire would be tightly affiliated to Germany.

Until the military conflict began to flare up, the vast majority of Czech politicians considered the Austro-Hungarian confederation of states as a natural and generally acceptable governmental framework for the application of Czech national interests. The outbreak of the war meant the collapse of all the existing Czech political ideas and programs. All political trends were forced to find new outlets. However, only certain individuals from the ranks of leading Czech politicians began openly to oppose the empire at the outset of the war. Based on their knowledge of international politics, they observed that the participation of Austria-Hungary as a member of the Triple Alliance in the war against a broad alliance of states concentrated around the allied superpowers represented an extraordinary opportunity to begin the fight for Czech emancipation, leading up to the establishment of an independent national state. Of course, achieving their ultimate goal required the utter defeat of the Triple Alliance (or Central Powers), in which the Czech nation would contribute both militarily and politically within the limits of its powers. They aimed their subsequent steps towards this goal, representing a major break in Czech politics.

The formulation of the radical program was most strongly influenced by the behaviour of the government regard to the Czech nation, the aggressive rise in German-Austrian nationalism and, not least, the growing dependence of the monarchy on the politics of Vilhelm's Germany. All this placed new emphasis on the question before Czech politics regarding the relationship of the nation to Austria-Hungary. Leading Czechs who saw the situation in this way included Karel Kramář, the longtime leader of the National Liberal Party (Young Czech Party [*Národní strana svobodomyslná* (*mladočeši*)]), and philosophy professor at Charles University in Prague, Tomáš Garrigue Masaryk. Both politicians believed in the defeat of Austria-Hungary in the war and were convinced that it was necessary to seek Czech national existence outside of this confederation of states. Their specific ideas on the methods and forms of fulfilling this goal were, however, diametrically opposed. While Karel Kramář, in the spirit of neo-Slavism, dreamed of the creation of a great Slavic empire under the leadership of the Russian Romanovs, of which the Czech state would be a part, Masaryk from the start was oriented towards fighting for an independent Czech state. Kramář's concept was fated to fail for several reasons and completely lost any real basis after the Russian revolution of 1917.

T. G. Masaryk, who until 1914 had preferred positive methods of fighting for national interests within the Habsburg Monarchy, came to the conclusion that this state had ceased to be a protective barrier against the pressure from a dynamic Germany and, furthermore, the monarchy's internal politics had become hostile towards the Czech nation. During his travels abroad in the autumn of 1914, he became well-versed in the international situation and outlined the first concept of an independent Czech state. He further refined his idea until finally coming up with a project for an independent Czech state. In addition to the Czech Lands, this state should also include the northern parts of the Hungarian Kingdom, which had been settled largely by Slovaks. Masaryk realized that to attain this goal it would be necessary to take part in the military defeat of Austria-Hungary and, on the basis of this, approved of the Entente powers for the radical transformation of central Europe.

Other than for K. Kramář and T. G. Masaryk, an immediate change of posture towards the Austro-Hungarian empire was almost unthinkable for the majority of Czech politicians. Some were bound by fear of imminent persecution, and so took a waiting stance, and the majority were optimistic and even expressed loyalty to the government, although possibly only formally. The Czech-Slavic Social Democrats (*Československá sociální demokracie*), in complete harmony with other parties of the Socialist International, were smitten with hopelessness and passivity. Not only did they not condemn the war, but they even ceased operations in an attempt to maintain an unchanged party organizational structure. In the spirit of the thinking of then-leader Bohumír Šmeral, who was already leaning towards a radical revolutionary ideology, some of their adherents even believed that the upcoming socialist revolution would bring with it the solution to the Czech question. The Agrarian Party (*Strana agrární*) behaved pragmatically: when necessary expressing loyalty to the state without hesitation, but was in discreet contact with the resistance organization, the so-called Mafia, which was established in the first months of the war and maintained foreign contacts. Other political streams were silenced by a wave of extreme persecution. Only the parties of political Catholicism expressed open support for the monarchy. Their stance was the result of the traditional ties between the Catholic church and the Habsburg Dynasty.

At the outset of the war, the military-bureaucratic regime felt itself to be so strong that it could not fully appreciate the moderate positions of the majority of Czech politicians. Not only distrust towards Czechs, but also the nationalist stance of the German ethnic elements, affected the regime's behaviour leading to the unleashing of harsh repression of all that was Czech. Czech books on the history of the Czech state were banned, textbooks and theatre repertoires were censored, and the Czech press was put under intensified oversight, with many Czech newspapers and magazines ceasing to publish. Czech journalists, writers, functionaries of Czech clubs, anti-militants, anarchists and even the executives of the Trade Bank, who were insufficiently eager to issue war loans, were all subjected to persecution. At the beginning of the autumn of 1914, the leaders of the National Socialist Party (*Národně-sociální strana*), Jaroslav Klofáč a Emil Špatný, and were arrested and interned. By the end of the year, the first death sentences for civilians were issued by a military court in Ostrava. Another wave of arrests occurred during 1915. Karel Kramář, Alois Rašín, and others were sentenced to death for high treason. However, in their case the execution of the sentences was delayed, and the changed situation after the death of Emperor Francis Joseph in 1916 no longer allowed for the sentences to be carried out.

2 Foreign Actions

Amidst the almost complete passivity of the vast majority of Czech politicians, only T. G. Masaryk left himself room for action. He had neither a strong political party backing him nor material resources. His authority rested only on his renown in the scientific world and the reputation he had gained in the pre-war Vienna parliament as a principled politician. Immediately after the outbreak of war, he discussed his ideas for future development with several politicians with similar ideals, with whose help he created the secret committee later known as the Czech Mafia. The great majority of its members were Marasyk's adherents from the small Realist Party (*Realistická strana*), but it also included individuals from other national parties. They maintained contact with Masaryk even after his departure from the country in December 1914, and kept him informed of the political situation at home and even sent him messages of interest to the political and military wings of the Entente. The only hope for Masaryk's resistance was a faith in the utter defeat of the Central Powers and in the will of the victorious Entente to agree to the new layout of central Europe. Masaryk himself felt most at home in the British political scene. He was aware that representatives of the Entente Powers did not have a comprehensive plan for the organization of post-war Europe, and that it would be advantageous to offer them a project that would be in accordance with the goal of the Czech resistance.

Masaryk's concept was completely original. He did not want the nation to beg for liberation; it needed to attract enough attention to itself so that after the war it would be impossible to ignore. The goal was not merely the assertion of the historic Bohemian state law, but the formation of a completely new Czechoslovak state. He was primarily led to join the Czech and Slovak emancipation efforts for pragmatic reasons. He realized that the German ethnic minority would be too strong within the historic Bohemian borders, consisting of about one third of the population, and furthermore would be completely surrounded by ethnic Germans. The connection with Slovakia would allow this state to free itself, at least partially, geopolitically from its grip. During his considerations on the issue, he was of course affected by his longtime close contacts with Slovakia and Slovak politicians, and naturally his consciousness of the closeness of the two languages and other factual and sentimental factors. In the atmosphere of the struggle for an ethnic state, the term *Czechoslovak nation* started to appear in foreign action concepts. It is not apparent from Masaryk's statements whether it represented a conscious simplification for Entente politicians who could not sufficiently orient themselves in central European international relations, or whether it was an attempt to form a future political nation. The goal of his concept of a unified nation was in no way an attempt to "Czechify" the Slovaks.

The idea of a common Czech and Slovak resistance immediately met with a great response among the groups of Czech and Slovak fellow countrymen living in France, Great Britain, Russia and in the USA. At that time, up to two million Czech and Slovak emigrants were living abroad, and in the environment after the outbreak of war there were attempts to form military units, which were to become the basis of the Czechoslovak foreign legion. The first agreement was reached during negotiations in Cleveland in the autumn of 1915, though, a number of questions remained unanswered, especially regarding the future relations between the nations. The leaders of the Slovak emigrants of course presumed that Slovakia would have wide autonomy in the future independent state.

Following complex negotiations abroad, T. G. Masaryk succeeded in founding the Czech National Committee, whose authority was recognized by many organizations of his countrymen. He did not publicly proclaim the fight against Austria-Hungary until July 6, 1915, in Geneva during a speech given on the occasion of the 500th anniversary of the burning at the stake of Czech religious reformer Jan Hus. Soon afterward, Masaryk was joined by Associate Professor of Sociology, Edvard Beneš, who emigrated in the autumn of 1915. Beneš quickly became the organizing force behind Czechoslovak foreign actions. Their centre was opened in Paris, and in 1916 the Czech National Council established, later changed into the Czechoslovak National Council. The third of the leaders who formed the core of this panel was Milan Rastislav Štefánik, a Slovak astronomer who had already been living in France for several years. Thanks to his close ties to prominent socialites in France and Italy, Štefánik significantly aided in making contacts and in the realization of Czechoslovak goals.

The first task of the foreign resistance was to change the notions of the Entente politicians regarding the political layout of post-war central Europe, and to place the breakup of Austria-Hungary, an empire firmly anchored in the consciousness of global politics, among the Entente's military goals. From the beginning, it was clear to the resistance leaders that the existence of the Czechoslovak forces could support their arguments. And so from the original modest beginnings, the Czechoslovak Legion began to form in co-operation with the Entente states. First in France and later in Russia, where it was necessary to overcome distrust towards prisoners of war (Austro-Hungarian soldiers of Czech or Slovak nationality), from whom the majority of the legion members were recruited. During the climactic phases after the Russian revolution of 1917, the number of legionnaires in Russia reached

60–70 thousand men. There were an additional ten thousand in France, and towards the end of the war another twenty thousand men joined the legions in Italy. The Czechoslovak force was active on both of the main fronts, the western (Arras) and eastern (Zborov, Bakhmach), but the legions did not play a significant role until 1918 as the political buttress for Czechoslovak foreign actions, when they intervened in internal developments in post-revolutionary Russia.

3 The Situation at Home During the War

In the meantime, however, Czech domestic politics were reaching the deepest stage of opportunism. Passivity was the norm and opportunity for nationalism in the German-Austrian environment was growing. Czech politicians could not find an effective defence against the concentrated pressure of German nationalists and the government. The need for the concentration of forces was obvious, but attempts to mobilize and unite Czech political parties met with failure. The first hopes for a change in the relations in internal politics came in the autumn of 1916. In October, the Prime Minister Count Karl Stürgk was assassinated in Vienna, and on November 21, 1916, Emperor Francis Joseph I died at the age of 86. The military-bureaucratic regime was weakened by the loss of these personalities, which allowed for the partial freeing up of the possibilities for the renewal of political life. The new Emperor, Charles I, pledged the renewal of operations of Parliament. In November 1916, the League of Czech Members of Parliament in the Reichsrat was begun, and the National Committee was established in Prague. Both Czech political bodies had, however, only worked up to expressions of loyalty towards the regime. The pinnacle of their opportunism towards the empire was the Czech League's statement on January 31, 1917, which condemned the declaration of the Entente and its military goals, among which was the liberation of "Czechoslovaks." This was a harsh blow for the Czech foreign mission, which had barely managed to get this demand into Entente documents.

It was at about this time that forces began to mobilize within the domestic scene to overcome the opportunism and passivity. The signs of returning to life, as was often seen in the Czech environment, were expressed outside of the political sphere. However, in places where politics failed or had been superseded, representatives of culture ascended. The portent of the renewal of Parliament and the unfortunate experiences with the actions of Czech politics from January 1917 onwards led a group of Czech intellectuals, in particular writers, to issue a manifesto to the Czech delegation at the Reichsrat (May 17, 1917), in which the signatories called on members of parliament to look after national interests and to endeavour to work towards a Europe of free nations. Up until then, the only request that had been made was for the autonomy of the Bohemian state within the Austro-Hungarian empire. Now for the first time, the thought of a constitutional alliance between the Czech Lands and Slovakia was openly expressed.

The second impulse leading to the renewal of political life originated in the social sphere. Starting in the spring of 1917, the catastrophic situation with the supply of goods set off a wave of strikes and protests. The state authorities reacted with ever-increasing brutality. In April, during a protest by workers in Prostějov, 23 people were killed in a hail of gunfire; in August in Moravská Ostrava 13 workers were killed, and so on. Even so it was evident that the situation was beginning to change. The protesters' boldness and their level of organization was growing. During the elections of shop stewards in the summer of 1917, primarily candidates who were not associated with the pro-Austrian politics of the Social Democrats were elected.

The year 1917 was also a turning point in the war. The balance of forces was slowly beginning to change on the front lines, especially when, in April 1917, the United States entered the war against the Central Powers. The situation for the Entente forces was temporarily complicated by the advance of Soviet Bolsheviks, who had ceased fighting on the eastern front and signed an independent peace treaty with Germany and Austria-Hungary in Brest-Litovsk on March 3, 1918. The German command was then able to move part of its forces to the western front, but the overall depletion of resources did not allow the Central Powers to reach a decisive turning point in the war. The year 1918 was beginning to portend the end of the war and the growing hopes for a new order in Europe, as was otherwise announced in a message from American President Woodrow Wilson on January 8, 1918, in which he went so far as to speak of the will to create new national states.

Political parties once again took up their roles in domestic political life in Czech society. Starting in 1917, within two years the majority of these underwent a certain transformation. Their first attempts at merging were not too successful. The principal political currents, which we know from the beginning of the 20th century, had survived the most critical period of political repression; they adapted to the period's current needs, occasionally absorbing smaller political parties. The most stable party was the Czech Agrarian Party (*Česká strana agrární*), which before the war had remade itself into a popular political party. Its professional, seemingly non-political, character allowed it to survive without great harm the most critical phases of persecution while maintaining its reputation as a patriotic force, although at the cost of pronounced opportunism. The Agrarian Party did in fact become the leading force of the domestic upheaval. The Czech Constitutional Democratic Party (*Česká strana státoprávně demokratická*) represented a continuity of the liberal trends in Czech politics from the 19th century. Its base was formed by the National Liberal Party (Young Czech Party), which at the beginning of 1918 merged with several smaller political parties and groups. Their political line was shaped by the original Young Czechs. The war left them with a relatively complicated legacy. Their ranks included political martyrs (K. Kramář, A. Rašín), active members of the Mafia, and even pro-Austrian opportunists. The Czech National Socialist Party (*Česká strana národně sociální*) also underwent interesting changes. At the beginning of the war, it was the target of the most extreme persecution, and under pressure from its members, who were socially hard hit by the war, shifted significantly to the left. Tendencies to join with the Social Democrats began to emerge, but were never actually followed through. In April 1918, the original national socialist cause joined with a number of liberal politicians (Czech Democrats), realists and with the Czech Federation of Anarcho-

Communists. And so the Czech Socialist Party (*Česká strana socialistická*) was formed, from 1926, it was known as the Czech National Social Party (*Československá sociálně demokratická strana dělnická*). The most important internal rebirth was undertaken by the Czech-Slavic Social Democratic Workers' Party. At the outset of the war, it had ceased all political activity for tactical reasons. Leadership of the party was assumed by Bohumír Šmeral, a lawyer and journalist, who among their leadership had the closest ties to revolutionary Marxism. He assumed a stance against the breakup of Austria-Hungary, captivated by the thought of the revolutionary transformation of this state into a federation of free socialist nations. During a wave of increasing resistance to the monarchy, control of the party was taken by a group of politicians with a more overt Czech constitutional program. Discord between the nationalist and socialist sides remained. In the meantime, the Czech Catholic parties stood aside from the political upheaval, having been associated too much with the Church, which supported the conservative forces in the Habsburg monarchy. The Catholics were to wait for their unification.

4 The Balance of Forces

At the beginning of 1918, a certain balance of forces between the state powers and the emancipation movements of the partially-fledged nations in the Habsburg empire was formed. As early as January 1918, the Czech political representation took the offensive and the state's authorities no longer had sufficient forces to suppress or quash the initiatives, which were further destabilizing the domestic situation. Visible signs of the growing instability were marked by the toothless reaction to an evidently seditious act, the Epiphany Declaration. The document was approved in Prague on January 6, 1918, during combined negotiations of Czech deputies of the Reichsrat and the Diets of the Kingdom of Bohemia, the Margraviate of Moravia and the Duchy of Silesia. The impulse which led to the issuing of the declaration was dissatisfaction with the official composition of the Austro-Hungarian delegation to the Russian peace negotiations in Brest-Litovsk. Foreign Minister Count Ottokar Czernin categorically refused to allow the representatives of the monarchy's individual nations to participate in the negotiations, he could not, however, prevent the public protest culminating in the requirement of an independent and fully-fledged Czech state, which would include part of the territories of the Hungarian Kingdom, settled by a national "Slovak branch." After this, the stream of concessions from the state powers was not to be stopped.

The Epiphany Declaration arose from deeper issues, not least of which was caused by the mottos of the Russian October revolution on peace and the right of nations for self-determination; this gave the national movements a new impulse. The declaration was at least one step ahead of the positions of the Entente at the time, where the notion of maintaining Austria-Hungary still survived. The goal was to separate it from Germany, which would then be easier to defeat. The position of the Entente on the efforts of unfledged nations of the monarchy towards political emancipation was best expressed by President Woodrow Wilson's address to American Congress on January 8, 1918. His Fourteen Points speech, stated among other things that the peoples of Austria-Hungary "should be accorded the freest opportunity of autonomous development," a position that could not at this stage satisfy the demands of the national movements.

After reaching a separate peace with Russia, the self-confidence of the governing circles in Vienna briefly grew. We can see evidence of this in one of Minister Czernin's statements, which quite arrogantly criticized Czech emancipation efforts – he spoke of the actions of "miserable Masaryks" at home and abroad – which provoked a sharp reaction from the Czech side. In front of a large assembly of Czech political, cultural and scientific representatives in the Municipal House in Prague on April 13, 1918, prominent Czech writer Alois Jirásek read a "national oath," in which he expressed a determination to continue the fight for independence to its successful conclusion. The state was again unable to react to this clearly seditious declaration, and the number of public demonstrations began to increase. The most effective of these were associated with the celebrations of the 50th anniversary of the laying of the cornerstone of the National Theatre on May 16–17, 1918. At this time, political movement had already begun in Slovakia, as is witnessed by the demonstration on May 1 in Liptovský Svätý Mikuláš, where the participants demanded the formation of a Czechoslovak state.

During the first half of 1918, evidence of the decline of the Habsburg empire was no longer merely political and culturally motivated demonstrations by the representatives of national movements. A mass social movement was developing in parallel. The winter of 1917–1918, marked by war, once again brought with it the depletion of human and material resources. Both raw materials and labour were lacking, and basic foodstuffs were in short supply. Production levels fell even in companies supplying the front lines. Not even militarization, or their subjugation to military administration and law, of the firms helped the situation. Poverty, hunger and societal illnesses caused by malnutrition drove workers to desperate acts. In January 1918, a massive new wave of strikes arose. It began in Lower Austria and spread to other Alpine land and even as far as the Czech Lands. Several hundred thousand workers took part, expressing not only social demands, but also calling for an end to the war, and in the Czech Lands their calls for national self-determination could be heard.

For the empire, however, the greatest danger was found in developments in the army. Desertion from the front was continual, soldiers either deserting to the enemy (on the Italian front), or going into hiding near their homes, and groups of deserters (the green echelon) were gathering in the forests. The increasing number of insurrections within military units was an even greater indication of the army's decay. The mutiny at the naval base in the Gulf of Kotor in the south of the Adriatic Sea set off a wave of unrest in the army. The crew consisted of members of multiple nationalities, and the mutiny was led by František Raš from Přerov (Moravia). The naval command was, however, able to isolate the mutineers and to put down the insurrection. In February 1918, some of the Czech companies on the Italian front went over, followed by Czech soldiers in Mostar (Herzegovina). On May 21, 1918, mutiny broke out in the company in Rumburk (Bohemia) and similar expressions of resistance to the war and against relations in the country were seen in dozens of places; as a rule, in places where the personnel came from partially-fledged nations (Czechs, Slovaks, Slovenians and Italians). For example, in June 1918, 44 soldiers of Slovak origin were executed in Kragujevac (Serbia) for mutiny. In the summer months, the breakup of the army became an avalanche and could no longer be stopped.

5 The Agony of the Habsburg Empire and the Czechoslovak Resistance

The peace accord reached in Brest-Litovsk gave the governing circles of the Central Powers hope for a positive turn in the war. Amid scandalous circumstances, Austria-Hungary strengthened its dependence on Germany. At the time, secret peace negotiations between Entente diplomats and the Austro-Hungarian government were underway, but after Minister Czernin offended the honour of French Prime Minister George Clemenceau in a speech in April 1918, French sources revealed information on the negotiations. Germany immediately took advantage of the scandal, which became known as the Sixtus Affair, to pressure its allies. Emperor Charles I was forced to pledge loyal friendship and a part of the Austro-Hungarian army was placed under German command. So nationalist groups within the monarchy were able to use the situation to further increase the influence of the German and Hungarian ethnic groups. By government order, a regional system was put in place which reflected long-term plans to divide the country along ethnic lines. It was precisely these events that convinced the Entente that it would not be possible to lessen the dependence of the Habsburg monarchy on Germany, and began to be indifferent to the fate of Austria-Hungary. Clearly, this changed the standing of the political representation of the servile nations, including the Czechoslovak foreign mission, which began to bear the fruit of its tireless propagation and even the results of its efforts in the creation of the sizable Czechoslovak legions.

Czechoslovak military units proved themselves on the western front in the defence of France and were also significant on the eastern front, but most of all they began to play an exceptional role in the plans of the Entente to quash the revolution in Russia. In March 1918, the Czechoslovak legions joined the Red Army against the Central Powers' offensive in the Ukraine at the Battle of Bakhmach. However after the Brest-Litovsk peace accord came into effect and the Russian front ceased to exist, the "Czechoslovaks" were to be redeployed to the western front. Due to the balance of power in the western parts of Russia, their only path led through Siberia and the Far East and from there by sea to Europe.

During the evacuation of the legions along the Trans-Siberian railway, on May 14, 1918, a chance incident occurred in Chelyabinsk between the soldiers of one of the legionnaires' echelons and the local soviet. The animosity quickly spread, and in a short time the legionnaires controlled the entire Trans-Siberian railway all the way to Vladivostok. The Entente powers expressed a desire to use the well organized and trained Czechoslovak troops to intervene against Soviet power. Individual military units were drawn into local conflicts on the side of the anti-revolutionary forces, but fatigue from the long war and a feeling of the senselessness of remaining in Russia began to be evident in the legions. The units' morale began to decline and it was ever more urgent to quickly evacuate them to the Pacific Ocean and arrange their transport to Europe.

In spite of the fact that the Entente's plan to make use of the legions was unsuccessful, the very existence of this force increased the authority of the Czechoslovak National Council and sped up its diplomatic recognition by the Entente. At the end of June 1918, the French government recognized the right of the "Czechoslovak" nation to independence and the National Council as the basis for the coming Czechoslovak government. In August, the British government proclaimed the Czechoslovak nation an ally and the Czech National Council as the highest representatives of the future state, followed in September by similar proclamations by the government of the USA.

After his return from Russia, T. G. Masaryk lived in the USA, and took part in negotiations between Czech and Slovak expatriate organizations there. During a meeting in Pittsburgh on May 30, 1918, their representatives signed an agreement approving the confederation of Czechs and Slovaks in an independent state, and Slovakia was to gain autonomy with its own administration and assembly. The details were left to be worked out by the legally elected representatives of both nations in the new state.

The process of Habsburg empire's disintegration picked up speed in the summer of 1918. It was accompanied by defeats on all fronts, growing social pressure within the state and increasingly strong cries from the various national movements to achieve the complete political emancipation of their nations. The Czech political representation also resolved to take decisive preparatory steps in this direction. After the individual Entente powers had gradually proceeded to recognize the Czechoslovak National Council as the representative of the future nation, the domestic political scene became more active. The leaders of Czech political parties decided to create a coordinating body, which would be in charge of the further development of Czech politics and, at the appropriate time, take control of the government in the regions specified by the constitutional program, which had already been formulated in general terms at the beginning of the war in Masaryk's plans.

At the initiative of the leader of the Czech Agrarians, Antonín Švehla, after reaching an accord with the secret political committee, the Mafia, the Czech National Committee, an association of the representatives of Czech political parties, was renewed on July 13, 1918. The key to its assembly were the results of the elections to the Reichsrat in 1911. In its first phase, the National Committee had 38 members and elected as its chairman Karel Kramář, the leader of the Czech Constitutionalist Party (originally the leader of the Young Czech Party), who held considerable authority in the Czech public after escaping the death penalty. Antonín Švehla and Czech Socialist Václav Klofáč were elected vice-chairmen and Social Democrat František Soukup served as secretary. The National Committee set as its mission to assemble, organize and conduct all intellectual, moral and material forces of the nation towards achieving the right to self-determination in an independent, democratic Czechoslovak state with its own administration and under its own sovereignty. Indeed, it already considered itself to be a "Czechoslovak" body, and its creators naturally counted on the representation of Slovaks. In the meantime, however, the majority of representatives were Czech public figures, who were well known adherents of Czech-Slovak solidarity. Representatives of the burghers' parties held a majority in the National Committee. In spite of the fact that the influence of socialist thinking visibly increased during the war, the socialist parties did not attain commensurate representation, and so on September 6, 1918, in the interest of coordinating their policies, they created a united body, the Socialist Council, which nonetheless fully recognized the authority of the National Committee. Both bodies for the moment adopted a wait-and-see policy.

However, a crucial turn in the war had already occurred. In the summer of 1918, Entente armies succeeded in breaking through the German defence on the western front and began an extensive offensive; at the beginning of that September, the Austrian army suffered defeat on the Italian front and several days later Bulgaria, ally of the Central Powers, capitulated. The Austro-Hungarian Foreign Ministry subsequently, and in agreement with Berlin, approached all of the warring nations with an offer of peace. At that time the Vienna government was obviously losing control of the domestic situation. The supply system collapsed, threatening to unleash an explosion of socially motivated unrest. In as much as the government considered relations with the Alpine lands to be the most important, especially in Vienna, the central authorities began looting other parts of the state to try to calm the situation there. Trains filled with coal and the remainder of the grain supply were exported, primarily from Bohemia and Moravia. The Prague National Committee emphatically protested against the export of essential necessities. The Socialist Council also took the step of organizing a general strike in protest of the government's policy.

The strike, which took place on October 14, 1918, culminated in a number of towns as a political action and the declaration of an independent Czechoslovak Republic, and, in isolated cases, of a socialist republic. The National Committee immediately clamped down on these tendencies, however the impression left behind by the massive declarations of the Czech public's will was impossible to ignore. The emperor tried one last time to save his disintegrating empire. In his manifesto dated October 16, 1918, he proposed transforming Austria (Cisleithania) into a federal state, in which each nation would form a state unit within its borders. He also urged the national councils founded by representatives of individual nations to cooperate in the transformation of the empire. It was, however, already a hopeless gesture. The empire's disintegration could no longer be stopped.

The Czech foreign mission once again sprang into action. Edvard Beneš, who had feared the constant hesitation of Entente on the fate of the Habsburg Empire, on October 14, 1918, announced to the governments of the Entente states that the Czechoslovak National Council in Paris had become the provisional Czechoslovak government and requested diplomatic recognition. T. G. Masaryk stood at the head of the provisional government, along with members Edvard Beneš and Milan Rastislav Štefánik. Furthering Beneš's steps, T. G. Masaryk, while still living in the USA, issued the Declaration of Independence of the Czechoslovak Nation on October 18, 1918. In accordance with the place from which it was issued, this document is known as the Washington Declaration. One might assume that it influenced the negative response of the American president to the offer of peace from the Austrian emperor.

Still, Vienna was not ready to surrender. Representatives of the Austrian Germans, though, no longer believed that the efforts of the government and court to save the empire would succeed. On October 21, 1918, the German-Austrian National Council was founded in the spirit of the emperor's manifesto, and were composed of representatives of the Reichsrat from the Austrian Alpine lands and German representatives from Bohemia, Moravia and Silesia, which attempted to save at least the position of the German environment in Cisleithania. In the meantime, Prague was waiting for the appropriate moment to make a crucial statement.

Bibliography

BENEŠ, Edvard: *Světová válka a naše revoluce*, I–III, Praha 1927–1928.
Česká společnost za velkých válek 20. století. Pokus o komparaci. Jan Gebhart – Ivan Šedivý (eds.), Praha 2003.
DEJMEK, Jindřich: *Edvard Beneš. Politická biografie českého demokrata*, I–II, Praha 2006 and 2008.
GALANDAUER, Jan: *Slovník prvního českého odboje 1914–918*, Praha1986.
GALANDAUER, Jan: *Karel I. Poslední český král*, Praha 1997.
GEBHART, Jan – ŠEDIVÝ, Ivan (eds.): *Česká společnost ze velkých válek 20. století*. Pokus o komparaci, Praha 2003.
HADLER, Frank (ed.): *Weg von Österreich! Das Weltkriegsexil von Masaryk und Beneš im Spiegel ihrer Briefe und Aufzeichnungen*, Berlin 1995.
HAJŠMAN, Jan: *Česká Maffie. Vzpomínky na odboj doma*, Praha 1932.
HANISCH, Ernst: *Österreichische Geschichte 1890–1990. Lange Schatten des Staates. Gesellschaftsgeschichte im 20. Jahrhundert*, Wien 1994.
HLAVAČKA, Milan: *Podivná aliance*, Praha 1987.
HRONSKÝ, Marián: *Slovensko pri zrode Československa*, Bratislava 1987.
JINDRA, Zdeněk: *První světová válka*, Praha 1984.
KALVODA, Josef: *The Genesis of Czechoslovakia*, New York 1985.
KALVODA, Jiří: *The Czechoslowak Declaration of Independence. A History of Document*, Washington D. C. 1985.
KALVODA, Jiří: *Masarykův triumf. Příběh konce velké války*, Praha 1991.
KUČERA, Martin: *Rakouský občan Josef Pekař*, Praha 2005.
MASARYK, T. G.: *Die Weltrevolution. Erinnerungen und Betrachtungen 1914–1918*, Berlin 1925.
PAULOVÁ, Milada: *Dějiny Maffie. Odboj Čechů a Jihoslovanů za světové války 1914–1918*, I–II/1, Praha 1937.
PAULOVÁ, Milada: *Tajný výbor (Maffie) a spolupráce s Jihoslovany v letech 1916–1918*, Praha 1968.
PETRÁŠ, J.: *Československé legie a první světová válka*, České Budějovice 2002.
PICHLÍK, Karel: *Bez legend. Zahraniční odboj 1914–1918. Zápas o československý program*, Praha 1991.
PICHLÍK, Karel – Klípa, Bohumil – Zabloudilová, Jitka: *Československé legie 1914–1920*, Praha 1996.
PROKŠ, Petr: *Politikové a vznik republiky 1914–1918*, Praha 1998.
První světová válka a vztahy mezi Čechy, Slováky a Němci. Hans Mommsen, Dušan Kováč, Jiří Malíř (eds.), Brno 2000.
ŠEDIVÝ, Ivan: *Češi, české země a Velká válka 1914–1918*, Praha 2001.
TOBOLKA, Zdeněk: *Politické dějiny československého národa IV*, Praha 1937.
ZEMAN, Zbyněk: *The Break-up of the Habsburg Empire 1914–1918*, London–New York–Toronto 1961.

JOSEF HARNA

XV. First Czechoslovak Republic (1918–1938)

President T. G. Masaryk's return to his homeland after four years in emigration.
Welcome at the station in České Budějovice on December 21, 1918.

1 The Building of a State

In mid 1918, the prevalent opinion in the Prague National Committee was that the essential questions concerning further development had already basically been decided and that the time had come to coordinate the policies of the domestic political representation with the foreign mission. On October 26, 1918, a delegation of Czech politicians travelled to Geneva with the approval of the Vienna government for negotiations with Edvard Beneš, representing the provisional Czechoslovak government, and was joined by Constitutional Democrat Karel Kramář, chairman of the National Committee, his vice-chairman Czech Socialist Václav Klofáč, Social Democrat Gustav Habrman, representative of the Trade Bank Jaroslav Preiss and others. While they reached complete agreement in Geneva, especially concerning the future republican state foundation, composition of the government and on the future president, events in Prague took an unexpected turn.

On October 28, 1918, a diplomatic note from Austrian Foreign Minister Count Gyula Andrássy was made public, in which agreement was expressed with the conditions of American President Wilson for truce negotiations. The inhabitants of Prague interpreted this note as the final and general surrender of the monarchy and began to spontaneously declare the independence of the Czechoslovak state. Representatives of the National Committee had at that time started an orderly takeover of the Grain Institute, but on hearing the news on the situation in the streets immediately took the lead in the revolution that was breaking out. They announced to the Land Vice-regency that they were taking control over the administration of the country. They sent spokesmen out into the streets to explain the situation, organized groups to ensure public order, primarily consisting of volunteers from the Sokol organization. In an attempt to prevent unrest and violence they supported the celebratory atmosphere of the day. Musical groups performed in the streets, people rejoiced and enthusiastically greeted the fall of the Habsburg empire.

Later that evening the leadership of the National Committee issued a proclamation which stated that the "Czechoslovak State had come to life." This de facto first law of the new state was signed by representatives of the National Committee – chairman of the Agrarian Party Antonín Švehla, one of the leaders of the Constitutional Democrats Alois

Rašín, for the Social Democrats journalist František Soukup, and also the vice-chairman of the Czech Socialist Party Jiří Stříbrný, also a journalist by trade, and for the Slovak representation Vavro Šrobár, all now to be known in history as the "Men of October 28th." Their ability to act quickly was admirable. They were able to organize a fundamental coup d'état without major conflicts, maintained order and the next day negotiated with the Land Military Command to rule out army intervention into events and began to immediately assert the general authority of the National Committee.

The situation in which the Czechoslovak National Committee took over power was extraordinarily complex. Furthermore, the leaders of the coup had virtually no resources on hand for the inexhaustible number of tasks facing them. They were lacking the means of asserting their authority, there was no administrative apparatus, the state borders were undefined, there were no international guarantees. The war had exhausted material resources, the economic disruption continued, supply lines were clogged, hundreds of thousands of men were returning from the front lines looking for work, and the unbearable social tension was growing. In spite of this, several brave men set to work very energetically. Immediately on October 28, the National Committee expanded to approximately three times its original size and declared itself to be the legislative body of the new state. Its primary interest was in calming the situation and agitated moods. At first they were able to make use of the vigour of the Czech population, who of course completely subjugated themselves to its authority, as did the state apparatus and self-governing bodies in regions with a majority Czech population. Its support base was formed by the majority of Czech political parties.

In the area of legislation, the National Committee concentrated on ensuring the basic functions of the state. On November 13, they declared themselves to be the Revolutionary National Assembly. It first divested the Habsburg Dynasty of its rights to the Bohemian throne and set up a republican form of government. One day later, on November 14, 1918, they elected T. G. Masaryk the president of the republic and named the first Czechoslovak government headed by Karel Kramář. The government of the nation-wide coalition was supported by almost all Czech and Slovak political parties. At the end of December 1918, president T. G. Masaryk (1850–1937) took office, having finally returned from emigration. He was triumphantly greeted as the creator of national independence. He gained considerable political and moral authority during the war, and with his knowledge and experience greatly exceeded the average for the politics of that day. Furthermore, he could rely on extensive contacts abroad. At home he was not associated with any prominent political party, which allowed him to act as a unifying personality.

One of the urgent tasks of the first government was to ensure the effectiveness of the legal system and the functioning of the state administration. Important tasks were the ratification of the provisional constitution from November 13, 1918, and the passing of the "Reception Act," which adopted the existing Austro-Hungarian legal system and assured the continuity of the legal system. The problem was in the dual nature of the former monarchy's legal system. The Czech Lands used the laws of the former Cisleithania, while the Hungarian system was used in Slovakia and in the later annexed Subcarpathian Ruthenia. A ministry for the unification of laws was established to overcome this disadvantage. Its work, however, went slowly and the office was abolished as unnecessary at the end of the 1920s.

In February 1920, the parliament ratified the Constitution of the Czechoslovak Republic. The document's origin can be seen in several legal examples (the French, Swiss and American constitution, even domestic traditions) and assured a wide range of democratic rights and freedoms. At the same time as the constitution, laws were passed on the use of languages in official communications and on the organization of state administration, which established districts (*župy*) as a middle layer of state administration. The district law was never put into force. Districts remained in use only in Slovakia from the era of the Hungarian state, while the Czech Lands remained under the Land system.

The Czech public generally expected that the Czechoslovak state would include the Czech Lands within its traditional borders, to which would be added the northern areas of the Hungarian Kingdom occupied by inhabitants of Slovak nationality. The most serious problem was of course the fact that the German population living primarily in the border regions of the Czech Lands completely refused the newly emerging state. Their political representatives, Nationalist Rudolf Lodgman von Auen, Social Democrat Josef Seliger and others took part in the creation of a National Council for German Austria in Vienna and simultaneously organized the creation of separate regions in the border areas of the Czech Lands, which they declared as part of German Austria; they expected that this territory would, along with Austria, be affiliated with Germany. The largest of these regional units, *Deutschböhmen* (German Bohemia), whose Land seat was in Liberec, contained the majority of northern Bohemia; similarly the *Sudetenland* was formed in northern Moravia and Silesia, with its seat in Opava. Not long after, the *Böhmerwaldgau* (*župa Český les*) in southern Bohemia and the *Deutschsüdmähren* in southern Moravia were established. The German leaders continued in the tradition of attempting to stake out a closed German-speaking territory, persisting at least from the times of the ethnic struggles following the Austro-Hungarian stabilization (1867), but with the difference that this time they relied on the right of nations for self-determination. Neither the Czech political representation nor public could reconcile with this stance. The idea of separation of extensive territories which had always been considered to be a integral part of their homeland was utterly incomprehensible for the Czech public. It was a desperate attempt by the German side, in which many believed, but which in reality never had a chance to succeed. It was made impossible not only by political obstacles, but even geopolitical, in particular economic. The border regions of the Czech Lands along with the interior regions formed an organic whole which could not be broken up without serious economic, supply or communications problems. In addition to this, international conditions were not favourable either. "Czechoslovaks" were an allied nation and it would be absurd for the victorious Entente to allow regional concessions in favour of the defeated Germany or Austria, especially at the expense of an ally.

Not even this favourable combination of circumstances however allowed the Czech political representation to ignore the existence and stances of the large German population living in the territories of the emerging nation. During the war, T. G. Masaryk had of course counted on the participation of Germans in the government and representatives of the National Committee attempted to make contact with the German leadership immediately after the coup. The German side however uncompromisingly refused the offer to take part in building the state. The breakaway regions in the meantime met with a number of problems. Problems with supply increased, social tensions grew, only with difficulty was the state administration able to fulfil its function and maintained order only at the cost of maximal effort. The Prague National Committee, having failed to reach an agreement, began to immediately occupy the border regions. Czechoslovak army units took town after town. The German Land governments gradually relocated to Vienna and the local administrative bodies subjugated themselves without much resistance to the new state. The occupation of the entire border regions of the Czech Lands was completed by the end of December 1918.

Another principal problem that the state leadership had to solve was the integration of Slovakia. In comparison with the Czech Lands, the process of liberating Slovakia proceeded under substantially more difficult conditions. Slovakia remained a primarily agrarian land, the number of the intelligentsia and burghers was low and they were rather weak. In addition to this, there was a much more severe national pressure in Hungary, which made it almost impossible to organize any type of opposition to the Hungarian state administration. Even so, political life in the Slovak environment slowly began to come to life during the year 1918. Impressed by external events, the guiding political force, the Slovak National Party (*Slovenská národní strana*), called an assembly on October 30, 1918, in Turčiansky Svätý Martin, which elected the Slovak National Council and passed the Declaration of the Slovak Nation. The assembly's participants, without knowledge of the events in Prague, declared the independence of the Slovak Nation and their desire to incorporate in the Czechoslovak state. Even though some of the formulations in the Martin Declaration are ambiguous, it still represented a constitutional document of utmost importance. Doubts were later raised by the formulation in which the Slovak nation was declared to be "part of the linguistic and cultural-historic unified Czechoslovak nation." However it was rather just a result of imprecise terminology. No one could doubt the fact that the Slovaks at this point were a wholly independent nation. It was significant that the political leaders of the Slovak nation, in issuing the Martin Declaration, had freely expressed their will to co-operate with the Czechs in the building of a common state.

The resolution of the Martin assembly, however significant, was now necessary to be put into effect. Slovakia was still under the control of the Hungarian administration and was occupied by Hungarian forces. The situation did not change either after the coup in Budapest on October 31, 1918, or after the official end of the First World War on November 11, 1918. The new Hungarian government insisted on the indivisibility of the former Hungarian territories, and so the only remaining possibility to integrate Slovakia into the Czechoslovak state was the use of military force. Not even in this situation did the Prague National Committee delay. On November 4, 1918, the Committee named a provisional Slovak government headed by Vavro Šrobár and charged it with taking the necessary steps to assert the authority of the Czechoslovak state in Slovakia. The jurisdiction of this body was later taken on by a Ministry with full authority over Slovakia's administration, also under Šrobár's leadership. The first attempt to occupy Slovakia by the underarmed and for the most part volunteer forces of the Czechoslovak army ended in failure. Military actions under the command of Italian officers to expel the Hungarian units did not begin until January 1919. The advance of the Czechoslovak army stopped at the provisional demarcation line, which was later more fully specified and recognized at the peace conference as the Czechoslovak-Hungarian state border. By the end of February 1919, Slovakia was already a part of the Czechoslovak state.

The definitive demarcation of the borders and their international recognition was linked to the signing of accords at the Paris peace conference, specifically the peace treaty signed with Germany in Versailles (July 28, 1919), the treaty with Austria in Saint Germain (September 10, 1919) and the treaty signed with Hungary in Trianon (June 4, 1920). The border with Germany and Austria, in comparison with the former lands borders, saw just minor changes in favour of the Czech Lands (Hlučín, Valtice, České Velenice regions); the Slovak-Hungarian border was completely new, leading from Bratislava along the Danube river to the junction with the Ipeľ river, and on to the east to the Tisa river.

The dispute with Poland over the Těšín region (Teschen Silesia; Cieszyn in Polish) was complicated. Both states asserted rights over the entire historic territory of the Duchy of Těšín. The Czechoslovak side emphasized the fact that Těšín had been a part of the lands of the Bohemian Crown. The Poles relied on the fact that the inhabitants of the disputed territory were primarily of Polish nationality, and referred to their right to self-determination. Of course interest in the coal reserves in the Ostrava-Karviná basin was firmly in the background of the dispute. The Košice-Bohumín railway, which crossed this territory and represented one of the only connections between the western part of the country with Slovakia, was also important for Czechoslovakia. The dispute, which had threatened to grow into a protracted military conflict, was essentially solved by a decision by the superpowers that divided the Těšín territories between both states. Minor corrections were made to the border between Slovakia and Poland in 1924. Several villages in the Orava and Spiš regions were ceded to Poland. The dispute however brought constant tension into relations between Czechoslovakia and Poland.

With the approval of the Entente, Czechoslovakia also gained the Subcarpathian Ruthenia, consisting of a rather extensive territory (12,694 km² with 600,000 inhabitants), lying to the east of Slovakia in the large Carpathian Arch, inhabited primarily by Rusyns (now the Transcarpathian Ukraine, part of the Ukrainian Republic). The Entente powers thus complied with the wishes of the Rusyn countrymen's organizations in the USA, whose representatives had already discussed this question before the end of the war with T. G. Masaryk.

Czechoslovakia with its total area of 140,394 km² and 13 million inhabitants belonged among the smaller European states. The creation of this state was the culmination of the national liberation goals of the Czech and Slovak nations. With regards to the complex borders, especially due to the fact that diffusion of ethnic groups was typical for Central Europe, the structure of settlements by nationality was extraordinarily diverse.

The constitution of 1920 guaranteed not only Czechs and Slovaks, but also members of other nationalities full rights – they had their own education system, the full possibilities for cultural development and approximately equal conditions for development of the political life. Even though the extent of minority rights was in comparison to other states in Central Europe distinctly larger, it was not possible to satisfactorily solve all ethnic problems and attain the acceptance of the Czechoslovak state as the permanent framework of their existence.

A unique relationship developed between the Czech and Slovak nations. The initial bilateral enthusiasm from the attained freedom was replaced by the disappointment of Slovaks in their position in the new state. The cause of the problem was primarily in the official theory of a unified *Czechoslovak people*. In the atmosphere of general enthusiasm for the right of people to self-determination, Edvard Beneš made use of it at the Paris peace conference to prove that the nascent Czechoslovakia was a state of one people, or that even with the existence of numerous ethnic groups the "Czechoslovak" people had a majority (65%). During this phase the ethnic theory was slowly changing into an attempt to construct a political (state) ethnic, which would contain two equal parts, Czech and Slovak. The concept of a unified nation was not objectively a barrier to the cultural development of the Slovaks. The Slovak language was used alongside Czech as an official language, and was the language used in all Slovak schools. The principle of a unified nation was not intended to suppress the national identity of the Slovaks, but in reality the numeric, political and cultural prevalence of Czech society began to exert itself. This prevalence began to show in the mutual relations of both nations, along with the inconsiderate stance of some of the political and cultural representatives towards the distinct historical and cultural traditions, and towards the living conditions in Slovakia. At first it evoked a feeling of dissatisfaction which changed to calls for the autonomy of Slovakia, leading up to separatist tendencies. For a number of Slovaks, these feelings completely overshadowed the positive contribution of Slovakia's belonging to a democratic state, and negated the positive work in state

Ethnic composition of inhabitants of CSR from the 1921 census

Ethnicity	Number (in thousands)	%
Czechs*	6842	50.3
Slovaks*	1977	15.2
Germans	3123	23.4
Hungarians	745	5.6
Poles	76	0.6
Rusyns (Russians, Ukrainians)	462	3.4
Jews	25	1.3
Other	25	0.2

* From a later calculation of the proportion of Czechs and Slovaks. Czechoslovak statistics used only the Czechoslovak nationality.

administration, health care, education, industry and elsewhere by Czech specialists who came to Slovakia in the first years after the revolution.

The relationship between Czechs and Germans was more transparent. It was dominated by distrust, which could not be masked by numerous examples in everyday life of peaceful co-existence. The German political leaders in the Czech Lands took an unambiguously negative stance towards the republic, and made their opinions clear when possible. They filed a protest at the Paris peace conference and expressed their averse relations to the CSR at home as well. In March 1919, on the occasion of the commencement of the Austrian Parliament, there were demonstrations and clashes between the German population and the armed state powers. During the army intervention several dozen demonstrators were killed (most in Kadaň and Šumperk). These events worsened even further the stance of Germans towards Czechs and the Czechoslovak state. The other ethnic minorities were numerically weaker, basically lived in the border regions of the state and essentially could not influence the internal political situation.

The economic character of the First Republic also held great significance for the further development of relationship between ethnicities in the new state. With regards to the territorial disposition of industrial production in the defunct Habsburg empire, Czechoslovakia from the start belonged to the industrially developed European nations. It had only 21% of the area of the former empire (140,394 km^2) and 26% of its population, however between 60 and 70% of the manufacturing capacity of Austria-Hungary was located in its territory. In certain branches this ratio was even higher, for instance the mining of anthracite, glass production, the textile and shoe-making trades. The ironworks and machinery industries were at a high level. The distribution of industry in the new state was uneven as well. Slovakia was primarily agrarian, and Subcarpathian Ruthenia was from an economic standpoint the least developed part of the state. Although these easternmost regions of the state experienced an "industrial revolution" in the ensuing years, they were not able to overcome the economic deficiency. The differences in the economic levels of individual regions was among the most serious problem inherited from the past, second only to the ethnic dispositions in the regions. Then there were additional problems arising from the shrinking of the domestic market. The pressure caused by increased competition within the Czechoslovak economy grew disproportionately, and the poorer and less technically and technologically developed enterprises, primarily seated in Slovakia, could not compete in this situation. The Slovak economy was also harder hit by all of the fluctuations caused by crises, the effects of which were felt not only in the social but also in political areas.

Currency reform and the separation of the Czechoslovak currency from the Austro-Hungarian currency was of fundamental importance for the rapid consolidation of the economy. The state's fiscal policy, put in place by the first post-war Finance Minster Alois Rašín, was successful in maintaining the crown's high exchange rate. Measures were also put into place to prevent the outflow of capital abroad. Foreign capital groups were forced to relocate their centres to Czechoslovakia. This allowed the transfer of a large part of the stock of Czechoslovak companies into the hands of domestic capital (domestication of stocks).

The above-mentioned economic measures had a positive effect on the rise of production, and were measurably felt in the socially weaker layers of the population. Social problems had grown into inconceivable proportions as a result of the war. The danger of social unrest was growing stronger, and a significant part of the work force was becoming more radical. The government therefore immediately took at least some partial social measures. The eight-hour work day was set in law in industry, and unemployment support was enacted. The excess workforce continued to be solved by mass emigration, largely to the USA. The stream of emigrants was stronger from Slovakia and Subcarpathian Ruthenia.

Even so, society did not avoid a wave of social conflicts. In particular, 1919 was characterized by a menacing number of strikes, demonstrations and hunger riots, which grew into the looting of stores and warehouses. The workers were sensitive to the level of social and political conflicts that shook neighbouring states. In Slovakia and Subcarpathian Ruthenia, the attempt at a Bolshevik revolution in Hungary met with a certain response. Troops of the Hungarian Soviet Republic crossed into Czechoslovak territory and on June 16, 1919, under their auspices the Slovak Soviet Republic was established for an interim period with its seat in Prešov. It was abolished when under pressure from Entente diplomats the Hungarian units withdrew from Czechoslovak territory. In the Czech Lands the expansion of social struggles was held in check by governmental countermeasures, but it acted as a constant reminder of the threat that social unrest could lead to the loss of the newly acquired state independence.

2 On the Path to Prosperity

By 1920, the process of stabilization of international relations had made significant progress. A number of treaties had been signed, forming the "Versailles Peace System," named according to the most important treaties signed between the victorious powers and Germany. This system was to become the basis for international coexistence and security in Europe. From the very beginning, however, it suffered from a number of compromises, which weakened its effectiveness. As Czechoslovak Foreign Minister, Edvard Beneš went to great efforts to assert specific Czechoslovak requirements not only with regards to the determination of state borders, but he also concentrated on strengthening allied ties with the Entente. The failure of the Soviet offensive in Poland in the summer of 1920 and especially the creation of the League of Nations, in which Czechoslovakia had been heavily involved from the beginning, were all important towards calming the situation.

A number of problems however remained in relations with neighbouring nations. Poland could not come to terms with the forced compromise on Těšín and so the tense relations with Czechoslovakia persisted. The relationship with Germany was at first without problems. The republic was interested in improving contacts due to the fact that the majority of foreign trade was with neighbouring Germany. But when the domestic political situation in Germany had stabilized and a new expansion of German capital abroad had began, these relations began to be more complicated.

Czechoslovakia's relations with Austria were particularly sensitive. There were numerous relationships from older periods and there was an evident attempt to create proper relations between both new states. Czechoslovakia also took part in solving Austria's oppressive economic situation after the end of the war, but the overall intensity of contact was lessened. Hungary's adversarial position towards Czechoslovakia remained even after the fall of the Hungarian Bolshevik government and the rise of Admiral Miklós Horty's regime. During the year 1921, two attempts by former Emperor Charles I to return to the Hungarian throne raised tensions between both countries. Fears of Hungarian demands to revise the state borders were renewed in Czechoslovakia, Yugoslavia and Romania. These states therefore signed a series of alliance treaties, which formed a defensive pact later known as the Little Entente. The main initiator of the Little Entente, Edvard Beneš, saw in it not only a defensive formation against the territorial demands of Hungary, but even an adequate tool for asserting greater authority of the member states of the pact in European politics. The overall level of relations between young Czechoslovakia and its neighbours was not encouraging. Truly friendly relations were developed only with Romania, which however shared only a short border with eastern Czechoslovakia.

The orientation of foreign politics towards France was definitive. The relationship with Great Britain was more complicated, as it gave precedence to Hungary in the central European region. Developing relations with Russia was of great importance to all of Europe. Thanks to Masaryk, the principle of non-intervention into Russian affairs was asserted in Czechoslovak foreign policy. The Czechoslovak legions gradually withdrew from Siberia. Their retreat was not completed until 1920 with the departure of the last units back to the homeland. The de jure recognition of the Soviet government had not yet been granted, but in 1922, under pressure from industrial circles a commercial agreement was reached which facilitated the export of Czechoslovak products into Russia.

The most serious problems in anchoring the new state in Europe had just been solved, when the first weakening of the Versailles System occurred. During negotiations in Locarno in 1925 between the superpowers and Germany and outside the framework of existing agreements, Germany's western borders were reconfirmed and guaranteed. Similar guarantees for the eastern borders were refused. Poland and Czechoslovakia were therefore supposed to regulate their relations with Germany by means of bilateral agreements. The superpowers thus indicated to Germany that it had a free hand in this region, forming a new threat of potential instability in Central Europe.

In the meantime, relations at home were becoming calmer. In May 1920, the first democratic parliamentary elections were held. For the first time in the Czech Lands and in Slovakia, the public voted with a truly broad and equal franchise, including suffrage for women. The usage of proportional representation allowed a realistic proportion of strength between the individual political parties in parliament, the composition of which was quite diverse. And so representatives of all nationalities living in Czechoslovakia were seated. The best results were attained by the Czechoslovak Social Democrats, receiving almost 1.6 million votes (26% of the valid total votes). It was an extraordinary success, as the second most powerful party, the German Social Democrats, gained 11% and the Republican (Czechoslovak Agrarian) Party (*Republikánská [československá agrární] strana*) received just under 10% of the vote.

The victory of the Czech and German Social Democrats was of course a problem. Both parties were already internally divided by the culminating battle between the social reform and revolutionary wings endorsing the Communist International. A special congress was called to address the growing differences within the Czechoslovak Social Democratic Party. In September 1920, only supporters of the so-called Marxist Left were in attendance and they elected new party leadership. The original executive committee refused to resign, and so for a certain amount of time there were actually two parties fighting over members and supporters.

On the evening before the congress, the Marxist left wing split from the Social Democrats, and quit the government coalition following agreements with other parties and after a meeting with T. G. Masaryk. Vlastimil Tusar's government resigned and the president shortly thereafter named a caretaker government, which was supposed to ride out the crisis that had developed. In December 1920, a controversy between the two Social Democratic factions over the party's property escalated. The interference of state in favour of the original reform leadership provoked the Marxist left to urge workers to call a general strike. The insufficiently prepared action met with a response only in certain places (Kladno, Rosice--Oslavany, Hodonín regions). In Prague during the occupation of the Social Democrats' seat, the People's House, there were several skirmishes between workers and the police. After several days, all of the focal points of the strike had been suppressed.

The defeat of the December general strike ended a period of political instability in the state, and at the same time accelerated the transformation of the Social Democrats' Marxist left wing into an independent party. During its next congress in May 1921, the left wing declared itself the Communist Party of Czechoslovakia (*Komunistická strana Československa*). In the autumn of the same year, other left-leaning groups professing the Communist International united on its foundations. The Czechoslovak and also German Social Democrats during this period lost the larger part of their members and were put on the defensive against the civic parties. The Agrarian Party took over the role of the largest political party in the country.

The division of the Social Democrats had a positive influence towards clarifying the political scene. It was necessary to cement "state-bearing" forces against the opposition, which was reaching dangerous proportions. The caretaker government, named in September 1920, was only seemingly politically independent. During the breakup of the red-green coalition, the so-called *Pětka* (Czech for "five"), an informal political panel composed of the representatives of the five most important Czech and Czechoslovak parties, which were to coordinate the policies of the "state-bearing" forces in parliament and influence the government's politics, was formed. In 1922, following Beneš's provisional government, a new coalition government was named. It was based on the parties of the *Pětka*, and truly represented a nationwide coalition. Antonín Švehla, leader of the Agrarian Party, became its Prime Minister. From that moment on, the Agrarian Party regularly held this post in all coalition governments. They were distinguished by their internal consolidation, solid backing in specific strata of the population and positions in prominent economic institutions. The Agrarian Party intensified its co-operation with the Catholic Czechoslovak People's Party (*Československá strana lidová*) in the renewed coalition. The National Democratic Party (*Strana národnědemokratická*), representing the interests of Czech industrialists and financial circles joined the government with the intention of asserting direct influence on the economic policies of the state. But it was an unstable component of the coalition, always prepared to switch to the opposition. The position of both socialist parties changed significantly. The Czechoslovak Social Democrats were weakened by the loss of parts of its membership base to the communists. The stances of the Czechoslovak Socialist Party (*Českosovenská strana socialistická*) were unstable. Officially this party supported reform socialism, but its core was more and more inclined towards the political centre. The "state-bearing" bloc was supplemented by the Czechoslovak Tradesmen-Business Professional Party (*Československá živnostensko-obchodnická strana středostavovská*), which for the time being remained outside the coalition. The number of its supporters was visibly growing at the expense of the National Democrats and Socialists. Its political positions were near those of the Agrarian Party.

All of the remaining political currents stood in opposition not only to the government, but the majority were essentially in opposition to the Czechoslovak state. The political stances of the Catholic Slovak People's Party (*Slovenská ľudová strana*) was a serious problem. After first welcoming the creation of a common state of Czechs and Slovaks, immediately in 1919, it went into the opposition and its calls for Slovak autonomy grew ever more emphatic. This was met by the resistance of Czech politicians, who feared that any weakening of the centralized state could cause an avalanche of separatist demands, especially from the Czechoslovak Germans. Other Slovak parties, the Slovak Farmers' Party (*Slovenská rolnícka strana*) and the Slovak Social Democrats merged with their Czech counterparts.

The stance of the German political camp was a second serious domestic political problem. The German parties were established following the failure of the separatist attempts at the end of 1918. They originated in part from the Austria-wide parties that found themselves within Czechoslovak territory. They adopted a sharply negative stance towards Czechoslovakia. For strictly pragmatic reasons, and even due to the fact that the democratic regime allowed their political development, some of them gradually subdued their nationalist positions. They were making contact with similar political parties in the Czech environment. At the beginning of the 1920s, this tendency was already being seen in the German Agrarian Party (*Bund der Landwirte*), and the German Christian-Social People's Party (*Deutsche christlich-soziale Volkspartei*). This reversal similarly occurred in the German Social Democratic Workers' Party (*Deutsche sozialdemokratische Arbeiterpartei in der ČSR*), although for different reasons. The development of the so-called activist currents in the German environment showed great promise for the future. Even so the position of German nationalism was still strong and the activist currents felt constant pressure from them. The German National Socialist Workers' Party (*Deutsche nationalsozialistische Arbeiterpartei*) and the German National Party (*Deutsche Nationalpartei*) retained their strictly anti-state stance. The Hungarian political camp experienced similar differentiation as in the German environment.

The Communist Party of Czechoslovakia (CPCz) was a different opposition force. Although its founder Bohumír Šmeral originally expressed the position, that the communists considered the republic as a "natural basis for development of the class war," the majority of the party evaluated the republic in the spirit of the Third International. According to it, Czechoslovakia was the product of the imperialist Versailles System, which was declared a staunch enemy by the Communists. Shortly after its establishment, the CPCz was a sizable party, but it suffered from internal instability, and its negativistic stance was not acceptable for a number of members, who recognized certain values of the independent national state. The CPCz often suffered from internal party crises, which attenuated its numbers. After the victory of the Bolshevik wing (Klement Gottwald, Rudolf Slánský, Jan Šverma, Václav Kopecký and others), the party adapted itself to the dictate of the Communist International and became utterly dependent on Moscow.

Political and public life in the Czechoslovak Republic was not concentrated only in political parties. An endless number of professional, special-interest, cultural, sports and labour organizations pursued activities which gave people specific possibilities to take part in forming and influencing society. The Czechoslovak Legionnaire Community, an association of former members of the Czechoslovak foreign military forces, was unique in both its number and overlap from the special-interest spheres to the political spheres. A similar position was enjoyed by the Czechoslovak Sokol Community, the most prominent physical education organization, founded on a "state-bearing" and national ideology.

At the beginning of the 1920s, it was apparent that the republican system had been successfully stabilized. All of the governing bodies had been properly established. In spite of the strong opposition, the existing regime was not threatened by serious internal political danger. The political scene had just started to calm, when the post-war economic crisis began to affect the development of society. Immediately after the war, it seemed that Czechoslovakia would relatively easily survive the problems of transforming to peace-time production. However, between 1921–1923 as a consequence of the Europe-wide crisis, a sharp reduction in demand and production was felt in the CSR. The crisis brought on a worsening of material living conditions for the workers and other weaker social layers of the population. At the same time, the process of capital concentration had accelerated, productivity of work and effectiveness had increased. Assembly-line manufacturing began to be implemented in Czechoslovakia, and the electrification of the countryside continued. Changes in the structure of industrial production were slower, and in particular the development of certain prospective branches (chemical production, electrical industry) was delayed.

The problems that accompanied the crisis from the beginning of the 1920s highlighted the social role of the labour organizations. However the organizational fragmentation complicated their economic defensive battles. Each of the more significant political parties set up their own labour headquarters, in which a seemingly endless number of professional unions were involved. And so the labour organizations were able to coordinate their activities only with difficulty, and the results of their actions was of partial significance. The strongest headquarters, that of the Social Democratic Czechoslovak Labour Federation (*Odborové sdružení československé*), was weakened by the creation of the International Labour Organization organized by the Communists. The problems of mass unemployment which accompanied the crisis could be solved by neither the unions or the state. At the height of the crisis in 1922, there were up to 400,000 registered unemployed. Unemployment benefits paid by the individual labour organizations were of only partial aid. It was not until 1925 that the so-called Ghent system of unemployment benefits was enacted, allowing unions to receive financial grants from the state towards the payment of unemployment benefits.

The second parliamentary elections held in 1925 confirmed the considerable shifts in the political orientation of voters. The socialist parties emerged from the elections weakened, while the number of votes for the civic parties grew. The Agrarian Party won, but continuing discontent of part of the voters with the social situation was reflected in the relatively large success of the CPCz. It became the second most powerful party in the republic. After the elections the "all-national" coalition was restored for a short while. The Agrarian Party's growing pressure to enact protective customs duties on the import of agricultural goods however forced the socialist parties to leave the coalition in the spring of 1926. The socialists as representatives of consumer interests could not agree with the new customs policy, because it meant, among other things, the preservation of high prices for foodstuffs. T. G. Masaryk again solved the temporary governmental crisis by naming the second caretaker government.

The Agrarian Party in the meantime was looking for a new coalition. They reached agreements with the People's Party, pledging support to enact a congruence law, which would once again provide state contributions for church expenses. It had also enlisted the support of the Tradesmen's Party, but the agreement with the German Agrarians and the German and Hungarian Christian Social Parties was of fundamental importance. In the autumn of 1926, a new coalition government was named. Due to the fact that the socialists were not represented in it, the government was labelled the government of the civic or gentlemen's coalition. In addition to the above mentioned parties, later on the National Democrats and for a short while even the Slovak People's Party were gained into the coalition. The fundamental difference was the fact that for the first time representatives of the German population had a say during the formation of state policy. There were two German ministers in the government, Franz Spina (Bund der Landwirte) and Robert Mayr-Harting (Deutsche christlich-soziale Volkspartei). The socialist parties joined the so-called loyal opposition, which unlike other opposition movements in the CSR held state-supporting positions. The new government energetically continued to consolidate state power. It enacted a law excluding members of the armed forces from the right to vote and a law reorganizing state administration. The district law of 1920 was repealed and, effective from the start of 1928, a Land system was put in place. Czechoslovakia was still further administratively divided into Bohemia, Moravia, Slovakia and Subcarpathian Ruthenia. The rights of self-governing bodies were partially limited.

The gentlemen's coalition government started with an extraordinarily positive situation. Resistance towards its measures was lessened by the coming phase of economic prosperity. Czechoslovakia at the time was ranked between the 10th and 15th place among nations of the world in a number of industrial and living standard indexes. The easing of social tensions also allowed the government to limit the extent and scope of certain social measures. A deep crisis within the CPCz also dulled the edge of political battles. However, the Slovak calls for autonomy could not be accommodated, but for now this fact did not have a deeper influence on relations between Czechs and Slovaks. By international standards, reaching an agreement on relations with the Vatican (*modus vivendi*) was a success for Czechoslovakia. And so in spite of a number of problems, the tenth anniversary of the founding of the republic could be held in a celebratory atmosphere and belief in further positive development.

3 Cultural Life in the Conditions of Democracy

Since the times of the national revival, the cultural sphere had played a special role in the Czech environment. It was a phenomenon that at first was required for its creation, and eventually influenced the development of the modern Czech nation. In a smaller measure this applied to the Slovaks as well. Culture also functioned as a significant national identifier in this area even among the other national communities. It was closely tied to politics and in some situations even substituted for politics. The creation of the independent Czechoslovak state in 1918 changed the conditions for the development of cultural life, however it did not diminish its importance in the lives of the nations and nationalities that were living within the territories of the new state. The high level of education inherited from the times of Austria-Hungary was to a certain extent a necessary condition for the cultural quality of life in the Czech Lands. The Czechoslovak state expended enormous efforts to raise the level of education in Slovakia and in Subcarpathian Ruthenia. The network of universities was also expanded. The Czech and German universities in Prague were supplemented by a new Czech university in Brno and a Slovak university in Bratislava. Two Czech and two German technical universities remained in operation, as did several specialized universities.

The wide extent of democratic rights and freedoms formed a favourable framework for the full development of all national cultures, which however made only limited use of these conditions for meetings and mutual enrichment. The survival of the barriers between Czech and German culture was especially noticeable. Closer relations were formed only between the Prague Czech and Jewish-German environments. Prague could not replace Vienna in this respect, even though a number of German cultural institutions were located there (the German university, technical university, theatre, opera, several publishers, newspaper and magazine editorial offices among others). The German minority in Prague felt isolated and besieged, as the Czech culture in the capital city was unambiguously prevalent. Other towns with a majority German population were scattered in the regions, which lived their own lives. In spite of all of the efforts to develop German culture, its provinciality instead only deepened.

The founding of the republic indisputably represented the greatest contribution for the development of Slovak culture. While in the final decades of the monarchy Slovaks had tenaciously resisted Hungarization, and then after the revolution fought with a lack of creative forces (only a few members of the intelligentsia claimed Slovak nationality) and with major problems in allocating material resources for cultural development. The democratic republic, however, removed the political pressures slowing down the development of Slovak culture, and mainly ensured the development of the Slovak education system and the necessary cultural financing, and the Slovaks made full use of these conditions. The concept of a unified "Czechoslovak" ethnic in no way weakened nor slowed down the process of Slovak cultural development; on the contrary, the tight contacts with the Czech environment provided unexpected possibilities to make use of Czech culture to enrich cultural life in Slovakia. The Czech arts were a source of inspiration, Czech artists were active in Slovakia and in some areas helped to lay the foundation for Slovak production (theatre, music, film). The aid of Czech teachers in the initial stages of development of the Slovak education system played an immense role.

The cultures of the ethnic minorities, Hungarians and Poles, suffered from undue isolation, even in spite of the above-mentioned democratic conditions. Both minorities naturally felt cultural unity with their nations abroad, but due to the fact that relations between Czechoslovakia and Hungary and Poland were not developing especially positively, state policy was not particularly disposed to minority cultural contacts with those states. Neither ethnic group was sufficiently large to be able to develop its own full cultural life in all respects.

The Rusyns living as a overwhelming majority in the Subcarpathian Ruthenia found themselves in a peculiar situation, in a territory that had up to that time been among the least developed, both culturally and economically, regions in Europe. The primary problem faced during the development of the Rusyn national culture was to raise the level of basic education and to foster the intelligentsia. At the time, however, the Rusyns were also just starting to face the problem of finding their national identity. This process was not completed even during the entire twenty years of existence of Subcarpathian Ruthenia in the Czechoslovak state. During this entire time, there were conflicts between political streams declaring the region's population as either a part of the Russian or Ukrainian ethnic, or as part of the unique Rusyn ethnic. The large Jewish minority there was in complete isolation. In spite of all of these barriers, during the first years of the Czechoslovak Republic, the Rusyns underwent a literally decisive phase in their cultural rebirth.

Czech culture assumed a key role in the cultural life of the First Republic, and not only because the Czech people had become a nation in its own state, but primarily because of their intrinsic values. They profited from the existence of a large creative intelligentsia and could rely on the vast background and intensive interest of the Czech public in culture and art. Even prior to the war it had been open to the world and in the new conditions continued in active contacts with the centres of European culture (Paris, Munich, Berlin and London). Culture could not fully begin to fulfil its mission until after the founding of the state. The responsibilities of the national defence disappeared and new tasks to represent the state increased the number of possibilities to make use of artistic works and brought additional material resources into culture. Primarily it was true of architecture and sculpture. In the majority of cases the artists were able to assert challenging aesthetic viewpoints even in state commissions. This resulted in a number of projects of lasting architectural value, which were to represent the state, such as the reconstruction of the Prague Castle, completion of St Vitus' Cathedral, new government offices, banks, schools and cultural and economic institutions, along with many interesting works of fine and applied arts – monuments and statues from Czech history, artistic designs for national emblems, banknotes, postal stamps and so on. Positive conditions for the development of Czech culture were formed by a number of other factors. The highly-developed industry and advanced agriculture required a sizable educated workforce with sufficient general and specialized education, who regarded culture as an essential part of their living necessities. The dense population centres with mature transportation systems and rapid technological progress eased the spread of information and works of art (advances in literary culture, radio, and the beginnings of reproduction technology). Sport was becoming a part of the lifestyle.

At that time, certain phenomena related to the specificities of the nation's historical development in Czech culture had matured, but others had also passed. Culture had finally broken free from the grasp of politics and became an independent component of society. Artists were interested in political and social happenings for their own reasons, and not in order to substitute for the political sphere. In fact, dual personalities could be observed in many of them. Their artistic development proceeded separately from their personal political alignment. It is especially apparent in the works of artists leaning to leftist streams, who became the bearers of avant-garde, often exclusive artistic experiments. Liberation from politics allowed the cultural sphere to more sensitively perceive stimuli from European culture and use them for its enrichment.

One of the defining characteristics of Czech culture from the First Republic was the tight coupling between life and the problems of wide strata of the population. This characteristic of Czech art can be observed more in the selection of subject matter than in the actual works of art themselves. It is also reflected in the conscious raising of moral categories which were attributed to the "people," even though it was an indivisible part of the humanist understanding of man and his place in society – sense of justice, conviction of the equality of people, distrust of authorities, refusal of the use of violence, the desire to free man from moral and social poverty, and so on. In addition to works with high artistic value, pop culture began to develop as well. The 1920s were filled with experiments which accompanied the stormy development in all areas of artistic production. From the beginning of the 1930s on, however, the social situation changed sharply and culture was once again to a large extent drawn into the political sphere.

The situation in Czech literature after the First World War can be called the meeting of the generations. The generation from the 1880s, Alois Jirásek, Antal Stašek, Jan Herben and others, were just culminating their works, and the mature representatives of Czech

Modernism, Josef Svatopluk Machar, František Xaver Šalda and Antonín Sova were accorded great authority. The decadents, such as Jiří Karásek ze Lvovic, the naturalists Karel Matěj Čapek-Chod and Anna Marie Tilschová, and the so-called rebels from the pre-war years, Fráňa Šrámek, Stanislav Kostka Neumann, Karel Toman, Jiří Mahen, Viktor Dyk, Marie Majerová, Ivan Olbracht and others, were continuing to produce works. At the same time the generation of young artists was just coming of age, setting the tone for literary development in the coming period. However it is almost impossible and always a simplification to try to assign them to specific artistic movements and genres. Many of them extended into the most diverse artistic spheres, underwent development, changed artistic methodologies; others presented completely distinctive personalities which were above all attempts at classification.

The turbulent revolutionary atmosphere of that time most deeply affected the sizable generation of young writers and poets. It was expressed in their selection of themes and also in their inclination towards leftist political streams. For a short time these themes crystallized in so-called proletarian poetry, which reached a high level of artistic values in the works of Jiří Wolker and also S. K. Neumann, representing the older generation. In a short period of time, the literary avant-garde arose from this circle, which also provided the foundation for the single originally Czech artistic movement – Poetism. Reactions to the avant-garde streams in world literature were to follow, Dadaism, Surrealism or Socialist Realism; all of which were to appear in Czech literature, although individual writers were affected differently by the rapidly changing styles (Josef Hora, Jaroslav Seifert, Vítězslav Nezval, Konstantin Biebl, František Halas, Vladimír Holan, Vladislav Vančura and others).

It is possible to trace several of the more important circles in the sizable collection of literary themes. The first is a reaction to the wartime experience. A number of poetry collections and works of prose came about on this theme (Jaromír John, Viktor Dyk and others). Jaroslav Hašek's crowning work, the Good Soldier Švejk and His Fortunes in the World War, stands out among them. A specific group was formed by the authors of the so-called legionnaires' literature (Jaroslav Kratochvíl, František Langer, Josef Kopta, Rudolf Medek), depicting the experiences of the members of the Czechoslovak forces in Russia.

The Ruralists, a large group of authors following the breakdown of traditional forms of country life with a certain nostalgia (Josef Knap, František Křelina and others), interpreted a restricted set of subjects. Adherents of socialist realism stood apart from them, aesthetically undetermined but unilaterally leftist ideologically, inspired by Soviet literature (Ivan Olbracht, Marie Majerová and Marie Pujmanová). In addition to the leftist stream, a pronounced democratic humanist stream was developing. Its most prominent representative was Karel Čapek, who in the 1920s was heavily influenced by the role of science and technology in the human life and society. Unlike the predominant concept of the time, he developed a rather pessimistic vision of an over-technologicized society. He searched for an escape from this feeling in the small everyday pleasures of a simple person. Eduard Bass and Karel Poláček largely shared his views. The Christian Catholic depiction of human existence

(Jaroslav Durych, Jan Zahradníček, Jan Čep) also cannot be overlooked in the diverse palette of literary happenings. A number of authors of psychological (Egon Hostovský), relativistic and literature of other intellectual orientations swayed between the main movements. As a whole, Czech literature from the period of the First Republic was on par with the artistic values of a number of large world literary scenes.

A picture of the literary life of the Czech Lands after World War I would not be complete without mentioning literature written in German. After the founding of Czechoslovakia, the isolation of German writing Jewish authors in Prague only increased. Their production basically was coming to its end. Several of them were searching for an escape of this ethnic "ghetto" by emigrating to Austria (Franz Werfel) or to Germany (Egon Erwin Kisch), while others attempted to make closer contact with Czech culture. Franz Kafka stands out above them all, a personality whose life was ended early by illness. He came from a Jewish family and spoke fluent Czech, but wrote in German. He was the embodiment of a possible but never fulfilled symbiosis of Czech, German and Jewish culture in the Czech Lands.

The majority of German literary writers in the Czech Lands underwent a similar ideological and thematic artistic differentiation as the Czech writers. And so poet, author of prose and dramatist, Louis Fürnberg sympathised with the communist movement, as did journalist and publicist E. E. Kisch or Franz Carl Weiskopf, a novelist and translator. Max Brod, a novelist, poet, literary critic, who was a friend of Kafka's, held Zionist opinions. We can find the humanist sentiments in the works of Oskar Baum. Hans Watzlik, awarded the Czech Literary Award in 1931 for his literary work, was an adherent of nationalistic, anti-Czech opinions, as were many German writers in the Czech Lands, who were captivated by Nazi propaganda in the 1930s. Johannes Urzidil, writer and journalist, was a representative of the minority, which was trying for Czech-German understanding up until the tragic end of the First Republic.

Immediately after the First World War, the interest of the Czech public in theatre sharply increased. The National Theatre in Prague maintained its representative position. Another mature artistic corps was active in the City Theatre in Královské Vinohrady. Further professional Czech scenes could be found in Brno, Plzeň, Olomouc and Kladno. In addition to this there were several private theatres in Prague. Also cabarets attracted much attention. Travelling theatre troops held irregular showings in smaller towns, and the abundant activities of the amateur groups began to revive as well.

During the nationalist unrests in 1920, the Estates Theatre was violently taken from German hands. Similarly, Czech professional theatre troops took over the buildings of German theatres in České Budějovice, Olomouc, Moravská Ostrava and Brno. During the 1920s, new theatres were built in many towns, and elsewhere theatre halls were adapted from existing structures. A number of stages of course met with a constant shortage of finances. Nurturing of the upcoming artists was taken over by newly founded dramatic sections in the conservatories in Prague and Brno. The era of impressionism and symbolism in theatre direction and scenography was brought to a close in the National Theatre under the influence of Jaroslav Kvapil. In contrast, Karel Hugo Hilar in Vinohrady developed his expressionist concept, which allowed a reaction to the tastes of theatre audiences enchanted by the revolutionary disturbances in society.

A diverse repertoire was introduced into the scenes of the professional theatres. In addition to world classics and modern works, older Czech dramatic works were staged and modern Czech production began to develop. Little of it however was to demonstrate a longer life span. The dramas of Karel Čapek loomed high above the average, captivating in their emphasis on humanistic ideals (The Robber, R.U.R., The Makropulos Affair). The Insect Play, written in co-operation with Josef Čapek, also received a great reception.

The theatre also received a great opportunity to experiment. Leftist oriented enthusiasts used the series of dramatic sketches for their political agitation. A different stream however proved to be more perspective, variety shows consisting of sketches with current themes, primarily developing on the stages of Prague cabarets. Their contribution was mainly in satiric sketches. In association with this, it is necessary to mention the activities of singer and composer of popular hits Karel Hašler in the Lucerna cabaret in Prague. The most thought-provoking, at least according to number of themes, was the program of the Seven of Hearts (*Červená Sedma*) cabaret, which began in October 1918. A number of well-known personalities performed there, such as Jiří Červený, Eduard Bass, Vlasta Burian or Jaroslav Hašek. The most prominent act in the area of theatrical arts was the founding of the Liberated Theatre (*Osvobozené divadlo*). It was formed from the artistic avant-garde thanks to three original personalities, Jiří Frejka, Jindřich Honzl and Emil František Burian. A fundamental break in the work and scope of the Liberated Theatre occurred in 1927 after the arrival of new, essentially synthetic artistic types, Jiří Voskovec and Jan Werich. The effectiveness of their expression was significantly underscored by co-operation with composer and pianist Jaroslav Ježek.

In the first decade of the republic, the older generation of composers maintained their decisive position in musical composition, which before the war had belonged primarily to Czech music modernism. Leoš Janáček and Josef Bohuslav Foerster both composed their crowning works, and even Josef Suk, Vítězslav Novák or Otakar Ostrčil made contributions to musical culture. Bohuslav Martinů, who mostly lived abroad, achieved world fame. In addition to styles that built upon the traditions of Czech music, after the war the influence of West European musical expressionism could be seen (Alois Hába). This orientation in the Czech environment was propagated by the Society for Modern Music in co-operation with the Club of Moravian Composers.

After the founding of the republic, the conditions for the development of the musical arts were greatly improved. In addition to the opera at the National Theatre in Prague, opera ensembles were established in Moravská Ostrava, Olomouc, České Budějovice, and the corps at the National Theatre in Brno reached a high standard. The activities of the Czech Philharmonic Orchestra in Prague were expanding, and other bodies performing orchestral or chamber music were being formed. Starting in 1923, the radio provided a great opportunity for musicians to reach audiences.

Musical life, of course, was not limited merely to classical or avant-garde music; popular music remained in favour. Hundreds of bands performed dance music of various genres. Great many singers performed popular hits. In some places the traditions of folk music and songs maintained their positions. A great response was also received by jazz, which inspired also original composer Jaroslav Ježek.

Immediately after the war, architecture was influenced by the founder of modern Czech architecture Jan Kotěra. For a short time the construction of government buildings was heavily influenced by the Viennese school of architecture with its decorativeness. Several of Kotěra's students, Josef Gočár, Pavel Janák, and Dušan Jurkovič, attempted to found a Czech variant of the architecture by making use of decorative elements taken from folk art. They soon abandoned this trend, and began to be oriented towards the simplification of forms – towards Constructivism, emphasizing the construction itself as a creative element, and towards Functionalism, which stressed the functionality of the buildings. German architect Adolf Loos, born in Brno, was a leading personality of world renown, who both in theory and in actual buildings attained an almost extreme simplification of form. He was mostly active abroad (Vienna, Paris, Chicago), but several of his buildings are in Bohemia (Prague). New styles of architecture were promoted primarily by young architects, Josef Chochol, Bedřich Feuerstein, Jaroslav Fragner, Josef Havlíček, Karel Honzík and others, who grew up in close contact with European developments. In addition to the Prague centres, a large group of outstanding architects was active in Brno, several of whom took part in the preparations for the exhibition of contemporary culture in 1928 (Bohuslav Fuchs, Josef Polášek, Jiří Kroha). Many other architects worked in a number of other places, leaving behind a quantity of artistically valuable buildings. In addition to the realization of new buildings, the renovation of certain historical structures was under way, of which the most important was the renovation of the Prague Castle by Slovenian architect Josip Plečnik and the completion in puritanical style of St Vitus' Cathedral (Kamil Hilbert). Larger urban projects were also to be seen, such as the construction of parts of Hradec Králové, Zlín, and the housing development in Prague's Baba quarter. Czechoslovak architecture in the 1930s attained European levels.

After the death of Josef Václav Myslbek in 1922, the leading role in Czech sculpture was taken by Jan Štursa, who further developed the tradition of monumental art. Other artists, especially students of Rodin, expressed a departure from impressionism to a more realistic style (Josef Mařatka, Bohumil Kafka). Ladislav Kofránek excelled in portraits, while Otakar Španiel attained world renown in the making of medals. František Bílek, with his pronounced mysticism, and Ladislav Šaloun, marked by symbolism, both steered clear of officialdom. Modern sculpture was influenced by the current social situation, the development of technology and opinions of its purpose. Otto Gutfreund, who developed a new definition of realism and captured the civility of life with a modern expressive shortcut, became a decisive personality of this direction. He found a number of successors in this style (Karel Pokorný, Jan Lauda, Karel Dvořák and others).

Unlike sculpture, which was marked by official commissions, painting developed without these influences. The complete lack of any unifying element led to the existence of a number of groups and diversity of artistic forms. In 1925, Vojtěch Hynais died, and the reigns were taken by Max Švabinský, who was best able to react to the sparse commissions of a grandiose character. Alfons Mucha, who had gained several official state commissions for the design of banknotes, postal stamps, and the state seal, did not abandon the Art-Nouveau style. The other painters of the older generation can be categorized by style only with difficulty. František Kavan and Antonín Hudeček were interested in themes from nature, while Jóža Úprka captured the folklore of Moravian Slovakia. Emil Filla worked his way into the forefront of the movement, which arose from Expressionism and further developed Cubistic forms. Otakar Kubín (Coubine) went from Cubism to modern European classicism. The Stubborn Group (*Tvrdošíjní*), which formed in the spring of 1918, first embraced Cubism, but gradually expanded both thematically and in expression. Václav Špála with his lavish colours was close to folk art. Josef Čapek became a distinctive painter of the urban periphery, while Jan Zrzavý found his own completely new dreamy depiction of the world. A third distinctive movement took a liking to the realistic depiction of the Czech countryside (Václav Rabas, Vlastimil Rada, Vojtěch Sedláček).

Naturally, artists searching for the meaning of modern art by experimentation were to be found in Czech paining as well. They quickly went through a number of fashionable trends which had captivated the West. Jindřich Štýrský, Toyen (Marie Čermínová) and František Muzika all found their own path to Surrealism. But not just these painters, there was an entire plethora of other, not less-talented Czech artists. Among the German painters, high renown was achieved by Oskar Kokoschka, who became acquainted with the Czech environment during his stay in Prague. Egon Schiele, born in Český Krumlov, made a name for himself in Austria.

The impulses affecting all of the areas of fine arts were also reflected in the sphere of applied arts. Book illustrations, metal casting, ceramics, glass making and textile production all attained admirable technical perfection. Modern art was reflected in the production of posters, tapestries, stage design, and in book and magazine graphics. All of this was heavily connected with an approach to the environment and life style.

4 The Economic Crisis Reflected in the Social and Political Spheres

The period of economic prosperity was reaching its peak by the end of the 1920s. Impressive results were achieved in the overall volume of production and other indicators. Industrial production in 1929 exceeded its pre-war levels by over 40%, while for the same period agricultural production grew by 28%. The economic integration of the state was showing progress. Largely due to the development of the domestic market, Czechoslovakia was transforming into a unified economic block, although its regions were not yet completely balanced. Bohemia played the majority role in this development, while Slovakia and Subcarpathian Ruthenia were still falling behind. The domestic market was limited, and industry was dependent on export, where it faced a difficult battle with strengthening competition.

Industrial production from Germany, which was undergoing an exceptional economic boom thanks to foreign capital investments, was an especially unpleasant competition. The fight for market share forced entrepreneurs to optimize production, but the ability to compete in foreign markets was attained at the cost of lower wages and profit margins, which limited the amount of further investments.

Only certain firms, the Baťa shoe factories, Škoda and other producers of armaments, were able to keep pace with world trends in the modernization of production, which helped them to overcome the disadvantages of small-scale production. The structure of industry was almost constant; the production of consumer goods was prevalent, and the automotive and aeronautical industries were also growing. Technological progress consisted primarily of the use of electricity as a decisive driving force, which was reflected in the extensive construction of power plants. Older factories were being modernized and expanded, with only sporadic construction of new plants. Unlike in Germany, investments were financed from internal sources, while some of the capital was flowing abroad. Rationalization of production was not being attained by the introduction of modern machinery and technologies, but also by increasing the intensity of work. The first wave of mechanization in agriculture was coming to a peak. Agricultural farms were being reconstructed, with extensive improvement of the soil, and the blanket electrification of the countryside continued.

During 1929, the first problems with sales afflicted the overall favourable development. It primarily affected the consumer goods industry (textiles, glass, ceramics) and certain branches of agricultural production (grain, sugar beets). The production of heavy industries was kept afloat by the culminating wave of investments. The world economic crisis, which began with the stock market crash in New York on October 24, 1929, appeared after a certain delay. The reduction in production was gradual, and the sharp break did not occur until the middle of 1931. The world credit and currency crisis had already disrupted international trade; all nations were hit with falling demand and the tendency towards economic autarky grew stronger. Czechoslovak foreign trade during 1932 practically collapsed, shrinking to 1/3 of its previous levels. Industrial production in Czechoslovakia fell to just 60% of its pre-crisis level.

Compared to western Europe, only in 1934 did a somewhat delayed and relatively slow increase in production come about. The credit and agricultural crises continued. All in all the economy fell into a depression. The renewal of export was a necessary condition for a more rapid revival of production. The products of Czechoslovak industries were, however, being driven out of a number of advantageous nearby markets by German industry. It became necessary to orient towards more distant and less advantageous markets, such as South America or the Far East. The increase in production was also influenced by the export of weapons and state commissions for the army. Building industry focused on constructing border fortifications, the interest in building and reconstruction of roads increased, and work on waterworks also expanded. The greater extent of investments was also apparent in Slovakia. The renewal came to a peak in 1937, but even then production levels had not reached their highest pre-crisis levels from 1929. The economic cycle did not have time to

416

cross back into prosperity. In 1938, the world markets again met with problems, which were reflected in a slight decrease in production in Czechoslovakia.

In 1929 during the time of the impending economic crisis, domestic politics was met with a new reorganization of forces. The departure of Prime Minster Antonín Švehla from political life represented a serious loss; the reason was his worsening health, and he died in 1933. He was to be replaced as Prime Minister by another Agrarian leader, one of the founders of the party František Udržal, by trade a farmer from the Pardubice region; Udržal was a politician with experience from the Vienna Reichsrat, parliament and the government of the Czechoslovak Republic.

Shortly after the start of Udržal's government, the coalition was weakened. Hlinka's Slovak People's Party left the coalition, upset by the ongoing court proceedings against party ideologue Vojtech Tuka, who was charged with collaboration with Hungarian irredentism. Early parliamentary elections in October 1929 confirmed certain changes in the stances of voters. The Agrarian Party remained even after the elections the strongest political party, however the socialist parties were visibly strengthened. After complex negotiations, a government was created with the participation of eight political parties, a rainbow coalition; of this six parties were Czech, or Czechoslovak (Agrarians, Social Democrats, National Socialists, People's Party, and the Tradesmen's Party), and two were German (Agricultural Union, German Social Democrats). Hlinka's Slovak People's Party went permanently into opposition. Under pressure from the Czech National Democrats, the activist German Christian Social Party, which was prepared to continue in positive politics, was excluded from the coalition, which can be marked as a political error.

The new government had just taken up their new functions when problems connected to the impending economic crisis began to mount. The worsening standard of living for the majority of the population caused tension in society, which threatened to expand from the social to the political level. The decline in production caused a sharp rise in unemployment. According to official data, during the deepest decline in production levels in 1933, the number of unemployed in Czechoslovakia reached almost one million. In reality this number was probably about 300 thousand higher. Consumption levels generally fell, which multiplied the problems of production. The reduced consumption of foodstuffs led to falling prices for agricultural products, the lowering of farmers' income, restriction of investment and stagnation in agricultural production. The state budget was also noticeably affected by a reduction in income. The government was forced to limit expenditures for social benefits and other budget items. Unemployment, poverty and hunger all raised the radical moods among wide strata of the population.

The government of Jan Malypetr, another Agrarian politician who had taken over the reigns of the government from František Udržal in 1932, did not have sufficient resources to effectively solve either the causes or effects of the worsened state of society. Government on the one hand took legislative measures, whose goal was to make the organisation of social protests more difficult, and on the other hand attempted to solve the crisis with governmental interventions in the economy. None of these measures were effective enough to stop the decline in production and bring about a change in economic development. Several of these measures were preferential to the interests of agriculturalists than for the needs of society as a whole. Immediately in 1930, the agricultural customs duty was raised, approval proceedings for the import and export of agricultural goods were implemented, the government intervened in the credit and currency politics (deflation) and a grain monopoly was created. This entire package of measures was crowned by a law on special executive powers, which temporarily empowered the government to take economic measures without the approval of parliament.

The harsh social situation evoked varied forms of protest, ranging from polemics in the press and parliament, hunger marches and workers' demonstrations, up to strikes. These grew into clashes with the police and gendarmerie that even resulted in the loss of human lives. The public again reacted to it with sharp protests. Expressions of solidarity with the workers were quite often seen in the ranks of the leftists intelligentsia. The reaction to the shooting into a march of workers in Dolní Lipová during the Frývald strike (November 25, 1931) is among the best known. At that time, up to 70 Czech scientists, journalists and artists vigorously protested in the press.

The culmination of the social battles in the years of the great economic crisis was the strike in Most in spring 1932. Up to 25,000 miners from the Most mining district went on strike in protest of being laid off from work. Other local inhabitants joined up with them in a show of solidarity, as did miners from other districts. The strike drew a special attention of intellectuals and political circles. The conflict was settled when the unity of the strikers was broken by combined pressure from entrepreneurs and governmental offices. During 1934, the social conflicts began so slowly subside with the change of the crisis into the phase of depression.

Even so social conflicts of greater impact increased tension in the political sphere and contributed to the radicalization of society. The position of the communists was growing stronger, but right-wing extremist and fascist streams were also coming back to life. The CPCz following its fifth congress in 1929 began to orient its members towards the preparation of a proletarian revolution, even though it was clear that it was in fact merely an unrealistic political adventure. Their destructive position was clearly illustrated by the motto "No Masaryk, but Lenin!", which was propagated before the presidential elections in 1934. Some of their functionaries, including party chairman Klement Gottwald, fled from criminal prosecution for a time to Moscow.

Both extremes, left and right, were without a doubt a threat to parliamentary democracy. Even more serious were the multiplying voices in the government coalition speaking of the weakening of liberal democracy and calling for limits to certain political freedoms. The greatest danger to the democratic regime at that time was the growth of nationalism. It was at least partially encouraging that nationalism and its related Czech fascism in Czech society was held in check by a wide spectrum of democratic forces. The Czech fascist movement was fragmented and expressed itself outwardly very loudly, but did not gain greater acceptance. They often held anti-Jewish and anti-German actions. Czech fascists watched the rise of the Nazi movement in Germany with mixed feelings. On the one hand, they admired the violent methods used by the German Nazis, but on the other hand, being Czech nationalists, they followed with fear every expression of growth of German forces and aggressiveness.

Among the Czech fascists, the largest organization was the National Fascist Community (*Národní obec fašistická*). Its leader was former Legionnaire and demoted General of the Czechoslovak Army Radola Gajda. In January 1933, their supporters organized an attack on the barracks in Brno-Židenice, which was intended to be the start of a fascist putsch. It was however an isolated act which was easily suppressed. The growing anti-democratic moods in the ranks of National Democracy were more serious. Some of their leaders advocated the introduction of a "strong-hand government." In 1934, in protest against the devaluation of the crown, the National Democrats left the government and attempted to consolidate forces among the radical political right. They joined up with Jiří Stříbrný's National League (*Národní liga*) and with other fascist groups, forming a party with the provocative name National Unification (*Národní sjednocení*). But within the atmosphere of sharp polarization of opinions, the Czech fascists did not succeed in attaining mass influence even after this attempt.

In comparison with the Czech Lands, the impact of the economic crisis in Slovakia was even more harshly felt. Dissatisfaction there increased over the position of Slovakia in the Czechoslovak state and calls for autonomy grew in emphasis. In 1933, Hlinka's Slovak People's Party used the occasion of the 1100th anniversary of the founding of the first Christian church by Prince Pribina in Nitra to hold a demonstration, which was of an extremely nationalist and anti-Czech orientation.

From the perspective of the further development of society, the impact of the crisis on the political orientation of Germans in Czechoslovakia was most dangerous. Light industry located mostly in the Bohemian and Moravia-Silesian border areas, inhabited primarily by a population of German nationality, was harder hit by the crisis. It was evidenced there in higher unemployment and its negative effects. This cleared the way for the sharp growth in nationalism and a new worsening of relations of the German population with the Czechoslovak state. Social problems were not the only cause of this development. At the same time, the rise of the Nazis to power in neighbouring Germany also affected the situation. In Czechoslovakia, efforts were undertaken by a number of German educational, cultural, sports, political and in general "patriotic" organizations to mould the nationalist sentiments of citizens of German nationality. Many of them had ties with Nazi, or all-German institutions with headquarters in Germany. This was demonstrated in the process with the Volkssport organization in 1932. The provocative expressions by supporters of the German National Party (*Deutsche Nationalpartei*) and the German National-Socialist Workers' Party (*Deutsche nationalsozialistische Arbeitspartei*) forced the government to pass a law banning and breaking of political parties. Both parties, however, dissolved before the law could be applied by state offices. Before then however, on October 2, 1933, Konrad Henlein, chairman of the German Sports Federation (Deutscher Turnverein), announced the formation of the Sudeten German Patriotic Front (Sudetendeutsche Heimatfront). Members of both banned German parties began to join it in droves. Prior to the parlamentary elections in April 1935, Henlein's Patriotic Front transformed into the Sudeten German Party (Sudetendeutsche

Partei, or SdP), which strove to expand its influence over all of the German population of the Czech Lands. In Slovakia, Germans joined up with the Carpathian German Party (Karpatendeutsche Partei). Democratic political streams found themselves on the defensive against the rise of aggressive nationalism.

5 The Threat to Democracy

For several years it seemed that the first weakness of the Versailles Peace System, the Locarno Treaties of 1925, would not have more serious consequences. Czechoslovakia, which was especially dependent on the stability of relations in Europe, however followed with trepidation the changes in the orientation of the superpowers' foreign policy and also in the balance of forces between democracy and totalitarianism in a number of European states. The creator of Czechoslovak foreign policy Edvard Beneš saw a solution in building closer ties between Czechoslovakia and France, and also in strengthening the ability to act and the cohesion of the Little Entente states. As a result of his endeavours, at the beginning of 1933, the Little Entente Organizational Pact was reached, resulting in the creation of a Permanent Council, Secretariat, and an Economic Council. He was active in the disarmament conferences of the League of Nations, but felt the limited effectiveness of these actions. So he settled on the thought of collective security in Europe and on the plan for an eastern pact from 1934, the brainchild of French Foreign Minister Louis Barthou. The plan was never put into effect, running into fundamental opposition from Germany and Poland, whereas Germany and Poland reached a non-aggression pact. It was the first significant step leading towards the international isolation of Czechoslovakia. The remainder of the eastern pact in the end was represented by a triangle of bilateral agreements – the Czechoslovak-French agreement and the newly signed French-Soviet and Czechoslovak-Soviet agreements from May 1935. The admission of the Soviet Union to the League of Nations (1934) opened the path to these agreements, and also to the subsequent diplomatic recognition by the Czechoslovak government. The Little Entente allies however reacted to these steps with a further lessening of interest in co-operation with Czechoslovakia.

Nazi Germany in the meantime continued to systematically strengthen its positions. It reached an agreement with Great Britain outside the framework of the peace treaty allowing it to rebuild its war-time naval forces (1935). The incursion of the German Army into the demilitarized zone in the Rhine province (1936) was a violation of the Versailles Treaty. Germany also ended the Rhine security pact (Locarno Treaty), and allied with Mussolini's Italy, with which it actively participated in the civil war in Spain on the side of Franco's fascists. All of the steps aimed at strengthening its position as a superpower were taken either with countenance or outright approval of the western superpowers. Great Britain and France adopted the politics of appeasing Germany, and clearly lost interest in the fate of Central Europe, where they left Germany a free hand in its efforts to expand its "living room." The Versailles System of European organization, on which Czechoslovakia was dependent, was falling apart.

The progressive isolation of Czechoslovakia in the international scale and the ever more confident expressions of anti-democratic forces within the state led to a mobilization of forces to the defence of democracy and the republic. The actual balance of forces was revealed by the parliamentary elections in 1935. They showed that fascism in the Czech environment remained on the periphery of political life. National Unification, in which the extreme right-wing streams were concentrated, gained only 6% of the vote, and not all of the supporters of the former National Democratic Party were disposed towards totalitarianism. This confirmed the stable influence of the democratic parties. However, several of these parties were unable to reach a unified opinion on either the further orientation of Czechoslovak foreign policy or the solution of domestic political questions. Sympathy towards the growing totalitarian regimes in Europe and efforts to reach an agreement with Nazi Germany appeared even in the Agrarian Party, whose leader had been, since the death of Antonín Švehla in 1933, longtime General Secretary Rudolf Beran. Milan Hodža, leading personality of the Slovak Agrarians and Czechoslovak Prime Minister since 1935, was of a different orientation. His policies were marked by efforts to overcome the isolation of Czechoslovakia in the international sphere by establishing closer co-operation of the Danube states. Hodža's plan did not however have a large chance to succeed. It ran into the categorical opposition of Germany and Italy, but the main obstacle was in the different interests of the already existing authoritarian regimes in the states of that region (Poland, Hungary, Austria, Bulgaria and Yugoslavia).

The position of Hlinka's party in Slovakia was strengthened, but the greatest surprise, which evoked panic in democratic circles, were the movements in the German political camp. The immense dominance of influence of the Sudeten German Party was confirmed, receiving over 1.2 million votes, or approximately 2/3 of the German voters. On a nationwide scale it became the strongest party and the Agrarian Party, only thanks to the supplementary awarding of mandates in the second and third election counts, attained a one mandate lead, which gave it the Prime Minister's seat in accordance with the customs of the time. German political parties which took a positive stance towards the state suffered catastrophic losses. They attempted to dampen further losses of their influence by means of "neo-activism," or an increased emphasis on asserting the requirements of the German population (Wenzel Jaksch, Gustav Hacker, Hans Schütz). In February 1937, they reached agreements with the government on a national settlement, the goal of which was to improve the economic and social situation in the border areas and to ensure the staffing of government offices according to ethnic ratios. As was later to be seen, the efforts of the neo-activists to maintain their positions were futile. The Sudeten German Party more and more emphatically took the position of fighting for the "rights" of the Czechoslovak Germans. It was changing into an effective instrument of Nazi expansionist politics leading to the disruption and subjugation of Czechoslovakia.

At the end of 1935, there was yet another measuring of forces between the democratic and anti-democratic fronts. Due to health reasons T. G. Masaryk resigned from the presidency. He recommended Edvard Beneš, who was foreign minister at that time, as his successor, because in him he saw a guarantee of continuation of the democratic line of development in society and the state. Beneš's opponents, largely from the ranks of the Agrarians and National Democrats attempted to assert their own candidate, a totally non-political personality, Charles University Professor Bohumil Němec. He however, upon learning that he was a pawn in a political fight, gave up his candidacy and Edvard Beneš was elected the second president of the Czechoslovak Republic on December 18, 1935. In the following period he became the deciding personality, around which the fragmented democratic forces would be organized. The boundaries between those who were sounding the alarm and those who were resigned to searching for a new starting point in an agreement with the aggressive anti-democratic forces crossed across parties and clubs. The Czech public for the most part stood for the defence of democracy and the democratic republic. The democratic camp in Slovakian society was weakened by the unresolved standing of Slovakia in the state and the supporters of democracy in the German environment (Social Democrats, leftist intellectuals, etc) were subjected to the immense pressure by the Sudeten German nationalism.

The Communist Party of Czechoslovakia in this phase held a specific position. While in 1934 the communists were still sharply criticizing the relations in the republic and searching for ways to overturn the existing political system, during 1935 they took up the role of defenders of the state from the growing fascist threat. The change in their stance came from the general trends in the development of the modern communist movement. In the summer of 1935, the 7th Congress of the Communist International took place in Moscow, which among other topics addressed the question of the growing influence of fascism. The congress designated it as an actual threat for the working class and the communist movement. Czechoslovak communists began to make use of the tactic of "people's fronts." The term covered all forms of co-operation with democratic (civic) streams against fascism. This party line met with a positive response among Czechoslovak communists. Many members of the CPCz welcomed this party line, because it at least partially allowed them to overcome the disparity between their internal relationship to the homeland and the previous official line of the Communist International. Later it of course came to be seen that the tactics of the 7th Congress of the Communist International was not without ulterior motives. The fight against fascism was primarily meant to be a means for the communist movements to gain decisive influence in society and to prepare the way for the "proletarian" revolution. Some CPCz leaders did not understand this and were instructed in how to apply the new tactics after the return of Klement Gottwald from Moscow in 1936. In this concrete situation, however, their stance supported the position of democratic forces.

Social conflicts related to the economic crisis and the threat to democracy could not remain unresponded to in the circles of the Czech intelligentsia. The severe interventions of state power against socially motivated protests became the target of harsh criticism by the intellectuals regardless of their ideological orientation or political affiliation. Any and all indications of limiting democratic freedoms evoked substantial attention. A crisis of democracy was talked about in general terms. The deepening of this crisis was confirmed by developments in a number of European states, in which totalitarian regimes or even fascist dictatorships were coming to power. In particular, the Czech intelligentsia considered the rise of the Nazis to power in Germany as the most dangerous.

The leadership of the Czech intelligentsia reacted to the mobilization of anti-democratic forces in two ways. First, many intellectuals intensively entered into politics, and second, they reacted to the new situation in the artistic creations. The number of protests against the Nazi's treatment of democratic forces in Germany increased, but specific activities aimed at helping the German anti-fascists, who were seeking asylum from the Nazis in Czechoslovakia, were far more effective. After the fascist coup in Austria in 1934, similar aid was offered to Austrian refugees.

By the end of the 1930s, up to 10,000 German emigrants had passed through Czecho-slovakia, the vast majority of which were members of the democratic or leftist intelligentsia. Thanks to the stance of the Czech intellectuals, for a time Czechoslovakia became not only an exile country, but a base for the survival of German democratic and humanist culture. Largely due to many Czech organizations, clubs, anti-fascist committees and even certain communities, refugees from Germany and Austria received material aid, and sometimes found working opportunities here. With the support of publishing houses, editorial staffs and artistic organisations, newspapers were published by the German emigrés, German plays were performed in theatres, and exhibitions of German art were organized. Several German cultural organizations and political parties began to be active in Czechoslovakia (German Social Democratic and Communist parties). Under pressure from the Czech cultural public, in 1934 citizenship was granted to German writer Heirich Mann and later in 1936 to his brother Thomas Mann, laureate of the Nobel Prize for Literature.

The civil war in Spain was also a mobilizing factor for the Czech intelligentsia. A wide movement for the defence of democratic Spain was established, which concentrated on propagation of the fight against fascism and enlisting volunteers for the international bri-gade fighting on the side of the Spanish Republican Government. Intellectuals took part in organizing international movements against the dangers of war. They saw the only hope to maintain the security and independence of the Czechoslovak Republic in keeping the peace. The leftist-oriented and Communist members of the cultural front anchored their hopes in an alliance with the Soviet Union, from which their interest in Soviet culture and its propagation in Czechoslovakia arose.

In the area of artistic production this time the most rapid reaction to the growing threat came from the theatre. The productions of Jiří Voskovec and Jan Werich in the Liberated Theatre played an utterly exceptional role. It is sufficient to recall a series of their produc-tions (The Donkey and the Shadow, The Executioner and the Madman, A Rag Ballad, Heavy Barbara) from 1933–1938, in which they revealed, in biting satire, the basis for fas-cism and urged the Czech public to actively oppose it. The dramas of Karel Čapek (The White Disease, Mother), although of a different genre, spoke to the public with a similar message, as did his allegorical novel War with the Newts. Poetry reacted similarly, along with painting, film and other elements of Czech artistic production. The movement of the

Czech intelligentsia for the defence of democracy and the republic also met with a certain response among the Slovak intelligentsia. For German democrats and leftist intellectuals the anti-fascist activities were associated with great personal risk. Only several of the bravest joined this movement (writer Luis Fürnberg, journalist Egon Erwin Kisch, Franz Carl Weiskopf, journalist and writer Ludwig Winder, journalist Walter Tschuppik, editor-in-chief of the Prager Presse Arne Laurin, painter and graphic artist Oskar Kokoschka, poet, journalist and publicist Rudolf Fuchs and several others).

During 1937, Czechoslovakia found itself ever more internationally isolated. It was basically the last refuge of democracy in Central Europe, surrounded on all sides by totalitarian and fascist regimes. This was visibly reflected in the domestic political situation. The atmosphere of uncertainty and fears for the future was further accentuated by the death of former president T. G. Masaryk (September 14, 1937). He had not interfered in political happenings since his resignation in 1935, he was, however, considered to be the moral support for democracy and a symbolic guarantee of the further existence of the republic. Problems in the political sphere were already culminating at the beginning of the year. Ethnic compromise, attained during government negotiations with the German activist parties in February1937, brought few results.

The Sudeten German Party (SdP) had assumed the role of fighter for the rights of the German population, and tendencies to accept its roles as the spokesman for the German population in later talks in the governmental coalition were strengthening. This was caused in part by the conviction, that in a democratic system it is not possible to overlook the strongest German party, and was also an expression of the internal instability of the governmental coalition, in which the wing prepared to make concessions to the nationalist parties of the German camp was asserting itself. A fundamental error in these considerations was in the hope that it was possible to reach an agreement with the Henlein's supporters without violating the integrity of and losing the sovereignty of the state. The SdP was already unambiguously acting under directions from Berlin. Its mission was to contribute to the breakdown of the republic from within and to create a pretext for an external intervention. It is not surprising therefore that the negotiations between Prime Minister Milan Hodža and Konrád Henlein in the autumn of 1937 foundered as did other attempts at reaching an understanding.

The interest of parts of the Czech political scene in co-operation with the SdP was confirmed by the initiative of the Chairman of the Agrarian Party Rudolf Beran at the beginning of 1938, when Beran even suggested winning the SdP to enter into the government coalition. This stance was met with a massive wave of outrage in the Czech public. The requirement to form a government that would be a true guarantee of democracy and defence of the republic grew in strength. While other coalition parties (Social Democracy, National Socialist and People's) refused to make concessions to Henlein's movement, they were not able to make use of the mass support from below to strengthen their positions. The Agrarian Party on the other hand made use of the depression, which had engulfed Czech society after the Austrian Anschluss in March 1938, and enacted several changes which heightened its leading position. Domestic politics was met with shifts weakening the democratic camp. The government coalition was strengthened by the entrance of a representative of the National Unification Party (*Strana národního sjednocení*) (František Ježek) into the government. In the meantime, the German activist parties, supporting the democratic orientation of the government, had collapsed. In March 1938, the Sudeten German Party absorbed the German Federation of Farmers (*Svaz zemědělců*), the German Christian Social Party and the Tradesmen's Party. The German Social Democrats also left the government coalition. Its new leader, Wenzel Jaksch, who had replaced the decidedly democratic oriented Ludwig Czech, even consulted this step with Konrád Henlein. The SdP had finally become the dominant political force among the German population of the Czech Lands. Democratic forces found themselves on the defensive, and their only ally was the Communists, who continually urged the creation of a people's anti-fascist front. The Communists were of course just looking after their own interests, since they were well aware that a parliamentary democracy gave them considerably more room to assert their political aims than an authoritarian or fascist regime.

The congress of the SdP in Karlovy Vary, held on April 23–24, 1938, brought about new commotion in the turbulent domestic political atmosphere. It formulated demands, the implementation of which as Henlein himself admitted would mean the creation of a new legal system. In any case the border regions would be placed under the power of the SdP. The danger of this demand evoked, at least for a short time, a new wave of resolve to face the dangers of fascism.

After the annexation of Austria to Germany, a ban on public assemblies was put in place. The government justified this measure as an attempt to maintain national unity and from fears of unnecessarily provoking the Sudeten German movement. The government offices in the Czech regions enforced the adherence to this ban, while Henlein's movement at the same time held dozens of demonstrations and manifestations without any interference. The ban on assembly was revoked just at the end of April 1938 so that the traditional May 1 manifestations could take place. The May celebrations, which were usually organized by the individual parties separately, had this time been changed into a common display of the resolve of all of the anti-fascist forces to defend democracy and the republic. It was also a mobilization of the public to the upcoming municipal elections.

The municipal elections, in comparison to previous elections into self-governing organs, held extraordinary meaning. This time they were not deciding simply who would lead the municipal governments, but it represented an overall measuring of forces between the advocates of democracy and fascism. Henlein's supporters expected that the elections would allow them to at least take control of the border areas. In regions where they held a majority, they used various forms of pressure, from mass agitations and intimidation through various forms of terrorizing the democratic thinking voters. Just before the elections, terrorist commando units organized by the SdP broke up meetings of anti-fascist organizations, attacked Nazi dissenters, attempted assassinations at the homes of republic-minded people regardless of whether they were Czech or German; they also enforced a boycott of merchants who were known to be anti-fascist. Fascist businessmen fired anti-fascists from work and the unemployed of the same orientation were deprived of benefits, and other forms of economic and psychological pressure were being used. Henlein's press openly designated the nearing elections as the Sudeten German "Anschluss." All actions of this type were inspired and supported by the German Reich. At the same time, Germany attempted to influence the results of the expected measuring of forces by the demonstrative redeployment of military forces to the Czechoslovak border.

While the government showed ever more indecisiveness, the dominant elements of the democratic camp concentrated on counteractions. The manifesto by the representatives of Czechoslovak culture known under the name "We shall Remain Faithful" held considerable weight even in the international scale. The acute situation in the border areas and news of the concentration of German forces near the Czechoslovak border finally forced the government to take action. On May 21, 1938, it called up two years worth of military reservists. Units of the Czechoslovak army occupied the border fortifications and within several hours had the situation in the border areas under control. The Nazi armed commandos were completely powerless, and their members fled in confusion to the Reich. This action by the Czechoslovak government left an overwhelming impression around the world, in Germany itself and even in other countries. Hitler had for the first time run into true resistance while putting his plans into effect. The government circles in Great Britain and France, completely smitten by the thought of appeasement, took the mobilization of the Czechoslovak army extremely negatively at first. The world democratic public, however, greeted this measure. Mass expressions of support for Czechoslovakia finally forced the French government to confirm that in the event of aggression it would fulfil its obligations arising from the Czechoslovak-French alliance treaty. The British government finally expressed support, although grudgingly.

The mobilization evoked feelings of relief and hope among the Czech public. It was seen as the beginning of a decisive policy of the government against the expanding fascism. Confidence in the government grew, which was reflected in the number of votes cast for government parties. The last large demonstration of the stance of the Czech public was the 10th "All-Sokol Gathering" (mass gymnastics rallies by the Sokol gymnastics organization), held at the beginning of July 1938 in Prague. It took place in a mood of great enthusiasm. The Czech public regarded the event as an expression of national strength and resolve to defend the republic even at the cost of extreme sacrifice.

The successful mobilization and the results of the elections in the Czech regions visibly calmed the tense atmosphere. Unfavourable developments however continued in the political lobbies. For the SdP the May elections were a triumph. The movement openly taking the side of Hitlerism gained more than 90% of the German voters. It took control of the majority of municipalities in the border areas and began to implement its politics there. It stepped up pressure on the government, which was making ever more concessions. In the meantime the diplomatic pressure from the western powers, which ended in a hypocritical offer to play the impartial go-between, who would after examination of the situation propose a solution to the problem of the German minority. The Czechoslovak government agreed, and so on August 3 Lord Walter Runciman, a zealous supporter of appeasement, came to Prague. There was no doubting his mission. He behaved very reservedly towards the government, while making active contacts among representatives of the pro-Nazi oriented groups of German businessmen and nobility. Regardless of the result of Runciman's mission, the western superpowers took further steps to avoid responsibility for the situation in central Europe. The major obstacle in applying this policy was the system of alliance treaties, which were supposed to ensure aid for Czechoslovakia in the event of foreign aggression. The Sudeten German problem became secondary under these circumstances. It served only as a pretext to increase pressure.

Even so the Czechoslovak side, in order to not cause a conflict, attempted to put forward yet another proposal for a national statute. President Beneš himself took part in the preparation of the "Third Plan." But even he did not meet with success. The radical wing, represented by Karl Hermann Frank, was coming to the forefront of the SdP. He acted in accordance with Hitler's directives, according to which it was necessary to refuse all proposals of the Czechoslovak government and constantly increase demands. After the refusal of the Third Plan, Prime Minister Hodža presented representatives of the SdP with the "Fourth Plan," which in essence fully accepted the demands of the Karlovy Vary Congress (Karlsbad Congress). The SdP found itself under pressure, but found a way out of the situation. Its supporters provoked an incident on September 9, 1938 in Ostrava, which the leadership of the party used to discontinue negotiations.

Not long after that, on September 12, 1938 at the congress of the Nazi party in Nuremberg, Adolf Hitler once again bluntly accused Czechoslovakia of suppressing national rights and promised to ensure the liberation of the Sudeten Germans and annexation of the Czechoslovak border regions to the Greater German Reich. For the Sudeten Germans it was a signal to attempt a putsch. A new wave of terror began in the Czech border regions, which the SdP wanted to use to take power into its own hands. The situation was far worse than that in May. Acts of violence occurred in over seventy places. The Sudeten Germans' fanatic storm troopers (militia, Freikorps) attacked and demolished Czech minority schools, political offices, police stations and other public buildings. The Czech population was subjected to brutal violence, and on the Czech side there were a number of injured and even losses of human life. Finally in this situation the Czechoslovak government resolved to take a radical step. On September 13, 1938, it declared martial law in the border regions and on September 16, dissolved the SdP. The party leaders fled to the Reich. The army and units of the national guard were sent to the centres of unrest. The effectiveness of this measure was immediate. The terrorist acts ceased, members of the terrorist bands took refuge on the other side of the border. The reaction of Czechoslovak organs formed such a strong impression, that even the representatives of Hlinka's Slovak People's Party, who had been negotiating with SdP over co-operation, found it necessary to distance themselves from it and issue a declaration of loyalty to the republic.

It was as if the declaration of martial law had exhausted the resolve of the government. It immediately expressed a willingness to return to negotiations. They did not even attempt to make a case for Czechoslovakia in the international arena, while it was exactly there that decisive events had begun to take place. Soviet delegate to the League of Nations Maxim Litvinov expressed support for Czechoslovakia. He demanded the use of collective action to dissuade the prospective aggressor, and made assurances that the Soviet Union would fulfil its obligations from the alliance treaties with Czechoslovakia. French diplomacy however searched for a way out of its obligations. One of the possibilities was to remove the entire problem from the League of Nations into the level of direct negotiations with Hitler. In this situation, British Prime Minister Neville Chamberlain took the initiative.

The British Prime Minister visited Adolf Hitler on September 15, 1938 in his seat at Berchtesgaden. It was there that he first publicly expressed agreement with the secession of the border areas of the Czech Lands. And so on September 19, the German demands were transmitted to the Czechoslovak government in the form of a joint English-French diplomatic note. The note stated that the border areas populated by Sudeten Germans could no longer remain a part of Czechoslovakia, as it threatened the interests of the CSR and of European peace. If Czechoslovakia were to refuse to solve this problem, then it could not expect the aid ensured it by its alliance treaties with France.

In this situation President Beneš made one final, likely only formal, attempt to extricate the republic from international isolation. He turned to the Soviet government with a question, whether the Soviet Union would provide immediate assistance, if the French were to honour their alliance obligations. Even though he knew the stance of the French government, he did not miss the opportunity to remind them of the clause in the Czecho-slovak-Soviet treaty, which obliged the Soviet Union to aid Czechoslovakia only in the event that France were to do so as well. This likely reflected Beneš's fear of committing to unilateral co-operation with the Soviet Union. The answer of the Soviet government to Beneš's question was positive, although it was apparent even to the Soviets that the request was merely formal in nature. At the same time, however the Soviet delegate to the League of Nations once again proposed collective support for Czechoslovakia.

In Prague following complex negotiations in the so-called political committee and in the government, at Beneš's request a negative response to their diplomatic note was transmitted to the English and French governments. Shortly after this on September 19, ambassadors of both superpowers undertook a demarche with the president, during which they presented an ultimatum to unequivocally accept the previous propositions, or else Great Britain and France would leave Czechoslovakia to its fate. After consideration of all of the circumstances, on September 21, the government gave in to the coercion.

The acceptance of the English-French ultimatum evoked an explosion of resistance in the Czech public, too aggravated from the long-term tension. Immediately in the afternoon hours of September 22, 1938, first demonstrations broke out in Prague. Regardless of their political affiliation, the Czech population refused to accept the given situation. Supporters of democratic parties and Communists alike spoke out together. Even some of the adherents of right-wing nationalism (National Democrat Ladislav Rašín) supported the defence of the republic.

428

Pressured by demonstrations and other forms of protest, Hodža's government resigned on September 22. Edvard Beneš became the decisive personality for the political control of the state. The Czech public placed the most hope in him as well. At that time, he of course took on more responsibility than that to which he was entitled by the constitution. First, after consulting with the major parties, he named a new semi-caretaker government, with representation of all of the parties of the previous government coalition. General Jan Syrový, a man with the aura of a national hero from the First World War, where he had fought in Russia in the ranks of the Czechoslovak legions, was named the head of the government. The hopes placed in the new Prime Minister were however unwarranted. He was an apolitical personality, who in the extreme situation could not fulfil expectations.

In the west, after a certain delay a spontaneous movement for the defence of Czechoslovakia started, and Hitler constantly threatened war. On September 22 and 23, Neville Chamberlain met with him again in Godesberg in the hopes of limiting a further escalation of demands. He was not successful and Hitler expanded the German demands, and what is more conveyed territorial demands of Poland and Hungary. As soon as news of the results of these negotiations reached Prague, the Czechoslovak government declared mobilization.

The mobilization took place in unbelievably rapid and disciplined fashion. After its declaration, Czech society was overcome by a noticeable relief and the mass resolve to defend the country even at the price of heavy casualties was strengthened. Military units deployed into the border fortifications and took up positions for the event of attack. The government circles were still permanently in a state of confusion and hesitation. Western diplomacy continued in the appeasement of German, while Hitler continually escalated the war psychosis. Then at the suggestion of Neville Chamberain and Édouard Daladier, Italian dictator Benito Mussolini entered the negotiations. He urged Adolf Hitler to a meeting of the representatives of German, Italy, Great Britain and France. The four-powers conference took place on September 29 1938, in Munich. Its participants signed an "agreement" on the ceding of the border territories of the Czech Lands to Germany. The Czechoslovak representatives were not even invited to the negotiations, they were accorded only the final version of the document. Both in its content and the method of its acceptance the Munich Agreement represented an unprecedented breach of international law and the sovereignty of an independent state, and the trampling of all rules of civilized behaviour between states. A wave of indignation again broke out in Czechoslovakia along with the resolve to face the new pressure. The pressure of making decisions at this time fell on the shoulders of President Beneš. The problem before him was all the more unsolvable, as he knew all aspects of the situation, and the strengths and weaknesses of the Czechoslovak position.

The primary decisive factor at the time was the quality of the Czechoslovak army. In general the high quality of its infantry weapons was recognized, as well as the quality armaments of the artillery; there were also the border fortifications that could be used in case of attack. In comparison with the German army, the motorization of the army had fallen behind as had the military aspects of aeronautical technology. The construction of the fortifications was not anywhere near complete on the German border, and had barely begun on the Austrian border. After the Austrian Anschluss, the border with Germany was extended from 1539 km to 2117 km. The confidence in the fortifications came from the ideas, that based on the fighting in the First World War, future wars would be fought in the trenches, despite the fact that modern technology and the fighting in the most recent local wars indicated a more dynamic method of fighting. Also, the territory of the ČSR was extended and from a strategic standpoint disadvantageous. Attack aircraft could easily fly over, and the country could easily be split in two by a concentrated ground offensive in the country's narrowest location (Kłodzko region – South Moravia).

The soldiers' training was at a good level, while the question of their resolve to fight was more complex. There was no doubt about the soldiers of Czech and Slovak nationality. However on the basis of a general defence law, almost 1/4 of the serving soldiers in the Czechoslovak army were of German nationality. The most ardent Nazis avoided the mobilization, but it was not clear how those that did join the army would react. It is also possible to speculate on the quality and preparedness of the German army. It is clear that they did not hold sufficiently trained reserves, and there are indications that their command had doubts whether the proper time to start the war had arrived. In any case it was necessary to take into account an almost two-to-one advantage in the number of soldiers on the German side, even without the advantage of Germany's economic potential. In addition to this, there was always the threat that Poland and Hungary would weigh in on the side of Germany. After consideration of the facts the General Staff estimated that the Czechoslovak army would be able to defend itself for approximately three weeks.

As far as the political side of the defence of the state goes, one must take into consideration that there was a lack of unity in the political leadership of the state. Not even the defenders of democracy acted with due emphasis. And primarily the international political standing of Czechoslovakia was unfavourable. With the exception of the Soviet Union, no state officially came to its defence. But even the possibility of the Soviet aid in the event of war would meet with a number of problems. The Soviet army was in general not sufficiently prepared for war, and although the danger was acute, it was not even in a state of sufficient military readiness. It was not clear, where and how the Soviet army would intervene. A crossing into Czechoslovakia had not been secured and a common border between Germany and the Soviet Union did not at that time exist. Also the question remained as to what reaction the entry of the Soviet (Bolshevik) army into Central Europe would have evoked in the world. The hope that the politics of the western powers would be reversed in the event of aggression by Nazi Germany against Czechoslovakia was no more than illusory. And finally the morality of either defence or surrender remained, as it was clear that in the event of a military conflict between Czechoslovakia and Germany with other neighbouring countries the bare existence of the nation was at stake. After consideration of all of these factors, the Czechoslovak government capitulated in the given situation. The political, economic and even moral impact was catastrophic. The trauma of Munich remained in the Czech consciousness for decades.

The blame for the capitulation fell unequivocally on President Beneš, who explained his stance arguing that it was just a temporary concession. According to him, in the given situation Czechoslovakia did not have a chance to successfully fight the war, but he was convinced that in a short time a great European conflict would arise, in which the question of Czechoslovakia would be addressed. After consultations with the government, and definitely with a heavy heart, he conceded and accepted the Munich Dictate on September 30, 1938. The army was ordered to evacuate the border areas and German units began to immediately on October 1 occupy Czechoslovak territory according to the dictated zones. The Polish army without delay occupied the Czechoslovak part of the Těšín region. The budding resistance to the capitulation was stifled. While cheering crowds of Sudeten Germans greeted the Nazi units and even Adolf Hitler himself, who had visited several towns in the ceded border regions, in Czech society the initial outrage was replaced by resignation and feelings of hopelessness. On October 5, 1938, President Beneš resigned from his function. The first Czechoslovak Republic had come to an end after not even twenty years of existence.

Bibliography

Azyl v Československu 1933–1938, Praha 1983.

BARTOŠ, Josef – TRAPL, Miloš: *Dějiny Moravy, díl IV. Svobodný stát a okupace*, Brno 2004.

BOREK, David: *Židovské strany v politickém systému Československa 1918–1938*, in: Moderní dějiny 11, 2003, pp. 65–201.

BOSL, Karl (Ed.): *Die „Burg". Einflußreiche politische Kräfte um Masaryk und Beneš*, I–II, München–Wien 1973–1974.

BOSL, Karl (Ed.): *Die demokratisch-parlamentarische Struktur der Ersten Tschechoslowakischen Republik*, München–Wien 1975.

BOSL, Karl (Ed.): *Die Erste Tschechoslowakische Republik als multinationaler Parteienstaat*, München–Wien 1975.

BOSL, Karl (Ed.): *Handbuch der Geschichte der böhmischen Länder, IV, Der Tschechoslowakische Staat im Zeitalter der modernen Massendemokratie und Diktatur*, Stuttgart 1970.

BOSL, Karl – SEIBT, Ferdinand (eds.): *Kultur und Gesellschaft in der Ersten Tschechoslowakischen Republik*, München 1982.

BOYER, Christoph: *Nationale Kontrahenten oder Partner? Studien zu den Beziehungen zwischen Tschechen und Deutschen in der Wirtschaft der ČSR*, München 1999.

BROKLOVÁ, Eva: *Československá demokracie. Politický systém ČSR 1918–1938*, Praha 1992.

BROKLOVÁ, Eva: *Politická kultura německých aktivistických stran v Československu 1918–1938*, Praha 1999.

BRÜGEL, Johann Wolfgang: *Ludwig Czech: Tschechen und Deutsche 1918–1938*, Wien 1967.

BRÜGEL, Johann Wolfgang: *Tschechen und Deutsche, 1*, München 1967.

BŘACH, Radko: *Československo a Evropa v polovině dvacátých let*, Praha 1996.

CÉSAR, Jaroslav – ČERNÝ, Bohumil: *Politika německých buržoazních stran v Československu v letech 1918–1938*, I–II, Praha 1962.

ČAPEK, Emil: *Politická příručka ČSR*, Praha 1931.

ČELOVSKÝ, Boris: *Mnichovská dohoda 1938*, Šenov u Ostravy 1999.

ČECHUROVÁ, Jana: *Česká politická pravice*, Praha 1999.

Československá vlastivěda, I–X, Praha 1929–1935.

Československo 1918–1938. Osudy demokracie ve střední Evropě, I–II, Jaroslav Valenta, Emil Voráček, Josef Harna (eds.), Praha 1999

DEJMEK, Jindřich: *Edvard Beneš. Politická biografie českého demokrata, 1–2*, Praha 2006, 2008.

DEJMEK, Jindřich: *Československo, jeho sousedé a velmoci ve XX. století (1918–1922)*, Praha 2002.

DEJMEK, Jindřich: *Historik v čele diplomacie: Kamil Krofta. Studie z dějin československé zahraniční politiky v letech 1936–1938*, Praha 1998.

DEJMEK, Jindřich: *Nenaplněné naděje. Politické a diplomatické vztahy Československa a Velké Británie (1918–1938)*, Praha 2003.

Die Beneš-Dekrete. Nachkriegsordnung oder ethnische Säuberung: Kann Europa eine Antwort geben?, Heiner Timmermann, Emil Voráček, Rüdiger Kipke (eds.), Münster 2005.

DOSTÁL, Vladimír: *Agrární strana. Její rozmach a zánik*, Praha 1998.

GAWRECKÁ, Marie: *Československé Slezsko mezi světovými válkami 1918–1938*, Opava 2002.

HARNA, Josef: *Krize evropské demokracie a Československo 30. let 20. století*, Praha 2006.

HARNA, Josef – KAMENEC, Ivan: *Na společné cestě. Česká a slovenská kultura mezi dvěma válkami*, Praha 1988.

KÁRNÍK, Zdeněk: *České země v éře první republiky, I–III*, Praha 2000, 2002, 2003.

KLEPETAŘ, Harry: *Seit 1918…Eine Geschichte der Tschechoslowakischen Republik*, Mährisch Ostrau 1937.

KLIMEK, Antonín: *Boj o Hrad, I–II*, Praha 1996, 1998.

KLIMEK, Antonín, *Velké dějiny zemí Koruny české, XIII, XIV*, Praha–Litomyšl 2000, 2002.

KOLÁŘ, František et al.: *Politická elita meziválečného Československa 1918–1938. Kdo byl kdo za první republiky*, Praha 1998.

KOVTUN, Jiří: *Republika v nebezpečném světě. Éra prezidenta Masaryka 1918–1935*, Praha 2005.

KUČERA, Jaroslav: *Minderheit im Nationalstaat. Die Sprachenfrage in den tschechisch-deutschen Beziehungen 1918–1938*, München 1999.

KURAL, Václav: *Konflikt místo společenství? Češi a Němci v československém státě 1918–1938*, Praha 1994.

KVAČEK, Robert: *Nad Evropou zataženo. Československo a Evropa 1933–1937*, Praha 1966.

KVAČEK, Robert: *Osudná mise*, Praha 1958.

LACINA, Vlastislav: *Formování československé ekonomiky 1918–1923*, Praha 1990.

LACINA, Vlastislav – SLEZÁK, Lubomír: *Státní hospodářská politika v ekonomickém vývoji první ČSR*, Praha 1994.

LACINA, Vlastislav: *Zlatá léta československého hospodářství (1918–1929)*, Praha 2000.

LIPTÁK, Lubomír: *Slovensko v 20. storočí*, Bratislava 1998.

LEMBERG, Hans: *Porozumění. Češi – Němci – východní Evropa 1848–1948*, Praha 1999.

LUKEŠ, Igor: *Československo mezi Stalinem a Hitlerem. Benešova cesta k Mnichovu*, Praha 1999.

LVOVÁ, Míla: *Mnichov a Edvard Beneš*, Praha 1968.

MAREK, Jaroslav: *Česká moderní kultura*, Praha 1998.

MALÍŘ, Jiří – MAREK, Pavel et al.: *Politické strany. Vývoj politických stran a hnutí v českých zemích a v Československu, I. 1861–1938*, Brno 2005.

MILLER, Daniel: *Antonín Švehla. Mistr politických kompromisů*, Praha 2001.

OLIVOVÁ, Věra: *Dějiny první republiky*, Praha 2000.

PASÁK, Tomáš: *Český fašismus 1922–1945 a kolaborace 1939–1945*, Praha 1999.

PEKNÍK, Miroslav et al.: *Pohľady na slovenskú politiku*, Bratislava 2000.

PEROUTKA, Ferdinand: *Budování státu, I–IV*, 3. vydání, Praha 1991.

Politické strany na Slovensku, 1860–1989, ed. Lubomír Lipták, Bratislava 1992.

Politický systém a státní politika v prvních letech existence Československé republiky (1918–1923), Josef Harna (ed.), Praha 1990.

PRŮCHA, Václav: *Hospodářské a sociální dějiny Československa 1918–1992, I. díl*, Praha 2004.

RYCHLÍK, Jan: *Češi a Slováci ve 20. století. Česko-slovenské vztahy 1914–1945*, Bratislava 1997.

SEIBT, Ferdinand: *Deutschland und die Tschechen*, München 1995.

SOUBIGOU, Allain: *Tomáš Garrigue Masaryk*, Praha 2004.

ŠEBEK, Jaroslav: *Mezi křížem a národem. Politické prostředí sudetoněmeckého katolicismu v meziválečném Československu*, Brno 2005.

ŠVORC, Peter: *Zakletá zem. Podkarpatská Rus 1918–1946*, Praha 2007.

TEICHOVÁ, Alice: *Mezinárodní kapitál a Československo v letech 1918–1938*, Praha 1994.

TEICHOVÁ, Alice: *The Czechoslovak Economy, 1918–1980*, London–New York 1988.

WINKLER, Martina: *Karel Kramář (1860–1937)*, München 2002.

ZEMKO, Milan – BYSTRICKÝ, Valerián (eds.): *Slovensko v Československu (1918–1939)*, Bratislava 2004.

432

XVI. Czechoslovakia in the years after the Munich Agreement and in the Second World War (1938–1945)

A motif from the title page of an issue of an illegal magazine *V boj* [Into Battle]. Painter and graphic artist Vojtěch Preissig (1873–1944), who drew the motif, was a member of anti-Nazi resistance. He was arrested in 1940 and died in 1944 in the Dachau concentration camp. The illegal magazine *V boj* was published by resistance members in the Protectorate of Bohemia and Moravia from May 1939 to the turn of 1940/1941.

1 The Consequences of the Munich Agreement on the Divided Territory

In accord with the decision of representatives of the four Great Powers and the acceptance of the terms and conditions of the Munich Agreement by the Czechoslovak government, the first German units began occupying the surrendered territories on 1st October, 1938. They first entered South Bohemia and by 10th October they had annexed the remaining three territorial zones in Bohemia and northern and southern Moravia. By the start of November 1938, Germany had secured the annexation of more than one hundred Czech towns in the Jilemnice, Český Dub and Chodsko regions, which included not only the de facto fifth, but also the not-agreed-upon 'sixth zone' of annexation. When the Czechoslovak delegation at the international commission negotiations failed to overturn the advance into yet another zone, a Czechoslovak-German protocol on a new state boundary was signed on 20th November, 1938. The next day this was confirmed by an international committee in Berlin whose workings were under the total control of Adolf Hitler, his political allies and generals. The territorial losses were made all the more severe, as Poland and Hungary also pressed claims on parts of Czechoslovakia.

In furtherance of this act, there was issued a 'law on the reunification of the Sudeten German territory with the German Reich,' which from the German legal standpoint completed 'the return of the Sudeten Germans to the Reich.' The Czech Lands' occupied territories had a total area of 28,942.66 km². Approximately 78% of this territory was given to the newly created Sudetenland Reichsgau, while the remainder was attached directly to the German Reich, specifically to Upper Silesia (the Hlučín region), Lower Bavaria and to the Austrian districts of Upper and Lower Danube (the south Bohemian and south Moravian territories). Estimates of the number of citizens who lived on the detached lands have not yet been precisely determined, but it is most commonly cited that 3.4 million Sudeten Germans 'returned to the Reich.' The annexed territories represented approximately 38% of the total area of the Czechoslovak Republic and 36% of the population living in the Czech Lands. The number of Czechs who remained in the detached borderlands is estimated at not quite 400 thousand and, of these, 291 thousand in the Sudetenland Reichsgau.

From a geographical perspective, the territories that were now absorbed into Germany were disjointed, but they had one common trait. They mostly consisted of hilly, mountainous terrain, formerly the borderlands of Bohemia, Moravia and Silesia, which had a fundamental strategic and military significance for the CSR (the length of the Sudetenland Reichsgau border with the Czecho-Slovak Republic measured 435 km). The general geographic conditions were markedly expressed in the unfavourable soil and climatic conditions which were necessarily reflected in the economy. The geographically disjointed shape of the occupied territories and the fact that it had never existed as a historical whole required the German Reich to search for new means to effectively administer the land. The German military was the first to take on an administrative role in the newly formed Sudetenland Reichsgau. A short period known as the Military Administration lasted from 1st October to 20th October.

Following Hitler's decision, the decisive role in the administration of the Sudeten territories fell to the then Sudeten German leader Konrad Henlein, who on 1st October, 1938, was named 'Reich Commissar for the Sudeten German territories.' One of his first decisions concerned the dissolution of all political parties and the prohibition of all published newspapers and magazines. On the basis of his order of 10th October, 1938, a ban on all assemblies was also put into effect, though, for the time being, this did not apply to the SdP and its affiliates; on 16th October, 1938, the last party congress of the SdP took place in Ústí nad Labem. Two weeks later, Hitler announced the creation of an NSDAP Sudetenland Reichsgau, subordinate to the Reich leadership of the Nazi Party in Munich. In line with the principles of the National Socialist totalitarian regime, the NSDAP was granted final say in all aspects of life of the Sudetenland Reichsgau. On 5th November, the SdP formally ceased to exist. Despite the fact that only some members of the SdP joined the ranks of the NSDAP over the following months, the number of Sudeten German members of the NSDAP was estimated at roughly 520 thousand, which placed the district at the forefront in the entire Reich in terms of membership in the Nazi Party. In connection with this, Henlein was commissioned by Hitler to become a Reich Governor, was promoted to SS-Obergruppenführer, and took the position of District Leader of the NSDAP in the party hierarchy. By-elections to the Reichstag took place on 4th December, 1938. These concluded the fundamental political changes, and the Sudeten lands were transformed into 'a new part of the German Reich.' The changes in the political structure and public life were guided by four basic principles: the identification of the central and local government, the leader principle, the unification of the NSDAP and state personnel, and the totalitarian manipulation of all social life.

The process of constituting the administration of the German Reich meant the immediate liquidation of all democratic elements of the previous Czechoslovak administration and local government. They were replaced with a totalitarian, dictatorial leadership principle, fully established in the law on the structure of the Sudetenland Reichsgau, which divided the territory of the Sudetenland Reichsgau into three districts of government with headquarters in Karlovy Vary, Ústí nad Labem, and Opava, effective as of 15th April, 1939. Individual districts, administered by ruling governors, were further divided into rural counties, roughly approximating the pre-Munich structure, run by offices of the Landrats (53 in the entire district) and urban counties in the five largest cities, administered by head mayors. The majority of the district's population lived in small towns and villages. With 69,195 citizens, Liberec became the largest city and was chosen as the headquarters of the Reich Governor and District Leader of the NSDAP Konrad Henlein.

Operational divisions of the security police (Gestapo) entered the borderlands at the same time as the Nazi army units. Their first task was to undertake so-called cleansing actions, that is, preventive arrests of all opponents and adversaries to the new regime. This took place in the period of military administration from about 1st to 20th October, 1938. In the first months, approximately ten thousand people were arrested, roughly one-third of which the Nazis transported to concentration camps. The attention of the Gestapo also began to focus on those of Jewish origin. From the first days of taking power, the Nazis applied the racist Nuremberg laws to the territories of the Sudetenland Reichsgau. The aim of the police and especially the Gestapo was to force Jews to leave the Reich territories. The process of the expulsion of Jews had assumed great dimensions by October 1938; pressure gradually increased and grew into the direct detention of Jewish citizens in improvised camps and anti-Jewish pogroms such as Kristallnacht on 9th–10th November, 1938. The anti-Semitic persecutions had economic in addition to racial motives. The Nazis concentrated their attention on factories, businesses, finance capital, and other valuables held by Jewish owners. The process of Aryanization which took place in the German Reich from the end of 1937 quickly spread to the areas of the Sudetenland Reichsgau. The anti-Semitic campaign stretched to the end of 1938 and the beginning of 1939 and led to a sudden wave of Jewish emigration to the interior of the Czecho-Slovak Republic. The Nazis succeeded in expelling the majority of the Jewish population from the borderlands, with Aryan citizens occupying Jewish flats, businesses, and medical and legal offices. This reality casts into doubt the claims of some Sudeten German historians and journalists that the local populace did not know of and had nothing to do with the persecution of the Jews.

The Nazi administration devoted special attention to the Czech minority which remained in Sudeten territory, who were generally regarded as unreliable and unfriendly to the Reich. Prior to the entrance of the Wehrmacht and police units, roughly 120 thousand Czechs fled to the interior in fear of repression and persecution and by the end of 1938, the number of refugees with Czechoslovak citizenship rose to 200 thousand, many of whom had left behind their property (especially real estate, but also the furnishings of apartments, businesses, and so on). By that point, less than a half of the original Czech population remained on the occupied territory. This represented roughly 12–13% of the entire population that lived on the detached territories in the autumn of 1938. Immediately after the occupation, all Czech political parties and organizations ceased to exist; only fire brigades under German direction remained. The majority of Czech schools, including primary schools, were closed and, in the remaining primary schools that taught in Czech, teaching was conducted according to the Nazi curriculum with the aim of Germanization.

Czechs were not allowed to attend any Czech secondary or tertiary schools and no Czech press was published, no theatre, radio, nor film played. There was no guaranteed space for Czech national or cultural life. The Czech population lost representation in all spheres of administrative, political, economic, and cultural life. In sum, one can say that while the German national minority before Munich invoked national rights and autonomy, the Nazis in the Sudetenland Reichsgau took the exact opposite position towards the Czechs and assigned them the role of a de facto work force with no guaranteed rights.

The situation in the Hlučín region, with an area of 316 km² and 38 municipalities, developed along broadly similar, though not identical, lines. It became part of the Altreich (German Old Reich), specifically the county of Racibórz in the Opole district of the Reich province of Silesia (from 1941, called Upper Silesia). Even after the German annexation, Hlučín remained the seat of both county court and, in 1939–1940, the Gestapo. The town was also home to a financial and postal office, the county inspectorate of schools, branches of the labour and cadastre offices, and the county hospital and social welfare home. Reich legislation was implemented in the Hlučín region on 1st July, 1939, completing the transition to Nazi administration. The most significant political event was the by-elections to the Reichstag on 4th December, 1938. That the 99.2% turnout of legal voters in the Hlučín region gave 99.8% of their votes to the Nazi regime testifies to the totalitarian nature of the elections. Government offices began to organize the teaching of German, which many residents barely knew, and began a campaign against Czech signs and names. Public use of Czech was subject to fines and public officials were not allowed to use it even in private. The penalty for violating the ban was the loss of trade, the revocation of license, and police detention. The evacuation of unreliable citizens, a list of whom was verified in the Landrat, was prepared. In April 1941, however, Hitler decided that the deportation of these persons would occur only after the war.

An absolute majority of residents (roughly 52,900) automatically received German citizenship, with all the rights of Reich citizens. Under the terms of the option agreement, Czechs had until March 1940 to move, but they had to leave behind their property, which was for many unacceptable; despite this, about 8,600 people, mostly Czechs, moved to the interior. There they did not have the rights of Reich citizens, but instead merely German citizenship which was enough to retain their property. They received the same food ration coupons and salaries as Germans. They could not, however, hold managerial posts or send their children to higher studies. Unlike their fellow Reich citizens, however, they did not have to serve in the German army, which many came to value later. During the war, approximately 12 thousand men from the Hlučín region were called up to serve in the Wehrmacht (over three thousand perished and perhaps five thousand who later returned from captivity were injured or crippled).

Unlike the neighbouring Opava region in the Sudetenland Reichsgau, Czech schools in the Hlučín region were closed without exception and teaching was conducted in 46 newly organized German primary schools in which, initially, the teachers were those who had to leave the Těšín region annexed by Poland. Czech cultural life was forbidden. Czech books were withdrawn from municipal and school libraries and were sometimes publicly burned; in Kravaře, for example, this was accompanied by music and dance. Estimates suggest that 20 thousand Czech books were destroyed.

2 The Second Republic

The Munich Agreement fundamentally changed the existence of the Czech and Slovak nations in the remaining territory of the republic as well. Developments after Munich constituted a catastrophe for the Czechoslovak state as it cast doubt on the decisive aspects of state sovereignty. For Czechs, it meant a national catastrophe as well because they – unlike the majority of Slovaks, Germans, Ruthenians, Hungarians, and Poles – considered this state identical not just with their national, but also state, aspirations. The shock to Czechoslovak statehood was so deep that doubts about the legitimacy of the origin and existence of the state were again revived. Even though contemporaries did not immediately notice it, a nearly seven-year period of subjugation arrived in which two basic phenomena that had pervaded Czech history came into conflict: on the one hand, efforts to build democracy; on the other, totalitarian social and political developments. The rivalry and interpenetration of elements of continuity and discontinuity with prior historical developments became an integral part of this fundamental conflict.

The crisis which struck Czechoslovakia after Munich touched all imaginable areas and dimensions of social life. Wide strata of the population suffered intense depression, disappointment and bitterness over the betrayal of their allies and shock that after a mere twenty years of independent statehood, its existence and future were shaken to its very foundations. Masaryk's idea of a Czechoslovak state collapsed as Munich did not mean only a fundamental change in the boundaries and international position of the republic, its pervasive economic weakening, but it also brought with it considerable shocks to the democratic state's internal structure. It also cast into doubt the reigning system of ideological and moral values. This was all amplified by feelings of existential uncertainty and anxious worry about the future of the nation and state, springing from the forthcoming fundamental changes in the nature of the Czechoslovak state and, especially, the position of Slovakia and Subcarpathian Ruthenia, which had to come to terms with the oppressive consequences of the First Vienna Arbitration of 2nd November, 1938. The arbitration verdict gave Hungary custody of a part of the territory of Slovakia and Subcarpathian Ruthenia measuring 41,098 km^2.

The idea of making fundamental changes to the existing political system and the arrangement of power quickly began to dominate political life. In the phraseology of the time, this idea was given names like 'reconstructing' or 'simplifying' political life. In reality, they were talking about a fairly radical break with the existing liberal democratic arrangement of political power, which in the opinion of the leaders of the time had failed at a critical moment and was not able to defend basic national and state interests. A coming 'revolution' was to replace it, initiated and led by nationalist conservative forces who saw an opportunity to work their way to power.

On 4th October, 1938, the caretaker government of General Jan Syrový submitted its resignation, which was accepted by President Beneš and the following day he named a new government, again with General Syrový as its Prime Minister. The same day President Beneš abdicated and, on 22nd October, he flew as a private citizen to London. The process of simplifying political life accelerated at the start of October in Slovakia where, on 6th October in Žilina, Hlinka's Slovak People's Party (HSĽS) proclaimed the autonomy of Slovakia on the basis of an agreement with other political parties. The establishment of an autonomous government with Jozef Tiso at its head followed and three days later politicians in Subcarpathian Ruthenia formed an autonomous government with Andrej Brody at its head.

The second half of October and November 1938 passed under the sign of building a 'new', Second Republic. The political system was simplified until two new political groups were established, mutually connected by a loyal opposition: the governing Party of National Unity, headed by Rudolf Beran, and the National Labour Party, presided over by Antonín Hampl. The lawyer Emil Hácha was elected the new president on 30th November, 1938. Soon after, on 1st December, 1938, President Hácha named a new 'central' government, again of politicians and experts, with Rudolf Beran as Prime Minister. This was the first government of Czecho-Slovakia because it was formed under the constitutional law of 22nd November, 1938, on the autonomy of Slovakia and Subcarpathian Ruthenia. Ministers in the autonomous governments of all the part of the Czecho-Slovak Republic were members of the central government and together decided questions of finance, defence and foreign policy, while contending with numerous domestic and foreign policy problems. The domestic political process of 'simplifying' democracy grew to the passage of an authorizing law, passed by the National Assembly on 15th December, 1938, which gave the government the authority to carry out legislative functions and to go so far as to alter or change the constitution by means of government decrees for a period of two years.

For the entire months-long existence of the Second Republic, the central and simultaneously most sensitive point of politics was its relations with the German Reich, whose representatives were already preparing the destruction of Czecho-Slovakia. Even though events in and around the Second Republic became on the surface more complicated in many respects, by the start of spring 1939, they approached the final denouement. The results of Foreign Minister František Chvalkovský's negotiations in Berlin on 21st January, 1939, were an omen of later developments. The conditions which the representatives of the Nazi Reich formulated at the meeting revealed their dissatisfaction with developments up to that point and resulted in forcible pressure being exerted on the Czecho-Slovak government. The government was asked to renounce its alliances and fully proclaim the neutrality of Czecho-Slovakia, withdraw from the League of Nations, adopt a foreign policy in line with the German Reich and join the Pact against the Comintern, abolish the remains of the Beneš regime, issue anti-Jewish laws according to the Nuremberg example, demobilize the army, reduce the military budget and the size of the army to a minimum, as well as satisfy the demands of the Germans who remained on the republic's territory.

On the domestic side, Czecho-Slovak relations became more complicated, which more and more predetermined the relation of the Nazis to HSLS. By the end of 1938, after the electoral victory of HSLS in Slovakia and the start of Slovak Assembly operations in the middle of January, 1939, the relationship of Bratislava and Prague had worsened. The policies of HSLS were being enacted in Slovakia and separatist tendencies pushing for the dissociation of Slovakia from the Czech Lands were strengthening within the party. All of these developments suited Berlin and found direct support with political representatives there. The activities of HSLS radicals, some of whom had, with the knowledge of Jozef Tiso, the Prime Minister of the autonomous government, negotiated in Berlin about the break-away of Slovakia, had not passed unnoticed in Prague. Czech members of the 'central' government searched for ways to straighten out the growing misunderstandings with an agreement, but their efforts did not meet with the expected reception in Bratislava; on the contrary, Vojtech Tuka's audience with the Reich Chancellor Adolf Hitler in Berlin on 12th February, 1939, and further negotiations indicated that efforts to ensure the break-away of Slovakia under the patronage and direction of Berlin were growing.

The Prague government tried to take measures which would prevent the looming breakup of the state. Prime Minister Beran proposed to President Hácha that in case of disagreement with their Slovak partners in the expected negotiations on 9th–10th March, he relieve Tiso's government of executive power and name a caretaker administration for Slovakia before a new government was formed according to the constitution. The army and police were to prevent any violent acts of Hlinka's Guard and anti-state activities by other Slovak figures, arresting them if necessary, so that the existing constitutional organization of Czecho-Slovakia was not breached. Military actions immediately began in Slovakia, starting with President Hácha's abolition of the existing Slovak government delegates' functions and the declaration of martial law by the commander of the 7th Corps in Banská Bystrica, Bedřich Homola, and ending in the formation of two new autonomous governments in Slovakia, both lasting only a few days, led first by Jozef Sivák and then by Karol Sidor.

In an attempt to fortify state ties and prevent the disintegration of the republic, Prime Minister Beran decided on 6th March to intervene in Subcarpathian Ruthenia where the autonomous government was reorganized. Though the Greek Catholic priest and People's Party politician Augustin Voloshin remained Prime Minister, General Lev Prchala was named Minister of Finance, Transportation, and the Interior, while the agrarian politician Stepan Klochurak was to assume the post of Minister of Agriculture, Public Works, Health, Industry, Business, and Trade.

Despite all these 'central' government measures, the situation in Slovakia developed differently from the assumptions in Prague. When Karol Sidor rejected the German offer of the break-away of Slovakia on 12th March, radicals from HSLS, vehemently supported by emissaries from Berlin and pressure from Germany, made contact with Jozef Tiso. He received an invitation to Berlin where 'Slovak matters' were to be resolved as rapidly as possible. On 13th March, the Slovak autonomous government expressed agreement with Tiso travelling to 'appraise the situation in Berlin,' but he was not to commit to anything without the agreement of the Slovak assembly. Tiso was welcomed to Berlin with all the honours appropriate to the highest state representatives, but this was followed by clear demands for the immediate secession of Slovakia. Tiso, however, recognized the seriousness of the moment and did not surrender to the pressure to immediately declare Slovak independence while in Berlin and simultaneously asked for German protection. He was allowed to telephone Bratislava and Prague and request that the Slovak assembly be convened the next day. Upon his return to Bratislava on the morning of 14th March, the government first discussed the results of Tiso's mission and, at 11 o'clock, debate began in the Slovak parliament. Sidor submitted the resignation of his government and Tiso reported on the results of his journey to Berlin. Several minutes after 12 o'clock, the Slovak parliament approved independence and declared a Slovak state. A new government was named with Jozef Tiso again as the Prime Minister. Czecho-Slovakia had broken apart, while the situation in the easternmost part of the country had also changed. Though Voloshin's Subcarpathian government announced a pledge of loyalty to the Czecho-Slovak Republic on the morning of 15th March, only a few hours later and under the influence of news from Bohemia and Moravia, it proclaimed an independent state of Carpatho-Ukraine. Its existence did not last long as the Hungarian army began to occupy its territory and a day later captured its capital, Khust.

On 13th March, the Minister of Foreign Affairs Chvalkovský visited Prime Minister Beran and informed him that he had suggested to President Hácha to personally visit Berlin and 'gauge Hitler's intentions.' After diplomatic negotiation, it was agreed that the President of the Czecho-Slovak Republic would go to Berlin at Hitler's invitation. In the meantime, the German army had already occupied Moravská Ostrava, Místek, and other surrounding locations. In the course of a late-night conversation, Hitler alerted Hácha of his decision to occupy militarily the rump of Bohemia and Moravia and demanded his assent. Hácha asserted that he could not decide without the knowledge and agreement of his government; however, after threats and extortion, and a phone-call with Prime Minister Beran, he and the Minister of Foreign Affairs Chvalkovský signed a German-Czech Declaration designed by Berlin. On 15th March, the German army occupied the remaining Czech Lands' territory and, on 16th March an order was issued on the formation of the Protectorate of Bohemia and Moravia.

After twenty years of co-existence, the fates of the Czech and Slovak nations once again took different paths. Despite their divergent and sometimes bitter experiences, and the new conditions imposed on them, however, the idea of Czechoslovak statehood continued on. For many social classes, resistance groups, and even individuals, the restoration of Czechoslovakia as an independent and sovereign state within its pre-Munich borders became the unifying element of their activities and their ultimate goal.

3 The Protectorate of Bohemia and Moravia

Adolf Hitler's order of 16th March, 1939, formally guaranteed the Protectorate autonomy and its own administration, though 'in conformity with the political, military, and economic needs of the Reich.' The Protectorate had neither its own representation abroad nor rights to an independent army. The government's army was assigned a symbolic role and filled only ancillary services. Parliament was dissolved and political life was simplified. The Protectorate's administration was represented by the state president (a function Emil Hácha served for the entire period) and the Protectorate government led by its Prime Minister. After a month of military administration, a Reichsprotektor assumed direction of the administration of the German occupation; his task was to defend and assert the interests of the Reich in relation to the Protectorate. The Sudeten German Karl Hermann Frank held the important position of state secretary in the office of the Reichsprotektor; at the end of April 1939, he was also named a higher leader of the SS and police in the Protectorate. He gradually assumed a privileged position in the occupation administration and then, after Hitler named him the German State Minister for Bohemia and Moravia on 20th August, 1943, he assumed de facto all executive authority in the occupation regime.

The basic level of the occupation's administration was the Oberlandrats whose main task was to oversee the activity of the local Protectorate administration. They controlled the Protectorate authorities, and had the authority to overturn their decrees and replace them with their own statutes. The police and security departments of the extensive repressive apparatus (Geheime Staatspolizei – Gestapo, SD – Sicherheitsdienst, Sipo – Sicherheitspolizei, Kripo – Kriminalpolizei) formed the core of the occupying forces with the task of suppressing all activities 'unfriendly to the Reich.'

The German Reich and occupation authorities represented the real holders of state power, while the Czech authorities of the Protectorate functioned as their subsidiary executive organs. The appearance of an autonomous administration allowed for more effective governing of the population to the Reich's advantage and ensured the desired developments in the life of the Protectorate. The aim was to ensure the organized Germanization policy of the Czech nation's annihilation and the incorporation of the rest of the Czech Lands into the German Reich. The Germans could not, of course, achieve this 'final aim' during the war as they needed to exploit both the economic potential of the Protectorate and the Czech workforce for its war plans.

The subjection of the Czech Lands to the Reich's interests manifested itself most conspicuously in the economy. From the first days, the occupiers systematically began introducing a wartime-focused economic system, leading to a change felt throughout the entire economy. Germany further improved its international economic position and balance of payments with the surpluses of export goods and gold reserves of the former republic; it used its own companies to take control of the most important weapons manufacturers and the Protectorate's banks, and seized the dissolved Czechoslovak army's armaments. In terms of social development, the organized deployment of the labour force (the forced-labour regime), which later became the forced assignment of work both in Germany and the Protectorate, had fundamental significance. The Czech Lands represented one of the most important industrial and weapons arsenals of Germany for the entire course of the WWII.

In the framework of Aryanization, Jewish property came under German administration and fell into German hands. A June 1939 decree from the Protector allowed the anti-Semitic

Nuremberg laws to be applied against the Jewish populace within the territory of the Protectorate. So began the 'final solution to the Jewish question.' In November 1941, a Jewish ghetto was established in Terezín; in reality, it was merely a transfer station on the path to the death camps in the east where, after mass transports from January 1942 to October 1944, the vast majority of Jews from the Czech Lands perished in gas chambers. Jews from Slovakia and Subcarpathian Ruthenia met the same fate.

The application of race theory led the Nazi occupiers to preparations and later the realization of the 'final solution to the gypsy question.' The lives of violently abducted Czech and Moravian Roma and Sinti ended in the concentration and death camps of Auschwitz, Buchenwald and Ravensbrück. Roughly four and a half thousand Roma men and boys, women and girls and an undetermined number of other Roma and Sinti, were sent there from the Protectorate, of which only 538 Roma prisoners survived the Holocaust.

4 Anti-Nazi Resistance at Home and Abroad

As early as the spring and summer of 1939, when apparent peace prevailed in Europe, the first seeds of resistance emerged in the Protectorate of Bohemia and Moravia. The events of March caused shock and trepidation regarding the nation's existence, along with bitterness and expressions of spontaneous defiance from the widest sections of the Czech populace. All this provoked Czech national solidarity as a self-preservation instinct which began to express itself in various forms and became a unifying element. The essentially negative anti-German attitude gradually grew into more and more flagrant actions of defiance to the occupation of the Czech Lands. The return to a traditional national and cultural past created a distinctive atmosphere. Every major action (the burial of the remains of Karel Hynek Mácha in Prague's Slavín cemetery, the celebration of the memorial to Master Jan Hus, the reverential ceremony at the tomb of Bedřich Smetana, and most notably the national summer pilgrimages and celebrations to various locations of Bohemia and Moravia) possessed an aspect of resistance. With the participation of thousands, they expressed the nation-wide spirit of resistance and became tests for further displays which culminated in a boycott of public transport on 30. 9. (1st anniversary of the Munich Agreement) and organized demonstrations throughout the Protectorate on 28. 10. (St Wenceslas Day), 1939.

Open repression by the occupiers soon followed. The medical student Jan Opletal was fatally wounded during anti-German student demonstrations on 28th October. The demonstration at his funeral became an excuse for the closing of Czech universities on 17th November, 1939, the abduction of more than a thousand university students to concentration camps, and the execution without trial of nine functionaries of the Student Association. This harsh approach was not a haphazard reprisal, but part of a thought-out campaign of annihilation of Czech intelligentsia, schools, and culture.

At the same time as the mass demonstrations, an organized resistance was also building. The birth of resistance centres reflected the new stratification of social and political forces in the Protectorate. A group of Beneš's close associates (including Prokop Drtina and Jan Jína), who initiated and designed the pattern of co-operation with him before his flight from the republic in October 1938, and other young politicians, journalists, and state bureaucracy employees, the Political Central (PÚ) was created. Its leadership consisted of a committee composed according to the pre-Munich governing coalition line-up (Přemysl Šámal, Ladislav Rašín, Jaromír Nečas, Ferdinand Richter, František Hála, Ladislav Feierabend). The military Defence of the Nation organization (ON), a hierarchically organized underground army, was built along the same lines as the organizational structure of the Czechoslovak army. The central command of the ON (Generals Sergej Ingr, Josef Bílý, Bedřich Neumann, Hugo Vojta) assumed that it would rise up in the decisive phase of the military defeat of Germany, with the aim of restoring the republic within its pre-Munich borders and ensuring its continuance. Another significant resistance centre was the Petition Committee We Will Remain Faithful (PVVZ), which counted among its ranks a relatively wide political and social spectrum. From a political perspective, it formed a kind of centrist leaning of the Czech resistance. Its organizers (Wolfgang Jankovec, Václav Běhounek, Josef Friedl, Josef Fischer, Karel Bondy, Vojtěch Čížek, Karel J. Beneš) not only built an illegal network throughout the Protectorate, but also formulated their own political program for the restoration of the republic. Publishers of illegal magazines (including *V boj*, Rise up for Battle; *the ISNO, RČS*, and *Signál*) around which distinctive illegal structures had gathered, often overlapping with already existing resistance networks, significantly added to the process of creating a resistance in the same manner.

While noticeable political, ideological, and social diversity was exhibited in the PÚ, ON, and PVVZ, the Communists entered the resistance as a Leninist-style organized party. Not even under conditions of the occupation did they resign their goal of gaining power through a Bolshevik revolution, but they temporarily accepted the idea of a struggle against the occupiers, for the restoration of state sovereignty and the independence of the republic, so as not to betray their ultimate aim. While in the first months of the occupation, the Communists shared the common base with the Czech resistance, after the signing of the Soviet-German Non-Aggression Pact and the start of the war in September 1939, the situation changed. When the Comintern called the war 'imperialist and unjust for which the bourgeoisie of all warring states can be blamed,' the Communists assumed the firm, class-based and international position dictated by Moscow. The change in their position broke the heretofore unity of the anti-German resistance and led to its fissure. The split deepened when the Communists used illegal propaganda to attack not just the Western powers, but also the representatives of international Czechoslovak resistance, especially Beneš. Confusion was sown among the rank and file, which was expressed in sectarian opinions, naturally stronger in Slovakia than in the Czech Lands. The end of the dual-track resistance and the isolation of the Communists came only with another change in the Comintern policy after the outbreak of war between Germany and the USSR in June 1941. Illegal central leaderships replaced one another at the head of the party structure. The leadership managed lower network cells through instructors and transmitted instruction which came from the directives of the Communist International.

With breaks of various lengths, the CPCz published the illegal paper *Rudé právo* until May 1945.

From the beginning, the Czech resistance clashed with the security apparatus of the occupiers (Gestapo, SD, and so on). Several waves of arrests in the ranks of the resistance from the end of 1939 to the spring of 1940 affected their activities. The shared headquarters of the PÚ, ON, and PVVZ resistance groups, created in spring 1940 and called the Central Leadership of the Home Resistance (ÚVOD), were not spared in these attacks. Despite considerable problems caused in 1939, for example by the Soviet-German Non-Aggression Pact, the unfavourable development of the war, and especially the fall of France, Czech resistance achieved remarkable results by the end of 1941; the illegal network continued to function, illegal press continued to be published, successful intelligence-gathering activities developed, and a wide-ranging political program for the post-war renewal of Czechoslovakia was prepared under the title 'For Freedom. Towards a New ČSR.' This became the common ideological basis of the resistance on the territory of the Protectorate.

From the beginning, Czechoslovak resistance abroad played an unusually significant role. The first wave of emigration took place shortly after the Munich Agreement and those leaving included prominent political representatives, Communists, and members of the wealthier class of the Jewish population, who feared racial persecution. Another wave followed after the March 1939 occupation. Many left their homeland with the aim of joining the foreign resistance; some were sent by resistance organizations, others were inspired by the tradition of the Legionnaires from the First World War, and still others fled from the terror of the occupation. Many of them were soldiers who – in the same way as twenty years earlier – saw their task as the creation of a foreign army. The Czechoslovak exile movement began its activities in unfavourable conditions. Great Britain and France kept to the principles of the Munich Agreement and the Soviet Union recognized the Slovak Republic. Gradually three main centres of exile were formed: in Poland, France, and the USA, in the last of which Czech immigrant organizations played a positive role. After the 1939 return of Beneš to Europe from the USA, the main centres were transferred to Paris and London which drew both older politicians (Jan Šrámek, Jaroslav Stránský, Rudolf Bechyně and others) and younger followers of Beneš (Hubert Ripka, Eduard Outrata) along with a group of high officers (Sergej Ingr, Rudolf Viest, František Moravec) and former MP Jan Masaryk. From the beginning, the activities of the Czechoslovak exile movement developed along two lines – political and military.

Until the middle of 1939, considerable disagreements in political opinions showed themselves, caused both by competition for key positions and differing opinions on future relations between the Czech and Slovak nations. Only gradually did the politics of Edvard Beneš win out over the opposition of Štefan Osuský and Milan Hodža. Its foundation was the theory of the legal continuity of the pre-Munich ČSR and its main goal was to press for the restoration of an independent state with its pre–1938 borders in the international community. Its main means were the diplomatic, military, and intelligence and propaganda activities of the resistance abroad and at home.

As early as December 1938, the Communists established foreign leadership in Moscow (which included Klement Gottwald, Václav Kopecký, Bohumír Šmeral and Jan Šverma), whose activities were subordinated to the Comintern, which directed and organized the activities of Communists both abroad and at home. On the order of Moscow, a foreign secretariat of the CPCz was established in May 1939, and functioned until the fall of France. The task of Jan Šverma, Viliam Široký, Bruno Köhler, and from June 1939 Vlado Clementis was co-operation with the French and British Communists.

In the middle of October 1939, after futile attempts to induce France to allow the creation of a provisional government, politicians in exile agreed to establish a Czechoslovak National Committee (ČSNV) with its headquarters in Paris. The war, along with news of the resistance in the Protectorate, the demonstration on 28th October, 1939, and persecution by the occupiers led to certain changes in the previously reserved attitude of French politicians. Of all days, on 17th November, 1939, the French government recognized the ČSNV, though only with limited powers and not as a government in exile. The British government took a similar position. The ČSNV was to represent the Czech and Slovak nation abroad as well as direct and organize military units.

The formation of a Czechoslovak army abroad influenced the process of recognizing the right of Czechoslovakia to revive itself. The army's foundations were laid at the end of October 1939 in Polish territory, and a considerable portion left on board the naval transports bound for France before the outbreak of war. Only after the invasion of Germany did the Polish government acknowledge the Czechoslovak legion, led by General Lev Prchala, with approximately 1,000 men. It shared in the Polish army's defensive battle, and a considerable portion of the legion including the commander, Lt. Col. Ludvík Svoboda, were captured by the Red Army in the course of the Soviet occupation of the eastern regions of Poland and transferred to an internment camp. Most foreign military volunteers gathered in 1939 in France. Because France had refused their applications to enter the regular army, Czechoslovak volunteers joined the Foreign Legion, and that included those who left in the summer of 1939 from Poland with the intention of joining Czechoslovak legions in the event of war. Only pilots were directly accepted into the French air force.

Czechoslovak soldiers and pilots later contributed to the defence of France at the start of the summer of 1940, and after France's capitulation, four thousand soldiers were evacuated to Great Britain where Germany then concentrated its attack in preparation for an invasion of the islands. From the middle of July 1940, pilots were rapidly organized for the defence of England. Gradually, three Czechoslovak wings were formed (310 Fighter Squadron, 311 Bomber Squadron, and 312 Fighter Squadron); their members were engaged in battle by the end of August. Beyond these men, other Czechoslovak pilots worked in the British and Polish fighter squadrons. Their results in battles placed the Czech pilots among the most successful in the Battle of Britain, which deflected the attack and foiled the German invasion of Britain.

Over the following years, Czechoslovak soldiers and pilots contributed to battles in Europe and over the Atlantic. Infantry units of the Czechoslovak independent brigades fought to defend the English coast, and guarded airports and various important locations. Czechoslovak soldiers also participated in battles in the Middle East and North Africa. In British Palestine, the Czechoslovak 11th Infantry Battalion – East was formed under the leadership of Lieutenant Colonel Karel Klapálek. Its ranks were made up of exiles who had come through the Balkans and after the fall of France had not travelled west, and of soldiers from the Soviet Union who were allowed to leave holding camps there. After being assigned to battles as part of the British army, their paths led them from Alexandria and the Libyan deserts, through Syria to Tobruk. There, from the end of October 1941, Czechoslovak soldiers helped to defend the strategic port that was surrounded by German and Italian armies. In May 1942, the brigade was reorganized as the 200th Czechoslovak anti-aircraft regiment. After the end of fighting in North Africa in May 1943, the soldiers transferred to Great Britain where they reinforced the local units. At the beginning of September, a Czechoslovak independent armoured brigade was formed there. In August 1944, it transported to the continent and joined the Allies in the siege of the fortified port city of Dunkerque. In May 1945, Alois Liška, the commander of the brigade and operational commander of the allied armies accepted the surrender of the German defenders.

In the summer of 1940, Great Britain recognized the provisional Czechoslovak government and with it the entire provisional state organization of the ČSR in exile, which consisted of President Edvard Beneš, the government in exile led by Msgr. Jan Šrámek and the State Council, an advisory organ of the President and government. Due to the absence of a law-making parliament, the state organization in exile passed legal acts in the form of decrees by the President of the Republic, just as other governments in exile did. The international recognition of the government in exile allowed preparatory work leading to the formation of a post-war Czechoslovak-Polish confederation. This idea, however, was shipwrecked in 1942 by the negative position of the Soviet Union.

Due to the changes in the war situation in the summer of 1941 (the invasion of the Soviet Union, the start of a war coalition), the pre-requisites for definitive recognition of the Czechoslovak government in exile improved. As early as spring 1941, a military mission headed by Colonel Heliodor Píka went to Moscow and their diplomatic negotiations culminated on 18th July with the signing of a Czechoslovak-Soviet agreement on the exchange of envoys and mutual support in the war, including consent to the creation of Czechoslovak military units on Soviet territory. The agreement recognized the republic in its pre-Munich form, without restrictions or conditions. On the same day, the Czechoslovak government in exile was also recognized by the British government. Despite the official British position not accepting the legal continuity and borders of the republic, British recognition opened new possibilities. The United States of America then recognized the Czechoslovak government in exile on 31st July, 1941.

On the basis of the Czechoslovak-Soviet agreement, Czechoslovak military units began to be formed on Soviet territory. The first was started in Buzuluk at the beginning of February 1942. The foundations of the 1st Czechoslovak Independent Field Battalion were on the one hand the remainder of the former so-called Czechoslovak legion released from internment and on the other Czechoslovak citizens gradually arriving, especially Subcarpathian Ruthenians freed from Soviet prisons and forced labour camps by a requested amnesty. In January 1943, a battalion under the command of Ludvík Svoboda left for the front and, in March, participated in the defence of the Ukrainian village of Sokolovo. At the beginning of that May the battalion, which had suffered heavy losses in battle, was withdrawn to Novochopersk where the 1st Czechoslovak Independent Brigade was formed. After training had been completed at the end of September 1943, it left for the front and was deployed to the battle for Kiev, Ruda, Biela Tserkov, and Zhashkov.

Changes in international political relations and the military situation were reflected in the resistance inside the Protectorate. A series of strikes and numerous acts of sabotage in industry and transport occurred in the summer of 1941. There were fundamental changes in efforts to unify the Czech resistance forces which, after the reversal in Stalin's policies, accepted the Czech Communists. ÚVOD and the new central leadership of the CPCz directed by Jan Zika reached an agreement at the end of 1941 on the creation of a common resistance organ, the Central National Revolutionary Committee of Czechoslovakia (ÚNRVČ). From then on, the increasingly popular but easily exploited idea of a unified national front became the foundation of the Communist strategy and tactics in their effort to take over the main power centres in the new republic, and began to permeate all their other actions.

However, the efforts of the Czech resistance and its attempts at unification were at odds with the occupation administration and Berlin's vision of calm and order in the Protectorate. It was for this reason that Reichsprotektor Konstantin von Neurath was replaced by Reinhard Heydrich, General of the SS and Police and head of the Reich Central Security Office in Berlin. He took office on 27th September, 1941, and immediately announced a civil emergency (martial law) to take effect the next day; it ended on 20th January, 1942. The Prime Minister of the Protectorate government, General Alois Eliáš, was arrested on 27th September, 1941, and was tried and executed for his contacts with Czechoslovaks in exile and the resistance. Heydrich's approach – arrests, military courts, executions and, later, effective social demagoguery and further safeguards in the administration of the economy – were intended to radically alter the situation. The weeks and months of martial law were accompanied by hundreds of executions (among them the leading representatives of the Defence of the Nation organization and members of the Communist central leadership) and thousands of people imprisoned in concentration camps. The forces of the resistance were to be liquidated, intimidated and restricted in their activities. The arrests severely affected ÚVOD's illegal networks; the heretofore regular radio contacts between the Protectorate and London were lost.

The politicians and soldiers of the Czechoslovak government in exile knew that they had to overcome the crisis that had set in and were further exposed to reproofs from the Soviets that the home front was passive. In co-operation with the British, they resolved this situation by sending trained and technically equipped parachutists into the Protectorate. Their mission was to reorganize and revive the damaged networks, renew and maintain contacts, develop intelligence, and undertake acts of sabotage on the territory of the Protectorate. Two of the soldiers deployed at the end of December of 1941 and the spring of 1942 – Jan Kubiš and Jozef Gabčík (operation Anthropoid) – parachuted into the Protectorate with one task: to assassinate Reinhard Heydrich. After several months of preparation in co-operation with resistance organizations (most importantly the Sokols) and with the help of another parachutist, Josef Valčík, they carried out the assassination in Prague on 27th May, 1942; the Reichsprotector died as a result of his wounds several days later.

This action, extraordinary in Europe at the time, triggered a widespread response and a wave of sympathy among the anti-Nazi coalition nations. As early as the afternoon of 27th May, the occupiers proclaimed martial law and unleashed a previously unseen wave of terror against the Czech nation and the resistance. Martial law ended on 3rd July, 1942, and its final count was appalling. More than 1,500 people were executed, more than three thousand were arrested, the villages of Lidice and Ležáky were destroyed and their citizens slaughtered. Both the assassins and other parachutists paid for the act with their lives when, on 18th June, 1942, they died in a heavily outnumbered battle in an Orthodox church on Prague's Resslova Street. This second period of martial law, known as the Heydrichiad, noticeably affected the Czech domestic resistance. Only small groups remained from the ÚVOD networks; the Gestapo completed the destruction of the Communist central leadership, yet despite this, by the start of autumn 1942, signs of new resistance activity began to appear.

The beginning of August 1942 concluded another phase in the struggle for the restoration of Czechoslovakia's international standing. The validity of British commitments stemming from the Munich Agreement was annulled and, at the end of September, the French National Committee representative in London, General Charles de Gaulle, also declared the Munich Agreement invalid from the start.

The question of the Sudeten Germans' future in post-war Czechoslovakia was closely related to the annulment of the Munich Agreement. By July 1942, Great Britain withdrew from its pre-war support for national minorities and accepted the general principle of the transfer of German minorities out of the lands of Central and South-Eastern Europe. During President Beneš's visit to the USA in the spring of 1943, the American president Franklin Delano Roosevelt assented to the transfer of Germans out of Czechoslovakia, with the Soviet Union immediately taking the same position. From there a direct path led to concrete negotiations on the mechanics of the transfer, culminating in the Potsdam Agreement of the Allied Great Powers in the summer of 1945, which in Article XII approved the transfer of the German population of Poland, Czechoslovakia and Hungary.

5 Czech Culture during the War

Despite the efforts of the German occupiers to limit and mould to their own needs all aspects of culture and Czech national life, Czech culture continued to advance. The dozens of measures of the occupiers, from censorship of the press, radio, publication, film production, and the removal of the works of Czech and foreign authors from libraries, to direct bans on the issuing of literature, the showing of films, and the operation of theatres; all this did not prevent art from speaking to the sorely tested nation and its readers, viewers, and listeners from finding encouragement, enlightenment, and entertainment in various aspects of culture. Books which echoed the nation's past, the traditions of Czech culture and language, and reinforced patriotic consciousness spoke particularly strongly to a wide circle of readers (beyond the classics of Czech literature, these included the prose of Vladislav Vančura, František Kubka, František Kožík, and Eduard Bass and the poetry of František Halas, Josef Hora, Jaroslav Seifert, Vítězslav Nezval, and František Hrubín). Psychologically attuned prose began to appear in Czech literature at the start of the 1940s, but it fully emerged only in the period after 1942. It was foreshadowed by the novels Black Light (*Černé světlo*, 1940) by Václav Řezáč and *Helimadoe* (1940) by Jaroslav Havlíček. One can add to this Karel Konrád's novel Beds without a Canopy (*Postele bez nebes*, 1939) and Egon Hostovský's works written in exile. The writer Jarmila Glazarová also published her masterpieces in these years, particularly the novel *Advent* (1939).

A literary movement inspired by the tradition of folk story-telling, folk literature and folklore also began to emerge in Protectorate-era prose. Apart from Josef Štefan Kubín, known as a collector of folklore from the Krkonoše region, Jan Drda and Jaromír John also attracted attention in this genre. Drda successfully introduced himself to Czech literature with his debut novel Town in the Palm of the Hand (*Městečko na dlani*, 1940) and John's novel Wise Engelbert (*Moudrý Engelbert*, 1940) was also popular. A new generation of poets also began to mature, concentrated around Václav Černý's Critical Monthly *(Kritický měsíčník)*. Its spokespersons included Kamil Bednář and Zdeněk Urbánek, while Ivan Blatný and Jiří Orten were among its leading representatives. Book publishing did not lose its function even with the censorship restrictions (mainly after 1941) because books that had been published earlier remained with readers.

During the occupation, film was the most sought-after and compelling cultural medium. Despite the growing dominance of German productions, new Czech films also appeared on cinema screens. Despite censorship and the attempts at Germanizsation, a series of films focused on national themes and, through historical reminiscences, strengthened the Czech nation's self-awareness and defiance. The films featured numerous allusions, allegories and parables, understandable only to Czech film-goers. The other end of the spectrum was represented by comedies, adventures and crime films which offered entertainment and the opportunity to extricate oneself for a moment from the oppressive daily life in the Protectorate. A similar tendency emerged on the theatre stages, as well as in visual art and music. Artists' work expressed worries about the fate of the nation along with faith in its future; they tried to personify its rights in its struggle for survival. Painters and sculptors (František Muzika, František Tichý, Jaroslav Král, Václav Tikal, Jindřich Wielgus, Karel Pokorný and members of the younger generation in groups like Seven in October, Ra and Group 42) were involved in both classic and modern art movements.

6 The Final Stage of the War
and the Restoration of Czechoslovakia

The real possibility of the defeat of Germany and its allies on the European battlefield first appeared in the second half of 1943. At this time, decision making about the post-war form of Czechoslovakia moved to political negotiations abroad, which visibly reflected changes in the relations of the great powers in the anti-Hitler coalition. This fully emerged during Beneš's journey to Moscow in December 1943. In signing a Czechoslovak-Soviet Pact of Friendship, Mutual Aid and post-war Co-operation, E. Beneš affirmed the new elements of Czechoslovak foreign policy, in which the Soviet Union was to be the primary supporter of independence after the war and the guarantor of the secure position of a reborn Czechoslovak Republic in regard to Germany; all this naturally assumed co-operation between East and West. In a series of conversations with representatives of the Czechoslovak Communists, conceptions and plans for the future organization of domestic political relations in Czechoslovakia were crystallized and clarified. President Beneš realized the political risks he was taking on himself, but he assumed that the next government would be a government of the democratic majority, in which he included the Communists. He had no illusions about their attempt to take advantage of post-war radicalism and the growing influence of the Soviet Union. He relied, however, on the fact that a portion of the responsibility for governing would dampen the Communists' revolutionary bolshevism. He also assumed that their participation in government would protect the republic from disruption or, even worse, a civil war. He incorrectly expected that the Soviet Union would not – in accord with the signed agreement – interfere in the affairs of the renewed republic, and had faith in its gradual democratization.

The Moscow negotiations showed both agreement and disagreement between the representatives of the democrats and Communists, the two main currents of the anti-fascist resistance. They agreed that the post-war republic would be founded on the principle of a national front. The left, a bloc of CPCz, ČSD, and ČSNS, would predominate. The Communists objected to the Agrarian Party being represented, so that right from the start, an opposing and moderating political force was weakened. The Communists also demanded the confiscation of the property of traitors and the installation of state administration in large businesses and joint-stock companies. E. Beneš expressed an understanding of these opinions. Controversies emerged during discussions on the character and authority of the new administrative organs – the national committees. Beneš doubted their democratic character, considered them an accommodation to the Soviets, and saw them as a means for the Communists to assert their power; for all these reasons he did not commit himself to a more concrete declaration. The discussion on the question of the Slovak nation's position in the post-war republic was also marked by a degree of disagreement. The Communists took up the justified demand of the Slovaks that the post-war government should recognize Slovak national specificity, while Beneš continued to uphold the notion of a Czechoslovak nation.

JAN GEBHART

The content and breadth of the problems that were negotiated, despite not leading to binding agreements, to a large degree foreshadowed the shape of Czechoslovakia's post-war organization and the possibilities of co-operation between democratic and Communist forces. Though the coming together during the conversations was in the spirit of compromise, their consequence was to predetermine Czechoslovakia's place in the Soviet sphere of influence. In foreign and domestic resistance, the Communists' path to the seizure of unlimited power was opened. The weight of the Communists in the general struggle against the occupiers rose in the final years of the war as a consequence of developments at the front, changes in international relations, and a general social shift to the left. This ideological shift reflected the beliefs of the time regarding the future permeation and co-existence of socialism and democracy.

Even before the war had ended, the democratic and Communist visions of the reborn Czechoslovakia clashed directly on the territory of the Protectorate of Bohemia and Moravia and Tiso's Slovak Republic. The future lives of millions of people, beleaguered by wars and occupations were being decided.

At the start of 1943, the German armies suffered a crushing defeat in Stalingrad which the Czech population of the Protectorate greeted with satisfaction and hope for a quick end to the war and liberation. Otherwise, life in that year was characterized by both a further tightening of the occupation regime (forced labour, K. H. Frank's consolidation of power) and an increase in resistance activities. After overcoming the consequences of the Heydrichiad, the illegal networks were renewed and resistance activity was revived. In comparison to the preceding period, partisan guerilla tactics were taken to a higher level. The activities of the Communists, directed by their 3rd illegal central leadership, influenced this process. They tried to bring the new strategy of a political power struggle to life in the Protectorate. According to the directives of the CPCz's foreign leadership, the partisan movement represented (in accordance with Soviet experiences and orders) not just a form of armed combat, but a tool for the widening of Communist political influence and a means of controlling the emerging national front and, after the war, the state itself. On the initiative of the Communists, partisan units arose in the Brdy region and Moravia in 1943; instructors from the foreign leadership of CPCz were to secure the organization of these units. The rise of the partisan movement was, however, considerably limited by the actions of the occupation security and repressive apparatus from the end of 1943 to the autumn of 1944.

Czechoslovak military units in London also began to intensify their activity at the beginning of 1944. The Staff for the Construction of a Defence Force orchestrated new directions for the preparation and execution of a rebellion, whose realization was entrusted to Czechoslovak parachutists and other waves of parachute units organized in co-operation with the British. The fates of individual parachute units and their members varied. Some were not able to create the necessary base for their activities due to Gestapo harassment; rather under the direction of the Gestapo, they became a means for what became known as radio ploys and the spread of Gestapo's own so-called decoy networks. Others, however, made radio connection with the London central office soon after they landed and, with local illegal organizations (especially with the many-branched and wide-spread Council of Three), created an active and useful network. In the middle of September 1944, parachutists from Operation Wolfram were among the latter group. They were expected to become the core leadership organ of the partisan groups in the northern regions between the Protectorate and Slovakia.

Relations between the individual streams of the Czechoslovak domestic and foreign resistance were most complicated during the preparation and course of the Slovak National Uprising, which was supposed to prepare the ground for a new Slovak future. The consequences of the Bratislava government's many decisions (Slovakia joining the war against the Soviet Union, the break-up of the Slovak army on the eastern front, the worsening of the economic situation and its consequences for Slovak society, the fate of Jewish citizens), along with the erosion of the initial harmony between the majority of the Slovak nation and the domestic authoritarian regime had already started to manifest themselves negatively. The worsening situation was principally caused by the development of the war and the prospect of Germany's defeat. Though opponents to the regime had a difficult time coming together, their rapprochement occurred at the end of 1943, and the idea of a rebellion continued to gain a wider endorsement. At the same time, it illustrated the necessity of resolving conflicts which divided the leadership of individual resistance movements. Of key importance for future developments was the coming together of parts of the national civic resistance from the agrarians (Ján Ursíny), the democrats (Jozef Lettrich, Vavro Šrobár), and the Communists (Karol Šmidke, Gustáv Husák, Laco Novomeský), who concluded a Christmas agreement on the formation of a Slovak National Council (SNC) in December 1943. The political program of the SNC spoke of the battle against German and domestic dictatorship, the assumption and the execution of SNC power, co-operation with the Czechoslovak government in London and the entire Czechoslovak foreign resistance. At the same time, it wrote of a unified state of Czechs and Slovaks based on the equality of the two nations and called for the democratic organization of the future republic.

The uprising in Slovakia was supposed to break out when the Soviet army approached the former Czechoslovak border and the Slovak army was to play a key role. Preparations initially developed along two independent paths, progressing slowly and in secret. The Czechoslovak government in London made contact with both Czechoslovak groups (V. Šrobár) and with officers of the Czechoslovak army (Lieutenant Colonel Ján Golian). The uprising started before all the necessary preparations were made. Co-ordination with the Red Army and with the actions of the partisans acting on their own orders was still not resolved. In the middle of August 1944, partisan units were operating in central and eastern Slovakia and the Slovak regime was not able to suppress them by itself. After the capture and destruction of the German military mission in Martin, the Slovak government gave its assent for the German army to intervene. On 29th August, 1944, the German army started to occupy Slovakia and on the same day Lieutenant Colonel Golian gave the order to fight. Banská Bystrica was the centre of the uprising. A broad territory found itself under the control of the rebel army. After the foiling of the plan to open a Carpathian pass, the territory remained cut off and besieged in the rear of the frontline. Political power was taken by the reconstructed SNC. At the start

454

of October, the leadership of the newly established 1st Czechoslovak army in Slovakia was entrusted to General Rudolf Viest, who had come from London. At the end of September, the 2nd Czechoslovak Independent Paratroop Brigade and the airborne 1st Independent Czechoslovak Fighter Regiment joined the battle.

The rebels' military position became critical in late September and early October of 1944. They lacked heavy weapons and the German army took advantage of its superiority. On 18th–20th October, 1944, German units in Slovakia launched a general offensive. On 27th October, the centre of the uprising, Banská Bystrica, fell; the next day General Viest gave the order to switch to a 'partisan struggle.' The organized rebel territory ceased to exist and with it the rebel army. Over the following months, fierce battles continued in Slovakia. Reprisals by the German occupiers occurred under the watch of official Slovak institutions and representatives, and lasted until the arrival of Soviet units. Partisan leadership was provided by staff directed by Communists, Soviet partisans, and military instructors working towards Soviet interests. The Slovak national uprising represented a fundamental break in developments. With their actions, its participants rejected the Slovak Republic's collaborating regime and committed themselves to a common state of Czechs and Slovaks. Despite its defeat, the uprising contributed to the victory over Germany and laid the foundation of political-power relations in post-war Czechoslovakia.

From 8th September, 1944, the Soviet armies undertook the Carpathian-Dukla operation to aid the Slovak National Uprising, but ran into well-prepared German defences which inflicted heavy losses on the attacking Soviet units and the 1st Czechoslovak Army Corps. The corps originated in the spring of 1944 in Volhynia where the 1st Czechoslovak Independent Brigade had matured and grown with many members of the local Czech colony and Slovak soldiers who had earlier transferred to the ranks of the Red Army and Soviet partisan groups. During the summer, this army corps grew to 16 thousand men under the leadership of General Jan Kratochvíl. In accordance with Soviet directive and under Moscow's influence, Ludvík Svoboda took command of the corps during the deployment in Dukla.

The entrance of Czechoslovak soldiers to the territory of the homeland on 6th October, 1944, was paid for with thousands fallen and wounded. Together with the 38th Soviet army and troops of the 4th Ukrainian front, Czechoslovak soldiers took part in the difficult winter battles in North-Eastern Slovakia until the defensive positions on the Ondava River were captured in December 1944. Czechoslovak soldiers shared in other exacting and sacrifice-filled liberation battles in Slovakia (Liptovský Mikuláš, the battle of the Malá Fatra mountains), where the corps was greatly aided by a mobilization on the liberated territory. At the end of April 1945, a tank brigade and a mixed airborne division of the corps was deployed in the Ostrava operation of the Soviet troops, who had entered and liberated the north Moravian industrial region. As an uprising broke out in the Protectorate, the remaining corps were approaching the borders and, shortly afterward, participated in the cleaning out and liberation of Moravia and Bohemia.

The first weeks of the Slovak National Uprising had provoked a considerable response in the Protectorate of Bohemia and Moravia's territory and saw a new intensification of the activities of resistance forces. From September to October 1944, members of the partisan-organizing parachute units from the USSR landed in the Protectorate. With the help of the local populace, they began to build a partisan region, first in the Czech-Moravian highlands, though a similar region simultaneously emerged in North-Eastern Moravia. Though the interventions and arrests of the Gestapo handicapped the partisans in the winter of 1944 and 1945, the occupiers were not able to stop the development of the partisan movement in the Protectorate. Further parachute units landed in the Protectorate in the spring of 1945.

At the end of 1944 and in February and March 1945, Czechoslovak intelligence agents sent by the London Ministry of National Defence in co-operation with their English-American allies, parachuted in and soon after participated in the preparations and battles of the uprising. In the course of the uprising, Captain Jaromír Nechanský worked in the Czech National Council. However, partisan organizers sent by the commander of the Soviet troops and security organs landed in Bohemia and Moravia in much larger numbers. Most were tasked with reconnaissance, though they simultaneously fulfilled their partisan-organizing role and prepared the installation of a post-war regime governed by the Communists. At the end of March and the beginning of April, new units formed around the parachute brigades whose members arrived at their predetermined sites. At the end of April 1945, new areas of partisan control existed in the Brdy region and in Eastern, Southern, and Northern Bohemia and in South Moravia. Though the partisans did not succeed in organizing a unified staff due to the constant pressure of the occupiers, an increased concentration of German troops, and the movement of the front line, they did in various places influence the rebellion and the liberation of Moravia and Bohemia.

At the end of April 1945, the war in the territory of the Protectorate entered its final phase. The front line moved between the areas of Brno-Vyškov-Žilina and Ostrava. In the west, the first American formations crossed the frontiers of the pre-Munich republic on 18th April and over the following days and after regrouping their forces, they continued their push into the interior of Bohemia. The German command and the occupation administration tried to create conditions that would prevent internal unrest and allow them to continue to battle on the territory of Moravia and Bohemia. To this end, they prepared a defensive plan for the occupied territory, with particular emphasis on the Ostrava region and Prague. Scorched earth tactics began to be applied to territories governed by Germany and everything available was thrown into battle. Starting on 25th April, 1945, all command authority in the Protectorate was transferred to Field Marshal Ferdinand Schörner, the commander of the Central group of armies. Apart from this, representatives of the occupying administration, especially K. H. Frank, tried through political and diplomatic activity (including creating a new Protectorate government, attempts to negotiate with the Americans) to contain the consequences of their military defeat and prevent the eruption of a rebellion.

Preparations for an armed rebellion went forward in several lines: the Czech National Council (Speaker Prof. Albert Pražák), the military command, including Alex (General František Slunečko), Bartoš (General Karel Kutlvašr and Lieutenant Colonel František

456

Bürger), the Communists, and the partisan Council of Three. They were, however, unable to co-ordinate and events overtook them. News of Hitler's suicide, the fall of Berlin, and the reputed presence of the Americans in Prague increased tension, especially in the countryside. At the same time, a crisis was occurring within the occupying regime.

A communication alleging the end of the war served as the impulse for an uprising in Přerov on 1st May, which was put down by the occupiers. In the following days, this spread to Central and Eastern Bohemia, the submountaineous Krkonoše and Brdy regions, and the Plzeň region. A different situation was created in North-Eastern and Southern Moravia in regions around the front lines where partisans launched armed appearances. They succeeded in forming connections with the advancing units of the Red Army, and the Romanian and Polish soldiers who participated in military operations in the company of Soviet troops and, in the case of the town of Vsetín, with soldiers of the 1st Czechoslovak Army Corps.

The spontaneous armed ascent culminated on 5th May with an uprising in Prague headed by the Czech National Council (CNC), presided over by Albert Pražák and a broad range of representatives established at the end of April 1945. Co-operation by the CNC with the Military Command of Greater Prague and employees of both transport authority and radio had considerable significance. Czech Radio broadcasts not only gave the signal for a general uprising both in Prague and throughout the remainder of the occupied lands, but also served as the co-ordinator of the rebel forces. Rebels in Prague achieved a series of victories on the first day; they used the advantage of surprise and put the German forces on the defensive. The 3rd American army launched a push into Bohemia on the morning of 5th May. On that day, its soldiers entered Domažlice, Tachov, and Klatovy, and on the following day, they took Strakonice, Plzeň, and Mariánské Lázně. On 4th May, the Commander of the Expeditionary Forces of the Allies, General Dwight D. Eisenhower, proposed to the Soviet high command that American formations would proceed to the Vltava and Labe rivers. His proposal was rejected and he was told that Soviet troops would begin their Prague operations on 6th May. General Aleksei Innokentievich Antonov asked the Americans to halt their advance along the České Budějovice-Plzeň-Karlovy Vary line. Eisenhower agreed as he respected the position of politicians, who understood the significance of Prague's liberation for the further evolution of Czechoslovakia but feared a rupture in the wartime coalition and, most importantly, the imperilment of further co-operation with the Soviets against Japan in the close of the war.

The uprising in Prague and other areas threatened the plans of the German commanders and the new government of Grand Admiral Karl Dönitz for the rapid withdrawal of forces from the eastern front to the west. In an attempt to ensure a line of retreat, and especially a transport junction in Prague, German units moved in to counter-attack on 6th May, and the situation began to develop badly for the rebel forces. Units of the SS dislocated in Bohemia and several parts of the forces of the Central army group headed to the aid of the isolated German formations in Prague; their advance against the enemy was characterized by pillaging, brutality, and the murder of both prisoners and civilians. Over the following days, the uprising passed a critical period in both Prague and other regions. In the afternoon hours of 6th May, the Vlasov army (the Russian liberation army which had until then fought on the German side) and the formations of the 1st division (Commander Sergei Bunyachenko) intervened in the battle in Prague. They permitted the co-ordination of the German attack on Prague and helped to fortify the defence against the uprising on the left bank of the Vltava on 7th May, the most difficult day. As a result of conflicts with the CNC when they tried to act as an independent political body, they began their exit to the west on the morning of 8th May.

On 7th May, representatives of the Third Reich signed a document of capitulation in Rheims which, after ratification, would come into effect in the first minute of 9th May. In Prague, however, the battles continued on the barricades and not just in outlying districts, but also in the centre of the city itself. Only on 8th May did the consequences of the Rheims capitulation and news of the advance of the Red Army begin to be heard, primarily outside Prague where the unrelenting battle continued to rage. On the afternoon of 8th May, representatives of CNC and, on the German side, General Rudolf Toussaint signed a protocol regarding the implementation of the German armed forces' surrender in and around Prague, which allowed their retreat to the west. This was not in conflict with the Rheims capitulation, as it allowed the movement of German forces until 9th May; what is more, there lay open the genuine danger of an uncontrolled advance of the enemy, especially in the centre of Prague, and of further irreplaceable losses. Ultimately, even the plenary CNC agreed to the protocol. Nevertheless, battles did not stop immediately after the signing of the protocol; violations of the conditions more than once flowed from lack of knowledge of the protocol's contents and from efforts of soldiers to forge the fastest possible path out of Prague.

In the early hours of 9th May , the day after the unconditional surrender of Germany, the first Soviet tanks entered Prague from the north-west. They were soon followed by other units advanced from the north, and behind these formations followed the main tank forces of the Red Army, intent on destroying and cleaning out the remaining pockets of resistance and block all retreat paths. At the end of the day, the 1st, 2nd, and 4th formations of the Ukrainian front met in Prague. On the same day, the first Czechoslovak foreign soldiers stood in Prague; airplanes of the 1st Czechoslovak Mixed Airborne Division landed in Kbely, and a day later members of the 1st Czechoslovak Tank Brigade arrived. On 10th May, the Czechoslovak government, established in the first days of April 1945 in the eastern Slovak town of Košice, flew to Prague and took executive power from the CNC the following day, according to the agreement of the representatives in exile.

The war had ended on the European continent. The basic aim of the Czechoslovak resistance was achieved – the rebirth of the Czechoslovak Republic. The functioning of the President and the new government in the liberated state, however, was to prove to have been predetermined by the symbolic reality that its representatives travelled to Prague not by way of London, but through Moscow and Košice.

JAN GEBHART

Bibliography

AUSKÝ, Stanislav: *Vojska generála Vlasova v Čechách*, Praha 1996.

BORÁK, Mečislav: *Transport do tmy. První deportace evropských židů*, Ostrava 1994.

BRANDES, Detlef: *Der Weg zur Vertreibung 1938–1945. Pläne und Entscheidungen zum "Transfer" der Deutschen aus der Tschechoslowakei und aus Polen*, München 2001.

BRANDES, Detlef: *Großbritannien und seine osteuropäischen Alliierten 1939–1942*, München 1988.

BRANDES, Detlef: *Die Tschechen unter deutschem Protektorat*, I–II, München 1969–1975

BROD, Toman: *Moskva, objetí a pouto. Československo a Sovětský svaz 1939–1945*, Praha 1992.

BURIAN, Michal – KNÍŽEK, Aleš – RAJLICH, Jiří – STEHLÍK, Eduard: *Atentát. Operace Anthropoid 1941–1942*, Praha 2002.

CORNWALL, Mark and EVANS, R. J. W. (eds.): *Czechoslovakia in a nationalist and Fascist Europe (1918–1948)*, Oxford, 2007.

ČELOVSKÝ, Boris: *Mnichovská dohoda 1938*, Praha 1999.

ČERMÁK, Vilém: *Muž proti okupaci. Portrét štábního kapitána Václava Morávka*, Praha 2007.

ČERVINKA, František: *Česká kultura a okupace*. Praha 2002.

DALLEK, Robert: *Franklin D. Roosevelt and American Foreign Policy (1932–1945)*, New York–Oxford 1979.

DEJMEK, Jindřich: *Edvard Beneš. Politická biografie českého demokrata. II. Prezident republiky a vůdce národního odboje (1935–1948)*, Praha 2008.

GEBEL, Ralf: *„Heim ins Reich!" Konrad Henlein und der Reichsgau Sudetenland (1938–1945)*, München 1999.

GEBHART, Jan – KUKLÍK, Jan: *Druhá republika 1938–1939. Svár demokracie a totality v politickém, společenském a kulturním životě*, Praha 2004.

GEBHART, Jan – KUKLÍK, Jan: *Velké dějiny zemí Koruny české, XV, 1938–1945*, Praha–Litomyšl 2006–7.

GLETTLER, Monika – LIPTÁK, Lubomír – MÍŠKOVÁ, Alena (eds.): *Nacionálno-socialistický systém vlády. Ríšská župa Sudety. Protektorát Čechy a Morava. Slovensko*, Bratislava 2002.

HAASIS, Helmut G.: *Tod in Prag. Das Attentat auf Reinhard Heydrich*, Hamburg 2002.

HANÁK, Vítězslav: *Muži a radiostanice tajné války*, Dvůr Králové 2002.

JANEČEK, Jiří: *Válka šifer. Výhry a prohry československé vojenské rozvědky (1939–1945*, Olomouc 2001.

JELÍNEK, Zdeněk: *Operace Silver A*, Praha 1992.

KAPLAN, Jan – UHLÍŘ, Jan B.: *Praha ve stínu hákového kříže*, Praha 2005.

KÁRNÝ, Miroslav: *Konečné řešení. Genocida českých židů v německé protektorátní politice*, Praha 1991.

KÁRNÝ, Miroslav – MILOTOVÁ Jaroslava – KÁRNÁ Margita (eds.): *Deutsche Politik im Protektorat Böhmen und Mähren unter Reinhard Heydrich 1941–1942*. Eine Dokumentation, Berlin 1997.

KLIMEŠ Miloš – LESJUK Petr – MALÁ Irena – PREČAN Vilém (eds.): *Cesta ke Květnu. Vznik lidové demokracie v Československu*. Dokumenty, I–II, Praha 1965.

KOKOŠKA, Stanislav: *Praha v květnu 1945. Historie jednoho povstání*, Praha 2005.

KOPEČNÝ, Petr: *Pozor parašutisté*, Praha 1993.

KOSTA, Jiří – MILOTOVÁ, Jaroslava – ZUDOVÁ-LEŠKOVÁ, Zlatica: *Tschechische und slowakische Juden im Widerstand 1938–1945*, Berlin 2008.

KOURA, Petr: *Podplukovník Josef Balabán. Život a smrt velitele legendární odbojové skupiny „Tři králové"*, Praha 2003.

KRÁL, Václav (ed.): *Die Deutschen in der Tschechoslowakei 1933–1947*. Dokumentensammlung, Praha 1964.

KUKLÍK, Jan (Jr.): *Mýty a realita takzvaných „Benešových dekretů". Dekrety prezidenta republiky 1940–1945*, Praha 2002.

KUKLÍK, Jan (Jr.) – NĚMEČEK, Jan: *Proti Benešovi! Česká a slovenská protibenešovská opozice v Londýně 1939–1945*, Praha 2004.

KURAL, Václav: *Vlastenci proti okupaci. Ústřední vedení odboje domácího 1940–1943*. Praha 1997.

KURAL, Václav – RADVANOVSKÝ, Zdeněk et al.: *„Sudety" pod hákovým křížem*, Ústí nad Labem 2002.

LUŽA, Radomír: *The Hitler Kiss*, Baton Rouge 2002.

LUŽA, Radomír: *The transfer of the Sudeten Germans*, London 1964.

MAMATEY, Viktor – LUŽA, Radomír (ed.): *A History of the Czechoslovak Republic 1918–1948*, Princeton–New York 1973.

MARŠÁLEK, Pavel: *Protektorát Čechy a Morava. Státoprávní a politické aspekty nacistického okupačního režimu v českých zemích 1939–1945*, Praha 2002.

MASTNÝ, Vojtěch: *The Czechs Under Nazi Rule 1939–1942*, New York 1971.

MATÚŠŮ, Marie: *Muži pro speciální operace*, Praha 2004.

MILOTOVÁ, Jaroslava et al.: *Židovské zlato, ostatní drahé kovy, drahé kameny a předměty z nich v českých zemích 1939–1945. Protiprávní zásahy do majetkových práv, jejich rozsah a následné osudy tohoto majetku*, Praha 2001.

NĚMEČEK, Jan: *Od spojenectví k roztržce. Vztahy československé a polské exilové reprezentace 1939–1945*, Praha 2003.

NĚMEČEK, Jan: *Soumrak a úsvit československé diplomacie*, Praha 2008.

NĚMEČEK, Jan (ed.): *Mnichovská dohoda. Cesta k destrukci demokracie v Evropě. – Munich agreement. The way to destruction of democracy in Europe*, Praha 2004.

NĚMEČEK, Jan et al. (ed.): *Od rozpadu Česko-Slovenska do uznání československé prozatímní vlády 1939–1940. 16. březen 1939–15. červen 1940*, Praha 2002.

NĚMEČEK, Jan – NOVÁČKOVÁ, Helena – ŠŤOVÍČEK, Ivan – KUKLÍK, Jan (eds.): *Československo-francouzské vztahy v diplomatických jednáních 1940–1945. Dokumenty*, Praha 2005.

NĚMEČEK, Jan – NOVÁČKOVÁ, Helena – ŠŤOVÍČEK, Ivan – TEJCHMAN, Miroslav (eds.): *Československo-sovětské vztahy v diplomatických jednáních 1939–1945. Dokumenty*, I–II, Praha 1998–1999.

PASÁK, Tomáš: *JUDr. Emil Hácha (1938–1945)*, Praha 1997.

PETRŮV, Hana: *Právní postavení židů v Protektorátu Čechy a Morava (1939–1941)*, Praha 2000.

PREČAN, Vilém (ed.): *Nemci a Slovensko. Dokumenty*, Bratislava 1971.

PREČAN, Vilém (ed.): *Slovenské národné povstanie. Dokumenty*, Bratislava 1965.

PROCHAZKA, Theodor: *The Second Republic: The Desintegratin of Post-Munich Czechoslovakia (October 1938–March 1939)*, New York 1981.

RAJLICH, Jiří: *Jediný československý maršál. Životní osudy Air Marshala a armádního generála (in memoriam) RNDr. Karla Janouška, KCB (1893–1971)*, Brno 2002.

ŠŤOVÍČEK, Ivan – VALENTA, Jaroslav (eds.): *Czechoslovak-Polish Negotiations on the Establishment of Confederation and Alliance. 1939–1944. Czechoslovak Diplomatic Documents*, Prague 1995.

TESAŘ, Jan: *Mnichovský komplex čili Příspěvek k etologii Čechů*, Praha 2000.

TESAŘ, Jan: *Traktát o „záchraně národa". Texty z let 1967–69 o začátku německé okupace*, Praha 2006.

TOMÁŠEK, Dušan – Kvaček, Robert: *Generál Alois Eliáš. Jeden český osud*, Praha 1996.

VONDROVÁ, Jitka (ed.): *Češi a sudetoněmecká otázka: 1939–1945. Dokumenty*, Praha 1994.

ZÁMEČNÍK, Stanislav: *Český odboj a národní povstání v květnu 1945*. Praha 2006.

ZIMMERMAN, Volker: *Die Sudetendeutschen im NS-Staat. Politik und Stimmung der Bevölkerung im Reichsgau Sudetenland (1938–1945)*. Essen 1999.

ZUDOVÁ-LEŠKOVÁ, Zlatica (ed.): *Československá armáda 1939–1945 (plány a skutečnost)*, Praha, 2003.

BUDOVATELSKÝ PROGRAM GOTTWALDOVY VLÁDY — PROGRAM CELÉHO NÁRODA

Projevy poslanců

R. SLÁNSKÉHO, G. KLIMENTA a J. NEPOMUCKÉHO

v Ústavodárném národním shromáždění v rozpravě o vládním prohlášení

10. VII. 1946.

Vydalo kulturně propagační oddělení Ústředního výboru KSČ, Praha

Title page of a brochure published by the Department of Propaganda and Agitation of the CPCz's Central Comittee, which contains the agenda of the government formed under the leadership of Klement Gottwald after the 1946 election (Reconstruction Plan of the Gottwald's Government – A Plan of the Whole Nation) and transcripts of speeches of several communist deputies in the Constituent National Assembly during the government declaration debate. The CPCz's victory created favourable conditions for the party in the decisive fight for the power in the country.

1 Post-war Changes

The years 1945 to 1948 represent a pivotal period in the history of Czechoslovakia. The foundations were laid for the regime of a people's democracy, characterized during its relatively brief duration by three distinctive features: a) it was a new model of regulated democracy, which, for pragmatic reasons, the Soviet Union allowed to exist in its sphere of influence; b) the strongest political party in post-war Czechoslovakia – the Communist Party – openly regarded the new regime as a temporary model on a journey towards Soviet style socialism and to acquiring absolute power; c) the nature of the post-war people's democracy was based on Czechoslovakia's prior historical experience, and was a practical realization of the resistance groups' ideas about rebuilding post-war Czechoslovakia.

From day one, the construction of this regulated democratic system entailed a large number of systemic changes in political, economic and social spheres. They were supposed to do away with the imperfections that the previous liberal system had not been able to cope with, including dangerous political phenomena and social-economic upheavals in particular. Yet, three years of rebuilding Czechoslovakia did not lead to 'democracy with socialist overtones' – a term often used by President Edvard Beneš and his political friends – but culminated in the coup d'état carried out by the Czechoslovak Communists in February 1948.

This historic process of change had been triggered by the liberation of Czechoslovakia in May 1945 and by the renewal of a state shared by Czechs and Slovaks and its political and territorial autonomy (now including the border region, but excluding Subcarpathian Ruthenia). At the time, many Czechoslovak people anticipated major societal transformations that would bring about a welfare state and social justice, democracy and freedom, while ensuring the country's political autonomy. A large number also believed that they were about to see their ideal of a socialist society – a notion they associated with the political line of the CPCz (the Communist Party of Czechoslovakia) – become a reality.

By the spring of 1945, the victory of the anti-Nazi allies over Hitler's Germany, combined with a logical increase of the Soviet Union's influence, as well as its foray into Central Europe, had created conditions conducive to fundamental changes in the political nature of Czechoslovakia. The Czechoslovak-Soviet wartime treaty of alliance signed in Moscow on 12th December, 1943, became one of the defining factors of the country's political transformation. The treaty not only created room for the Soviet Union's Eastern European policy to be modified to promote Soviet interests, but in relation to post-war Czechoslovakia, it mainly provided a boost to the political influence of the Communists. President Beneš and his many political collaborators perceived the treaty as an 'act of diplomacy, complementing and concluding our entire wartime political liberation line,' and as such considered it an important instrument for keeping the political aspirations of the Communists in check.

The transformation of the political face of post-war Czechoslovakia was also significantly determined by the talks held in Moscow about the new Czechoslovak government and its plan. The initiators and driving force behind these talks were the Czechoslovak Communists, who presented their own draft of the government's mission and how the first cabinet was to be made up. The circumstances and location of the talks were heavily influenced by the international developments which had resulted from the outcome of war-time operations, as well as the interests of the anti-Hitler coalition powers; furthermore, they reflected a more profound transformation process taking place in the Czechoslovak exile community. The impending end of WWII and the military engagement of the Red Army in Slovakia and its foray into the Czech Lands marked a significant shift in the focus of Czechoslovak political interests from London to Moscow. This put President Beneš and the Czechoslovak democratic representation in exile in London at a disadvantage. The USSR's growing interest in shaping the foreign and domestic policy of Czechoslovakia as one of the countries belonging to its sphere of interest (the existence of which was by now indisputable) was becoming more and more obvious. All these developments combined to provide a boost to the morale of the Czechoslovak Communists in Moscow. Their hopes of acquiring a significant or majority percentage of power in the reinstated republic – a claim to which they had earned by their active participation in the national resistance movement – were further reinforced in the spring of 1945 by Soviet accomplishments in both international politics and military fronts.

Both Czech and Slovak societies had been profoundly transformed as they entered the peaceful era at the end of spring 1945. The events of the preceding decade had left a deep mark on people's political consciousness. As well as shared or similar experiences, the two nations were dealing with their own distinctive experiences. Together, they had suffered the social consequences of the Great Depression in the early 1930s and lived through the 1938 Munich Agreement and its aftermath, sharing their disappointment over the attitude of the Western allies. In contrast, the complete destruction of Czechoslovakia in March 1939 and its split into two entirely separate territories – the occupied Protectorate of Bohemia and Moravia, and the Slovak Republic – and the ensuing different political experiences, contributed little to the two nations' mutual trust. Nonetheless, the events of the final year of the war, most notably the Slovak National Uprising, breathed new life into the concept of a unified country and of Czechoslovak statehood.

Many citizens' political consciousness had undergone a shift to the left and towards socialism (no matter how different their respective notions of socialism were). This shift occurred for several reasons: the revolutionary atmosphere reigning in Europe and Czechoslovakia before and after the end of WWII; the bleak experience of the 1930s' Great Depression, which had created a demand for a welfare state, associated with socialism by many; the Munich and resistance experience; and the part played by the Soviet Union in defeating the Nazi Germany. Together, they reinforced the people's conviction that the country's foreign policy must be rooted in an alliance with the USSR and that socialism held both great benefits and a great future. The arrival of new social groups – particularly the socially disadvantaged – on the political scene and their rise to power were likewise significant, for it was these groups that associated the improvement of their social status with socialism. Furthermore, the majority of political parties, hobby organizations and public figures professed their support for socialism in their manifestos after the war. Those parties which presented themselves as non-socialist, including the Democratic Party of Slovakia (DS) and the Czechoslovak People's Party (ČSL), claimed to be socially-reformist and even endorsed a number of socialist policies. Nevertheless, the notions that citizens, political parties and public figures harboured about socialism and the character it should eventually assume in Czechoslovakia differed significantly across the board and tended to be vague.

Nationalism, working on a number of levels and in several directions, was a distinctive feature of Czech and Slovak society's political thinking in 1945. It reflected, or perhaps triggered, the rise of a nationalist wave – both nations' reaction to the events and outcomes of the war. Czech society had been profoundly affected by six years of occupation and the loss of national autonomy, while the Slovaks were dealing with the experience of their status in pre-war Czechoslovakia; and both were revelling in an overblown sense of war triumph. Czech nationalism was predominantly characterized by a very intense anti-German sentiment, while Slovak nationalism was for the most part anti-Hungarian. In both cases, nationalist sentiment was highly aggressive and often vented in a way incompatible with democratic principles, particularly with respect to the German and Hungarian ethnic minorities. A strand of Czech nationalism characterized by a lingering Czechoslovakism was also still alive, while many Slovaks harboured fairly strong anti-Czech, as well as anti-Semitic, feelings. Nationalism was expressed not only in ethnic intolerance and mistrust between the two nations, their hostility against Germans and Hungarians, or even their turning towards national histories, but also in overestimating the role of Czechoslovakia in Europe and its historic task of testifying to the viability of fusing the ideas and political systems of the East and West, of democracy and socialism.

Discussions regarding the make-up of the new post-war Czechoslovak government and its programme were held from 22nd to 29th March in Moscow. Among the participants were delegations from the three political parties which had expressly voiced their adherence to socialism in their manifestos: the Communist Party of Czechoslovakia (CPCz), the Czechoslovak Social Democracy (ČSD) and the Czechoslovak National-Socialist Party (ČSNS).

Representatives of the ČSL were also invited, and a delegation representing the Slovak National Council (SNC), including members of the Slovak Communist Party (KSS) and the newly-established Slovak Democratic Party (DS), attended talks concerning Slovakia. One of the outcomes of the talks was an agreement concerning the line-up of the first post-war cabinet. Communists were to take eight ministerial positions; three each went to ČSD, ČSNS and the ČSL; the DS secured four departments, and the cabinet included four independent ministers. Excepting the Slovak ministers, the cabinet members were exclusively enlisted from among exile politicians. The promise that representatives of the Czech national resistance would be added to the line-up was fulfilled neither before nor after liberation. The CPCz took control of important departments, including the Ministries of Interior, Agriculture, and Information. The former Czechoslovak Ambassador to the USSR, Social Democrat Zdeněk Fierlinger, was appointed Prime Minister. The new government of the National Front of Czechs and Slovaks was appointed by President Beneš in Košice on 4th April, 1945. It was also there that the cabinet adopted its agenda on 5th April, 1945; hence its title, The Košice Government Programme.

The new government's plan of action was created by the Communists, who had thoroughly and comprehensively designed it while in their Moscow exile. Representatives of other Czech political parties who took part in the Moscow talks concerning the first post-war government's programme in March 1945 failed to present their own draft. While the London-based Czechoslovak government-in-exile, including its organizational framework, had been in the process of drawing up action plans for the first months after the end of WWII, most were unusable. The leadership-in-exile of the ČSNS and the ČSD did little more than adopt general principles for the set-up of the liberated republic in January and February 1945, listing a number of social reforms that did not contradict the Communist scheme draft.

In his speeches, President Beneš also pushed for the necessary reforms. They were in accordance with his policy of a 'Munich redress,' which had been gradually put together during the war and featured three dominant points: the renewal of Czechoslovakia to its 1937 borders; foreign policy based on an alliance with the USSR as a shield against the German threat; and political and socio-economic reforms that would safeguard the country against another 'Munich.' The most crucial reforms included constructing a new state of Czechs and Slovaks, resolving the issue of ethnic minorities, nationalizing the property of Germans, collaborators and traitors, and eliminating any fragmentation of the political party system by limiting the number of parties. In this respect, Beneš's vision for post-war changes did not go against Communist concepts, and he accepted their government agenda draft with little reservation.

Few passages of the Communist draft aroused disagreement or discussion. Talks were primarily focused on fine-tuning the text wording and on additions to the agenda. An argument of some seriousness occurred in connection with the status of and elections for national committees, and a conflict of great intensity flared up over Slovakia and its national political organs. On 2nd March, 1945, the Presidium of the SNC issued a list of instructions to be followed by its delegation in the talks, based on a federal arrangement of the country. The ČSNS and ČSL representatives contested the SNC's proposal as dangerously dualistic and hazardous for Czechoslovak national unity. Indeed, they went so far as to break off negotiations, thus endangering the government's plan of action. The dispute ended in a compromise. The SNC delegation surrendered their federal idea, leaving it for the parliament to decide, and the opponents accepted a formulation regarding the recognition of the autonomy of the Slovak nation and its national authorities, bestowing upon them great legislative and executive powers. The National Socialists in particular argued for limiting the powers of the SNC, and did not regard the existing Slovak national authorities as a definitive solution. Politically, their resistance was rather short-sighted, as it raised concern among the Slovaks, contributed little to overcoming past disagreements and mistrust between the two nations, and prevented Czech parties from taking 'political root' in Slovakia. Participants in the talks agreed that until the Provisional National Assembly convened, legislative acts were to be enacted by the government and the President in the form of decrees. Thus, a majority of societal reforms that shaped the new regime were enacted and implemented in this manner.

The Czechoslovak government flew to Prague on 10th May, 1945, only hours after the war had ended in Europe. President Beneš arrived in Prague on 16th May. Both the government and the President returned to Prague in the midst of a revolution in the liberated republic. The political atmosphere was characterized by a great wave of civic activity, reflecting the people's joy at the end of the war and the renewal of a free state, as well as their hopes and expectations for future societal changes that were to become central to the revolution. Yet a part of the population – mostly private business owners, including both prominent businessmen and some middle-class entrepreneurs – was apprehensive about the future of the country.

The governmental scheme declared in Košice came to serve as a basis for profound and extensive changes in both political and social-economic domains. It was far from being a recipe for rebuilding and perfecting parliamentary democracy: rather, it was a Communist project for the construction of a new regime. It not only warranted a transition toward rebuilding Czechoslovakia, but was also an attempt to respond to domestic political matters and to deal with the issue of guarantees for the country's security and autonomy. These issues were addressed in statutes concerning, respectively: a foreign-policy oriented towards the Soviet Union; national committees as the new administrative and executive bodies; Czech-Slovak relations; the confiscation of the property of enemies and traitors; and societal purification, along with certain restrictions on democracy. Other important points formulated included the need for economic revitalization, employment guarantees and the provision of a welfare system and health care.

Among the major tasks facing the new Czechoslovak government was the territorial reinstatement of the country following six years of Nazi occupation. The country's borders were eventually renewed, though not in their exact pre-Munich form, as former Subcarpathian Ruthenia was ceded – under Soviet pressure – to the USSR after the war. This act was confirmed by a Czechoslovak-Soviet treaty signed on 29th June, 1945. The process of reconstituting the republic's territorial integrity was marked by further obstacles regarding settling the border-area and ethnic-relation issues. For example, a major Czechoslovak-Polish border dispute, chiefly concerning the Těšín region, was to remain unresolved. The Czechoslovak government was likewise unsuccessful in its efforts to incorporate areas inhabited by Lusatian Serbs in Germany, while Austria's response to Czechoslovak territorial demands within Austria was similarly negative.

The traditional democratic model of the division of power was significantly circumscribed and modified after 1945. The National Front had become a new political basis for the regime of people's democracy in Czechoslovakia, and a distinctive feature of the new political system was the non-existence of opposition. Furthermore, the government, President and provisional parliament (as elected in delegation elections on 28th October, 1945,) were not the only organs of political power in Czechoslovakia: they were now complemented by Slovak national authorities, including the SNC and Board of Commissioners (BC); lastly, a specific role in the nascent post-WWII political system was played by national committees.

The existence of the SNC and BC, and the power they exercised, were supposed to reflect the equal status of the Slovak nation within the country. Ever since the Slovak National Uprising, these organs had enjoyed great legislative and executive authority, which was now being curbed and passed to central authorities. In conclusion, although most issues concerning the position of Slovakia in the Czechoslovak state remained unresolved after 1945, the recognition of equality of both the Slovak nation and its political organs represented a new element in the political hierarchy, or political system, of the post-war republic.

A network of local government organs was growing throughout the country (district and local community committees, along with two provincial committees in the Czech Lands, between 1945 and 1948), which were both a new and characteristic feature of the new regime's political system. The government tried to limit their activity to following its agenda, insofar as major societal transformations were concerned. The degree of power enjoyed by these local organs was, nevertheless, significant: in addition to having decision-making authority, they also controlled the executive administrative apparatus. National committees became a major arena for political battles. Until the parliamentary elections in May 1946, representation of political parties on the committees was parity-based; after the elections, the national committees were configured based on election results.

In a system in which such major changes in power distribution were taking place, the government's position could not remain unaltered. Extensive powers were now concentrated in its hands: unlimited political power and, following the nationalization of the industrial and banking sectors in October 1945, a decisive share in economic power. The Provisional National Assembly convened on 28th October, 1945, creating a single chamber; the previously-existing Senate was not renewed. After the elections in May 1946, it was renamed the Constituent National Assembly and charged with the responsibility of designing, discussing and adopting a new constitution which would entrench all the post-war changes.

A significant tool and an emergency measure in the country's post-war reconstruction were the Decrees of the President of the Republic, issued between 1940 and 1945. They had the power of laws and were issued to aid in solidifying the autonomy of Czechoslovakia, to rectify the wrongs of the war, to ensure the country's security, and to implement important economic and social changes. The period of decree legislation, which had been necessitated by wartime conditions and in which the government played an active legislative role, was limited to the duration of WWII and the ensuing post-war period, until the formation of the Provisional National Assembly in October 1945.

Many of the presidential decrees issued in 1945 were largely concerned with rebuilding both political and public life, and their execution affected the atmosphere in post-war Czechoslovak society. Along with the nationalization decrees, those related to penal law and confiscations were of great importance. The latter dealt primarily with the issue of Germans and Hungarians living in Czechoslovakia, but were also directed at punishing Czech and Slovak traitors and Nazi collaborators.

The penal law decrees introduced retribution as a method of punishing crimes committed during the war and under Nazi occupation. Emergency people's courts were set up for just this purpose. The most notable people's court trial was the K. H. Frank trial, held in the spring of 1946 in Prague. For special cases concerning particularly prominent, high-ranked offenders on the home front (such as members of protectorate governments, or the Slovak President Jozef Tiso), National Courts were set up, one in Prague and another in Bratislava. A majority of the prominent trials handled by the National Court and emergency people's courts were marked by institutional political interference in their preparation and proceedings, particularly by the government and the SNC. In a number of cases, matters related to retribution lawsuits became a subject of contention between representatives of the existing political parties in these institutions. The most intense disputes regarding punishment level and sentence length were elicited during trials of Protectorate cabinet members and the trial of Jozef Tiso.

The period of retribution trials in Czechoslovakia proceeded in three stages: the first and principal stage ended in the Czech Lands on 4th May, 1947, and in Slovakia on 31st December, 1947; the second phase, in which the authority of the retribution courts was passed to regular courts, ended on 1st January, 1948; the last stage was carried out entirely under the baton of the CPCz, which, after the February coup, decided, for reasons relating to power politics, to make the retribution decrees retroactive for one year, from 2nd January to 31st December 1948. During the first phase up to May 1947, as many as 22,078 people received sentences, including 713 death penalties; in Slovakia, of a total of 8,055 sentences, 65 were death penalties. In the entire period to the end of 1948, the total number of sentences based on retribution norms was 33,463, of which 819 death penalties were imposed by the end of 1948. Of the total number of persons convicted between 1945 and 1948 due to the retribution decrees, nearly 30% were Czechs and Slovaks, 53% Germans, with the rest comprising other nationalities, mostly Hungarian. The National Court in Prague tried 83 persons and handed down 18 death sentences, as opposed to 17 death sentences out of a total of 83 trials for the Bratislava National Court. While the retribution trials were a rightful way to punish indisputable transgressors, they also became a platform for the dangerous settling of personal and political scores.

The post-war Czechoslovak political system acquired a major political organ in the form of the National Front. It became one of the most important political factors in the country, while functioning as a foothold of, and the most important element in, the new political system. The National Front had been formed during WWII as a base for establishing connections between the anti-fascist forces and providing a platform for their collaboration both at home and abroad. When the war ended, the National Front became a specific government coalition, and the CPCz attempted to transform it into a politically powerful institution with a fixed organizational structure. The Communists suggested that prominent mass organizations – particularly those over which they held sway, such as trade unions and unions of guerrilla fighters – should become its members. They met with resistance from their political partners, and failed to achieve their objective until February 1948. The CPCz was similarly unsuccessful in its efforts to create a socialist core in the National Front, in the form of a bloc of three socialist parties. The existence and sphere of activity of this core was intended to oblige the ČSD and ČSNS and to champion revolutionary measures in both the government and National Front. By eliminating the principle of opposition, the National Front put strict limitations on one of the pillars of democracy. Its superior power position was also reinforced by the fact that it stood apart from both the Parliament and democratic control mechanisms.

The few political parties operating in the reborn Czechoslovakia followed either a socialist or socially-reformist agenda, or were not prepared to stand in the way of post-war transformations, regardless of their own critical view of many social processes and changes in the system. Opposition was non-existent, though nominally considered an option. The respective simplified party systems were different in the Czech Lands and Slovakia. In May 1945, four Czech parties resumed their activities in full: the ČSNS, ČSL, ČSD and the CPCz. These parties had been active before 1938 and their new leaderships had been formed in exile during WWII. In Slovakia, there had been two political parties in existence before the end of WWII, with the DS a new-comer. It had been formed in the autumn of 1944 during the Slovak National Uprising, out of a political movement known as the Civic Bloc. Then there was the Communist Party of Slovakia (KSS), which operated as a formally independent party from 1939 until 1948. The party system in Slovakia had earlier, during the Slovak uprising, undergone reduction and simplification. The DS was formed out of several resistance groups and movements, all of which shared a non-communist characteristic. In 1944, the KSS merged with a part of the Slovak Social Democratic Party. The formation of a number of small Slovak parties prior to the 1946 elections did not bring any change or solution to this state of affairs; the Liberty Party, with pro-Czechoslovak and Christian democratic leanings, and the Labour Party, with social democratic tendencies, could not seriously threaten the position of the non-communist DS. Neither right-wing parties, nor parties representing ethnic minorities, were re-established in either part of the country.

Post-war political parties formed the National Front government and also had a significant bearing on state policies. Their mass membership at the time testifies to their influential position in society: the CPCz recruited over a million members in a short time, the ČSNS had over half a million members, the ČSL boasted a membership of around 400,000, the ČSD had some 350,000 members, and the DS had nearly 300,000 members.

Four of the above political parties adhered to socialism in their agendas; however varied their understanding of the term may have been, they all regarded it as a socially just system that had won the hearts of many people in post-war Czechoslovakia. The Communists had embraced the current Soviet, Stalinist model of totalitarian communism; in 1946, however, they were still – for tactical reasons – publicly endorsing a specifically Czech route to socialism, free of the dictatorship of the proletariat or revolutionary violence. The Social Democrats talked of 'democratic socialism' based on the public ownership of manufacturing industry on the one hand, and of small and medium private enterprises on the other, as well as of land reform and an extensive welfare state, all rooted in parliamentary democracy. The National Socialists put primary emphasis on the provision of basic civil liberties and political rights, and were advocates of the nationalization of major manufacturing enterprises and natural resources, while consistently insisting on the protection of individual private property and on the support of entrepreneurship. The two non-socialist parties – the ČSL and the DS – did not reject the necessary social reforms and they supported their implementation, though not without qualification.

A new element was added to the political system of post-war Czechoslovakia in the form of hobby and mass social organizations. Members of the resistance had agreed that political parties would no longer set up their own party-affiliated hobby organizations, and that these should instead be organized in a non-partisan, nationwide fashion. The principle of administrative unity endowed them with an impressive political and social momentum. At the same time, political parties began to fight each other over both political control of these organizations and the assumption of important positions in their administration. The Revolutionary Trade Union Movement, the most powerful mass organization with nearly two million members (mostly factory workers and professionals), and deeply influenced by the CPCz, became a major political force. Some trade unionists were calling for making trade unions equal partners to the government – a demand supported by a number of cabinet officials. Resistance organizations were another important player in the political arena, and the list of major mass organizations further included two agriculture unions (one Czech and one Slovak), the Union of Czech Youth, which survived for only a year, and sports and physical education clubs, which were, however, never united under one umbrella. The non-Communists maintained their influence in the agrarian organization known as the United Syndicate of Czech Agricultural Workers, and in physical-education organizations, particularly the large Sokol movement.

A major issue of Czechoslovak domestic and foreign policy in the first years after WWII was finding a solution to the problems concerning ethnic minorities. In particular, the idea of the expulsion of Germans seemed to act as a unifier for the National Front. The Potsdam

Conference resolution of August 1945, which validated the expatriation of Germans from Czechoslovakia, was, nevertheless, preceded by the 'wild expulsion' or forced migration of the German population. This was accompanied by violent acts against Germans. The most notorious anti-German excesses included what became known as the Brno Death March of 30th May, 1945, when over 20,000 Germans were forced to leave the city immediately and march to the Austrian border (hundreds of people died, primarily of dysentery); the massacre of Horní Moštěnice near Přerov on 18th June, with 265 German civilians shot to death; and the anti-German pogrom in Ústí nad Labem, which took place on 31st July, 1945. Disturbingly, similar acts of violence, both small- and large-scale, were occurring in many other places.

At the time, the Czechoslovak government declared that 2.5 million ethnic Germans must be expatriated, even though this was clearly going to cause an economic loss. The organized expulsion of Germans from the Czechoslovak Republic was carried out, for the most part, during 1946, under the supervision of the allied Control Commission. 'Additional transfer' was carried out between 1947 and 1948, with the goal of uniting divided families. In total, nearly 3 million Germans left Czechoslovakia after the war. This included some 660,000 persons driven out during the 'wild expulsion' – a series of acts halted by the Czechoslovak government in late June 1945, after protests from the American and British governments. Nearly 2,250,000 persons were expatriated as part of the organized transfer, and an additional 80,000 Germans left during the later transfer. By the end of 1948, some 185,000 ethnic Germans were left on Czechoslovak soil – mostly anti-fascists, several tens of thousands of 'indispensable professionals' (including glassmakers, miners, textile workers, and agricultural workers, who were excluded from the transfer for economic reasons), as well as people from mixed marriages. A large number of these people subsequently opted for voluntary emigration, especially to the Federal Republic of Germany.

The tense anti-German atmosphere in Czechoslovakia after the war was first and foremost a direct public and political response to the recent attempted genocide of the Czech nation and the subsequent persecution of the public. However, it was also an expression of a post-war nationalist sentiment, stemming from long-standing Czech-German discord. Between 1938 and 1945, some 360,000 Czechoslovak nationals lost their lives through the actions of the German occupiers. This number included people killed in concentration camps, persons who died prematurely due to the harsh living conditions, civilian casualties of bomb attacks and front line advancement through Czechoslovak territory, as well as citizens executed during reprisal campaigns. Added to all this were the Czechs, Slovaks, and members of other ethnicities who died as a result of direct military engagement with the enemy on various WWII fronts and in guerrilla operations, the Slovak National Uprising in the fall of 1944, and the May 1945 uprising in the Czech Lands. In addition to causing a grievous loss of life and depriving the nation of its freedom, Nazi occupation militarized and germanized the Czech economy, planned a 'final solution' to the Czech question, restricted the Czech school system and culture, and racially persecuted Jews and Roma, orchestrating their mass murder in murderous concentration camps. In the Protectorate of Bohemia and

Moravia alone, 80,000 Jews fell victim to Nazi persecution, along with 70,000 Slovak Jews and tens of thousands of Jews from the Hungarian-occupied territories of southern Slovakia and Subcarpathian Ruthenia. Of the total of 19,000 Roma murdered in the Auschwitz-Birkenau concentration camp, nearly 5,000 were Czech nationals.

Another issue relating to political power that remained unresolved in February 1948 was finalizing the new design of the Czech-Slovak relations and their institutional organization. The conditions were unfavourable for the Slovak proposal to organize the country on a more or less federative basis. The Czech National Council, formed shortly before the end of the war as the supreme body of resistance and power in the Czech Lands, was – to all intents and purposes – destroyed at the instigation of the Soviets. The Czech ministers were very much opposed to the idea of federation, apprehensive of an institution that would potentially curb the power of the government. As a result, Czech-Slovak relations were arranged asymmetrically. Slovak national organs, including the SNC and the BC, exercised their authority in Slovakia, while the Czech Lands were governed by the central state government, which was able to use the asymmetry to both regulate and limit the power of the Slovak organs.

At first, the Slovak organs had extensive power at their disposal, a fact acknowledged in the First and Second Prague Agreements, signed in June 1945 and April 1946, respectively, by the government and the SNC. Major modifications were introduced after the 1946 general election, which the DS won in Slovakia by a wide margin. Communists cleverly took advantage of the Czech political parties' fears, which saw in Slovakia's emancipation efforts the threat of dualism that could undermine the country's unity. The Third Prague Agreement of June 1946 dramatically restricted the Slovak authorities' power, in favour of the central institutions, while in November 1947, during a staged political crisis in Slovakia, the Communists pushed through further restricting amendments to the Third Prague Agreement.

The Košice Government Programme's economic division emphasized several major tasks that lay ahead: ensuring a speedy recovery for the national economy, which had been devastated during the war; laying foundations for a new social policy 'to the benefit of all strata of the working class;' and converting to governmental ownership the property of 'Germans, Hungarians, collaborators and traitors,' with the exception of German and Hungarian anti-fascists. Land confiscated from traitors was to be subjected to land reform. The government declared its utmost determination to 'bring before a court of law the traitors amongst bankers, industrialists, and big land owners,' as well as the urgent need to 'bring the entire financial and credit system, key industrial enterprises, the insurance industry, and natural and energy resources under the general administration of the state.' Although not explicitly requested in the agenda, nationalization was generally expected to take place, while its scope and manner were to be decided once the entire country was liberated.

The property of enemies and traitors came under national administration and was managed either by individuals (tradesmen's workshops, stores and farmsteads) or collective organs (major businesses).

In industry alone, with the exception of crafts, as many as 9,045 businesses with 923,000 employees had been placed under national administration by the end of August 1945. National administration was also imposed in cases where the functioning of businesses was at risk owing to the absence of owners who had not yet returned from exile, concentration camps, etc. A large percentage of property under national administration was subsequently confiscated in October 1945. Land owned by traitors had already been expropriated in June 1945. There were two ways to administer confiscated property – it could be either nationalized, or re-privatized. The decision slowly crystallized to transfer small and medium-sized agricultural, crafts, and commercial businesses into the private hands of new owners or co-operative societies, while large businesses were to be nationalized. This decision corresponded to the overall economic philosophy of the ongoing revolution, which envisaged the existence of a multi-sector economy when the time was right: it was to be a combination of the public sector, small-scale production units, and limited private, capitalist entrepreneurship.

As of mid-1945, the political issue of the day was a push for the nationalization of major non-agricultural private property. This demand was most notably championed by the Communists, Social Democrats and the Revolutionary Trade Union Movement. When the nationalization decrees were being drawn up – a process in which representatives of various political parties participated – it appeared that their ratification by the cabinet would go smoothly and the president would sign them before 20th September, 1945. However, cabinet discussions on the decrees in September and October 1945 indicated serious objections on the part of the non-socialist parties, concerning primarily the scale, pace, and form of nationalization.

The ministers representing the National-Socialist, People's and Slovak Democratic parties were not prepared to pass the proposals in a routine manner, as the Communists and Social Democrats had hoped, and they tried to introduce changes. As for the scope, the CPCz and ČSD championed large-scale nationalization that would yield a strong, comprehensive economic sector which would play a decisive role in the economy. The other parties were at first in favour of a 'national limit' – in other words, a scope of nationalization that would only affect major enterprises owned by Germans, collaborators, and traitors. Arguments against large-scale nationalization were partly based on a fear of the resulting monopoly of the nationalitzed sector and its natural tendency to restrict economic competition and the spirit of enterprise; a concern that it would pose a threat to private entrepreneurship and the existence of mid-sized businesses; and qualms about the bureaucracy involved in managing the nationalized sector. Opponents were also concerned that a powerful state sector with strong monopolistic tendencies would support identical tendencies in the domain of power politics, that it could strengthen the government's power and become a threat to the democratic principles of governance. They were also concerned about the technical and organizational perspective. The problem of providing qualified personnel, expertise and an organizational framework for the nationalization process was a recurring theme, and even staunch proponents of large-scale nationalization admitted the validity and seriousness of such concerns.

Another contentious issue was the pace of nationalization. Originally, all political parties and President Beneš believed the process should proceed in stages, but they differed widely on the particulars. Both Communists and Social Democrats soon changed their minds and began pushing for a one-step act. The rest were in favour of carrying out the 'national scope' first, and only then – based on experiences drawn from it – determine the next step.

The form of nationalization presented a third point of controversy. Proponents of nationalization as the only option stood against supporters of the idea that minor businesses be taken over by co-operatives or national committees. Eventually, the Communists and Social Democrats managed to push through nationalization as the sole option, against ministers from the other parties and Václav Majer, the Social-Democratic Minister of Nutrition. The dispute concerning compensation for nationalized property was handled reasonably smoothly by the government. Some economists representing the Central Council of Trade Unions and the CPCz championed the idea of nationalization without compensation. In the end, the government agreed to nationalize the property of Germans, collaborators and traitors without compensation, and other property with compensation.

Nationalization took place based on four presidential decrees of 24th October, 1945. The first provided a basis for nationalizing key and major industries, while the other decrees nationalized the food industry, joint-stock banks, and insurance companies. The film industry, including the import, export, and distribution of films, had been nationalized earlier. In the industrial sector, nationalization affected all enterprises operating in key domains, as well as other large businesses (those with 150–500 employees). In some domains, the limit for nationalization was determined by the production facilities' capacity. In particular, mines, independent power plants, gas works, steelworks, rolling mills, munitions factories, cement works, pulp mills, and major chemical industries were nationalized in full.

The total number of nationalized enterprises amounted to 3,000, employing 61% of the industrial workforce in March 1947. The production capacity of the nationalized enterprises represented nearly two thirds of the Czechoslovak industrial potential. The actual share of the public sector in industry was even higher, if the communal and co-operative owned businesses, which had been state-owned before, are taken into account. A final decision was still pending as to the fate of those industrial seizures, now state-administered, which were smaller in size than the limit set for nationalization. Their re-privatization would have strengthened the capitalist sector, since they employed roughly 15% of the industrial workforce. In 1947, the government passed a resolution ordering that all confiscated industrial property remaining was to be preferentially incorporated into national enterprises or placed under municipal administration.

The nationalization of banks and insurance companies also had a major economic impact. All joint-stock banks and private insurance houses were gradually placed in state hands, leaving only co-operative and publicly owned financial institutions un-nationalized, as far as the financial sector was concerned.

The management and activities of national enterprises in the first post-war years were essentially under the control of workers and other employees, imposed through workers' councils, trade union organizations, and direct representation on the enterprises' management boards. The wide-ranging powers of the workers' councils were guaranteed by a decree that came into force alongside the nationalization decrees. According to the decree, the CEOs of national enterprises could not be appointed without the approval of the Central Council of Trade Unions. Also, a third of the members of every managing board were selected from among and elected by employees, and two thirds were appointed by super-ordinate organs, following a consultation with the Central Council of Trade Unions.

The organizational structure of national enterprises at that time boasted many advantages when compared to the post–1948 practice. Employees were involved in the decisions made by activities of their companies and did not feel alienated, as they one day would. The national enterprises were run as commercial businesses, with their respective economic results, profits, and possible losses and subsidies being public knowledge. Nationalization was perceived as an act of social justice and resulted in better work ethic – a fact reflected in the success of post-war industrial reconstruction. The agenda of the new government formed after the 1946 election included a statement explaining that the government considered the nationalization of manufacturing industry completed. This was supposed to create a stable perspective for private entrepreneurship in the industrial domain, but it also hinted at the possibility of nationalising the sphere of exchange – in other words, foreign trade, mass trade, and the largest department stores.

A major component of the economic transformation in post-war Czechoslovakia was land reform. It was implemented in three stages, two of which were legislated before February 1948. The first phase was centred around the expropriation of land owned by Germans, Hungarians, collaborators, and traitors (regardless of the acreage) and its subsequent re-distribution to Czech and Slovak applicants (from 1945 to 1946 in the Czech Lands, and from 1945 to 1948 in Slovakia). The confiscated farming land was, for the most part and in accordance with the strong tradition of private ownership, turned into smallholdings. State farms and cattle-breeding co-operatives began cultivating some of the expropriated land, located mainly in the less fertile, foothill areas of the Czech border region.

With the exclusion of Hungarian farmers' land, which was exempt from confiscation in 1948 and 1949, land reform affected 2,946,000 hectares (ha) of land, including 44% of forests; this area represented nearly a fourth of Czechoslovakia's total area. A total of 1,241,000 ha of land were acquired by 303,000 persons, while the remaining land, mostly forests, went to the state, municipalities, and co-operatives. In places with enough land (the Czech border region in particular), medium-sized farming estates were being established, with an area of about 10 ha each, while the maximum allotment size was 13 ha. All those who acquired land through this reform were obliged to cultivate it themselves; leasing and alienation of land were prohibited. In the Czech Lands, the first stage of the reform resulted more or less in a demise of the agricultural working class employed on large private farm-steads, as these workers became free farmers. The first stage of land reform most notably affected the conditions in the Czech border region, where the majority of the land seized from expatriated Germans was located, and the area became an attractive destination for some Slovaks who had been disenchanted by the small scale of land reform in Slovakia. Indeed, land reform took a different course in the two parts of the country: in the Czech Lands, it affected 28% of agricultural land, compared to a mere 9% in Slovakia, where the anticipated expatriation of ethnic Hungarians did not take place. The course and outcome of the first phase of agricultural reform became a controversial issue. Non-communist parties criticized the Communists for using the reform to their own partisan advantage and later also highlighted the economic losses, the low capability of the settlers, the excessively large area of fallow land, and the insufficient allotment size.

The 1946 government plan of action envisaged the implementation of the second stage of land reform, that is, a re-examination of the pre-Munich land reform by the consistent application of legal measures from the years 1919 to 1921. According to a bill passed in July 1947, the area of any private or church-owned farming estate was to be limited to 150 ha of farming land, or 250 ha of all land (including forests). In addition to that, residual estates were to be either liquidated or significantly reduced, as their formation was not in keeping with the letter of the law passed after WWI. Land confiscation based on the bill passed in 1947 was implemented partly before and partly after 25th February, 1948. According to aggregate data from March 1949, over one million hectares of land had been taken over, 28% of which was farming land. The tenure of 61,000 ha of farming land was left to the original owners, while the rest went to small-scale farmers, state farms, municipalities, and agricultural co-operatives. Most forest land was acquired by the state.

2 Life in Post-war Czechoslovakia

The everyday life of the Czechoslovak population was heavily politicized, in part by the euphoria of victory – a natural consequence both of the country's liberation and the defeat of the brutal and despised German Nazi regime – that lasted several months. New economic and political developments enjoyed widespread, enthusiastic support, yet there were also voices of concern and doubts about what such changes might bring about.

Surely, the quotidian post-war reality was influenced above all by the dismal state of the country's economy and its problems, mainly concerning the supply of goods and the provision of essential social security for the population. War-time bank deposits made by the population were blocked by the banks, and goods all over the country were still being supplied through a controlled rationing system. The shortage of flour, sugar, eggs, and cooking fat continued. The supply of meat was similarly complicated, making it necessary for nearly all Protectorate regulations concerning the management of livestock production, distribution, meat processing, and rationing to be kept in effect through 1946. The situation went from bad to much worse after a poor harvest and drought of the summer 1947.

Among the pre-requisites for the successful rebuilding of the country's economic life was the monetary reform of November 1945. A single currency was reinstated, and the remainder of the war-time separate currencies was partly eliminated and blocked; until this time, following the end of the war, the money circulating in Czechoslovakia included

Protectorate notes, money issued by the former Slovak State, German marks, Hungarian pengös, as well as 'crown vouchers' that had been issued by the Czechoslovak Monetary Authority after liberation and used by both the allied armies and the Czechoslovak army and authorities.

The government increased the salaries of women and youths and, in November 1945, carried out wage reforms. The reform measures were, however, directed toward wage levelling, thereby disrupting the existing wage structure that had respected the employees' qualifications. In December 1945, child benefits and a Christmas salary bonus were introduced, and the paid-time-off package was extended by 7 to 12 days. Bolder interventions aimed at restoring the currency, as suggested by experts, were not implemented for fear of social consequences. The plan to gradually valorize the population's wartime savings, both blocked and depreciated, also came to nothing. The simultaneous increase of both prices and wages, on the other hand, aroused discontent and social tension. The volume of production at the time was only half the level of the pre-war years, indicating that production had not yet managed to yield enough value to cover the cost of the social measures that were being introduced.

The defeat of Nazi Germany brought a collapse of its forced labour system. Immediately after liberation, hundreds of thousands of employees left their prescribed jobs. Women returned to their households, and a percentage of the country's youth embarked on secondary-school and university studies that had been interrupted or made impossible by the occupation. Many employees returned to their former workplaces or looked for other, better jobs. The reconstruction of the economy required a large labour force. Both the labour market and the make-up of post-war society were deeply affected not only by the expulsion of Germans and the resettlement of the border region by the Czech and Slovak population, but also by the repatriation of persons formerly deported – either for forced labour or to concentration camps and prisons – to Germany; by the re-immigration of countrymen from Volhynia in the USSR, Romania, Hungary, Yugoslavia, and some Western European countries; and, last but not least, by the arrival of a relatively small number of guest workers from abroad. In October 1945, a decree regarding the work duty of Czechoslovak citizens came into force, allowing for any man or woman to be hired for urgent jobs for up to 12 months, without their original employee contract expiring. Two related decrees followed, concerning the work duty of the Germans and Hungarians who had lost their Czechoslovak citizenship, as well as those Czechs and Slovaks who had applied for German or Hungarian citizenship during the occupation era. In the summer months of 1946, when approximately 14,000 Germans were being expatriated from the country daily, tension in the job market reached its peak, as the existing, more-or-less voluntary forms of labour force distribution proved insufficient. A particularly critical situation arose in agriculture, resulting in numerous voices calling for slowing the expatriation of Germans; as a result, a small number of the German workforce was exempt from expulsion, precisely for the above reasons.

Particularly memorable for people in Czechoslovakia were the free supplies delivered by the UNRRA (United Nations Relief and Rehabilitation Administration), which had been founded in 1943 with the purpose of providing economic and humanitarian aid to countries damaged during WWII. The UNRRA campaign's role was irreplaceable both in terms of food and clothing aid, and in boosting the post-war reconstruction of the Czechoslovak national economy. Between 1945 and 1947, as part of the food programme alone, the UNRRA delivered nearly 800,000 tonnes of various commodities. Fifty percent of the total was made up of grains and flour, followed by meat, canned meat and fish, milk, soap, coffee, and cocoa. The local people's diet was enriched by foods which had been completely unavailable during the war, such as rice, spaghetti, peanut butter, cinnamon, and different kinds of tea. Children received chocolate, peanuts, sweets, as well as canned fruit, fruit juice, apple sauce, and jam. Powdered milk was available on prescription. Furthermore, the UNRRA deliveries covered nearly 33% of the national demand for edible fat and oil. Of great importance was the free supply of medical equipment and medications. Penicillin, which was not produced in Czechoslovakia at the time, was particularly appreciated. The ethical aspect of the campaign, it should be noted, also played an important part.

The great pre-WWII ethnic variety of the Czechoslovak population had changed beyond recognition. A majority of the Jewish community had been exterminated, and most Germans expatriated; only the expulsion of Hungarian citizens was not carried out, partly due to the protests of Western heads of states. By February 1946, lengthy negotiations had given rise to a Czechoslovak-Hungarian agreement on population exchange, but it failed to meet the expectations it had raised. In contrast, a re-Slovakization campaign, instructing Hungarians to profess Slovak nationality, was carried out on a mass scale. This practice was criticized by the international community, as was the following attempt at domestic colonization by relocating Hungarian citizens from Southern Slovakia to the Czech border region. The efforts to destroy the Hungarian minority resulted in more than 300,000 Hungarians being re-Slovakized, over 70,000 of them 'exchanged,' and more than 44,000 forcibly relocated. The steps taken by the government created tension and sometimes open hostility in Czechoslovak-Hungarian relations, accompanied by feelings of national injustice and dissatisfaction on the part of the victims of the unfair treatment.

After WWII, the Polish ethnic minority in Czechoslovakia was concentrated primarily in the ethnically mixed part of the Těšín area. Their situation during the years 1945 to 1947 was heavily influenced by the Czechoslovak-Polish border dispute over this region, which remained a part of Czechoslovakia, and the dispute over former German territories that had been given to Poland (the Kłodzko, Glubczyce, Racibórz, and Koźle regions.) This tension was perpetuated by ethnic squabbles and minor border incidents, as well as various manifestations of power and unresolved issues on both sides. These included a major Polish propaganda campaign for incorporating the Těšín region into Poland; the return of Czech repatriates; preparations for the expatriation of some 6,000 so-called Polish invaders – Polish people who had settled in the Těšín region during Polish annexation between 1938 and 1939 – and the unsuccessful attempts to resume the activities of Polish clubs. The situation did not improve until 10th March, 1947, when Czechoslovakia and Poland, prompted by the USSR, signed the Treaty of Friendship and Mutual Aid. Among other things, the treaty allowed another two years for the final determination of the hitherto disputed state border (though the dispute was not, in fact, resolved until the late 1950s). The treaty was accompanied by an appendix determining the rights of the Polish ethnic minority in Czechoslovakia, including the right to establish the Polish Association for Culture and Public Education and the Polish Youth Association, the right to develop a Polish-language school system, Polish co-operatives, etc.

Czechoslovak citizens who professed Ukrainian, Ruthenian, or Russian nationality after 1945 had often participated in the domestic and foreign anti-fascist resistance movements. They secured numerous positions in both district and local national committees in Northeast Slovakia and were hired for state service. They not only enjoyed all civil rights but – unlike the other minorities – obtained some additional minority rights. The Ukrainian National Council of Priasevcina (UNCP) was founded on 1st March, 1945. After a brief period where the incorporation of Northeast Slovakia into the Soviet Socialist Republic of Ukraine was considered, the Council assumed a pro-Czechoslovak stance, and maintained a parliamentary presence in both the Provisional National Assembly and the SNC until the 1946 elections. Until 1951, the UNCP published its own paper, actively participated in developing a school system for its ethnic group, and was active in the spheres of culture and public education. It played a positive role in war damage repair and in the region's reconstruction. Yet, despite a great effort on the part of its leaders, neither the UNCP nor other institutions of this ethnic minority managed to be incorporated into the country's legal system.

The reintegration of the Jewish population into the life of Czech and Slovak society was marked by difficulties of its own. Many Jews who had been imprisoned in concentration camps but declared to be of German nationality were, upon their return, treated by some officials as any other Germans, regardless of the fact that German and Hungarian Jews with Czechoslovak citizenship had been persecuted by Germans and made considerable sacrifice. A number of German Jews even left Czechoslovakia in 'regular' transports during the initial phase of organized expatriation.

Openly antisemitic actions were not unheard of in post-war Czechoslovakia, although they were more common in Slovakia than in the Czech Lands. They tended to be associated with the restitution – or rather, thwarting the restitution – of property seized during the war to persons of 'Jewish origin'. Even though Czechoslovak authorities stood up against the discrimination of Jews, the settling of issues associated with Jewish property rights was accompanied with numerous difficulties. Beginning in 1945, the Czechoslovak state even placed under national administration that part of Jewish property that had been seized by Germans, or by institutions created by Germans, during the occupation. When returning Jews began laying claim to such property to which the confiscation regulations did not apply, they were up against numerous obstacles.

In spite of all the political issues and economic problems, the first years after WWII were a period of a rapid scientific and cultural progress. Immediately after its liberation, Czechoslovakia opened itself up to the world. Traditional scientific institutions quickly resumed their pre-war contacts with partner organizations, both in Europe and overseas, while also establishing relations with scientific institutions in the USSR. People could freely keep in touch with international cultural developments. Works of contemporary world literature were being translated. Theatres produced plays by modern playwrights such as Jean-Paul Sartre. Alongside movies made in Hollywood, Britain and France, cinemas offered screenings of Soviet avant-garde films by directors such as Sergei Eisenstein. Major classical music personalities visited Czechoslovakia, and the Prague Spring International Music Festival was organized for the first time in 1946.

Czechoslovak culture did not get left behind. Many of its exponents professed left-wing political views, in keeping with the pre-war tradition, and a number of prominent cultural figures accepted positions as ministerial officials. Ivan Olbracht and Vítězslav Nezval, to name but two, worked at the Communist-controlled Ministry of Information. There were also significant opposing voices heard, arguing emphatically – yet still freely – against the left-wing, revolutionary concept of culture: Pavel Tigrid and Ivo Ducháček, for example, voiced their views in the ČSL's Revue Horizons (*Obzory*), others published in Václav Černý's Critical Weekly (*Kritický týdeník*) or Ferdinand Peroutka's Today (*Dnešek*). In addition to visual artists, filmmakers were forging ahead on both domestic and international scenes, after overcoming initial obstacles caused by the 1945 nationalization; among them were Karel Steklý, Václav Krška, and Martin Frič. Likewise, the famous Czech school of animation (including Jiří Trnka and Hermína Týrlová) was rising from the ashes. And finally, the post-war Czechoslovak music scene was dominated by jazz, which was particularly appreciated by young people.

Freedom of religion in Czechoslovakia was reinstated after May 1945, and religious life blossomed as a result. Churches, especially the Roman Catholic Church, faced new conditions in post-war Czechoslovakia. People of faith continued to claim affiliation to a great variety of church and religious organizations after 1945. Based on a 1950 report by the Ministry of Interior, the country registered twelve religious denominations, some thirty religious societies, and over 1,400 religious associations. The Roman Catholic Church continued to be the most influential of all denominations in Czech and Slovak society after 1945. In 1950, following the expulsion of Germans and the forced dissolution of the Greek Catholic Church, the number of Czechoslovak Catholics was estimated to be around 9 million – approximately 76% of the total population. The strongest membership base amongst non-Catholic denominations after 1945 continued to be ascribed to a number of Protestant churches (associating about 1,000,000 believers, or 7.8% of the population in 1950) and the Czechoslovak Hussite Church, with around 900,000 members after 1945.

After WWII, the Roman Catholic Church remained a major player in both cultural and social fields, significantly shaping the character and life of the people in Czechoslovakia. Good relations between the state and the Holy See in the Vatican were essential for maintaining its social role and mission. These relations had been put on a firm footing by the Modus Vivendi – an agreement between the Holy See and the Czechoslovak Republic signed in February 1928 – which was still in effect.

While the government proclaimed, and in practice also guaranteed, freedom of religion after 1945, some of the reforms implemented by the political system of people's democracy had a negative impact on the church, its structure and activities. Church schools and property were a case in point, as were the consequences of the merging – at that stage either intended or being implemented – of community organizations, including trade unions, youth and women's organizations, and sports associations. The political influence of the Roman Catholic Church was thus reduced, partly due to changes in the distribution of power among the political parties.

The Roman Catholic Church entered the post-war era in Czechoslovakia with enormous moral capital. With a few exceptions, its clergy had shown courage during the Nazi occupation; many of its members participated in the national resistance movement, over five hundred clergymen were imprisoned, with more than a fifth of these paying the highest price for their actions. Among the leading church figures after the war were some former concentration camp inmates, such as Archbishop Josef Beran.

The church found itself in a more complicated post-war situation in Slovakia, where it played a more major role in the social and political life than in the Czech Lands. It did not help that both the government-in-exile and the post-war Czechoslovak cabinet declared that the establishment and support of the Slovak State, which existed between 1939 and 1945 and was partially reliant on Roman Catholic clergy, was an act targeted against the interests of Czechoslovakia. Moreover, the National Court of Bratislava passed a death sentence – which was subsequently carried out – on the former President of the Slovak State, Roman Catholic priest Jozef Tiso in the spring of 1947.

Between 1945 and 1948, the Czechoslovak Roman Catholic Church had around seven thousand clergy members , two archdioceses – one in Prague, presided over by Archbishop Josef Beran from 1946 to 1949, and one in Olomouc, led by Archbishop Leopold Prečan until 1947 – as well as dioceses in Hradec Králové, Litoměřice, Brno, Spiš, Banská Bystrica, Nitra and Rožňava, and apostolic administrations in Český Těšín, Košice and Trnava.

As many as 1,051 monasteries, convents, and church homes were home to 2,800 monks and 12,000 nuns, who were primarily engaged in social and charity work, as well as culture-oriented religious services. The education of priests was provided by three theological faculties, with 327 students in the academic year of 1947–1948, and over 530 students attended a total of thirteen theological seminaries. The Roman-Catholic Church had numerous clubs and institutions with which it operated in association, including an extensive network of 133 church and religious journals, youth and women's organizations, the Orel physical education organization, and Marian and St Wenceslas' religious companies. One of the major church institutions was Charity (*Charita*), managing as many as 268 asylums until the year 1950.

The religious, cultural, and social activities of the church were primarily financed from its own resources or gifts. Only one out of three clergymen received the congrua – a state-provided remuneration for administrative acts such as maintaining birth registries or teaching religion. The church owned extensive property, including some 319,000 hectares of farming and forest land, and over 200 estates and agricultural or lumber-production companies – mainly breweries, distilleries, mills, and sawmills.

Church-state relations during the years 1945 to 1948 were marked by mutual respect and peaceful co-existence, ensuring favourable conditions for the churches' activities. Still, the relations were tainted by two controversial issues: the nationalization of church schools and the application of the post-war land-ownership emendations and reforms to church property.

The post-war land reform had a deep impact on the Roman Catholic Church. The revision of the first land reform affected its assets to a degree which put it at the mercy of the state, thus endangering its social mission. The subsequent permanent land-ownership amendment bill – i.e., the new land reform of March 1948 – left in the hands of subordinate church institutions a maximum of 30 hectares of land, and only on condition that this land was not claimed by the local farmers' commissions.

3 The Struggle to Maintain Democracy in Czechoslovakia

26th May, 1946 marked the day of the general elections with the participation of several political parties – the last democratic elections for decades to come. The implications of the elections were far-reaching. They determined not only the distribution of seats among political parties in the elected institutions, but also the future division of power between the Communists on the one hand, and democratic forces on the other. The majority of non-communist parties had expected the Communists to suffer defeat. Non-Communists were convinced that the positions of power seized by Communists immediately after WWII did not correspond to their real-life influence on the population. They failed to recognize the impact of the effective CPCz-designed scheme of socio-economic measures and demands, which appealed to a large portion of the population. In the country, the border region in particular, the Communists won over the local population by handing out land allotment decrees.

The CPCz's sweeping victory, weakened only slightly by the success of the DS in Slovakia, confirmed its standing as the strongest political party in the Czechoslovak Republic. The new Government of National Front was appointed on 2nd July, 1946, led for the first time by a Communist Prime Minister, Klement Gottwald. In addition, Communists took the positions of presidents and security officials in both provincial national committees in Prague and Brno, 127 presidencies of district national committees, and – to their even greater advantage – the positions of district security officials. Furthermore, over a half of all local national committees were now led by Communists.

The elections significantly contributed to the differentiation of the Czechoslovak political system. Political parties, both Communist and non-communist, gradually abandoned the idea of a tightly-knit National Front. The CPCz came to regard its partners, excepting the Social Democrats, as potential opposition. Simultaneously, forces determined to stop the ongoing departure from the traditions of parliamentary democracy were gaining ground in some parties, particularly the National-Socialist Party, but also ČSL and the Slovak Democrats. In many instances, the new parliament refused the dictates of the National Front.

After the parliamentary elections were over, the non-communist parties assumed that the revolutionary era was also over and that it was time to continue building a political regime in which the principles of parliamentary democracy would be extensively applied. They acted more boldly and presented themselves more openly as the opponents of the Communists. In the course of the year 1947, co-operation between political parties became ever less intensive and the number of disputes grew exponentially.

In many respects, the year 1947 was a turning point in the post-war history of Czechoslovakia. The economy began to send out distress signals. The country faced a growing number of domestic difficulties, while – independent of this – profound changes swept across the international scene. The demand for higher wages and lower prices continued, both among factory workers and a large number of state officials. Small business owners

Results of general election in Czechoslovakia held on 26th May, 1946.

Number of ballots in %:

Political parties	Czech Lands	Slovakia	National count
CPCz	40.17	–	31.05
Slovak Communist Party (KSS)	–	30.37	6.89
National Socialists (ČSNS)	23.66	–	18.29
Social Democracy (ČSD)	15.58	–	12.05
People's Party (ČSL)	20.24	–	15.64
Democratic Party (DS)	–	62.00	14.07
Liberty Party	–	3.73	0.85
Labour Party	–	3.11	0.71
White ballots	0.35	0.79	0.45

Results of general election in Czechoslovakia held on 26th May, 1946.

Absolute numbers of ballots

Political parties	Czech Lands	Slovakia	National count
CPCz	2,205,697	–	2,205,697
Slovak Communist Party (KSS)	–	489,596	489,596
National Socialists (ČSNS)	1,298,980	–	1,298,980
Social Democrats (ČSD)	855,538	–	855,538
People's Party (ČSL)	1,111,009	–	1,111,009
Democratic Party (DS)	–	999,622	999,622
Liberty Party	–	60,195	60,195
Labour Party	–	50,079	50,079
White ballots	19,453	12,724	32,117

JIŘÍ KOCIAN

complained about the shortage of both raw materials and labour, which were preferentially supplied to state-owned enterprises. The economic result of new medium-sized farms in the border region – for the first time operating without the contribution of the German workforce – was poor. The impending obligation to pay the first instalment for the property allotted to them further aggravated their situation, and the effects of the drought in the summer of 1947 made it extremely dire. The drought directly affected the provision of supplies to the population. The government lowered food rations and although the black market burgeoned, most employees' low wages prevented them from shopping there. The situation in Slovakia was exceptionally difficult, to a degree which became critical. The drought caused the socially disadvantaged classes to sink even lower into destitution. In the autumn of 1947, the consequences of the recent bad harvest stirred up political conflict concerning the so-called millionaires' tax. Following a turbulent political campaign and heated negotiations in the government, the CPCz pushed through this one-time property tax affecting the wealthiest social class. The tax yield was subsequently used to cover some of the losses caused to farmers by the poor harvest.

Another reason for the political tension of the moment stemmed from the parties' different views on dealing with property issues. In 1947, almost all the parties took a stand on agricultural policies. The CPCz published its Hradec Agenda in April 1947, which called for the launch of a third stage of land reform. The other parties rejected the demand and the bill enacting the final stage of land reform was not passed until March 1948. Yet another major crisis occurred during talks about implementing the second stage of land reform in mid-1947, despite it having been part of the government reconstruction plan, approved by all political parties in July 1946.

The 1947 black-market wholesale profiteering scandals were used as a pretext for demanding the liquidation of private enterprises in that sphere. Early in 1948, privately-owned textile wholesale was eliminated and replaced by state textile distribution centres, which controlled the movement of goods from the production line to the retail network. The demand for further nationalization in the production sphere, presented by the trade unions and later also the CPCz in the autumn of 1947, went beyond the limits set by the government agenda; it called for reducing the size of capitalist enterprises to no more than 50 workers. In support of the demand, a National Congress of Workers' Councils was called to Prague for late February, 1948.

Social tension seeped into the political arena, with an increasingly negative influence on the relationships between the National Front parties. There were, however, other issues that further strained relations. Although co-operation still predominated, disputes threatening to develop into open conflict were more and more common. Tension increased in the Czech-Slovak relationship: in the autumn of 1947, the CPCz launched a new campaign against the DS, to prepare the ground for later changes in the distribution of political power in Slovakia. Disputes in the National Front, which began to create a serious political and later governmental crisis in January and February 1948, indicated what the future course of events would be.

As early as the second half of 1946, there were indications that the East-West relations were beginning to deteriorate – an omen of the forthcoming cold war. The United States cut off Czechoslovakia's access to previously approved credit and did not renew the pre-war trade agreement. Promising negotiations regarding an International Bank loan were halted. The US suspended the return of Czechoslovak gold seized by Germany during the war, and in 1947 refused to give permission for the export of two thirds of facilities earmarked for Czechoslovakia as the German indemnity quota for the year. Any other potential discrimination measures from the West presented a risk for Czechoslovakia in 1946 and 1947, when 80% of the country's foreign trade turnover came from trading with the West (while the share of the USSR was only 7%).

The launch of the Marshall Plan in June 1947 lent new urgency to the question of Czechoslovakia's economic direction. This American initiative played a truly crucial role in the post-war reconstruction of European economies. The Marshall Plan offered a helpful solution and an auspicious path to overcoming the post-war economic troubles of the countries invited to participate, among them Czechoslovakia. This was primarily why the Czechoslovak government accepted the American offer, as well as an invitation to a conference on the Marshall Plan, scheduled to take place in Paris. To Soviet leaders, however, this decision signalled the potential escape of an economically and strategically important Central European country from its sphere of influence, and they regarded it as an unacceptable threat to Soviet interests. Therefore, when a Czechoslovak government delegation visited the USSR in early July 1947, Stalin personally requested that Czechoslovakia should withdraw its participation from the Paris conference, and the Czechoslovak government immediately, if grudgingly, obeyed. Non-Communists, surprisingly, did not try to use the issue of participation in the Marshall Plan to start a major confrontation on the domestic political front. Yet nothing less than the country's sovereignty, economic prosperity, and standard of living was at stake; in other words, issues where Communist views did not enjoy majority popular support.

The year 1947 saw the relations between the allied powers deteriorate. The Czechoslovak absence from the Marshall Plan talks in July 1947 – the result of Stalin's personal intervention – represented both an actual and symbolic turning point in the development of Czechoslovakia. In mid-1947, the USSR adopted a new concept of its European foreign policy. Its tenets were first presented by Soviet officials at the constitutional meeting of the Information Bureau of Communist and Workers' Parties (Cominform) in Poland in September 1947. The Soviet delegation presented the main outlines of its policy, designed to weaken the influence of the USA in Europe, with the ultimate goal of pushing it out of the region. The change of Soviet political focus from Germany towards the USA as its enemy had a far-reaching and perhaps key implication for Czechoslovakia, both in terms of foreign policy orientation and maintaining agreements in the National Front. Another major point made at the Cominform meeting was the rejection of a parliamentary path to socialism, with critical comments made about the Czechoslovak Communist Party's course of action. At that point in time, Czechoslovakia was the last country in the Soviet sphere of influence in which the Communist monopoly of power had not yet been established. This fact, along with the internal situation in Czechoslovakia, pushed the country to the forefront of Soviet political attention. Moscow's power plan and the power plan of the Czechoslovak Communist Party had become one. The Soviets seemed to very strongly favour a definitive and speedy solution to the power relations in Czechoslovakia.

The non-Communist political parties in Czechoslovakia were too slow to understand the implications of the Soviets' change of heart in their European policy and, most importantly, did not grasp them fully. Their existing post-war foreign policy strategy was falling apart. The effectiveness of the Czechoslovak alliance with the USSR as a barrier against the German threat was beginning to erode. On the international level, the Czechoslovak non-Communist parties found themselves in a vacuum. The Soviet Union, which they still held in high esteem as a friend and ally, was globally – in the countries of its sphere of influence – plotting for their destruction as a political force. The Western powers, from which they expected help in their struggle against the Communist efforts to seize a monopoly on power, promised nothing more than moral support. This unfavourable international position significantly weakened the non-Communist parties in their fight against the CPCz – a fact later confirmed by the course and outcome of the February 1948 coup. In contrast, the Communists were well aware of the changes on the international scene and acted accordingly. They were gearing up for a decisive power clash, during which they hoped to rely on the well-respected and virtually unchallenged position of Moscow in its sphere of influence, as well as on Moscow's stake in Czechoslovakia's entry into the new bloc that was being formed at the time. The existing and continuing foreign policy orientation made Czechoslovakia's inclusion in the bloc all the easier: Czechoslovakia entered without resistance.

At a time of profound changes in international relations, though almost independent of them, Czechoslovakia was facing an increasing number of domestic troubles. The country was now on the verge of a full-blown crisis. Growing discontent, particularly among those social groups that formed the social backbone of the regime, was a source of tension. It was reflected in the pressure exerted on political parties, and more importantly, created fertile ground for radicalism, which was quickly gaining momentum. Radical tendencies intensified among the social classes lifted onto the political scene by the revolution; they were characterized by extensive and incessant activity – the cornerstone of Communist politics. They contained a radical movement, which had so far been muffled by the CPCz leadership; by mid-1947, the time had come to take advantage of it. Social unrest was also expressed on the political scene, where it affected relations between the National Front parties. The social card was being played with increasing intensity in the disputes and hostilities between the political parties.

Parties were increasingly at odds, both during cabinet talks and in the National Front. In the autumn of 1947, the CPCz began to consider several alternative methods of how to seize power and thus achieve its main objective – a monopoly on power. Disputes within the National Front escalated into a major political and, later, governmental crisis during the first two months of 1948, indicating that people's democracy in Czechoslovakia had reached a dead end. The foundations on which it had been built and was able to function were either disturbed or utterly abandoned.

The political tension had an increasing influence on the decisions made by the opposing parties. Over time, hopes of reaching a consensus between coalition partners waned, as points of disagreement multiplied and each one threatened to burst into open conflict. Lengthy debates, arguments and mutual finger-pointing took place at both the upper and lower levels of political life. Such a state of affairs paralyzed administrative performance and slowed down the legislative efforts launched in the autumn of 1946.

In 1947, CPCz's pressure focused primarily on weakening the position of the DS in Slovakia. Above all, the Communists took advantage of their dominant positions at the Ministry of Interior and in the police. Some DS functionaries were criminalized. The police force in Slovakia claimed to have uncovered conspiratorial networks, allegedly linked to the ČSL representation-in-exile and posing a hazard to the unity of the state. The Communists also tried to profit from the situation when the remainder of the Ukrainian Insurgent Army attempted a retreat through Slovakia. They demanded substantial police reinforcements and the deployment of army units in the region, as well as the re-armament of the former guerrillas, most members of which were Communist sympathizers. The Communists organized political strikes and demonstrations against the DS, and worked on splintering it from the inside. The Slovak crisis eventually fizzled out without a clear result, mainly because of the Communists' inability to garner support of Czech non-Communist parties at the right time, though they were otherwise usually appealing to their Czechoslovakism (especially in the case of the National Socialists). The DS did come out of the crisis somewhat weakened but, for the time being, the Communists had failed to eliminate it as a major political force in Slovakia.

The non-Communist parties looked with hope towards the next election, scheduled for the spring 1948, hoping it would weaken the power of the CPCz, even though they were not planning on ousting it from the government or the National Front. As the main issues of the election campaign, they put forth the struggle for maintaining democratic principles, against a police state, and for control over security forces that would ensure that they did not serve a single party's interest. The Communists' activity in the police had become so extensive and assumed such characteristics, that it began to threaten the functionaries and even the very existence of non-Communist parties. Attacking the DS and instigating the Slovak crisis were cases in point, but Communists had also begun using similar practices with increasing frequency in the Czech part of the country.

Political tension in Czechoslovakia had further escalated. And yet, what proved crucial for the country's future development was the situation in the institutions wielding political power, particularly in the last month of the existence of the people's democracy in Czechoslovakia. In late January and early February, the cabinet discussed several major contentious issues, in which a number of serious aspects were reflected, such as the rate and degree of tension between individual members of the coalition, as well as the likelihood of their future cooperation.

The controversial issues included: the outline of a bill to permanently settle farmland ownership matters and form a government commission that would oversee the partition of farming estates; the adjustment of the salaries of state and public employees, according to which higher-ranked and better-qualified officials would receive a raise; the proposal for a bill addressing work obligation for military servicemen; and, last but not least, the unlawful impinging of the security forces on the life of non-Communist parties and their functionaries. A major dispute eventually developed over the replacement of several Prague police district commanders – a step which drove the National Socialist cabinet members to request revocation of the command by the Minister of Interior. The Communist ministers turned down their request.

Bibliography

ALTE, Rudiger: *Die Außenpolitik der Tschechoslowakei und die Entwicklung der intenationalen Beziehungen 1946–1947*, München 2003.
ABRAMS, Bradley F.: The *struggle for the soul of the nation: Czech culture and the rise of communism*, Lanham 2004.
BIRKE, Ernst –NEUMANN, Rudolf: *Die Sowjetisierung Ost-Mitteleuropas: Untersuchungen zu ihrem Ablauf in den einzelnen Ländern*, Frankfurt am Main 1959.
BLOOMFIELD, Jon: *Passive revolution: politics and the Czechoslovak working class, 1945–1948*. New York 1979.
BROD, Toman: *Cesta československých komunistů k moci v letech 1945–1948*. I. *Operace Velký podvod*. II. *Triumf a zkáza*, Prague 1990–1991.
ČAPKA, František – SLEZÁK, Lubomír – VACULÍK, Jaroslav: *Nové osídlení pohraničí českých zemí po druhé světové válce*, Brno 2005.
CHURAŇ, Milan: *Potsdam und die Tschechoslowakei: Mythos und Wirklichkeit*, Dinkelsbühl 2007.
CORNWALL, M. – EVANS, R. J. W. (eds.): *Czechoslovakia in a nationalist and fascist Europe, 1918–1948*, Oxford 2007.
COUDENHOVE-KALERGI, Barbara –RATHKOLB, Oliver (eds.): *Die Benes-Dekrete*, Wien 2002.
DEJMEK, Jindřich: *Edvard Beneš: Politická biografie českého demokrata. Část druhá: Prezident republiky a vůdce národního odboje*, Praha 2008.
DEJMEK, Jindřich – KUKLÍK, Jan (Jr.) – NĚMEČEK, Jan: *Historické, právní a mezinárodní souvislosti dekretů prezidenta republiky*, Prague 2003.
Erzwungene Trennung: Vertreibungen und Aussiedlungen in und aus der Tschechoslowakei 1938–1947 im Vergleich mit Polen, Ungarn und Jugoslawien, Detlef Brandes, Edita Ivaničková, Jiří Pešek (eds.), Essen 1999. (Veröffentlichungen der Deutsch-Tschechischen und Deutsch-Slowakischen Historikerkommission; Bd. 8)
FAURE, Justine: *L'ami americain: la Tchécoslovaquie, enjeu de la diplomatie americaine, 1943–1968*, Paris 2004.
FEJTÖ, François: *Le coup de Prague 1948*, Paris 1976.
FEJTÖ, Francoise: *Histoire des démocraties populaires. l'Ere de Stalin 1945–1952*, Paris 1979.
FROMMER, Benjamin: *National Cleansing: Retribution Against Nazi Collaborators in Postwar Czechoslovakia*, Cambridge 2005.
KALINOVÁ, Lenka: *Východiska, očekávání a realita poválečné doby: k dějinám české společnosti v letech 1945–1948*, Prague 2004.
KALINOVÁ, Lenka: *Společenské proměny v čase socialistického experimentu. K sociálním dějinám v letech 1945–1969*, Praha 2007.
KAMIŃSKI, Marek K.: *Polska i Czechoslovacija w polityce Stanów Zjednoczonych i Wielkiej Brytanii 1945–1948*, Warszawa 1991.
KAPLAN, Karel: *The short march: the communist takeover in Czechoslovakia, 1945–1948*, New York 1987.
KAPLAN, Karel: *Das verhängnisvolle Bündnis: Unterwanderung, Gleichschaltung und Vernichtung der Tschechoslowakischen Sozialdemokratie 1944–1954*, Wuppertal 1984.

KOSTA, Jiří Jindřich: *Abriß der sozialokonomischen Entwicklung der Tschechoslowakei 1945–1977*, Frankfurt am 1978.

KUČERA, Jaroslav: *„Der Hai wird nie wieder so stark sein": tschechoslowakische Deutschlandpolitik 1945–1948*, Dresden 2001.

LOBKOWICZ, Nikolaus – PRINZ, Friedrich (eds.): *Schicksalsjahre der Tschechoslowakei 1945–1948*, München – Wien 1981.

LUŽA, Radomír: *The Transfer of the Sudeten Germans. A Study od Czech-German Relations, 1933–1962*, New York 1964.

LUŽA, Radomír – MAMATEY, Victor (eds.): *A History of the Czechoslovak Republic 1918–1948*, Princeton, New Jersey 1973.

MYANT, M. R.: *Socialism and democracy in Czechoslovakia, 1945-1948*, Cambridge 1981.

National policy in the countries of the forming Soviet bloc, 1944–1948, Moscow 2004.

RAGEAU, Jean-Pierre: *Prague 48: le rideau de fer s'est abattu: 1948*, Bruxelles–Paris 1981.

RUPNIK, Jacques: *Histoire du Parti Communiste Tchécoslovaque: des origines à la prise du pouvoir*, Paris 1981.

STANĚK, Tomáš: *Internierung und Zwangsarbeit: das Lagersystem in den böhmischen Ländern 1945–1948*, München 2007 (Veröffentlichungen des Collegium Carolinum ; Bd. 92).

STANĚK, Tomáš: *Verfolgung 1945: die Stellung der Deutschen in Böhmen, Mähren und Schlesien (außerhalb der Lager und Gefängnisse)*, Wien 2002.

STANĚK, Tomáš: *Odsun Němců z Československa 1945–1947*, Prague 1991.

STEVENS, John N.: *Czechoslovakia at the crossroads: the economic dilemmas of communism in postwar Czechoslovakia*. Boulder 1985.

ULLMAN, Walter: *The United States in Prague 1945–1948*, New York 1978.

VOLOKITINA, Tatiana Viktorovna – MURAŠKO, Galina Pavlovna – NOSKOVA, Albina Fiodorovna: *Narodnaja děmokratija: Mif ili reálnost? Obščestvjenno-političeskije procesy v Vostočnoj Evropě, 1944–1948*, Moskva 1993.

ZEMAN, Zbyněk A. B.: *The life of Edvard Beneš 1884–1948: Czechoslovakia in peace and war*. With Antonín Klimek, Oxford 1997.

ZINNER, Paul E.: *Communist strategy and tactics in Czechoslovakia, 1918–48*, New York 1963.

XVIII. The Establishment and First Crisis of the Communist Regime in Czechoslovakia (1948–1958)

The head from the monument of Stalin in Prague. The monument was officially unveiled in 1955 and demolished in 1962. There were dozens of similar monuments around Czechoslovakia, albeit not so monumental. Also many public spaces were named after Stalin. Most monuments and names disappeared mostly as early as at the turn of the 1950s and 1960s, although some not until 1989.

1 The Coup d'état of February 1948

Political tension, which had been gradually on the increase in Czechoslovakia, came to a climax in early 1948. The Communists took advantage of having their man, Václav Nosek, running the Ministry of Interior, and were set on assuming complete control of this important government department. One by one, they appointed members of their party to top positions in the National Security Corps (the police force, known as the SNB) and State Security (the secret police, or StB), thereby transforming the state's security apparatus into a vehicle for their political line. It was one of these steps that triggered a deep government crisis, far graver than any that had afflicted Czechoslovakia in the post-WWII era.

At a government meeting on 13th February, 1948, while the National-Socialist Minister of Justice Prokop Drtina was reading a report about complaints regarding the activities of the police, he coincidentally received fresh information that an SNB regional commander had just dismissed another eight Prague police district commanders and transferred them to administrative service. None of the dismissed officers was a member of the Communist Party (CPCz); in fact, the majority of them were affiliated to the National-Socialist Party. This information upset to the point of outrage all the ministers except those representing the CPCz. The ministers representing the democratic parties unanimously adopted a resolution calling for the Interior Minister to revoke the regional commander's order, and for the dismissed officers to be reinstated to their posts until the cabinet had discussed the complaints regarding police activities and had issued an appropriate resolution. When the cabinet reconvened four days later, however, the Interior Minister was absent, excusing his absence on grounds of illness. Under the circumstances, the non-Communist ministers refused to proceed with the daily agenda, and the PM ended the meeting prematurely.

Following the unsuccessful government session, a separate meeting was held by representatives of the Czechoslovak National-Socialist Party, the Czechoslovak People's Party (ČSL) and the Democratic Party of Slovakia (DS). They agreed not to give in to Communist aggression under any circumstances, to insist that the government resolution of 13th February be brought into effect, and to leave the government rather than to succumb to Communist pressure. After much deliberation, they concluded that the Social Democratic ministers were not likely to support their cause and resign their posts, but their stance nonetheless remained unchanged. That same evening, another meeting was held by the Presidium of the Communist Party's Central Committee (CC CPCz), at the end of which a resolution was adopted, characterizing the current state of affairs as 'serious,' and accusing the non-Communist parties of escalating it. At the same time, the document called upon CPCz members and supporters to be prepared to 'nip in the bud any subversive schemes of Reaction.' A similar document, entitled 'The Onslaught of the People Will Thwart Reactionary Designs,' was released by the Communist Party of Slovakia (KSS). Simultaneously, CPCz leaders mobilized their local organizations across the country and put them on alert. The democratic parties' concern over the Communist Party's gaining control over the police force was not unfounded – a fact illustrated by such things as the state of alert declared within the Prague division of the StB, and by the Interior Minister in intelligence departments around the country. Eight border patrol regiments were put on alert, and selected sections of these were deployed in Prague.

The next two days saw frenzied negotiations within the National Front, which also involved the Czechoslovak President. Each of the two camps assumed an unyielding position: the National-Socialists, the ČSL and the Slovak Democrats insisted that the government resolution must be implemented, their positions backed by President Beneš himself – all of them unaware of the measures to seize power taken by the Communists in the meantime, in which the CPCz leaders had further radicalized their positions. They were concerned that after recent events in France, Czechoslovakia could become another country to oust the Communists from government. As a result, they adopted a resolution proclaiming that they would not yield 'a single position' to their political rivals. At the same time, the leadership decided to organize a general strike, if necessary. In formulating their tactics, the Communists decided to make use of the Factory Council Representatives' Congress, which had been slated – before the government crisis broke out – for 22nd February. The Social Democrats took up a compromise position: they declared their resolve not to join an anti-Communist government, while turning down an offer from the Communists jointly to create a bi-partisan cabinet with them and against all the others. The Social Democratic Party's presidium meeting, held on 19th February, 1948, adopted a resolution calling for an effort to calm the situation, hold talks with other parties and settle their disagreements, and to prevent the crisis from escalating further. However, the Social Democratic proposal had missed their window of opportunity for success: the positions of both camps had been so polarized as to become completely unyielding, and those who were once political rivals had become enemies, gearing up for a decisive power clash.

The direction in which Czechoslovakia was heading was also a matter of concern for other countries – a fact illustrated by an unexpected visit from Valerian Zorin, Secretary of the USSR's Minister of Foreign Affairs, who flew in to Prague on 19th February. He was familiar with the Czechoslovak political milieu, having served as a Soviet ambassador in the Czechoslovak Republic between 1945 and 1947. The official reason for his visit was to monitor the state of grain deliveries from the Soviet Union, though in fact he held talks with both

Communist and Social Democratic ministers. He passed on Stalin's message to Gottwald, urging the Communists not to delay the onset of the decisive power battle any longer and to forge ahead with the utmost determination. On the same day, US Ambassador Laurence A. Steinhardt returned to Prague after a long period of sick leave and, in meeting the press after leaving the plane, he expressed the conviction that democracy would prevail in Czechoslovakia. A police informer, who had been in his presence during a reception held at the Italian embassy that same evening, reported, however, that the ambassador was very nervous and almost green in the face. 'It is unclear whether the reason (for his physical and mental state) was the flight to Prague or the reports he received over here,' writes the informer.

Indeed, the latest developments had been unfavourable for the country's democratic forces. Their ministers' filibustering attempts in government proved ineffective and actually prompted the Communists to adopt an even more steadfastly inflexible stance. Yet the democratic politicians were resolved to hold their own. They did not attend the government assembly arranged for 20th February, and they responded to Prime Minister Gottwald's summons with a letter saying that they were present in the government presidium building and would come to the meeting as soon as they 'receive word that the Interior Ministry has implemented the government resolution of 13th February, 1948.' Since they never received that information, they decided to resign their posts, undaunted by the fact that only twelve of twenty-six ministers would resign, representing less than a half of the cabinet.

Only after reaching such an important decision did the ministers for the National-Socialist, People's and Democratic Parties choose to inform the other non-Communist ministers – which were the Social Democrats, as well as Jan Masaryk (Minister of Foreign Affairs) and Ludvík Svoboda (Minister of Defence), who stood apart from these parties – and invite them to express solidarity, but their hopes came to nothing. The Social Democrats chose to continue to play the role of stabilizer in the unsteady National Front; Jan Masaryk categorically rejected their initiative, and General Svoboda sided with the Communists. The twelve democratic ministers therefore sent the President a letter announcing their resignation from their posts, regardless of the other ministers' stance. It was late afternoon, 20th February, 1948.

Prime Minister Klement Gottwald had no more intention of conceding now than before. On the contrary, he chose to use the inflamed situation to deal a major blow to what was left of parliamentary democracy in Czechoslovakia and ensure that his party would seize power in the country, as had always been the Communists' goal. The fact that the democratic politicians timed their actions so close to the upcoming elections may have surprised, but did not paralyse, Gottwald. As soon as he made sure they went through with their resignation, he decided to use it to his own advantage.

His plan was simple: the government had only lost a minority of its members, and it was now crucial to make sure that the President accepted that minority's resignation and fill their seats with a new set of ministers nominated by Gottwald himself.

He had no shortage of candidates. For many years, the Communists had been setting up their own intelligence services in other National Front parties. They operated by persuading members who were either discontented with their parties' policies or leadership, or frustrated by unfulfilled aspirations, to cooperate with them; or they went even further, sending their own party members on a mission to assume party positions, report on the non-Communist parties' activities, and influence their activities and standpoints in favour of the CPCz. It was from these people that Gottwald was now going to select new ministers to fill the seats of those who had resigned.

Without delay, the Communists organized a massive demonstration of their supporters in the Prague's Old Town Square on 21st February, 1948. The huge attendance numbers – both in Prague and other cities – were evidence of the support they enjoyed. The CPCz leaders capitalized on the fact that one of their members, Václav Kopecký, ran another crucial government department – the Ministry of Information – and they arranged for the demonstration to be broadcast on the national radio. In addition, Communist organizations outside of Prague organized collective sessions to listen to the broadcast in large factories, mines, and the squares of major cities, giving rise to spontaneous and unpremeditated nationwide demonstrations in support of Communist politics. According to official records, attendance at the demonstrations topped one million citizens. Gottwald's speech, regarded by Communists as a roadmap for their future course of action, was heard by several million people. In his speech, the Prime Minister and Chairman of the CPCz repeated his own recipe for resolving the cabinet crisis: the ministers' resignation must be accepted and their seats must be filled with new ministers; the names of the new ministers would be selected by Gottwald himself, regardless of anything the 'treacherous' parties had to say. Equally serious was Gottwald's appeal to his cabinet's supporters – regardless of party affiliation – to establish "Action Committees" of the National Front that would 'purge' the public arena of all supporters of the resignation. Democratic party representatives underestimated the gravity of the situation and appealed for calm to those of their members who expressed concern over the Communist offensive and rejected the idea of organizing their own counter-rallies. The only thing they agreed to do was to speak at public meetings at various places across the country. None of those meetings, however, came even close in size or significance to the Communists' Prague rally.

While the CPCz was on alert, the leadership of the democratic parties did not meet and their central secretariats did not begin to operate non-stop until the evening of February 21st. Democratic leaders still acted as though this were merely a normal government crisis that takes place from time to time in parliamentary democracies, and that sooner or later it would be resolved using standard political means. Their steps were characterized by an effort to maintain negotiations on the level of the National Front's top party officials, consultations with the President and possibly in the Parliament, but they obstinately refused to allow the resolution of the issue to take place 'in the street.' For the same reason, they prevented their members from organizing their own mass meetings and anti-Communist rallies.

The Factory Councils Representatives' Congress, which took place on Sunday, 22nd February, 1948, had among its participants representatives of factories around the country. Since 1945, the trade unions had been in Communist hands, a fact that had grave consequences in these crucial moments. The congress was run completely under the Communist baton. Keynote speakers included Antonín Zápotocký (Chairman of the Central Council of Trade Unions, Cabinet Vice-Chairman, and member of the CPCz's Presidium), and Klement Gottwald. Zápotocký made new radical demands concerning both social and economic fields, and Gottwald reiterated his plan for a solution to the crisis. The congress put forward a number of resolutions based on both speeches, which were adopted almost unanimously, with only three members of the Central Council of Trade Unions and a small minority of the entire assembly of several thousand participants voting against. The key conclusions of the congress included the resolution to organize a warning general strike in support of Gottwald's cabinet on 24th February. The proceedings and conclusions of the Factory Councils Representatives' Congress caught the attention of the whole of society and pushed into the background such momentous events as the Appeal to the Czechoslovak Public, released on the same day by some 80 public figures, in which the signatories expressed their concern over the political practices of the Communists and called for truly free and democratic elections to be held.

The Communist-controlled Interior Ministry put all police divisions on full alert and, late at night, bridges, important buildings, the radio building and post offices in Prague began to be secured by armed and reinforced patrols. Police units from the surrounding areas began to concentrate in the capital, while units from Moravia and Slovakia were deployed to Bratislava. Representatives of the democratic parties did not have the slightest notion that any of this was happening, and so completely failed to respond. Their top party officials did not meet; indeed, many of their high-ranked functionaries were talking at public assemblies outside Prague. The Communists certainly did not lag in holding their own – much more numerous – meetings all around the country.

Monday, 23rd February, was perhaps the most crucial day of the whole crisis. The Communists set up The Central Action Committee of the National Front that began coordinating the activities of local National Front Action Committees, which in turn had begun springing up all across the country as early as 21st February, encouraged by the Communists. Nobody appointed their members or authorized their establishment, yet they acted on behalf of self-appointed 'progressive' forces, and succeeded in preventing lawful, properly elected authorities and their official representatives from doing their job. It was a tragic irony that the Action Committees were joined not only by Communists and left-leaning Social Democrats, but also by some members of the full spectrum of the democratic parties. In the course of time, the NF Action Committees became the key instrument of the Communist coup, and they gradually assumed real power.

The success of the coup was further aided by the armed forces. The ministers who had handed in their resignations were under constant police surveillance, quite openly followed by StB agents, who even stood guard on the doorsteps of their offices and homes. Police units performed a search of the building at the National-Socialist Party headquarters in Prague and participated in an open coup d'état in Bratislava. The first coup attempt there took place on 21st February, when Gustáv Husák – the Communist chairman of the Board of Commissioners (BC) – sent a letter to those colleagues who represented the Democratic Party, informing them that they were removed from office, on the grounds that their party members' resignation from the government was considered to be also a resignation from the BC. DS leaders refused to accept Husák's arguments, which in turn propelled the Communists to use force against them: on 23rd February, with the help of armed 'guerrilla fighters,' they seized the DS headquarters and prevented the party from publishing its own newspaper, Time (Čas), along with other periodicals.

On 23rd February, university students rose up in defence of democracy in Prague, at a spontaneous rally held outside the National-Socialist Party headquarters and a subsequent march to Prague Castle, where their representatives were seen by the Czechoslovak President. It was he who had become the Czechoslovak democrats' only hope. They expected him to persist, turn down Gottwald's proposal for a solution of the crisis, and perhaps suggest steps that would help calm the situation. However, Edvard Beneš found himself in the direst of straits, with little or no room to manoeuvre; the Communists were meanwhile mounting an increasingly open attack. They managed to defer the parliamentary session at the National Assembly until the crisis had been brought under control. It must be noted at this point that the National Assembly was a key instrument of the democratic state, which could have helped the democratic forces avert the impending catastrophe. Furthermore, the CPCz armed its own paramilitary troops – known as the People's Militia – the formation of which had been launched on 21st February.

The Interior Ministry released a memo ordering – in a manner quite out of keeping with the Constitution – that all subordinate units were to confiscate printed material 'assailing the National Security Corps.' The police order was carried out immediately and comprehensively, with almost all non-Communist publications in circulation falling victim. Similarly, the Ministry of Information took the initiative of halting paper deliveries to non-Communist parties. Added to this were the unlawful actions of Communist workers in many printing houses after 22nd February, when they refused to print any newspapers and magazines that were not Communist-oriented. Thus, the democratic parties were not only unable to respond to false accusations of treason made against them by the Communists, but had also been driven into almost complete isolation. Another ordinance issued by the Interior Ministry on 23rd February obliged all national committees in the Czech Lands to 'disregard notifications of assemblies if organized by the National-Socialist Party,' and, only a little later that day, an executive order was issued that banned all resigning parties from holding any public meetings whatsoever.

The crisis was inevitably drawing to a close. A nationwide general strike in support of Klement Gottwald's politics was held on Tuesday, 24th February from 12 to 1 p.m. Two and a half million people participated, while only a tiny fraction of the workforce refused to take part (although in most cases, this fraction was forced to stop working as well and most of those involved were later punished). Wherever fair means failed, Communists did not hesitate to use the armed forces, which were under their control. The Social Democrats, whose support they needed to carry out their plans, were now split. Besides pro-Communist collaborators such as Zdeněk Fierlinger there were party officials who were unwilling to participate in a coup d'état and refused to give their consent to their party joining a Communist government. The party's left wing, aided by the People's Militia and police, took over the People's House in Prague – the seat of the Social Democratic leadership – as well as the printing office and newsroom of The Right of the People *(Právo lidu)* newspaper. After the objectors against collaborating with the Communists had been isolated, the presidium of the Social Democratic Party decided to support Gottwald's cabinet. Over the course of the day, the police had taken over the headquarters of democratic parties almost everywhere in the country and carried out unlawful searches of their buildings, arresting party functionaries and holding them in custody. Ane Action Committee was set up in Melantrich, the press works of the National-Socialist Party, and appointed a new leadership. A similar coup took place in the non-partisan Free Newspaper *(Svobodné noviny)*, whose editor-in-chief, Ferdinand Peroutka, was high-handedly relieved of his position and replaced by the communist writer Jan Drda.

Everyone's hopes were now pinned on Prague Castle in the form of President Edvard Beneš, who was still refusing to accede to Gottwald's plan for resolving the crisis. He assured a delegation representing the DS that he would only appoint the new government if there was a consensus of all parties, and should the Communists continue to be obstinate, he would talk to the nation and explain his standpoint. Despite these assurances, the Slovak politicians left in low spirits, particularly disheartened 'by the crippling impression left on them by the President,' as one of them put it. Others were left with the impression that at this point 'he was only talking for history's sake' and that 'the President is only saving himself, not the situation.' What was more, upon returning to Bratislava, they found the DS with a newly-formed opposition wing, which had set up its own Action Committee and was prepared to enter into talks with the Communists. Like their Czech counterparts, the Slovak democrats were stripped of any chance to maintain contact with their organizations and other supporters. The exclusive sources of information regarding new developments for citizens all over the republic were the Communist-controlled state radio station, and newspapers and journals that either directly belonged to the CPCz, or were controlled by them through their people in editorial offices. Simultaneously, the police continued (entirely unlawfully) to arrest and isolate non-Communist party secretaries, seizing and closing down their district and local headquarters. When opponents of the CPCz attempted to organize a demonstration in Prague later that evening, it was peremptorily dispersed by the police.

The situation reached its final resolution on the following day, 25th February. As with everywhere else, collaborators with the CPCz were elbowing their way to power in democratic parties. Early the next morning, they took over the headquarters, political office and press works of the ČSL. The party chairman, Monsignor Jan Šrámek, tried to stop the activities of the pro-Communist elements by ordering that all party activities be halted, but his gesture met with a cool reception, and many ČSL Parliamentary deputies began offering to cooperate with the self-appointed party leadership. Similar developments took place in other parties: The DS was buffeted by dual leadership, with the official leadership increasingly isolated. The National-Socialist Party, too, had an Action Committee formed within its ranks under the auspices of the Communists, which was gearing up to seize the party's central secretariat. A ferocious battle over what the future course of the party should be was being waged within the Czechoslovak Social Democracy (ČSD), where a group around minister Václav Majer was still holding on, refusing to surrender willingly to Communist aggression. In support of the position of the resigned ministers, Majer and his party colleague Franrišek Tymeš handed in their resignation on 25th February, 1948. This made them the thirteenth and fourteenth Czechoslovak ministers officially to resign, and resulted in Gottwald and his henchmen losing their cabinet majority; however, this gesture came too late and had no effect.

The Communists were aware that the last obstacle to their sweeping victory was the President's resistance, and so at this point directed their pressure to him. A CPCz delegation paid him a visit before noon and urged him to make a speedy decision and accept the resignation of the democratic ministers. Beneš, now a sick and worn-out man, who could not see a viable solution to the deepening crisis, who realized the helplessness of the non-Communist parties, and who had a horror of civil war, eventually succumbed to their intense and continuous pressure. He accepted the resignation and appointed a new cabinet, including only Communists, left-leaning Social Democrats, and Communist collaborators from other National Front parties; the latter accepted government membership of their own accord, against the wishes of their parties' official authorities.

Prior to this turn of events, the CPCz leadership had organized a massive demonstration in Prague, planning to bring the demonstrators to the Castle should the President turn down their request, or, should he accept, to express their thanks to him by sending over a special delegation. In addition, they had several thousand armed People's Militia troops on alert in Prague factories, which were to take control of the city centre in the event of the chief of state sticking to his guns. In the end, the Communists did not need to resort to violence. The demonstrators, whose numbers have been estimated between one and two hundred thousand, filled Wenceslas Square to the brim and received with cheers Gottwald's information that the President had accepted all of his proposals exactly as they had been presented to him. The defeat of democracy could not have been averted by the demonstration of university students who were now on their way to the Castle; four to five thousand young people clashed with the police, who were intent on stopping them at any cost. The academics eventually managed to send their own delegation to the President, but the President failed to meet them. The deputation of five was received by Chancellor Smutný, who gave them a vapid answer. 118 participants were arrested during the demonstration and received administrative sentences, and one was accidentally wounded by police gunfire.

The government crisis, which shook Czechoslovakia from 20th to 25th February 1948, led to the fall of democracy and the establishment of a totalitarian regime, which lasted more than 40 years. A sad coda to this drama was provided by the session of the National Assembly on 11th March, 1948, during which 230 out of a total of 300 deputies accepted the Gottwald's new cabinet's programme, appointed on 25th February by President Beneš, and thus authorized its legal status. Eleven deputies left the House prior to voting in order to express their disapproval. Nobody voted against.

2 Fundamental Changes in the Political and Economic Nature of the Country

The seizure of power by the CPCz in February 1948 dealt a deep and fatal blow to the political, economic and social life of the country. The destruction of the existing democratic mechanisms, dovetailed with the elimination or isolation of prominent political figures holding different political views, prepared the ground for a complete remake of the society into a Soviet-style totalitarian system. The critics and dissenters of the Communist regime, most of whom participated in the power clash with the Communists, used the term 'putsch' to describe the events of February 1948, though contemporary historians who have studied this watershed moment in the post-war history of the Czechoslovak society prefer the term 'political coup d'état' or 'takeover.'

The development of the power clash in February 1948 once again proved the CPCz's unique position in the society at the time. The popular support of the party was formally expressed in the general elections held on 30th May, 1948. The elections were far from free, but voters at least had a choice between the 'united ballot of the National Front' and a 'white ballot.' Even though the official election results were probably somewhat embellished by the CPCz, they still illustrate the atmosphere in the country at the time. According to the CPCz, only 9.32% of voters in the Czech Lands and 13.98% of voters in Slovakia submitted white ballots. In any case, the deputies of the new parliament were exclusively those with ties to the CPCz who supported its political line. The Communists also took all of the top state offices. Beginning on 25th February, 1948, they dominated the government, since – in addition to the ministers who publicly professed affiliation with the CPCz – only those members of other parties who were either prepared to give unequivocal support to Communist policies or had already been doing so for some time were appointed to ministerial positions. Among them were National-Socialists Emanuel Šlechta and Alois Neuman, the ČSL's Alois Petr and Josef Plojhar, and Social Democrats Zdeněk Fierlinger and Ludmila Jankovcová. The election victory in May 1948 launched Dr. Oldřich John into the position of the National Assembly chairman; though himself a Social Democrat, he had collaborated closely with the CPCz, and after the ČSD was incorporated into the CPCz, he became a member of its top leadership. Following the resignation of President Edvard Beneš on 7th June, 1948, Klement Gottwald took over the highest office, ceding the position of Prime Minister to another prominent CPCz member, Antonín Zápotocký. The Communists also seized other top offices in the country, further contributing to the destruction of the democratic system.

The high esteem that the CPCz continued to enjoy with a large part of the Czechoslovak population after February 1948 enabled the party to introduce many profound changes to public life, without facing major resistance. Above all, the Communists took violent steps to consolidate the unlimited power they had just seized. Using the National Front Action Committees as a tool, they made certain that those functionaries of non-Communist parties who refused to collaborate with the new regime were dismissed from their organizations, state authorities, and various associations. The number of people affected thus can only be estimated; according to some sources, it was as high as 250,000. Nearly 60,000 members of non-Communist parties were removed from the national committees at all levels, over 20,000 inconvenient persons were stripped of their trade union positions, and some 15,000 functionaries were dismissed by screening commissions from the Czech Sokol Organization. About 11,000 officials lost their jobs on the basis of their pre-February political affiliation. Nearly half – 294 out of 600 – CEOs of nationalized enterprises had to leave their positions, immediately followed by an unknown number of employees of the SNB and StB (that is, the police force and secret police), particularly those who had served during the First Republic. The army lost 28% of its officers. Similarly, some university professors were let go, and 18% of 48,000 university students fell victim to the political purge. The vacant positions were re-filled with the CPCz's own people, completely devoted to the party and ready to serve it without reservation. All this was accomplished in a very short period of time immediately following the February coup. A substantial part of the population endorsed these steps, while most citizens passively accepted them as a fact.

Another step towards consolidating the Communist power consisted of eliminating democratic political parties. After dismissing the idea of disbanding them altogether, the CPCz leadership ascribed a new role to the parties including the ČSNS, the ČSL, the DS, and the Liberty Party. They were to be transformed into organizations of people ready to support the politics of the CPCz, into bodies fully dependent – both politically and financially – on the totalitarian state whose construction was in progress at the time, and governed by the reorganized and (in a term coined by the propaganda of the period) 'reformed' National Front. The CPCz achieved its objective. Some parties went so far as to change their name (for example, the Czechoslovak National-Socialist Party dropped 'national' from its name), and all of them became, as it were, transmission levers of Communist power: they were financed from the state budget, their new members were accepted only upon the approval of the National Front, and the apparatus of each was staffed with people screened by Communist organs, some of whom were StB collaborators.

A different fate was planned for the ČSD: a merger with the Communist Party. The deal was sealed on 27th June, 1948, in Prague. The CPCz itself controlled which members of the ČSD would be accepted into its fold, and only those who had previously shown a readiness to cooperate with the CPCz and supported its politics were allowed to join its ranks, along with previously passive members. By 4th January, 1949, as many as 118,104 Social Democrats became members of the CPCz, a total of about one third of the former ČSD member base. The rest were under occasional surveillance by the secret police, and former ČSD functionaries sometimes became the target of oppression and victims of trumped-up trials.

Communists, or people prepared to support their politics without reservation, took top positions in various organizations, some of which had already existed and some which had been , while others were newly established to aid in controlling the society. They included the Union of Czechoslovak Journalists, founded in October 1948. The party's ideologist, Gustav Bareš, essentially defined the Union's mission when he declared at its constituent congress: 'For journalists [...] to do their job [...], they cannot rely solely on their own judgment, but need to go and learn from workers in factories and from the CPCz leaders.' Bareš also spoke of the need to send journalists to factories on 'educational fellowships' and to educate them politically and ideologically, and stressed the necessity to capitalize on experience gained in the Soviet Union. The Union of Czechoslovak Writers was founded in March 1949 as a selective organization for authors who supported the politics of the CPCz in their works, and Communist author Jan Drda became its chairman. The former 'Writers' Syndicate' was transformed into a new organization. At the request of the CPCz's Cultural Committee and following the screening commission's decision, the original member base of the Syndicate of 1,711 members was reduced to about 300 full members and 120 candidates for membership. Similarly, the Union of Czechoslovak Composers and Music Artists was established in May 1949, followed by the Union of Czechoslovak Visual Artists in March 1950. In April 1949, a unified youth organization known as the Union of Czechoslovak Youth was formed in Prague, and the 'Pioneer Organization,' based on the Soviet model, was founded for children. Those with unswerving loyalty to the CPCz became their leaders. All other youth and children's organizations ceased to exist.

Enormous pressure was exerted on churches, particularly the Roman Catholic Church. From the regime's perspective, this was a fairly logical step. Once all the organizations representing a political, and later also spiritual, alternative to the ruling Communist Party and its ideology were successfully eliminated, the churches remained the only organisms in society to maintain their autonomy and, unlike other organizations, to escape the controlling grip of the CPCz. They constituted a legal (albeit merely temporarily tolerated) spiritual alternative and, in point of fact, an opposition to the all-pervading Marxist-Leninist worldview. In addition, the Catholic Church was part of a global, supranational community. After a brief period attempting to maintain the coexistence of the regime and church, it became clear that the Catholic Church could never be separated from the Vatican and the regime launched severe repressive measures. Soon after 1950, practically all of the Catholic Church's prelates found themselves either in prison or internment camps. In 1950, religious orders were disbanded and monasteries overrun by the police and the People's Militia, with monks sent to labour camps or the army and nuns assigned to hard labour. During the first half of the 1950s, nearly five hundred priests and thousands of laymen were imprisoned. The Greek Catholic Church, which had a particularly strong base in Eastern Slovakia, was completely wiped out and its churches passed on to the Orthodox Church.

In an effort to undermine the existing relationship between the citizen and the state and dispel traditions as much as possible in favour of the emerging 'people's democracy' or 'socialist' society, the Communist leadership wasted no time and, in early 1949, abolished the provincial system that had been in use for a millennium. The existing historical provinces of Bohemia, Moravia and Silesia, to which Slovakia had been added in 1918, were replaced by a system of regions. They, nonetheless, proved so inefficient that before long the CPCz found it necessary to reorganize them and reduce their number.

In the early 1950s, full civil rights were restored to those members of the German minority who had managed to avoid the post-WWII expatriation. The significance of this act was negligible, however, and most Germans living in Czechoslovakia at the time began to attempt emigration to West Germany. Ethnic minority organizations, if they existed at all, were under Communist sway to the same degree as all other social organizations, functioning as no more than transmission levers for the CPCz.

Top management and functionaries were being replaced throughout the public sector. The new regime created its own elites, which in turn served it unconditionally, as they owed their prestigious social standing, as well as the material benefits that came with it, solely to the Communist takeover. The main exponent of this concept was Rudolf Slánský, the then General Secretary of the CPCz; at the CPCz's Central Committee meeting held on 17th and 18th November, 1948, he made it the party's aim to train workers and peasants to become the new intelligentsia. To quote him, 'the first task in this (i.e. personnel-related) domain is to create our own management staff in the state and economic apparatus, and army and police officers, who will share a working-class background and devotion to the party.'

The job of putting Slánský's ideas into practice fell to Ladislav Kopřiva, the CPCz's Central Personnel Office Secretary, who maintained that 'workers are the most reliable guarantee that we shall march vigorously forward. Our personnel politics should therefore always be geared towards strengthening the working-class element, ensuring that its number corresponds to the party's needs and the historical mission of the proletariat. [...] The working-class personnel is the mainstay of the party.'

Prior to the CPCz's 9th Convention in 1949, the industrial domain had no more than a handful of 'working-class CEOs.' It took less than a year after Slánský laid his plan of creating a dependable elite with an appropriate class background for their numbers to soar to 28% – and later to 30% – of all CEOs of national enterprises. In addition, the Communists appointed working-class personnel to key positions in the state administration authorities, from government ministries, through to national committees, to top ranks in the army, police, and the judiciary, but also to positions of foremen and what were termed production chiefs in industrial and agricultural establishments. Among the tools used by the CPCz to breed its own new personnel were centralized schools for the working class, formed after authorization from the CPCz's Central Committee Secretariat in October 1949. The original number of 17 schools rose to 24 in 1951, with an enrolment of 1,750 students. Their graduates began replacing the old functionaries, many of whom had socially or politically unacceptable backgrounds.

The judiciary is a good example of a domain in which the new regime felt an urgent need to dismiss 'old experts,' who often harboured anti-Communist convictions, and replace them with its own people. As qualified lawyers who also adhered to the Communist ideology were few and far between, the regime set about breeding a new class of lawyers, recruited from among the working class. For this purpose, the party set up the Workers' Law School, accepting students who could often boast only a primary school degree. This fact was brushed aside; what was important was their political dependability. By 1952, more than three out of four leadership positions in the judiciary were taken by graduates of this institution.

As has been said, the working class was supposed to be the mainstay of the newly-installed regime in Czechoslovakia. In addition to recruiting as many members of the proletariat as possible to replace old and unreliable experts in all domains of public life, the Communists took great pains to win the favour of those workers who remained in the factory halls. Their efforts were aided by a new wave of nationalization, launched after the takeover. As early as 28th April, 1948, the Communist-controlled National Assembly passed a series of bills concerning the nationalization of wholesale, foreign-trade enterprises, travel agencies, medical institutions, construction, transportation and printing works, and other companies with over 50 employees. Similar nationalization measures continued to be taken until the autumn of that year. The already existing national enterprises played a central role in nationalization, using the process to knock out potential competition by demanding the nationalization of enterprises with under 50 employees, even though this was in violation of the current law. By the end of 1948, over 5,000 industrial enterprises had been national-ized, of which only some 2,700 employed more than 50 people. All in all, the new wave of nationalization in Czechoslovakia left only 3,848 enterprises in private hands, with as few as 48,342 employees – or 3.8 % of the total industrial workforce. What is more, their existence was rather uncertain, as the CPCz openly declared its intention to nationalize all 'means of production,' a concept which soon became reality.

The post-February wave of nationalization was first and foremost a political act, un-substantiated by economic need. In fact, it was becoming clear that the development of the sector nationalized after 1945 and its economic results were unfavourable and did not economically justify its further extension. The new nationalization wave in 1948 aggravated this unfavourable trend, resulting in the demise of tri-sector economy in the Czechoslovak Republic. Privately-owned businesses virtually ceased to exist, and the state's position in the economy assumed the character of a monopoly. The nationalized enterprises were be-ing integrated into enormous organizations, which thus found it very easy to advance their own narrow interests. In consequence, nationalization and the subsequent monopoliza-tion of the state economy led to the annihilation of competition and to the suffocation of all entrepreneurial initiatives. All these facts had a negative impact on the future of the Czechoslovak economy, making it ineffective and contributing to the chronic economic crisis of the Communist regime.

Incidentally, the efforts of the Communist regime to gain complete control over the economy did not end with nationalising enterprises with more than 50 employees. The party went on a quest, soon crowned with success, to eliminate small businessmen, private craftsmen and shopkeepers. The collectivization of agriculture was another major shift in the development of the country. Despite the Communists' assurances before the February takeover that 'no kolkhozes will be set up' in Czechoslovakia, and although they even continued to distribute land among small and medium farmers thereafter, the National Assembly passed a bill on 23rd February 1949 regarding the formation of Standard Farming Co-operatives. Even though the law presumed that the private farmers would join the co-operatives voluntarily, the Communists in fact used any measures necessary to make them join, including brutal violence.

As a result of the continuing nationalization, all workers became employees of national enterprises. This made ownership and employment relations in Czechoslovakia notably simpler, and enabled the state to implement its social and wage policies more easily. They were characterized by a tendency towards social levelling. The primary feature of the social and wage policy package was preferential treatment of workers both in the wage domain and in terms of social prestige. From 1948 to 1953, workers' nominal wages rose by 56% (from 734 to 1,145 CZK), compared to a 26% increase (from 1,214 to 1,527 CZK) for engineers and technical professionals and a 15.2% increase (from 914 to 1,053 CZK) for administrative workers. Concurrently, the social prestige of the intelligentsia as a group plummeted, as a lack of appreciation for education became widespread. This fact was also reflected in the social and wage domain. While, in 1948, the wages of engineers and technical professionals were 66% higher (and administrative workers' wages 24% higher) than those of factory workers, by 1953 they were respectively 33% higher and 8% lower. Though the wages of industrial employees rose continuously, wages in other domains either stagnated or fell. Another feature of the social and wage policy of the day was wage levelling based on underestimating qualified blue-collar work; on deliberately reducing the differences in the remuneration of qualified versus unqualified workers. Most workers, regardless of their qualifications, were placed in medium-wage categories, the differences between the individual categories being so small that 45% of workers' monthly wages were within a 200 CZK range of the average wage. A third feature of the policy entailed various benefits for factory workers, including a greater share in social consumption and the privileged provision of supplies.

The social and wage levelling in favour of factory workers, especially the preferential treatment of some of its groups, was a political factor, working to stabilize the Communist regime. A host of other measures also contributed to winning the working class' support for the Communist politics; most workers now felt a heightened sense of social security and enjoyed the right to a job, doubly guaranteed by a shortage of available workers in the market; in addition, the new social measures implemented by the party worked primarily to their advantage. Quality of life of the working class increased in comparison with the pre-war period: between 1949 and 1953, the nominal wage rose by 54% (or 418 CZK) for construction workers and by a massive 59% (430 CZK) for industrial workers. The real value of working-class wages was further increased by a number of social and child-care benefits, low prices of services, cheap meals available at the workplace, cheap rents (around 40% of workers owned their houses, the rest lived in rented flats with rents ranging from 5 to 7% of their wages.) Still, the increase in workers' wages was differentiated and income levels in most priority domains of heavy industry far exceeded the national average. The raise affected around 400,000 workers, who also enjoyed highly preferential provision of supplies.

The CPCz focused much attention on the issue of supply provision. The rationing system had been in effect since 1945, enabling the National Front government to deliver sufficient supplies of food and consumer goods to its citizens, while differentiating between people holding jobs and pensioners, between single people and family providers, and so on. After the February coup, the CPCz had several reasons for creating a free market. Most importantly, the party felt it was time for a populist gesture. There was also the need to reduce the surfeit of money in circulation, and the fact that some other countries in the Soviet Bloc had achieved considerable success in this area certainly played a part. Therefore, beginning on 1st January 1949, Czechoslovakia introduced a free market, which co-existed alongside the already established closed market and offered certain types of goods without limitation, although for much higher prices. The free market proved highly effective, leading the CPCz to further extend the range of goods supplied freely as of 1st June, 1949, immediately after the party's 9th Convention.

The 9th Convention of the CPCz, held from 25th to 29th May, 1949, was the first for the party after its victorious coup d'état. A new era for the country's development was ushered in, and a 'general line of socialist construction in the Czechoslovak Republic' was inaugurated. In their speeches to Czechoslovak citizens, the Communist leaders promised many things, including: a significant improvement in the quality of the people's lives; the construction of state-owned machinery and tractor stations in the countryside, designed to lighten the burden of labour for the farmers; the elimination of 'anti-people, anti-state and reactionary elements' from the state administration, army and security forces; and, last but not least, a reform of the secondary-school and university system which would create opportunities for the enrolment of working-class and peasant youth, while preventing the 'Reaction' from studying. Needless to say, it was reiterated that unemployment, poverty and exploitation were finished once and for all.

As previously mentioned, the Communist government was primarily trying to win the hearts of as many of the proletariat as possible after the February coup. In addition, the party also sought the favour of the other social classes. The Communist propagandists launched a major campaign designed to convince the public that the party was open to 'all Czechs and Slovaks of good character.' This rhetoric was noted by Pavel Tigrid, a prominent figure of the Czechoslovak democratic exile, when he said that it was evident after February 1948 that 'the CPCz put on "velvet gloves" to win over – or at least neutralize – those classes of the population that would never have thought of following it...' The result was astounding: by November 1949, the CPCz had 2.6 million members, representing 22% of the total population, or one of every three Czechoslovak adults. There are indications that for a few months after the takeover, the CPCz leadership did in fact pay attention to its influence on the public and to the popular response to its steps. An example of this was that the CPCz received weekly reports, starting in 1949, from its intelligence bureau about the situation and state of opposition in the country. This proves that the party was eminently interested in being informed of societal reactions.

At the same time, the Communist regime severely and harshly punished anybody who dared stand up against it. On 6th June, 1948, the new National Assembly passed bill No. 231/48 Coll. about the protection of the people's democratic republic, which gave the green light to imprisoning thousands of people considered inconvenient by the regime. Another bill, adopted on 12th June, 1950, sanctioned the establishment of forced labour camps in Czechoslovakia, to which inconvenient persons could be sent based entirely on the decision of the national committees – no court order was required. Enormous power was now enjoyed by the secret police, which had set about constructing a network of informers throughout the country.

In 1949, the first political trials of prominent figures of the defeated democratic regime took place. On 21st June, 1949, the life of General Heliodor Píka, the former head of the Czechoslovak Military Mission to the USSR, ended on a scaffold. Other show trials soon followed, with members of the clergy and with the so-called leaders of an evil conspiracy against the republic, featuring the former National-Socialist Member of Parliament Milada Horáková and other figures. The trials were designed in such a way that would make them as shocking as possible for the public. All of them followed a script and were staged in front of politically vetted audiences; the victims were selected to suit the political needs of the regime, and the sentences – particularly cruel – were determined in advance by political organs; the courts merely passed these on to the accused.

Besides using violent means to break the backbone of the nation, the Communists also strove to subdue its spirit. They had controlled the Ministry of Information since 1945, which enabled them to dominate the radio and use it to spread their propaganda and curb the dissemination of objective information. While the February coup was still in progress, the Ministry of Information placed a ban on importing Western press to Czechoslovakia and left the ban in effect after the governmental crisis was over and a new cabinet had been appointed. To make matters worse, censorship was introduced, fettering all Czechoslovak dailies, journals, books, and films, and causing the works of inconvenient authors to be removed from public libraries. Simultaneously, the borders were closed, preventing Czechoslovak citizens from travelling abroad. In time, the entire country was surrounded by an intricate system of barriers topped with barbed wire and, later, surrounded by mine fields and other obstacles. The borders were guarded by special armed units known as the Border Patrol, members of which were selected from families with favourable political and class backgrounds.

At the same time it was transforming public life, the CPCz set about rebuilding the economic structure of the country. One of the main tenets of its policy was a plan-based management of the national economy – the mainstay of the Soviet Union's economic policy, which the CPCz had embraced as its own. For this reason, Soviet advisors were appointed to key positions in virtually all national economic departments. Following the Soviet example, the course of the economy was to follow a cycle of five-year plans. The first of these plans, delineated by the years 1949 to 1953, entailed a major overhaul of the Czechoslovak economy. It had been designed by a team of Czechoslovak experts before the coup d'état, its outline having been drawn up separately by different parties' experts on national economy. After February 1948, those who represented political parties other than the CPCz were removed from key positions.

The first five-year plan of economic development of the Czechoslovak Republic, as it was officially called, waited until 27th October, 1948, to be passed by the National Assembly as Bill No. 241 Coll. Its very first article proclaimed that it was designed 'to develop and rebuild the Czechoslovak economy' and 'significantly improve the quality of life for all strata of the working people both in urban and rural areas.' Article No. 2 specified that this objective 'should be achieved by the full and continuous development of productive forces in such a way as to increase the national income by 50%,' as well as by 'economic co-operation with countries with centrally planned economies,' that is, countries of the Eastern Bloc. The bill openly declared that the defensive power of the country would be strengthened once these goals were reached.

The targets of the first five-year plan were highly ambitious. It set the growth rate of industrial production from 288 billion in 1948 to 454 billion CZK by 1953, which amounted to a 57% growth, when all the tasks defined by the plan were to have been fulfilled. The increase of output was set at 35% for the coal mining industry; 52% for power engineering; 49% for metallurgy; 62% for the chemical industry; 59% for construction materials and ceramics production, and an astounding 93% for metal-manufacturing industry, among others. The five-year plan put a clear priority on developing heavy industry to the detriment of service industries. Monumental growth was also planned for agriculture (11% for the cultivation of crops and 86% livestock farming), the construction industry, and the transportation and trade industries. The five-year plan also determined the pace of development of the material and cultural maturity of the people, planned an advancement in social welfare, improvement in health care delivery, and culture- and education-related services, and for maximising private consumption. The centrally-planned economy also allowed for channelling investments into those regions of the country that had so far been under-industrialized – mainly Slovakia, but also southern Bohemia and the Highlands.

From the start, the implementation of the first five-year plan encountered unexpected political obstacles, stemming from the nature of the Communist regime. Soviet disapproval led to the CPCz leadership abandoning their original intention of 1947 to create a harmonious fusion of planned and market economies. Furthermore, the continuing militarization of the economy, characteristic of the early 1950s, presupposed a higher-than-usual degree of centralization in the national economy. Building a large army required the construction of new munitions factories, new investments, and qualified staff; all this hindered the implementation of tasks planned in other sectors of the national economy. In addition, agriculture struggled against the negative consequences of forced and unscrupulous collectivization.

The Cold War economy called for the mobilization of the entire work force – another step made possible by the new approach to economic management. In the early 1950s, heavy industry drew in more than 400,000 new workers, most of whom had formerly worked in the service industry, agriculture, state administration, or had been homemakers. Investment cuts in light industry resulted in a loss of traditional markets abroad, causing both economic losses and a shortage of consumer goods in the domestic market, which in turn aggravated popular discontent. The economic strategy adopted by the country was uneconomical, allowing enterprises to carry on production regardless of both primary cost and actual profits. Other factors contributing to the unprofitability of the Czechoslovak economy included the fragmentation of investment, a high number of unfinished construction projects, extensive geological investigation, and unprofitable extraction and processing of raw materials. The concept of Czechoslovakia as a mechanical engineering power, imposed by the Soviet Union, overestimated its economic potential, thus sending the economy into recession. The regime responded by increasing centralizsation, which it apparently believed to be a cure-all. By 1953, it was clear that while the original targets set by the five-year plan had been achieved, the enhanced tasks later added failed to be fulfilled.

One of the instruments of the gradual subjection of Czechoslovak economy to the economic and political interests of the Soviet Union – a course set after 1948 – was the country's membership in the Council for Mutual Economic Assistance, or COMECON. This was an international organization designed – according to its statute adopted as late as 1959 – to 'increase multilateral economic co-operation and facilitate the development of economic integration.' COMECON was founded on 5th-8th January, 1949, in Moscow, with its first members being Czechoslovakia, Albania, Bulgaria, Hungary, Poland, Romania and the USSR; the German Democratic Republic joined in 1950.

It should not be overlooked that part of the Czechoslovak population rejected the Communist takeover and openly protested the new order imposed by the CPCz. The first large demonstration against the new regime took place in July 1948 during the 9th Sokol gathering in Prague, and was followed by a demonstration on the occasion of President Beneš's funeral in September of the same year. Nonetheless, there were far fewer opponents of the new regime than there were proponents of the 'regenerated people's democracy' – a term coined by the new regime. Many people opted to leave the country and settle in democratic countries abroad; an overwhelming majority of them were convinced that the Cold War would soon precipitate into a 'hot war' and that crossing the border would ultimately give them the chance to help liberate the country as members of Western armed forces. The precise number of exiles who left after February 1948 has not been determined, but a combination of various sources has allowed historians to estimate that more than 60,000 people went into exile during the first two decades of Communist rule. A considerable number of Czechs and Slovaks decided to fight the Communist usurpers on the domestic front, some of them ready to pick up arms. The 'third resistance,' or the resistance movement against the CPCz government, has yet to be researched in great detail, however, it is clear that the StB infiltrated the movement with its agents and clamped down with great efficiency. Most participants in the struggle for democracy ended up in prison and many were executed. The secret police carried out pre-emptive arrests of those citizens who may not have actively participated in the resistance, but were nevertheless considered potential dissenters.

510

Family members of the persecuted citizens, exiles, and people whose behaviour did not correspond to the norms set by the regime, were not spared from victimization. In order to prevent their ascent in society and the improvement of their social status, and to make sure that only 'reliable' people were assigned to managerial positions, the regime introduced a 'personnel policy code,' which applied to virtually all Czechoslovak citizens.

The politics of personnel played a decisive role in the Communist power mechanism. The regime used it to fill key and leadership positions with people who either endorsed the Communist ideology or were for various other reasons willing to carry out orders and assignments from the CPCz. The rule of personnel nomenclature was introduced, based on the parallel existence of state and party authorities: on specific levels of the political hierarchy, party authorities controlled who was assigned to positions within the state administration (that is, the district committees of the CPCz filled the leadership positions of the district national committees, as well as all the economic, cultural and educational organizations controlled by the national committees.) It follows that higher-level party organs had more power, and determined staffing for more prominent positions. The CPCz's personnel politics also greatly affected the make-up of the legislative organs of the state, which in democratic societies are normally independent. In effect, in order to have the chance of a seat in parliament, one had to be favoured by the party and be prepared to carry out its orders wholeheartedly. In turn, this meant that the parliament only passed bills that further enhanced the power of the CPCz and its 'leadership role.' The regime used the police, which was of course also under Communist control, to enforce observance of these laws. The personnel politics of the Communist state also affected the admission policies of secondary schools and universities and the conferment of scientific degrees, as well as many similar aspects of life.

From the early 1950s, the policies of the CPCz increasingly conflicted with the interests of an ever larger segment of the population. Disapproval of the regime was becoming widespread and came not only from groups that had rejected Communism from the very start out of principle, but also from part of the working class, and even the new elites bred by the party after February 1948. The Communist regime now faced a deep political and economic crisis.

3 First Crisis of the Communist Regime and Its Resolution

After the CPCz government had been installed and began implementing its programme, one of the consequences was the severance of the country from its traditional trade and economic relations with Western states and – after the Soviet-Yugoslav dispute in the summer 1948 – also with Yugoslavia. As a result, the Czechoslovak economy suffered considerable troubles, which were very hard to overcome. The speedy militarization of society, as ordered by the Kremlin, proved even more taxing. In an effort to meet Soviet demands and prepare the country for a new armed conflict, the Prague Communist leadership decided in the early 1950s to add more items to the list of tasks set for the economy; these proved, however, impossible to fulfil. As the Czechoslovak Republic inherited an advanced armament industry from both the pre-war and war periods, the demands imposed by the Soviet General Staff were very high. Czechoslovakia was to become the blacksmith of the Eastern Bloc, supplying weaponry not only to its own army, but also the armies of other Soviet allies. However, building up the military according to Moscow's blue-print required significant intervention in the economy, which in turn had a detrimental effect on non-military sectors and on the quality of life of the population.

The total cost of building a large army and police force between 1949 and 1953 came to 235.7 billion CZK, making up half of all economic investments of the time. In 1953, the share of defence expenditure reached 18% of national income (compared to 6% in 1950) and 20% of officially acknowledged state-budget spending. Defence-related investments amounted to 24.88% and 34%, respectively, of total investment volume in 1952 and 1953. From 1950 to 1953, armament production rose from 100% to 453%, its volume exceeding that of all mechanical engineering production combined in 1948. The armament engineering industry grew sixteen-fold between 1948 and 1953, making up 32.3% of total engineering production volume. In addition to the construction of new military industry enterprises and adequate investments, the programme of building a large army also called for the supply of good-quality and rare raw materials, qualified staff, and enormous funds. All of these factors required a reduction in civil production, thus preventing the fulfilment of the five-year plan. In addition, in 1953 alone, the army appropriated 15.88% of textile consumption, 30.7% of clothes production, 16.9% of underwear production, 5.3% of leather footwear production, 7.4% of meat production, and 8.3% of lard production, to name but a part of their toll.

The investments and raw materials consumed by the army elsewhere became scarce, most notably in the process of the much-needed modernization of Czechoslovak industry and the construction of non-military enterprises; the appropriated goods were also in short supply in the domestic market. Yet, judging by their payroll checks alone, the population would have had no notion of how badly the economy was doing. The salaries and wages of employees, factory workers in particular, had marked a continuous increase since 1948. On the one hand, the shortage of consumer goods disgruntled workers: beginning in 1950, the police registered growing discontent across all sides of the working class, including the new working-class elite, so meticulously created by the regime after 1949. On the other hand, the impossibility of purchasing quality products prevented money from returning to the state treasury, causing financial capital to accumulate in private hands.

The government responded to the unfavourable situation by lowering workers' wages. Political pressures prevented it from cutting wages directly; instead, in November 1951, it discontinued Christmas bonus payments, which had been awarded annually at the end of each year. This measure saved the state approximately 2.5 billion CZK, but saving the money was not in itself a priority. As Prime Minister Antonín Zápotocký said in a radio address on 22nd November, 1951: 'This is a sum that worries us. The challenge is not how to raise the funds; the challenge is how to provide something for those funds.' He thereby admitted the disastrous shortage of consumer goods that plagued the Czechoslovak domestic market in the early 1950s: waiting lines outside of stores became longer and popular discontent increased. The Communist regime tried to save the day by tightening its grip on the already strictly controlled economy. The rationing system was re-applied to all groceries and imposed on a wide range of commodities that had previously been freely available. As a result, the black market flourished and the gulf between the regime and the population continued to deepen.

The discontinuation of the Christmas bonus, combined with a crisis in the provision of supplies, ignited a major wave of unrest. On 21st and 22nd November, 1951, strike action swept across major enterprises in Brno and many other places in the region, and tens of thousands of demonstrators flooded the streets of the Moravian capital, where they came up against an armed People's Militia. This was the first major workers' protest against the Communist regime in Czechoslovakia since February 1948, but it was not to be the last for long. Strike action spread to other factories and mines around the country, especially in the Ostrava and Kladno regions. The state was unable to respond in any way other than through reprisals and persecution. In short, the Communist regime in Czechoslovakia faced a deep economic, social and political crisis in the early 1950s, which prevented it from achieving the objectives it had set itself, namely to enhance the quality of life of the Czechoslovak population and help increase its cultural and educational level, and ultimately establish a just, class-free society.

The situation was further aggravated by the state of terror that reigned in Czechoslovakia in the early 1950s. It was no longer directed only at people who were considered the regime's natural enemies – members of pre-February political parties, clerics and former entrepreneurs – but affected also other strata of the population, including, curiously, some members and functionaries of the CPCz. The prospect of a speedy collectivization of agriculture led to the use of unscrupulous, brutal methods of breaking private farmers' resistance to joining the co-operatives. Similar aggression was used to pressure private craftsmen and shopkeepers still holding on to their companies into disbanding them. Persecution was directed at members of foreign military units, particularly those who had fought in the West, but also soldiers of the Czechoslovak Army Corps in the USSR, Volhynia Czechs, who had recently returned to their old homeland, and members of international brigades who had fought on the side of the Republican Army in the Spanish Civil War. Stalin's thesis, which had recently been put forward, concerning the aggravation of the class struggle and 'discovering the enemy in our own ranks,' led to the arrest and incarceration of many Communist functionaries. Inspired by the great political trials that had occurred in the USSR, Albania, Bulgaria and Hungary since the late 1940s, Czechoslovakia embarked on its own search for 'traitors,' who had allegedly wormed their way into the party in order to harm it from within. Their elimination and the trial preparation were overseen by Soviet advisors, whose numbers were quickly rising. This new wave of terror resulted in the trials of CPCz exponents who had, until recently, been revered. Most prominent of all was the trial of the 'anti-state conspiracy against the Republic,' which was held from 20th to 27th November, 1952, following months of preparation. Fourteen high-ranking party officials faced charges, including CPCz's former Secretary General Rudolf Slánský, the Minister of Foreign Affairs Vladimír Clementis, the Deputy Minister of National Defence Bedřich Reicin, two Deputy Ministers of Foreign Affairs, three Deputy Ministers of Foreign Trade, and several officials of the party's Central Committee and Regional Secretaries of the CPCz. Eleven of these were sentenced to death and subsequently executed, and three received life in prison.

The wave of arrests was not limited to those convicted in the Slánský trial. Dozens and hundreds of other Communists were simultaneously or subsequently tried, while others were never brought to court and were eventually released, after spending a long time in unlawful detention. These events left both society and the party shaken to their foundations. Positions had to be relinquished not only by those arrested and investigated by the StB, but also by their closest collaborators. Hundreds of people were affected. Both top officials and rank-and-file members of the CPCz were wracked with insecurity, which brought chaos to the party's tightly-knit phalanx. The investigation of top party officials, most of them previously highly-respected and venerated, and charges of the most heinous crimes brought against them, undermined the trust of people from all walks of life in the politics of the CPCz; in many cases, even circles previously considered to be the power base of the Communist politics were now rejecting official propaganda and questioning the arguments put forth by the party leaders.

Party members and, to an extent, the general public, now looked to the Chairman of the CPCz and Czechoslovak President Klement Gottwald as their only certainty. However, Gottwald, who had enjoyed unshaken authority in the party, died on 14th March, 1953, shortly after the demise of Joseph Vissarionovich Stalin, the revered leader of the world's proletariat. The Communist regime in Czechoslovakia had suffered too many blows, and the political, economic and social crisis which it had been facing came to a head.

The Presidium of the CPCz met on 20th March, 1953, the day after Gottwald's funeral, and agreed that the best candidate for the post of the Czechoslovak President was Antonín Zápotocký, hitherto the Prime Minister. They were rather more hesitant in picking the new party leader. After lengthy discussions, the Presidium decided to abolish the position of party chairman and instead appoint Antonín Novotný Secretary of the Central Committee of the CPCz (CC CPCz), as head of its Central Secretariat. This new position did not receive the title of 'First Secretary' until the CC CPCz meeting on the 4th and 5th September, 1953 and, incidentally, was not warranted by party statutes. During the meeting held on 21st March, 1953, the party's Central Committee passed all motions. On the same day, the National Assembly went ahead and elected Zápotocký the country's new head; Viliam Široký became the new Prime Minister, and Antonín Novotný immediately took up the position of the leader of the party's apparatus.

The haste with which the CC CPCz Presidium filled the leadership positions was not unwarranted. As one of its members, Jaromír Dolanský, put it, the situation required 'that the leaders show their decisiveness,' a claim he was able to back up with plausible argument. Indeed, instances of outright disapproval of the Communist regime had begun to multiply. In connection with Stalin's death and on the anniversary of T. G. Masaryk's birthday, for example, a bomb attack directed at the Secretariat of the CPCz's Municipal Committee was carried out in Hostinné, East Bohemia, with anti-Communist slogans appearing around town. The biggest anti-regime demonstration, with hundreds of participants, took place only a little later, on 10th April, in Prostějov, Central Moravia. In May, strike action was called in the workshops of the Czechoslovak Railways in Česká Lípa. These events may well have been isolated and the police were able to track down their instigators shortly afterwards; but they nonetheless indicated that relations between the controllers and the controlled were impaired, and suggested that popular discontent might eventually be expressed in a more riotous fashion. The party leadership therefore strove to find a solution to the regime's crisis.

Among the steps taken to resolve the crisis was the monetary reform instituted on 31st May and 1st June, 1953, with the following key measures:

1) Based on a newly passed amendment, the monetary unit – the Czechoslovak crown – was backed by gold and tied to the Soviet ruble.
2) All hitherto-used means of payment were replaced by new ones printed in the USSR. Citizens were advised to exchange old money for new money based on exchange rates tailored to the amount of money and savings at their disposal.
3) The rationing system was abolished and replaced by a free market for all commodity types.
4) Price differences between the individual types of closed- and free-market commodities were equalized by decreasing the former free-market prices and increasing the closed-market prices.

A great many other measures were taken, all designed to contribute to strengthening the economy, but their practical impact was not immediately obvious to the population. Above all, people wanted to know how and at what rate they could exchange their money. They were shocked to find out that no more than CZK 300 could be exchanged at the rate of 5:1; the rest of their money was subjected to an exchange rate of 50:1. (The 5:1 rate was not even available for some population groups, such as private farmers, who were obliged to use the 50:1 rate exclusively.)

The monetary reform had an unfavourable impact on all strata of the population, but people with savings in banks were hit the worst. Savings were exchanged on the basis of a sliding scale system, with increasingly unfavourable rates imposed on higher deposits. The Communist state made a fortune in the reform, acquiring not only the population's savings, but also the yield of their fixed deposits and life insurance policies. The overall profits were used to help ameliorate the gargantuan national debt. This 'great monetary robbery,' as the reform was nicknamed by the Western press, not only helped the Communist regime solve its pressing economic problems, but also created sizeable financial reserves that would cover the grandiose social gestures planned for the near future. The monetary reform impoverished a wide spectrum of the population, some of whom were deprived of their entire life savings. The upside was that the government succeeded in taking the first step towards improving the situation in supply provision by decreasing the population's purchasing power.

Outraged citizens launched strikes against 129 enterprises, and riots swept across many cities. The most intense anti-Communist disturbance took place in Pilsen, where the workers at the V.I.Lenin Works (formerly the Škoda Works) took to the streets and seized the city centre, the city hall, and the prison. It took the police, the People's Militia and the Border Patrol until evening to quash the uprising. Harsh reprisals ensued: 256 people were brought before the court in Pilsen alone, facing charges in a total of fifteen trials. Likewise, representatives of striking Ostrava miners were sent to jail, as were malcontents from other parts of the republic. The newly-elected president Antonín Zápotocký made no secret of his intention to take strong action against anybody who complained about the Communist regime, regardless of their class background. At the same time, he tried to calm the situation down by using a conciliatory tone, especially as he began to feel the effect of the changes in the USSR following Stalin's death. The new leadership of the Communist Party of the Soviet Union (CPSU) and of the country inaugurated 'the New Course,' which made it a priority to produce consumer goods for the Soviet population and brought about a degree of liberalization on the domestic political scene, resulting in the release of the first political prisoners from the Siberian gulags.

Antonín Zápotocký attempted to apply the New Course to the Czechoslovak condition. His first goal was to appease the rural parts of the country, which had been shaken by forced collectivization. In a speech made at the Klíčava Dam near Prague on 1st August, 1953, he admitted that peasants had often been violently forced to join the co-operatives. He declared that this practice was now over and that the CPCz and the government would not prevent anybody from leaving the co-ops, should they choose to do so. His assurances led to a major outflow of workers from the co-ops, many of which had to be disbanded as a result. Zápotocký remained isolated with his programme of partial liberalization. Most notably, his anti-collectivization views met with the fierce opposition of Antonín Novotný, who – backed by the Soviets – managed to push Zápotocký to the side and gradually accumulated power in his own hands. While countries such as the USSR, Hungary, and Poland were experiencing the Communist regime's political thaw, no such attempts were made in Czechoslovakia.

Instead, the CPCz leaders preferred to focus on the social advancement of the society and on increasing the population's quality of life. Their efforts were mostly manifested in a series of price cuts. The first retail price cut came on 1st October, 1953, followed by six more before the end of 1956. As a result, the price of groceries dropped by 18% in a relatively short period of time. However, price cuts were not the only measure taken by the CPCz leaders to improve the social conditions of the general public. Nearly every meeting of the CPCz leadership had on its agenda a new social measure designed to make life easier for the people. The resulting increase in the population's quality of life made the political and social climate in the country more favourable for the regime in power. It became apparent that the damage caused by the Communist policies in people's minds up to this point was rectifiable and that a consensus between the governing and the governed in Czechoslovakia could be reached after all. Nikita Sergeyevich Khrushchev, among others, commended the CPCz's social policies at a meeting of the Presidium of the CPSU's Central Committee held on 24th October, 1956, calling on other Communist countries to learn from their example.

Social policies favourable to the working population were made possible by the Soviet Union's political shift. The new leadership at the Kremlin abandoned the politics of pursuing war-like conflict with the West, instead promoting the peaceful co-existence of states with different political systems. This new trend was accompanied by cuts in armament spending, a decrease in troop numbers, and a reduction in armament production both in the USSR and the other Eastern Bloc countries. This was another reason the Communist regime in Czechoslovakia could afford to invest more money than before in social projects and light industry, to support the production of goods until then in short supply, and to provide a financial boost to collectivized agriculture. It was now, figuratively speaking, able to make caterpillar tractors and combine harvesters instead of tanks, and lift the burden from rural Czechoslovakia.

The improved economy and quality of life in the country gradually lifted the spirits of the workers, who no longer felt inclined to question their traditional left-wing politics. In turn, the Communist leadership no longer felt obliged to abandon the existing Stalinist line, regardless that Stalinism had, by and large, been relinquished in the USSR and other socialist countries, where the unlawful practices of the past began to be exposed and calls for rectification were heard. Czechoslovakia, however, continued to stage trumped-up political trials even after Stalin's and Gottwald's deaths, including one with a group of Slovak 'bourgeois nationalists' (among them Gustáv Husák, who received a long prison term in this trial), and did not stop carrying out executions (including that of Osvald Závodský, former head of the Communist StB, in 1954.) To top it all, on the occasion of the 10th anniversary of the liberation of Czechoslovakia, the regime unveiled a gigantic monument of Joseph Stalin, which rather anachronistically stayed put for another seven years until 1962, when it was pulled down.

A new test of the firmness of the Communist regime came in 1956. The world was astir over Khrushchev's speech at the 20th Convention of the CPSU, about the 'cult of personality and its consequences,' in which he exposed the criminal practices of J. V. Stalin. In consequence, the CPCz was encouraged to follow in the Soviet footsteps and pursue de-Stalinization to a degree tailored to Czechoslovak conditions. However, the country's Stalinist leadership, inextricably linked to the crimes of the previous years, was neither able nor inclined to do so. Instead, it focused on suppressing the spontaneous democratization efforts that had swept across the whole of society, including within the CPCz itself, in the spring of 1956. Heated discussions over the results of the CPSU's 20th Convention were held in primary party organizations in March and April, which subjected the CPCz leadership to strong criticism. Calls for convening an unscheduled party convention, which would lay the foundation of a new political line, were more and more common. The recent practices were roundly berated at the 2nd Czechoslovak Writers' Congress, held from 22nd to 29th April, 1956. The demands heard during the congress included the democratization of society, the abolishment of censorship, and justice for writers who were banned from publishing. Critical voices were also heard during students' rag days, which were permitted once again after years of bans in many university towns.

The CC CPCz Presidium did its best to resist the Czechoslovak public's pressure. Although some functionaries exercised self-criticism, all the blame for the Communist 'deformations' of the previous years was ultimately pinned on Alexej Čepička, the Minister of National Defence and Deputy Prime Minister, who also happened to be the late President Gottwald's son-in-law. By order of the CC CPCz, he was dismissed from all public offices and went into seclusion. Instead of the unscheduled convention demanded by the primary party organizations, the 2nd national conference of the party took place from 11th till 14th June, 1956; the delegate selection mechanism was such that it ensured no dramatic change of the party's political line would be introduced during the conference. Indeed, all major criticism was muffled during the event. The conference issued a resolution stating that the 'general line of the construction of socialism in Czechoslovakia is correct' and the 'minor deformations' of the previous years would be rectified.

The conclusions of the CPSU's 20th Convention received a much more enthusiastic response in Poland and Hungary than in Czechoslovakia. At first, the Czechoslovak public followed the ongoing democratization process in these countries with approval; but when the anti-Communist revolution broke out in Hungary in 1956, accompanied by a wave of terror that caught Czechs and Slovaks unprepared, they were unable to respond to it in any way other than by rejection. The few brave people who tried to use the occasion of 28th October, 1956, for anti-Communist demonstrations and then follow them with an uprising similar to that in Hungary ended up in police custody. Reports of atrocities in Budapest were shocking to the rest of the population, leading them to reconsider their objections to the Communist regime and ask themselves what was better – socialism as they knew it, which guaranteed them a relatively comfortable life and social security, or political uncertainty, or even the collapse of the socialist system, followed by a return to the pre-Munich conditions.

The CPCz leadership noted with appreciation that party members acknowledged during their meetings that 'the CPCz's Central Committee took the right course after the 20th Convention of the CPSU by not allowing the dictatorship of the proletariat to be undermined by various so-called democratization measures.' Some primary party organizations, which had requested an unscheduled party convention a short time before, were now eating humble pie and backtracking on their demand. At a meeting held at the S. K. Neumann Theatre in Prague, they declared that 'it was not until the latest events in Poland and Hungary that they had come to fully appreciate the potential threat to the unity of the CPCz, if other members of the party held the same views as [the insurgents in Poland and Hungary].' Party meetings were held with employees of universities and theatres, the Czechoslovak Academy of Sciences, with film-makers and writers. According to party documents of the period, 'the discussions confirmed that the party core was sound and solid across all the departments where meetings were held,' and that 'it had become even more consolidated in the recent period.'

The discussions of the political situation held in the autumn of 1956 were entirely different from those held in the spring: 'On reflection, concrete events brought our comrades to appreciate that the course determined by our party is correct. They openly talked about their errors during discussions and self-critically admitted having made mistakes in their party activities so far.' Without exception, Czechoslovak magazines that were culturally oriented informed their readers of the development of the Hungarian revolution in the same spirit as the rest of the press, that is to say, with a one-sided, biased, and frightened slant.

The defeat of the Hungarian revolution brought about by Soviet military intervention, coupled with the victory of forces opposed to democratization in Poland, put a stop to any further discussions concerning the internal democratization of socialist society and the rejection of Stalinist politics in Czechoslovakia once and for all.

Bibliography

BARTOŠEK, Karel: *Les aveux des archives: Prague–Paris–Prague 1948–1968*, Paris 1996.
BEER, Fritz: *Die Zukunft funktioniert noch nicht: ein Porträt der Tschechoslowakei 1948–1968*, Frankfurt am Main 1969.
BLAIVE, Muriel: *Une déstalinisation manquée: Tchécoslovaquie 1956*. Préf. de Krzysztof Pomian, Bruxelles 2005.
CONNELLY, John: *Captive university: the Sovietization of East German, Czech, and Polish higher education*, Chapel Hill 2000.
COTIC, Meir: *The Prague trial: the first anti-zionist show trial in the communist bloc*. Introduction by Karel Kaplan, New York 1987.
DUPAL', Peter: *Kommunistische und kirchliche prokommunistische Propaganda in der Tschechoslowakei von 1948 bis 1968: mit besonderer Berucksichtigung des slowakischen Landesteils in ihrem geschichtlichen Kontext*, Hamburg 2004.
FRENCH, Alfred: *Czech writers and politics 1945–1969*, Boulder 1982.
GOLDSTÜCKER, Eduard: *Prozesse: Erfahrungen eines Mitteleuropaers*, München–Hamburg 1989.
HODOS, George Hermann: *Schauprozesse: stalinistische Säuberungen in Osteuropa 1948–1954*, Berlin 2001.
HOFFMANN, Roland J.: *Die Anfänge der Emigration aus der Tschechoslowakei nach der kommunistischen Machtergreifung vom Februar 1948 und die provisorische Aufnahme der Flüchtlinge in der amerikanischen Besatzungszone Deutschlands*, Praha 1996.
JIRÁSEK, Zdeněk – ŠŮLA, Jaroslav: *Velká peněžní loupež v Československu 1953 aneb 50:1*, Ostrava 1992.
KALINOVÁ, Lenka: *Společenské proměny v čase socialistického experimentu. K sociálním dějinám v letech 1945–1969*, Praha 2007.
KAPLAN, Karel: *The Communist Party in power: a profile of party politics in Czechoslovakia*. Ed. and transl. by Fred Eidlin, Boulder 1987.
KAPLAN, Karel: *Political persecution in Czechoslovakia, 1948–1972*. Köln 1983.
KAPLAN, Karel: *Report on the murder of the general secretary*, Columbus 1990.
KAPLAN, Karel: *The overcoming of the regime crisis after Stalins death in Czechoslovakia, Poland and Hungary*. Introduction by Zdeněk Mlynář, Köln 1986.
KAPLAN, Karel: *The short march: the communist takeover in Czechoslovakia, 1945–1948*, New York 1987.
KAPLAN, Karel: *Die politischen Prozesse in der Tschechoslowakei 1948–1954*, München 1986.
KAPLAN, Karel: *Staat und Kirche in der Tschechoslowakei: die kommunistische Kirchenpolitik in den Jahren 1948–1952*, München 1990.
KAPLAN, Karel: *Das verhängnisvolle Bündnis: Unterwanderung, Gleichschaltung und Vernichtung der Tschechoslowakischen Sozialdemokratie 1944–1954*, Wuppertal 1984.

KAPLAN, Karel: *1952 procès politiques à Prague*, Paris 1980.

KAPLAN, Karel: *Dans les archives du comité central: trente ans de secrets du bloc sovietique*, Paris 1978.

KAPLAN, Karel: *Pět kapitol o únoru*, Brno 1997

KOSTA, Jiří Jindřich: Abriß *der sozialokonomischen Entwicklung der Tschechoslowakei 1945–1977*, Frankfurt am Main 1978.

KRAKOVSKÝ, Roman: *Rituel du 1er mai en Tchécoslovaquie, 1948–1989*, Paris 2004.

LIŠKA, Ondřej: *Jede Zeit ist Gottes Zeit: die Untergrund-Kirche in der Tschechoslowakei 1948–1989*, Leipzig 2003.

LÖFFLER, Emil F.: *Kirche auf dem Kreuzweg: 40 Jahre Christenverfolgung in der Tschechoslowakei*, Thaur 1993.

LONDON, Artur: *Ich gestehe: der Prozeß um Rudolf Slansky*, Berlin 1968.

Maderthaner, Wolfgang – Schafranek, Hans – Unfried, Berthold: *"Ich habe den Tod verdient": Schauprozesse und politische Verfolgung in Mittel- und Osteuropa 1945–1956*, Wien 1991.

MATTHEWS, John P. C.: *Majales: the abortive student revolt in Czechoslovakia in 1956*, Washington 1998.

MATTHEWS, John P. C.: *Tinderbox: East-central Europe in the spring, summer, and early fall of 1956*. Tucson 2003.

OREN, Mordechai: *Prisonnier politique à Prague, 1951–1956*, Paris 1960.

PELIKÁN, Jiří: *Pervertierte Justiz: Bericht der Kommission des ZK der KPTsch über die politischen Morde und Verbrechen in der Tschechoslowakei 1949–1963*, Wien–München–Zürich 1972.

PÉTERI, György: *Intellectual life and the first crisis of state socialism in East Central Europe: 1953–1956*, Trondheim 2001.

PYNSENT, Robert B.: The *phoney peace: power and culture in Central Europe 1945–49*, London 2000.

RAŠKA, Francis D.: *Fighting communism from afar: the Council of Free Czechoslovakia*, Boulder 2008.

RÉTI, Tamás: *Soviet economic impact on Czechoslovakia and Romania in the early postwar period: 1944–1956*, Washington 1987.

SLÁMA, Jiří: *Die sozio-ökonomische Umgestaltung der Nachkriegs- Tschechoslowakei: zur politik des kommunistischen Machtmonopols*, Wiesbaden 1977.

SUDA, Zdeněk: *Zealots and rebels: a history of the Communist Party of Czechoslovakia*, Stanford 1980.

ŠIK, Ota: *Das kommunistische Machtsystem*, Hamburg 1976.

TÁBORSKÝ, Eduard: *Communism in Czechoslovakia, 1948–1960*, Princeton 1961.

ZAND, Gertraude: *Totaler Realismus und peinliche Poesie: tschechische Untergrund-Literatur 1948–1953*, Frankfurt am Main 1998.

XIX. Communist Czechoslovakia on a Journey from a Consolidation of Totalitarianism towards a Liberalization of the Regime (1959–1967)

ÚSTAVA

ČESKOSLOVENSKÉ SOCIALISTICKÉ REPUBLIKY

PRAHA 1960

STÁTNÍ PEDAGOGICKÉ NAKLADATELSTVÍ

Title page of the Constitution of the Czechoslovak Socialist Republic. The new constitution was passed in 1960 and socialism was proclaimed in Czechoslovakia (as the second country in the world after the USSR). At the same time, the name of the country was changed by adding the adjective "socialist".

1 The Consolidation of the Totalitarian Regime in the Late 1950s

The Stalinist leadership of the Communist Party of Czechoslovakia (CPCz) began to persecute harshly any spontaneous attempts to liberalize public life in 1956. First it chose to assail the Second Conference of the Czechoslovak Writers' Union held in April of that year. Initially, objections raised by the Politburo of the Central Committee of the Communist Party of Czechoslovakia (CC CPCz) were fairly restrained, and even the *Rudé Právo* newspaper took a long time to take a significant stand on the message of the conference. While it was under way, the paper only published abridged versions of the keynote speeches and a brief summary of the papers presented, while refraining from any sort of assessment of the conference and its outcome. It was not until 10th June that the first public attack was made against Jaroslav Seifert: in his article entitled 'On Bratislava and the Writers' Conference,' reporting on the Slovak Writers' Conference held on 1st June, Josef Rybák concluded that 'the gentlemen at Radio Free Europe are enthusiastically applauding' Seifert for his conference paper.

In contrast, the New Mindset – a theoretical and political journal of the CC CPCz – published a whole-heartedly positive assessment of the Writers' Conference, entitled 'Purifying the Atmosphere for Creative Work,' in June 1956. It even went so far as to suggest that 'the key benefit of the conference [...] has been that it fully ushered in the spirit of free creative discussion, of a frank exchange of views. The views have not only been declared, but also already put into practice.'

A more fundamentally positive assessment of the Writers' Conference came from the Politburo of the Communist Party of Slovakia's Central Committee. Its resolution mentioned the altered political situation under which the conference had been held, and added 'That is, in fact, the reason the conference served as a test of our writers, a test which they have so far passed with honourable, flying colours.' In short, it seems clear that the assessment of the 2nd Czechoslovak Writers' Conference changed over time, that it was not initially dismissive, although later the Communist propaganda labelled the conference a prototypical attack by 'anti-socialist forces.' The different opinions on the conference were still evident within the CPCz in the spring and summer of 1956. The assessment of the 2nd Writers' Conference can be regarded as a kind of barometer of the spirit of freedom in the country.

The speech made by Václav Kopecký at the state-wide conference of the CPCz held from 11th to 15th June, 1956, made it clear that the Stalinists were lining up to counter-attack. At the time, Kopecký was not only a Deputy Prime Minister of the Czechoslovak government, but, more importantly, a member of the Politburo of the CC CPCz, as well as the party's chief ideologist and a highly dogmatic propagandist. At the party's conference, he presented a scathing critique of the Writers' Conference, including its very first public rebuff. He branded its entire proceedings – with the exception of several Communist functionaries' contributions – as oppositional and aimed against the regime. Kopecký's attack received support from the party conference, and was even interrupted several times by cheers from the floor. The speech surprised everyone, including the Politburo, which had not yet condemned the conference in an official statement. However, as Kopecký's views corresponded with those of the other Politburo members and had been endorsed by the state-wide conference, the Politburo decided to give their blessing to the speech, albeit with a caveat that 'it is not a criticism of the intelligentsia as a stratum of working people.'

The events of the second half of 1956, particularly the bloodshed in Hungary, were damaging for the democratization efforts in Czechoslovakia. The resulting political shift was reflected, for instance, in the proceedings and conclusions of the CC CPCz meeting held on 5th and 6th December of that year. During the meeting, Antonín Novotný went so far as to label the criticism of the cult of personality 'an argument of reactionary propaganda,' and voices were heard attacking the proponents of 'anti-party, liberalist tendencies.' The struggle against such people became the focus of the CPCz's political and ideological activities in the upcoming period and was also manifested in a series of authoritarian interventions in the public life, as well as in the persecution of the most active advocates of de-Stalinization and democratization tendencies. The 12th November meeting of the Politburo passed a draft resolution to the CC CPCz, requesting that only 'those Communists who have not wavered in implementing the political line of the party and government' be elected as leaders of the CPCz's organizations during the party meetings and conferences held between December 1956 and March 1957.

The Politburo of the Communist Party of Slovakia (KSS) was the first to perform an about-turn. Along the lines of the new political trend, its members focused their attention on the situation in 'a part of the intelligentsia,' as early as March 1957. Primarily, they zeroed in on the political views of Ondrej Pavlík, Chairman of the Slovak Academy of Sciences and, since 1954, a member of the Presidium of the KSS's Central Committee, who authored a number of very broad-minded articles published in Cultural Life *(Kultúrny život)* magazine; they also probed the opinions of Juraj Špitzer, Editor-In-Chief of Cultural Life, Ctibor Štítnický, Chief Secretary of the Slovak Writers' Union, and Ivan Kupec, Editor-In-Chief of The Slovak Writer *(Slovenský Spisovateľ)* Publishing House. The leadership of the KSS accused them of straying into 'erroneous positions,' and decided to punish them: Kupec and Špitzer received a party reprimand, with Špitzer also being removed from his editorial position, while Pavlík was expelled from the CPCz. These sanctions were approved by a regular congress of the KSS, held from 26th to 28th April, 1957. It validated the anti-democratization course taken by the party, denounced the 'erroneous attitudes directed against the party' among the intelligentsia, condemned the 'negative' attitude towards the results of the construction of socialism, and some of its speakers even insisted that there was a connection between the Hungarian 'counter-revolution' and reformist efforts in Czechoslovakia. Although these events took place in Slovakia, they had a major impact on developments in the Czech Lands. This was because they directly affected the atmosphere of the whole country, and because the functionaries who had helped prepare and organize the events were all highly influential throughout the country, holding top positions in both the KSS and the state-wide leadership of the CPCz.

On a national level, events took the same course as in Slovakia. The CC CPCz meeting, convened for 13th and 14th June, 1957, was dedicated to the issues of ideological struggle. The key speech was delivered by the Central Committee Secretary, Jiří Hendrych, who referred to 'revisionism' as the primary danger of the moment. He illustrated his point by citing once again the Second Writers' Conference, this time dismissing its proceedings and conclusions quite unequivocally: 'In our country, the same as elsewhere, there have been people who would have liked to raise doubts about our party's platform and political line, who sought to create an atmosphere of widespread defamation and distrust. Bear in mind the various radical and bourgeois platforms that were being formed, the voices that were heard – and I mean political voices – at the Second Writers' Conference, at some universities, and even some central institutions. These voices elicited some response, they were welcomed and endorsed by foreign propaganda, and would surely have grown to greater proportions if left to sprout, as experience in the neighbouring countries has taught us'. The meeting adopted a resolution calling for more intensive education of the masses to inculcate 'socialist consciousness,' to do everything to ensure that 'all intelligentsia adopt the Marxist worldview and overcome all anachronisms of the past,' and focus on the struggle against religion. In other words, the resolution once again validated the power monopoly of the CPCz, provided a platform for persecuting inconvenient people, and clearly indicated the party's determination to put an end to all discussions regarding both the past and the CPCz's future political course.

Experiences from 1956 contributed to the restoration of the class-based doctrine in the CPCz's personnel management. The top functionaries once again reassured themselves that the one and only true pillar of their regime was the working class. It followed that the workers' leadership position in the society must be reinforced and their needs given priority. At the same time, they concluded that it was imperative to punish the critics of the political course so far, as well as those who had not been sufficiently fervent or active back in 1956. The means they employed to reach this end were the so-called 'screening tests of class and political reliability,' conducted in state and economic institutions. The screenings were launched on 10th December, 1957 by the Political Bureau of the CC CPCz, which prescribed the following rules: the state apparatus was to be purged of all former factory owners, landowners, merchants, and the like, as well as their closest relatives, collaborators with the Nazi occupants during WWII and members of fascist organizations, functionaries of non-Communist political parties from the 1918–1939 period, high-rank officials of the pre-Munich era, pre-war army, police and gendarmerie officers, CEOs of big corporations, but also people expelled from the CPCz or trade unions, as well as relatives of exiles and of people serving time in prison for anti-Communist activities. The original idea was to conduct the screening in all government ministries and central authorities, with the exception of the ministries of interior and national defence, but its scope was soon extended to include regional and district organs, as well as the management, technical-support, projection, and administration departments of some enterprises and factories, and the field of education including universities.

The screening was carried out in early 1958. At government ministries and central organs, it was conducted by special commissions appointed by the corresponding department of the CC CPCz. The results were subsequently discussed by the Politburo on 25th April, 1958, and found satisfactory: the screening was supposed to 'purge the state apparatus of all politically undependable elements, prevent undependable elements from infiltrating into other important positions, and create favourable personnel conditions for re-organization of the state and economic apparatus;' all those demands were met. The leaders were pleased to acknowledge that 'the screening boosted the authority of the party, its organs and organizations.' Based on the data collected by the CPCz leadership, a total of 28,686 persons were vetted; based on their trespasses thus ascertained, 14.7% were transferred to lower-rank positions in the state and economic apparatus, 3.7% were made to retire, and 3.1% were removed from the state apparatus and assigned to other jobs. The screenings also had a detrimental effect on the retirement pensions of those who were made to leave their jobs. A high number of people who were vetted or somehow affected by the screenings were officials at the regional and district levels and in Slovak national organs. Historians estimate that the total number of people subjected to the screenings all over Czechoslovakia amounted to fifty thousand.

18th to 21st June, 1958 were the dates set for the 9th Congress of the CPCz held in Prague. Prior to its commencement, the regime made a point of demonstrating its power and resolve. The screening tests of class and political reliability were being carried out simultaneously with the district party conferences, which were above all meant to show 'the tight formation of the party ranks,' as well as the party's determination to continue the struggle against 'various anachronisms and influences of bourgeois ideologies that still affect our workers.' The same spirit of resolve pervaded the regional conferences and, in May 1958, the Congress of the KSS, which adopted a resolution declaring a struggle 'against the residues of Hlinka's People's Party (HSĽS) ideology and bourgeois nationalism.' On 15th April, 1958, the Politburo of the CC CPCz adopted a resolution about the 'continued development and intensification of the ideological effectiveness of public education,' affecting all leisure-time domains of the working people of Czechoslovakia.

Shortly before the congress opened, the party leadership had commissioned a detailed report about manifestations of enemy activity against the Communist regime in Czechoslovakia. The report was presented to the Politburo by the Minister of Interior Rudolf Barák on 13th June, 1958. Although it gave an assurance that no specific activities directed against the congress had been detected, it insisted that the police had registered a surge in activity among both foreign and internal enemies of the regime, and provided a list of examples. Concurrently, the Communist leadership had to tackle a problem with which it had no prior experience: the first television broadcast occurred in 1953 and the number of TV sets owned by the population had been on the rise ever since. By 1958, the police was obliged to report to the Politburo that, the number of viewers watching broadcasts from Austria and Bavaria was rising, in proportion to the growing number of TV sets in people's living rooms. They deemed the foreign broadcast harmful to the interests of Czechoslovakia and other Communist countries. Members of the Politburo assumed that they could use the same weapons against the troublesome television as they did against foreign radios, and asked the Minister of Telecommunications Alois Neumann to work out a method of blocking foreign TV broadcasts from the Czech territory. But neither Neumann nor his successors managed to accomplish the task.

The intimidating ideological crusade against actual and potential enemies or simply critics of the Stalinist regime in Czechoslovakia did not end with the 9th Congress, and drove the CPCz to include the Ministry of National Defence in the purge. This was on account of the fact that most of those who had requested an exceptional party congress back in 1956 were, surprisingly, this ministry's employees. For instance, on 20th July, 1958, the Politburo discussed the results of the screening at the Military Political Academy. The submitted documents demonstrated that the atmosphere at the institution was permeated 'by extremely unhealthy views bordering on revisionist tendencies,' the roots of which were traced by the screening commission back to 1956. It had been then, the document suggested, that 'a majority of the academy members, professors of social sciences in particular, ardently supported the convention of an unscheduled party congress,' a fact attributed to their 'bourgeois-radical misinterpretation of the conclusions of the 20th Congress of the CPSU.'

At the end of the day, however, the CPCz leaders were most wary of the intellectual, artistic and cultural circles as the main source of potential danger to the regime. To keep them in check, they focused on working with individual art unions. In February 1959, the leadership initiated the 2nd Congress of the Czechoslovak Composers' Union. Although the Politburo appreciated the union's backing the party line in 1956, it now requested that the Czechoslovak musicians once again declare their adherence to the principles of socialist realism in music, including its composition and reproduction. For it was the steady departure from the method of socialist realism, a doctrine perceived by the Communist regime as the one and only, that the party leadership considered the main cause of revisionist and ideological deviations, which had – in their opinion – perpetually plagued the Czechoslovak intellectual front. In early March 1959, a nationwide conference of the Czechoslovak Writers' Union was convened for the same reason, featuring Ladislav Štoll, member of the

CC CPCz and former Minister of Education and Culture, as the keynote speaker. In his contribution, Štoll went back to the 2ⁿᵈ Writers' Conference held in 1956 and once again rejected it, this time to the cheers of many ambitious authors. But the keepers of the Czechoslovak literature's ideological purity had to grapple with a number of new vexing phenomena, besides reckoning with the past. As the main object of their criticism, they picked the May (*Květen*) literary magazine, which had the reputation of being a mouthpiece of the young generation of writers, and as such was subsequently banned by the order of the party authorities. Another sign indicating that the regime was not truly willing to loosen its grip on culture was the condemnation of Josef Škvorecký's novel The Cowards (*Zbabělci*). His portrait of life in a small Czech town at the end of WWII was a far cry from the canonized, black-and-white, heroic style used up to that point in Czech literature, film and theatre to depict that era. Criticism by President Novotný himself instigated a witch hunt on the book. Still, although the regime temporarily tightened its grip on culture, it was a domain that proved increasingly harder to regulate and presented a growing number of problems and frictions as time went by.

The Czechoslovak Writers' Union Conference took place in the midst of preparations for the Congress of Socialist Culture, organized on 8ᵗʰ to 11ᵗʰ June, 1959. Officially, it was supposed to discuss the tasks of 'the cultural revolution in the process of completing the construction of socialism,' while in reality it was an attempt to once again manacle the Czechoslovak culture with the socialist-realist doctrine. But although the regime's campaign, aimed at crushing all attempts at reform and democratization, was initially successful, it was halted as early as 1959 by the serious difficulties that hit the Czechoslovak economy and negatively affected the views and beliefs of the working class that had remained calm up to that point. The leadership of the Communist Party was facing obstacles of major proportions.

2 Attempts to Reform the Economy and Liberalization of the Regime in the Mid-1960s

In the late 1950s, the CPCz leadership pushed through the main objectives of its political platform, under the command of Antonín Novotný (in the autumn of 1957, after Antonín Zápotocký's death, he came to hold both the office of the First Secretary of the CC CPCz and the President of the Republic). As tension diminished on the international scene and the 1953 monetary reform and other domestic policy measures had been put into effect, the economic and social situation in the country had plateaued. In addition, the regime had successfully completed the collectivization of agriculture. Indeed, the conditions had become more favourable for collectivization than they had been several years before. Many co-ops had reached a point of making a good profit, the industry had the capacity to produce sufficient farming equipment, and the government was able to invest considerable sums in constructing agricultural buildings and facilities. Simultaneously, more and more farmers were no longer able to take the pressure from the authorities and perpetual harassment from the regime. In result, co-operatives farmed on 65.7% of all farmland, the government and state farms controlled 85.2% of all land, and, in time, the collectivized agriculture became an anchor of the Czechoslovak economy.

The Communist leadership also managed to avoid making the kind of eccentric moves that had been so characteristic of the early 1950s. The public show trials were over, and the open terror against people of different beliefs had taken a back seat. At this point, the pressure exerted by the regime on its opponents was chiefly bureaucratic: inconvenient people were prevented from holding public offices, and positions of consequence were filled exclusively with the party faithful. Yet, although open violence was not on the day's agenda, the police remained vigilant and was constantly reminded of its own key role in ensuring the consolidation of the power of the working class in the country. The staunchest enemies of the Communist dictatorship had been eliminated: they were in prison or under police surveillance, or had gone into exile. The rest were either intimidated or tired, while the majority of the population had resigned and considered the regime as a reality they could not change in the near future.

On 23rd September, 1959, Antonín Novotný declared at the meeting of the CC CPCz: 'If we summarize everything that has been accomplished in our country, the victory of socialism in Czechoslovakia has essentially been achieved.' Only a little later, on 11th July, 1960, the National Assembly passed a new constitution, which characterized Czechoslovakia as a 'socialist' state, and adopted a new name for the country – the Czechoslovak Socialist Republic (CSSR) – as well as a new state symbol.

The struggle against revisionism in economy led to the renewal of the 'steel-based concept' of the construction of the country. The formerly discontinued construction of the HUKO metallurgy complex near Košice was resumed in 1958, and work began on building the Eastern-Slovakia ironworks. The economy's demand for energy and raw-material thus increased, which in turn caused the country to fall even more behind developed countries in applying modern technologies. In chemical industry, for example, Czechoslovakia trailed 5 to 10 years behind the world's leading level.

In 1960, the National Assembly passed legislation concerning the 3rd consecutive five-year plan for the period of 1961–1965. The regime put a lot of hope into this venture. At the 3rd plenary session of the Central Council of Trade Unions, organized on 12th and 13th October 1959, the Council Chair František Zupka declared: 'The third five-year plan will solidify the commanding position of industry – the cornerstone of our economy. During the period in question, the gross industrial product is estimated to grow by 50.8%, or by 101.3% in comparison with the year 1957. With this overall growth in mind, the industrial development shall be focused on its main component, that is to say, mechanical engineering, which is expected to help utilize the existing raw material resources and open new ones, and also initiate a growth spurt in chemical industry. Consumption and food industries should cover the increased level of domestic consumption, and as such the pace of their production increase has been set to meet that demand. The basic factor of the industrial production growth will be the production of production means, whose volume will increase by 61.8%, and the production of consumer products by 31.6%, compared to 1960. [...] By 1965, industrial production will have grown six times compared to the pre-war level, meaning that in 1965, we will match the production volume of the entire year 1937 in only two months.'

In their megalomania, the Communist leadership envisioned tasks that were utterly unrealistic. The objectives that the economy was supposed to achieve disregarded the unsatisfactory legacy of the second five-year plan. To make matters worse, both the government and the CC CPCz intensively supported the international workers' movement, to a degree that exceeded their actual means. Another adversity came in the form of a discontinuation of trade relations with China, a consequence of the Sino-Soviet split. The first serious problems occurred the following year. The winter of 1961/1962 brought a failure in coal supply, which in turn led to a shortage of electric energy. Power outages lasting for hours were common not only in households but also in factories, causing further economic losses. The problem became even more pressing in the winter of 1962/1963. The shortage of coal and electricity paralysed the railway system, and the government – in an attempt to save money – declared 'coal holidays' that lasted for several weeks. In addition, the provision of supplies lagged behind the demand: the already notorious shortage of meat was now accompanied by a scarcity of milk, butter, cheese, and eggs. It was in this period that prominent economists recorded Czechoslovakia's steep fall in the world's economic charts. Up to that point, the country had boasted the strongest economy of all COMECON countries. In the early 1960, this position was ceded to the German Democratic Republic and, of non-communist countries, Czechoslovakia was outpaced by Japan and Austria. It was becoming clear that the country was facing a crisis of major proportions, caused by a transformation of the national economy into one centralized, nationalized whole, which was – to make matters worse – run by unprofessional managers.

This realization was not lost on the top-level party functionaries: at the meeting of the CC CPCz on the 15th to 17th November, 1961, the party's First Secretary Antonín Novotný conceded: 'The first year of the third five-year plan has revealed many negative phenomena, consisting mainly in failing to meet the requirements related to technological development and investment construction projects, in failing to produce the prescribed line of products and meeting the liabilities, as well as in failures in agricultural production. The poor economic performance, primarily in the third quarter of 1961, has seriously undermined the implementation of a large number of measures in the national economy.' In other words, the plan for the year 1961 failed to be accomplished.

The 3rd five-year plan was discreetly withdrawn and replaced by a sequence of annual plans, which, however, proved to be an inadequate solution. The authors of the plans did not search for reasons for the existing troubles and did not try to find a remedy. The economy faced similar issues a year later, in the form of failures in gas and electricity supply, accompanied by glitches in transportation, scarce retail supplies – primarily meat, followed by dairy products, eggs and fruit – and the situation failed to improve in the following year. In consequence, the national income dropped by 2% in 1963. The decrease in economic growth, which occurred for the first time since 1945, alarmed the CPCz and country leaders to the highest degree. The economic stagnation did not have serious social consequences or cause social unrest only thanks to the system of re-distribution, which had been introduced in Czechoslovakia and enabled the government to borrow from the future for a while. Nonetheless, it was a major warning for those in power. What was important was that in 1963, the state of the economy did not improve. The national income in standard prices was 862 million CZK lower than in 1961, while the monetary income of the population increased in the same period by an incredible seven billion crowns. The drop in production and national income was dealt with at the expense of accumulation and some international debt. Scarcity in consumer products caused regular shopping crazes and growing popular discontent.

In the end, the CPCz leadership – constantly pressured by the worsening state of the economy, influenced by a number of initiatives of prominent political and scientific figures (notably Ota Šik) and inspired by the example of other communist countries which were also striving to improve their economies, above all the USSR – began to consider a profound reform of the Czechoslovak economy. This was not the first time a change in the existing course was suggested: attempts at decentralizing public life had been made back in 1956 and again in 1959, when there had also been efforts to introduce changes in the management style of industrial enterprises, restructure the system of workers' wages and, most importantly, to improve the system of planning the national economy. However, these attempts were short-lived and unsuccessful.

The guiding principles of the new reform, which was much more radical and thorough than the previous one, had been formulated in 1963. The CPCz leadership accepted them in 1965, and in the same year gave the project the go-ahead. The steps that had been taken put some elements of the reform into effect as early as 1966, and the restructuring of prices was launched on 1st January, 1967. Subsequently, the rapidly accelerating democratization in 1968, affecting all domains of public life, facilitated the implementation of the reform's third stage. Its success depended on profound changes in the understanding of 'socialist' ownership, national economy management, planning, everyday activities of production enterprises, as well as on the attitude of the general public. The new work and management styles – a prerequisite of the reform – required from the employees a much higher degree of personal commitment and participation in management. The trade union movement was supposed to help effect this change, but suggestions were being made for using other tools, such as workers' councils. The economic reform that was launched in Czechoslovakia in the mid-1960s had far-reaching political, social and cultural consequences, and contributed more than a little to the radicalization of events, which culminated in an attempt at a profound social reform in the period of 1968–1969. In turn, the gradual shift in political climate influenced the efforts to rebuild the national economy, sped up the reform steps taken in the economy, and allowed for them to be more fundamental.

At a meeting of the CC CPCz organized on 18th and 19th December, 1963, Director of the Economic Institute Ota Šik presented his criticism of the unprofessional economic management style and the dogmatic way of thinking in that domain. He emphasized that in order to ensure a healthy development of the socialist economy, it was imperative to introduce market relations and create a consumer market. The highly unsatisfactory results of the national economy, coupled with the critical words coming from the CPCz leadership members themselves, gave rise to the decision to try and resolve the situation by partial economic reforms. They were formulated in the document entitled 'The Principles of Improving the Plan-Based Management of the National Economy,' adopted by the Presidium of the CC CPCz and published in the *Rudé Právo* paper on 17th October, 1964. The solutions may have been half-hearted, yet their medicinal effect on the economy soon became obvious. Another measure that had a positive impact on the economy was granting the agricultural co-ops a higher degree of decision-making freedom than before. Before long, the co-ops managed to overcome their shortcomings and became the most efficient domain of the Czechoslovak economy.

Searching for new ways to improve the state of the economy initiated changes in the ideological work and political practices of the CPCz. Originally, the party leadership had agreed to loosen reins on the economy but tighten them in the political and ideological domains. But things took a different, unexpected course. The solution required gradual, unobtrusive liberalization measures in other domains of public life, allowing for the atmosphere in the country to become more relaxed. In the first half of the 1960s, this shift was manifested in a marked transformation of the CPCz's political thinking and ideology. Opening the country's doors to the world, combined with the Eastern Bloc's newly-adopted strategy of peaceful co-existence with countries with different political systems and its acceptance of every country's right to its own specific journey to socialism, required relinquishing the cherished dogmas and searching for answers to new questions. The state of society and the easing up of censorship allowed for the discussion to spread into many nooks and crannies of the society. This was also the period when the 'revisionist philosophers' (Karel Kosík, Ivan Sviták) and other critically-thinking philosophers (Ivan Dubský, Robert Kalivoda, Jiřina Popelová, Ladislav Tondl) reached their creative prime. Thinkers in other fields including law, economy, literary science, and sociology, were also highly active, producing works characterized by a critical reflexion of the Marxist-Leninist party line and political practice and of socialist realism in arts (authors such as Zdeněk Mlynář, Zdeněk Jičínský, František Šamalík, Július Strinka, František Kožušník, Eduard Goldstücker, Miroslav Drozda and many others).

The loosening up of the regime was manifested in the gradual lifting of censorship and concessions in personnel management: managerial positions were now filled with more emphasis on qualifications and less on political loyalty; students from families with unfavourable personnel profiles were allowed to study at secondary schools and universities, and borders were gradually opened for travel to capitalist countries. No matter how isolated they were, cases such as these they had been absolutely unthinkable before. After a plenary session of the CC CPCz in January 1963, censorship became considerably less stringent. Changes in this area were advocated by the Committee Secretary Jiří Hendrych, reputably the second-in-command in the country. In 1963, Jiří Pelikán was appointed general manager of Czechoslovak Television. Under his leadership, the station began broadcasting a lot more discussion shows and current news analyses that helped search for solutions to the most pressing problems. More current-affairs talk shows were contributed by the Czechoslovak Radio. The society was bustling with public debate, increasingly more frank, about all the serious problems that had gone unresolved for years and weighed down on people's minds. Scientific magazines and later also the daily press began publishing discussions about the Czechoslovak past and about topics that had until recently been taboo – such as T. G. Masaryk, the legionnaires, the First Republic, and increasingly more often the political trials of the 1950s, their victims and perpetrators.

The leadership of the CPCz, whose positions were further influenced by the internal development in the USSR characterized by another wave of de-Stalinization, could not leave this rising surge of criticism without response. In 1960, the CC CPCz declared an extensive amnesty for most political prisoners, and was even compelled to set up an inquiry and review commission to probe into the political trials. Its findings were published in the daily press on 22nd August, 1963. The *Rudé Právo* daily had to admit that the Communist Party had committed crimes. Slánský and his associates were cleared of all charges and for some of them the verdict was repealed. A total of 481 cases of judicial persecution were reviewed and most victims were subsequently acquitted, pardoned, or had their sentences commuted. But this was only the first step towards justice. Simultaneously, a number of people who had not qualified for amnesty back in 1960 were now released from prison. In October 1963, Bishops Vojtaššák, Zela and Hlad, incarcerated since the early 1950s, were absolved from the rest of their sentences, and Bishop Karel Skoupý was discharged from internment.

A significant social upheaval was also under way in Slovakia. The young generation of Slovak Communists began pointing out with growing frequency the discrimination of Slovakia in relation to the Czech Lands. The CPCz leadership eventually handled the situation by firing the most compromized functionaries, most of whom happened to be Slovaks. Besides Bruno Köhler, who was an ethnic German, the officials who were made to leave included the Slovaks Viliam Široký and Karol Bacílek, who lost the position of the First Secretary of the KSS, and Július Ďuriš. The vacant position of Prime Minister was filled with Josef Lenárt, and Alexander Dubček became leader of the KSS.

All these changes ran like a vitalizing current through the veins of the Czechoslovak culture. In 1963, a Franz Kafka conference of international consequence was organized at the Liblice Castle by Eduard Goldstücker, Professor of German Literature at Charles University. Books by previously banned foreign authors were back in print, as were fundamental works in scientific fields that had before been mocked as 'bourgeois pseudo-sciences:' Norbert Wiener's Cybernetics, Adam Schaff's Introduction to Semantics, but also works like Alexander Solzhenitsyn's One Day in the Life of Ivan Denisovich. In addition, new original writings of Czech and Slovak authors were once again available at bookstores, including Dominik Tatarka's Demon of Conformism (*Démon súhlasu*), written in 1956 and therefore long awaited, Ladislav Mňačko's Belated Reports (*Oneskorené reportáže*), and Karel Kosík's Dialectics of the Concrete (*Dialektika konkrétního*). In 1963, Bohumil Hrabal, already a man of mature years, published his first work Pearls of the Deep (*Perličky na dně*). In the same year, readers got their hands on A Busy House (*Rušný dům*), the first opus by Ludvík Vaculík, who was to become so polemical in the years to come, and Arnošt Lustig's new novel Nobody Will Be Humiliated (*Nikoho neponížíš*). In 1964, Ivan Klíma first published his Lovers for One Night (*Milenci na jednu noc*) collection of stories, and A Dictionary of Czech Writers came out, which for the first time officially mentioned many names that the Communist regime had had taken great pains to erase from the nation's memory. In 1966, Ludvík Vaculík's The Axe (*Sekyra*) and Milan Kundera's The Joke (*Žert*) caused quite a stir, the latter soon reaching worldwide renown. A great many plays were written and new theatres were suddenly thick on the ground, including mostly small-form theatres and various other non-traditional ensembles. Kundera's drama The Owners of the Keys (*Majitelé klíčů*) had already been put on in 1962, followed by Ivan Vyskočil's 'text-appeal' Why, It's Easy to Fly! (*Vždyť přece létat je snadné*) a year later, and the staging of Václav Havel's absurdist dramas Garden Party (*Zahradní slavnost*) and The Memorandum (*Vyrozumění*) in the same period drew international attention. In 1964, the Brno Evening Theatre (*Večerní divadlo Brno*) staged Milan Uhde's King Vávra (*Král Vávra*), a play then considered an unconcealed criticism of the current political situation.

In response to the public demand for answers to the pressing questions of the past and present, journalism was undergoing a similar boom as belles-lettres. A new genre of 'non-fiction fiction' was born, championed on the home market in the works of Miroslav Ivanov. Magazines that had until recently had very limited readership – e.g., Literary Newspaper (*Literární noviny*) and History and the Present (*Dějiny a současnost*) were now appreciated by the general public. The Czechoslovak society's isolation, so successfully crafted by the Communist regime in the early 1950s, was now a distant memory. The radio and also television, which was quickly becoming a mass medium, began to broadcast fresh, objectively delivered information, as well as shows featuring Western pop music. Young people turned to Western fashions both in clothing and hairstyles, driving their teachers and orthodox functionaries round the twist. Furthermore, the Czechoslovak cinema experienced its golden age, giving rise to a great many films that came to win international acclaim, among them the first Czech musical The Hop Pickers (*Starci na chmelu*) and Loves of a Blonde (*Lásky jedné plavovlásky*), the latter containing daring nude scenes that made the film the talk of the day. In 1965, the movie Shop on Main Street (*Obchod na korze*) was released and came to be the first Czechoslovak film to win an Academy Award. A large number of movies thematically focused on life at the present time came out shortly afterwards.

Authorities took great pains to put a stop to the new wave. In 1963, they reprimanded the magazine Cultural Life (*Kultúrny život*); a year later, the regime dismissed and replaced the entire editorial staff of the History and the Present (*Dějiny a současnost*); Jiří Müller and Jiří Holeček, the spokesmen of the Prague university students, were expelled in the 1965/1966 academic year; and, last but not least, author Jan Beneš was charged with espionage, sentenced and put in prison in 1966. But since the Communist government no longer used brutal violence against its opponents, its chances to curb their activities were smaller than small. The surge of criticism came to a head in 1967, at the 4th Czechoslovak Writers' Confer-

534

ence, which came to symbolize a search for new horizons towards which the society should march and for the democratization of life as it was known. In their contributions, Ludvík Vaculík, Milan Kundera and others spoke the hearts and minds of almost everybody in the country. This time, however, the CPCz leadership felt directly threatened and clamped down on the writers with a vengeance. The conference organizers and the keynote speakers were subject to social discrimination by the regime and lost their CPCz membership, their works were banned again after a long period of being tolerated, and the Literary Newspaper was seized from the Czechoslovak Writers' Union and put under the wings of the Ministry of Culture to make sure it would publish regime-approved articles.

Isolated steps such as the ones taken against writers and students had little chance of ending the crisis in the society, as neither students nor writers had caused the crisis to happen in the first place. Additionally, the CPCz leadership lacked sufficient determination and unity for a consistent use of force. Before long, the Prague Spring took the country by storm. It was the year 1968.

Bibliography

Aufbruch in die Zukunft: Die 1960er Jahre zwischen Planungseuphorie und kulturellem Wandel. DDR, CSSR und Bundesrepublik Deutschland im Vergleich, Haupt, Heinz-Gerhard – Requate, Jorg –Kohler-Baur, Maria (eds.),Weilerswist 2004.

BARTOŠEK, Karel: *Les aveux des archives: Prague-Paris-Prague 1948–1968*, Paris 1996.

BEER, Fritz: *Die Zukunft funktioniert noch nicht: ein Porträt der Tschechoslowakei 1948–1968*, Frankfurt am Main 1969.

GRAY, Elizabeth: *The fiction of freedom: the development of the Czechoslovak literary reform movement 1956–1968*, Clayton 1991.

KALINOVÁ, Lenka: *Společenské proměny v čase socialistického experimentu. K sociálním dějinám v letech 1945–1969*, Praha 2007

KAPLAN, Frank L.: *Winter into spring: the Czechoslovak press and the reform movement, 1963–1968*, Boulder 1977.

KAPLAN, Karel: *Kořeny československé reformy 1968*, I–II Brno 2000.

KAPLAN, Karel: *Kořeny československé reformy 1968*, III–IV, Brno 2002.

KEANE, John: *Vaclav Havel: A political tragedy in six acts*, London 1999.

KOSTA, Jiří: *Abriß der sozialökonomischen Entwicklung der Tschechoslowakei 1945–1977*, Frankfurt am Main 1978.

KOSTA, Jiří: *Die tschechoslowakische Wirtschaftsreform der sechziger Jahre*, Marburg 1993.

KUSIN, Vladimir V.: *The intellectual origins of the Prague spring; the development of reformist ideas in Czechoslovakia, 1956–1967*, Cambridge 1971, 2nd edition 2002.

LIŠKA, Ondřej: *Jede Zeit ist Gottes Zeit: die Untergrund-Kirche in der Tschechoslowakei 1948–1989*, Leipzig 2003.

MYANT, M. R.: *The Czechoslovak economy, 1948–1988: the battle for economic reform*, Cambridge 1989.

PAGE, Benjamin B.: The *Czechoslovak reform movement, 1963–1968: a study in the theory of socialism*, Amsterdam 1973.

PUSTEJOVSKY, Otfrid: *In Prag kein Fenstersturz: Dogmatismus 1948–1962, Entdogmatisierung 1962–1967, Demokratisierung 1967–1968, Intervention 1968*, München 1968.

SUDA, Zdeněk: *Zealots and rebels: a history of the Communist Party of Czechoslovakia*, Stanford 1980.

TEICHOVÁ, Alice: *The Czechoslovak economy: 1918–1980*, London 1990.

XX. The Half-Life: the Communist Regime's Greatest Crisis (1967–1971)

Soviet armoured vehicles and crowds of protesters in Wenceslas Square in the centre of Prague in the morning of August 21, 1968. Scenes like this occurred on that day in hundreds of places around Czechoslovakia. Photograph by Štěpán Šandrik.

1 The Prague Spring

Early in 1968, events in Czechoslovakia picked up tremendous speed and momentum. The public, which only a few months before had been generally disaffected with the political and economic state of the country, yet inert and resigned to its fate, suddenly came to life in an outburst of creative activity. Week by week, profound changes were transforming public life, the media, and even the Communist party itself beyond recognition. This dramatic process was happening on various levels that conditioned, influenced and energized each other. To begin with, it was an attempt at a far-reaching reform of the Communist system, carried out from within the Communist party, conducted by reformist politicians and party intellectuals harbouring increasingly critical and unorthodox views. However, its reach was broader than that: it was a spontaneous movement involving the entire population, towards a free and open society. A movement which, though partly overlapping with the agenda and vision of the Communist party reformers, had implications that far exceeded the scope of change that the reformist CPCz leaders were prepared to accept. As might be expected, the movement aspired to loosen up and ultimately tear down the foundations of the Communist system, and as such it was a potential – or certain – source of conflict between society and the CPCz leadership. That such a conflict never came to pass, and its contours remained hidden in the cloud of possible future (but unrealized) alternatives, was mainly caused by external factors. For the events in Czechoslovakia were from the start shaped by external forces, namely the efforts of the USSR and other Eastern Bloc countries to maintain the status quo. This pressure from the outside made everything else matter less, while bringing the positions of the CPCz leadership's reformist wing and the majority population closer together. It became clear only later that this unity was a partial delusion.

The swirling ferment that engulfed Czech and Slovak society in 1968 had several different sources. Popular discontent with the current state of affairs, perceived by and large as discontent with the current national and party leadership, was on the increase both in society and within the party's ranks. More and more people were becoming conscious of the unsatisfactory social and economic development, their discoveries reinforced by the newly acquired opportunities for extensive travel, including to capitalist countries. They were able to see with their own eyes the degree to which Czechoslovakia lagged behind the countries west of its borders, countries that only a generation earlier had been more or less its equals. While they may not have pinned the blame for this unfavourable development directly on the Communist system, they certainly attributed it to the heavy-handed, inefficient governance of their current leaders.

Within the CPCz's ranks, the desire for change was represented mainly by the middle-aged generation of intellectuals, thinkers, and artists. That is to say, people who had, in their youth back in the post-war years, been staunch, enthusiastic proponents of Communist ideology and the construction of a new social system, but who over time had assumed a critical stance, realizing the risks involved in Czechoslovakia's fatal setback in many domains. On a number of levels, including social organizations, media, scientific institutions, state administration and the party, people of this generation had already acquired considerably prominent positions. Now they were searching for new alternatives, but always within the framework of the system, never against it.

In the period immediately preceding the Prague Spring, the cultural and artistic scene was an area of perpetual tension and both minor and major friction. The palpable relaxation of the atmosphere after 1963 gave rise to hopes of further liberalization. The regime's attempts at regimentation, such as the interference in the status of The Literary Newspaper (Literární noviny), and the renewed efforts to impose censorship on films, met with considerable resistance.

In the autumn of 1967, the immediate catalyst for open dispute between the opposing camps of CPCz leaders was 'the Slovak question.' The post-war decades saw Slovak society go through an economic and cultural boom, though its circumstances were deformed in myriad ways by the Communist regime. By the 1960s, Slovak society equalled Czech society in many ways. In turn, this led a large part of the Slovak nation, including members and functionaries of the Communist Party, to engage in an ever-more-open discussion on the need for constitutional changes that would guarantee genuine powers for Slovak national organs. Antonín Novotný's approach to the Slovak wishes and claims was particularly insensitive, and during his trip to Slovakia in the late summer of 1967, it would have been hard to find one person he did not manage to insult.

In the fall of 1967, a rather unhomogeneous coalition, united primarily by their aversion to the party's First Secretary, formed within the CPCz leadership. It featured staunch reformers who feared that Novotný would put a stop to the reforms – economic reform in particular – that had already been launched. Other members of the coalition included the majority of the Slovak representatives, as well as individuals with their own personal reasons for joining the group. By this point, the party's First Secretary and President of the country, Antonín Novotný, became – in the eyes of the population and a part of the CPCz leadership – the main obstacle to further reforms and the embodiment of the mistakes and crimes of the past. This was somewhat paradoxical and unfair, as in fact he had opened the door to major changes years before in the early 1960s, and realized that certain reforms were indeed necessary. However, by 1967, some consequences of the changes he had helped to implement began to frighten him and, combined with the pressure exerted on him by the reformist camp, he drifted closer to those members of the leadership who categorically rejected change of any sort.

The Central Committee CPCz (CC CPCz) meeting in October 1967 unfolded in a highly unusual way, diametrically different from the pattern that had years before become a rut. The customary expressions of unanimity and paeans to the success of socialism's construction gave way to polemic discussions culminating in a conflict, however enshrouded it may have been in ideological rhetoric and esoteric party jargon. Alexander Dubček, the then First Secretary of the Communist Party of Slovakia (KSS), was both the target of Novotný's attack and one of the most open critics of the current practices. At the October plenary session, Novotný's critics were still in a minority and so the session ended without resolution. In the meantime, both camps were bracing themselves for the next plenary session slated for December.

The conflict within the party leadership unfolded behind closed doors, without any information available to the public (at least, the non-Communist public) in the media or elsewhere. Rumours swirled nonetheless, including one from the winter of 1967, according to which Novotný was preparing a series of harsh measures to eliminate his critics, which counted on a significant involvement by the army.

The situation, particularly in Prague, was aggravated by what became known as 'the Strahov events.' On 31st October, the students' disgruntlement over glitches in the operation of their newly-constructed Strahov dormitory complex escalated into open protest. A power outage – quite common in those days – induced the students to organize a demonstration and march down Strahov Hill and into downtown Prague. It was more-or-less a spontaneous event, more along the lines of a student happening, but the nervous regime responded inappropriately. The march was brutally suppressed by the police, who later also took action on the dormitory grounds. Many students were savagely beaten, a number were arrested, and suggestions were made regarding exemplary punishment. The Strahov events caused outrage, and created a desire for revolt among students, mainly in Prague. At the time, the student movement was already well-organized, with the college committees of the Union of Czechoslovak Youth – the regime's official youth organization – mostly in the hands of student radicals. Nevertheless, the students decided against holding a general strike in November 1967, and the regime refrained from further persecution. Yet the Strahov events became one of the first points of massive public criticism of the regime which erupted several months later. By 1968, the student movement became one of the most radical and well-organized parts of the awakening Czechoslovak society, equipped with the most refined plan of action.

In early December 1967, before the plenary session, Novotný made an attempt to reverse the course of events in his favour by inviting Leonid Brezhnev, General Secretary of the Communist Party of the Soviet Union, in the hope of winning his support. But Brezhnev, being neither a big fan of Novotný, nor well informed of the Czechoslovak situation, remained neutral. Yet, in light of the events that followed, his statement 'eto vashe delo,' meaning 'it's your affair' – later the frequent subject of quotes and comments – acquired a tragically comic flavour, to say the least.

Both camps were now gearing up for a decisive battle. The Central Committee Presidium was essentially evenly divided into two equally robust halves. When the time came, the December session of the CC CPCz lived up to the expectations by being full of conflict, but like the previous session, it failed to yield a conclusion. The proceedings were suspended for Christmas and resumed after New Year's Day. The January session brought a compromise solution, which nevertheless signalled Novotný's ultimate defeat. Once again, the two top positions in the country and party were separated. Novotný managed to hold onto the presidency, but was bound to surrender the most politically influential position in the country: on 5th January, he resigned from his post as the CPCz's First Secretary, and was replaced by the newly-elected Alexander Dubček.

Dubček, as a moderate reformist and one of the first people to dare enter into a public debate with Novotný in October months before, was a reasonably natural choice to represent the above-mentioned anti-Novotný coalition with its incoherent plan of action. In 1968 and, even more so in the years that followed the defeat of the Prague Spring, he came to personify and symbolize the movement, both at home and abroad. His symbolic value was, however, somewhat unjustified. For Dubček was not a fighter for democracy and national independence, although he gained that reputation, particularly in the West: he was much rather a hardcore Communist and a faithful ally of the Soviet Union. Still, he had undeniable charisma which set him apart from the drab apparatchiks who led the CPCz before and after him. He enjoyed not only the support of, but also considerable affection from the Czechoslovak population. Dubček hoped to introduce many changes, but he could hardly be called radical, and in early 1968 he surrounded himself with people, some of whom later became avowed enemies of the process of liberalization and democratization. For example, Dubček's circle of collaborators at the time included Vasil Biľak, who eventually replaced him as the First Secretary of the Central Committee of the KSS.

Part of the arrangement reached at the January plenary session resembled an armistice agreement between the two camps, and included a pledge of silence to ensure no information about the party leadership disputes was leaked. While probably few people were sorry to see Novotný go, at the same time, few people saw the party leader's replacement as the beginning of far-reaching changes. The initial reaction in both Czech and Slovak societies was to view the new First Secretary through a nationalist prism, as this was the first time since the formation of Czechoslovakia fifty years before that the most prominent political position in the shared country was assumed by a Slovak, rather than a Czech.

The post-January 'armistice,' turned out to be quite unsteady and unsustainable, and society was soon fully engaged in the ongoing party dispute. Novotný's camp was preparing a counter-offensive, and the President himself used his public speeches – particularly those held in large factories – to criticize the economic reform and to incite the workers to rebel against it. Likewise, the members of the opposing camp were more and more forthright about their views, among them Josef Smrkovský, who later became Speaker of Parliament, and Ota

Šik, the architect of the economic reform and a Deputy Prime Minister of the government after the spring of 1968. In their statements for the media, they rather frankly described the need for more changes, including personnel replacements. In February, highly critical words about the current situation were heard from Dubček himself, and he was among those who called for major reforms. The catalyst in the intensification of the public discussion and general politicization of the atmosphere was the decision to abolish censorship, pushed through by the pro-reform members of the party leadership at the turn of February and March.

Their campaign was based on the premise, which turned out to be correct, that a censorship-free media would assume a critical stance toward Novotný, thus providing a counter-balance to the influence still exerted by Novotný's camp over the law-enforcement arm of state power. They also assumed that, after twenty years of strict media control by the regime, and with the overwhelming majority of journalists being members of the CPCz, the media would continue to advance the Communist leadership's agenda even after censorship was abolished. Further, the reformists regarded the public in the same way. They were convinced that the Czechoslovak public was, with few exceptions, generally devoted to socialism and that, no matter how much it was calling for the whole system to be humanized and rationalized, there was little risk of any major discord. Both these assumptions turned out to be fatally wrong. The media, now free of censorship and regulation, became an independent player on the political field in a matter of days, as well as – for several months in the spring and summer of 1968 – something of a dominator of political development, to which the party leadership had to adapt. The role of the mass media in the Prague Spring convincingly testifies to the importance of the media in modern society.

Right at the genesis of the censorship-free era, the media happened to receive particularly shattering ammunition for their criticism of Novotný, in the form of 'The General Šejna Affair.' Jan Šejna, once a small-time officer, had used his scheming and opportunistic skills, as well as his personal relationship with Novotný and his family, to launch himself on a spectacular career trajectory in the Czechoslovak army after 1956. In addition to a high-ranking position at the Ministry of Defence, he was also a member of both the CC CPCz and the National Assembly. He led a life of opulence, financed partly by his machinations with army property. When a number of his colleagues – or rather, his accomplices – were arrested in February 1968 and the prosecutor's office asked the parliament presidium to lift his parliamentary immunity, Šejna fled the country, but not before equipping himself with photographs of many top secret documents from the General Staff of the Czechoslovak Army. By way of Hungary and Yugoslavia, he got to Italy and eventually, with help from the CIA, to the United States. Šejna was one of the most prominent military defectors to have ever switched sides from the Soviet Bloc to the United States, and the information and documents he provided to the Americans were of extraordinary importance. At the end of February 1968, the press released startling front-page reports of General Šejna's escape. The terminology used in the articles was in itself quite surprising, signalling that something was indeed in the air: terms such as 'affair' or 'scandal' had once been reserved for reporting the situation in the imperialist West, or in the bourgeois First Republic. By this point, however, the media began speaking openly about domestic ills, and the Šejna Affair was perfect material. A high-ranked official, a schemer, Novotný's personal friend, a thief and a deserter, Šejna perfectly represented the degeneration, corruption, and ineptitude of the regime. Since he was also a top functionary in the army, his escape suggested a murky connection with potential secret plans for using the army against Novotný's critics.

The daily influx of new and shocking information soon metamorphosed into a direct critique of Novotný, bringing about demands for his departure from public life. And the media went further: every day, they broke new taboos, venturing into territory previously proscribed, such as the Strahov events, the lack of efficiency in the centrally managed economy, restrictions to both cultural and artistic spheres, and – with growing frequency and openness – they delved into the issue of the crimes committed by the regime in the first years of its existence, and their victims. The criticism was directed not only at Novotný, but also affected a large number of prominent functionaries in Novotný's (or, more precisely, the anti-reformist) camp, who were labelled as 'conservatives.' In March and April, the campaign prompted a series of resignations from political positions, and even drove a number of people to suicide: the crimes committed by the regime were not yet ancient history, and the perpetrators' bad consciences, coupled with the fear of being held accountable, became too strong to deny. Meetings were organized in Prague and other places around the country, with thousands of mostly young people in attendance. Politicians, artists, and other public figures frankly answered open questions from the audience, which sometimes responded with thunderous applause and sometimes by expressing disapproval. The atmosphere at the meetings was entirely different from that of the mandatory gatherings of the recent past. The 'new' meetings were broadcast live on the radio and electrified the public. A wave of interest in politics, personal engagement, and public mobilization was sweeping through Czechoslovakia.

President Novotný finally resigned on 21st March, and the National Assembly elected Ludvík Svoboda to replace him on 30th March. As a person who had fought for the formation and renewal of Czechoslovakia in both world wars, and as someone who had fallen victim to the regime's persecution in the early 1950s, General Svoboda enjoyed the respect and support of the public. Somewhat naively, people saw in him a figure capable of restoring the prestige of the president's office that had once been held by Masaryk and Beneš. On the other hand, Svoboda was not expected to intervene in the daily political agenda. The public was proven wrong on both counts: in August 1968, General Svoboda made a very significant and very unfortunate intervention in the country's politics.

Another meeting of the CC CPCz convened in early April. More personnel changes were made in both state and party positions, inaugurating Oldřich Černík as the new Prime Minister, and Josef Smrkovský as the new Speaker of Parliament. Both gentlemen had been long-standing CPCz functionaries, with all the twists and turns involved in such a career under the Communist regime, but by this point they had become advocates of the reforms. At the same time, many top positions in the state apparatus and the party were still filled with people who were either reform-averse from the start, or were happy with the scope of reforms that had been carried out since January, but felt apprehensive about

OLDŘICH TŮMA

further liberalization. In the spring, however, the party leadership was not yet split into two clearly antagonistic camps of reform proponents and opponents. Instead, various personal alliances and factions were temporarily formed and transformed in an atmosphere of disputes over various issues. The party leadership meeting minutes reveal that even some of those politicians who later opposed Soviet interference and promoted the reforms were at this point making harsh comments about the new course, warning against overly rapid and spontaneous development, and even openly considering the use of tanks and weapons of the People's Militia against the enemies of socialism.

The key outcome of the Central Committee's April session was the adoption of the Party Action Plan. This document had been in preparation since the beginning of 1968, but also contained some last-minute amendments designed to keep up with the fluid situation and the expectations of the Communist and non-Communist public. Even though the Action Plan remained within the framework of the Communist ideology and used predominantly traditional Marxist vocabulary, it generally endorsed the continuation of reforms and a certain degree of liberalization. It promised to ensure legal security, civil liberties, liberalization in culture, media and science, and to reconcile relations between Czechs, Slovaks and other nationalities. It also sanctioned the implementation of an economic reform based on combining the advantages of state ownership and market forces. The role of central planning in the economy was intended to be significantly restricted; businesses were to receive much more independence, and the principle of profit maximization was to regain respect. Private initiative and entrepreneurship in services and commercial trade were to be given increasingly more room. However, the development of the political system was addressed in a vague, inconsistent manner. On the one hand, it was mentioned that the party would no longer assert its authority by means of administrative, let alone repressive, methods, but instead continuously try to gain and renew the genuine trust and support of the public. On the other hand, nobody asked, let alone answered, the question of what ought to be done if society stopped supporting the CPCz's political line.

In fact, reality overtook the Action Plan, and had outmatched it by the time it was adopted. Various components of the Communist regime quickly disintegrated, albeit under the banner of renewal and restoration, not the abolishment, of the system. Mass and hobby organizations emancipated themselves from servitude to the CPCz. Once the proverbial 'transmission gears' of the regime (the trade unions, associations of artists, scientists, veterans of anti-Nazi resistance and many others) were turning into authentic representatives of various layers of society. Non-Communist parties in the National Front, after twenty years of wretched existence as puppets in the hands of the CPCz, were now at least partially regaining their independent status. The youth organization dissolved completely, giving rise to dozens of free-standing children's and youth organizations, including the independent and highly radical University Students' Union, and the Scout organization resumed operation. Other newly-established organizations were directly political, such as The K-231 – an association of former political prisoners named after a notorious legal article, under which most of them had once been convicted. The Club of Committed Non-Party Members (KAN) was an intellectual discussion club rather than anything else; but despite its name, it inherently tended towards becoming an independent force or, more precisely, political opposition. In the same spirit, the first issue of the reinstated Writers' Union weekly, now known as Literary Gazette *(Literární listy)*, published Václav Havel's essay on the potential and benefits of political pluralism. There was also a broad initiative finally launched to restore the existence of the Czechoslovak Social Democracy, which had been forcibly merged with the CPCz in 1948. None of the earlier-mentioned political bodies, including the K-231, KAN, and particularly the renewed Social Democracy, had been officially registered and their operation was somewhat conditional and tentative. The existence of the renewed Social Democracy was especially unacceptable, and even the ardent reformists among the CPCz leaders went out of their way to convince the Social Democrats of the detrimental effects of their efforts. The party leadership, including the reformists, planned on taking aggressive steps to prevent the reinstatement of the Social Democracy, should the situation require them.

In the end, such steps were unnecessary, as Czechoslovakia's domestic affairs brought the country deeper and deeper into the shadow of indignation, interference and threats from abroad. This growing pressure from the surrounding Communist countries, the Soviet Union in particular, created a justifiable feeling that national unity was at stake, and that it was imperative to keep a low profile and let the reformist CPCz leaders do their job of negotiating with the allies. In early summer, largely of their own accord, the K-231, KAN and ČSD temporarily reduced their activity to the minimum. The Communists in the surrounding countries try to hide their chagrin over the course taken by Czechoslovakia. As early as February, Brezhnev's objections induced Dubček to rewrite his speech on the occasion of the 20th anniversary of the Communist takeover. A truly fierce attack came at the end of March, during the Dresden talks of the heads of the Communist Warsaw Pact countries. Although the scheduled agenda of the meeting was entirely different, the CPCz's delegation was surprised to realize that discussions revolved around a single topic, namely the situation in Czechoslovakia, and the new CPCz leadership received a lot of flak for losing control over events and for creating a platform for forces hostile to socialism. The most scathing critics, perhaps even more merciless than the USSR's delegation, were Władysław Gomułka and Walter Ulbricht, the respective heads of the Communist parties in Poland and East Germany. Their position did not substantially change in the following months, as the Polish and East-German Communists felt apprehensive of the influence that the Czechoslovak example might have on their societies, and in time they began to suggest radical measures.

The CPCz leadership's tentative response indicated what the Czechoslovak attitude would be in the coming months. Dubček and his entourage essentially conceded that the domestic political situation in Czechoslovakia became a matter of negotiations, thereby accepting external interference in the country's internal affairs. They were not even able to insist on including the leaders of Romania, another Warsaw Pact state, in the talks. Regrettably, Romania's presence could have helped their cause as it was at the time jealously protecting its hard-earned greater independence from the Soviet Union, and would have broken the united anti-Czechoslovak front in the group talks. And the last thing the Czechoslovak reformers would have dreamt of doing was to seek help against the Soviet pressure from still other foreign countries. Western countries were completely out of the question, even though their support would have only been symbolic. While the Western public and media followed developments in Czechoslovakia with great interest and approval, their leaders stuck to the strategy of expressing no official support for Czechoslovakia, fearing it might lead the Soviet Union to surmise that they were trying to play the Czechoslovak card to change the balance of power in Europe. When asked to name the best thing the West could do for Czechoslovakia at this time of mounting pressure, Willy Brandt, the then Minister of Foreign Affairs for the Federative Republic of Germany, answered 'Nothing at all.' His laconic words perfectly summarized the overall attitude of the West. Added to this, the USA was too caught up in the Vietnam War to even so much as try to formulate a policy related to the growing crisis in Czechoslovakia. Added to this, it was quite beyond Dubček and the others' imagination to use the disputes within the Communist movement to their advantage, and perhaps try to find a common platform with the Chinese Communists. While the Chinese Communists would have had little sympathy for the Czechoslovak reforms, they were likely to side with anybody who was causing grief to the USSR, China's rival in an impending military conflict. The foreign policy of the Prague Spring leaders remained based on repeated assurances that Czechoslovakia would honour its commitments to its allies, as well as on a last-minute effort to manifest good mutual relations with Romania and Yugoslavia. Both the Yugoslav President Tito and the Romanian leader Ceauşescu visited Prague in August, both received a warm welcome, and both expressed their pro-Czechoslovak feelings, but the significance of such actions was, at best, symbolic. In the decisive bilateral and multilateral talks in the spring and summer of 1968, the CPCz leadership remained a lone player facing five future invaders.

During both Dresden and other talks, it was always Dubček's goal to explain to the allies that the situation in Czechoslovakia was far from being as dramatic as it seemed to them, that the new CPCz leadership enjoyed the support of society, and that if there were any hostile forces, their potential was very limited. Nonetheless, during negotiations, the reformists accepted some of the criticism directed at them and pledged to take appropriate steps. What's more, upon their return, they informed neither the public nor (fully) the party leadership of the pressure to which they had been subjected. Their approach was understandable insofar as it helped prevent the anti-reformists from strengthening their position, but they were nonetheless deceiving the public. In the spring, the CPCz leadership was not even able to turn down the Soviet proposal to hold military manoeuvres involving Soviet troops in the summer of 1968 in Czechoslovakia, although they had originally been slated for 1969.

Czechoslovakia thus ended up hosting Soviet staff and troops from late May until early August. The Šumava allied exercise was, however, only a cover-up, and the Soviet military presence in Czechoslovakia had two real purposes. First, the Soviet troops constituted a reserve force to assist in suppressing the social movement that the Soviets perceived more and more clearly as an advancing counter-revolution, if Dubček and the CPCz leadership could be prevailed upon to take that route. Should such a situation arise, Soviet troops would be on hand to either intimidate or crackdown on potential protests and disturbances. The Soviet leaders long harboured the hope that such a plan would eventuate, and the military designs and preparations for an invasion to Czechoslovakia that had been formulated as early as April were tailored to that scenario. The alternative that the CPCz leaders would not come to their senses and that intervention in Czechoslovakia would have to be carried out against their will, to Moscow seemed, for many reasons, to be a last resort that was likely to cause many complications. Still, it had remained on the list of options ever since April, and the Soviet troops used the summer military exercise to probe the situation and to reconnoitre terrain, which would later aid them in carrying out the actual invasion. Indeed, during the August invasion, many officers and staff returned to the locations they had recently scouted as part of the Šumava exercise. The August intervention and the events that preceded it are unique in the history of military campaigns, in that the future invader was able to simulate its attack on the territory of its future victim and, what is more, with the victim's consent.

In April and May, an invasion by the USSR became a contingency to be reckoned on, particularly in view of the Hungarian experience of 1956. Still, even to pessimists it seemed quite improbable, for in spite of the increasingly frequent remarks by Soviet-Bloc politicians and media about the onset of a counter-revolution in Czechoslovakia (it was labelled 'creeping counter-revolution'), more than anything else, it was the comparison to Hungary that had a lulling effect. There was no violence going on in Czechoslovakia, nor – with few exceptions – were there any street demonstrations. The Prague Spring played out primarily in discussions during meetings and public gatherings and in the media, rather than in the street. People were truly interested in things political and bought tonnes of newspapers and magazines, but they were also avid consumers of the growing choice of cultural and entertainment events, and jumped at the chance to travel abroad more freely. The reverse was also true, with foreign tourists and journalists flooding into Czechoslovakia.

As the spring advanced, the forces that felt uneasy about the direction things were going and whose assessment of the situation essentially matched that of the critics from the Soviet Bloc, somewhat consolidated their positions in the party. As could be expected, the ever clearer and sterner declarations from the USSR, Poland, and East Germany emboldened them and pulled them out of the tight corner they had been pushed into since early March by the mighty mobilization of public opinion. It should be noted that this group still held key positions in CPCz central, regional, district, and local organizations. During the May session, these forces managed to incorporate into the final resolution a clause warning against two dangers and the necessity of fighting not only against 'conservatives', but also, and perhaps more importantly, against the danger coming from the right. Concurrently, the party leadership agreed to hold an irregular 14th Congress of the CPCz on 9th September. The idea of an irregular congress had the support of Moscow and the consensus of all factions within the party leadership, however, as the summer delegate elections at district and regional conferences came to indicate, the congress would have significantly changed the balance of power within the party leadership. Zdeněk Mlynář, one of the leading theoreticians and political strategists of the reform, estimated that some 80% of the elected delegates were adherents of Dubček's wing: advocates of thorough, albeit moderate and cautious, reforms. Another ten percent were delegates whose vision had fundamentally – if not expressly – left the framework of the communist system, and only the remaining ten percent were opponents of the reforms and upholders of the course pushed by Moscow.

Unlike the congress, which was supposed to be held earlier than planned, elections for representative bodies, slated for 1968, were postponed. The argument that it was unthinkable to hold elections in the usual absurd manner involving a unified ballot was correct, but politically short-sighted. The election delay meant that the parliament (as well as the SNC) retained its original 1964 line-up, including a strong representation of deputies who looked more than suspiciously on the direction taken from January 1968. It was somewhat ironic that the parliament subsequently extended its own term of office until the elections in autumn of 1971, which were conducted in the old style. Equally peculiar was the manner in which the Czech National Council (CNC) was constituted in the summer. Its formation was the first step towards overcoming the asymmetrical arrangement of the country, principally the fact that in addition to central authorities, there were mirror Slovak national bodies, but no Czech ones. The CNC was elected by the parliament, not by the Czech citizens in a popular election. Despite this, its line-up corresponded much more closely with the situation-to-date and public preferences.

The improvised formation of the CNC was necessitated by the Slovak National Council (SNC)'s need to have a formal partner in negotiations regarding changing the country's constitutional arrangement. The Slovak Question was one of the catalysts of the crisis that led to Novotný's downfall, and to all intents and purposes, the constitutional changes were supported by the Czech public, although Czechs saw them as less essential than did Slovaks. The plan for the constitutional changes, which the public translated for themselves as the formation of a federation, was a political priority in Slovakia. As early as the spring 1968, Gustáv Husák managed to garner significant influence by emphasizing that the Slovaks needed to grab the bull by the horns, as they might never have a second chance. While in the Czech Lands, Husák – as someone who had spent nearly ten years in a Communist prison and was well-known for his vitriolic criticism of Novotný and his cabinet in public debates – enjoyed the reputation of a reformist, Slovaks looked to him mainly as a defender of Slovak national interests. In reality, neither view was accurate. More than anything else, Husák was a pragmatist, a cold-blooded schemer, and a brilliant orator. The spring of 1968 marked a major turning point in the turbulent and remarkable career path of this politician who was both a Communist and a Slovak nationalist. His appointment to the position of Deputy Prime Minister in April launched his steep ascent to the highest offices.

Husák's slogan 'Federalization first, democratization later!' exemplified almost perfectly the atmosphere that reigned in Slovakia in the spring and summer 1968. Indeed, the movement towards liberalization was far slower in Slovakia than in the Czech Lands, after the effort of some Slovak intellectuals to explain to the public that, without thorough democratization, federalization would only be superficial, was not entirely successful. The year 1968 was neither the first (nor last) period in modern history when the political situation in the Czech and Slovak nations, so close to each other linguistically, culturally and otherwise, took divergent routes and paces. The result of such dissimilar development in the Czech and Slovak societies was that both Moscow and the staunch Communists at home had Slovakia pegged as a suitable base for reversing the unfavourable course. Symptomatically, some Czech anti-reformist functionaries with minuscule chances of becoming delegates in the 14th party congress – including the Central Committee Secretary Alois Indra, otherwise the most prominent collaborator with Moscow among the CPCz leaders – were subsequently elected in Slovakia.

The actual negotiations on constitutional changes moved ahead relatively quickly and were largely unobstructed. The only significant point of controversy came with the effort of some Moravian representatives to introduce a three-member federation. This proposal was unacceptable for the Slovak camp, as a federation based on a geographical, not ethnic, principle would have prevented them from achieving their key objective: full national emancipation. The tenets of the federal arrangement were eventually drawn up in the summer 1968 and passed as a constitutional bill in October, and they came into force on 1st January, 1969. The bill gave rise to two national republics (the Czech Socialist Republic and the Slovak Socialist Republic), each with its own government and parliament (Czech and Slovak National Councils). The state-wide federal government and Federal Assembly – a successor to the National Assembly – were shared. The Federal Assembly was divided into two chambers, including the House of the People (with 101 deputies elected in the Czech Lands and 49 in Slovakia) and the House of Nations (with 75 deputies for each republic). Key legislation was subject to separate voting in each chamber, and constitutional bills required a three-out-of-five majority vote by each national group of deputies in the Chamber of Nations. Such an arrangement effectively prevented the Slovaks from being outvoted: at the same time, two thirds of the Slovak deputies in the Chamber of Nations, who represented fewer than 15% of voters of the country, were able to block any ruling. While this did not matter under Communism, when all decisions of any consequence were made by the Presidium of the CC CPCz, political practice after 1989 showed the impracticality of this complicated system. In 1968, the formation of a federation was celebrated in Slovakia with a deep sense of satisfaction, while the Czechs accepted it with an indulgent smile.

It was with great chagrin that the public noted that the liberalization trend might be slowing down, due to criticism and pressure from abroad, coupled with the fact that the party hardliners had found a new footing. The media coverage looked critically upon the international context of the Czechoslovak situation, but their approach only made the Soviet-Bloc Communist leaders more furious, confirming their suspicion that the CPCz no longer had a grip on the direction in which the country was heading. The publication of the 'Two Thousand Words' manifesto in late June 1968 only added fuel to the fire. The

OLDŘICH TŮMA

manifesto was precisely a reaction to that power realignment within the CPCz leadership, as well as an expression of the fear that the reforms might be suspended or completely terminated. It was initiated by a group of leading Czech scientists, written by author Ludvík Vaculík, and signed by a few dozen prominent figures of Czech public life (collecting Slovak signatures simply did not occur to anybody). The text was published simultaneously in several newspapers and magazines on the same day, which added to its urgency. The 'Two Thousand Words' analysed the status quo, warned against slowing the pace of reform, and appealed to the public to show commitment and take the initiative, mainly on a community level and in the workplace. The manifesto sparked an infuriated response from the Soviets and the Communist hardliners at home, to whom it sounded like a call to counter-revolution. Merciless criticism rolled in from Moscow, East Berlin and Warsaw, appealing to the CPCz leaders to take immediate action, which they deemed long overdue. Similar calls to action came from the anti-reformers in the CC CPCz and National Assembly. Interestingly, even the protagonists of the reform course, including Josef Smrkovský and Dubček himself, initially assumed a critical attitude towards the manifesto. The reaction of the public, in contrast, was completely opposite, and within days the 'Two Thousand Words' received hundreds of thousands of signatures. The reform leaders were thus forced to tone down their objections, and the Two Thousand Words controversy was soon over – at least on Czechoslovak soil. Smrkovský's and Dubček's about-face, which was indeed instigated by their reflection on the vox populi, was rather typical of the reformers' behaviour in the summer of 1968. After the defeat of the Prague Spring, its protagonists were reproached for yielding to public opinion, which was seen as a manifestation of spineless and opportunist politics (Josef Smrkovský earned the nickname 'two-faced politician'). Admittedly, the reformists may have sometimes been guided by expediency, and the politicians' popularity ratings, published regularly by the media, did have a bearing on the behaviour of the leading CPCz politicians. Much more importantly, though, political life began assuming features which were distancing it from the standards of the Communist regime and bringing it closer to standards known in democracy: a critically-thinking citizenry, acting as an independent force; the media playing the role of a corrective of politics; and the politicians realizing the importance and significance of public feedback.

As of early July, the centre of gravity in Czechoslovakia's political development shifted once and for all to the international level. Gomułka and Ulbricht pushed relentlessly for a radical solution. Moscow basically gave up hope that the CPCz leaders could be induced as a group to reverse their course to Moscow's liking, and instead focused on collaborating with those opponents of the reforms who had more or less formed into a firm group. Although a final decision had not been made, the Kremlin saw military intervention as more and more plausible, carried out in coordination and concurrence with political action from the conservatives amongst the CPCz leaders. The role of chief mediator between the conspirators and the Soviets went to Vasil Biľak. The military preparations had also been essentially completed. Massive, practically non-stop manoeuvring of troops was underway in the Western part of the USSR, Poland, East Germany and Hungary, and large invasion forces were concentrated along the Czechoslovak borders. Coverage from Czechoslovakia became front-page news in the world press, and remained so for weeks.

The situation escalated dramatically in mid-July. The CPCz leaders received an invitation to Warsaw for a summit of the Communist party leaders of Warsaw Pact countries, again with the exclusion of Romania; however, they refused to send a delegation, arguing that it would be put before a tribunal. While this would have been correct, their decision to boycott the summit robbed the CPCz of the opportunity at least to try and prevent the formation of a unified front of five states. Before the Warsaw summit took place, Hungary's stance had been more differentiated, but once in Warsaw, János Kádár agreed to close ranks with the others. The Warsaw summit attendees, namely the USSR, Poland, the GDR, Hungary and Bulgaria, sent the CPCz a collective letter, which assessed the internal political situation in Czechoslovakia as critical, and called for immediate rescue action to save socialism, described as the common responsibility of all socialist countries. The CPCz leaders discussed a reply to the communiqué on 17th July, which was then unanimously ratified by the Central Committee. In the reply, the leaders defended the post-January course with a degree of determination, but again accepted the premise that Czechoslovakia's internal affairs should be a subject of talks between East European Communist parties. The CPCz proposed holding bilateral talks, during which it hoped to demonstrate to the allies that their assessment of the situation was off the mark. And they insisted that such talks should be held on Czechoslovak territory.

Tension mounted ever more in the second half of July. The Soviet secret service staged, and the Soviet media dramatically reported on, the discovery of secret arms dumps in Czechoslovakia. The goal was to create the illusion that both domestic and foreign enemies of socialism were preparing an armed takeover, which would provide a neat pretext for a strike from without. Moscow still hesitated to make the final decision at this point, fearing the repercussions that a military intervention might have on the policy of détente. They were aware that Dubček had the unanimous support of the Czechoslovak public. They also took into account that, in the matter of the Warsaw letter, the reformists managed to push through a united line, endorsed by everybody including the anti-reform faction. The leaders of strong Western European Communist parties, particularly the Italian and French parties, made it clear that they would not support a strike on Czechoslovakia. In the end, the Soviets conceded to holding bilateral talks on Czechoslovak territory, even if the location was a train station in Čierna nad Tisou, only several hundred yards from the Czechoslovak-Soviet border. The meeting was preceded by another massive mobilization of the Czech and Slovak public to shore up the reform course and Dubček's leadership. Under the headline 'Socialism – Alliance – Sovereignty – Freedom,' (contradictory though this might have been), the Literary Gazette published the text of a letter addressed to the CPCz leaders, signed by millions of people within a matter of days.

The talks in Čierna at the turn of July and August dragged on for four days. They were attended by all the members of the presidiums of both Communist parties, and the Czecho-

OLDŘICH TŮMA

slovak side also invited President Ludvík Svoboda. The negotiations demonstrated just how deep the rift was within the CPCz leadership.

Part of the delegation supported the Soviet stance and their critique of the state of affairs in Czechoslovakia almost unequivocally in their statements. In contrast, the reform-oriented members of the CPCz leadership who enjoyed the respect of the population (apart from Dubček and Smrkovský, these were primarily the Prime Minister Oldřich Černík and the Chairman of the National Front's Central Committee František Kriegel) defended the positions of the CPCz as laid out in the reply to the Warsaw letter. There was a point when open conflict seemed inevitable, but after a one-on-one conversation between Dubček and Brezhnev, and a subsequent talk attended by a limited number of the respective parties' leaders, a compromise solution was reached, although it was interpreted somewhat differently by each party later. An indisputable outcome of the talks was an agreement to hold a joint meeting of the Warsaw Pact party and country leaders, to demonstrate their newfound unity and future co-operation. It is, however, evident that the CPCz – while perhaps not directly accepting them – did not expressly reject the Soviet demands for resuming control over the media, for some personnel changes, for banning the clubs and organizations outside of the National Front (i.e. K-231, KAN, and Social Democracy), and for making the State Security (StB) an independent organization, with the goal of disengaging this political police force from the control of the reform-oriented Minister of the Interior, Josef Pavel. At any rate, a definite outcome of the talks in Čierna was to hold off military intervention for the time being.

On 3rd August, an ostentatious meeting took place in Bratislava of the Communist leaderships of Czechoslovakia, the USSR, Poland, East Germany, Hungary, and Bulgaria – five aggressors and their future victim. A declaration was solemnly adopted, defining in broad terms the relations between socialist countries and their future cooperation. It also contained passages describing the joint responsibility of all socialist states to defend socialism (or: the Communist regime) in each individual country. The Czechoslovak public and foreign media concluded that the immediate threat of intervention had been averted. This turned out to be the case for only a few weeks. The radical part of the Czech population, as well as the media, regarded the outcome of the talks with suspicion, and requested information about the real nature of the commitments that the CPCz had taken upon itself in Čierna nad Tisou, plus a clear indication that such commitments would not lead the country towards curbing fundamental liberties and reforms. Spontaneous demonstrations took place in Prague practically every day, and petitions with similar demands were being signed. The reform leaders issued repeated assurances, which were at least partially in contradiction with reality, that no commitments related to Czechoslovak internal affairs had been made in either Čierna nad Tisou or Bratislava.

Dubček seems to have hoped that by agreeing to a compromise in Čierna, he had gained the time necessary to carry out the 14th Congress of the CPCz. At the same time, he realized that the public would by no means tolerate some of the agreed-upon measures, including restrictions on media freedom. The Soviets, however, were relentless in requesting that their demands be fulfilled immediately, with Brezhnev sending out frequent reminders, either by phone or through Ambassador Chervonenko. When he realized that Dubček was once again playing for time (a recording of his and Dubček's phone call from 13th August aptly illustrates such tactics and their limitations), he decided to take action. For even the Soviets recognized that any interference in Czechoslovakia's domestic affairs after the 14th Congress would be far harder to pull off. The clock was ticking, as the Congress of the KSS was scheduled for an even earlier date, 26th August. A meeting of the Central Committee of the CPSU was hurriedly convened in Moscow from 15th to 17th August, where the decision was finally made to carry out a military intervention in Czechoslovakia. On 18th August, representatives of the five countries that were to participate in the intervention met in Moscow and gave their ultimate consent, while also learning the details of the invasion from Brezhnev.

The military aspect had been taken care of, with the intervention armies already lined up on the border. Key was the political scenario, in which the crucial role was to be played by conspirators within the CPCz. These were politicians whom Moscow considered 'healthy forces,' while the Czechoslovak public referred to them as 'conservatives,' and later 'traitors.' When the Presidium of the CC CPCz convened on the 20th August, during a discussion about a report on the political situation in the country, the plan was to form a majority, in which those who knew of the invasion would join forces with the conservative members of the presidium. As soon as a majority agreed to describe the political situation in the country as critical, it would not be a problem to take the next step: request military assistance from the Warsaw Pact countries to suppress the impending counter-revolution. The Soviets expected that such a request – if presented as a *fait accompli* – would be backed by President Svoboda, as well as most members of the government and the Presidium of the National Assembly. The military operations that would by then have been launched would be presented to the Czechoslovak and foreign public as an act fully legitimized by the request of Czechoslovak constitutional and political figures. At the onset of the intervention, the pro-Moscow conspirators were also supposed to take control of the Ministry of the Interior, electronic media, and the Czechoslovak Army Command.

Obviously, it remains a question why the proponents of reform among the CPCz leaders failed to respond to this turn of events. At the very least, the massive and long-term concentration of armed forces along the Czechoslovak border could not have escaped their attention. Most likely, their life experience and beliefs simply made them unwilling or unable to accept reality. They were all avowed Communists and could not even conceive of a foreign policy based on anything other than a firm alliance with the USSR. They refused to accept that Moscow could send intervention troops to Czechoslovakia to overthrow *them*, who genuinely believed they were rehabilitating socialism, not destroying it. They interpreted the military manoeuvres as a component of psychological and political pressure, and so raised no objections. In seeking an answer to the question of whether Czechoslovakia should have defended itself in August 1968, it should not be overlooked that the Czechoslovak army was not, in fact, the army of a sovereign state at that point; rather, it was part of a broader military coalition, fully controlled and commanded by Soviet marshals. The

Soviets knew everything about the arsenal, training, line-up procedures, and deployment of the Czechoslovak units. The Czechoslovak army had been trained, in accordance with Soviet military doctrine, for offensive operations in Western Europe, not for defending its own territorial integrity. It was positioned to face west, with its forward echelons deployed in Western Bohemia and the training and reserve divisions in the rest of the country. A last-minute order to put up armed resistance would have been risky business indeed, and would have provided the invaders with the perfect excuse of a fight provoked by a counter-revolution; after all, Brezhnev had not ruled out local skirmishes when he laid out his intervention plan. Still, with the above-said, it does not necessarily follow that the reformist CPCz leaders could not and should not have made it clear in good time that they were prepared to defend Czechoslovakia's sovereignty and prevent anybody from interfering in its internal affairs. Chances are such a well-timed, unambiguous attitude would have made it much harder for the Soviets to go ahead with the invasion.

2 The August Invasion and Its Consequences

On the morning of 20th August, as the meeting of the CC CPCz Presidium unfolded, the commencement of the military operations was only hours away. The scenario of the political utilization of the intervention began to collapse at the very beginning, as the conspirators failed to move the domestic political situation to the top of the agenda, and discussion on other issues dragged on in the usual unstructured way until the evening. The report in question came up for discussion at about 8 p.m. It elicited intense debate that had not yet finished when Prime Minister Černík announced at half past eleven that the Czechoslovak border had been crossed in several places by foreign troops half an hour previously. No majority willing to support the invasion was created. On the contrary, those members of the presidium who had been opposed to the reform, but had not been told of the invasion plan, were surprised and disoriented, and in the ensuing discussion over what the party leadership's response should be, the conspirators and proponents of the invasion remained a minority.

In the initial phase, Czechoslovakia was invaded by some 165,000 troops, with more than 4,000 tanks, hundreds of fighter jets and transport aircraft, and other equipment pouring across the border from East Germany, Poland, the Soviet Union, and Hungary in several major streams. They were followed by more forces over the next few days. Participants in the intervention included Soviet, Polish and Hungarian divisions. The Bulgarian army was represented only symbolically by two regiments. The East German army divisions stopped at the border, sending in only their minor communication and liaison units. The respective tank columns set off in different directions and reached key administrative and industrial hubs of the country before the night was over. Special Soviet planes had landed at the Prague and Brno airports in the evening. Their crews then secured the airports at around 11 p.m., and prepared the ground for the landing of dozens of Soviet transport aircraft, bringing with them more soldiers and military equipment. One of the priority tasks in the first hours of the invasion was to take over key buildings in Prague. As for the headquarters of the CC CPCz where the meeting of the presidium was under way, troops arrived later than planned and expected by the conspirators. From a strictly military perspective, the intervention was successful, although the troops lost their way in some locations and so were somewhat delayed. Logistical issues also piled up in the days that followed when the Czechoslovak army refused to supply food and fuel. The Czechoslovak units were consigned to their barracks, but they resisted all attempts at disarmament.

The elements of the operation that were the responsibility of the 'healthy forces' in Czechoslovakia were only partially successful. Karel Hoffman, Director of the Central Communications Authority, did not manage to get a prepared text legitimizing the intervention on the air via the electronic media, and later also failed to cut off their broadcast. A palace coup of sorts had begun in the late afternoon on 20th August at the Ministry of the Interior, under the baton of StB Chief Viliam Šalgovič; during the coup, Minister of the Interior Pavel was deposed, and officers loyal to him detained or sequestered. At the Ministry of Defence, the Soviet liaison officers forced the minister, General Dzúr, to issue orders to the Czechoslovak army not only to refrain from resistance and retire to their barracks, but also to provide the arriving foreign troops with all manner of support. The latter part of the order was universally ignored. When the Soviet Ambassador informed President Svoboda of the intervention, Svoboda refused to endorse it. Most importantly, however, the Presidium eventually adopted a proclamation by a seven-to-four vote, in which they resolutely rejected the invasion; they managed to communicate the story to the media, and the radio broadcast it without delay.

The political scenario of the invasion broke down completely on the very first night. By the time the Soviet paratroopers ambushed the CC CPCz headquarters and arrested the leading reformist politicians, the streets had flooded with people. People were protesting all around the country, trying to stop the troops from advancing by building barricades or even with their own bodies. Resistance was equally strong both in the Czech Lands and Slovakia. The Soviet soldiers opened fire in many places, killing dozens and injuring hundreds of civilians. The shooting continued in the days that followed. The most intense clashes took place on 21st August in the centre of Prague, particularly around the headquarters of Czechoslovak Radio, which was continuing to broadcast news. The Soviets failed to cut off the broadcast even after seizing the building, as the coverage continued from alternate locations. Radio and television transmitters from other parts of the country joined in during the day. Although the editorial and printing offices of major dailies had been seized, newspapers and magazines kept on publishing special editions and anti-invasion flyers and had them distributed around the country. The whole country was covered with posters and signs, traffic signposts and street names were removed in a matter of hours, to make orientation harder for the intervention troops. The resistance, although non-violent, was very imaginative and quite impressive. In this atmosphere of general resistance, the intervention was also rejected by the government, the Presidium of the Parliament, and other central, regional and local authorities. In the first days after the invasion, the interventionists gained military control over Czechoslovakia, but remained politically isolated. At a meeting of the representatives of five states, held on the 24th August in Moscow, Brezhnev complained that 'the healthy forces failed to take action and acted like cowards.' Gomułka added that – as the example of Czechoslovakia illustrated – 'counter-revolution can be carried out even in the presence of Soviet troops.'

On 22nd August, some 80% of the delegates of the 14th Congress gathered in an industrial complex in Vysočany, Prague. Quite in keeping with the party statutes, they pronounced their gathering a party congress and thus ensured that another of the key political goals of the invasion failed, namely preventing the party congress from happening. The congress categorically rejected the intervention, elected a new party leadership that featured all the reformists, including those held in Soviet captivity. In contrast, those who had collaborated with the Soviets were not elected. For several days in August 1968, the CPCz seemed to be implementing policies in the interest of, and in accordance with, the wishes of Czechoslovak society. The CPCz, as the only political force in a position to put up resistance against the occupation of the country, was now being joined by people who had never subscribed to Communist ideology.

The pro-Soviet wing of the party leadership was unable to face this challenge. After the failure of the plan that expected them to take the reins of the party, the alternative option involving the creation of a provisional government of workers and peasants also fell through. After two days of talks at the Soviet embassy, during which none of the pro-Moscow group members stepped forward to take responsibility, Ambassador Chervonenko pressed the plan for a provisional government, which President Svoboda refused to accept. This presented the interventionists with a serious dilemma: backing out was naturally out of the question, but neither were they ready to set up an occupation regime, launch an extensive arrest campaign, or break public resistance through brutal force. They wished to avoid uncontrolled bloodshed and an even greater international scandal. Since their allies in Czechoslovakia, who – it turned out – represented nobody and were unable to fulfil their tasks, the Soviets were obliged to return to the strategy they had abandoned in early summer, and try to teach obedience to those who enjoyed the public's genuine trust: the reformers. For those politicians, by this point glowing with the aura of martyrs, had just reached the absolute pinnacle of their popularity, and every public announcement made by Czechoslovak institutions, organizations and spontaneous public rallies demanded their return to Czechoslovakia and to their constitutional and political positions. Dubček, Smrkovský, Černík, Kriegel, and others were arrested at the CC headquarters on 21st August and, before the day was over, flown to the USSR, where they were held in custody. Two days later, the prisoners with an uncertain destiny regained their political status and were flown to the Kremlin to participate in talks. President Svoboda, who had taken it upon himself to save the situation and in the face of the constitutional organs' doubts, travelled to Moscow on the 23rd August, where he helped to forge a suitable arrangement. While he was determined to bring the detained politicians home, he was also determined to make them come to an agreement with the Soviets.

Beginning on 23rd August, the Kremlin hosted a series of arduous talks. The make-up of the Czechoslovak delegation changed over time, as more and more politicians were transported to Moscow. The Soviets' demands had not greatly changed from the previous negotiations held in the spring and summer. In addition, they now pressed the Czechoslovak leaders to put a stop to the public's anti-occupation resistance and, above all, to have the 14th Congress of the party declared invalid. As could be expected, the Soviet demands were acceptable not only to the pro-Moscow group, but also, significantly, to President Svoboda. Gustáv Husák advertized himself to the Soviets as a politician with 'a sense of reality.' Dubček and the others initially resisted, but the constant pressure, open threats of bloodshed, and the lack of reliable information about what was going on in Czechoslovakia eventually caused them to buckle. The 'Moscow Protocol' was signed on 26th August and rather than any kind of compromise, established the reformers' capitulation. According to this document, which was supposed to remain top secret, the CPCz leadership acceded to practically all the Soviet demands in exchange for a guarantee that they could resume their positions, a vague hope that at least some of the reforms might be implemented, and a promise that as soon as the situation in Czechoslovakia was normalized (in other words, when the state-wide resistance against the presence of foreign troops was stopped), the gradual withdrawal of troops would be launched, particularly from large cities, where the risk of incidents was the highest.

When the Czechoslovak delegation returned home, Dubček, Smrkovský and Černík were at first welcomed as heroes, but as soon as information leaked out about the true nature of the Moscow deal, the public began to grumble and the media – at the time still free – asked serious questions. Tension was mounting, but Dubček's emotional radio address on the afternoon of 27th August finally broke the people down. From that day, life in Prague and other cities gradually returned to its old groove. Husák took it upon himself to get the 14th Congress declared invalid, and went about his task very shrewdly. He used – as he would do a few more times in the autumn and in the spring of the following year – an argument based not on a general political, but a national, issue. The Congress of the KSS began in Bratislava on 26th August and, on day one, endorsed the conclusions of the 14th Congress held in Vysočany, Prague. Husák addressed the congress on the 27th August, upon his return from Moscow, and convinced the delegates that the 14th Congress could not be considered valid on the grounds that it had only a handful of participants from Slovakia. This was actually true, but only because the conditions of an occupied country prevented the delegates from reaching the location. Also true was that the Slovaks were still proportionally represented in the new leadership (which now included Husák, who had never before held a party position, but the Vysočany congress elected him into the presidium of the CC), and that the congress assumed that as soon as the situation calmed down, its talks would be resumed and completed with a full Slovak delegation. Husák's argument received support in Slovakia. The Czech side, having no interest in destroying the Czech-Slovak unity, found it very hard to object, much more so than it would have in the event of a full frontal attack. In summary, the 14th Congress was declared invalid and the CPCz revoked what may have been the one redeeming moment in its history. The leading party positions were reinstituted, after a limited number of the 'Vysočany' functionaries had been co-opted into them, including Husák, who held onto his membership in the Presidium and, on top of this, became First Secretary of the KSS.

After returning from Moscow, the reformers assumed that there was still a chance to save at least a part of the reform package, and hoped that a speedy withdrawal of the foreign troops could be ensured. It soon turned out that the Kremlin was planning nothing of the sort. True, the Soviet troops were withdrawn from Prague and most big cities, their numbers in Czechoslovakia were gradually reduced, and the intervention troops from all the other countries were gone by the autumn; the Soviets, however, made it clear during the September talks that they intended to keep some of their units in Czechoslovakia permanently. They requested that a number of military barracks and premises used by the Czechoslovak army be vacated, and made Dubček's leadership agree to the temporary presence of Soviet forces in Czechoslovakia. When the agreement was ratified by the parliament in October, the presence of the Soviet forces was legalized. The troops then remained 'temporarily' in the country until 1991.

There was still a chance to fight back against the unrelenting Soviet pressure. As Václav Havel said at the session of Co-ordination Committee of Artists' Associations in the autumn of 1968, a reality that must be counted upon was not only the presence of a foreign army in the country, but also the continuing enthusiasm and resolve of the vast majority of the public to defend their freedom and to do anything to prevent the return to the pre-January–1968 state of affairs. Indeed, the civic society's power remained considerable. While the re-introduction of censorship, enforced by the Moscow talks, imposed on the media a list of taboo topics, freedom of speech was still merely restricted, not liquidated. The media were still an important element in the development of public affairs. Students' and artists' organizations and trade unions were determined to back the reformers. Workers' committees for the defence of freedom of speech were set up, and co-operation between workers and the University Students' Union was intensified. Protest demonstrations were organized on the national holiday of 28th October and again on 7th November, and a general strike action of secondary-school and university students, lasting several days, was called in the second half of November. However, Dubček and most reformist leaders cared little for such support. They did not wish for society to be mobilized, hoping instead that things would calm down and allow them to reach at least a limited number of objectives through cabinet negotiations. This, however, was merely more wishful thinking on their part, as was demonstrated in the run-up to the November session of the CC. The Kremlin vetoed several resolution proposals, and a thesis had to be incorporated into the session's conclusions that the primary danger was coming from the right and that the party was obliged to combat this. On top of that, the unity of the reformist wing began to split at the seams. Husák, and many others by now, were trying to find a common language with the Soviets and, in an effort to maintain their careers, were prepared to make more and more concessions. Every chance to lean on the support of society and to resist the Soviet pressure was wasted. When the Federal Assembly was being set up in early 1969, Husák once again employed his tried-and-true tactics: asserting that, since both the President and Prime Minister were Czechs, the parliament should be presided over by a Slovak, rather than another Czech, Josef Smrkovský. What he was really trying to do was to strip Smrkovský of any consequential position, as the Soviets perceived him to be a prominent opponent of the occupation. This time, however, Husák's arguments fell short of the mark even in Slovakia, and gave rise to protest rallies in the Czech Lands. Students and the strongest trade unions organized a strike. In the end, it was the reformists who gave in and Smrkovský personally requested that the protests in support of him be called off. On the 16th January, in protest of the increasingly defeatist politics of the Czechoslovak leaders, a Charles University student by the name Jan Palach committed self-immolation in the centre of Prague. His act and, three days later, his death, once again stirred the public to action. But yet again, the power of the mobilized society was used to no productive end. Although hundreds of thousands of people participated in Palach's remembrance ceremony and funeral, things eventually returned to the routine. The repeated build-up of tension and the pointless offers of protest actions and mobilization which never came to anything began to wear the public down and their spirit of resistance began to wane.

It is something of a paradox that the decisive turning point was not triggered by a political event, but by the games of the ice-hockey world championships. Although the 1969 championships had been planned to take place in Prague, a decision was made to move them to Sweden due to the August invasion. Ice-hockey matches between Czechoslovakia and the USSR have always had an undertone of something more than a sports event, and this was particularly true in March 1969. In the minds of Czechs and Slovaks, the matches against the Soviets turned into an opportunity to retaliate for the August invasion. In the two matches against the USSR, Czechoslovakia came out the winner. Especially after the second game against the Soviets on 28th March, the nation erupted in spontaneous joy and massive celebration. Husák later expressed his outrage when he said that 'half a million people took to the streets that night.' In the recently occupied country, the celebration could not have been apolitical. The demonstrations, and especially the fact that they involved attacks on Soviet buildings, including the vandalizing of the Aeroflot Airlines office in Prague's Wenceslas Square were used by the regime as an excuse to step up the strong Soviet pressure on Dubček's already declining administration. It should be noted that the Aeroflot attack was likely a provocation of the already 'normalized' StB, which had thus manufactured a spectacular pretext for escalating the crisis. Still, the ardour and hatred in the streets were spontaneous and authentic, and it could hardly have been otherwise. Soviet buildings were attacked in twenty locations around the country (the USSR's army was stationed in 36 cities). There were places where the situation came to a very dramatic head, as in Mladá Boleslav, where the crowds in the streets came face to face with Soviet transport vehicles aiming machine guns at them.

OLDŘICH TŮMA

Events took a quick turn after the Stockholm Championships. Without the knowledge and consent of the Czechoslovak government (which is exactly what the agreement regarding the troops' temporary presence stipulated), the Soviets sent new reinforcements to Czechoslovakia, and the Soviet Minister of Defence Grechko and Deputy Minister of Foreign Affairs Semyonov flew in uninvited. *Pravda*, the Moscow daily, began once again publishing stories about counter-revolution in Czechoslovakia. Latent and open threats were accompanied by behind-the-scenes negotiations and a successful breaking up of the pro-reform wing of the CPCz leadership. The Soviets were now determined to dispose of Dubček and replace him with their new favourite, Gustáv Husák, who had a secret meeting with Brezhnev on 13th April in Ukraine. As usual, Dubček eventually buckled, without trying to capitalize on public support. The 17th April session of the CC CPCz started with Dubček's resignation, and continued with Husák winning a clear majority vote to become the new party leader. Up until several days earlier, it had seemed that the only imaginable response of the public to Dubček's removal from the highest office would have to be a general strike; eventually, however, the protests were limited to strikes at several universities. The party leadership received a thorough reconstruction during the April plenary session, with the reformers retaining only a fraction of their former positions. A political overthrow – in a way, a finalization of the August invasion – was carried out, although not everybody saw it that way at the time. Many people considered Husák a guarantee that Czechoslovakia could not return to what it had been prior to January 1968. They were soon to learn that this was nothing more than wishful thinking. Admittedly, Husák's own plans and ideas could have been somewhat different from reality, and he had little room to manoeuvre, with Vasil Biľak and Alois Indra – obvious agents of Moscow – breathing down his neck from top party positions. It was not what he wanted to do that mattered, but what he did do: a few months after Husák took office, the country could clearly see that all the values, liberties, ideals, and achievements of the Prague Spring were quickly being buried in the past.

If in the several months that have been discussed, the energy of society had been squandered in support of those who were unable or unwilling to use it, and if it was not always clear who deserved to be trusted and who should be defied, things acquired very clear contours after a few months of Husák's government. The first anniversary of the invasion in August 1969 saw the final open clash between the consolidating regime and the last remaining part of the public that refused to capitulate or admit defeat without a fight: mostly the young people. The impending August anniversary of the occupation gave them a substitute – but significant – opportunity to show their determination to prevent a complete reversal of direction, or at least protest against it. In July and August '69, the country was flooded with signs and flyers, and appeals for passive resistance, respectful tributes to the victims of the occupation, and symbolic strikes. The regime, however, was living in fear of the anniversary, and would not be caught off guard. On 10th July, 1969, during a meeting at the People's Militia headquarters, Husák declared: '…we will mercilessly crush those who dare put up active resistance in the streets or anything like that, whatever the cost.' The regime welcomed the fact that the major wave of resistance against the onset of normalization (a term then coined to describe regime consolidation) took place not after Dubček's downfall, but much later in August. The time lapse gave it time to build, train, and equip special police squads for suppressing public protests. Special army units were also selected and trained, and the People's Militia was undergoing training. Special headquarters, information systems, and emergency plans were set up. The regime took the preparations seriously, acting as though it expected a civil war. Eventually, the clash between the Communist regime and the public in August 1969 unfolded in a rather inverse order when compared to other instances of street unrest. In 1953, 1956, 1970, among other cases, large demonstrations had erupted suddenly in, respectively, Eastern Germany, Hungary and Poland, taking the regimes by surprise and precipitating widespread crisis. Not so in Czechoslovakia in 1969, where the regime anticipated the protests and had enough time to thoroughly prepare, and where the protests themselves represented the final stage of what was by then a practically hopeless battle.

The centre of Prague was hit by turbulent demonstrations on the 19th and especially on the 20th August. The security forces, particularly the People's Militia, were brutal in their reprisals, and in some cases went so far as to open fire at demonstrators, leaving two dead and several injured. On the 21st August, rallies were organized at dozens of locations around the republic. Hundreds of thousands of people heeded the appeal for passive resistance and boycotted public transport, the daily press, shopping, cinema and theatre. Dozens of factories went on strikes of varying duration. The demonstrations, particularly those in Prague, Liberec and Brno, were suppressed by the security forces with only the utmost exertion. Army reinforcements were called to Prague and Brno, including a tank regiment for the capital city. Again the militia opened fire, with another casualty in Prague and two more in Brno. About 2,500 people were arrested and taken to police stations and prisons, where most of them were badly mistreated. The demonstrations continued in Brno and several other locations in Moravia on the 22nd August, when the Federal Assembly adopted 'A Legal Measure for Maintaining Public Peace and Order.' Alexander Dubček, who at the time still presided over the parliament, played an infelicitous role in creating the document. He let himself be manipulated into signing it, although it was unconstitutional in both form and spirit. Thousands of people were later persecuted on the basis of a measure signed by the man whom they had once celebrated in the streets, sometimes at their life's peril. The document provided the regime with the legal tools it needed to subject society to an intensive pacification campaign. The Legal Measure was in effect a small-scale state of emergency, which allowed the regime to detain its opponents for weeks without a court order, increase penalties for certain offences, simplify and speed up court proceedings, use a simple procedure to stop the publication of selected periodicals, dissolve social organizations, and dismiss people from jobs and universities. By the end of 1969, about 1,500 people were convicted on the basis of Legal Measure articles, although most of the sentences were suspended or pecuniary.

3 The Restoration of Order

'Counter-Revolutionary Forces Crushed in Open Confrontation,' was the triumphant banner headline on the front page of *Rudé Právo* on 25th August, 1969. The August confrontation, which – given the distribution of power at the time – could not have had any other outcome, was indeed a major turning point. Husák's regime and his by now completely blatant dismantling of all the achievements of the Prague Spring faced very little organized resistance. The regime, which had all the machinery of propaganda and power at its disposal, was from now on opposed only by individuals with strong moral values and conscience – weapons often too weak to pose a real threat.

All the rudiments of a civil society created during 1968 were being stamped out. The University Students' Union was abolished in June, immediately after the semester finished, and was followed by other youth organizations. Trade unions and other organizations were gradually brought back under the yoke of the CPCz. Some other associations, such as the Writers' Union, continued to fight a tenacious retreating battle, though no longer in the public eye, but they were normalized or abolished and replaced by new, obedient ones a year or two later. Media control became much more effective and many periodicals were discontinued. In May and June 1969, this fate befell The Reporter (*Reportér*, published by the Journalists' Association), The Gazette (*Listy*, published by the Writers' Union), and The Students' Gazette (*Studentské listy*, published by the University Students' Union) – three weeklies with an combined circulation of several hundred thousand and with enormous influence on public opinion. A whirlwind of personnel replacements followed in the electronic media and the daily press came next in the summer and autumn. Censorship was now running at full steam. The September 1969 session of the CC brought about an open, concentrated attack on the remaining reformers' positions. Disobedient parliament deputies, especially in the CNC, were disposed of by the regime in a peculiar manner: they were either forced to resign, or the parliaments dismissed them and co-opted others in their stead. The key anti-invasion resolutions of the state and party organs from August 1968 were revoked in the autumn, while October brought with it the abolishment of the still relatively liberal regulations governing travel to the West.

1970 was the year of screening tests and purges within the CPCz, as a result of which nearly half a million members (28%) lost their membership in one way or another (some left of their own accord, others were expelled). In subsequent or concurrent purges, tens of thousands of these people – along with many others who had never been members of the CPCz – were stripped of their positions, jobs, or a chance to work in their field of expertise. The majority of these purges were completed in 1970 and 1971, but many continued longer. Very often this was a gradual procedure, by which people were at first made to trade their prominent positions for less prominent ones, e.g. leave political positions for jobs at scientific institutions or abroad, or trade a senior for a junior position. The illusion that the purges would stop there was short-lived: more persecution would follow only months later, usually involving a transfer to manual labour. The prototype of such a gradual downfall was, in fact, Alexander Dubček – a symbol of the Prague Spring. He was forced to resign his position of First Secretary in April 1969, lost his CC Presidium membership in September and his membership of the CC in January 1970, and in June of that year he was expelled from the party. Dubček moved from presiding over the Federal Assembly between April and September 1969, to serving as Ambassador to Turkey from January to June 1970, to becoming an official of the Forestry Service of Western Slovakia in December 1970.

It was in the same period that the repressive authorities managed to eradicate most of the groups which – after the opportunity to express publicly non-conformist views was lost – tried to continue their resistance in other ways. In late 1969, dozens of arrests were carried out (with most of those arrested later convicted) among adherents of the Revolutionary Youth Movement. This group, mostly comprised of students, radically stood up against the course that the country had taken since Autumn 1968; at first, it did so openly, and after the spring of 1969, with a degree of conspiracy. In 1970 and 1971, opposition groups which had mostly formed around erstwhile Communist reformers were wiped out, including a very active group based in Brno that was mainly made up of members of National Front Czechoslovak Socialist Party. This stage of police and court reprisals culminated in an arrest campaign on the eve of the 1971 general elections, and once again in 1972 with what is known as 'the summer of trials.' Fortunately, the fears of another 1950s did not materialize: the court and police reprisals of the early 1970s were selective, affected only dozens of people, and handed out sentences much lower than those of twenty years earlier – mostly up to five years of imprisonment. It is not quite clear why the regime abandoned the idea of a more massive retaliation (occasionally, as in the case of the student leaders or the signatories of the '10 Points' protest petition from August 1969, the prosecution was prepared, only to be suspended at the last minute). This becomes all the more interesting in view of the fact that there were voices in the CC itself calling for punishing the leaders of the Prague Spring, including Dubček. Some credited the relatively moderate course to Husák and his personal experience as a long-term political prisoner in the 1950s. What was perhaps more significant was the attitude of the Soviets, who were reluctant to attract the world's attention to Czechoslovakia during the détente period. There was also the complex manoeuvring and latent conflict between individual factions of the CPCz's normalization leadership; and the issue of punishment for 1968 was one of the fields in which such battles were waged. In the end, the reprisals were certainly much more selective and moderate than they had been in the first years after 1948. To make up for this, the regime launched a far more elaborate and extensive social discrimination campaign. Hundreds of thousands of people's lives were affected, either through the loss of their jobs or by having their professional careers curbed in some way. In some fields (the media, academia, scientific institutions, and some state-administration sectors), the purges affected up to 50% of all employees. Another highly effective tool to enforce obedience was to affect the lives of people's children: in the early 1970s, but later as well, thousands of gifted young people were prevented from receiving a university education because of their parents' stance.

At the turn of the 1960s and 1970s, dissident activities were confined almost exclusively to the Czech Lands. Slovakia was barely touched by the protests, including the most turbulent ones in August 1969; the regime was consolidated at a faster pace there, and Slovak society was exposed to much milder reprisals than Czech society after 1968. On top of this, the federalization of the country and the formation of Slovak national authorities as part of the package, was the only significant achievement of the 1968 reform year to survive the onset of normalization. Although Slovak society unequivocally rejected the August intervention, the year 1968 was branded somewhat differently in its collective memory, and the Slovaks entered the 1970s in a slightly different spiritual climate than Czech society. In a way, this continued to be the case for the twenty years that followed.

At the end of 1970, the CC CPCz adopted a text which provided a binding interpretation of the 1968 events, known as Lesson Drawn from the Crisis Development in the Party and Society. In 1971, the long-overdue party congress could finally take place, as could elections, by then fully under the control of the CPCz. To use the words of Milan Šimečka, the era's insightful analyst of the Communist regime's re-consolidation, order was restored. The kind of order involving the reconstruction of the Communist party, intimidating the public, resuming control over the media, bringing social organizations into line, and crushing what was left of political opposition, had been achieved by the end of 1971.

Viewed from a different perspective, however, the Prague Spring seems to have taken longer than that to burn out. Until the early seventies, books that had been prepared for publication during the Prague Spring, by both domestic and foreign authors, continued to be published. Sadly, after only a few months in the catalogues, they were later either summarily destroyed or removed from libraries for the next twenty years. Movies were still being made based on scripts authorized a year of two before; but they were no longer destined for distribution. Most importantly, society still was not prepared to admit that normalization was to be something more than a temporary slip off the most logical course towards a more humane, liberal, and rational interpretation of socialism. This conviction (or subconscious wish) regarding the temporary nature of normalization was terribly strong. In less sophisticated circles, rumours spread about a pending international agreement that would make Czechoslovakia neutral, and prophecies were uttered, based on the most improbable evidence, of changes that were to take place in the USSR. Quite possibly the fact that all the changes for the worse were perceived as temporary may have lulled society into resisting with less determination. The reality was far worse: the milieu created in Czechoslovakia in the early 1970s changed only very slowly and remained in operation for almost two more decades.

Bibliography

BENČÍK, Antonín: *Rekviem za Pražské jaro*, Praha 1998.
BRACKE, Maud: *Which socialism? whose detente?: West European communism and the Czechoslovak crisis, 1968*, Budapest–New York 2007.
BISCHOF, Günter – KARNER, Stefan – RUGGENTHALER, Peter (eds.): *The Prague Spring and the Warsaw Pact Invasion of Czechoslovakia in 1968*, Lanham 2009.

LITTEL, Robert (ed.): *The Czech Black book*, New York 1969.

MASTNY, Vojtěch (ed.): *Czechoslovakia: crisis in world communism*, New York 1972.

DAWISHA, Karen: *The Kremlin and the Prague Spring*, Berkeley 1984.

DUBČEK, Alexander: *Hope dies last: the autobiography of Alexander Dubcek*, New York 1993.

EIDLIN, Fred H.: *The logic of "normalization": the Soviet intervention in Czechoslovakia of 21 August 1968 and the Czechoslovak response*, Boulder 1980.

FAURE, Justine: *L'ami americain: la Tchécoslovaquie, enjeu de la diplomatie americaine, 1943–1968*, Paris 2004.

HEJZLAR, Zdeněk: *Czechoslovakia, 1968–1969*, New York 1975.

KAPLAN, Frank L.: *Winter into spring: the Czechoslovak press and the reform movement, 1963–1968*, Boulder 1977.

KEANE, John: *Vaclav Havel: a political tragedy in six acts*, London 1999.

KUN, Miklós: *Prague spring – Prague fall: blank spots of 1968*, Budapešť 1999.

KURAL, Václav et al.: *Československo 1968, 1: Obrodný proces*, Praha 1993.

KUSIN, Vladimir V.: *Political grouping in the Czechoslovak reform movement*, New York 1972.

FEJTÖ, Francois – RUPNIK, Jacques (eds.): *Le Printemps tchécoslovaque 1968*, Brussels 1999.

MENCL, Vojtěch et al.: *Československo roku 1968, 2: Počátky normalizace*, Praha 1993.

MLYNÁŘ, Zdeněk: *Nightfrost in Prague: the end of humane socialism*, New York 1980.

MYANT, M. R.: *The Czechoslovak economy, 1948–1988: the battle for economic reform*, Cambridge 1989.

NAVRÁTIL, Jaromír et al. (eds.): *The Prague Spring 1968. National Security Archive Documents Reader*, Budapest 1998.

OSCHLIES, Wolf: *Demokratisierungsprozess und Herrschaftstechnik in Partei und Gewerkschaften der Tschechoslowakei*, Trittau/Holst. 1970.

PAGE, Benjamin B.: *The Czechoslovak reform movement, 1963–1968: a study in the theory of socialism*, Amsterdam 1973.

PAUER, Jan: *Prag 1968: der Einmarsch des Warschauer Paktes: Hintergründe – Planung – Durchführung*, Bremen 1995.

PITHART, Petr: *Osmašedesátý*, Praha 1990.

PRAVDA, Alex: *Reform and change in the Czechoslovak political system: January–August 1968*, Beverly Hills 1975.

PRIESS, Lutz – KURAL, Václav – WILKE, Manfred: *Die SED und der "Prager Frühling" 1968: Politik gegen einen "Sozialismus mit menschlichem Antlitz*, Berlin 1996.

RETEGAN, Mihai: *In the shadow of the Prague Spring: Romanian foreign policy and the crisis in Czechoslovakia 1968*, Iaşi 2000.

RYCHLÍK, Jan: *Češi a Slováci ve 20. století: Česko-slovenské vztahy 1945–1992*, Praha 1998.

SCHNEIDER, Eleonora: *Prager Frühling und Samtene Revolution: soziale Bewegungen in Gesellschaften sowjetischen Typs am Beispiel der Tschechoslowakei*, Aachen 1994.

SHAWCROSS, William: *Dubcek: Dubcek and Czechoslovakia 1968–1990*, London 1990.

SKILLING, H. Gordon: *Czechoslovakia's interrupted revolution*, Princeton 1976.

SKOUG, Kenneth N., jr.: *Czechoslovakia's lost fight for freedom, 1967–69: an american embassy perspective*, Westport 1999.

TANTZSCHER, Monika: *Massnahme "Donau" und Einsatz "Genesung": die Niederschlagung des Prager Frühlings 1968/69 im Spiegel der MfS-Akten*, Berlin 1998.

TŮMA, Oldřich et al.: *Srpen '69*, Praha 1996.

VALENTA, Jiří: *Soviet intervention in Czechoslovakia, 1968: anatomy of a decision*, Baltimore 1991 (1st ed. 1979).

WENZKE, Rudiger: *Die NVA und der Prager Frühling 1968: die Rolle Ulbrichts und der DDR- Streitkrafte bei der Niederschlagung der tschechoslowakischen Reformbewegung*, Berlin 1995.

WILLIAMS, Kieran: *The Prague Spring and its Aftermath: Czechoslovak politics, 1968–1970*, Cambridge 1997.

OLDŘICH TŮMA

XXI. The Second Consolidation of the Communist Regime and the Descent into Collapse (1972–1989)

POUČENÍ
z krizového vývoje ve straně
a společnosti
po XIII. sjezdu KSČ

★

**Rezoluce k aktuálním otázkám
jednoty strany**

VYDALO ODDĚLENÍ PROPAGANDY A AGITACE ÚV KSČ

Title page of a brochure published by the Department of Propaganda and Agitation of CC CPCz. *Lesson Drawn from the Crisis Development in the Party and Society after XIIIth Congress of the CPCz* was passed by the CPCz's leadership at the end of the 1970s. It was an attempt for a radical analysis and interpretation of the regime's crisis at the end of the 1960s and determined the main strategic line of the CPCz's policies through the end of the 1980s.

1 The Normalization Regime

The defeat of the Prague Spring ushered in the second half of the Communist regime's existence in Czechoslovakia. It lasted for about as long as the first half and can be said to have traced – at least in broad contours – the same arc of development. In 1948, the Communists seized power, crushed the opposition, and used force to consolidate their regime. In the ensuing era, however, the system as a whole was increasingly frequently confronted with phenomena that contradicted its fundamental premises. Over time, it became more liberal, giving up on an aspect of society that it was no longer able to control. By the second half of the 1960s, the whole edifice eventually slumped into a deep crisis, which the regime survived only by virtue of military intervention from abroad. In the post-1968 era, following the reversal of power launched and enabled by the August occupation, the regime once again crushed the opposition and managed to consolidate itself from within. Once again, it gradually proved unworkable. Its widespread degeneration became ever more obvious, and culminated in a crisis and the rapid disintegration of the system in the late 1980s. The difference being that, at that point in time, there were no foreign armies available to ensure the regime's survival.

It is highly interesting to compare the gradual weakening of the CPCz control over mass organizations in both eras, as the course of development was very similar both times. The most obvious example was that of the youth organizations, the ČSM (the Czechoslovak Youth Union) in the 1960s and the SSM (the Socialist Youth Union) in the 1980s. After the Communist regime was inaugurated in 1948, it aspired to eliminate all youth hobby organizations and, if possible, organize all young people in the single, Komsomol-type, youth association it permitted to exist. The same thing happened after the onset of normalization. In both eras, the objective was essentially achieved within a few years, but later the 'transmission gear' and 'the party's reserve' began to assume – at least on the level of basic organizations – the characteristics of an authentic organization for young people, who used it to engage in all sorts of leisure activities. Over time, the management of the basic organizations was placed in the hands of genuinely elected figures who enjoyed respect and authority among their peers.

This was particularly evident at universities. As early as around 1965, the leadership positions of most faculty organizations were secured by highly critical student radicals, and after the August invasion the Students' Union (formed in 1968) became the most radical opponent of the return to the old order. In a similar fashion, the second half of the 1980s was a time when top positions in faculties went to people who used them to publish daring student magazines and organize critical discussions on topics that had until recently been taboo, and they did so – unlike the dissidents – on unquestionably legal platforms. The repeated history of youth organizations in Czechoslovakia in the 1960s and 1980s illustrates that although the regime was temporarily able to control society (or a segment thereof) by force and strict organization, it did not hold sway spiritually, and its aspiration for full control and thorough systemization was, by its very nature, self-contradictory and counter-productive.

This becomes all the more striking given that, in the 1970s and 1980s, the CPCz leadership made a very thorough and careful analysis of the experience made in the first half of its existence, particularly as regards the 1960s, and gave it a very concrete form in the above-mentioned 'The Lesson Drawn from the Crisis in the Party and Society after the 13th Congress of the Communist Party of Czechoslovakia.' The document assessed and analyzed the course of events in Czechoslovakia before and during the Prague Spring, and the CPCz leaders would not change a single letter of it until 1989. Having experienced a situation when the regime all but ceased to exist and was saved only by means of a massive international military campaign, was an essential formative element of the CPCz leaders' political reasoning during the Husák era. The maxim and fairly simple strategy of this reasoning was to prevent, at any cost, the mistakes that the leaders believed had brought about the 1968 catastrophe. In other words, they were prepared to do their best to maintain party unity, eliminate any internal disputes regarding future tactics or past mistakes, and ergo to avoid any reform ideas. If required to preserve stability, reprisals were to be conducted in measured doses. It was also imperative to maintain close co-operation with the Soviet leadership (in other words, to toe the line set by Moscow and never to digress); to allow no social structures to be formed that would be independent of the party – including the domains of politics, economy and culture; to deal with any social subject exclusively from a position of the country's leader; and to maintain permanent supervision and control over mass organizations. Furthermore, as it proved impossible to keep Czechoslovak society in complete isolation from the West (which was not entirely possible particularly in the arts, culture, and science, but also, to some extent, travelling), contact with the West would be allowed, but only to a small degree and under strict control. Last but not least, it was necessary to ensure at least moderate growth in the standard of living and to maintain social welfare, at least for the most important social groups; primarily for the working class. Put simply, the course of the day was to make no reforms, allow no liberalization, take no risks, and maintain the status quo. Indeed, immobility was a basic trait of Czechoslovak life long after the early 1970s. Nobody as much as dared utter the word 'reform' and, later, during the Gorbachev era, the CPCz found it hard to translate the word 'perestroika.'

OLDŘICH TŮMA

Maintaining personal continuity in the CPCz leadership, and preserving a stability which bordered on sterility within the party, were successful for a long time. Few replacements – apart from those dictated by natural causes – were made in top party positions, and in the late 1980s, the country was essentially still run by the same set of people who had seized power after the defeat of the Prague Spring. Younger politicians, whose career was not associated with the crisis of the late 1960s, began breaking into the top positions only very slowly and only when the two decades in question were drawing to an end. Though a number of changes were introduced in 1987, they were primarily changes only of names, rather than changes in political line. For over 18 years, the party was run by Gustáv Husák, who also replaced the ailing Svoboda as Czechoslovak President in 1975. The post of Prime Minister was held by Lubomír Štrougal from 1970 until the autumn of 1988. Alois Indra's era as Speaker of the Federal Assembly ended only with the Velvet Revolution in November 1989. However, as could be expected, the party leadership was not completely unanimous even after 1969. Balance between the influence and power of the pragmatists such as Husák and Štrougal on the one hand, and Biľak, Indra, and other pro-Moscow conspirators of 1968 on the other, was not easy to maintain. The 'old Communist fanatics' who had openly declared their support for the invasion as early as autumn 1968 and who had called for uncompromising fight against the counter-revolution, had tended to play the role of useful idiots, who served as a 'propagandist battering ram' against the reformers, but once no longer needed for this purpose, they became a burden and were discarded.

Husák's regime fundamentally gave up on keeping up the pretence that it enjoyed public support, and with few exceptions (as when Charter 77 was released in 1977), it did not try to mobilize society's consent. It settled for loyalty, whether genuine or feigned. Needless to say, the majority of society decided to play the game and let their lives be controlled in this manner. Society's general ethos had indeed changed beyond recognition. For some time after the August intervention, the notion that things could return to the pre–1968 status quo seemed completely absurd. If nothing else, the sense of unity that characterized society felt unbreakable, and it seemed preposterous to think that a regime installed by the Soviets could ever find enough collaborators. It was certainly conceivable that a regime such as that could persecute people it considered unacceptable, imprison them or take away their jobs; but it appeared unthinkable that enough people would be willing to fill the vacancies left by the fired and harassed people. By the time the 1970s were in full swing, things had changed considerably, and careers that were launched in precisely this manner could have been counted in hundreds and thousands.

It should be noted that in pondering the Husák era, one may sometimes be subject to an optical illusion. The whole system of empty rituals, careerism, false loyalties and stagnation seemed like a repugnant anomaly, most especially to those Communists who after the reform attempt failed, found themselves in opposition or on the periphery of society. In their eyes, once so enthusiastic but later more and more critical, the pre-1968 situation appeared strikingly different from the dullness of the 1970s, but what had changed more profoundly than anything else was their own role and status. To those who had never been

ardent supporters of the construction of socialism or the critical yet untouchable reformers thereof, may not have perceived the Novotný and Husák eras as so different from each
other. In explaining the temporary stabilization in Husák's period, there may be no need for
sophisticated models of social contract, in which society voluntarily gave up any attempts to
make a difference in politics and retreated into private lives in exchange for an acceptable
standard of living. Having been confronted with the enormous power of the Soviet Union
and its army, with the perpetual concessions of those they had trusted and to whom they
repeatedly offered support (namely the reformers who rejected the support time and time
again and who continued to compromise and surrender), and with the indifference of the
West, which would not allow one unfortunate accident (the August intervention) stop the
flow of traffic on the road (the Détente), it is little wonder that people eventually gave
up on engaging in public affairs. This does not deny the existence of both inexcusable and
unacceptable motivations, such as cowardice, lack of faith and opportunism, at individual
and collective levels. Thus, the gradual de-politicization, resignation, scepticism and focus
on private lives were not entirely incomprehensible reactions. The opposite side of the
situation was that the regime depended more and more on loyalty and obedience for the
sake of maintaining careers and living standard, rather than on support based on personal
belief. Of course, such support was no tower of strength.

In summary, the pillar on which the regime's power rested was certainly not the secret
agents of State Security (StB), as might seem to observers of Czech discussions on dealing
with the past in later decades. Rather, it was those who were bound to the regime by the
bonds created by social benefits and who served it publicly and openly: a host of directors,
secretaries, functionaries of the CPCz and the Socialist Youth Union's basic organizations,
and secret police officers, among others, who considered it their right to make decisions regarding other people's lives; TV commentators, journalists, teachers, and academics, official
establishment and others, who were always ready to put on an arrogant smile and reiterate
things they well knew to be untrue. The shared principle of their mental attitude was
not their endorsement (half-hearted to greater or lesser degrees) of Communist ideology,
but above all their conviction that they knew how to play the game, that they knew what
conduct was reasonable and what conduct was pointless. They also shared a disparaging or
patronizing attitude to those who tried to fight the regime in one way or another; people
who went to great lengths to avoid party membership or attendance at the rigged elections
and political celebrations, were in their eyes naive simpletons at best, and those who took
even greater risks were 'surely' doing it for money or for some unclear, dark reasons. Still,
the majority of society tried to belong to neither extreme – the camp of people who sponged
off the regime and served it, nor the one that tried to oppose it.

The normalization regime in Czechoslovakia did not even begin to try introducing
economic reforms similar to those in Poland and Hungary. Certain measures taken in the
mid-1980s were nothing more than cosmetic changes, rather than an attempt to transform
the existing model. Any ideas of granting entry to private initiative and entrepreneurship
remained essentially taboo until 1989. The Czechoslovak regime perhaps was not entirely

OLDŘICH TŮMA

unsuccessful in its effort to maintain a certain acceptable living standard, with special attention paid to the working class. Prime Minister Štrougal expressed it in crude yet accurate terms, when he declared 'let's hope the workers don't get pissed off.' Indeed, when all problems and obstacles are considered, Czechoslovakia did not experience any socially-motivated unrest before 1989. The Czechoslovak working class enjoyed a uniquely privileged social status in Eastern Europe. The standard of living increased in the first half of the 1970s. The state provided young families with children with generous social benefits. Problems began piling up in the late 1970s, but neither then nor later did the provision of goods in general (let alone groceries specifically) become as catastrophic as in Poland or Romania. People waited only months, compared to years in East Germany, to buy a car. Again unlike Poland and Hungary, the government did not go into debt abroad. The main lines of the underground managed to be constructed in Prague against all odds, and the same was true of the motorway system's basic grid, and Prague, Brno and Bratislava were connected by expressways. In all these areas, Czechoslovakia was not so badly off when compared to the other Soviet satellites, but it did lag decades behind Western Europe, with the gap increasing rather than decreasing over time. Housing continued to be a pressing problem. In the early 1970s, despite the government investing huge sums into constructing new blocks of flats and creating large neighbourhoods of grey concrete buildings that enveloped Prague and other big cities, and also irreversibly destroying the beauty of most quaint towns and even villages, the housing shortage continued. On the one hand, there was a complicated system of flat distribution, and on the other, a housing black market with a great deal of money involved. In fact, the grey economy gained more and more ground in areas where the centrally managed economy was unable to function. The supply of goods in chronic short supply (a category that included some types of groceries, white goods, Western fashions and, surprisingly, even books), illegal but ubiquitous foreign currency exchanges, as well as other services – all contributed to the gradual formation of affluent groups of people. Much as they perhaps treaded a thin line between legal and illegal, they were also slowly gaining financial independence of the regime, and their social status was not based on their loyalty to the regime.

The regime's effort to control and manipulate science, culture and art in this period evolved in much the same way as it had in the first twenty years after 1948. It only took one major campaign to restrict art, divest disobedient artists of their opportunity to communicate with the public, to take their jobs away, to ban their books from libraries and their films from distribution. Husák's regime went about this task even more systematically and thoroughly than the post-1948 authorities. Hundreds upon hundreds of artists lost all chance of presenting their works to the public. This was all the more painful, as in the late 1960s, Czechoslovak culture flourished in many fields and artists had begun to achieve international renown. These included new wave film directors, such as Jiří Menzel (his Closely Watched Trains, adapted from a novella by Bohumil Hrabal received Czechoslovakia's second Academy Award in 1968, while the film Larks on a String, also based on a short story by Hrabal, was finished in the same period, but had to wait until the late 1980s to be distributed), Miloš

Forman, Věra Chytilová, Vojtěch Jasný, Jan Němec (who, as well as his avant-garde feature films, also made the documentary Oratorio for Prague, depicting the August invasion), and Ivan Passer. This list continues with authors Ludvík Vaculík, Josef Škvorecký, Milan Kundera, and Ivan Klíma, poets Jaroslav Seifert, Jan Skácel, Antonín Brousek, and many others. Václav Havel was at the time already a playwright of world renown, and every new drama by Pavel Kohout caused a stir in theatres abroad, most certainly in German-speaking countries. This sort of harassment also affected those artists – actors, visual artists, musicians – who would not have tried to extol any political message, but whose civic attitudes made them inconvenient nonetheless. The same was particularly true for science, at least in respect to some humanities and social sciences such as historiography and sociology.

A number of these artists, including Bohumil Hrabal and the filmmakers Jiří Menzel and Věra Chytilová, were later allowed to resume creative work, but only on certain conditions (which sometimes included public repentance or self-censorship of their own works). There were some exceptional cases, such as Jaroslav Seifert, who received the Nobel Prize for Literature in 1984, whom the regime could not afford to ignore forever, unless it was prepared to upset the international public. Still, many others remained silenced or had to resort to the samizdat, apartment exhibitions, and other non-standard distribution channels for the whole twenty years. A great number emigrated. It should be noted that many Czech and Slovak scientists and artists, for example the author Milan Kundera, truly made a name for themselves abroad. In any case, their contribution to the development and refinement of domestic society was fundamentally lost. The exception tended to be when the artists' careers abroad were tolerated, as in the case of the world-famous filmmaker Miloš Forman, and the theatre director Otomar Krejča. In the Czech context (the situation in Slovakia was, yet again, somewhat different), the early 1970s brought the country into a cultural abyss, or in a term of the time, 'a spiritual Biafra.'

Over the years that followed, however, some artists and scientists whose activities were by definition individualistic, authentic, and resistant to the manipulation that had worked so well in thousands of other instances, tried to win back at least some of the public ground they had lost. The regime was unable to resist the pressure forever, unless it wanted to keep mobilizing the public and launching campaigns in the style of the Cultural Revolution – something the Czechoslovak regime was loath to do, preferring instead to boast of its merits in consolidating the situation and to pretend to both the domestic and international public that everything was normal. It was not entirely irrelevant that the demand for access to banned works of art of both domestic and – even more often – foreign provenance was part and parcel of the claims of a higher standard of living, and as such was also made by social groups that were either politically loyal to the regime or on which the regime actually depended. Needless to say, the wishes of such social groups had to be accommodated.

As in the 1950s, the regime sought to curb the influence of churches, which had also experienced a brief period of relatively free development in the second half of the 1960s. A regime that wanted to appear to a foreign observer as though it were giving free reign to religious life had to use more sophisticated and refined methods. The regime's primary tool for manipulating the Catholic Church was the Pacem in Terris association, which some of the clergy had joined. The goal was to limit the churches' potential impact to strictly religious matters and to eliminate any form of their influence on society as a whole. In the Czech Lands, with the exception of South Moravia, the regime's efforts were somewhat aided by the fact that Czech society was, for a number of reasons, heavily secularized. This trend had advanced considerably since the 1950s, and the Czech nation's level of religious devotion was very low in comparison to other European countries. Things were again very different in Slovakia, where the Catholic Church managed to retain most of its leverage over society, although often at the cost of great compromise with the regime. Dozens of 'inflexible' clergymen were stripped of their state license for pastoral work. As an agreement with the Vatican did not seem to be near to hand, the vacated positions of bishops and archbishops remained unfilled, and most dioceses were provisionally run by administrators. The Catholic Church assumed a very compromised and defensive position, something that only began to change with the inauguration of the Polish Pope John Paul II. It was partly his influence that led the head of the Catholic Church in Czechoslovakia, Cardinal František Tomášek, to assume a much more unyielding attitude.

In the field of international politics, the status of Husák's Czechoslovakia changed little over the twenty years in question. Czechoslovakia always followed Moscow and stayed completely clear of any potential problems nor caused trouble, and the West perceived it as one of Moscow's faithful vassals, which could not for a second be considered an independent country. Czechoslovakia backed the Soviet invasion of Afghanistan, as well as other interventions by the USSR in the Third World (not only in terms of propaganda, but also by offering more economic and other aid than did other countries of the Eastern Bloc), and it obediently boycotted the 1984 Olympic Games in Los Angeles. During the Polish Communist regime's crisis, it came very close to repaying the Poles for their 'fraternal assistance' of August 1968: in December 1980, two reinforced Czechoslovak divisions were deployed, along with Soviet and East German units, to the Polish border, and it was through no merit of Husák's administration that Moscow eventually desisted from the planned operation. Quite the contrary: at that point, the CPCz felt rather anxious about Poland's recent course, and this time it was the Czechoslovak side that kept pushing for severe measures. Relations with the West were intermittent, and Czechoslovakia lagged far behind its Communist neighbours in economic indicators and mutual trade. In 1973, a pact was finally signed and diplomatic relations established with West Germany. Admittedly, the talks between Prague and Bonn were complicated and also took much longer than in the case of other Eastern European countries. Alongside Husák's inflexible administration, for which Brandt's 'Ostpolitik' was a complication rather than an opportunity to improve relations, the burden of the past's painful legacy played a part. Many of the issues that caused Czechoslovak and West German negotiators' efforts to fail in the early 1970s returned to the table in the 1990s, during talks between the unified Germany and the Czech Republic, when it became clear that very little had changed.

Another thing which Husák's regime congratulated itself on was the signing of the Helsinki Final Act in the summer of 1975. The passages relating to human rights left the regime unmoved and, judging by its victorious and jubilant official response, it expected no major inconvenience. The media gave extensive coverage to the Helsinki Conference (for example, an entire issue of the *Rudé Právo* newspaper was dedicated to the subject after the signing of the Final Act), and a commemorative stamp was issued to honour the event. In the summer of 1975, Gustáv Husák welcomed the Helsinki Act as a contribution to the improvement of international relations based on the co-existence of states with different political systems. Normalization leaders saw Helsinki as yet another step towards the reinforcement and international legitimization of their position which, as they had to admit to themselves, had been shaken by the events of 1968 and the manner in which they had seized power. This feeling of satisfaction – that their isolation was broken once and for all – certainly outweighed any fears they would have had of potential discussions on human rights and cultural and interpersonal relations.

2 A New Type of Anti-regime Opposition

And yet, in 1975 – the year Husák seemed to have reached the peak of his career, when the situation in the country seemed completely stabilized, when the few attempts at resistance and opposition were crushed, when Husák received the symbolic confirmation of his status by becoming President of the Republic – new problems and new dangers began to appear on the horizon. Voices began to be heard which the regime had considered silenced forever, and later merged into a new type of opposition, initially rather frail but ultimately successful: the same opposition whose protagonists eventually received a grudging handshake from Husák before his own resignation when he appointed them to be government ministers. It might seem that factors quite external to the Czechoslovak situation were at play here: the thawing of international tension, which eventually assumed a different dimension, the Helsinki Final Act, the Third Basket, human rights and the international supervision of their observance. Yet while all these factors had their undeniable significance, an equal and possibly greater part was played by domestic causes.

It turned out that the normalization regime failed to pacify society completely. True, the first 'echelon' of opposition had been suppressed before the end of 1971 by force – that is the police force, but the normalization society, while passive and depoliticized, was not loyal – a fact that generated a degree of potential for future opposition. It can even be said that the regime created such potential through its own acts. The 'party of the expelled' with half-a-million members, occasionally described in the analyses by political planners in the Central Committee apparatus as the basis of a potentially dangerous opposition, was in fact a complete fiction as a social force. However, there were thousands and thousands of people who had been pushed to society's margins, who lost every chance of a professional career (yet the regime could and would not dispose of them in the manner of the1950s), who had nothing to lose and nothing to gain from the regime. Society featured various enclaves over which the regime had no control whatsoever.

One of them was a relatively broad youth community, known as 'the Underground', which was essentially a free association of people following a few rock bands. Rock music was very popular in Czechoslovakia, and until 1969 the rock music scene had been very rich and colourful. Later the problems began. The regime looked upon rock music with suspicion, considering it an import of Western culture with a detrimental effect on young people, but it was also hard to accept for its authenticity and aesthetic dissimilarity from regime-dictated standards. In the early 1970s, rock bands were subjected to humiliating exams, during which the musicians were tested not only on music theory, but also on their knowledge of Marxist-Leninist philosophy. It was not until after they had passed such exams and their repertoire had been officially approved that they were allowed to continue plying their trade – usually for no more than a year, at the end of which the entire procedure was repeated. Moreover, the groups thus authorized faced further pressure and obstacles. English band names and long hair were out of the question. More and more concerts were being cancelled 'for technical reasons,' and more and more bands were banned from touring, either in certain regions or anywhere.

There were bands, including the already iconic 'Plastic People of the Universe,' which refused to succumb to such pressure; they gave up seeking an official approval and tried to perform on various informal occasions. This decision on the part of the Plastic People sprang primarily from the influence of the band's leader, art theoretician and poet Ivan M. Jirous, known as 'Magor' (the Loony). In his activities and lyrics, Jirous shaped the character of the Underground as a free environment, independent of the establishment. The community of musicians and their large audiences, who followed them to unauthorized concerts organized intermittently in various god-forsaken village dance halls, was not at all primarily oppositional or political, but doggedly tried to defend and maintain the freedom to choose their entertainment, lifestyle, and aesthetic values. At the same time, the movement made no secret of its aversion to and condescending contempt for the normalization establishment, including the character and form of its daily operation. While the Underground scene had been increasingly in the sights of the state's repressive apparatus, in early 1976, the regime decided to teach the non-conformist youth a lesson, along with anybody else planning for a similarly independent lifestyle. In February that year, the members of the Plastic People, along with a group of about twenty of their followers, were arrested. Simultaneously, a media campaign was launched, depicting the accused as drunkards and layabouts, and their art works as the convergence of vulgarity and obscenity. A big show trial was in the works. It was evident that the regime expected no major difficulties in this matter, which was a misjudgement. A wide range of prominent figures from Czech culture expressed their solidarity with the arrested musicians; this included people who had made a great impact in art, society, and – eventually – politics in the 1960s, people who were not allowed by the normalization regime to work and create in freedom, who were almost completely erased from the public consciousness, but who enjoyed too much international renown to be brought to court or sent to jail.

Somewhat paradoxically, it was this special status of 'protected animals' – a term coined by Václav Havel – that made them feel unable to hold their tongue when the regime was attempting to persecute young unknown artists, in whose case it feared no international repercussions. The support of prominent cultural figures from across the world in defence of the arrested group managed to be garnered. In the summer of 1976, the protests and acts of solidarity became more and more frequent, both at home and abroad, forcing the regime to step back. Most of the detained individuals were released, only four (including Jirous) were eventually put on trial in September, and the sentences were – while certainly undeserved – probably extremely moderate in comparison to the original plan. The solidarity campaign with the Plastic People was crowned with at least partial success and showed that the regime could be induced to make concessions after all.

The atmosphere of co-operation and solidarity, as experienced in the autumn of 1976 and sealed by the relative success of confronting the regime, was not destined to fade away from the independent community. Discussions were led in early winter as to what should next be done. A decision was finally made to make use of the right to petition guaranteed by the constitution and to prepare a declaration. It was to be neither a political opposition's manifesto, nor a petition in defence of a persecuted individual (the type that had been sent to the authorities many times in the early 1970s), but rather a major position concerning the state of human rights in Czechoslovakia. The declaration leaned on the Final Act of the Helsinki Process and the fact that Czechoslovakia was a signatory of international covenants on the observance of human rights, which had become a formal part of the Czechoslovak legal system. The declaration, while openly criticizing the status quo, offered the state authorities (at least formally) an opportunity to start a dialogue and co-operation. At the same time, it was made clear that the Charter 77 document was not a one-time act, that the community of signatories was resolved to voice their opinions on the major issues of life in Czechoslovak society. To that purpose, the initiative created a rudimentary (yet permanent) structure: the positions of spokespersons. Every year, three people were elected to fill the positions, starting with Václav Havel, philosopher Jan Patočka, and former Minister of Foreign Affairs Jiří Hájek, becoming spokespersons for 1977. The initial declaration of Charter 77 had 243 signatories.

The regime found itself in a difficult situation it had not anticipated. By its nature, it could not possibly tolerate such an act on the part of the opposition, but neither could it very well apply the toughest possible reprisals. With regard to the international public, it was not feasible to stage a mass arrest campaign and imprison people who called for the regime to observe the commitments it had only recently made at Helsinki's international conference. The regime opted for an alternative strategy that involved ostracizing the Charter signatories, intimidating potential sympathizers, and hindering any further opposition activities in every way possible. As a result, the signatories suffered all manner of persecution, including losing their jobs, having their phone lines cut off, and their driving licences and car registration documents taken away; they were also threatened, repeatedly detained for hours-long interrogations and kept in custody for 48 hours. The trump card

OLDŘICH TŮMA

of the regime's strategy, however, consisted in an extensive media campaign, designed to discredit Charter 77 and its signatories in the eyes of the Czechoslovak public and to create the illusion that the government had the unconditional support of the public. For weeks on end, Czech and Slovak dailies were filled with belligerent and slanderous articles, and most of the prime-time TV news programme featured attacks on the Charter 77. The aggressive, disparaging tone remained a characteristic attribute of the massive campaign throughout its duration, and the entire campaign has come to represent one of the most deplorable and pitiable episodes in Czechoslovak media history. The regime, however, was not content with a mere media campaign. It needed to mobilize – at least ostensibly – the public as well. Mass campaigns were launched at workplaces, producing resolutions against the Charter that were passed by acclamation or by individual vote. The paradox of these campaigns was that people were expected to object to a text which they did not and could not officially know. A model for such condemnatory actions was the meeting at the National Theatre of figures from the cultural scene, and a declaration known as the Anti-Charter that they signed in their hundreds either on the spot or over the following few days.

Charter 77 was opposition of a new type, uncompromisingly insistent on its own legal status and its open operational style. That said, it goes without saying that at least some of the association's activities, technical support and finances had to be run in a somewhat conspiratorial manner. Above all, it was important that Charter 77 managed to survive the regime's campaigns and the harsher reprisals that soon followed (a great many of the Charter's protagonists ended up in jail after all, particularly in the early 1980s), and became a permanent fixture in the Czechoslovak situation, even if only marginally in the context of general society. Charter 77 received undoubtedly significant support from the Czechoslovak exile community, to which it owed at least some of its success. The exiles spread word in the West about opposition activity in Czechoslovakia, organized countless events in its support, and managed to provide the association with substantial material and financial support. While the solidarity and media coverage of the Czechoslovak opposition's activities was significant, the financial support from abroad was equally important. It was sufficient to neutralize, at least in part (though a statistically significant part), the most common reprisal method used by the communist regime in the 1970s and 1980s: social persecution.

At its very core, Charter 77 was a major political act, although the association refused to call itself political opposition. By calling for human rights to be observed, it effectively questioned the regime itself and its legitimacy, while causing it continuous trouble on the international scene. The existence of Charter 77 created a horizon of sorts, which shielded other independent activities and lent them a deeper purpose. The end of the 1970s gave rise to a new, growing wave of independent cultural and artistic creation, distributed mostly in the samizdat. Although it mostly had to rely on very primitive technical forms, and focused primarily on disseminating belles-lettres and scientific literature, it reached and influenced a significant number of people. In 1978, another crucial oppositional activity was born within the Charter 77 community: the Committee for the Defence of the Unjustly Persecuted (known as the VONS). In the twelve years of its existence, the VONS monitored hundreds of cases of political persecution, strove to provide the persecuted persons with legal advice and financial aid, and organized solidarity campaigns.

While the Charter signatories were certainly subject to persecution, many were forced to emigrate and many were put in prison, it is also true that the regime refrained from the ruthless 'blanket' persecution used in the 50s. A specific pattern developed as a result: Charter 77 repeatedly analysed and criticized the regime's practices across the spectrum of its operation, published its positions and suggestions, proposed carrying out a dialogue – an offer which was, unsurprisingly, never taken up. The truly active core of the Charter was limited to a maximum of hundreds of people, living mostly in Prague and Brno, but awareness of its activities and the credit it enjoyed in society was probably greater than its protagonists would have thought. Without a doubt, a specific 'situation segment' was established in the late 1970s, which resurfaced and was put to good use ten years later, during a new acute crisis of the regime.

3 Degeneration and Collapse

It was not until the mid-1980s that the monotonous routine began to change. The international situation was again in flux, this time including the Eastern Bloc. The Polish Communist regime faced ever more pressing challenges, as the scope for freedom and the opposition's influence were evidently on the rise. Czechoslovakia watched the development in Poland with a great interest, and the Polish events were highly influential – likely thanks to the close ties between the Czechoslovak opposition and its obviously stronger Polish counterpart. Last but not least, the events that shook the Soviet Union, particularly the developments after 1987, had a tremendous impact on the situation in Czechoslovakia. Gorbachev's reforms were followed with a mixture of approbation and scepticism, but they certainly aroused hope that change was possible and furnished the critics of the motionless situation in Czechoslovakia with useful arguments. The regime failed to respond appropriately to the rapidly changing situation both at home and abroad, in the same way as it was unable to adequately address the problems caused by its political and economic strategy (such as the catastrophic state of the environment). It was unable to step out of its own shadow, which had always been characterized by unquestioning obedience to the centre of the Communist movement, and as such it now had to subscribe – at least on paper – to the course set by Moscow. While this was inevitable, it was also highly unpleasant, and required an ever greater degree of tightrope walking between words and action.

The minority attempt of some of the CPCz leaders, especially Prime Minister Štrougal, to take advantage of the situation in the spring of 1987 and – with reference to the Soviet example – launch a new course of reform, came to nothing, and eventually cost Štrougal both his ministerial seat and his position in the party presidium. He was replaced as Prime Minister by Ladislav Adamec, who eventually came to understand the urgent need for reforms better than anybody else in the leadership. It seemed as though the position of Prime Minister predestined its holder to a pro-reform perspective; this may have been because it was the position of Prime Minister in which direct responsibility for the deteriorating, reform-hungry economy was most palpable. In 1987 and 1988, the CPCz leaders took the plunge and carried out a number of personnel changes, but their effect was ambiguous, to say the least. Husák was made to quit the position of First Secretary (although he held on to his Presidency), but he was replaced by Miloš Jakeš, who was associated even more closely than Husák with the unfortunate legacy of the August occupation and the destruction of the Prague Spring. In early 1988, a degree of hope was primarily focused on Miroslav Štěpán, the new and relatively young member of the Central Committee Presidium, who was unconnected to the events of 1968. Štěpán, who also took on the position of Secretary of the Municipal Committee of the CPCz in Prague, was for a while the prime candidate of domestic and foreign speculations for the position of the 'Czechoslovak Gorbachev'. Before long, however, Štěpán's popularity dove sharply, his exceptionally arrogant manner and his role in suppressing demonstrations in Prague making him – along with Jakeš – the most unpopular member of the CPCz leadership. Until the very last minute, the regime employed tactics it considered well-tested by the past twenty years, and refused to accept the opposition as a partner in negotiations.

From 1987, the spectrum of independent initiatives and organizations widened considerably. Charter 77 and the Committee for the Defence of the Unjustly Persecuted (VONS) were complemented by an array of other groups. Most of them overlapped at least partly (and some completely) with the Charter, but they were groups with a more defined platform. Very close to the core of the Charter was the Movement for Civic Freedom, established in the autumn of 1988. In contrast, a somewhat critical alternative to the Charter was represented by the Democratic Initiative, which strove to accentuate – in addition to human-rights and moral issues – problems in both the social sphere and economy, and hoped to spread its influence among those groups in society that had so far been beyond the opposition's reach. The group Revival (*Obroda*), mostly made up of former Communists, sought to pick up the threads of the 1968 reform attempt. The Independent Peace Initiative and the group known as Czech Children were primarily made up of young people. While the two groups emphasized somewhat marginal issues (pacifism in the case of the Independent Peace Initiave and an at least formally declared leaning towards monarchism in the case of the Czech Children), it was crucial that both groups made it their priority to engage in political, openly oppositional activity, which involved organizing street protests. The opposition was now able to use far better communication and technical facilities than before, some of which were supplied from abroad. In this respect, it is worth noting that the post-August political and cultural émigrés managed to maintain contacts with their homeland and continued to influence the situation in Czechoslovakia to a much greater degree than the post-February exile had done after 1948. Samizdat novels and poems circulating in dozens of carbon copies were now replaced by periodicals (some of them monthlies) with circulation in the hundreds or even thousands, focused on current affairs. The People's Newspaper *(Lidové noviny)* had been published and distributed monthly since the autumn of 1987. The younger generation, mostly people who as teenagers had been beaten in the streets and prisons in August

1969, now took the floor. This generation was much more radical than its predecessors in its approach to the regime and choice of strategy. The magazine *Sport*, issued by this group in 1989, was designed as a platform for political agitation, and it was the first community to declare itself anti-Communist. Broadcasts to Czechoslovakia from abroad had also become much more flexible and efficient. The Vienna-based studio of the Voice of America managed to provide its listeners with immediate feedback on current developments in the country, including recorded telephone interviews with prominent dissidents and recordings from protest rallies in the streets of Prague. In the beginning of 1989, international covenants that the Czechoslovak government had to adopt as a result of talks following the Helsinki conference made it possible for Czechs and Slovaks to listen to the unjammed broadcasts of Radio Free Europe.

From 1988, street demonstrations became a common expression of the growing level of public discontent. Although limited to Prague and with only several thousand participants, they were recurrent and frequent. Minor street protests had been taking place ever since the mid-1980s (some were held on 8th December to commemorate the death of John Lennon), but the first truly major demonstration took place on 21st August, 1988, on the 20th anniversary of the Warsaw Pact invasion. Its size and the fact that it came to pass surprised not only the regime, but even the traditional opposition, who had known nothing of the plan and had not participated in the preparations. Instead, the event was organized by the Independent Peace Initiative and the Czech Children, and a large role was played by spontaneity and the 'itch' in part of the public that 'the time had come to do something.' Before the end of the year, more street protests had taken place, but this time Charter 77 participated in announcing and preparing them. The approach of the regime and the traditional opposition to the demonstrations held in 1988 and 1989 was intriguing and symptomatic in more ways than one. The regime was naturally bothered by them as open acts of resistance, and although it always managed to restore order to the streets (sometimes by resorting to very brutal measures), it failed to prevent them from recurring. It did not dare use reprisals of the 1969 kind, which would probably have been sufficient to intimidate the public. The traditional opposition's approach to the demonstrations was somewhat ambivalent: it was determined – in the words of Václav Havel – always to stand up for the citizens' right to freedom of speech and assembly, but it was reluctant to organize demonstrations and use them as a means of clearly articulated political pressure on the regime.

In 1989, things took a quick turn – quicker than the established opposition was able to take in. Street protests continued, and protest petitions now had not hundreds, but tens of thousands of signatories. In January, during the days near the anniversary of the death of Jan Palach, the centre of Prague was stricken with demonstrations for six days in a row. A petition for the release of Václav Havel, who had been arrested and kept in jail until May in connection with these demonstrations, was signed by hundreds and thousands of cultural figures, scientists and other publicly active people. The Several Sentences petition, drawn up in the summer by Václav Havel and containing relatively moderate demands by the

582

opposition that were nonetheless still completely unacceptable to the regime, was signed by almost 50,000 people by autumn. The opposition's power and influence grew rapidly. The situation was also changing in Slovakia, although there independent activities would have borne fewer characteristics of genuine political opposition, and were more concerned about issues such as religious freedom and environmental problems. Such were also the concerns of the Slovak samizdat, and the single major Slovak demonstration prior to November 1989 – the 'candle demonstration' held in the spring 1988 – was an act in support of freedom of religion.

Prior to November 1989, attempts to create an integrated co-ordinating body that would unify the opposition had failed. This was partly owing to disputes between individual oppositional initiatives and figures, and likely also due to the disruptive activities of the StB. The non-existence of such a body was, to a degree, redeemed by the authority of Václav Havel, whose stature was becoming ever more indisputable. Moreover, the opposition was not sufficiently flexible in adjusting its tactics and still relied on the pattern of requesting a dialogue with the state authorities or, more precisely, round table talks (following the successful Polish model), and did not seek to abolish the regime. The lack of homogeneity and decisiveness surfaced in August 1989. The upcoming anniversary of the 1968 intervention seemed to both a part of the radicalized public and a part of the opposition (mostly young people) to be a suitable opportunity for a new confrontation with the regime. The regime itself was highly apprehensive of the looming anniversary. The core of the traditional opposition, including Václav Havel, eventually appealed to the public to refrain from street protests. Their appeal was motivated by a fear of potential harsh reprisals, which in turn had been influenced by the recent bloody suppression of the oppositional protests in China. 21st August thus did not become a turning point. While a demonstration did take place in Prague, it was not nearly as sizeable as the January protests, and the dispute over 21st August affected the opposition's unity and readiness for action for weeks to come.

The situation in society and the popular mood became radical nonetheless. The change of atmosphere in the autumn of 1989 was greatly influenced by concurrent events in the neighbouring countries, particularly East Germany. This was all the more so as the downfall of the East German Communist regime unfolded before the very eyes of the Czechoslovak public: the exodus of tens of thousands of East Germans, who in several waves sought asylum at the West German embassy in Prague, accelerated a change in the atmosphere, particularly in the capital city. The impact of the East German development on the situation in Czechoslovakia culminated in the fascinating TV coverage of the fall of the Berlin Wall on 10th November and the days that followed. A certain form of glasnost had, after all, reached Czechoslovakia in the late 1980s, compelling the media to present more objective reports providing basic facts, even if accompanied with the standard, strictly pro-regime commentary. Citizens were now able to get basic information from their domestic media, and did not need to rely so much on foreign broadcasts.

Symptomatically, when the final and crucial crisis broke out, it was beyond the scope of traditional opposition activity. Prague university students organized a gathering on the

17th November to commemorate the Nazi reprisals against Czech students in 1939. Preparations for the demonstration were not run by the opposition initiatives, but exclusively by 'independent' students, who maintained close ties with the opposition and organized the event in co-operation with official student organizations at individual faculties. In the turbulent atmosphere of the day, it was impossible for the demonstration not to turn into an anti-regime protest, the biggest of its time. Up to 50,000 people participated in the final march to the city centre. Eventually, the demonstration was dispersed with exceptional brutality; for a while, a rumour circulated that one student had been killed – which seemed quite probable, given the severity of the crackdown. 17th November and the uproar caused by the brutality of the police became not the proverbial pebble, but the boulder that started a landslide of such proportions and speed that nobody could have anticipated it in their wildest dreams.

Bibliography

BLEHOVA, Beata: *Der Fall des Kommunismus in der Tschechoslowakei*, Vienna 2006.

BUGAJSKI, Janusz: *Czechoslovakia, Charter 77's decade of disent*, New York 1987.

CÍSAŘOVSKÁ, Blanka – PREČAN, Vilém: *Charta 77: Dokumenty*, Praha 2007.

DAY, Barbara: *The velvet philosophers*, London 1999.

DEVÁTÁ, Markéta – SUK, Jiří – TŮMA, Oldřich (eds.): *Charter 77: from the Assertion of Human Rights to a Democratic Revolution, 1977–1989*, Prague 2007.

FALK, Barbara J.: *The dilemmas of dissidence in East-Central Europe: citizen intellectuals and philosopher Konga*, Budapest 2003.

FIDELIUS, Petr: *L'esprit post-totalitaire*, Paris 1986.

GOETZ-STANKIEWICZ, Marketa (ed.): *Good-bye, samizdat: twenty years of Czechoslovak underground writing*, Evanston 1992.

GRAEVENITZ, Karoline von: *Die "Untergrunduniversität" der Prager Bohemisten: ein Fallbeispiel für Parallelkultur in der "normalisierten" ČSSR*, Bremen 2008.

KEANE, John: *Vaclav Havel: a political tragedy in six acts*, London 1999.

KENNEY, Padraic: *A carnival of revolution: Central Europe 1989*, Princeton 2002.

KRAKOVSKÝ, Roman: *Rituel du 1er mai en Tchécoslovaquie, 1948–1989*, Paris 2004.

KUSIN, Vladimir V.: *From Dubček to Charter 77: a study of "normalization" in Czechoslovakia, 1968–1978*, New York 1978.

LIŠKA, Ondřej: *Jede Zeit ist Gottes Zeit: die Untergrund-Kirche in der Tschechoslowakei 1948–1989*, Leipzig 2003.

LUTZ, Annabelle: *Dissidenten und Bürgerbewegung: ein Vergleich zwischen DDR und Tschechoslowakei*, Frankfurt am Main 1999.

MCRAE, Robert Grant: *Resistance and Revolution: Václav Havel's Czechoslovakia*, Ottawa 1997.

MINK, Georges – SZUREK, Jean-Charles: La *grande conversion: le destin des communistes en Europe de l'Est*, Paris 1999.

NOVÁK, Miroslav: *Du printemps de Prague au printemps de Moscou: les formes de l'opposition en URSS et en Tchécoslovaquie de janvier 1968 a janvier 1990*, Genf 1990.

OTÁHAL, Milan: *Der rauhe Weg zur "samtenen Revolution": Vorgeschichte, Verlauf und Akteure der antitotalitären Wende in der Tschechoslowakei*, Köln 1992.

OTÁHAL, Milan: *Opozice, moc, společnost 1968/1989*, Praha 1994.

OTÁHAL, Milan – VANĚK, Miroslav: *Sto studentských revolucí: studenti v období pádu komunismu – životopisná vyprávění*, Prague 1999.

RUBEŠ, Jan: *Vaclav Havel, un révolutionnaire de velours*, La Tour-d'Aigues 1999.

SALFELLNER, Hafale – WNENDT, Harald: *Das Palais Lobkowicz: ein Ort deutscher Geschichte in Prag*, Prague 1999.

SCHNEIDER, Eleonora: *Prager Frühling und Samtene Revolution: soziale Bewegungen in Gesellschaften sowjetischen Typs am Beispiel der Tschechoslowakei*, Aachen 1994.

SKÁLA, Jan: *Die ČSSR: vom Prager Frühling zur Charta 77: mit einem dokumentarischen Anhang*, Berlin 1978.

SKILLING, H. Gordon: *Charter 77 and human rights in Czechoslovakia*, London 1981.

ŠIMEČKA, Milan: *The restoration of order: the normalization of Czechoslovakia 1969–1976*, London 1984.

ŠIMEČKA, Milan: *Das Ende der Unbeweglichkeit: ein politisches Tagebuch*, Frankfurt am Main 1992.

TUCKER, Aviezer: *The philosophy and politics of Czech dissidence from Patočka to Havel*, Pittsburgh 2000.

TŮMA, Oldřich: *Zítra zase tady! Protirežimní demonstrace v předlistopadové Praze jako politický a sociální fenomén*, Praha 1994.

VANĚK, Miroslav: *Nedalo se tady dýchat. Ekologie v českých zemích v letech 1968 až 1989*, Praha 1996

WHEATON, Bernard – KAVAN, Zdeněk: *The Velvet Revolution: Czechoslovakia, 1988–1991*, Boulder 1992.

XXII. Czechoslovakia's Return to Democracy (1989–1992)

Poster published by the Civic Forum at the end of 1989. Along with a wish of peaceful Christmas ("Peaceful Christmas with the Civic Forum"), the picture in the poster carries a hidden message: after the fall of the communist regime, the path is open to abundance and prosperity – or to the consumer society. Offset print. Designed by Michal Cihlář.

1 The Velvet Revolution

In the second half of the 1980s, the Soviet Communist empire that was supposed to last 'forever' went through changes that led to its dissolution and brought about a new division of power and values in the world. For the most part, what used to be Czechoslovakia played only a passive role in these changes, except for a brief period at the turn of 1989 and 1990, when it became an important agent in shaping the character of the new era.

The peaceful student demonstration in Prague on 17th November, 1989 – harshly suppressed by the police – became the seminal event that triggered the revolutionary process. Immediately after the police crackdown, the university students contacted intellectuals, artists, and theatre and film actors, and went about forming the first active centres of civic discontent. A strike movement was launched. Starting on 18th November, almost all theatres in Prague went on strike, joined by theatres in the provinces over the following days. Dozens of theatre auditoria became spaces open for public discussions. Strike action was launched at universities on Monday, 20th November, soon followed by most secondary schools. Demonstrators overran the Prague city centre on 19th November, while the police squads more or less retreated. The area at the top of Wenceslas Square turned into anti-regime agitation headquarters. And every afternoon, beginning on 20th November, hundreds of thousands of people gathered on a daily basis in the centre of Prague, followed by millions of other demonstrators in most Czech, Moravian and Slovak towns and cities.

The Civic Forum (OF) was founded at the Drama Club (Činoherní klub) on Sunday, 19th November, as a political movement uniting dissident groups and all discontented and outraged citizens, including some members of the CPCz and of National Front parties. Václav Havel, Central Europe's most well-known dissident, became a universally respected leader of the OF. At the same time, a parallel civic movement was formed in Bratislava, the capital of Slovakia, which became known as the Public Against Violence (VPN). The roles of the people's tribunes went to environmental activist Ján Budaj and the popular actor Milan Kňažko. The OF and the VPN made it their objective to enter into negotiations with the state powers on the liberalization and democratization of totalitarian Czechoslovakia. The Communist authorities eventually yielded to the unrelenting pressure of the crowded streets and squares that culminated in a mass general strike on 27th November, and by the end of the first revolutionary week, the cabinet led by Prime Minister Ladislav Adamec engaged in talks with the opposition.

The political talks gave rise to the first liberalization steps. These included the release of political prisoners, the abolishment of the article of the constitution that established the leading role of the Communist Party in society and the closed circle of the National Front, legalizing oppositional initiatives and granting them media access, etc. The OF and the VPN initiatives demanded crucial changes in the make-up and platform of the cabinet, but they were still hesitant to share power. Their reluctance to join the government stemmed from the civic movements having been set up too hastily, not until after 17th November, 1989, and they needed time to form organizational structures and draw up their political platforms. The precipitous development of events took them by surprise. Prime Minister Adamec took advantage of the opportunity offered him and, on 3rd December, presented a new cabinet, again dominated by the Communists, who secured 15 out of 20 seats. Nonetheless, the mobilized public remained the key shaper of events, and rejected the Communist-dominated government in a fierce gesture. The protests were thunderous but noble, and did not degenerate into violence. The events of the next few days brought the opposition to the realization that unless it was prepared to fail, it was time to accept governmental responsibility. Prime Minister Adamec, having no room left to manoeuvre, resigned. The 'Government of National Understanding,' led by a sympathetic Communist named Marián Čalfa, was joined by seven members of the OF, who took up ministerial positions in key economic and legislative departments, but not the ministries of interior or defence; importantly, the Public Against Violence was entirely unrepresented in the cabinet. Such a significant imbalance in taking over the government that escaped notice and consideration in the hectic revolutionary days was an omen of a crisis in containing the repressive forces of the Communist regime, as well as in the sphere of Czech-Slovak relations.

On 10th December, the day the new federal cabinet was appointed and Gustáv Husák resigned his presidency, the OF and Public Against Violence initiatives announced that their joint candidate for the presidential office was Václav Havel. This candidacy was artfully opposed by the Communists. In the Federal Assembly (FA) – the top-most legislative body of the Czechoslovak federation – they had a comfortable majority and decided to push for a direct election, in which they expected the victory of their own candidate, former Prime Minister Ladislav Adamec. All political parties and social organizations in Slovakia rejected Havel in favour of Alexander Dubček, the political symbol of 1968. A paradoxical situation ensued: the OF as a revolutionary political movement wanted to honour the constitution and for the president to be elected by the Federal Assembly, while the Communist Party, for expediency's sake, pressed for a presidential system, which would have made a fundamental constitutional change, something the OF was determined to prevent. However, the 'round table' negotiations over this issue failed repeatedly. The democrats proclaimed readiness to work for the benefit of the country and, driven by fear of constitutional destabilization, they chose to take over the state and political structures and procedures. They refused to protract the non-constitutional, revolutionary period. They did not, however, have a single seat at the FA, and this 350-member legislative body was beyond their control. They had no formal tools at hand. All that was left for them to do was to mobilize the public once again, but they feared another wave of discontent that might wreck the parliament and block the presidential election. This was an undesirable alternative for the democrats, as they were not prepared for an unconstitutional development.

A way out of the deadlock was offered to presidential candidate Havel by Prime Minister Čalfa during a private meeting at the Office of the Government Presidium on 15th December. They agreed to take co-ordinated steps, with the goal of persuading the majority of the FA deputies to elect Havel for President of the Republic before the end of 1989. Čalfa's adept interventions in the parliament led a number of Communist deputies to abandon the idea of a direct election and to express their willingness to vote for Havel. Concurrent to the Prime Minister's backstage interventions, students demonstrated daily outside of the parliament building in support of Havel. This double pressure – from both above and below – was something the Communist deputies found themselves unable to resist.

To prevent a crisis in Czech-Slovak relations after the presidential election, it was key to eliminate to mutual satisfaction any tension between the Czech and Slovak candidates for the position, namely Havel and Dubček. The two men met several times over this issue. The complicated negotiations, complemented by the simultaneously held round-table talks of political parties, resulted in an agreement on staffing the top state positions: on 28th December Alexander Dubček was elected Speaker of the FA, and Václav Havel became Czechoslovak President a day later, both in unanimous votes. It was not until after the election ceremony, ended by a Te Deum celebratory mass at St. Vitus Cathedral, that the university students – the driving force and symbol of the protest movement since 17th November – terminated their strike.

2 Political Development in the Period of Transition (January–June 1990)

The abolishment of the articles of the constitution establishing the leading role of the Communist Party in the political system and society, the taking over of the key federal ministries, and the election of Václav Havel for President of the Republic broke the CPCz's political supremacy. At the turn of January and February 1990, the Communist Party also lost its dominance in the top legislative bodies, although it held on to its strategic position in politics until the free elections. The division of power in the period following the 'Velvet Revolution' is well-illustrated by the numbers co-opted into top legislative bodies. The scope and manner of this was agreed upon by so-called 'decisive political forces' that had held round-table meetings since 8th December. These 'decisive political forces' formed a situational conglomerate assembled from political parties, movements and organizations of major, minor and negligible consequence. They included the parties of the pre-November National Front (the CPCz, the Socialist Union of Youth, the Czechoslovak People's Party – ČSL, the Czechoslovak Socialist Party – ČSD, the Liberty Party and the Party of Slovak Revival), as well as the new political movements, including the OF and the Public Against Violence; some talks were attended by others as well.

The main change in the make-up of the Czechoslovak Federal Assembly of 350 deputies was made on 30th January, 1990. A total of 122 of the 242 CPCz deputies either resigned or were removed from office (with the CPCz keeping 120 seats); the OF and the VPN took 114 seats (while 6 seats remained unfilled); independents retained 41 out of 64 seats, and the ČSL, the Czechoslovak Socialist Party and the Liberty Party took four each. In early February 1990, the Czech and Slovak National Councils went through a similar makeover, with one major anomaly: the VPN only secured 21 co-opted mandates of a total of 150, while the Communists held on to 65. The Slovak democratic movement failed to take control of the state authorities of their republic. The VPN continued to emphasize the civic politics of ethos over party-based politics of interests, and made the wrong assumption that this course would be effective until free elections were held.

In February 1990, negotiations moved from the 'round table' to the reconstructed legislative bodies (which later also including local and district representative authorities around the country, which co-opted new members by the end of March). Parliamentary democracy was formally reinstated in post-totalitarian Czechoslovakia, while the existing constitution and state authority structures retained their legal force. Discord in their own ranks, coupled with disagreement with the VPN, the OF failed in its attempt to push through a fundamental restructuring of the federation, proposed by Josef Vavroušek and Petr Pithart – representatives of the OF Coordination Centre Council – and backed by Havel. Their proposal's objective was to ensure the smooth functioning of communication channels and efficient state authorities – Czech, Slovak and federal – in the oncoming conditions of democracy and political plurality. However, their attempt to effect a major change had to give way to the inertia of constitutional continuity, championed by FA functionaries (especially its new deputy speaker Zdeněk Jičínský, a co-author of the 1960 'socialist' constitution and the Czechoslovak Federation Bill of 1968) and Slovak politicians (including VPN activists), who considered the federated state a historic conquest and any potential changes to it was for them deeply unnerving.

What was the character of parliamentary democracy in this transitory period? The country's complex constitutional apparatus, performing under the baton of the dominant CPCz, presented a rather complicated matrix for the new politics. The federation was represented by over 50 ministers in three cabinets (Czech, Slovak and federal) and 700 deputies in three legislative assemblies (the FA, and the Czech and Slovak National Councils). The complex constitutional system featured elements of confederation. It did not anticipate institutional co-operation between the national councils and the federal parliament, nor between the respective national councils; between the Czech, Slovak and federal governments and the individual ministries. The issue of competencies suddenly became urgent, yet was not approached systematically.

The reconstructed cabinets and parliaments operated in a rather peculiar fashion. The nature of the transition to democracy was influenced by distinctive political types, with a majority of politicians associated to a greater or lesser degree with Communist or Socialist ideology: ex-Communists (former Communist reformers) who returned to politics after an involuntary break of twenty years, including FA Speaker Alexander Dubček and FA Deputy Speaker Zdeněk Jičínský; neo-Communists as representatives of the post-November CPCz, such as Vasil Mohorita, Jozef Stank, Peter Weiss and Pavol Kánis; the old-style Communists who had kept their convictions and political style mostly left top political positions or were removed from office; post-Communists – political pragmatists who had turned away from the Communist Party and its doctrines, usually in order to embrace another political doctrine, including, among others, the Prime Minister of the Federal Government Marián Čalfa, Deputy Prime Minister of the Federal Government Vladimír Dlouhý, Speaker of the SNC Rudolf Schuster, and Prime Minister of the Slovak Government Milan Čič. Some counterbalance was provided by two main types of politicians representing the civic approach to politics: non-Communist civic activists who had risen from the dissident movement or the 'grey zone' (such as President Václav Havel, the Czech Government's Prime Minister Petr Pithart, the Federal Minister of the Interior's First Secretary Jan Ruml); and, last but not least, the pragmatic activists who had entered politics at the moment of the revolution (Federal Finance Minister Václav Klaus, Federal Minister of Employment and Social Affairs Petr Miller, as well as activists from district and regional committees of the OF and Public Against Violence).

Such was the setup in which swift liberalization and democratization of political, social and economic life was launched. On 23rd January, 1990, the FA enacted the 'small bill on political parties,' ushering in a free, pluralist political system. This was a boon to the already established political parties of the pre-November National Front, including the CPCz, as they automatically and without limitation became part of democratic political life. The only political bodies to bring a new element into the new system were the OF and the Public Against Violence. In addition to these parliamentary bodies, numerous other political parties were being founded, hoping to break through in the January and February co-options and, most importantly, in the June and November elections. According to the new election bill enacted on 27th February, the elections were to be run based on the formula of proportional representation, in 12 constituencies, with a 5% election threshold (3% for the SNC); representatives would be elected for a two-year term of office, and the politicians' key task would be to adopt new constitutions, consolidate democracy, and reform the economy.

Key laws confirming civil liberties, including the freedom to associate, the right to assemble and petition, amendments to the Press Law and the Civil Code, were enacted by the parliament between 27th and 29th March, 1990. The basic conditions for the forthcoming economic changes were to be laid by the law equalizing all forms of ownership, as well as bills on joint-stock companies, individual businesses of natural persons, and state enterprises were passed in the second half of April. The respective parliaments adopted bills on new names of the state and new state symbols. In actual terms, this meant relieving the names of the two republics of the 'Socialist' modifier, whereby they became the Czech Republic (the CR) and the Slovak Republic (the SR), and the shared state got the new name the Czech and Slovak Federal Republic (the CSFR). In early May, parliament abolished the death penalty, passed an amendment to the bill regarding the elementary and secondary school system, and adopted a new bill on universities, bestowing academic communities with freedom and autonomy.

Changes in foreign policy orientation were also dynamic, indicating that Czechoslovakia was leaving 'the world of yesterday' and returning to Europe and the world. This tendency was symbolically emphasized by two unusual foreign visitors coming to the country: Tenzin Gyatso, the 14th Dalai Lama and a recent Nobel Peace Prize laureate, came on 2nd February, followed by Pope John Paul II, who visited Bohemia, Moravia and Slovakia on 21st and 22nd April. As early as 2nd January, President Václav Havel – hailed around the world as a symbol of the peaceful transition from totalitarianism to democracy – paid a visit to both German states to endorse their unification and express his regret for the wild expulsion of Germans from post-war Czechoslovakia. His visit to the United States from 19th to 23rd February was concluded in Congress, where he received a triumphant welcome. Three days later in Moscow, the governments of Czechoslovakia and the Soviet Union signed the Agreement on the Withdrawal of Soviet Troops from the Territory of Czechoslovakia (the last soldier left on 27th June, 1991).

Czechoslovak foreign policy was built on the premise that both military bloc systems – NATO and the Warsaw Pact – would be gradually disbanded and replaced by a collective security system under the aegis of the Organization for Security and Co-operation in Europe (OSCE). The Confederation of European States would come next, which in turn might develop into the United States of Europe. The Czechoslovak Minister of Foreign Affairs, former dissident Jiří Dienstbier, presented this bold proposal at the Royal Institute of International Affairs in London, on 3rd April. The Warsaw Pact member states' meeting held on 6th June in Moscow yielded an agreement on the gradual dissolution of the Soviet military pact. Czechoslovakia expressed an interest in co-operation with Western institutions, and was granted special guest status by the European Commission on 7th May. On the same day, the 'Agreement on Commercial and Economic Co-operation' with the European Union was signed by a Czechoslovak delegation in Brussels.

It should be noted that the politics of the transitional period were far more complex than it might seem from the simple list of laws enacted, triumphant visits abroad, and bold proposals and visions. Some bills passed through the parliament with surprising speed (although practical application later revealed their many flaws), others were stuck for weeks or months (although nothing had originally seemed easier than passing them). The politics of anti-totalitarian consensus was quickly giving way to the politics of vested interests. Various coalitions were being formed by those with power in the new hierarchy, now free of the Communist Party dictate, with the previously-mentioned political types coming together or breaking apart based on situational parameters and pragmatic formulas. Disputes and disagreements arose, such as the dispute between the proponents of the neo-liberal strategy and advocates of the welfare state, or the disagreement about the best way to eliminate the State Police. Ideas and ideologies returned to politics. With a certain degree of simplification, it can be said that Czech society was astir with disputes over economic reform and over the manner and extent to which they should redress the past wrongs of the CPCz; meanwhile, the issue of the day in the Slovak part of the country was Slovak national interests and Slovakia's unsatisfactory position in the Czechoslovak federation. To give an example, against the background of these events, the Slovak neo-Communists and ex-Communists teamed up in expedient coalitions against the civic politicians of the VPN, by whose expected rise they felt threatened. The first call for an autonomous Slovak state came as early as January 1990.

The victorious movements failed to make the issue of Czech-Slovak relations in the unified state a key topic for political discussions. Instead, the issue spread to the public arena in an unrestrained manner, and escaped political control for months. An impulse for the dispute between Slovak politicians and Czech and Slovak public opinion came with the question of a new name for the shared country. On 23rd January, 1990, President Václav Havel suggested to the FA that the word 'socialist' should be dropped from the name, which would have meant a return to the traditional 'Czechoslovak Republic.' However, quite against Havel's expectations, his proposal did not make it through parliament. Moreover, it caused an immediate uproar in Slovakia, and the decisions made by Slovak politicians were affected by a host of historical reminiscences – both real and purely expedient – on the complicated relations between Czechs and Slovaks since 1918. The Slovaks refused to accept any alternative that was reminiscent of the centralistic concept of the First Republic's Czechoslovakism. On the other hand, the Czech side assumed a patronizing stance, considering the 'Hyphen War' petty and irrelevant. It failed to recognize that the reason the Slovaks were suggesting peculiar variations for the name (Czecho-Slovakia, Federation Czecho-Slovakia, the Czecho-Slovak Republic, and the like) was that they wanted to finally accentuate the statehood they had been denied for a very long time. Finally on 19th April, 1990, following numerous lengthy negotiations and dramatic disputes, often directly influenced by the pendulum swings of public opinion, the FA adopted a compromise and with it a rather complicated solution to the name issue: the Czech and Slovak Federal Republic. The Czechs, having failed to comprehend the Slovak desire for their own underived statehood, began to suspect the Slovaks of separation intentions, when they ought to have expressed generous empathy. In Slovakia, the hyphen dispute stirred up nationalist sentiment manifested in various ways, from political utilitarianism to the first instances of racial and nationalist intolerance.

The parliament, composed mainly of Communist deputies, elected Václav Havel President of the Republic at the end of 1989, in return for being respected by the OF as a fully-fledged subject of the nascent political pluralism. In spite of this, anti-Communism became one of the fundamental issues in the upcoming period. In January, February and March 1990, it was 'born' in the Moravian capital of Brno. The Brno branch of the OF, led by ex-

Communist and Charter 77 signatory Jaroslav Šabata, wanted to keep CPCz member Josef Pernica in the prestigious and representative post of mayor. However, they met with stout resistance from the Brno public and local OF branches, with dissident and former political prisoner Petr Cibulka their torch-bearer. Although the Brno-based radicalism was subdued, anti-Communism could not be prevented from seeping into the OF's political line, where it began to play the role of a major facet and divider. As a suitable tool in the struggle for greater influence, it was mostly appropriated by the 'revolutionaries of the final hour:' the district and regional branches of the OF used it as a powerful instrument in their fight with the local 'Communist mafia' and 'nomenclature brotherhoods', which had started to transfer their political, social and financial capital into the sphere of private enterprise.

In mid-April 1990, Prague state prosecutor Tomáš Sokol (OF), came forward with an initiative to make the CPCz illegal. The proposal sparked great tension between the OF Co-ordination Centre, which was willing to compromise, and the regional OF branches, which became more and more radical. Anti-Communist sentiment gained strength with the looming elections, and the request to ban the CPCz won the approval of even those parties that had spent decades collaborating with it in the National Front. Other groups endorsing the ban included political prisoners, whose desire to impose legal measures on the CPCz was completely and undeniably legitimate. It was at their suggestion that, on 24th April, the FA enacted a law on court rehabilitations, which was essentially a copy of a similar bill from 1968. This fact also defined its limitations: the law sought to revoke wrongful verdicts and to create conditions for providing compensation to the victims of judicial abuse, without defining Communist totalitarianism as criminal and allowing for the prosecution of specific perpetrators. It was clear that this would not do as a manner of settlement.

The State Security (StB) issue made political headlines throughout the transitional period. The Ministry of the Interior immediately became the focus of attention for several interest groups, while the OF and the VPN had no decisive influence on developments in the department. The new Minister of the Interior, Richard Sacher (ČSL), initially received full backing by President Havel and the OF Co-ordination Centre, but it was not long before Sacher's concept of personal continuity became a matter of fierce, unscrupulous dispute with the OF, as it was in direct contradiction with their vision that all StB agents should be dismissed without delay. The leitmotif of the non-public activities at the Ministry of the Interior was to get hold of the information capital buried in the ministerial archives. Behind the doors of registries and secretariats, the first, unofficial lustrations were carried out (probing into the vetted politician's connections to the Communist regime's power structures), which have been associated not only with the idea of purging public life of police informers, but also with attempts at prefabrication and the expedient use of compromising material against public and political figures. Such an uncontrolled, dubious process – the personal files of some 15,000 key informers were destroyed or stolen in the early days of the revolution – led to an official pre-election lustration campaign involving screening the candidates running for political parties and movements. In Slovakia, a number of influential, nationalist-reoriented post-Communists and former Communists united in their suspicion of, and aversion towards, the civic politicians representing liberal and federative ideas, and they tampered with some files to their advantage. Needless to say, similar things went on in Prague as well.

The transformation of the economy became another hot issue. For some time after the inauguration of the 'government of national understanding,' it may have seemed an issue reserved for experts, but the first months of the new year proved that the economy would be a political matter par excellence. An informal contest for the best 'economic reform scenario' was launched at the instigation of the OF, attracting various groups and schools. Naturally, concepts more influential than any others had been drawn up by economic experts of the three governments. The reform project developed by a Czech government team of experts affiliated with the Czech cabinet (and led by the cabinet's First Deputy Prime Minister František Vlasák) shared some features with the policy drawn up by the federal government's economic experts led by the Finance Minister Václav Klaus. However, the relations between the Czech and federal teams were marked by competitive animosity, which prevented their co-operation. The Slovak perspective on economic reform developed in parallel fashion, without any reference to the Czech and federal plans. It was mostly based on the idea of Slovakia's specific journey towards a market economy, which was closely connected to the notion of state autonomy and self-sufficiency. The alarming lack of overlap between the Czech and Slovak visions went unnoticed by the OF and VPN until shortly before the elections, when it was too late to begin effective co-operation.

In spite of further problems and complications (such as the sky-rocketing crime rate following a general presidential amnesty), the government enjoyed relatively high popularity ratings. The population – still drunk on its newly acquired freedom – projected their desires and expectations onto the most prominent politicians. President Václav Havel represented an alternative kind of politics, one that addressed taboo topics in ingenious, non-bureaucratic ways and that was garlanded with moral appeals. The Minister of Foreign Affairs, Jiří Dienstbier, was associated with the new, pro-Western foreign policy leanings of Czechoslovakia. The Finance Minister, Václav Klaus, came to represent – as early as in the transitional period – a radical economic reform fraught with promise. In Slovakia, the most popular politicians included the Slovak Prime Minister Milan Čič and Rudolf Schuster, Speaker of the SNC, their connection with the pre-November Communist establishment presenting no obstacle. Their skilful rhetoric and gestures, by which they managed to persuade the public of their ability to be strong defenders of Slovak interests, certainly played a role in this.

The popularity of and trust in political symbols were closely connected with three post-November myths. The myth of 'tightening our belts' was fodder to the people's trust that temporary restraint and modesty would lead to a speedy and marked increase in living standards and prosperity of the whole society. Politicians were given the green light to take unpopular measures. The second myth had to do with 'the return to Europe' and bolstered the belief that Czechoslovakia would pick up the threads of its pre-WWII democratic and economic success and quickly catch up with the 'first world' Western countries. And last but not least, the third myth promised the Slovaks that the 'Velvet Revolution' finally opened the door to achieving their national and state autonomy.

3 The 1990 Parliamentary Elections. Seeking a Solution to the Czech-Slovak Question. The Principal Problems of the Renewed Democracy (June 1990–June 1992)

The eagerly awaited parliamentary elections held on 8th and 9th June, 1990, with a turnout of nearly 90% of registered voters; they were the first opportunity after more than half a century for Czech and Slovak citizens to freely elect their favourites out of dozens of politi-

Results of elections in the CSFR held on 8th and 9th June, 1990

The Federal Assembly, the Chamber of the People

Political party	Czech Republic		Slovak Republic	
	% of votes	Number of seats	% of votes	Number of seats
Civic Forum (OF)	53.15	68		
CPCz	13.48	15	13.81	8
Movement for self-governing democracy (HSD) –Society for Moravia and Silesia (SMS)	7.89	9		
Christian and Democratic Union (KDU)	8.69	9		
Public Against Violence (VPN)			32.54	19
Coexistence + Hungarian Christian and Democratic Union			8.58	5
Slovak National Party (SNS)			10.96	6
Christian Democratic Movement (KDH)			18.98	11

The Federal Assembly, the Chamber of Nations

Political party	Czech Republic		Slovak Republic	
	% of votes	Number of seats	% of votes	Number of seats
Civic Forum (OF)	49.96	50		
CPCz	13.80	12	13.34	12
Movement for self-governing democracy (HSD) – Society for Moravia and Silesia (SMS)	9.10	7		
Christian and Democratic Union (KDU)	8.75	6		
Public Against Violence (VPN)			37.28	33
Coexistence + Hungarian Christian and Democratic Union			8.49	7
Slovak National Party (SNS)			11.44	9
Christian Democratic Movement (KDH)			16.66	14

JIŘÍ SUK

cal parties and movements in the running. The 'feast of democracy' was tainted with two scandals, associated with Josef Bartončík, leader of the ČSL, and Ján Budaj, leader of the VPN, both of whom were branded StB collaborators. Budaj's name appeared on the list of positively lustrated candidates and he removed his name from the VPN ballot, but not until he denied ever having collaborated with the StB. The VPN backed him wholeheartedly, and challenged the legitimacy of the lustration process that had been designed in haste and was accompanied by dubious practices at the Ministry of the Interior. Bartončík, on the other hand, was not on the list of positively screened candidates for the ČSL. Based on the testimony of a former StB employee and ambiguous data in the StB's registry of files, the federal deputy interior minister Jan Ruml (OF) labelled him a major StB collaborator of many years' standing. The ČSL, Christian Democratic Party (KDS) and the Slovak KDH called it an unlawful and politically-motivated attack of the OF during the pre-election cease-fire, and saw it as an attempt to lessen the electoral gain of the Christian-oriented parties. The scandal subsequently affected the post-election coalition talks.

The OF was expected to win in the Czech Lands; the victory of the VPN in Slovakia had been somewhat uncertain, but was ultimately a sweeping one. The democratic political movement, born spontaneously in November 1989 in the squares of Czech and Slovak cities, emerged triumphant in the elections.

The deputy groups of the winning movements in the three legislative bodies were large. The 200-member CNC now had 127 deputies for the OF, and the SNC housed 48 deputies for the VPN of the total 150 council members. In the Czech section of the Federal Assembly's Chamber of Nations, the OF won 50 of the 75 seats, while the VPN won 33 of

The Czech National Council

Political party	% of votes	Number of seats
Civic Forum (OF)	49.50	127
CPCz	13.24	32
Movement for self-governing democracy (HSD) – Society for Moravia and Silesia (SMS)	10.03	22
Christian and Democratic Union (KCDU)	8.42	19

The Slovak National Council

Political party	% of votes	Number of seats
Democratic Party (DS)	4.40	7
CPCz	13.35	22
Green Party	3.49	6
Public Against Violence (VPN)	29.39	48
Coexistence + Hungarian Christian and Democratic Union	8.66	14
Slovak National Party (SNS)	13.49	22
Christian and Democratic Union (KDU)	19.21	31

75 total seats in the Slovak section. Bearing the pre-election anti-Communist surge in mind, the CPCz's election result was a success, although the party had lost a substantial number of seats in comparison to the transitory period. The CPCz moved into opposition. The period commentators expected that it would be disbanded soon, but the years that followed proved them wrong. The surprising election result of the Movement for Self-Governing Democracy – Society for Moravia and Silesia (HSD-SMS) indicated that, in addition to the Slovak question, the November revolution had raised the historical Moravian-Silesian issue. The Christian and Democratic Union (KDU), made up of a coalition of the ČSL and KDS, felt that its interests had been harmed by the Bartončík affair, and refused to join the federal government.

The Christian and Democratic Union (KDU), led by Ján Čarnogurský, considered its election result a failure, as it had expected to become a dominant political force in Slovakia. The KDU decided not to participate in the federal government-formation talks, and only joined the Slovak government, thus sending a clear message about its priorities. The election result of the Slovak Democratic Party was a great success and a cogent testimony to the nationalization of Slovak politics, given that the party had originated only two months before the elections, amidst the turmoil of the 'Hyphen War.'

The election results determined the character of coalition negotiations, and the new cabinets were introduced to the public at the end of June. Despite the OF's disapproval, the seat of Prime Minister again went to Marián Čalfa (formerly CPCz, now VPN), who received a strong backing from President Havel. The cabinet had 16 members including the Prime Minister, (9 OF, 5 VPN, 1 independent, and 1 CPCz member). Pavel Rychetský (OF) became first Deputy Prime Minister, Jiří Dienstbier (OF) took the position of Minister of Foreign Affairs, Václav Klaus became Minister of Finance, the seat of Minister of Economy went to Vladimír Dlouhý (formerly CPCz, now OF) and Ján Langoš (VPN) became Minister of the Interior, to name a few members. The Czech cabinet, led by Petr Pithart (OF), had another 21 appointed ministers (14 OF, 3 KDU, 2 independents, and 1 HSD-SMS). The Slovak cabinet had 23 members (12 VPN, 8 KDU, 3 DS), with Prime Minister Vladimír Mečiar (VPN) and First Deputy Prime Minister Ján Čarnogurský.

The seat of the Speaker of the Federal Assembly went again to Alexander Dubček (VPN), and Zdeněk Jičínský became First Deputy Speaker. Dagmar Burešová (OF) became Speaker of the FA, and František Mikloško (VPN, later KDU) Speaker of the SNC. Post-election talks culminated in the election of the new Czechoslovak president on 5th July, 1990. In a secret ballot, the FA elected Václav Havel, the only candidate, by a total of 234 votes with 50 deputies abstaining. A glance at the makeup of the governments and legislative bodies suggests that democratic forces took power as many as seven months after the fall of the Communist regime. Their victory in local government elections held on 23rd and 24th November was not as overwhelming; the OF won with 36% of the vote, followed by the CPCz with 17%, and another 11.5 % going to the ČSL. The turnout in these elections was nearly 75% of all registered voters.

600

The election triumph also had its dark side: the instability of the political movements. The OF and the VPN were not represented in politics by a single leader enjoying general respect, but by a free association of figures with differing views. The non-elected leadership teams of both co-ordination centres tried to prolong the life of 'consensual politics,' but their efforts were unproductive amidst the inevitable split in opinions. Calls for centrist politics devoid of party loyalties – shielded by President Havel's authority – began to be off-target after the elections. There was no internal or external force able to keep the over-pressured OF and VPN together. The time came for the movements to start splitting. A great difference in opinion heralded the incoming split of the OF and the VPN into ideologically separate political groups. The differences crystallized and deepened, particularly in debates over the previously-mentioned issues of the Czech-Slovak dispute, economic reform, and approaches to dealing with the Communist past.

The first conflict came directly after the elections. Right-wing parliamentary deputies for the OF, who formed a very small minority in the OF's Coordination Centre, voiced scathing criticism of the practice of appointing some Communists to top positions in the parliament. The unelected leadership of the OF, convinced by their election success that nothing significant in the existing political practice had to be changed, were being criticized by their own members. The legitimacy and self-confidence of the critics now rested on the mandate granted in the elections, which helps explain why the split began in the parliaments. In September, as a result of disputes over the character of economic reform, the Inter-Parliamentary Club of the Democratic Right (MKDP) was formed, associating the Club of Right Wing Deputies in the CNC, led by Jan Kalvoda (ODA – Civic Democratic Alliance), and a similar club in the CNC, led by Daniel Kroupa (also ODA). In reaction to the formation of the MKDP, those OF deputies who were against splitting the movement, founded the Liberal Club in mid-December, which drew in most ministers of the Czech and federal governments (including Jiří Dienstbier, Pavel Rychetský, Dagmar Burešová, and Petr Miller).

The OF's fundamental and inevitable transformation was drawing near. The congress held on 13th October, 1990 was not successful for those who hoped the OF would continue to function as a politically indistinct, centrist formation until the 1992 parliamentary elections. The will of most district and regional OF branches launched the charismatic Finance Minister Václav Klaus into the position of chairman. Klaus made no secret of his intention to turn the OF into a right-wing political party with a distinct platform and fixed membership, which he hoped to use as a source of support in pushing through the radical economic reform. Despite President Havel's disapproval – the movement's founder and the most influential political figure of the time – the OF congress on 12th and 13th October ratified Klaus's intention. A number of minor, mostly left-wing parties had to leave the Forum, which was now ready to undergo a profound transformation. On 10th February, 1991, President Havel summoned OF representatives to the presidential Lány Château, with the intent to make a joint decision on the future of the movement, particularly as regards the form it should assume for the period until the next general elections. The reasoning behind this was to maintain the pro-government majority in the Czech part of the Federal Assembly and the CNC, which in turn would preserve the current makeup of the Czech and federal cabinets. The two apparent successors of the OF made a deal to carry out a parity-based redistribution of seats in the parliamentary presidia, committees and governments. The final statewide congress of the OF was organized in Prague on 23rd February. It was there that a decision was passed to divide the OF into the Civic Democratic Party (ODS) with the Finance Minister Václav Klaus as the leader, and the Civic Movement (OH), informally led by Jiří Dienstbier, the Minister of Foreign Affairs. The ODS, which subsequently drew in the majority of the regional Forum branches, soon gained considerable clout in the political arena, and became an influential parliamentary faction. In contrast, most ministers of the Czech and federal governments were OH affiliates, including the Czech Prime Minister Petr Pithart and the CNC Speaker Dagmar Burešová. This effectively turned the Czech government into a minority cabinet – yet another surprising paradox in the politics of 'broad constitutional consensus.'

The VPN was unable to resist the separatist tendencies within the movement and underwent a dramatic split into two political parties only weeks after the dissolution of the OF. This was due to a dispute between the liberal-oriented VPN leadership, represented by František Mikloško (the SNC Speaker), and a group around the authoritarian Slovak Prime Minister Vladimír Mečiar. On 5th March, 1991, the latter group, which included some Slovak ministers and deputies, created a platform within the Public Against Violence called 'For a Democratic Slovakia' (VPN-ZDS). After some further disputes, the VPN's Slovak Council declared that Prime Minister Mečiar and Minister of Foreign Relations Milan Kňažko no longer represented the VPN movement. The SNC then divested Mečiar of his ministerial position on 23rd April; seven members of the cabinet suffered the same fate.

The position of the Slovak Prime Minister went to the CDM chairman Ján Čarnogurský. Although formally speaking, the coalition of the VPN, KDU, DD and MNI (Independent Hungarian Initiative) remained as before, the change nevertheless caused confusion and a shift in the balance of power that remained disregarded though it resulted, for example, in the unplanned removal from office of some loyal ministers. On 24th April, 1991, a major demonstration was organized in Bratislava in support of the dismissed Prime Minister Mečiar, who had, in the meantime, received backing from most of the original VPN's prominent officials. In the months that followed, the original VPN characterized itself as a right-wing political party, and adopted a new name as the Civic Democratic Union – Public Against Violence (ODÚ-VPN), with Martin Porubjak as the leader. Mečiar's supporters organized a congress in Banská Bystrica on 22nd June, 1991, where the Movement for a Democratic Slovakia (HZDS) was founded and, as expected, the charismatic Mečiar was elected as its leader.

New political clubs were formed within the FA from the ruins of the OF and VPN. The right-wing centrist and straightforward right-wing bloc was quite a bit stronger than their left-wing counterpart: the ODS (OF) with 47 members; the KDU (VPN) with 30 members; the ODA (OF) with 11 members; the ChDP with 5 members; the Liberal-Democratic

Party (OF) with 5 members. The left-wing group, or even those with merely left-of-centre characteristics had 34 members; the MDS (VPN) with 18 members; the Social-Democratic Direction club with 13 members; the OF Independent Deputies' Club with 6 members. Only some 15 deputies were not organized in clubs, and 6 deputies joined the Club of Successor Political Parties (formed outside of the parliament).

Following the 1990 parliamentary elections, crucial political and legislative steps were taken towards the transformation of the Czechoslovak economy. In September and November, the FA adopted the scenario of a 'radical economic reform,' designed under the leadership of the Finance Minister and Chairman of OF-ODS Václav Klaus. An era of 'shock treatment' for the economy began. The government introduced restrictive macro-economic policies, made substantial cuts in state aid, and opened up the market. The devaluation of the Czechoslovak crown was carried out in three steps taken in January, October and December 1990, and devalued the savings of the population, and the price of labour and material capital by 54%. Reducing the exchange rate of the crown in proportion to its purchasing power parity, while favourable for domestic exporters, put domestic investors at a disadvantage in the upcoming privatization. Price liberalization was implemented as of 1st January, 1991. Following these measures, consumer prices skyrocketed. The government countered inflation through the strict regulation of wages and subsidies, which had the consequence of curbing development in the spheres of education and scientific research. The population, resigned to the temporary 'belt tightening', took it well. The economic reform – associated with the myth of a speedy attainment of Western prosperity levels – was accompanied by a popular surge in right-wing sentiment and the popularity of right-wing parties. The OF parliament deputy clubs split into political groups with distinctive views, the consensual politics of the 'Velvet Revolution' continued to break up, and the process of societal transformation found new dynamism.

The unprecedented return from the centrally-planned socialist economy towards a free-market-based capitalist economy was marked by a number of fundamental conceptual and ideological disputes, the least controversial of them being the issue of 'small-scale privatization.' The first public auctions of shops, restaurants, and other lesser enterprises were launched in late January 1991 and continued through to December 1993. In the first round, the auctions excluded foreigners, while the current managers of the businesses on offer had not been granted the right of first refusal. A total of 30,000 units with a book value of 32 billion crowns were auctioned off in the Czech part of the country. The 'small-scale privatization,' in spite of obvious problems (including many buyers using black economy funds to purchase property; putting auction units up for sale also broke down functioning commercial networks), was relatively successful, and contributed to loosening up the stagnating service industry in the first years of the transformation. The issue of restitution – restoring property nationalized after 25th February, 1948, to the original owners – brought about a clash of neo-liberal economists and politicians on the one hand (such as Václav Klaus and Dušan Tříska) with politicians and economists espousing conservative values (among them

Daniel Kroupa and Tomáš Ježek). The idea of 'rectifying some of the property-related wrongs' won, making restitution one of the crucial privatization methods. The state began restoring both movable and immovable assets to those who claimed them and were able to prove the validity of the claim. Nevertheless, the restitution process – launched in the name of historical justice – had its own series of problems. Naturally, not all of those who acquired property in restitution proved to be good caretakers; a lot of property failed to be returned to the Catholic Church (the reason being that church property did not have the status of private property, but instead that of 'public service property' – which is why it could not be returned in restitution, but rather through a change in ownership relations); Czechoslovak exiles, societies, associations, and other corporate bodies were excluded from the pool of claimants.

The greatest and frequently heated disputes were over the 'large-scale privatization' intended to place medium and large enterprises, including Czech and Slovak industrial giants, into private hands. The need for extensive privatization in this key sector was questioned by nobody but the Communists, but the million-dollar question was: how to privatize? Klaus's team at the federal Ministry of Finance, bearers of neo-liberal economic views, was intent on finding new owners as quickly as possible, leaving the rest – including the subsequent redistribution and accumulation of property – in the 'invisible hand of the market;' the team categorically rejected any attempts on the part of the government to restructure the enterprises once they had been privatized. Forty years of an absence of private ownership resulted in an insufficient amount of private capital to make it possible for the enterprises to be privatized in the standard manner – that is, sold to solvent buyers. And as the property was supposed to go primarily into Czech hands, the neo-liberals selected 'investment vouchers' as the primary method of 'distributing' state property. All Czech and Slovak adults were invited to partake in the 'voucher privatization' by purchasing a book of vouchers at the operating cost of CZK 1,000, and then use their discretion to invest the vouchers into one or more enterprises included in the privatization, or to sign them over to mutual funds which would invest in their name. The neo-liberals proposed that up to 97% of property be privatized by this method, thus showing their clear preference for the 'Czech path to capitalism' over foreign investors (who were only permitted to buy enterprises from Czech owner-winners of the voucher game).

The voucher concept, endorsed by the federal government, met with resistance from some members of the Czech government, especially the Minister of Economy Jan Vrba (OH). They thought it too risky and objected that a high-quality ownership structure could not be created in a voucher lottery. Instead, they expected it to create highly fragmented, unproductive ownership, and that foreign investors – indispensable to Czechoslovak industry – would lose all interest in entering such enterprises. The OH economists, generally rejecting the macroeconomic neo-liberal concept in favour of the microeconomic institutional approach, called for more caution and a differentiation in selecting a privatization method. For example, most major and key enterprises of the Czechoslovak economy were supposed to be privatized into the hands of respectable foreign investors. The Czech government's team considered it indispensable that some enterprises should undergo special preparation by being freed from unprofitable operations, debt stocks, and the like. In the period from mid-1991 to the parliamentary elections in June 1992, from which the ODS emerged victorious while the OH failed disastrously, a total of 60 major enterprises, including the Škoda Mladá Boleslav Auto Works, were privatized into the hands of foreign investors, following the lines of the Czech government's plan; without exception, foreign capital brought all of these enterprises to prosperity.

The complex set of questions and issues associated with transferring state-owned property into private hands was heavily politicized in the period from 1990 to 1992. What should have been the subject of expert discourse often became an excuse for ideological clashes. The neo-liberals with Václav Klaus at the helm labelled their opponents in the Czech cabinet (as well as those among independent scientists) as proponents of outdated state interventionism of the socialist grain and adherents of misleading 'third ways.' The OH's economists, on the other hand, underestimated the political dimension of the economic transformation, and failed to popularize their concept and push it through. Public opinion at the time was more on Klaus's side, with more trust in neo-liberal recipes and promises of rapid prosperity.

The first wave of 'voucher privatization,' in which the state put the shares of 988 enterprises with a seat in the Czech Republic up for sale, at the aggregate cost of CZK 350 billion, was launched on 1st November, 1991, with the registration of 'investment voucher holders' (IVH). Under the influence of government propaganda and commercial advertizing, six million Czech citizens (and 2.5 million Slovaks) registered for the first wave. Beginning on 18th May, 1992, all holders of voucher books could invest their vouchers either directly in enterprises under privatization, or sign them over to investment funds. Three out of four IVHs, convinced by the advertizing campaign and hoping to 'get rich quick' in the atmosphere of 'people's capitalism' consigned their voucher books to the funds. The next, smaller wave was carried out at the turn of 1993 and 1994, with 6 million participating Czech IVHs and the shares of 676 enterprises put up for sale. The voucher privatization was carried out without sound legal backing, and led to many cases of fraud and thievery over the years to come, which became known under their world-renowned neologism of 'tunnelling.'

In addition to restitution, and small- and large-scale privatization, mention ought to be made of the two remaining privatization programmes. One was the transformation of the system of co-operatives, applied mostly in agriculture and retail. The other was the transfer of state-owned property with an aggregate value of approximately 350 billion crowns to over six thousand cities and municipalities. In total, 47% of property was privatized through vouchers, 13% through voluntary conveyance by the state, and 12% was sold, while the state retained 27% of property through to the year 1997. The transformation of the Czech economy was a very complex process, partially successful and partially highly misguided. But it was not until the second half of the 1990s that the 'Czech path to capitalism,' characterized by shock therapy and voucher privatization, was shown to be a failure. The Czech economic prosperity in the first decade of the new millennium was primarily due to the continuing privatization of major banks and enterprises to foreign investors – an approach adopted by the social democratic government after 1998 – and the linking of the Czech economy to the economic structures of the European Union.

The winners of elections in the Czech and Slovak Republics wished to preserve the common state as a federation of two equal, autonomous nations. The principal difference of opinion, which eventually proved insurmountable, consisted in differing concepts of the common state. While the Czechs thought that the essential entity of Czechoslovak statehood was to be a strong federation essentially built from the top down, the Slovak perspective was entirely the opposite, seeing the two self-contained, autonomous states as the fundamental building blocks that would grant competencies to the federation at their full discretion. Such diametrically opposed views complicated and obstructed the Czech-Slovak negotiations. The roles of speakers on behalf of the two nations were played by the Czech and Slovak state representatives, above all Prime Minister Petr Pithart (OF-OH) and CNC Speaker Dagmar Burešová (OF-OH) on one side, and the Slovak Prime Minister Mečiar (to April 1991) followed by Ján Čarnogurský (KDU), and SNC Speaker František Mikloško (VPN-KDH) on the other.

The main procedural issue in enacting bills and constitutional laws in the FA was a ban on majoritization, which was applied in the Chamber of the Nations. The chamber consisted of the Czech (75 seats) and Slovak (75 seats) sections, with each section holding separate votes. In effect, in discussing a run-of-the-mill law requiring an absolute majority of the votes of the deputies present, 38 Czech or 38 Slovak deputies were able to obstruct the entire 300-member parliament; for constitutional laws, the required majority was even higher – 3/5 of the present deputies, making it possible for a mere 31 deputies of one or the other state in the Chamber of Nations to veto any constitutional amendment. It follows that the anti-majoritization mechanism, whereby all decisions were effectively made in the Chamber of Nations, gave rise to perpetual instability. The OF had taken 50 seats in the Chamber of Nations, which was 5 more than the required 3/5 majority. In the Slovak section of that chamber, however, things were much more complicated: the VPN only held 33 seats, and needed the support of the 14 KDU deputies to pass bills and constitutional laws. As mentioned earlier, the KDU had not joined the federal government, which was made up of a coalition of OF and VPN and as such could not do without the support of other, mostly Christian, political parties.

Other symptoms of the gradual Czech-Slovak separation soon followed. In November 1990, the CPCz split into the 'Party of the Democratic Left' (SDL) in Slovakia and the 'Communist Party of Bohemia and Moravia' (KSČM) in the Czech Republic. More organizations with nationalistic and separatist leanings were being established in Slovakia. Incomprehension and suspicion deepened in the Czech part of the country. In the second part of 1990, the nationalist forces locked horns with liberals in Slovakia over the form of the language law: the nationalists' effort to deny the Hungarian minority the right to use their mother tongue in dealing with local authorities was not yet successful, but the VPN as a

606

liberal and democratic movement lost further points and gained a reputation among Slovaks as an anti-national and pro-federal force. All problems were blown up as a consequence of an unclear distribution of competencies between the federal authorities on the one hand, and the organs of the respective republics on the other.

Following the 'Hyphen War,' the next act in the drama of the Slovaks' position in Czechoslovakia was the dispute over competencies. It was in this controversy that the VPN was obliged to show the agitated Slovak public its preparedness to defend national interests. In Trenčianske Teplice, a spa town in Slovakia, the Czech and Slovak governments' delegations led by Petr Pithart and Vladimír Mečiar held talks on 8th and 9th August, 1990. The delegations agreed on the principle of granting more competencies to the respective republics, as expressed in popular slogans including 'A Federation Built from the Ground Up' and 'Strong Republics Make for a Strong Federation.' The two diametrically opposed perspectives were the reason behind the difference between the Czech and Slovak viewpoints. Mečiar later interpreted the preliminary agreement to the SNC as crucial and binding, and bringing Slovakia the real prospect of independence; the federation was supposed to be only a superstructure, created out of the will of the sovereign republics. Pithart, in contrast, announced to the public that no binding agreement had been made in Trenčianske Teplice, and that what Mečiar was presenting as a fait accompli was nothing more than suggestions put forward by the Slovak delegation. The Slovak side began a coercive, populist campaign to push its vision, regardless of the real status of negotiations. The main proponent of this political battle style was the unpredictable Slovak Prime Minister.

The dispute over competencies culminated in December 1990. Arduous negotiations of all three governments produced a draft of a compromise solution that seemed acceptable to all parties. However, the question of who was going to have the final say remained. The Slovak representation requested that the position of the SNC – declared after the negotiations of the state delegations – be binding for the CNC and the FA as well. Quite expectedly, the deputies in these bodies rejected this notion, and went on to put forward their amendments. This created a situation of double conflict: one between the two respective national councils, and one between the SNC and the FA. A political crisis ensued. To make matters worse, the Slovak government and the SNC threatened to unilaterally declare the independence of the Slovak Republic. The right-wing FA deputies, members of the disintegrating OF, came out against the compromise solution and – contrary to the logic of the recent negotiations – came up with proposals based on Czechoslovak unitarianism. The competency law, enacted on 12th December, 1990, a result of talks fraught with conflict and tension, significantly enhanced the authority of the respective republics at the expense of the federation. The difference in the positions of Czechs and Slovaks in the shared state remained the same. The Czech side considered the competency law a major concession, while the Slovak side saw it as merely the first step on the way to a loose Czech-Slovak confederation, or even Slovakia's full independence.

After the removal of the controversial Mečiar from office in April 1991, the Chairman of the KDU, Ján Čarnogurský, was appointed Prime Minister. The Czech-Slovak negotiations moved on to the issue of three constitutions. The Slovak representatives deemed it appropriate that the national constitutions be drawn up first, and provide a basis for the subsequently designed federal constitution. All legislative acts were to be preceded by signing a 'state agreement' between the CR and the SR on the formation of a common state. This idea was presented by the Slovak Prime Minister, who did not try to conceal his desire for a completely independent Slovakia, although not immediately, but rather after Czechoslovakia had joined the European Union. Not surprisingly, the Czech side did not give the time of day to the concept of a provisional union that would only be designed to bring Slovakia safely into the harbour of Europe. At first, the Czech politicians were strictly opposed to the idea of the state agreement, objecting that such agreements are only made by sovereign states, which was not the case of Czechia and Slovakia. The Slovak politicians (including VPN), however, were adamant in their demand for the agreement, thus making it a subject of further talks. The talks were deeply paradoxical, as most parties (excluding the Slovak National Party), advocated the idea of a common state, but the concept of the common state was – as has been made clear – diametrically different for Czechs and Slovaks.

In the first months of 1991, President Havel took the initiative. He held recurrent negotiations with the Slovak, Czech and federal representatives in the presidential Lány Château, the Vikárka Restaurant in Prague, Budmerice in Slovakia, and Kroměříž in Moravia. During his 'travels' around the Czech and Slovak castles and châteaux, he presented various proposals, hoping they would help find a solution to the protracted crisis. His efforts were, mostly, to no avail. The newly appointed Constitutional Court with its federal jurisdiction could not become an arbitrator in Czech-Slovak disputes, as the Slovak side refused to confer that power on it. On 8th July, the FA passed a law on referendum, according to which the common state could be dissolved only if a majority of Czech or Slovak citizens voted for it. The chance to hold a plebiscite also bore no fruit, as an agreement could not be reached about the question that should be asked in it. Another political crisis loomed on the horizon.

President Havel therefore made an appearance in the Czechoslovak television on 17th November, 1991, announcing his intention to present a new set of draft laws to the FA, which would give him the power to hold a referendum without the prior consent of the FA, to dismantle the FA, and govern temporarily by means of presidential decrees. He also proposed that the 150-member Chamber of Nations be replaced with a 30-member Federal Council with a seat in Bratislava. After the dissolution of the OF and VPN, the federal government lost its majority in the Chamber of Nations, which rendered it unable to push through laws subject to the ban on majoritization. However, the President's proposals, designed to resolve the protracted crisis, did not make it through the parliament.

The presidia of the CNC and SNC met for talks on 5th September, 1991, in Bratislava, and agreed to attempt to design a draft agreement and to present it at the plenary sessions of the national councils. Still, the fundamental differences in the two camps' positions on the character of the common state continued. What is more, pro-federal parties in Slovakia lost a great deal of influence in the second half of 1991. The only parties to have the federative arrangement of the country in their platforms were the Hungarian parties and the

608   JIŘÍ SUK

VPN. The HZDS, SDL – Party of the Democratic Left (the former KSS), the KDH, and the Green Party leaned towards the idea of a Czech-Slovak confederation. They expected that both republics would first adopt an agreement, which would then give rise to a federal constitution, and subsequently the confederation itself. The Czech side rejected the confederative arrangement, suspicious that it would merely be a temporary step towards a final split; it was only prepared to accept one of two possibilities: either 'a functional federation,' or two completely independent states. The impasse deepened.

On 28th October, 1991, the 75th anniversary of the founding of Czechoslovakia, President Havel paid a visit to Bratislava, where supporters of Slovak independence 'welcomed' him by chanting disapproving slogans and throwing eggs. The 'egg scandal' was subsequently condemned by most Slovak politicians, but their position did not stem Czech feelings of disillusionment nor the fear that all negotiations were pointless. On 3rd November, the President invited representatives of the governments and parliaments to his weekend house in Hrádeček near Trutnov, where he presented his own draft of an agreement between the republics, as well as a timetable of the adoption of three constitutions; he also suggested a specific procedure that was supposed to culminate on 1st May, 1992, on the adoption of the constitutions. But not even the President's authority was enough to move the delegations to reach an acceptable compromise. The difference in their views of the basic function of the agreement proved irreconcilable: for the Slovaks, it represented a binding legal document ratified by two sovereign states and a basis for all subsequent constitutional amendments; the Czechs, in contrast, saw it merely as a political declaration with zero legal force (in other words, they defended the federal representation's right to interfere actively in the constituent process). Furthermore, no agreement was reached at the thirteenth meeting of the two delegations of both national councils at Častá-Papierničky, in the Lesser Carpathians on 11th November.

As the year 1991 drew to a close, responsible politicians began to realize that a two-year term of office was too short to solve the Czech-Slovak question. The upcoming elections inspired them to attempt to break the stalemate and find a compromise solution. From 3rd to 8th February, expert government and parliament commissions tried to find such a solution in Milovy, near Žďár nad Sázavou; they actually managed to draw up a draft agreement (between the people of the CR represented by CNC deputies and the people of SR represented by SNC deputies) on the formation of a common state. The Slovak side abandoned its original request that the agreement have permanent legal force and predetermine the contents of the federal constitution, and also agreed that any further amendments to the federal constitution would have to be ratified by the respective national councils. However, the proposed draft was flatly rejected by the Slovak National Party and the HZDS as a 'sell-out of Slovak national interests,' which in turn caused a rift in the Slovak government, and as the draft was also rejected by the 20-member presidium of the SNC (10:10), it was not even put to the vote in the SNC plenum. In the meantime, a nationalist faction split from the KDU, rendering the Slovak government coalition a minority in the SNC. The failure of the Milovy agreement induced the CNC Presidium to formulate a declaration on

5th March, 1992, that any further negotiations with the Slovaks would be futile, as there was 'nothing left to discuss.' The presidia of the national councils agreed to leave the decision on the form of Czech-Slovak co-existence up to the winners of the parliamentary elections slated for June.

Using the slogan 'Together with us into Europe,' the democratic movement entered parliamentary elections in June 1990 and its unequivocal orientation connected with the majority of voters. Other countries of 'captive' Europe, such as Poland and Hungary, also chose a direct path to the West. President Havel and Minister of Foreign Affairs Dienstbier visited both neighbouring states in January 1990. The Czechoslovak president spoke in the Polish parliament about the necessity of filling 'the political vacuum which emerged in Central Europe after the disintegration of the Habsburg Empire.' He recalled the distinctive cultural and spiritual dimensions of the heavily tested region which now had to be supplemented with a political dimension. He proposed that the Central European post-Communist countries closely coordinate their steps in the return to a free Europe. On February 15th, 1991, in the Hungarian town of Visegrad, the heads of state of Czechoslovakia, Poland, and Hungary signed a declaration of co-operation and for a common approach in their integration into the European Community and in the destruction of the Warsaw Pact.

Co-operation within the framework of the "Visegrad Troika" had its limits. The problem of the Hungarian minority in Slovakia weighed on Czechoslovak-Hungarian relations; and the Hungarian state considered itself an economic leader and gave priority to independent negotiations with Western Europe; Poland had similar thoughts and, after 1993, so did the Czech Republic. There was an informal competition over leadership in Central Europe, over who would best manage the economic transformation. Problems even accompanied mutual economic co-operation as illustrated in the complicated foundation of a Committee for Co-operation in Central Europe, which focused on the liberalization of trade ties. There was a great will for co-operation in the sphere of security, as the dissolution of the Warsaw Pact had left a power vacuum in Central Europe. The short period of euphoria after the fall of the Berlin Wall was followed by new worries and dangers. In August 1991, conservative Communist forces in the Soviet Union attempted a putsch; in Yugoslavia, the ethnic crisis deepened, the federation disintegrated, and its parts headed towards bloody slaughter; in the Persian Gulf, NATO intervened against Saddam Hussein's invasion of Kuwait. NATO began to re-evaluate its existing military-political strategy and this change was more welcoming to the countries of the Visegrad Troika. As early as 1st March, 1991, the CSFR had agreed to official military contacts with NATO and three weeks later, President Havel appeared before NATO's Council of Ministers in Brussels and declared that Czechoslovak foreign policy was abandoning the idea of collective security in favour of entry into the North Atlantic Alliance. In October at a meeting in Cracow, representatives of the three Central European states agreed to a common approach towards co-operation with NATO.

Along with closer relations with the North Atlantic Alliance, Czechoslovak diplomats were engaged in other activities. In September 1990, CSFR was again accepted into the

610

International Monetary Fund and the World Bank; it became a regular member of the Council of Europe in February 1991; in June, it signed an agreement of co-operation with Organization for Economic Co-operation and Development (OECD); and in December it signed an Association Agreement with the European Community. Complicated relations with its most significant historical neighbour, Germany, weighed down mainly by ghosts of the Nazi occupation of Czechoslovakia from 1939 to 1945 and the post-war exile of three million Germans, now, after the fall of Communism, had a new opportunity to be settled. At the level of declarations, represented by Presidents Havel and von Weiszacker, there was obviously mutual good will; nevertheless, the residue of the Sudeten problem continued to divide public opinion in both countries and was reflected in elite politics. Fertile co-operation developed, however, in many spheres and at many levels. For example, a dialogue of Czech and German historians was started, German foundations generously supported Czech education and science, in 1997 a Czech-German Fund for the Future was established, and so on.

At the beginning of the nineties, Czechoslovakia established very good relations with the world's superpower and the winner of the Cold War, the United States of America. The historic first visit of a US President to Czechoslovakia by George H. W. Bush took place on 17th–18th November, 1990. The following American presidents – Bill Clinton and George W. Bush – also visited Prague. The Czechoslovak and later Czech president Václav Havel was in return heartily welcomed in Washington. Good relations were helpful during the first expansion of NATO to include Central European countries in 1999. Represented by the former dissidents Havel and Dienstbier, the ideological orientation of Czechoslovak foreign policy in the years 1990 to 1992 emerged out of concern for human and civil rights. In January 1991, the Federal Assembly adopted a Charter of Fundamental Rights and Basic Freedoms and incorporated it into the Czechoslovak legal system. This act culminated the historical mission of Charter 77, the best known of the Helsinki initiatives for the defence of human and civil rights in the lands of the former Communist Bloc. After parliamentary elections in 1992, the victorious ODS took control of foreign policy: while appreciating the progress made so far, it nevertheless it had up to then valued the course, but favoured a more 'realistic' conception and rejected a 'messianic, globalist, and abstract' approach. It was sceptical of membership in various subsidiary regional groupings and prioritized building ties on a bilateral basis.

4 Parliamentary Elections 1992. The New Division of Power and the End of the Czech and Slovak Federal Republic (July–December 1992)

Czech and Slovak voters responded to the confusion and uncertainty which were the unavoidable toll of the gift of political plurality by electing strong personalities. In the preceding two and a half years, Czechoslovakia experienced the shock of freedom and severely lacked a firm anchoring in the new order. The process of political transformation was complicated and almost cried out for simplification. Vladimír Mečiar as the chairman of the Movement for a Democratic Slovakia and Václav Klaus as the chairman of the Civic Democratic Party (ODS) embodied clear ideas and promises: the first, the politics of national determination; the second, the politics of economic prosperity. It now depended on these personalities above all which direction negotiations on Czech and Slovak relations would take. Only a rapid and peaceful resolution to this unsettling controversy would open a path forward. The majority of representatives of the existing political elite – grouped in the Czech Civic Forum (OF) and the Slovak Civic Democratic Union – fell by the wayside in elections and did not win seats in either the federal or national parliaments.

On 7th June, President Havel entrusted the chairman of ODS, Václav Klaus, with the formation of a federal government. A day later, the election victors began negotiations in Brno. HZDS proposed creating a confederated system in which both republics would have their own central bank and their own international sovereignty (including diplomatic representation); ODS, however, rejected this as not being a common state but 'Slovak independence with a Czech insurance policy.' The space for compromise dramatically narrowed. After further negotiations on 11th and 17th June in Prague, it appeared that the chances of sustaining the united state were very low; Václav Klaus gave up his post of Federal Prime Minister and decided to seek the post of Prime Minister of the Czech Government. On 20th June, a 'political agreement' was reached in Bratislava in which ODS and HZDS could not agree on a structure for the state and agreed to resolve all problems through 'constitutional means' by 30th September. At this moment a united state lost its priority status, even for those representatives of ODS who sincerely desired to preserve one.

Results of elections in CSFR on June 5–6, 1992

The Federal Assembly, the Chamber of the People				
Political party	Czech Republic		Slovak Republic	
	% of votes	Number of seats	% of votes	Number of seats
Czechoslovak Social Democratic Party (ČSSD)	7.67	10		
Christian Democratic Union – Czech People's Party (KDU-ČSL)	5.98	7		
Liberal Social Union (LSU)	5.84	7		
Rally for the Republic – Republican Party of Czechoslovakia (SPR-RSČ)	6.48	8		
Left Bloc (LB)	14.27	14		
Civic Democratic Party – Christian Democratic Party (ODS-KDS)	33.9	48		
Movement for a Democratic Slovakia (HZDS)			33.53	24
Party of the Democratic Left (SDL)			14.44	10
Hungarian Christian Democratic Movement			7.37	5
Christian Democratic Movement (KDH)			8.96	6
Slovak National Party (SNS)			9.39	6

The Federal Assembly, the Chamber of Nations

Political party	Czech Republic		Slovak Republic	
	% of votes	Number of seats	% of votes	Number of seats
Czechoslovak Social Democratic Party (ČSSD)	6.80	6		
Christian Democratic Union – Czech People's Party (KDU-ČSL)	6.08	6		
Liberal Social Union (LSU)	6.06	5		
Rally for the Republic – Republican Party of Czechoslovakia (SPR-RSČ)	6.38	6		
Left Bloc (LB)	14.48	15		
Civic Democratic Party – Christian Democratic Party (ODS-KDS)	33.43	37		
Movement for a Democratic Slovakia (HZDS)			33.85	33
Party of the Democratic Left (SDL)			14.04	13
Hungarian Christian Democratic Movement			7.39	7
Christian Democratic Movement (KDH)			8.81	8
Slovak National Party (SNS)			9.39	9
Social Democratic Party in Slovakia (SDSS)			6.09	5

The Czech National Council

Political party	% of votes	Number of seats
Civic Democratic Alliance (ODA)	5.93	14
Czech Social Democratic Party (ČSSD)	6.53	13
Movement for self-governing democracy (HSD) – Society for Moravia and Silesia (SMS)	5.87	14
Christian Democratic Union – Czech People's Party (KDU-ČSL)	6.28	15
Liberal Social Union (LSU)	6.52	16
Rally for the Republic – Republican Party of Czechoslovakia (SPR-RSČ)	5.98	15
Left Bloc (LB)	14.05	35
Civic Democratic Party – Christian Democratic Party (ODS-KDS)	29.73	76

The Slovak National Council

Political party	% of votes	Number of seats
Movement for a Democratic Slovakia (HZDS)	37.26	74
Party of the Democratic Left (SDL)	14.70	29
Co-existence and Hungarian Christian Democratic Movement	7.42	14
Slovak National Party (SNS)	7.93	15
Christian Democratic Movement (KDH)	8.89	18

On 24th June, the SNC leadership appointed a Slovak government headed by Vladimír Mečiar in which HZDS held the majority of seats (though Slovak nationalists from SNS were also represented); SDL, the Communist successor, supported the government. A Czech government headed by Václav Klaus was appointed by the leadership of the Czech National Council (CNC) on 2nd July. It consisted of a coalition of ODS, KDU-ČSL, and ODA. The same day saw the naming of a reduced ten-member federal government led by Jan Stráský (ODS) and composed proportionally of ministers from ODS and HZDS. Naturally, the powers of federal organs were limited to the absolute minimum and the centres of power moved to the national governments. The leaning towards the end of a unified state deepened further on 3rd July, when the Federal Assembly did not elect Václav Havel President of the Republic, mainly due opposition by the HZDS and Slovak nationalists. On 17th July, the SNC passed a declaration of Slovak sovereignty with the votes of deputies from HZDS, SNS and SDL. The same day, Václav Havel stepped down from the post of President of the CSFR because he refused to be the head of a disintegrating state. On 26th August, the Prime Ministers of the Czech and Slovak governments agreed on a timetable for the breakup of the state, again meeting in Brno, halfway between Prague and Bratislava. On 1st September, the Slovak parliament approved a constitution for the independent state of the Slovak Republic; on 3rd September, the federal government adopted a proposal for a constitutional law on the breakup the Czechoslovak federation and three weeks later a proposal for a constitutional law on the division of the property of the federation between the successor states of CR and SR, with a 2 to 1 proportion.

Mečiar's HZDS was outflanked by the uncompromising position of ODS. The rapid division of the state was not its priority because it worried that Slovakia was still not fully prepared for independence. It was for this reason that it tried to slow the process. It used the positions of the Czech and Slovak oppositions (calling for a referendum as the only legitimate path to the preservation or breakup of the unified state) and through the chairman of the Federal Assembly, Michal Kováč (HZDS), began to negotiate the creation of a Czech-Slovak union, which was supported by a significant portion of HZDS parliament deputies. Divisions among HZDS parliamentarians seriously threatened the passage of the bill on the breakup of the federation, but on 1st October, it was rejected by the Federal Assembly. The opposition Czech Social Democrats took advantage of this opportunity and proposed setting up a commission for preparing the transformation of the federation into a Czech-Slovak union. Over the following days, Czech PM Václav Klaus emphatically repeated that a union was unacceptable for ODS. Delegations from ODS and HZDS resolved the looming split on 6th October in Jihlava. The negotiations were long and dramatic. ODS, supported by its Czech coalition partners, made it clear that if HZDS would not agree to the federal state's rapid and orderly breakup, then the CNC would declare the complete independence of the Czech Republic at an extraordinary session. In the end, HZDS acceded to the original agreement on the breakup of the CSFR in the Federal Assembly.

On 18th November, the Federal Assembly began to debate the new proposal of a constitutional law on the breakup of the federation. Only after feverish backroom negotiations, and under the threat that the National Councils would enact the breakup of the federation in a joint declaration, did the Federal Assembly narrowly approve the law on 25th November. Czechoslovakia as a unified state of Czechs and Slovaks ceased to exist on 31st December, 1992 despite the fact that – according to public opinion surveys – the majority of citizens in both republics did not desire its breakup. The winners of the elections did not consider a referendum acceptable as, in all probability, Czech and Slovak citizens would have supported the preservation of the unified state which would not change the diametrically opposed views of Czech and Slovak political representatives. Only new parliamentary elections could alter the stalemate and the victorious political parties wanted this least of all.

With the breakup of Czechoslovakia into an independent Czech Republic and an independent Slovak Republic, there disappeared a state which had survived 74 years in the dramatic conditions of Central Europe. It disappeared because, throughout its entire existence, it never managed to satisfactorily resolve its basic existential question. Because the post-Communist democratic elites considered it a priority to preserve the Czechoslovak state as their historic inheritance, its extinction was the most pronounced failure of the transition. On the other hand, the act of division itself proceeded peacefully, quickly, and orderly. In comparison to the bloody national settling of accounts in the former Yugoslavia, this must be judged an unequivocal success which positively influenced the peaceful development of Czechoslovak and Central European relations. It came to be called the 'velvet divorce.'

The second parliamentary elections of 1992 brought to completion return to parliamentary democracy with political parties in the dominant role. In this respect, the Czech Republic followed the political system of the first Czechoslovak Republic (1918–1938) with all its virtues and shortcomings. On one hand, free competition, on the other, partisan haggling and 'clientism,' which allowed the intentional interweaving of the political, media, and business spheres. Disquieting affairs and scandals began to accumulate and with them came a long-term decline in trust in both politics and politicians. In the second half of the nineties, many began to speak of a 'velvet hangover.' In this respect, however, the Czech Republic did not differ overly much from Western countries which also suffered a crisis of confidence.

The Czech path to capitalism begun with 'shock therapy' did not lead to success and, after a crisis in 1996–1997, was quickly forgotten. Faith in the traditional capability of 'Czech golden hands' and in the 'invisible hand of the market' showed its limits in the expansive tendency to rapid and easy enrichment, contradicting both laws and generally shared values. The rise of the Czech economy around the year 2000 was mainly due to its close ties to the economic and political structures of the West. The numbers of foreign investors in Czech banks and firms significantly increased and the standards of Western capitalism contributed to Czech consumer prosperity. There was a visible change in what had been one of the main causes of the fall of Communism – the unavailability of basic consumer goods and the low quality of services. General shortage was replaced by profuse abundance.

This prosperity allowed citizens to free themselves at least partially from the stereotypical mobilization strategies of political parties. The social element no longer so determined the political process as it had at the start of the nineties. However, new social problems which all countries of the wealthy West share, loom on the horizon – the general aging of the population, uncontrolled migration from the poor South and East, growing differences in citizens' incomes and, with all this, the fragility of the middle classes. A distinctive Czech problem is the long-term undervaluing of education and science.

The historic compromise of December 1989 complicated the prospect of facing the legacy of the Communist Party and its forty years of totalitarian rule. Since 23rd January, 1990, the CPCz has remained a fully legal parliamentary party which enjoys the continued support of approximately ten percent of faithful voters. The other democratic parties label it an extremist force, despite the fact that – for pragmatic reasons – they co-operate with it at both local and parliamentary levels. It is apparent that the resolution of the question 'What to do with the Communist past?' is marked by ambiguity. From this spring the long-standing difficulties and confusion regarding the return of the billions in property of the CPCz to the state and the unconvincing attempts to prosecute real criminals and traitors. A long series of de-Communizing acts and decisions were accompanied by controversies which dominate public debate of Communism to this day. Let us recall the basic landmarks of the controversial process: in 1990, a law was passed on judicial rehabilitation and a constitutional law on the return of property of the CPCz; in 1993, the victorious right-wing parties adopted a declarative law on the illegality of the Communist regime and resistance to it; in 1995, the establishment of the Bureau for the Documentation and Investigation of Communist Crimes offered investigators instruments for the legal prosecution of Communist-era crimes; in 1996, the Czech parliament passed a law on opening StB files which, six years later, was significantly expanded. The last de-Communizing act to date was the founding of the Institute for the Study of Totalitarian Regimes in 2007.

As regards foreign policy, the will to join the political, economic, and military structures of Western Euro-Atlantic civilization dominated. This formally culminated at the turn of the millennium with the entrance of the Czech Republic and other Central European countries into the North Atlantic Alliance in 1999 and, in 2004, into the European Union. It seems that with the return of a consolidated Russia to its place as a global superpower and the attempt of the US to engage its Central European allies directly without the mediation of the EU, the question of Central Europe as a crossroad of powerful interests is looming. Few now share the optimistic view of the 'end of history' of the early nineties.

616

Bibliography

ALAMIR, Fouzieh Melanie: *Der Präsident Vaclav Havel: seine politische Rolle im Spannungsfeld zwischen Verfassungsbestimmungen und politischer Kräftekonfiguration von 1990 bis 2003*, Potsdam 2003.

BLEHOVA, Beata: *Der Fall des Kommunismus in der Tschechoslowakei*, Wien 2006.

BŘACH, Radko: *Die Außenpolitik der Tschechoslowakei zur Zeit der "Regierung der nationalen Verständigung"*, Baden-Baden 1992.

DĚDEK, Oldřich et al.: *The break-up of Czechoslovakia: an in-depth economic analysis*, Aldershot 1996.

EAST, Roger: *Revolutions in Eastern Europe*, London 1992.

Eyal, Gil: *The origins of postcommunist elites: from Prague Spring to the breakup of Czechoslovakia*, Minneapolis 2003.

FALK, Barbara: *The Dilemmas of Dissidence in East-Central Europe: Citizen Intellectuals and Philosopher Kings*, Budapest 2003.

GARTON ASH, Timothy: *The Magic Lantern: The Revolution of ´89 Witnessed in Warsaw, Budapest, Berlin und Prague*, New York 1990.

GJURIČOVÁ, Adéla – KOPEČEK, Michal et al.: *Kapitoly z dějin české demokracie po roce 1989*, Praha–Litomyšl 2008.

HORSKÝ, Vladimír: *Die sanfte Revolution in der Tschechoslowakei 1989: zur Frage der systemimmanenten Instabilität kommunistischer Herrschaft*, Köln 1990.

KEANE, John: *Vaclav Havel: a political tragedy in six acts*, London 1999.

KENNEY, Padraic: *A Carnival of Revolution: Central Europe 1989*, Princeton 2002.

KRAUS, Michael – STANGER, Allison K.: *Irreconcilable differences?: explaining Czechoslovakia's dissolution*, foreword by Václav Havel, Lanham 2000.

LEVESQUE, Jacques: *The Enigma of 1989: The USSR and the Liberation of Eastern Europe*, Berkeley 1997.

MAYER, Françoise: *Les Tchèques et leur communisme: mémoire et identités politiques*, Paris 2004.

MINK, Georges: *La grande conversion: le destin des communistes en Europe de l'Est* , Paris 1999.

MOUNIR, Omar: *La partition de la Tchécoslovaquie = Rozpad Československa*, Gerpinnes 1998.

MYANT, Martin: *The Rise and Fall of Czech Capitalism. Economic Development in the Czech Republic since 1989*, Cheltenham, UK–Northampton, MA, USA, 2003.

RYCHLÍK, Jan: *Rozpad Československa. Česko-slovenské vztahy 1989–1992*, Bratislava 2002.

SAXONBERG, Steven: *The Fall: A Comparative Study of the End of Communism in Czechoslovakia, East Germany, Hungary, and Poland*. Amsterdam 2001

SCHWARZ, Karl Peter: *Tschechen und Slowaken: der lange Weg zur friedlichen Trennung*, Wien–Zürich 1993.

SUK, Jiří: *Labyrintem revoluce. Aktéři, zápletky a křižovatky jedné politické krize (Od listopadu 1989 do června 1990)*, Praha 2003.

WOLCHIK, Sharon L.: *Czechoslovakia in transition: politics, economics and society*, London 1991.

WEHRLE, Frédéric: *Le divorce tchèco-slovaque: vie et mort de la Tchécoslovaquie 1918–1992*, Paris 1994.

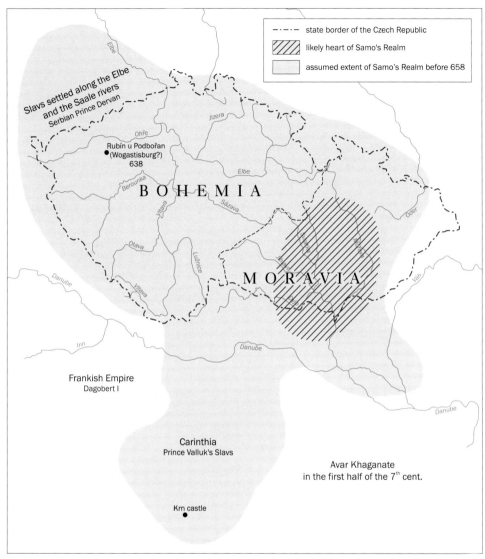

1. Samo's Realm in the first half of the 7th century
© Eva Semotanová, 2009
© Charles University in Prague, 2009

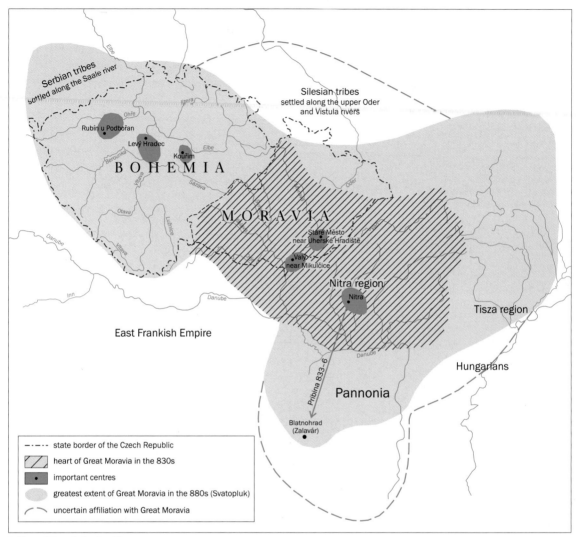

Serbian tribes
settled along the Saale river

Silesian tribes
settled along the upper Oder
and Vistula rivers

Rubín u Podbořan

Levý Hradec

Kouřim

B O H E M I A

M O R A V I A

Staré Město
near Uherské Hradiště

Valy
near Mikulčice

Nitra region

Nitra

Tisza region

East Frankish Empire

Přibina 833–6

Hungarians

Pannonia

Blatnohrad
(Zalavár)

Elbe
Ohře
Jizera
Elbe
Berounka
Vltava
Sázava
Oder
Otava
Lužnice
Danube
Vltava
Inn
Danube
Danube

- - - · - - -   state border of the Czech Republic

    heart of Great Moravia in the 830s

●   important centres

    greatest extent of Great Moravia in the 880s (Svatopluk)

    uncertain affiliation with Great Moravia

2. Great Moravia in the 9th century
© Eva Semotanová, 2009
© Charles University in Prague, 2009

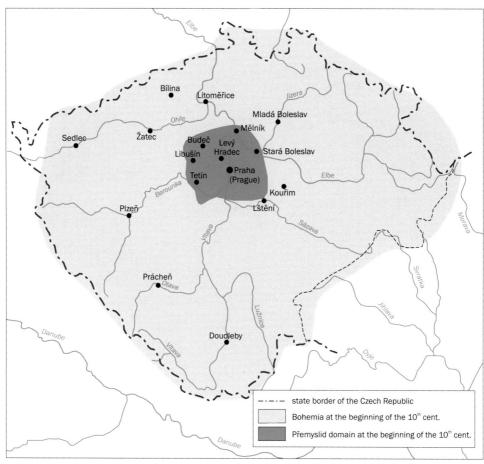

3. Bohemia at the beginning of the 10th century
© Eva Semotanová, 2009
© Charles University in Prague, 2009

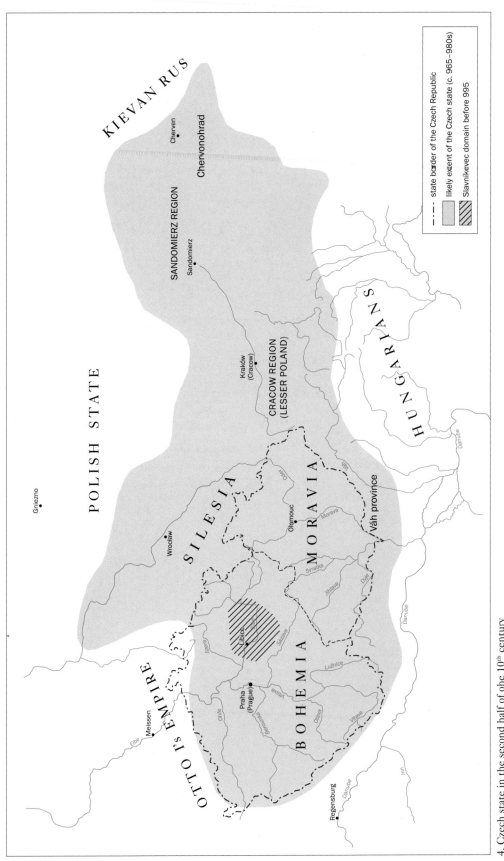

4. Czech state in the second half of ohe 10ᵗʰ century

© Eva Semotanová, 2009

© Charles University in Prague, 2009

© Eva Semotanová, 2009

© Charles University in Prague, 2009

Legend:
- state border of the Czech Republic
- likely extent of the Czech state (c. 965–980s)
- Slavnikevec domain before 995

KIEVAN RUS

Cherven

Chervonohrad

SANDOMIERZ REGION

Sandomierz

POLISH STATE

Gniezno

Kraków (Cracow)

CRACOW REGION (LESSER POLAND)

HUNGARIANS

Danube

Váh province

Danube

Váh

SILESIA

Wrocław

Odra

Olomouc

Morava

MORAVIA

Svratka

Jihlava

Dyje

Danube

BOHEMIA

Sázava

Libice

Cidlina

Jizera

Lužnice

Praha (Prague)

Vltava

Berounka

Otava

Ohře

OTTO I's EMPIRE

Meissen

Elbe

Regensburg

Danube

Inn

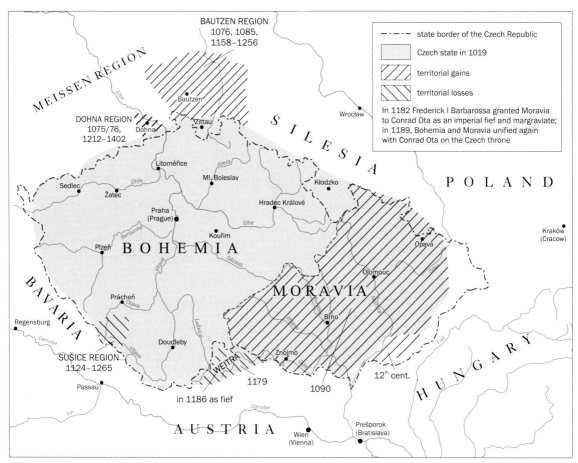

MEISSEN REGION

BAUTZEN REGION
1076, 1085,
1158–1256

DOHNA REGION
1075/76,
1212–1402

Dohna

Bautzen

Zittau

SILESIA

Wrocław

state border of the Czech Republic

Czech state in 1019

territorial gains

territorial losses

In 1182 Frederick I Barbarossa granted Moravia
to Conrad Ota as an imperial fief and margraviate;
in 1189, Bohemia and Moravia unified again
with Conrad Ota on the Czech throne

POLAND

Litoměřice
Sedlec
Žatec
Ohře
Ml. Boleslav
Kłodzko
Hradec Králové
Praha
(Prague)
Kouřim
Plzeň
BOHEMIA
Elbe
Sázava
Beroun ka
Opava
Kraków
(Cracow)

Vltava
Prácheň
Otava
MORAVIA
Olomouc
Regensburg
BAVARIA
Danube
Lužnice
Brno
SUŠICE REGION
1124–1265
Doudleby
Vltava
WEITRA
Znojmo
1179
1090
12th cent.
HUNGARY

Passau
in 1186 as fief
Inn
Danube
AUSTRIA
Wien
(Vienna)
Prešporok
(Bratislava)

5. Czech state in the 11th and 12th centuries
© Eva Semotanová, 2009
© Charles University in Prague, 2009

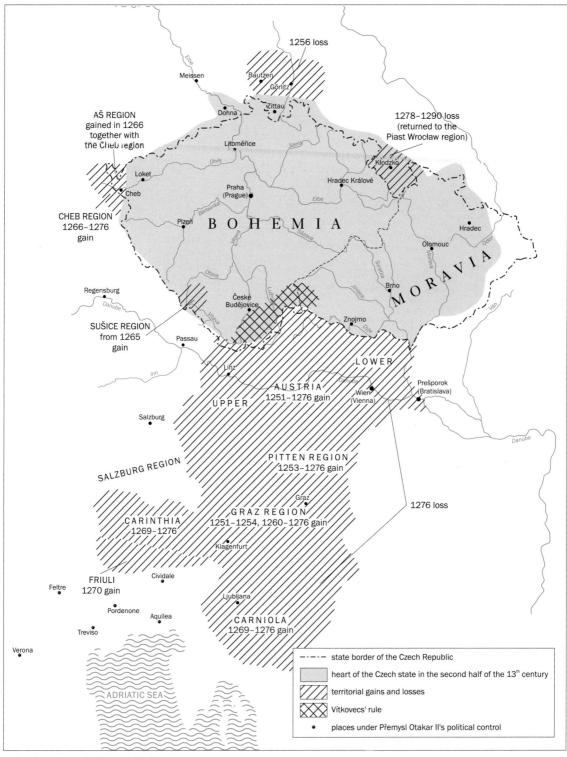

6. Czech state under Přemysl Otakar II
© Eva Semotanová, 2009
© Charles University in Prague, 2009

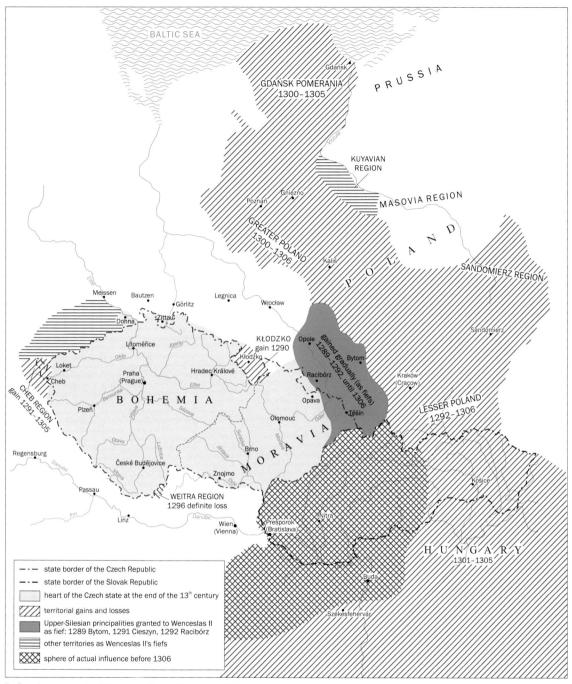

BALTIC SEA

PRUSSIA

Gdańsk

GDAŃSK POMERANIA
1300–1305

KUYAVIAN
REGION

Gniezno

Poznań

MASOVIA REGION

GREATER POLAND
1300–1306

Kališ

P O L A N D

SANDOMIERZ REGION

Meissen
Bautzen
Görlitz
Legnica
Wrocław

Sandomierz

Dohna
Zittau

Litoměřice
Jizera

KŁODZKO
gain 1290
Opole
Bytom

gained gradually
1289–1292, until 1306
(as fiefs)

Loket
Cheb

Kłodzko

Praha
(Prague)
Hradec Králové
Elbe

Racibórz

Kraków
(Cracow)

CHEB REGION
gain 1291–1305

Berounka

B O H E M I A
Opava

Regensburg
Danube

Plzeň

Sázava

Olomouc
Opava

Tešin

LESSER POLAND
1292–1306

Otava

Vltava
Lužnice
Jihlava
Svratka

Brno

Odra

M O R A V I A

Morava

České Budějovice
Jihlava
Dyje

Znojmo

Košice

Passau

Linz
Danube
Wien
(Vienna)

WEITRA REGION
1296 definite loss

Prešporok
(Bratislava)

Nitra

H U N G A R Y
1301–1305

Inn

Buda

Székesfehérvár

- · - · -   state border of the Czech Republic
- · - · -   state border of the Slovak Republic
▨   heart of the Czech state at the end of the 13ᵗʰ century
▨   territorial gains and losses
■   Upper-Silesian principalities granted to Wenceslas II
     as fief: 1289 Bytom, 1291 Cieszyn, 1292 Racibórz
▤   other territories as Wenceslas II's fiefs
▩   sphere of actual influence before 1306

7. Czech state under Wenceslas II and Wenceslas III
© Eva Semotanová, 2009
© Charles University in Prague, 2009

NEUMARK
1373–1402

Szczecin

BRANDENBURG
1373–1415

Brandenburg

Świdnica county
1353 through marriage
1368 as inheritance

1313–1409 via the ruler

LUXEMBOURG

Luxembourg

LOWER
LUSATIA
1368

Krosno

Cottbus

Żagań

Głogów

POLAND

SAXONY

UPPER
LUSATIA 1329
1319
Meissen   Görlitz
        Bautzen

Dohna region
lost 1402

Dohna

Zittau

Legnica

Jawor
county
1368

Wrocław

Świdnica
1353

SILESIA
1327–1335

Opole

CHEB REGION
gained 1322

Aš region
gained 1331

Litoměřice

Jizera

Kłodzko

Bytom

loss 1422

loss of part of Cheb
region c. 1400

Žatec   Ohře

Cheb

Hradec Králové

Elbe

Racibórz

Siewierz

Oświęcim

Zator

NEW BOHEMIA
(Bohemian
Upper Palatinate)
1353–1373

Berounka

Plzeň

Praha
(Prague)

BOHEMIA

Krnov

Opava

Vltava

Nürnberg

1353
1355
1401

BAVARIA

Otava

Sázava

Olomouc

Odra

UPPER
PALATINATE

Danube

Otava

Lužnice

Jihlava

Morava

MORAVIA

Svratka

Brno

Vltava

České Budějovice

Jihlava

Váh

Znojmo

Dyje

AUSTRIA

HUNGARY

Danube

8. Czech state in the Luxemburg period
© Eva Semotanová, 2009
© Charles University in Prague, 2009

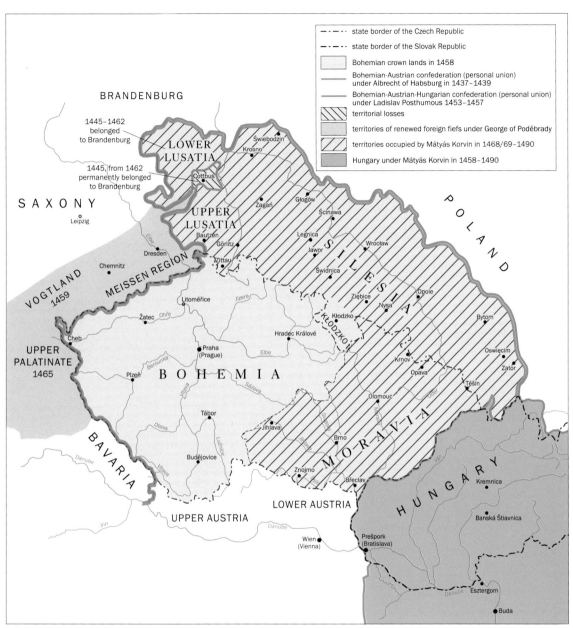

10. Czech state in the Jagiellon era
© Eva Semotanová, 2009
© Charles University in Prague, 2009

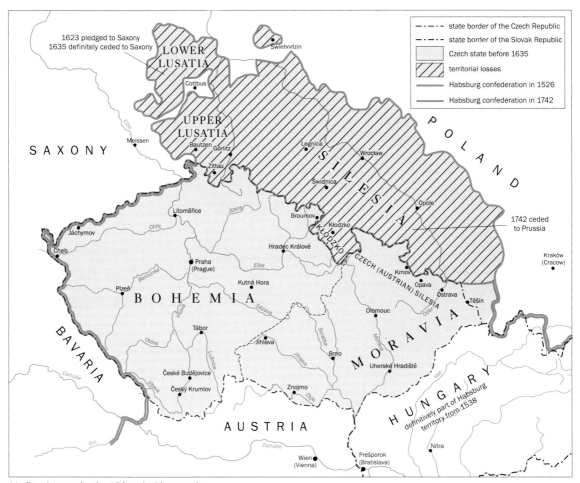

11. Czech state in the 17ᵗʰ and 18ᵗʰ centuries
© Eva Semotanová, 2009
© Charles University in Prague, 2009

RUSSIAN EMPIRE

GERMANY

BOHEMIA

Praha (Prague)

SILESIA

MORAVIA

GALICIA

Wien (Vienna)

VORARLBERG

UPPER AUSTRIA

LOWER AUSTRIA

SWITZ.

BUKOVINA

SALZBURG

STYRIA

TYROL

AUSTRIA-HUNGARY

CARINTHIA

GORIZIA

HUNGARY

CARNIOLA

ITALY

TRIESTE

ISTRIA

CROATIA–SLAVONIA

ROMANIA

BOSNIA–HERCEGOVINA

DALMATIA

SERBIA

ADRIATIC SEA

OTTOMAN EMPIRE

MONTENEGRO

——·— state border of the Czech Republic
——— international border of Austria-Hungary
——— border of Cisleithania and Transleithania
STYRIA internal provinces

12. The Czech Lands in Austria-Hungary after 1867
© Eva Semotanová, 2009
© Charles University in Prague, 2009

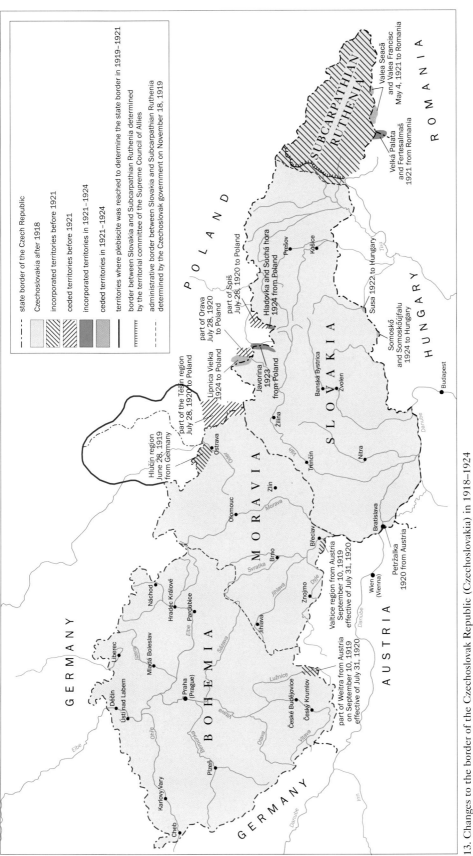

Legend:

- state border of the Czech Republic
- Czechoslovakia after 1918
- incorporated territories before 1921
- ceded territories before 1921
- incorporated territories in 1921–1924
- ceded territories in 1921–1924
- territories where plebiscite was reached to determine the state border in 1919–1921
- border between Slovakia and Subcarpathian Ruthenia determined by the territorial committee of the Supreme Council of Allies
- administrative border between Slovakia and Subcarpathian Ruthenia determined by the Czechoslovak government on November 18, 1919

Map labels:

GERMANY

POLAND

ROMANIA

HUNGARY

AUSTRIA

BOHEMIA

MORAVIA

SLOVAKIA

SUBCARPATHIAN RUTHENIA

Valea Seacă and Valea Francisc May 4, 1921 to Romania

Velká Palăta and Fertesalmaš 1921 from Romania

Susa 1922 to Hungary

Somoskő and Somoskőújfalu 1924 to Hungary

part of Spiš July 28, 1920 to Poland

Hladovka and Suchá hora 1924 from Poland

part of Orava July 28, 1920 to Poland

Javorina 1923 from Poland

Lipnica Vielka 1924 to Poland

part of the Těšín region July 28, 1920 to Poland

Hlučín region June 28, 1919 from Germany

Valtice region from Austria September 10, 1919 effective of July 31, 1920

part of Weitra from Austria on September 10, 1919 effective of July 31, 1920

Petržalka 1920 from Austria

Cities: Cheb, Karlovy Vary, Plzeň, Děčín, Ústí nad Labem, Liberec, Mladá Boleslav, Náchod, Hradec Králové, Pardubice, Praha (Prague), České Budějovice, Český Krumlov, Jihlava, Znojmo, Brno, Břeclav, Olomouc, Zlín, Ostrava, Wien (Vienna), Budapest, Žilina, Trenčín, Nitra, Bratislava, Banská Bystrica, Zvolen, Prešov, Košice

Rivers: Elbe, Ohře, Berounka, Vltava, Otava, Sázava, Lužnice, Dyje, Jihlava, Svratka, Morava, Odra, Váh, Danube, Tisa, Inn

13. Changes to the border of the Czechoslovak Republic (Czechoslovakia) in 1918–1924

© Eva Semotanová, 2009

© Charles University in Prague, 2009

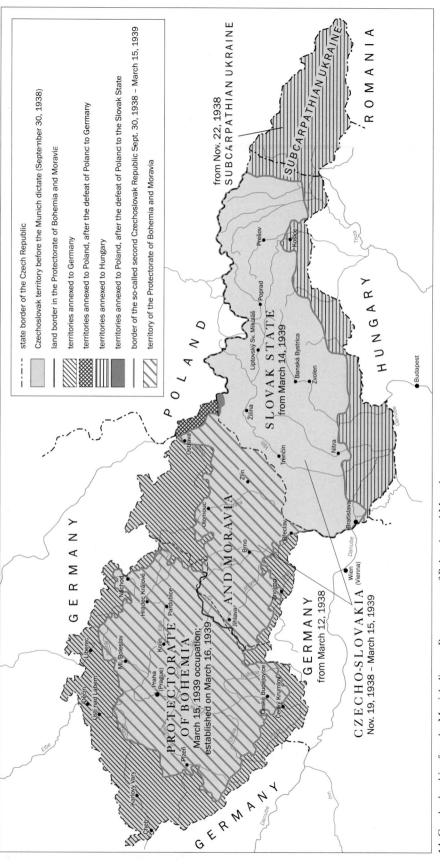

Legend:

- state border of the Czech Republic
- Czechoslovak territory before the Munich dictate (September 30, 1938)
- land border in the Protectorate of Bohemia and Moravia
- territories annexed to Germany
- territories annexed to Poland, after the defeat of Poland to Germany
- territories annexed to Hungary
- territories annexed to Poland, after the defeat of Poland to the Slovak State
- border of the so-called second Czechoslovak Republic Sept. 30, 1938 – March 15, 1939
- territory of the Protectorate of Bohemia and Moravia

GERMANY

POLAND

PROTECTORATE OF BOHEMIA

March 15, 1939 occupation;
established on March 16, 1939

AND MORAVIA

GERMANY
from March 12, 1938

CZECHO-SLOVAKIA
Nov. 19, 1938 – March 15, 1939

SLOVAK STATE
from March 14, 1939

SUBCARPATHIAN UKRAINE
from Nov. 22, 1938

HUNGARY

ROMANIA

Cheb, Karlovy Vary, Plzeň, Ústí nad Labem, Děčín, Liberec, Náchod, Ml. Boleslav, Praha (Prague), Kolín, Hradec Králové, Pardubice, České Krumlov, České Budějovice, Jihlava, Znojmo, Brno, Olomouc, Zlín, Ostrava, Břeclav, Wien (Vienna), Bratislava, Nitra, Trenčín, Žilina, Zvolen, Banská Bystrica, Liptovský Sv. Mikuláš, Poprad, Prešov, Košice, Budapest

Elbe, Vltava, Otava, Lužnice, Sázava, Jihlava, Dyje, Danube, Inn, Váh, Danube, Tisza

14. Czechoslovakia after the Munich dictate, Protectorate of Bohemia and Moravia
© Eva Semotanová, 2009
© Charles University in Prague, 2009

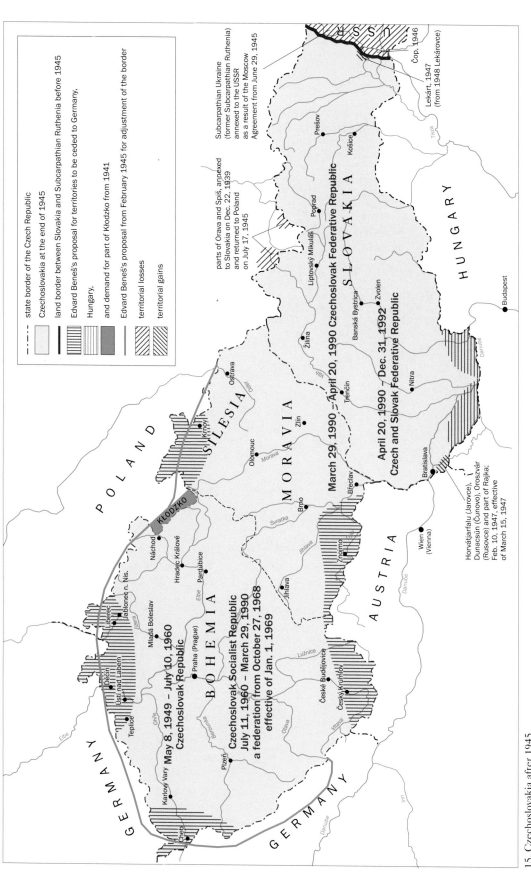

15. Czechoslovakia after 1945

© Eva Semotanová, 2009

© Charles University in Prague, 2009

Legend

- state border of the Czech Republic
- Czechoslovakia at the end of 1945
- land border between Slovakia and Subcarpathian Ruthenia before 1945
- Edvard Beneš's proposal for territories to be ceded to Germany, Hungary, and demand for part of Kłodzko from 1941
- Edvard Beneš's proposal from February 1945 for adjustment of the border
- territorial losses
- territorial gains

Subcarpathian Ukraine (former Subcarpathian Ruthenia) annexed to the USSR as a result of the Moscow Agreement from June 29, 1945

Čop, 1946

Lekárt, 1947 (from 1948 Lekárovce)

parts of Orava and Spiš, annexed to Slovakia on Dec. 22, 1939 and annexed to Poland and returned to Slovakia on July 17, 1945

March 29, 1990 – April 20, 1990 Czechoslovak Federative Republic

April 20, 1990 – Dec. 31, 1992 Czech and Slovak Federative Republic

May 8, 1949 – July 10, 1960 Czechoslovak Republic

Czechoslovak Socialist Republic July 11, 1960 – March 29, 1990 a federation from October 27, 1968 effective from Jan. 1, 1969

Horvátjárfalu (Jarovce), Dunacsún (Čunovo), Oroszvár (Rusovce) and part of Rajka; Feb. 10, 1947, effective of March 15, 1947

USSR

POLAND

GERMANY

BOHEMIA

SILESIA

MORAVIA

SLOVAKIA

AUSTRIA

HUNGARY

KŁODZKO

Ostrava
Krnov
Olomouc
Zlín
Žilina
Prešov
Košice
Poprad
Liptovský Mikuláš
Banská Bystrica
Zvolen
Trenčín
Nitra
Brno
Břeclav
Znojmo
Bratislava
Náchod
Hradec Králové
Pardubice
Jablonec n. Nis.
Liberec
Mladá Boleslav
Praha (Prague)
Ústí nad Labem
Děčín
Teplice
Karlovy Vary
Plzeň
Jihlava
České Budějovice
Český Krumlov
Wien (Vienna)
Budapest

Elbe
Ohře
Berounka
Vltava
Otava
Lužnice
Jihlava
Svratka
Morava
Odra
Jizera
Elbe
Váh
Tisá
Danube
Inn

16. Czech Republic since 1993
© Eva Semotanová, 2009
© Charles University in Prague, 2009

List of illustrations, tables and maps

Illustrations

Tables

Maps

620

List of Abbreviations

BC   Board of Commissioners (SP, Sbor pověřenců)
CC CPCz   Central Committee CPCz (ÚV KSČ, Ústřední výbor KSČ)
COMECON   Council of Mutual Economic Assistance (RVHP, Rada vzájemné hospodářské pomoci)
Cominform   Communist Information Bureau (Information Bureau of Communist and Workers' Parties)
Comintern   Communist International
CPCz   Communist Party of Czechoslovakia (KSČ, Komunistická strana Československa)
CPSU   Communist Party of the Soviet Union (KPSS, Kommunisticheskaya Partiya Sovetskogo Soyuza)
ČSD   Československá sociální demokracie (Czechoslovak Social Democracy)
ČSSD   Česká strana sociálně demokratická (od r. 1993; Czech Social Democratic Party, from 1993)
ČSM   Československý svaz mládeže (Czechoslovak Youth Union)
ČSL   Československá strana lidová (Czechoslovak People's Party)
ČSNS   Československá strana národně sociální (Czechoslovak National-Socialist Party)
ČSNV   Československý národní výbor (Czechoslovak National Committee)
DS   Demokratická strana Slovenska (Democratic Party of Slovakia)
FA   Federal Assembly (FS, Federální shromáždění)
Gestapo   Geheime Staatspolizei (Secret State Police)
HSDSMS   Hnutí za samosprávnou demokracii – Společnost pro Moravu a Slezsko (Movement for Self-Governing Democracy – Society for Moravia and Silesia)
HSĽS   Hlinkova slovenská ľudová strana (Hlinka's Slovak People's Party)
HZDS   Hnutie za demokratické Slovensko (Movement for a Democratic Slovakia)
IVH   Investment voucher holder (DIK, držitel investičních kuponů)
K-231   Klub bývalých politických vězňů (Club of former political prisoners)
KAN   Klub angažovaných nestraníků (Club of Committed Non-party Members)
KDU–ČSL   Křesťansko demokratická unie – Československá strana lidová (Christian Democratic Union – Czechoslovak People's Party)
KDH   Kresťanskodemokratické hnutie (Christian Democratic Movement)
KDU   Křesťansko-demokratická unie (Christian Democratic Union)
KDS   Křesťansko-demokratická strana (Christian Democratic Party)
Komsomol   Kommunisticheskiy Soyuz Molodyozhi (Communist Union of Youth)
Kripo   Kriminalpolizei (Criminal Police)
KSS   Komunistická strana Slovenska (Communist Party of Slovakia)
MKDP   Meziparlamentní klub demokratické pravice (Inter-parliamentary Club of the Democratic Right)
MNI   Maďarská nezávislá iniciativa (Independent Hungarian Initiative)
NSDAP   Nationalsozialistische Deutsche Arbeiterpartei (National Socialist German Workers' Party)
ODA   Občanská demokratická aliance (Civic Democratic Alliance)
ODS   Občanská demokratická strana (Civic Democratic Party)

ODÚ–VPN	Občanská demokratická unie – Verejnosť proti násiliu (Civic Democratic Union – Public Against Violence)
OECD	Organisation for Economic Development
OF	Občanské fórum (Civic Forum)
OH	Občanské hnutí (Civic Movement)
ON	Obrana národa (Defence of the Nation)
OSCE	Organization for Security and Co-operation in Europe
PÚ	Politická ústředna (Political Central)
PVVZ	Petiční výbor Věrni zůstaneme (Petition Committee We Shall Remain Faithful)
SD	Sicherheitsdienst (Security Police)
SDL	Strana demokratické levice (Party of the Democratic Left)
SdP	Sudetendeutsche Partei (Sudeten German Party)
Sipo	Sicherheitspolizei (Security Police)
SNB	Sbor národní bezpečnosti (National Security Corps)
SNC	Slovak National Council (SNR, Slovenská národní rada)
SNS	Slovenská národná strana (Slovak National Party)
SS	Schutzstaffel (Protective Squadron)
SSM	Svaz socialistické mládeže (Socialist Youth Union)
StB	Státní bezpečnost (State Security)
UNCP	Ukrainian National Council of Priasevcina
UNRRA	United Nations Relief and Rehabilitation Administration
ÚNRVČ	Ústřední národně revoluční výbor Československa (Central National Revolutionary Committee of Czechoslovakia)
ÚVOD	Ústřední vedení odboje domácího (Central Leadership of the Domestic Resistance)
VONS	Výbor na obranu nespravedlivě stíhaných (Committee for the Defence of Unjustly Persecuted)
VPN	Verejnosť proti násiliu (Public Against Violence)
VPN–ZDS	Verejnosť proti násiliu – Za demokratické Slovensko (Public Against Violence – For a Democratic Slovakia)

622

Czech Republic,
state representatives

SAMO'S REALM
623/4–658/9   Samo

GREAT MORAVIA
Mojmír Dynasty
830?–846   Mojmír I
846–870   Rastislav
870?–894   Svatopluk
894–906   Mojmír II

CZECH STATE
PRINCES
Přemyslid dynasty
?–894?   Bořivoj
?–915?   Spytihněv
915?–921?   Vratislav I
?–929/935   St Wenceslas (I)
929/935–967/972   Boleslav I
967/972–999   Boleslav II
999–1002   Boleslav III
1002–1003   Vladivoj
1003   Boleslav III
1003   Jaromír
1003–1004   *)Bolesław the Brave
    (Polish Prince and King 992–1025)
1004–1012   Jaromír
1012–1033   Oldřich
1033–1034   Jaromír
1034   Oldřich
1035–1055   Břetislav I
1055–1061   Spytihněv II
1061–1092   Vratislav II (king from 1085)
1092   Conrad I
1092–1100   Břetislav II
1101–1107   Bořivoj II
1107–1109   Svatopluk
1109–1117   Vladislav I

*) *the ruler does not belong to the dynasty*

1117–1120   Bořivoj II
1120–1125   Vladislav I
1125–1140   Soběslav I
1140–1172   Vladislav II (king from 1158)
1172–1173   Frederick
1173–1178   Soběslav II
1178–1189   Frederick
1189–1191   Conrad II Otto
1191–1192   Wenceslas II
1192–1193   Přemysl I Otakar
1193–1197   Jindřich Břetislav
1197   Vladislav Jindřich
1197–1230   Přemysl II Otakar (king from 1198)

KINGS
1197–1230   Přemysl I Otakar (prince until 1198)
1230–1253   Wenceslas I
1253–1278   Přemysl II Otakar
1278–1305   Wenceslas II (1300–1305 also King
    of Poland)
1305–1306   Wenceslas III (1301–1305 King
    of Hungary as Ladislaus V)
(the Přemyslid dynasty died out along the male line)
1306   *)Henry of Carinthia
1306–1307   *)Rudolf (I) of Habsburg
1307–1310   *)Henry of Carinthia

Luxemburg dynasty
1310–1346   John of Luxemburg
1346–1378   Charles IV (Roman King from 1346,
    Emperor from 1355)
1378–1419   Wenceslas IV (1363–1400 Roman
    King)
1419–1420   Sigismund of Luxemburg (Roman
    King from 1411, Emperor from 1433;
    also King of Hungary from 1387)
1420–1436   interregnum
1436–1437   Sigismund of Luxemburg
(end of dynasty)

1437–1439 *)Albrecht II of Habsburg (Roman King from 1437; also King of Hungary)
1439–1453 interregnum
1453–1457 *)Ladislav Posthumous (also King of Hungary)
1458–1471 *)George of Poděbrady (1452–1458 Land Administrator)

Jagiellon dynasty
1471–1516 Vladislav II (also King of Hungary from 1490)
1516–1526 Louis (also King of Hungary)

Habsburg dynasty
1526–1564 Ferdinand I (from 1556 Holy Roman Emperor; also King of Hungary)
1564–1576 Maxmilian II (also Holy Roman Emperor and King of Hungary)
1576–1611 Rudolf II (1576–1612 Holy Roman Emperor; 1576–1608 King of Hungary)
1611–1619 Matthias (Holy Roman Emperor from 1612; also King of Hungary from 1608)
1619 Ferdinand II (also Holy Roman Emperor and King of Hungary)
1619–1620 *)Frederick Palatine (1610–1622 as Frederick V Elector of the Palatinate)
1620–1637 Ferdinand II (also Holy Roman Emperor and King of Hungary)
1637–1657 Ferdinand III (also Holy Roman Emperor and King of Hungary)
1657–1705 Leopold I (also Holy Roman Emperor and King of Hungary)
1705–1711 Joseph I (also Holy Roman Emperor and King of Hungary)
1711–1740 Charles VI (also Holy Roman Emperor and King of Hungary)
1741–1745 *)Charles VII Albert of Bavaria (also Holy Roman Emperor)
1740–1780 Maria Theresa (also Queen of Hungary)

Habsburg-Lorraine dynasty (Habsburg-Lothringen)
1780–1790 Joseph II (Holy Roman Emperor from 1765; also King of Hungary)
1790–1792 Leopold II (also Holy Roman Emperor and King of Hungary)
1792–1835 Francis I (II) (also King of Hungary, Holy Roman Emperor until 1806 and Austrian Emperor from 1804)
1835–1848 Ferdinand V (also Austrian Emperor and King of Hungary)

1848–1916 Francis Joseph I (also Austrian Emperor and King of Hungary)
1916–1918 Charles I (also Austrian Emperor and King of Hungary)

PRESIDENTS OF THE CZECHOSLOVAK REPUBLIC
1918–1935 Tomáš Garrigue Masaryk
1935–1938 Edvard Beneš
1938–1939 Emil Hácha (1939–45 State President of the Protectorate of Bohemia and Moravia)
1939–1948 Edvard Beneš (1939–45 President of the republic in exile)
1948–1953 Klement Gottwald
1953–1957 Antonín Zápotocký
1957–1968 Antonín Novotný
1968–1975 Ludvík Svoboda
1975–1989 Gustáv Husák
1989–1992 Václav Havel

PRIME MINISTERS OF CZECHOSLOVAK GOVERNMENTS
1918–1919 Karel Kramář
1919–1920 Vlastimil Tusar
1920–1921 Jan Černý
1921–1922 Edvard Beneš
1922–1926 Antonín Švehla
1926 Jan Černý
1926–1929 Antonín Švehla
1929–1932 František Udržal
1932–1935 Jan Malypetr
1935–1938 Milan Hodža
1938 Jan Syrový
1938–1939 Rudolf Beran
1939 Rudolf Beran (Protectorate government)
1939–1941 Alois Eliáš (Protectorate government)
1941–1945 Jaroslav Krejčí (Protectorate government)
1945 Richard Bienert (Protectorate government)
1940–1945 Jan Šrámek (Czechoslovak government in exile)
1945–1946 Zdeněk Fierlinger
1946–1948 Klement Gottwald
1948–1953 Antonín Zápotocký
1953–1963 Viliam Široký
1963–1968 Jozef Lenárt
1968–1970 Oldřich Černík
1970–1988 Lubomír Štrougal
1988–1989 Ladislav Adamec
1989–1992 Marián Čalfa
1992–1993 Jan Stráský

624

PRESIDENTS OF THE CZECH REPUBLIC
1993–2003   Václav Havel
2003–   Václav Klaus

PRIME MINISTERS OF THE
CZECH REPUBLIC GOVERNMENTS
1993–1998   Václav Klaus
1998–1998   Josef Tošovský
1998–2002   Miloš Zeman
2002–2004   Vladimír Špidla
2004–2005   Stanislav Gross
2005–2006   Jiří Paroubek
2006–2009   Mirek Topolánek
2009   Jan Fischer

Frequently used geographical names

Czech	English	German
Dunaj	Danube	Donau
Dyje	Dyje / Thaya	Thaya
Labe	Elbe	Elbe
Odra	Oder	Oder
Ohře	Ohře / Eger	Eger
Tisa	Tisza	Theiss
Visla	Vistula	Weichsel
Vltava	Vltava	Moldau
Bílé Karpaty	White Carpathians	Weisse Karpathen
Českomoravská vysočina	Bohemian-Moravian Highlands	Böhmisch-Mährische Höhe
Jizerské hory	Jizera Mountains	Isergebirge
Krkonoše	Giant Mountains	Riesengebirge
Krušné hory	Ore Mountains	Erzgebirge
Lužické hory	Lužice Mountains	Lausitzer Gebirge
Orlické hory	Orlice Mountains Sudeten Mountains	Adlergebirge
Šumava	Bohemian Forest	Böhmerwald
Bratislava		Pressburg
Brno		Brünn
České Budějovice	České Budějovice / Budweis	Budweis
Český Těšín		Teschen
Cheb		Eger
Hradec Králové		Königgrätz
Jihlava		Iglau
Liberec		Reichenberg
Litoměřice		Leitmeritz
Karlovy Vary	Carlsbad	Karlsbad

Kroměříž		Kremsier
Olomouc		Olmütz
Opava		Tropau
Plzeň	Plzeň / Pilsen	Pilsen
Praha	Prague	Prag
Terezín		Theresienstadt
Znojmo		Znaim
Braniborsko	Brandenburg	Brandenburg
Budyšínsko	Bautzen	Bautzen
Čechy	Bohemia	Böhmen
Donínsko	Dohna	Dohna
Falc	Palatinate	Pfalz
Furlandsko	Friuli	Friaul
Halič	Galicia	Galizien
Kladsko	Kłodzko	Glatz
Korutansko	Carinthia	Kärnten
Kraňsko	Carniola	Krain
Lužice	Lusatia	Lausitz
Morava	Moravia	Mähren
Podkarpatská Rus	(Sub)carpathian Ruthenia	Karpatenrussland / Ruthenien
Sandoměřsko	Sandomierz	Sandomir
Slezsko	Silesia	Schlesien
Štýrsko	Styria	Steiermark
Svídnicko	Świdnica	Schweidnitz
Tyrolsko	Tyrol	Tirol
Vitorazsko	Weitra	Weitra
Zhořelecko	Görlitz	Görlitz
Žitavsko	Zittau	Zittau

A note on exonyms and Czech pronunciation – Throughout the book and in the maps we have used contemporary Czech geographical names, with the exception of available and well-known English exonyms (or German in some historical cases). For pronunciation of Czech names we refer to a detailed Guide to Czech Pronunciation, in: Velký česko-anglický slovník, Josef Fronek, Praha 2000, pp. XXIX–XLVII, or to http://en.wikipedia.org/wiki/Czech_language.

Index

A HISTORY OF THE CZECH LANDS

Prof. PhDr. Jaroslav Pánek, DrSc.,
PhDr. Oldřich Tůma, Ph.D.
et alii

English translation by Justin Quinn, Petra Key, Lea Bennis

Published by Charles University in Prague, Karolinum Press
Ovocný trh 3–5, 116 36 Prague 1, Czech Republic
http://cupress.cuni.cz
Prague 2011
Editor vice-rector Prof. PhDr. Ivan Jakubec
Edited by Martin Janeček
Proofread by Clea McDonald
Layout by Zdeněk Ziegler
Typeset by MU studio
Printed by Karolinum Press
First English edition

ISBN 978-80-246-1645-2